The Editor

MARIANNE DeKOVEN is Professor of English at Rutgers University. She is the author of *A Different Language: Gertrude Stein's Experimental Writing*; *Rich and Strange: Gender, History, Modernism*; and *Utopia Limited: The Sixties and the Emergence of the Postmodern*. She is the editor of *Feminist Locations: Global and Local, Theory and Practice*.

W. W. NORTON & COMPANY, INC.
Also Publishes

THE NORTON ANTHOLOGY OF AFRICAN AMERICAN LITERATURE
edited by Henry Louis Gates Jr. and Nellie Y. McKay et al.

THE NORTON ANTHOLOGY OF AMERICAN LITERATURE
edited by Nina Baym et al.

THE NORTON ANTHOLOGY OF CHILDREN'S LITERATURE
edited by Jack Zipes et al.

THE NORTON ANTHOLOGY OF CONTEMPORARY FICTION
edited by R. V. Cassill and Joyce Carol Oates

THE NORTON ANTHOLOGY OF ENGLISH LITERATURE
edited by M. H. Abrams and Stephen Greenblatt et al.

THE NORTON ANTHOLOGY OF LITERATURE BY WOMEN
edited by Sandra M. Gilbert and Susan Gubar

THE NORTON ANTHOLOGY OF MODERN AND CONTEMPORARY POETRY
edited by Jahan Ramazani, Richard Ellmann, and Robert O'Clair

THE NORTON ANTHOLOGY OF POETRY
edited by Margaret Ferguson, Mary Jo Salter, and Jon Stallworthy

THE NORTON ANTHOLOGY OF SHORT FICTION
edited by R. V. Cassill and Richard Bausch

THE NORTON ANTHOLOGY OF THEORY AND CRITICISM
edited by Vincent B. Leitch et al.

THE NORTON ANTHOLOGY OF WORLD LITERATURE
edited by Sarah Lawall et al.

THE NORTON FACSIMILE OF THE FIRST FOLIO OF SHAKESPEARE
prepared by Charlton Hinman

THE NORTON INTRODUCTION TO LITERATURE
edited by Alison Booth, J. Paul Hunter, and Kelly J. Mays

THE NORTON INTRODUCTION TO THE SHORT NOVEL
edited by Jerome Beaty

THE NORTON READER
edited by Linda H. Peterson and John C. Brereton

THE NORTON SAMPLER
edited by Thomas Cooley

THE NORTON SHAKESPEARE, BASED ON THE OXFORD EDITION
edited by Stephen Greenblatt et al.

For a complete list of Norton Critical Editions, visit
www.wwnorton.com/college/english/nce_home.htm

A NORTON CRITICAL EDITION

Gertrude Stein

THREE LIVES *and* Q.E.D.

AUTHORITATIVE TEXTS

CONTEXTS

CRITICISM

Edited by

MARIANNE DeKOVEN
RUTGERS UNIVERSITY

W. W. NORTON & COMPANY   *New York • London*

W. W. Norton & Company has been independent since its founding in 1923, when William Warder Norton and Mary D. Herter Norton first published lectures delivered at the People's Institute, the adult education division of New York City's Cooper Union. The Nortons soon expanded their program beyond the Institute, publishing books by celebrated academics from America and abroad. By mid-century, the two major pillars of Norton's publishing program—trade books and college texts—were firmly established. In the 1950s, the Norton family transferred control of the company to its employees, and today—with a staff of four hundred and a comparable number of trade, college, and professional titles published each year—W. W. Norton & Company stands as the largest and oldest publishing house owned wholly by its employees.

Copyright © 2006 by W. W. Norton & Company, Inc.

All rights reserved.
Printed in the United States of America.
First Edition.

Three Lives by Gertrude Stein is reprinted by permission of Peter Owen Publishers.

Q.E.D. by Gertrude Stein is from *Fernhurst, Q.E.D., and Other Early Writings.* Copyright © 1950 by Alice B. Toklas. Copyright © 1971 by Daniel C. Joseph, Administrator of the Estate of Gertrude Stein. Reprinted with the permission of Liveright Publishing Corporation, New York. All rights reserved.

Every effort has been made to contact the copyright holders of each of the selections. Rights holders of any selections not credited should contact W. W. Norton & Company, Inc., 500 Fifth Avenue, New York, N.Y. 10110 for a correction to be made in the next printing of our work.

The text of this book is composed in Fairfield Medium with the display set in Bernhard Modern.
Composition by Binghamton Valley Composition.
Manufacturing by the Maple-Vail Book Group, Binghamton.
Production manager: Benjamin Reynolds.

Library of Congress Cataloging-in-Publication Data

Stein, Gertrude, 1874–1946.
Three lives; and, Q.E.D.: authoritative texts, contexts, criticism /
Gertrude Stein; edited by Marianne DeKoven.
p. cm. — (A Norton critical edition)
Includes bibliographical references.

ISBN 0-393-97903-2 (pbk.)

1. Working class women—Fiction.   2. Stein, Gertrude, 1874–1946.
Three lives.   3. Working class women in literature.   I. DeKoven, Marianne, 1948–
II. Stein, Gertrude, 1874–1946. Q.E.D.   III. Title: Q.E.D.   IV. Title.   V. Series.
PS3537.T323T5 2005
813'.52—dc22   2005053924

W. W. Norton & Company, Inc., 500 Fifth Avenue,
New York, N.Y. 10110-0017
www.wwnorton.com

W. W. Norton & Company Ltd., Castle House,
75/76 Wells Street, London W1T 3QT

1 2 3 4 5 6 7 8 9 0

Contents

Preface

Gertrude Stein was one of the most prolific, important, and influential writers of the twentieth century. She published twenty-five books, approximately half of her body of work, during her lifetime; the other half was published after her death in 1946. She was at the center of several overlapping Parisian modernist and avant-garde movements of the first half of the twentieth century. Although she was not publically known as a lesbian—the social censure and opprobrium attached to homosexuality of that era made that impossible—she and her lifelong partner, Alice B. Toklas, were part of the loose network of lesbian writers and artists who lived on the Left Bank of Paris, in the free, tolerant avant-garde culture to which expatriate Americans fled, escaping both racial and sexual bigotry at home.

Gertrude and her older brother Leo Stein, with whom she expatriated to Paris in 1903, were among the earliest collectors of then-unknown painters such as Henri Matisse and Pablo Picasso and many others central to modernist art. Stein's collection of modernist painting, crowding the walls of her studio (where she wrote, longhand in French children's school notebooks, all night, often until dawn) at her Paris home, 27 rue de Fleurus, was an internationally-known mecca for those who wanted to see modernist painting. In the first decades of the century, modern art was not yet available either in museums or in reproduction; Stein's salon was one of the few places where a significant collection could be seen. News of Stein's collection traveled by word of mouth; people came from all over the world to see it at specific viewing times established by Stein. She and Picasso were at the center of the bohemian Paris she describes in vivid, humorous detail in *The Autobiography of Alice B. Toklas* (published in 1932). This book gave her the broader readership and reputation as a distinguished writer for which she had been longing since she began her career in 1903.

Stein was also at the center of the post–World War I scene of young American expatriate modernists, most notably Ernest Hemingway, F. Scott Fitzgerald, Sherwood Anderson, and Thornton Wilder, all of whom acknowledged her influence and importance. Hemingway credited Stein with the epigraph to his 1926 novel *The Sun Also Rises;* "You are all a lost generation" subsequently became one of the best-known characterizations of the era. (Several of Stein's sayings, in addition to "lost generation," have become staples of our culture—most notably, "there is no there there," which she said of her childhood home, Oakland, California, in *Everybody's Autobiography* (1937); and from "Sacred Emily" (1913), "Rose is a rose is a rose is a rose," which is usually quoted as "A rose is a rose is a rose is a rose.")

Nonetheless, despite her visibility, centrality, and enormous productivity, Stein remained an obscure writer, known more for her interesting life, her art collection, and her connections to other writers and artists than for her own work until various critical movements of the last decades of the twentieth century inspired a new, productive interest in her writing. The renaissance of the avant-gardes in the 1960s kindled an interest in Stein among both writers and critics. The structuralist, poststructuralist, and feminist movements in criticism and literary theory of the 1970s and 1980s inspired a flowering interest in Gertrude Stein, bringing to critical attention many of her most experimental, least conventionally accessible works. These include great works such as *Tender Buttons* (1914), *Four Saints in Three Acts* (1928), and *The Geographical History of America* (1935), and more obscure works such as the highly experimental, politically/ sexually significant long poems "Patriarchal Poetry" (1953) and "Lifting Belly" (unpublished until 1989)—works that had previously been almost entirely ignored. Starting in the late 1980s, and continuing until the present, critical discourses focusing on race, ethnicity and religion, gender and sexuality, and nation and location have produced a substantial body of work on Stein, particularly on *Three Lives* (1909). The chronological ordering of the excerpts and essays in the Criticism section intends both to reveal the historical progression of critical preoccupations, from biography and form, to gender and sexuality, to race, ethnicity, religion and class, and to give a sense of the ongoing dialogue within Stein criticism that addresses all these issues with varying emphasis.

Three Lives was Stein's first experimental work. Its three stories were not published in the order in which they were written: "The Good Anna" was written first, but "Melanctha" was actually written last, after "The Gentle Lena." Stein's departure from literary convention increases as she writes these three tales. "The Good Anna" is the most conventionally written; "Melanctha" is the most experimental, with its extended repetitions, its mysteriously emblematic, reduced vocabulary, and its intense focus on consciousness at the expense of plot. Much of the criticism included in this volume addresses the issues raised by Stein's style in *Three Lives*, particularly in "Melanctha."

"Melanctha" was an adaptation of an earlier novel, *Q.E.D.*

(1903; published in 1950 as *Things As They Are*), also included in this volume. Because of its overt, realistic, autobiographical lesbian content, *Q.E.D.* was not published until four years after Stein's death. Stein had in fact concealed the existence of *Q.E.D.*, presumably not wanting Alice B. Toklas to read it because it narrates Stein's earlier lesbian affair. Jefferson Campbell in "Melanctha" is a transformation of the character Adele, the stand-in for Gertrude Stein in *Q.E.D.*—many of his thoughts and significant portions of his dialogue are adapted directly from Adele's, and are quite recognizable. Adele, based closely on Stein's background and experiences— she is an upper-middle-class, Jewish lesbian and former medical student—becomes Jefferson Campbell, a middle-class, Christian, heterosexual, black doctor whose practice is among working-class black people. The character of Melanctha is based on May Bookstaver, the woman with whom Stein had a difficult and failed affair in Baltimore, where Stein attended the Johns Hopkins Medical School before moving to Paris. (Bookstaver was more committed to another woman, Mabel Haynes, who is Mabel Neathe in *Q.E.D.*, than to Stein. *Q.E.D.* narrates this triangle, its title an ironic reference to the closure of a geometric proof.)

The transformation of the upper-middle-class, white, lesbian women of *Q.E.D.*—women of Stein's own social-sexual milieu—into working-class and middle-class black (overtly) heterosexual characters in "Melanctha" is the subject of much of the criticism included in this volume. The other two stories of *Three Lives* focus on German Catholic, immigrant, working-class women. Issues of class, ethnicity, and immigration to America, as well as of race, gender, sexuality, and religion, are raised with increasing emphasis in criticism of *Three Lives*. Much of this criticism attempts to connect these issues to the formal experimentation that, along with the painfully blatant racism of "Melanctha" (both used and undercut by Stein, as are the ethnic and class stereotypes of the other two stories), constitute the most challenging features of *Three Lives*. Both this formal difficulty and this racism have made, and continue to make, *Three Lives* controversial. In this volume, I have attempted to represent the broad range of critical responses to these controversies, in the belief that it is better to address directly the challenges these works present than to turn away from them.

Stein composed *Three Lives*, as she explains and as many critics discuss, after beginning a translation of Gustave Flaubert's story "*Un coeur simple*," or "A Simple Heart," one of his *Trois contes*, or *Three Tales*. "A Simple Heart" has a servant as its protagonist. "The Good Anna" is clearly indebted to this story, but goes well beyond it in its refusal of sentimentality and literariness, as the differences in title alone make clear: "a simple heart" conjures a broad spectrum of moral sentiment, while the "good" in "The Good Anna" is highly ironic. The protagonist of "The Good Anna" is based on Lena Lebender, Stein's servant in Baltimore, from whom "The Gentle Lena" gets her name. Miss Mathilda, Anna's primary employer, is based on Stein herself. "Bridgepoint," the setting of all three stories, is a fictionalized version of Baltimore. Stein lived in a racially mixed neighborhood of Baltimore, and she met black patients at the hospital where she worked as a medical student.

Stein also acknowledges the influence of Paul Cézanne and Pablo Picasso on *Three Lives*. She sat under a Cézanne portrait of his wife, and also sat for Picasso's famous portrait of herself, a breakthrough work for Picasso into cubism—walking back and forth daily the long distance between the rue de Fleurus and Picasso's Montmartre studio—while she wrote these stories. In *The Autobiography of Alice B. Toklas*, Stein says that the ordinary Parisian lives she observed during these walks also influenced her writing of *Three Lives*. Portraits—inner consciousness in relation to the outer manifestations of individual lives—were central to Stein's work throughout her career. The radically new forms Cézanne and Picasso invented in painting also parallel the radically new forms Stein invented in writing, as many critics included in this volume discuss.

Stein attended the Johns Hopkins Medical School because she had been encouraged to do so by her teacher and mentor at Harvard, William James. He thought she would follow him and become a psychologist; in order to do that, as the profession was constituted at that time, she needed a medical education. She had been one of James's star pupils and she did brilliantly (though unevenly) at Hopkins as well, until, for various reasons, including the hostility toward women of several of the faculty members, her depression over the failure of her affair with May Bookstaver, and the waning of her own interest in the field, she dropped out of Hopkins only one course credit short of a medical degree. William James's influence on Stein, especially in his theories of time and consciousness, was crucial, and is apparent in *Three Lives*, as several critics included herein discuss.

Stein could not find a publisher for *Three Lives*, as she explains humorously in *The Autobiography of Alice B. Toklas*. She finally published it at her own expense with the Grafton Press in 1909. This press, unaware that Stein was American, and making assumptions based on her Parisian residence, sent a representative to Stein's home to ask whether she might need some help with her English. Since that time, *Three Lives* has become one of the most important works of literary modernism in any language.

Acknowledgments

I would like to express my enormous gratitude to Carol Bemis, Editor of Norton Critical Editions, for her remarkable patience, support, and helpfulness during the long process of gestation for this Norton Critical Edition. She is truly a remarkable and exceptional editor, as is Brian Baker, Assistant Editor of the series, whose unstintingly generous, thoughtful, and intelligent help with all the details and questions involved in the preparation of the manuscript has been invaluable. This edition could not have come into material existence without the invaluable help of my Research Assistant, Kelly Josephs.

Barry Qualls, currently Associate Dean for the Humanities of the Faculty of Arts and Sciences at Rutgers–New Brunswick, and formerly Chair of the English Department, helps me in every possible way. The Rutgers University English Department, particularly former Chair Cheryl Wall and current Chair Richard Miller, as well as the community of feminist scholars at Rutgers University, have also provided crucial material, intellectual, and moral support. First and last, I must thank my family, Julien, Maggie, Dan, and Phoebe Hennefeld, and my mother, Annabel DeKoven, for their love and support, the sine qua non of whatever I do.

The Texts of
THREE LIVES and *Q.E.D.*

A Note on the Texts

The text of *Three Lives* is the 1909 Grafton Press edition.
The text of *Q.E.D.* is the 1973 Liveright edition.

THREE LIVES[1]

STORIES OF THE GOOD ANNA,
MELANCTHA AND THE GENTLE LENA

---

1. Title is derived from Gustave Flaubert's *Trois Contes* (1877), or *Three Stories*, translated into English as *Three Tales*, the first story of which, *"Un Coeur simple"* ("A Simple Heart"), Stein was translating when she began writing "The Good Anna."

Donc je suis un malheureux et ce
n'est ni ma faute ni celle de la vie.
JULES LAFORGUE[2]

---

2. "So I am an unhappy person and this is neither my fault nor life's." This "quotation" from French Symbolist poet Jules Laforgue (1860–1887) may have been invented by Stein—it has not been found anywhere in Laforgue's work (see Carl Wood, "Continuity of Romantic Irony," in "Criticism," page 302).

CONTENTS

The Good Anna

Part I

THE tradesmen of Bridgepoint[3] learned to dread the sound of "Miss Mathilda", for with that name the good Anna always conquered.[4]

The strictest of the one price stores[5] found that they could give things for a little less, when the good Anna had fully said that "Miss Mathilda" could not pay so much and that she could buy it cheaper "by Lindheims."

Lindheims was Anna's favorite store, for there they had bargain days, when flour and sugar were sold for a quarter of a cent less for a pound, and there the heads of the departments were all her friends and always managed to give her the bargain prices, even on other days.

Anna led an arduous and troubled life.

Anna managed the whole little house for Miss Mathilda. It was a funny little house, one of a whole row of all the same kind that made a close pile like a row of dominoes that a child knocks over, for they were built along a street which at this point came down a steep hill. They were funny little houses, two stories high, with red brick fronts and long white steps.[6]

This one little house was always very full with Miss Mathilda, an under servant, stray dogs and cats and Anna's voice that scolded, managed, grumbled all day long.

"Sallie! can't I leave you alone a minute but you must run to the door to see the butcher boy come down the street and there is Miss Mathilda calling for her shoes. Can I do everything while you go around always thinking about nothing at all? If I ain't after you every minute you would be forgetting all the time, and I take all this pains, and when you come to me you was as ragged as a buzzard and as dirty as a dog. Go and find Miss Mathilda her shoes where you put them this morning."

3. "Bridgepoint" is based on Baltimore, Maryland, where Stein lived when she was a student at the Johns Hopkins Medical School from 1897 to 1901.
4. The character of Anna Federner is based on Stein's servant in Baltimore, Lena Lebender; Miss Mathilda is based on Stein herself.
5. Stores at which prices were fixed rather than subject to bargaining or haggling.
6. Based on Stein's house in Baltimore.

"Peter!",—her voice rose higher,—"Peter!",—Peter was the youngest and the favorite dog,—"Peter, if you don't leave Baby alone,"—Baby was an old, blind terrier that Anna had loved for many years,—"Peter if you don't leave Baby alone, I take a rawhide to you, you bad dog."

The good Anna had high ideals for canine chastity and discipline. The three regular dogs, the three that always lived with Anna, Peter and old Baby, and the fluffy little Rags, who was always jumping up into the air just to show that he was happy, together with the transients, the many stray ones that Anna always kept until she found them homes, were all under strict orders never to be bad one with the other.

A sad disgrace did once happen in the family. A little transient terrier for whom Anna had found a home suddenly produced a crop of pups. The new owners were certain that this Foxy had known no dog since she was in their care. The good Anna held to it stoutly that her Peter and her Rags were guiltless, and she made her statement with so much heat that Foxy's owners were at last convinced that these results were due to their neglect.

"You bad dog," Anna said to Peter that night, "you bad dog."

"Peter was the father of those pups," the good Anna explained to Miss Mathilda, "and they look just like him too, and poor little Foxy, they were so big that she could hardly have them, but Miss Mathilda, I would never let those people know that Peter was so bad."

Periods of evil thinking came very regularly to Peter and to Rags and to the visitors within their gates. At such times Anna would be very busy and scold hard, and then too she always took great care to seclude the bad dogs from each other whenever she had to leave the house. Sometimes just to see how good it was that she had made them, Anna would leave the room a little while and leave them all together, and then she would suddenly come back. Back would slink all the wicked-minded dogs at the sound of her hand upon the knob, and then they would sit desolate in their corners like a lot of disappointed children whose stolen sugar has been taken from them.

Innocent blind old Baby was the only one who preserved the dignity becoming in a dog.

You see that Anna led an arduous and troubled life.[7]

The good Anna was a small, spare, german[8] woman, at this time about forty years of age. Her face was worn, her cheeks were thin,

---

7. This repeated motif signals a key element not just of Anna's life but of the lives of the female protagonists of all three stories.
8. Stein frequently uses the lower case for nationality and ethnicity, signifying that it has no more weight or significance than other personal characteristics; here, "german" has the same descriptive status as "small" and "spare."

her mouth drawn and firm, and her light blue eyes were very bright. Sometimes they were full of lightning and sometimes full of humor, but they were always sharp and clear.

Her voice was a pleasant one, when she told the histories of bad Peter and of Baby and of little Rags. Her voice was a high and piercing one when she called to the teamsters[9] and to the other wicked men, what she wanted that should come to them, when she saw them beat a horse or kick a dog. She did not belong to any society that could stop them and she told them so most frankly, but her strained voice and her glittering eyes, and her queer piercing german english first made them afraid and then ashamed. They all knew too, that all the policemen on the beat were her friends. These always respected and obeyed Miss Annie[1] as they called her, and promptly attended to all of her complaints.

For five years Anna managed the little house for Miss Mathilda. In these five years there were four different under servants.

The one that came first was a pretty, cheerful irish girl. Anna took her with a doubting mind. Lizzie was an obedient, happy servant, and Anna began to have a little faith. This was not for long. The pretty, cheerful Lizzie disappeared one day without her notice[2] and with all her baggage and returned no more.

This pretty, cheerful Lizzie was succeeded by a melancholy Molly.

Molly was born in America, of german parents. All her people had been long dead or gone away. Molly had always been alone. She was a tall, dark, sallow, thin-haired creature, and she was always troubled with a cough; and she had a bad temper, and always said ugly dreadful swear words.

Anna found all this very hard to bear, but she kept Molly a long time out of kindness. The kitchen was constantly a battle-ground. Anna scolded and Molly swore strange oaths, and then Miss Mathilda would shut her door hard to show that she could hear it all.

At last Anna had to give it up. "Please Miss Mathilda won't you speak to Molly," Anna said, "I can't do a thing with her. I scold her, and she don't seem to hear and then she swears so that she scares me. She loves you Miss Mathilda, and you scold her please once."

"But Anna," cried poor Miss Mathilda, "I don't want to," and that large, cheerful, but faint hearted woman looked all aghast at such a prospect. "But you must, please Miss Mathilda!" Anna said.

Miss Mathilda never wanted to do any scolding. "But you must please Miss Mathilda," Anna said.

9. Drivers of vehicles burdened with goods, pulled by teams of horses or other animals. The Teamsters Union, based on this kind of labor, still represents commercial drivers.
1. Americanized version of Anna; Stein is pointing to the assimilation of immigrants.
2. Warning of intention to quit, generally given some weeks in advance.

Miss Mathilda every day put off the scolding, hoping always that Anna would learn to manage Molly better. It never did get better and at last Miss Mathilda saw that the scolding simply had to be.

It was agreed between the good Anna and her Miss Mathilda that Anna should be away when Molly would be scolded. The next evening that it was Anna's evening out, Miss Mathilda faced her task and went down into the kitchen.

Molly was sitting in the little kitchen leaning her elbows on the table. She was a tall, thin, sallow girl, aged twenty-three, by nature slatternly and careless but trained by Anna into superficial neatness. Her drab striped cotton dress and gray black checked apron increased the length and sadness of her melancholy figure. "Oh, Lord!" groaned Miss Mathilda to herself as she approached her.

"Molly, I want to speak to you about your behaviour to Anna!", here Molly dropped her head still lower on her arms and began to cry.

"Oh! Oh!" groaned Miss Mathilda.

"It's all Miss Annie's fault, all of it," Molly said at last, in a trembling voice, "I do my best."

"I know Anna is often hard to please," began Miss Mathilda, with a twinge of mischief, and then she sobered herself to her task, "but you must remember, Molly, she means it for your good and she is really very kind to you."

"I don't want her kindness," Molly cried, "I wish you would tell me what to do, Miss Mathilda, and then I would be all right. I hate Miss Annie."

"This will never do Molly," Miss Mathilda said sternly, in her deepest, firmest tones, "Anna is the head of the kitchen and you must either obey her or leave."

"I don't want to leave you," whimpered melancholy Molly. "Well Molly then try and do better," answered Miss Mathilda, keeping a good stern front, and backing quickly from the kitchen.

"Oh! Oh!" groaned Miss Mathilda, as she went back up the stairs.

Miss Mathilda's attempt to make peace between the constantly contending women in the kitchen had no real effect. They were very soon as bitter as before.

At last it was decided that Molly was to go away. Molly went away to work in a factory in the town, and she went to live with an old woman in the slums, a very bad old woman Anna said.

Anna was never easy in her mind about the fate of Molly. Sometimes she would see or hear of her. Molly was not well, her cough was worse, and the old woman really was a bad one.

After a year of this unwholesome life, Molly was completely broken down. Anna then again took her in charge. She brought her from her work and from the woman where she lived, and put her in a hospital to stay till she was well. She found a place for her as nurse-maid to a little girl out in the country, and Molly was at last established and content.

Molly had had, at first, no regular successor. In a few months it was going to be the summer and Miss Mathilda would be gone away, and old Katy would do very well to come in every day and help Anna with her work.

Old Katy was a heavy, ugly, short and rough old german woman, with a strange distorted german-english all her own. Anna was worn out now with her attempt to make the younger generation do all that it should and rough old Katy never answered back, and never wanted her own way. No scolding or abuse could make its mark on her uncouth and aged peasant hide. She said her "Yes, Miss Annie," when an answer had to come, and that was always all that she could say.

"Old Katy is just a rough old woman, Miss Mathilda," Anna said, "but I think I keep her here with me. She can work and she don't give me trouble like I had with Molly all the time."

Anna always had a humorous sense from this old Katy's twisted peasant english, from the roughness on her tongue of buzzing s's and from the queer ways of her brutish servile humor. Anna could not let old Katy serve at table—old Katy was too coarsely made from natural earth for that—and so Anna had all this to do herself and that she never liked, but even then this simple rough old creature was pleasanter to her than any of the upstart young.

Life went on very smoothly now in these few months before the summer came. Miss Mathilda every summer went away across the ocean to be gone for several months. When she went away this summer old Katy was so sorry, and on the day that Miss Mathilda went, old Katy cried hard for many hours. An earthy, uncouth, servile peasant creature old Katy surely was. She stood there on the white stone steps of the little red brick house, with her bony, square dull head with its thin, tanned, toughened skin and its sparse and kinky grizzled hair, and her strong, squat figure a little overmade on the right side, clothed in her blue striped cotton dress, all clean and always washed but rough and harsh to see—and she stayed there on the steps till Anna brought her in, blubbering, her apron to her face, and making queer guttural broken moans.

When Miss Mathilda early in the fall came to her house again old Katy was not there.

"I never thought old Katy would act so Miss Mathilda," Anna said, "when she was so sorry when you went away, and I gave her full wages all the summer, but they are all alike Miss Mathilda, there isn't one of them that's fit to trust. You know how Katy said she liked you, Miss Mathilda, and went on about it when you went away and then she was so good and worked all right until the middle of the summer, when I got sick, and then she went away and left me all alone and took a place out in the country, where they gave her some more money. She didn't say a word, Miss Mathilda, she just went off and left me there alone when I was sick after that awful hot summer that we had, and after all we done for her when she had no place to go, and all summer I gave her better things to eat than I had for myself. Miss Mathilda, there isn't one of them has any sense of what's the right way for a girl to do, not one of them."

Old Katy was never heard from any more.

No under servant was decided upon now for several months. Many came and many went, and none of them would do. At last Anna heard of Sallie.

Sallie was the oldest girl in a family of eleven and Sallie was just sixteen years old. From Sallie down they came always littler and littler in her family, and all of them were always out at work excepting only the few littlest of them all.

Sallie was a pretty blonde and smiling german girl, and stupid and a little silly. The littler they came in her family the brighter they all were. The brightest of them all was a little girl of ten. She did a good day's work washing dishes for a man and wife in a saloon, and she earned a fair day's wage, and then there was one littler still. She only worked for half the day. She did the house work for a bachelor doctor. She did it all, all of the housework and received each week her eight cents for her wage. Anna was always indignant when she told that story.

"I think he ought to give her ten cents Miss Mathilda any way. Eight cents is so mean when she does all his work and she is such a bright little thing too, not stupid like our Sallie. Sallie would never learn to do a thing if I didn't scold her all the time, but Sallie is a good girl, and I take care and she will do all right."

Sallie was a good, obedient german child. She never answered Anna back, no more did Peter, old Baby and little Rags and so though always Anna's voice was sharply raised in strong rebuke and worn expostulation, they were a happy family all there together in the kitchen.

Anna was a mother now to Sallie, a good incessant german mother who watched and scolded hard to keep the girl from any evil step. Sallie's temptations and transgressions were much like those of naughty Peter and jolly little Rags, and Anna took the same way to keep all three from doing what was bad.

Sallie's chief badness besides forgetting all the time and never washing her hands clean to serve at table, was the butcher boy.

He was an unattractive youth enough, that butcher boy. Suspicion began to close in around Sallie that she spent the evenings when Anna was away, in company with this bad boy.

"Sallie is such a pretty girl, Miss Mathilda," Anna said, "and she is so dumb and silly, and she puts on that red waist,[3] and she crinkles up her hair with irons[4] so I have to laugh, and then I tell her if she only washed her hands clean it would be better than all that fixing all the time, but you can't do a thing with the young girls nowadays Miss Mathilda. Sallie is a good girl but I got to watch her all the time."

Suspicion closed in around Sallie more and more, that she spent Anna's evenings out with this boy sitting in the kitchen. One early morning Anna's voice was sharply raised.

"Sallie this ain't the same banana that I brought home yesterday, for Miss Mathilda, for her breakfast, and you was out early in the street this morning, what was you doing there?"

"Nothing, Miss Annie, I just went out to see, that's all and that's the same banana, 'deed[5] it is Miss Annie."

"Sallie, how can you say so and after all I do for you, and Miss Mathilda is so good to you. I never brought home no bananas yesterday with specks on it like that. I know better, it was that boy was here last night and ate it while I was away, and you was out to get another this morning. I don't want no lying Sallie."

Sallie was stout in her defence but then she gave it up and she said it was the boy who snatched it as he ran away at the sound of Anna's key opening the outside door. "But I will never let him in again, Miss Annie, 'deed I won't," said Sallie.

And now it was all peaceful for some weeks and then Sallie with fatuous simplicity began on certain evenings to resume her bright red waist, her bits of jewels and her crinkly hair.

One pleasant evening in the early spring, Miss Mathilda was standing on the steps beside the open door, feeling cheerful in the pleasant, gentle night. Anna came down the street, returning from her evening out. "Don't shut the door, please, Miss Mathilda," Anna said in a low voice, "I don't want Sallie to know I'm home."

Anna went softly through the house and reached the kitchen door. At the sound of her hand upon the knob there was a wild scramble and a bang, and then Sallie sitting there alone when Anna came into the room, but, alas, the butcher boy forgot his overcoat in his escape.

You see that Anna led an arduous and troubled life.

Anna had her troubles, too, with Miss Mathilda. "And I slave and slave to save the money and you go out and spend it all on foolish-

3. Blouse or shirt; red hints at immodesty.
4. Curling irons.
5. Indeed.

ness," the good Anna would complain when her mistress, a large and careless woman, would come home with a bit of porcelain, a new etching and sometimes even an oil painting on her arm.[6]

"But Anna," argued Miss Mathilda, "if you didn't save this money, don't you see I could not buy these things," and then Anna would soften and look pleased until she learned the price, and then wringing her hands, "Oh, Miss Mathilda, Miss Mathilda," she would cry, "and you gave all that money out for that, when you need a dress to go out in so bad."[7] "Well, perhaps I will get one for myself next year, Anna," Miss Mathilda would cheerfully concede. "If we live till then Miss Mathilda, I see that you do," Anna would then answer darkly.

Anna had great pride in the knowledge and possessions of her cherished Miss Mathilda, but she did not like her careless way of wearing always her old clothes. "You can't go out to dinner in that dress, Miss Mathilda," she would say, standing firmly before the outside door, "You got to go and put on your new dress you always look so nice in." "But Anna, there isn't time." "Yes there is, I go up and help you fix it, please Miss Mathilda you can't go out to dinner in that dress and next year if we live till then, I make you get a new hat, too. It's a shame Miss Mathilda to go out like that."

The poor mistress sighed and had to yield. It suited her cheerful, lazy temper to be always without care but sometimes it was a burden to endure, for so often she had it all to do again unless she made a rapid dash out of the door before Anna had a chance to see.

Life was very easy always for this large and lazy Miss Mathilda, with the good Anna to watch and care for her and all her clothes and goods. But, alas, this world of ours is after all much what it should be[8] and cheerful Miss Mathilda had her troubles too with Anna.

It was pleasant that everything for one was done, but annoying often that what one wanted most just then, one could not have when one had foolishly demanded and not suggested one's desire. And then Miss Mathilda loved to go out on joyous, country tramps when, stretching free and far with cheerful comrades, over rolling hills and cornfields, glorious in the setting sun, and dogwood white and shining underneath the moon and clear stars over head, and brilliant air and tingling blood, it was hard to have to think of Anna's anger at the late return, though Miss Mathilda had begged that there might be no hot supper cooked that night. And then when all the happy crew of Miss Mathilda and her friends, tired with fullness of good health and burning winds and glowing sunshine in the eyes, stiffened

6. Stein was an avid art collector.
7. Stein dressed only for comfort, not for fashion.
8. This statement, like many others throughout *Three Lives*, is ironic; the narrator means exactly the opposite of what she says here.

and justly worn and wholly ripe for pleasant food and gentle content[9] were all come together to the little house—it was hard for all that tired crew who loved the good things Anna made to eat, to come to the closed door and wonder there if it was Anna's evening in or out, and then the others must wait shivering on their tired feet, while Miss Mathilda softened Anna's heart, or if Anna was well out, boldly ordered youthful Sallie to feed all the hungry lot.

Such things were sometimes hard to bear and often grievously did Miss Mathilda feel herself a rebel with the cheerful Lizzies, the melancholy Mollies, the rough old Katies and the stupid Sallies.

Miss Mathilda had other troubles too, with the good Anna. Miss Mathilda had to save her Anna from the many friends, who in the kindly fashion of the poor, used up her savings and then gave her promises in place of payments.

The good Anna had many curious friends that she had found in the twenty years that she had lived in Bridgepoint, and Miss Mathilda would often have to save her from them all.

Part II

THE LIFE OF THE GOOD ANNA

ANNA FEDERNER, this good Anna, was of solid lower middle-class south german stock.

When she was seventeen years old she went to service[1] in a bourgeois family, in the large city near her native town, but she did not stay there long. One day her mistress offered her maid—that was Anna—to a friend, to see her home. Anna felt herself to be a servant, not a maid, and so she promptly left the place.[2]

Anna had always a firm old world sense of what was the right way for a girl to do.

No argument could bring her to sit an evening in the empty parlour, although the smell of paint when they were fixing up the kitchen made her very sick, and tired as she always was, she never would sit down during the long talks she held with Miss Mathilda. A girl was a girl and should act always like a girl, both as to giving all respect and as to what she had to eat.

A little time after she left this service, Anna and her mother made the voyage to America. They came second-class, but it was for them a long and dreary journey. The mother was already ill with consumption.

---

9. Contentment.
1. Became a servant.
2. A "maid" is a lady's maid, who waits on her mistress personally; a "servant" takes care of the house. A maid is above a servant in the household hierarchy.

They landed in a pleasant town in the far South and there the mother slowly died.

Anna was now alone and she made her way to Bridgepoint where an older half brother was already settled. This brother was a heavy, lumbering, good natured german man, full of the infirmity that comes of excess of body.

He was a baker and married and fairly well to do.

Anna liked her brother well enough but was never in any way dependent on him.

When she arrived in Bridgepoint, she took service with Miss Mary Wadsmith.

Miss Mary Wadsmith was a large, fair, helpless woman, burdened with the care of two young children. They had been left her by her brother and his wife who had died within a few months of each other.

Anna soon had the household altogether in her charge.

Anna found her place with large, abundant women, for such were always lazy, careless or all helpless, and so the burden of their lives could fall on Anna, and give her just content.[3] Anna's superiors must be always these large helpless women, or be men, for none others could give themselves to be made so comfortable and free.

Anna had no strong natural feeling to love children, as she had to love cats and dogs, and a large mistress. She never became deeply fond of Edgar and Jane Wadsmith. She naturally preferred the boy, for boys love always better to be done for and made comfortable and full of eating while in the little girl she had to meet the feminine, the subtle opposition, showing so early always in a young girl's nature.[4]

For the summer, the Wadsmiths had a pleasant house out in the country, and the winter months they spent in hotel apartments in the city.

Gradually it came to Anna to take the whole direction of their movements, to make all the decisions as to their journeyings to and fro, and for, the arranging of the places where they were to live.

Anna had been with Miss Mary for three years, when little Jane began to raise her strength in opposition. Jane was a neat, pleasant little girl, pretty and sweet with a young girl's charm, and with two blonde braids carefully plaited down her back.

Miss Mary, like her Anna, had no strong natural feeling to love children, but she was fond of these two young ones of her blood, and yielded docilely to the stronger power in the really pleasing little girl. Anna always preferred the rougher handling of the boy, while Miss

3. Well-earned contentment.
4. At this period of her intellectual development, Stein subscribed to these gender stereotypes.

Mary found the gentle force and the sweet domination of the girl to please her better.

In a spring when all the preparations for the moving had been made, Miss Mary and Jane went together to the country home, and Anna, after finishing up the city matters was to follow them in a few days with Edgar, whose vacation had not yet begun.

Many times during the preparations for this summer, Jane had met Anna with sharp resistance, in opposition to her ways. It was simple for little Jane to give unpleasant orders, not from herself but from Miss Mary, large, docile, helpless Miss Mary Wadsmith who could never think out any orders to give Anna from herself.

Anna's eyes grew slowly sharper, harder, and her lower teeth thrust a little forward and pressing strongly up, framed always more slowly the "Yes, Miss Jane," to the quick, "Oh Anna! Miss Mary says she wants you to do it so!"

On the day of their migration, Miss Mary had been already put into the carriage. "Oh, Anna!" cried little Jane running back into the house, "Miss Mary says that you are to bring along the blue dressings[5] out of her room and mine." Anna's body stiffened, "We never use them in the summer, Miss Jane," she said thickly. "Yes Anna, but Miss Mary thinks it would be nice, and she told me to tell you not to forget, good-by!" and the little girl skipped lightly down the steps into the carriage and they drove away.

Anna stood still on the steps, her eyes hard and sharp and shining, and her body and her face stiff with resentment. And then she went into the house, giving the door a shattering slam.

Anna was very hard to live with in those next three days. Even Baby, the new puppy, the pride of Anna's heart, a present from her friend the widow, Mrs. Lehntman—even this pretty little black and tan felt the heat of Anna's scorching flame. And Edgar, who had looked forward to these days, to be for him filled full of freedom and of things to eat—he could not rest a moment in Anna's bitter sight.

On the third day, Anna and Edgar went to the Wadsmith country home. The blue dressings out of the two rooms remained behind.

All the way, Edgar sat in front with the colored man and drove. It was an early spring day in the South. The fields and woods were heavy from the soaking rains. The horses dragged the carriage slowly over the long road, sticky with brown clay and rough with masses of stones thrown here and there to be broken and trodden into place by passing teams. Over and through the soaking earth was the feathery new spring growth of little flowers, of young leaves and of ferns. The tree tops were all bright with reds and yellows, with brilliant

5. Elaborate cloth bedroom ornamentation, often used for windows ("window-dressing").

gleaming whites and gorgeous greens. All the lower air was full of the damp haze rising from heavy soaking water on the earth, mingled with a warm and pleasant smell from the blue smoke of the spring fires in all the open fields. And above all this was the clear, upper air, and the songs of birds and the joy of sunshine and of lengthening days.

The languor and the stir, the warmth and weight and the strong feel of life from the deep centres of the earth that comes always with the early, soaking spring, when it is not answered with an active fervent joy, gives always anger, irritation and unrest.

To Anna alone there in the carriage, drawing always nearer to the struggle with her mistress, the warmth, the slowness, the jolting over stones, the steaming from the horses, the cries of men and animals and birds, and the new life all round about were simply maddening. "Baby! if you don't lie still, I think I kill you. I can't stand it any more like this."

At this time Anna, about twenty-seven years of age, was not yet all thin and worn. The sharp bony edges and corners of her head and face were still rounded out with flesh, but ready the temper and the humor showed sharply in her clean blue eyes, and the thinning was begun about the lower jaw, that was so often strained with the upward pressure of resolve.

To-day, alone there in the carriage, she was all stiff and yet all trembling with the sore effort of decision and revolt.

As the carriage turned into the Wadsmith gate, little Jane ran out to see. She just looked at Anna's face; she did not say a word about blue dressings.

Anna got down from the carriage with little Baby in her arms. She took out all the goods that she had brought and the carriage drove away. Anna left everything on the porch, and went in to where Miss Mary Wadsmith was sitting by the fire.

Miss Mary was sitting in a large armchair by the fire. All the nooks and crannies of the chair were filled full of her soft and spreading body. She was dressed in a black satin morning gown,[6] the sleeves, great monster things, were heavy with the mass of her soft flesh. She sat there always, large, helpless, gentle. She had a fair, soft, regular, good-looking face, with pleasant, empty, grey-blue eyes, and heavy sleepy lids.

Behind Miss Mary was the little Jane, nervous and jerky with excitement as she saw Anna come into the room.

"Miss Mary," Anna began. She had stopped just within the door, her body and her face stiff with repression, her teeth closed hard and the white lights flashing sharply in the pale, clean blue of her

6. Plain dress worn in the morning.

eyes. Her bearing was full of the strange coquetry of anger and of fear, the stiffness, the bridling, the suggestive movement underneath the rigidness of forced control, all the queer ways the passions have to show themselves all one.

"Miss Mary," the words came slowly with thick utterance and with jerks, but always firm and strong. "Miss Mary, I can't stand it any more like this. When you tell me anything to do, I do it. I do everything I can and you know I work myself sick for you. The blue dressings in your room makes too much work to have for summer. Miss Jane don't know what work is. If you want to do things like that I go away."

Anna stopped still. Her words had not the strength of meaning they were meant to have, but the power in the mood of Anna's soul frightened and awed Miss Mary through and through.

Like in all large and helpless women, Miss Mary's heart beat weakly in the soft and helpless mass it had to govern. Little Jane's excitements had already tried her strength. Now she grew pale and fainted quite away.

"Miss Mary!" cried Anna running to her mistress and supporting all her helpless weight back in the chair. Little Jane, distracted, flew about as Anna ordered, bringing smelling salts and brandy and vinegar and water and chafing poor Miss Mary's wrists.

Miss Mary slowly opened her mild eyes. Anna sent the weeping little Jane out of the room. She herself managed to get Miss Mary quiet on the couch.

There was never a word more said about blue dressings.

Anna had conquered, and a few days later little Jane gave her a green parrot to make peace.

For six more years little Jane and Anna lived in the same house. They were careful and respectful to each other to the end.

Anna liked the parrot very well. She was fond of cats too and of horses, but best of all animals she loved the dog and best of all dogs, little Baby, the first gift from her friend, the widow Mrs. Lehntman.

The widow Mrs. Lehntman was the romance in Anna's life.

Anna met her first at the house of her half brother, the baker, who had known the late Mr. Lehntman, a small grocer, very well.

Mrs. Lehntman had been for many years a midwife.[7] Since her husband's death she had herself and two young children to support.

Mrs. Lehntman was a good looking woman. She had a plump well rounded body, clear olive skin, bright dark eyes and crisp black curling hair. She was pleasant, magnetic, efficient and good. She was very attractive, very generous and very amiable.

---

7. Midwives had primary responsibility for overseeing childbirth in this period.

She was a few years older than our good Anna, who was soon entirely subdued by her magnetic, sympathetic charm.

Mrs. Lehntman in her work loved best to deliver young girls who were in trouble. She would take these into her own house and care for them in secret, till they could guiltlessly go home or back to work, and then slowly pay her the money for their care. And so through this new friend Anna led a wider and more entertaining life, and often she used up her savings in helping Mrs. Lehntman through those times when she was giving very much more than she got.

It was through Mrs. Lehntman that Anna met Dr. Shonjen who employed her when at last it had to be that she must go away from her Miss Mary Wadsmith.

During the last years with her Miss Mary, Anna's health was very bad, as indeed it always was from that time on until the end of her strong life.

Anna was a medium sized, thin, hard working, worrying woman.

She had always had bad headaches and now they came more often and more wearing.

Her face grew thin, more bony and more worn, her skin stained itself pale yellow, as it does with working sickly women, and the clear blue of her eyes went pale.

Her back troubled her a good deal, too. She was always tired at her work and her temper grew more difficult and fretful.

Miss Mary Wadsmith often tried to make Anna see a little to herself, and get a doctor, and the little Jane, now blossoming into a pretty, sweet young woman, did her best to make Anna do things for her good. Anna was stubborn always to Miss Jane, and fearful of interference in her ways. Miss Mary Wadsmith's mild advice she easily could always turn aside.

Mrs. Lehntman was the only one who had any power over Anna. She induced her to let Dr. Shonjen take her in his care.

No one but a Dr. Shonjen could have brought a good and german Anna first to stop her work and then submit herself to operation, but he knew so well how to deal with german and poor people. Cheery, jovial, hearty, full of jokes that made much fun and yet were full of simple common sense and reasoning courage, he could persuade even a good Anna to do things that were for her own good.

Edgar had now been for some years away from home, first at a school and then at work to prepare himself to be a civil engineer. Miss Mary and Jane promised to take a trip for all the time that Anna was away and so there would be no need for Anna's work, nor for a new girl to take Anna's place.

Anna's mind was thus a little set at rest. She gave herself to Mrs. Lehntman and the doctor to do what they thought best to make her well and strong.

Anna endured the operation very well, and was patient, almost docile, in the slow recovery of her working strength. But when she was once more at work for her Miss Mary Wadsmith, all the good effect of these several months of rest were soon worked and worried well away.

For all the rest of her strong working life Anna was never really well. She had bad headaches all the time and she was always thin and worn.

She worked away her appetite, her health and strength, and always for the sake of those who begged her not to work so hard. To her thinking, in her stubborn, faithful, german soul, this was the right way for a girl to do.

Anna's life with Miss Mary Wadsmith was now drawing to an end.

Miss Jane, now altogether a young lady, had come out into the world. Soon she would become engaged and then be married, and then perhaps Miss Mary Wadsmith would make her home with her.

In such a household Anna was certain that she would never take a place. Miss Jane was always careful and respectful and very good to Anna, but never could Anna be a girl in a household where Miss Jane would be the head. This much was very certain in her mind, and so these last two years with her Miss Mary were not as happy as before.

The change came very soon.

Miss Jane became engaged and in a few months was to marry a man from out of town, from Curden, an hour's railway ride from Bridgepoint.

Poor Miss Mary Wadsmith did not know the strong resolve Anna had made to live apart from her when this new household should be formed. Anna found it very hard to speak to her Miss Mary of this change.

The preparations for the wedding went on day and night.

Anna worked and sewed hard to make it all go well.

Miss Mary was much fluttered, but content and happy with Anna to make everything so easy for them all.

Anna worked so all the time to drown her sorrow and her conscience too, for somehow it was not right to leave Miss Mary so. But what else could she do? She could not live as her Miss Mary's girl, in a house where Miss Jane would be the head.

The wedding day grew always nearer. At last it came and passed.

The young people went on their wedding trip, and Anna and Miss Mary were left behind to pack up all the things.

Even yet poor Anna had not had the strength to tell Miss Mary her resolve, but now it had to be.

Anna every spare minute ran to her friend Mrs. Lehntman for

comfort and advice. She begged her friend to be with her when she told the news to Miss Mary.

Perhaps if Mrs. Lehntman had not been in Bridgepoint, Anna would have tried to live in the new house. Mrs. Lehntman did not urge her to this thing nor even give her this advice, but feeling for Mrs. Lehntman as she did made even faithful Anna not quite so strong in her dependence on Miss Mary's need as she would otherwise have been.

Remember, Mrs. Lehntman was the romance in Anna's life.

All the packing was now done and in a few days Miss Mary was to go to the new house, where the young people were ready for her coming.

At last Anna had to speak.

Mrs. Lehntman agreed to go with her and help to make the matter clear to poor Miss Mary.

The two women came together to Miss Mary Wadsmith sitting placid by the fire in the empty living room. Miss Mary had seen Mrs. Lehntman many times before, and so her coming in with Anna raised no suspicion in her mind.

It was very hard for the two women to begin.

It must be very gently done, this telling to Miss Mary of the change. She must not be shocked by suddenness or with excitement.

Anna was all stiff, and inside all a quiver with shame, anxiety and grief. Even courageous Mrs. Lehntman, efficient, impulsive and complacent as she was and not deeply concerned in the event, felt awkward, abashed and almost guilty in that large, mild, helpless presence. And at her side to make her feel the power of it all, was the intense conviction of poor Anna, struggling to be unfeeling, self righteous and suppressed.

"Miss Mary"—with Anna when things had to come they came always sharp and short—"Miss Mary, Mrs. Lehntman has come here with me, so I can tell you about not staying with you there in Curden. Of course I go help you to get settled and then I think I come back and stay right here in Bridgepoint. You know my brother he is here and all his family, and I think it would be not right to go away from them so far, and you know you don't want me now so much Miss Mary when you are all together there in Curden."

Miss Mary Wadsmith was puzzled. She did not understand what Anna meant by what she said.

"Why Anna of course you can come to see your brother whenever you like to, and I will always pay your fare. I thought you understood all about that, and we will be very glad to have your nieces come to stay with you as often as they like. There will always be room enough in a big house like Mr. Goldthwaite's."

It was now for Mrs. Lehntman to begin her work.

"Miss Wadsmith does not understand just what you mean Anna," she began. "Miss Wadsmith, Anna feels how good and kind you are, and she talks about it all the time, and what you do for her in every way you can, and she is very grateful and never would want to go away from you, only she thinks it would be better now that Mrs. Goldthwaite has this big new house and will want to manage it in her own way, she thinks perhaps it would be better if Mrs. Goldthwaite had all new servants with her to begin with, and not a girl like Anna who knew her when she was a little girl. That is what Anna feels about it now, and she asked me and I said to her that I thought it would be better for you all and you knew she liked you so much and that you were so good to her, and you would understand how she thought it would be better in the new house if she stayed on here in Bridgepoint, anyway for a little while until Mrs. Goldthwaite was used to her new house. Isn't that it Anna that you wanted Miss Wadsmith to know?"

"Oh Anna," Miss Mary Wadsmith said it slowly and in a grieved tone of surprise that was very hard for the good Anna to endure, "Oh Anna, I didn't think that you would ever want to leave me after all these years."

"Miss Mary!" it came in one tense jerky burst, "Miss Mary it's only working under Miss Jane now would make me leave you so. I know how good you are and I work myself sick for you and for Mr. Edgar and for Miss Jane too, only Miss Jane she will want everything different from like the way we always did, and you know Miss Mary I can't have Miss Jane watching at me all the time, and every minute something new. Miss Mary, it would be very bad and Miss Jane don't really want me to come with you to the new house, I know that all the time. Please Miss Mary don't feel bad about it or think I ever want to go away from you if I could do things right for you the way they ought to be."

Poor Miss Mary. Struggling was not a thing for her to do. Anna would surely yield if she would struggle, but struggling was too much work and too much worry for peaceful Miss Mary to endure. If Anna would do so she must. Poor Miss Mary Wadsmith sighed, looked wistfully at Anna and then gave it up.

"You must do as you think best Anna," she said at last letting all of her soft self sink back into the chair. "I am very sorry and so I am sure will be Miss Jane when she hears what you have thought it best to do. It was very good of Mrs. Lehntman to come with you and I am sure she does it for your good. I suppose you want to go out a little now. Come back in an hour Anna and help me go to bed." Miss Mary closed her eyes and rested still and placid by the fire.

The two women went away.

This was the end of Anna's service with Miss Mary Wadsmith, and soon her new life taking care of Dr. Shonjen was begun.

Keeping house for a jovial bachelor doctor gave new elements of understanding to Anna's maiden german mind. Her habits were as firm fixed as before, but it always was with Anna that things that had been done once with her enjoyment and consent could always happen any time again, such as her getting up at any hour of the night to make a supper and cook hot chops and chicken fry for Dr. Shonjen and his bachelor friends.

Anna loved to work for men, for they could eat so much and with such joy. And when they were warm and full, they were content, and let her do whatever she thought best. Not that Anna's conscience ever slept, for neither with interference or without would she strain less to keep on saving every cent and working every hour of the day. But truly she loved it best when she could scold. Now it was not only other girls and the colored man, and dogs, and cats, and horses and her parrot, but her cheery master, jolly Dr. Shonjen, whom she could guide and constantly rebuke to his own good.

The doctor really loved her scoldings as she loved his wickednesses and his merry joking ways.

These days were happy days with Anna.

Her freakish humor now first showed itself, her sense of fun in the queer ways that people had, that made her later find delight in brutish servile Katy, in Sallie's silly ways and in the badness of Peter and of Rags. She loved to make sport with the skeletons the doctor had, to make them move and make strange noises till the negro boy shook in his shoes and his eyes rolled white in his agony of fear.

Then Anna would tell these histories to her doctor. Her worn, thin, lined, determined face would form for itself new and humorous creases, and her pale blue eyes would kindle with humour and with joy as her doctor burst into his hearty laugh. And the good Anna full of the coquetry of pleasing would bridle with her angular, thin, spinster body, straining her stories and herself to please.

These early days with jovial Dr. Shonjen were very happy days with the good Anna.

All of Anna's spare hours in these early days she spent with her friend, the widow Mrs. Lehntman. Mrs. Lehntman lived with her two children in a small house in the same part of the town as Dr. Shonjen. The older of these two children was a girl named Julia and was now about thirteen years of age. This Julia Lehntman was an unattractive girl enough, harsh featured, dull and stubborn as had been her heavy german father. Mrs. Lehntman did not trouble much with her, but gave her always all she wanted that she had, and let the girl do as she liked. This was not from indifference or dislike on the part of Mrs. Lehntman, it was just her usual way.

Her second child was a boy, two years younger than his sister, a bright, pleasant, cheery fellow, who too, did what he liked with his money and his time. All this was so with Mrs. Lehntman because she had so much in her head and in her house that clamoured for her concentration and her time.

This slackness and neglect in the running of the house, and the indifference in this mother for the training of her young was very hard for our good Anna to endure. Of course she did her best to scold, to save for Mrs. Lehntman, and to put things in their place the way they ought to be.

Even in the early days when Anna was first won by the glamour of Mrs. Lehntman's brilliancy and charm, she had been uneasy in Mrs. Lehntman's house with a need of putting things to rights. Now that the two children growing up were of more importance in the house, and now that long acquaintance had brushed the dazzle out of Anna's eyes, she began to struggle to make things go here as she thought was right.

She watched and scolded hard these days to make young Julia do the way she should. Not that Julia Lehntman was pleasant in the good Anna's sight, but it must never be that a young girl growing up should have no one to make her learn to do things right.

The boy was easier to scold, for scoldings never sank in very deep, and indeed he liked them very well for they brought with them new things to eat, and lively teasing, and good jokes.

Julia, the girl, grew very sullen with it all, and very often won her point, for after all Miss Annie was no relative of hers and had no business coming there and making trouble all the time. Appealing to the mother was no use. It was wonderful how Mrs. Lehntman could listen and not hear, could answer and yet not decide, could say and do what she was asked and yet leave things as they were before.

One day it got almost too bad for even Anna's friendship to bear out.

"Well, Julia, is your mamma out?" Anna asked, one Sunday summer afternoon, as she came into the Lehntman house.

Anna looked very well this day. She was always careful in her dress and sparing of new clothes. She made herself always fulfill her own ideal of how a girl should look when she took her Sundays out. Anna knew so well the kind of ugliness appropriate to each rank in life.

It was interesting to see how when she bought things for Miss Wadsmith and later for her cherished Miss Mathilda and always entirely from her own taste and often as cheaply as she bought things for her friends or for herself, that on the one hand she chose the things having the right air for a member of the upper class, and for the others always the things having the awkward ugliness that we call Dutch.[8] She knew the best thing in each kind, and she never in the course of her strong life compromised her sense of what was the right thing for a girl to wear.

On this bright summer Sunday afternoon she came to the Lehntmans', much dressed up in her new, brick red, silk waist trimmed with broad black beaded braid, a dark cloth skirt and a new stiff, shiny, black straw hat, trimmed with colored ribbons and a bird. She had on new gloves, and a feather boa[9] about her neck.

Her spare, thin, awkward body and her worn, pale yellow face though lit up now with the pleasant summer sun made a queer discord with the brightness of her clothes.

She came to the Lehntman house, where she had not been for several days, and opening the door that is always left unlatched in the houses of the lower middle class in the pleasant cities of the South, she found Julia in the family sitting-room alone.

"Well, Julia, where is your mamma?" Anna asked. "Ma is out but come in, Miss Annie, and look at our new brother." "What you talk so foolish for Julia," said Anna sitting down. "I ain't talkin' foolish, Miss Annie. Didn't you know mamma has just adopted a cute, nice little baby boy?" "You talk so crazy, Julia, you ought to know better than to say such things." Julia turned sullen. "All right Miss Annie, you don't need to believe what I say, but the little baby is in the kitchen and ma will tell you herself when she comes in."

It sounded most fantastic, but Julia had an air of truth and Mrs. Lehntman was capable of doing stranger things. Anna was disturbed. "What you mean Julia," she said. "I don't mean nothin' Miss Annie, you don't believe the baby is in there, well you can go and see it for yourself."

Anna went into the kitchen. A baby was there all right enough, and a lusty little boy he seemed. He was very tight asleep in a basket that stood in the corner by the open door.

"You mean your mamma is just letting him stay here a little while," Anna said to Julia who had followed her into the kitchen to see Miss Annie get real mad. "No that ain't it Miss Annie. The mother was that girl, Lily that came from Bishop's place out in the country, and she don't want no children, and ma liked the little boy so much, she said she'd keep him here and adopt him for her own child."

Anna, for once, was fairly dumb with astonishment and rage. The front door slammed.

"There's ma now," cried Julia in an uneasy triumph, for she was

8. Capitalized here perhaps because of its negative connotations: cheap, gaudy.
9. Scarf made of feathers.

not quite certain in her mind which side of the question she was on, "There's ma now, and you can ask her for yourself if I ain't told you true."

Mrs. Lehntman came into the kitchen where they were. She was bland, impersonal and pleasant, as it was her wont[1] to be. Still to-day, through this her usual manner that gave her such success in her practice as a midwife, there shone an uneasy consciousness of guilt, for like all who had to do with the good Anna, Mrs. Lehntman dreaded her firm character, her vigorous judgments and the bitter fervour of her tongue.

It had been plain to see in the six years these women were together, how Anna gradually had come to lead. Not really lead, of course, for Mrs. Lehntman never could be led, she was so very devious in her ways; but Anna had come to have direction whenever she could learn what Mrs. Lehntman meant to do before the deed was done. Now it was hard to tell which would win out. Mrs. Lehntman had her unhearing mind and her happy way of giving a pleasant well diffused attention, and then she had it on her side that, after all, this thing was already done.

Anna was, as usual, determined for the right. She was stiff and pale with her anger and her fear, and nervous, and all a tremble as was her usual way when a bitter fight was near.

Mrs. Lehntman was easy and pleasant as she came into the room. Anna was stiff and silent and very white.

"We haven't seen you for a long time, Anna," Mrs. Lehntman cordially began. "I was just gettin' worried thinking you was sick. My! but it's a hot day to-day. Come into the sittin'-room, Anna, and Julia will make us some ice tea."

Anna followed Mrs. Lehntman into the other room in a stiff silence, and when there she did not, as invited, take a chair.

As always with Anna when a thing had to come it came very short and sharp. She found it hard to breathe just now, and every word came with a jerk.

"Mrs. Lehntman, it ain't true what Julia said about your taking that Lily's boy to keep. I told Julia when she told me she was crazy to talk so."

Anna's real excitements stopped her breath, and made her words come sharp and with a jerk. Mrs. Lehntman's feelings spread her breath, and made her words come slow, but more pleasant and more easy even than before.

"Why Anna," she began, "don't you see Lily couldn't keep her boy for she is working at the Bishops' now, and he is such a cute dear little chap, and you know how fond I am of little fellers, and I thought

1. Custom or habit; standard practice.

it would be nice for Julia and for Willie to have a little brother. You know Julia always loves to play with babies, and I have to be away so much, and Willie he is running in the streets every minute all the time, and you see a baby would be sort of nice company for Julia, and you know you are always saying Anna, Julia should not be on the streets so much and the baby will be so good to keep her in."

Anna was every minute paler with indignation and with heat.

"Mrs. Lehntman, I don't see what business it is for you to take another baby for your own, when you can't do what's right by Julia and Willie you got here already. There's Julia, nobody tells her a thing when I ain't here, and who is going to tell her now how to do things for that baby? She ain't got no sense what's the right way to do with children, and you out all the time, and you ain't got no time for your own neither, and now you want to be takin' up with strangers. I know you was careless, Mrs. Lehntman, but I didn't think that you could do this so. No, Mrs. Lehntman, it ain't your duty to take up with no others, when you got two children of your own, that got to get along just any way they can, and you know you ain't got any too much money all the time, and you are all so careless here and spend it all the time, and Julia and Willie growin' big. It ain't right, Mrs. Lehntman, to do so."

This was as bad as it could be. Anna had never spoken her mind so to her friend before. Now it was too harsh for Mrs. Lehntman to allow herself to really hear. If she really took the meaning in these words she could never ask Anna to come into her house again, and she liked Anna very well, and was used to depend on her savings and her strength. And then too Mrs. Lehntman could not really take in harsh ideas. She was too well diffused to catch the feel of any sharp firm edge.

Now she managed to understand all this in a way that made it easy for her to say, "Why, Anna, I think you feel too bad about seeing what the children are doing every minute in the day. Julia and Willie are real good, and they play with all the nicest children in the square. If you had some, all your own, Anna, you'd see it don't do no harm to let them do a little as they like, and Julia likes this baby so, and sweet dear little boy, it would be so kind of bad to send him to a 'sylum[2] now, you know it would Anna, when you like children so yourself, and are so good to my Willie all the time. No indeed Anna, it's easy enough to say I should send this poor, cute little boy to a 'sylum when I could keep him here so nice, but you know Anna, you wouldn't like to do it yourself, now you really know you wouldn't, Anna, though you talk to me so hard.—My, it's hot to-day, what you

2. Dismal orphanage for poor unwanted children.

doin' with that ice tea in there Julia, when Miss Annie is waiting all this time for her drink?"

Julia brought in the ice tea. She was so excited with the talk she had been hearing from the kitchen, that she slopped it on the plate out of the glasses a good deal. But she was safe, for Anna felt this trouble so deep down that she did not even see those awkward, bony hands, adorned to-day with a new ring, those stupid, foolish hands that always did things the wrong way.

"Here Miss Annie," Julia said, "Here, Miss Annie, is your glass of tea, I know you like it good and strong."

"No, Julia, I don't want no ice tea here. Your mamma ain't able to afford now using her money upon ice tea for her friends. It ain't right she should now any more. I go out now to see Mrs. Drehten. She does all she can, and she is sick now working so hard taking care of her own children. I go there now. Good by Mrs. Lehntman, I hope you don't get no bad luck doin' what it ain't right for you to do."

"My, Miss Annie is real mad now," Julia said, as the house shook, as the good Anna shut the outside door with a concentrated shattering slam.

It was some months now that Anna had been intimate with Mrs. Drehten.

Mrs. Drehten had had a tumor and had come to Dr. Shonjen to be treated. During the course of her visits there, she and Anna had learned to like each other very well. There was no fever in this friendship, it was just the interchange of two hard working, worrying women, the one large and motherly, with the pleasant, patient, soft, worn, tolerant face, that comes with a german husband to obey, and seven solid girls and boys to bear and rear, and the other was our good Anna with her spinster body, her firm jaw, her humorous, light, clean eyes and her lined, worn, thin, pale yellow face.

Mrs. Drehten lived a patient, homely, hard-working life. Her husband an honest, decent man enough, was a brewer, and somewhat given to over drinking, and so he was often surly and stingy and unpleasant.

The family of seven children was made up of four stalwart, cheery, filial sons, and three hard working obedient simple daughters.

It was a family life the good Anna very much approved and also she was much liked by them all. With a german woman's feeling for the masterhood in men, she was docile to the surly father and rarely rubbed him the wrong way. To the large, worn, patient, sickly mother she was a sympathetic listener, wise in council and most efficient in her help. The young ones too, liked her very well. The sons teased her all the time and roared with boisterous pleasure when she gave them back sharp hits. The girls were all so good that her scoldings here were only in the shape of good advice, sweetened with new trimmings for their hats, and ribbons, and sometimes on their birthdays, bits of jewels.

It was here that Anna came for comfort after her grievous stroke at her friend the widow, Mrs. Lehntman. Not that Anna would tell Mrs. Drehten of this trouble. She could never lay bare the wound that came to her through this idealised affection. Her affair with Mrs. Lehntman was too sacred and too grievous ever to be told. But here in this large household, in busy movement and variety in strife, she could silence the uneasiness and pain of her own wound.

The Drehtens lived out in the country in one of the wooden, ugly houses that lie in groups outside of our large cities.

The father and the sons all had their work here making beer, and the mother and her girls scoured and sewed and cooked.

On Sundays they were all washed very clean, and smelling of kitchen soap. The sons, in their Sunday clothes, loafed around the house or in the village, and on special days went on picnics with their girls. The daughters in their awkward, colored finery went to church most of the day and then walking with their friends.

They always came together for their supper, where Anna always was most welcome, the jolly Sunday evening supper that german people love. Here Anna and the boys gave it to each other in sharp hits and hearty boisterous laughter, the girls made things for them to eat, and waited on them all, the mother loved all her children all the time, and the father joined in with his occasional unpleasant word that made a bitter feeling but which they had all learned to pass as if it were not said.

It was to the comfort of this house that Anna came that Sunday summer afternoon, after she had left Mrs. Lehntman and her careless ways.

The Drehten house was open all about. No one was there but Mrs. Drehten resting in her rocking chair, out in the pleasant, scented, summer air.

Anna had had a hot walk from the cars.[3]

She went into the kitchen for a cooling drink, and then came out and sat down on the steps near Mrs. Drehten.

Anna's anger had changed. A sadness had come to her. Now with the patient, friendly, gentle mother talk of Mrs. Drehten, this sadness changed to resignation and to rest.

As the evening came on the young ones dropped in one by one. Soon the merry Sunday evening supper was begun.

It had not been all comfort for our Anna, these months of knowing

3. Streetcar.

Mrs. Drehten. It had made trouble for her with the family of her half brother, the fat baker.

Her half brother, the fat baker, was a queer kind of a man. He was a huge, unwieldy creature, all puffed out all over, and no longer able to walk much, with his enormous body and the big, swollen, bursted veins in his great legs. He did not try to walk much now. He sat around his place, leaning on his great thick stick, and watching his workmen at their work.

On holidays, and sometimes of a Sunday, he went out in his bakery wagon. He went then to each customer he had and gave them each a large, sweet, raisined loaf of caky bread. At every house with many groans and gasps he would descend his heavy weight out of the wagon, his good featured, black haired, flat, good natured face shining with oily perspiration, with pride in labor and with generous kindness. Up each stoop he hobbled with the help of his big stick, and into the nearest chair in the kitchen or in the parlour, as the fashion of the house demanded, and there he sat and puffed, and then presented to the mistress or the cook the raisined german loaf his boy supplied him.

Anna had never been a customer of his. She had always lived in another part of the town, but he never left her out in these bakery progresses of his, and always with his own hand he gave her her festive loaf.

Anna liked her half brother well enough. She never knew him really well, for he rarely talked at all and least of all to women, but he seemed to her, honest, and good and kind, and he never tried to interfere in Anna's ways. And then Anna liked the loaves of raisined bread, for in the summer she and the second girl could live on them, and not be buying bread with the household money all the time.

But things were not so simple with our Anna, with the other members of her half brother's house.

Her half brother's family was made up of himself, his wife, and their two daughters.

Anna never liked her brother's wife.

The youngest of the two daughters was named after her aunt Anna.

Anna never liked her half brother's wife. This woman had been very good to Anna, never interfering in her ways, always glad to see her and to make her visits pleasant, but she had not found favour in our good Anna's sight.

Anna had too, no real affection for her nieces. She never scolded them or tried to guide them for their good. Anna never criticised or interfered in the running of her half brother's house.

Mrs. Federner was a good looking, prosperous woman, a little harsh and cold within her soul perhaps, but trying always to be pleasant, good and kind. Her daughters were well trained, quiet, obedient, well dressed girls, and yet our good Anna loved them not, nor their mother, nor any of their ways.

It was in this house that Anna had first met her friend, the widow, Mrs. Lehntman.

The Federners had never seemed to feel it wrong in Anna, her devotion to this friend and her care of her and of her children. Mrs. Lehntman and Anna and her feelings were all somehow too big for their attack. But Mrs. Federner had the mind and tongue that blacken things. Not really to blacken black, of course, but just to roughen and to rub on a little smut. She could somehow make even the face of the Almighty seem pimply and a little coarse, and so she always did this with her friends, though not with the intent to interfere.

This was really true with Mrs. Lehntman that Mrs. Federner did not mean to interfere, but Anna's friendship with the Drehtens was a very different matter.

Why should Mrs. Drehten, that poor common working wife of a man who worked for others in a brewery and who always drank too much, and was not like a thrifty, decent german man, why should that Mrs. Drehten and her ugly, awkward daughters be getting presents from her husband's sister all the time, and her husband always so good to Anna, and one of the girls having her name too, and those Drehtens all strangers to her and never going to come to any good? It was not right for Anna to do so.

Mrs. Federner knew better than to say such things straight out to her husband's fiery, stubborn sister, but she lost no chance to let Anna feel and see what they all thought.

It was easy to blacken all the Drehtens, their poverty, the husband's drinking, the four big sons carrying on and always lazy, the awkward, ugly daughters dressing up with Anna's help and trying to look so fine, and the poor, weak, hard-working sickly mother, so easy to degrade with large dosings of contemptuous pity.

Anna could not do much with these attacks for Mrs. Federner always ended with, "And you so good to them Anna all the time. I don't see how they could get along at all if you didn't help them all the time, but you are so good Anna, and got such a feeling heart, just like your brother, that you give anything away you got to anybody that will ask you for it, and that's shameless enough to take it when they ain't no relatives of yours. Poor Mrs. Drehten, she is a good woman. Poor thing it must be awful hard for her to have to take things from strangers all the time, and her husband spending it on drink. I was saying to Mrs. Lehntman, Anna, only yesterday, how I never was so sorry for any one as Mrs. Drehten, and how good it was for you to help them all the time."

All this meant a gold watch and chain to her god daughter for her birthday, the next month, and a new silk umbrella for the elder sister. Poor Anna, and she did not love them very much, these relatives of hers, and they were the only kin she had.

Mrs. Lehntman never joined in, in these attacks. Mrs. Lehntman was diffuse and careless in her ways, but she never worked such things for her own ends, and she was too sure of Anna to be jealous of her other friends.

All this time Anna was leading her happy life with Dr. Shonjen. She had every day her busy time. She cooked and saved and sewed and scrubbed and scolded. And every night she had her happy time, in seeing her Doctor like the fine things she bought so cheap and cooked so good for him to eat. And then he would listen and laugh so loud, as she told him stories of what had happened on that day.

The Doctor, too, liked it better all the time and several times in these five years he had of his own motion raised her wages.

Anna was content with what she had and grateful for all her doctor did for her.

So Anna's serving and her giving life went on, each with its varied pleasures and its pains.

The adopting of the little boy did not put an end to Anna's friendship for the widow Mrs. Lehntman. Neither the good Anna nor the careless Mrs. Lehntman would give each other up excepting for the gravest cause.

Mrs. Lehntman was the only romance Anna ever knew. A certain magnetic brilliancy in person and in manner made Mrs. Lehntman a woman other women loved. Then, too, she was generous and good and honest, though she was so careless always in her ways. And then she trusted Anna and liked her better than any of her other friends, and Anna always felt this very much.

No, Anna could not give up Mrs. Lehntman, and soon she was busier than before making Julia do things right for little Johnny.

And now new schemes were working strong in Mrs. Lehntman's head, and Anna must listen to her plans and help her make them work.

Mrs. Lehntman always loved best in her work to deliver young girls who were in trouble. She would keep these in her house until they could go to their homes or to their work, and slowly pay her back the money for their care.

Anna had always helped her friend to do this thing, for like all the good women of the decent poor, she felt it hard that girls should not be helped, not girls that were really bad of course, these she condemned and hated in her heart and with her tongue, but honest, decent, good, hard working, foolish girls who were in trouble.

For such as these Anna always liked to give her money and her strength.

Now Mrs. Lehntman thought that it would pay to take a big house for herself to take in girls and to do everything in a big way.

Anna did not like this plan.

Anna was never daring in her ways. Save and you will have the money you have saved, was all that she could know.

Not that the good Anna had it so.

She saved and saved and always saved, and then here and there, to this friend and to that, to one in her trouble and to the other in her joy, in sickness, death, and weddings, or to make young people happy, it always went, the hard earned money she had saved.

Anna could not clearly see how Mrs. Lehntman could make a big house pay. In the small house where she had these girls, it did not pay, and in a big house there was so much more that she would spend.

Such things were hard for the good Anna to very clearly see. One day she came into the Lehntman house. "Anna," Mrs. Lehntman said, "you know that nice big house on the next corner that we saw to rent. I took it for a year just yesterday. I paid a little down you know so I could have it sure all right and now you fix it up just like you want. I let you do just what you like with it."

Anna knew that it was now too late. However, "But Mrs. Lehntman you said you would not take another house, you said so just last week. Oh, Mrs. Lehntman I didn't think that you would do this so!"

Anna knew so well it was too late.

"I know, Anna, but it was such a good house, just right you know and some one else was there to see, and you know you said it suited very well, and if I didn't take it the others said they would, and I wanted to ask you only there wasn't time, and really Anna, I don't need much help, it will go so well I know. I just need a little to begin and to fix up with and that's all Anna that I need, and I know it will go awful well. You wait Anna and you'll see, and I let you fix it up just like you want, and you will make it look so nice, you got such sense in all these things. It will be a good place. You see Anna if I ain't right in what I say."

Of course Anna gave the money for this thing though she could not believe that it was best. No, it was very bad. Mrs. Lehntman could never make it pay and it would cost so much to keep. But what could our poor Anna do? Remember Mrs. Lehntman was the only romance Anna ever knew.

Anna's strength in her control of what was done in Mrs. Lehntman's house, was not now what it had been before that Lily's little

Johnny came. That thing had been for Anna a defeat. There had been no fighting to a finish but Mrs. Lehntman had very surely won.

Mrs. Lehntman needed Anna just as much as Anna needed Mrs. Lehntman, but Mrs. Lehntman was more ready to risk Anna's loss, and so the good Anna grew always weaker in her power to control.

In friendship, power always has its downward curve. One's strength to manage rises always higher until there comes a time one does not win, and though one may not really lose, still from the time that victory is not sure, one's power slowly ceases to be strong. It is only in a close tie such as marriage, that influence can mount and grow always stronger with the years and never meet with a decline. It can only happen so when there is no way to escape.

Friendship goes by favour. There is always danger of a break or of a stronger power coming in between. Influence can only be a steady march when one can surely never break away.

Anna wanted Mrs. Lehntman very much and Mrs. Lehntman needed Anna, but there were always other ways to do and if Anna had once given up she might do so again, so why should Mrs. Lehntman have real fear?

No, while the good Anna did not come to open fight she had been stronger. Now Mrs. Lehntman could always hold out longer. She knew too, that Anna had a feeling heart. Anna could never stop doing all she could for any one that really needed help. Poor Anna had no power to say no.

And then, too, Mrs. Lehntman was the only romance Anna ever knew. Romance is the ideal in one's life and it is very lonely living with it lost.

So the good Anna gave all her savings for this place, although she knew that this was not the right way for her friend to do.

For some time now they were all very busy fixing up the house. It swallowed all Anna's savings fixing up this house, for when Anna once began to make it nice, she could not leave it be until it was as good as for the purpose it should be.

Somehow it was Anna now that really took the interest in the house. Mrs. Lehntman, now the thing was done seemed very lifeless, without interest in the house, uneasy in her mind and restless in her ways, and more diffuse even than before in her attention. She was good and kind to all the people in her house, and let them do whatever they thought best.

Anna did not fail to see that Mrs. Lehntman had something on her mind that was all new. What was it that disturbed Mrs. Lehntman so? She kept on saying it was all in Anna's head. She had no trouble now at all. Everybody was so good and it was all so nice in the new house. But surely there was something here that was all wrong.

Anna heard a good deal of all this from her half brother's wife, the hard speaking Mrs. Federner.

Through the fog of dust and work and furnishing in the new house, and through the disturbed mind of Mrs. Lehntman, and with the dark hints of Mrs. Federner, there loomed up to Anna's sight a man, a new doctor that Mrs. Lehntman knew.

Anna had never met the man but she heard of him very often now. Not from her friend, the widow Mrs. Lehntman. Anna knew that Mrs. Lehntman made of him a mystery that Anna had not the strength just then to vigorously break down.

Mrs. Federner gave always dark suggestions and unpleasant hints. Even good Mrs. Drehten talked of it.

Mrs. Lehntman never spoke of the new doctor more than she could help. This was most mysterious and unpleasant and very hard for our good Anna to endure.

Anna's troubles came all of them at once.

Here in Mrs. Lehntman's house loomed up dismal and forbidding, a mysterious, perhaps an evil man.[4] In Dr. Shonjen's house were beginning signs of interest in the doctor in a woman.

This, too, Mrs. Federner often told to the poor Anna. The doctor surely would be married soon, he liked so much now to go to Mr. Weingartner's house where there was a daughter who loved Doctor, everybody knew.

In these days the living room in her half brother's house was Anna's torture chamber. And worst of all there was so much reason for her half sister's words. The Doctor certainly did look like marriage and Mrs. Lehntman acted very queer.

Poor Anna. Dark were these days and much she had to suffer.

The Doctor's trouble came to a head the first. It was true Doctor was engaged and to be married soon. He told Anna so himself.

What was the good Anna now to do? Dr. Shonjen wanted her of course to stay. Anna was so sad with all these troubles. She knew here in the Doctor's house it would be bad when he was married, but she had not the strength now to be firm and go away. She said at last that she would try and stay.

Doctor got married now very soon. Anna made the house all beautiful and clean and she really hoped that she might stay. But this was not for long.

Mrs. Shonjen was a proud, unpleasant woman. She wanted constant service and attention and never even a thank you to a servant. Soon all Doctor's old people went away. Anna went to Doctor and explained. She told him what all the servants thought of his new wife. Anna bade him a sad farewell and went away.

4. Performer of illegal abortions.

Anna was now most uncertain what to do. She could go to Curden to her Miss Mary Wadsmith who always wrote how much she needed Anna, but Anna still dreaded Miss Jane's interfering ways. Then too, she could not yet go away from Bridgepoint and from Mrs. Lehntman, unpleasant as it always was now over there.

Through one of Doctor's friends Anna heard of Miss Mathilda. Anna was very doubtful about working for a Miss Mathilda. She did not think it would be good working for a woman any more. She had found it very good with Miss Mary but she did not think that many women would be so.

Most women were interfering in their ways.

Anna heard that Miss Mathilda was a great big woman, not so big perhaps as her Miss Mary, still she was big, and the good Anna liked them better so. She did not like them thin and small and active and always looking in and always prying.

Anna could not make up her mind what was the best thing now for her to do. She could sew and this way make a living, but she did not like such business very well.

Mrs. Lehntman urged the place with Miss Mathilda. She was sure Anna would find it better so. The good Anna did not know.

"Well Anna," Mrs. Lehntman said, "I tell you what we do. I go with you to that woman that tells fortunes, perhaps she tell us something that will show us what is the best way for you now to do."

It was very bad to go to a woman who tells fortunes. Anna was of strong South German Catholic[5] religion and the german priests in the churches always said that it was very bad to do things so. But what else now could the good Anna do? She was so mixed and bothered in her mind, and troubled with this life that was all wrong, though she did try so hard to do the best she knew. "All right, Mrs. Lehntman," Anna said at last, "I think I go there now with you."

This woman who told fortunes was a medium.[6] She had a house in the lower quarter of the town. Mrs. Lehntman and the good Anna went to her.

The medium opened the door for them herself. She was a loose made, dusty, dowdy woman with a persuading, conscious and embracing manner and very greasy hair.

The woman let them come into the house.

The street door opened straight into the parlor, as is the way in the small houses of the south. The parlor had a thick and flowered carpet on the floor. The room was full of dirty things all made by hand. Some hung upon the wall, some were on the seats and over backs of chairs and some on tables and on those what-nots that poor people love. And everywhere were little things that break. Many of

5. Capitalized here as the name of a religion rather than as an ethnic identification.
6. Someone who communicates with the spirits of the dead.

these little things were broken and the place was stuffy and not clean.

No medium uses her parlor for her work. It is always in her eating room that she has her trances.

The eating room in all these houses is the living room in winter. It has a round table in the centre covered with a decorated woolen cloth, that has soaked in the grease of many dinners, for though it should be always taken off, it is easier to spread the cloth upon it than change it for the blanket deadener[7] that one owns. The upholstered chairs are dark and worn, and dirty. The carpet has grown dingy with the food that's fallen from the table, the dirt that's scraped from off the shoes; and the dust that settles with the ages. The sombre greenish colored paper on the walls has been smoked a dismal dirty grey, and all pervading is the smell of soup made out of onions and fat chunks of meat.

The medium brought Mrs. Lehntman and our Anna into this eating room, after she had found out what it was they wanted. They all three sat around the table and then the medium went into her trance.

The medium first closed her eyes and then they opened very wide and lifeless. She took a number of deep breaths, choked several times and swallowed very hard. She waved her hand back every now and then, and she began to speak in a monotonous slow, even tone.

"I see—I see—don't crowd so on me—I see—I see—too many forms—don't crowd so on me—I see—I see—you are thinking of something—you don't know whether you want to do it now. I see—I see—don't crowd so on me—I see—I see—you are not sure—I see—I see—a house with trees around it,—it is dark—it is evening—I see—I see—you go in the house—I see—I see you come out—it will be all right—you go and do it—do what you are not certain about—it will come out all right—it is best and you should do it now."

She stopped, she made deep gulps, her eyes rolled back into her head, she swallowed hard and then she was her former dingy and bland self again.

"Did you get what you wanted that the spirit should tell you?" the woman asked. Mrs. Lehntman answered yes, it was just what her friend had wanted so bad to know. Anna was uneasy in this house with superstition, with fear of her good priest, and with disgust at all the dirt and grease, but she was most content for now she knew what it was best for her to do.

Anna paid the woman for her work and then they came away.

"There Anna didn't I tell you how it would all be? You see the spirit says so too. You must take the place with Miss Mathilda, that is what I told you was the best thing for you to do. We go out and see her

7. Material used under tablecloths to protect the table or the woolen cloth that covers it.

where she lives tonight. Ain't you glad, Anna, that I took you to this place, so you know now what you will do?"

Mrs. Lehntman and Anna went that evening to see Miss Mathilda. Miss Mathilda was staying with a friend who lived in a house that did have trees about. Miss Mathilda was not there herself to talk with Anna.

If it had not been that it was evening, and so dark, and that this house had trees all round about, and that Anna found herself going in and coming out just as the woman that day said that she would do, had it not all been just as the medium said, the good Anna would never have taken the place with Miss Mathilda.

Anna did not see Miss Mathilda and she did not like the friend who acted in her place.

This friend was a dark, sweet, gentle little mother woman, very easy to be pleased in her own work and very good to servants, but she felt that acting for her young friend, the careless Miss Mathilda, she must be very careful to examine well and see that all was right and that Anna would surely do the best she knew. She asked Anna all about her ways and her intentions and how much she would spend, and how often she went out and whether she could wash and cook and sew.

The good Anna set her teeth fast to endure and would hardly answer anything at all. Mrs. Lehntman made it all go fairly well.

The good Anna was all worked up with her resentment, and Miss Mathilda's friend did not think that she would do.

However, Miss Mathilda was willing to begin and as for Anna, she knew that the medium said it must be so. Mrs. Lehntman, too, was sure, and said she, knew that this was the best thing for Anna now to do. So Anna sent word at last to Miss Mathilda, that if she wanted her, she would try if it would do.

So Anna began a new life taking care of Miss Mathilda.

Anna fixed up the little red brick house where Miss Mathilda was going to live and made it very pleasant, clean and nice. She brought over her dog, Baby, and her parrot. She hired Lizzie for a second girl to be with her and soon they were all content. All except the parrot, for Miss Mathilda did not like its scream. Baby was all right but not the parrot. But then Anna never really loved the parrot, and so she gave it to the Drehten girls to keep.

Before Anna could really rest content with Miss Mathilda, she had to tell her good german priest what it was that she had done, and how very bad it was that she had been and how she would never do so again.

Anna really did believe with all her might. It was her fortune never to live with people who had any faith, but then that never worried Anna. She prayed for them always as she should, and she was very

sure that they were good. The doctor loved to tease her with his
doubts and Miss Mathilda liked to do so too, but with the tolerant
spirit of her church, Anna never thought that such things were bad
for them to do.

Anna found it hard to always know just why it was that things
went wrong. Sometimes her glasses broke and then she knew that
she had not done her duty by the church, just in the way that she
should do.

Sometimes she was so hard at work that she would not go to mass.
Something always happened then. Anna's temper grew irritable and
her ways uncertain and distraught. Everybody suffered and then her
glasses broke. That was always very bad because they cost so much
to fix. Still in a way it always ended Anna's troubles, because she
knew then that all this was because she had been bad. As long as
she could scold it might be just the bad ways of all the thoughtless
careless world, but when her glasses broke that made it clear. That
meant that it was she herself who had been bad.

No, it was no use for Anna not to do the way she should, for things
always then went wrong and finally cost money to make whole, and
this was the hardest thing for the good Anna to endure.

Anna almost always did her duty. She made confession and her
mission[8] whenever it was right. Of course she did not tell the father
when she deceived people for their good, or when she wanted them
to give something for a little less.

When Anna told such histories to her doctor and later to her cherished Miss Mathilda, her eyes were always full of humor and enjoyment as she explained that she had said it so, and now she would
not have to tell the father for she had not really made a sin.

But going to a fortune teller Anna knew was really bad. That had
to be told to the father just as it was and penance had then to be
done.

Anna did this and now her new life was well begun, making Miss
Mathilda and the rest do just the way they should.

Yes, taking care of Miss Mathilda were the happiest days of all the
good Anna's strong hard working life.

With Miss Mathilda Anna did it all. The clothes, the house, the
hats, what she should wear and when and what was always best for
her to do. There was nothing Miss Mathilda would not let Anna
manage, and only be too glad if she would do.

Anna scolded and cooked and sewed and saved so well, that Miss
Matilda had so much to spend, that it kept Anna still busier scolding
all the time about the things she bought, that made so much work
for Anna and the other girl to do. But for all the scolding, Anna was

8. Charitable work.

proud almost to bursting of her cherished Miss Mathilda with all her knowledge and her great possessions, and the good Anna was always telling of it all to everybody that she knew.

Yes these were the happiest days of all her life with Anna, even though with her friends there were great sorrows. But these sorrows did not hurt the good Anna now, as they had done in the years that went before.

Miss Mathilda was not a romance in the good Anna's life, but Anna gave her so much strong affection that it almost filled her life as full.

It was well for the good Anna that her life with Miss Mathilda was so happy, for now in these days, Mrs. Lehntman went altogether bad. The doctor she had learned to know, was too certainly an evil as well as a mysterious man, and he had power over the widow and midwife, Mrs. Lehntman.

Anna never saw Mrs. Lehntman at all now any more.

Mrs. Lehntman had borrowed some more money and had given Anna a note then for it all, and after that Anna never saw her any more. Anna now stopped altogether going to the Lehntmans'. Julia, the tall, gawky, good, blonde, stupid daughter, came often to see Anna, but she could tell little of her mother.

It certainly did look very much as if Mrs. Lehntman had now gone altogether bad. This was a great grief to the good Anna, but not so great a grief as it would have been had not Miss Mathilda meant so much to her now.

Mrs. Lehntman went from bad to worse. The doctor, the mysterious and evil man, got into trouble doing things that were not right to do.

Mrs. Lehntman was mixed up in this affair.

It was just as bad as it could be, but they managed, both the doctor and Mrs. Lehntman, finally to come out safe.

Everybody was so sorry about Mrs. Lehntman. She had been really a good woman before she met this doctor, and even now she certainly had not been really bad.

For several years now Anna never even saw her friend.

But Anna always found new people to befriend, people who, in the kindly fashion of the poor, used up her savings and then gave promises in place of payments. Anna never really thought that these people would be good, but when they did not do the way they should, and when they did not pay her back the money she had loaned, and never seemed the better for her care, then Anna would grow bitter with the world.

No, none of them had any sense of what was the right way for them to do. So Anna would repeat in her despair.

The poor are generous with their things. They give always what they have, but with them to give or to receive brings with it no feeling that they owe the giver for the gift.

Even a thrifty german Anna was ready to give all that she had saved, and so not be sure that she would have enough to take care of herself if she fell sick, or for old age, when she could not work. Save and you will have the money you have saved was true only for the day of saving, even for a thrifty german Anna. There was no certain way to have it for old age, for the taking care of what is saved can never be relied on, for it must always be in strangers' hands in a bank or in investments by a friend.

And so when any day one might need life and help from others of the working poor, there was no way a woman who had a little saved could say them no.[9]

So the good Anna gave her all to friends and strangers, to children, dogs and cats, to anything that asked or seemed to need her care.

It was in this way that Anna came to help the barber and his wife who lived around the corner, and who somehow could never make ends meet. They worked hard, were thrifty, had no vices, but the barber was one of them who never can make money. Whoever owed him money did not pay. Whenever he had a chance at a good job he fell sick and could not take it. It was never his own fault that he had trouble, but he never seemed to make things come out right.

His wife was a blonde, thin, pale, german little woman, who bore her children very hard, and worked too soon, and then till she was sick. She too, always had things that went wrong.

They both needed constant help and patience, and the good Anna gave both to them all the time.

Another woman who needed help from the good Anna, was one who was in trouble from being good to others.

This woman's husband's brother, who was very good, worked in a shop where there was a Bohemian,[1] who was getting sick with a consumption. This man got so much worse he could not do his work, but he was not so sick that he could stay in a hospital. So this woman had him living there with her. He was not a nice man, nor was he thankful for all the woman did for him. He was cross to her two children and made a great mess always in her house. The doctor said he must have many things to eat, and the woman and the brother of the husband got them for him.

There was no friendship, no affection, no liking even for the man this woman cared for, no claim of common country or of kin, but in the kindly fashion of the poor this woman gave her all and made her

9. Stein deliberately uses grammatically incorrect formulations such as this to suggest the way an immigrant might speak English.
1. From what was then the country Bohemia, which is now part of the Czech Republic; lower on the class ladder than German immigrants; capitalized here perhaps derogatorily, as "Dutch" was.

house a nasty place, and for a man who was not even grateful for the gift.

Then, of course, the woman herself got into trouble. Her husband's brother was now married. Her husband lost his job. She did not have the money for the rent. It was the good Anna's savings that were handy.

So it went on. Sometimes a little girl, sometimes a big one was in trouble and Anna heard of them and helped them to find places.

Stray dogs and cats Anna always kept until she found them homes. She was always careful to learn whether these people would be good to animals.

Out of the whole collection of stray creatures, it was the young Peter and the jolly little Rags, Anna could not find it in her heart to part with. These became part of the household of the good Anna's Miss Mathilda.

Peter was a very useless creature, a foolish, silly, cherished, coward male. It was wild to see him rush up and down in the back yard, barking and bouncing at the wall, when there was some dog out beyond, but when the very littlest one there was got inside of the fence and only looked at Peter, Peter would retire to his Anna and blot himself out between her skirts.

When Peter was left downstairs alone, he howled. "I am all alone," he wailed, and then the good Anna would have to come and fetch him up. Once when Anna stayed a few nights in a house not far away, she had to carry Peter all the way, for Peter was afraid when he found himself on the street outside his house. Peter was a good sized creature and he sat there and he howled, and the good Anna carried him all the way in her own arms. He was a coward was this Peter, but he had kindly, gentle eyes and a pretty collie head, and his fur was very thick and white and nice when he was washed. And then Peter never strayed away, and he looked out of his nice eyes and he liked it when you rubbed him down, and he forgot you when you went away, and he barked whenever there was any noise.

When he was a little pup he had one night been put into the yard and that was all of his origin she knew. The good Anna loved him well and spoiled him as a good german mother always does her son.

Little Rags was very different in his nature. He was a lively creature made out of ends of things, all fluffy and dust color, and he was always bounding up into the air and darting all about over and then under silly Peter and often straight into solemn fat, blind, sleepy Baby, and then in a wild rush after some stray cat.

Rags was a pleasant, jolly little fellow. The good Anna liked him very well, but never with her strength as she loved her good looking coward, foolish young man, Peter.

Baby was the dog of her past life and she held Anna with old ties of past affection. Peter was the spoiled, good looking young man, of her middle age, and Rags was always something of a toy. She liked him but he never struck in very deep. Rags had strayed in somehow one day and then when no home for him was quickly found, he had just stayed right there.

It was a very happy family there all together in the kitchen, the good Anna and Sally and old Baby and young Peter and the jolly little Rags.

The parrot had passed out of Anna's life. She had really never loved the parrot and now she hardly thought to ask for him, even when she visited the Drehtens.

Mrs. Drehten was the friend Anna always went to, for her Sundays. She did not get advice from Mrs. Drehten as she used to from the widow, Mrs. Lehntman, for Mrs. Drehten was a mild, worn, unaggressive nature that never cared to influence or to lead. But they could mourn together for the world these two worn, working german women, for its sadness and its wicked ways of doing. Mrs. Drehten knew so well what one could suffer.

Things did not go well in these days with the Drehtens. The children were all good, but the father with his temper and his spending kept everything from being what it should.

Poor Mrs. Drehten still had trouble with her tumor. She could hardly do any work now any more. Mrs. Drehten was a large, worn, patient german woman, with a soft face, lined, yellow brown in color and the look that comes from a german husband to obey, and many solid girls and boys to bear and rear, and from being always on one's feet and never having any troubles cured.

Mrs. Drehten was always getting worse, and now the doctor thought it would be best to take the tumor out.

It was no longer Dr. Shonjen who treated Mrs. Drehten. They all went now to a good old german doctor they all knew.

"You see, Miss Mathilda," Anna said, "All the old german patients don't go no more now to Doctor. I stayed with him just so long as I could stand it, but now he is moved away up town too far for poor people, and his wife, she holds her head up so and always is spending so much money just for show, and so he can't take right care of us poor people any more. Poor man, he has got always to be thinking about making money now. I am awful sorry about Doctor, Miss Mathilda, but he neglected Mrs. Drehten shameful when she had her trouble, so now I never see him any more. Doctor Herman is a good, plain, german doctor and he would never do things so, and Miss Mathilda, Mrs. Drehten is coming in to-morrow to see you before she goes to the hospital for her operation. She could not go comfortable till she had seen you first to see what you would say."

All Anna's friends reverenced the good Anna's cherished Miss

Mathilda. How could they not do so and still remain friends with the good Anna? Miss Mathilda rarely really saw them but they were always sending flowers and words of admiration through her Anna. Every now and then Anna would bring one of them to Miss Mathilda for advice.

It is wonderful how poor people love to take advice from people who are friendly and above them, from people who read in books and who are good.

Miss Mathilda saw Mrs. Drehten and told her she was glad that she was going to the hospital for operation for that surely would be best, and so good Mrs. Drehten's mind was set at rest.

Mrs. Drehten's tumor came out very well. Mrs. Drehten was afterwards never really well, but she could do her work a little better, and be on her feet and yet not get so tired.

And so Anna's life went on, taking care of Miss Mathilda and all her clothes and goods, and being good to every one that asked or seemed to need her help.

Now, slowly, Anna began to make it up with Mrs. Lehntman. They could never be as they had been before. Mrs. Lehntman could never be again the romance in the good Anna's life, but they could be friends again, and Anna could help all the Lehntmans in their need. This slowly came about.

Mrs. Lehntman had now left the evil and mysterious man who had been the cause of all her trouble. She had given up, too, the new big house that she had taken. Since her trouble her practice had been very quiet. Still she managed to do fairly well. She began to talk of paying the good Anna. This, however, had not gotten very far.

Anna saw Mrs. Lehntman a good deal now. Mrs. Lehntman's crisp, black, curly hair had gotten streaked with gray. Her dark, full, good looking face had lost its firm outline, gone flabby and a little worn. She had grown stouter and her clothes did not look very nice. She was as bland as ever in her ways, and as diffuse as always in her attention, but through it all there was uneasiness and fear and uncertainty lest some danger might be near.

She never said a word of her past life to the good Anna, but it was very plain to see that her experience had not left her easy, nor yet altogether free.

It had been hard for this good woman, for Mrs. Lehntman was really a good woman, it had been a very hard thing for this german woman to do what everybody knew and thought was wrong. Mrs. Lehntman was strong and she had courage, but it had been very hard to bear. Even the good Anna did not speak to her with freedom. There always remained a mystery and a depression in Mrs. Lehntman's affair.

And now the blonde, foolish, awkward daughter, Julia was in trou-

ble. During the years the mother gave her no attention, Julia kept
company with a young fellow who was a clerk somewhere in a store
down in the city. He was a decent, dull young fellow, who did not
make much money and could never save it for he had an old mother
he supported. He and Julia had been keeping company for several
years and now it was needful that they should be married. But then
how could they marry? He did not make enough to start them and
to keep on supporting his old mother too. Julia was not used to working much and she said, and she was stubborn, that she would not
live with Charley's dirty, cross, old mother. Mrs. Lehntman had no
money. She was just beginning to get on her feet. It was of course,
the good Anna's savings that were handy.

However it paid Anna to bring about this marriage, paid her in
scoldings and in managing the dull, long, awkward Julia, and her
good, patient, stupid Charley. Anna loved to buy things cheap, and
fix up a new place.

Julia and Charley were soon married and things went pretty well
with them. Anna did not approve their slack, expensive ways of doing.

"No Miss Mathilda," she would say, "The young people nowadays
have no sense for saving and putting money by so they will have
something to use when they need it. There's Julia and her Charley.
I went in there the other day, Miss Mathilda, and they had a new
table with a marble top and on it they had a grand new plush album.
'Where you get that album?' I asked Julia. 'Oh, Charley he gave it to
me for my birthday,' she said, and I asked her if it was paid for and
she said not all yet but it would be soon. Now I ask you what business
have they Miss Mathilda, when they ain't paid for anything they got
already, what business have they to be buying new things for her
birthdays. Julia she don't do no work, she just sits around and thinks
how she can spend the money, and Charley he never puts one cent
by. I never see anything like the people nowadays Miss Mathilda,
they don't seem to have any sense of being careful about money.
Julia and Charley when they have any children they won't have nothing to bring them up with right. I said that to Julia, Miss Mathilda,
when she showed me those silly things that Charley bought her, and
she just said in her silly, giggling way, perhaps they won't have any
children. I told her she ought to be ashamed of talking so, but I don't
know, Miss Mathilda, the young people nowadays have no sense at
all of what's the right way for them to do, and perhaps its better if
they don't have any children, and then Miss Mathilda you know there
is Mrs. Lehntman. You know she regular adopted little Johnny just
so she could pay out some more money just as if she didn't have
trouble enough taking care of her own children. No Miss Mathilda,
I never see how people can do things so. People don't seem to have
no sense of right or wrong or anything these days Miss Mathilda,

they are just careless and thinking always of themselves and how they can always have a happy time. No, Miss Mathilda I don't see how people can go on and do things so."

The good Anna could not understand the careless and bad ways of all the world and always she grew bitter with it all. No, not one of them had any sense of what was the right way for them to do.

Anna's past life was now drawing to an end. Her old blind dog, Baby, was sick and like to die. Baby had been the first gift from her friend the widow, Mrs. Lehntman in the old days when Anna had been with Miss Mary Wadsmith, and when these two women had first come together.

Through all the years of change, Baby had stayed with the good Anna, growing old and fat and blind and lazy. Baby had been active and a ratter[2] when she was young, but that was so long ago it was forgotten, and for many years now Baby had wanted only her warm basket and her dinner.

Anna in her active life found need of others, of Peter and the funny little Rags, but always Baby was the eldest and held her with the ties of old affection. Anna was harsh when the young ones tried to keep poor Baby out and use her basket. Baby had been blind now for some years as dogs get, when they are no longer active. She got weak and fat and breathless and she could not even stand long any more. Anna had always to see that she got her dinner and that the young active ones did not deprive her.

Baby did not die with a real sickness. She just got older and more blind and coughed and then more quiet, and then slowly one bright summer's day she died.

There is nothing more dreary than old age in animals. Somehow it is all wrong that they should have grey hair and withered skin, and blind old eyes, and decayed and useless teeth. An old man or an old woman almost always has some tie that seems to bind them to the younger, realer life. They have children or the remembrance of old duties, but a dog that's old and so cut off from all its world of struggle, is like a dreary, deathless Struldbrug,[3] the dreary dragger on of death through life.

And so one day old Baby died. It was dreary, more than sad, for the good Anna. She did not want the poor old beast to linger with its weary age, and blind old eyes and dismal shaking cough, but this death left Anna very empty. She had the foolish young man Peter, and the jolly little Rags for comfort, but Baby had been the only one that could remember.

The good Anna wanted a real graveyard for her Baby, but this could not be in a Christian country, and so Anna all alone took her

2. A killer of unwanted rats.
3. From Jonathan Swift's *Gulliver's Travels*: large, slow, inactive, long-lived.

old friend done up in decent wrappings and put her into the ground in some quiet place that Anna knew of.

The good Anna did not weep for poor old Baby. Nay, she had not time even to feel lonely, for with the good Anna it was sorrow upon sorrow. She was now no longer to keep house for Miss Mathilda.

When Anna had first come to Miss Mathilda she had known that it might only be for a few years, for Miss Mathilda was given to much wandering and often changed her home, and found new places where she went to live. The good Anna did not then think much about this, for when she first went to Miss Mathilda she had not thought that she would like it and so she had not worried about staying. Then in those happy years that they had been together, Anna had made herself forget it. This last year when she knew that it was coming she had tried hard to think it would not happen.

"We won't talk about it now Miss Mathilda, perhaps we all be dead by then," she would say when Miss Mathilda tried to talk it over. Or, "If we live till then Miss Mathilda, perhaps you will be staying on right here."

No, the good Anna could not talk as if this thing were real, it was too weary to be once more left with strangers.

Both the good Anna and her cherished Miss Mathilda tried hard to think that this would not really happen. Anna made missions and all kinds of things to keep her Miss Mathilda and Miss Mathilda thought out all the ways to see if the good Anna could not go with her, but neither the missions nor the plans had much success. Miss Mathilda would go, and she was going far away to a new country where Anna could not live, for she would be too lonesome.

There was nothing that these two could do but part. Perhaps we all be dead by then, the good Anna would repeat, but even that did not really happen. If we all live till then Miss Mathilda, came out truer. They all did live till then, all except poor old blind Baby, and they simply had to part.

Poor Anna and poor Miss Mathilda. They could not look at each other that last day. Anna could not keep herself busy working. She just went in and out and sometimes scolded.

Anna could not make up her mind what she should do now for her future. She said that she would for a while keep this little red brick house that they had lived in. Perhaps she might just take in a few boarders. She did not know, she would write about it later and tell it all to Miss Mathilda.

The dreary day dragged out and then all was ready and Miss Mathilda left to take her train. Anna stood strained and pale and dry eyed on the white stone steps of the little red brick house that they had lived in. The last thing Miss Mathilda heard was the good Anna bidding foolish Peter say good bye and be sure to remember Miss Mathilda.

Part III

THE DEATH OF THE GOOD ANNA

EVERY ONE who had known of Miss Mathilda wanted the good Anna now to take a place with them, for they all knew how well Anna could take care of people and all their clothes and goods. Anna too could always go to Curden to Miss Mary Wadsmith, but none of all these ways seemed very good to Anna.

It was not now any longer that she wanted to stay near Mrs. Lehntman. There was no one now that made anything important, but Anna was certain that she did not want to take a place where she would be under some new people. No one could ever be for Anna as had been her cherished Miss Mathilda. No one could ever again so freely let her do it all. It would be better Anna thought in her strong strained weary body, it would be better just to keep on there in the little red brick house that was all furnished, and make a living taking in some boarders. Miss Mathilda had let her have the things, so it would not cost any money to begin. She could perhaps manage to live on so. She could do all the work and do everything as she thought best, and she was too weary with the changes to do more than she just had to, to keep living. So she stayed on in the house where they had lived, and she found some men, she would not take in women, who took her rooms and who were her boarders.

Things soon with Anna began to be less dreary. She was very popular with her few boarders. They loved her scoldings and the good things she made for them to eat. They made good jokes and laughed loud and always did whatever Anna wanted, and soon the good Anna got so that she liked it very well. Not that she did not always long for Miss Mathilda. She hoped and waited and was very certain that sometime, in one year or in another Miss Mathilda would come back, and then of course would want her, and then she could take all good care of her again.

Anna kept all Miss Mathilda's things in the best order. The boarders were well scolded if they ever made a scratch on Miss Mathilda's table.

Some of the boarders were hearty good south german fellows and Anna always made them go to mass. One boarder was a lusty german student who was studying in Bridgepoint to be a doctor. He was Anna's special favourite and she scolded him as she used to her old doctor so that he always would be good. Then, too, this cheery fellow always sang when he was washing, and that was what Miss Mathilda always used to do. Anna's heart grew warm again with this young fellow who seemed to bring back to her everything she needed.

And so Anna's life in these days was not all unhappy. She worked and scolded, she had her stray dogs and cats and people, who all asked and seemed to need her care, and she had hearty german fellows who loved her scoldings and ate so much of the good things that she knew so well the way to make.

No, the good Anna's life in these days was not all unhappy. She did not see her old friends much, she was too busy, but once in a great while she took a Sunday afternoon and went to see good Mrs. Drehten.

The only trouble was that Anna hardly made a living. She charged so little for her board and gave her people such good things to eat, that she could only just make both ends meet. The good german priest to whom she always told her troubles tried to make her have the boarders pay a little higher, and Miss Mathilda always in her letters urged her to this thing, but the good Anna somehow could not do it. Her boarders were nice men but she knew they did not have much money, and then she could not raise on those who had been with her and she could not ask the new ones to pay higher, when those who were already there were paying just what they had paid before. So Anna let it go just as she had begun it. She worked and worked all day and thought all night how she could save, and with all the work she just managed to keep living. She could not make enough to lay any money by.

Anna got so little money that she had all the work to do herself. She could not pay even the little Sallie enough to keep her with her.

Not having little Sallie nor having any one else working with her, made it very hard for Anna ever to go out, for she never thought that it was right to leave a house all empty. Once in a great while of a Sunday, Sallie who was now working in a factory would come and stay in the house for the good Anna, who would then go out and spend the afternoon with Mrs. Drehten.

No, Anna did not see her old friends much any more. She went sometimes to see her half brother and his wife and her nieces, and they always came to her on her birthdays to give presents, and her half brother never left her out of his festive raisined bread giving progresses. But these relatives of hers had never meant very much to the good Anna. Anna always did her duty by them all, and she liked her half brother very well and the loaves of raisined bread that he supplied her were most welcome now, and Anna always gave her god daughter and her sister handsome presents, but no one in this family had ever made a way inside to Anna's feelings.

Mrs. Lehntman she saw very rarely. It is hard to build up new on

an old friendship when in that friendship there has been bitter dis-
illusion. They did their best, both these women, to be friends, but
they were never able to again touch one another nearly. There were
too many things between them that they could not speak of, things
that had never been explained nor yet forgiven. The good Anna still
did her best for foolish Julia and still every now and then saw Mrs.
Lehntman, but this family had now lost all its real hold on Anna.

Mrs. Drehten was now the best friend that Anna knew. Here there
was never any more than the mingling of their sorrows. They talked
over all the time the best way for Mrs. Drehten now to do; poor Mrs.
Drehten who with her chief trouble, her bad husband, had really
now no way that she could do. She just had to work and to be patient
and to love her children and be very quiet. She always had a soothing
mother influence on the good Anna who with her irritable, strained,
worn-out body would come and sit by Mrs. Drehten and talk all her
troubles over.

Of all the friends that the good Anna had had in these twenty
years in Bridgepoint, the good father and patient Mrs. Drehten were
the only ones that were now near to Anna and with whom she could
talk her troubles over.

Anna worked, and thought, and saved, and scolded, and took care
of all the boarders, and of Peter and of Rags, and all the others.
There was never any end to Anna's effort and she grew always more
tired, more pale yellow, and in her face more thin and worn and
worried. Sometimes she went farther in not being well, and then she
went to see Dr. Herman who had operated on good Mrs. Drehten.

The things that Anna really needed were to rest sometimes and
eat more so that she could get stronger, but these were the last things
that Anna could bring herself to do. Anna could never take a rest.
She must work hard through the summer as well as through the
winter, else she could never make both ends meet. The doctor gave
her medicines to make her stronger but these did not seem to do
much good.

Anna grew always more tired, her headaches came oftener and
harder, and she was now almost always feeling very sick. She could
not sleep much in the night. The dogs with their noises disturbed
her and everything in her body seemed to pain her.

The doctor and the good father tried often to make her give herself
more care. Mrs. Drehten told her that she surely would not get well
unless for a little while she would stop working. Anna would then
promise to take care, to rest in bed a little longer and to eat more so
that she would get stronger, but really how could Anna eat when she
always did the cooking and was so tired of it all, before it was half
ready for the table?

Anna's only friendship now was with good Mrs. Drehten who was too gentle and too patient to make a stubborn faithful german Anna ever do the way she should, in the things that were for her own good.

Anna grew worse all through this second winter. When the summer came the doctor said that she simply could not live on so. He said she must go to his hospital and there he would operate upon her. She would then be well and strong and able to work hard all next winter.

Anna for some time would not listen. She could not do this so, for she had her house all furnished and she simply could not let it go. At last a woman came and said she would take care of Anna's boarders and then Anna said that she was prepared to go.

Anna went to the hospital for her operation. Mrs. Drehten was herself not well but she came into the city, so that some friend would be with the good Anna. Together, then, they went to this place where the doctor had done so well by Mrs. Drehten.

In a few days they had Anna ready. Then they did the operation, and then the good Anna with her strong, strained, worn-out body died.

Mrs. Drehten sent word of her death to Miss Mathilda.

"Dear Miss Mathilda," wrote Mrs. Drehten, "Miss Annie died in the hospital yesterday after a hard operation. She was talking about you and Doctor and Miss Mary Wadsmith all the time. She said she hoped you would take Peter and the little Rags to keep when you came back to America to live. I will keep them for you here Miss Mathilda. Miss Annie died easy, Miss Mathilda, and sent you her love."

FINIS

Melanctha

EACH ONE AS SHE MAY[1]

ROSE JOHNSON made it very hard to bring her baby to its birth.

Melanctha Herbert who was Rose Johnson's friend, did everything that any woman could. She tended Rose, and she was patient, submissive, soothing, and untiring, while the sullen, childish, cowardly, black Rosie grumbled and fussed and howled and made herself to be an abomination and like a simple beast.[2]

The child though it was healthy after it was born, did not live long. Rose Johnson was careless and negligent and selfish, and when Melanctha had to leave for a few days, the baby died. Rose Johnson had liked the baby well enough and perhaps she just forgot it for awhile, anyway the child was dead and Rose and Sam her husband were very sorry but then these things came so often in the negro world in Bridgepoint, that they neither of them thought about it very long.

Rose Johnson and Melanctha Herbert had been friends now for some years. Rose had lately married Sam Johnson a decent honest kindly fellow, a deck hand on a coasting steamer.

Melanctha Herbert had not yet been really married.

Rose Johnson was a real black, tall, well built, sullen, stupid, child-like, good looking negress. She laughed when she was happy and grumbled and was sullen with everything that troubled.

Rose Johnson was a real black negress but she had been brought up quite like their own child by white folks.

Rose laughed when she was happy but she had not the wide, abandoned laughter that makes the warm broad glow of negro sunshine. Rose was never joyous with the earth-born, boundless joy of negroes. Hers was just ordinary, any sort of woman laughter.

Rose Johnson was careless and was lazy, but she had been brought up by white folks and she needed decent comfort. Her white training

1. Pun on the name May Bookstaver, Stein's lover from 1900 through 1902, on whom the characters Melanctha, and Helen in *Q.E.D.*, are based. "Melanctha" was written last of the three stories, "The Good Anna" first, and "The Gentle Lena" second.
2. This is the first of a number of offensive racist stereotypes that appear throughout "Melanctha." Stein both uses and undercuts these stereotypes. The issues they raise are discussed in many of the essays and excerpts in "Criticism."

had only made for habits, not for nature. Rose had the simple, promiscuous unmorality of the black people.

Rose Johnson and Melanctha Herbert like many of the twos with
women were a curious pair to be such friends.

Melanctha Herbert was a graceful, pale yellow,[3] intelligent, attractive negress. She had not been raised like Rose by white folks but
then she had been half made with real white blood.[4]

She and Rose Johnson were both of the better sort of negroes,
there, in Bridgepoint.

"No, I ain't no common nigger," said Rose Johnson, "for I was
raised by white folks, and Melanctha she is so bright and learned so
much in school, she ain't no common nigger either, though she ain't
got no husband to be married to like I am to Sam Johnson."

Why did the subtle, intelligent, attractive, half white girl Melanctha Herbert love and do for and demean herself in service to this
coarse, decent, sullen, ordinary, black childish Rose, and why was
this unmoral, promiscuous, shiftless Rose married, and that's not so
common either, to a good man of the negroes, while Melanctha with
her white blood and attraction and her desire for a right position had
not yet been really married.

Sometimes the thought of how all her world was made, filled the
complex, desiring Melanctha with despair. She wondered, often,
how she could go on living when she was so blue.

Melanctha told Rose one day how a woman whom she knew had
killed herself because she was so blue. Melanctha said, sometimes,
she thought this was the best thing for her herself to do.

Rose Johnson did not see it the least bit that way.

"I don't see Melanctha why you should talk like you would kill
yourself just because you're blue. I'd never kill myself Melanctha just
'cause I was blue. I'd maybe kill somebody else Melanctha 'cause I
was blue, but I'd never kill myself. If I ever killed myself Melanctha
it'd be by accident, and if I ever killed myself by accident Melanctha,
I'd be awful sorry."

Rose Johnson and Melanctha Herbert had first met, one night, at
church. Rose Johnson did not care much for religion. She had not
enough emotion to be really roused by a revival. Melanctha Herbert
had not come yet to know how to use religion. She was still too
complex with desire.[5] However, the two of them in negro fashion

---

3. Light-skinned.
4. This is an inconsistency in the text: Melanctha's mother is "pale yellow" and "colored" like
   Melanctha, meaning that she is a light-skinned African American, or "mulatto"; Melanctha's father is very dark-skinned.
5. Melanctha's being "complex with desire"—Stein frequently describes her as "the complex,
   desiring Melanctha"—is a crucial character trait, related for her to "wandering," "knowledge," "wisdom," and "power"; the meanings of these words are primarily, but not at all
   exclusively, sexual in nature.

went very often to the negro church, along with all their friends, and they slowly came to know each other very well.

Rose Johnson had been raised not as a servant but quite like their own child by white folks. Her mother who had died when Rose was still a baby, had been a trusted servant in the family. Rose was a cute, attractive, good looking little black girl and these people had no children of their own and so they kept Rose in their house.

As Rose grew older she drifted from her white folks back to the colored people, and she gradually no longer lived in the old house. Then it happened that these people went away to some other town to live, and somehow Rose stayed behind in Bridgepoint. Her white folks left a little money to take care of Rose, and this money she got every little while.

Rose now in the easy fashion of the poor lived with one woman in her house, and then for no reason went and lived with some other woman in her house. All this time, too, Rose kept company, and was engaged, first to this colored man and then to that, and always she made sure she was engaged, for Rose had strong the sense of proper conduct.

"No, I ain't no common nigger just to go around with any man, nor you Melanctha shouldn't neither," she said one day when she was telling the complex and less sure Melanctha what was the right way for her to do. "No Melanctha, I ain't no common nigger to do so, for I was raised by white folks. You know very well Melanctha that I'se always been engaged to them."

And so Rose lived on, always comfortable and rather decent and very lazy and very well content.

After she had lived some time this way, Rose thought it would be nice and very good in her position to get regularly really married. She had lately met Sam Johnson somewhere, and she liked him and she knew he was a good man, and then he had a place where he worked every day and got good wages. Sam Johnson liked Rose very well and he was quite ready to be married. One day they had a grand real wedding and were married. Then with Melanctha Herbert's help to do the sewing and the nicer work,[6] they furnished comfortably a little red brick house. Sam then went back to his work as deck hand on a coasting steamer, and Rose stayed home in her house and sat and bragged to all her friends how nice it was to be married really to a husband.

Life went on very smoothly with them all the year. Rose was lazy but not dirty and Sam was careful but not fussy, and then there was Melanctha to come in every day and help to keep things neat.

When Rose's baby was coming to be born, Rose came to stay in

6. Fine sewing for a bride's trousseau.

the house where Melanctha Herbert lived just then, with a big good natured colored woman who did washing.

Rose went there to stay, so that she might have the doctor from the hospital near by to help her have the baby, and then, too, Melanctha could attend to her while she was sick.

Here the baby was born, and here it died, and then Rose went back to her house again with Sam.

Melanctha Herbert had not made her life all simple like Rose Johnson. Melanctha had not found it easy with herself to make her wants and what she had, agree.

Melanctha Herbert was always losing what she had in wanting all the things she saw. Melanctha was always being left when she was not leaving others.

Melanctha Herbert always loved too hard and much too often. She was always full with mystery and subtle movements and denials and vague distrusts and complicated disillusions. Then Melanctha would be sudden and impulsive and unbounded in some faith, and then she would suffer and be strong in her repression.

Melanctha Herbert was always seeking rest and quiet, and always she could only find new ways to be in trouble.

Melanctha wondered often how it was she did not kill herself when she was so blue. Often she thought this would be really the best way for her to do.

Melanctha Herbert had been raised to be religious, by her mother. Melanctha had not liked her mother very well. This mother, 'Mis' Herbert, as her neighbors called her, had been a sweet appearing and dignified and pleasant, pale yellow, colored woman. 'Mis' Herbert had always been a little wandering and mysterious and uncertain in her ways.

Melanctha was pale yellow and mysterious and a little pleasant like her mother, but the real power in Melanctha's nature came through her robust and unpleasant and very unendurable black father.

Melanctha's father only used to come to where Melanctha and her mother lived, once in a while.

It was many years now that Melanctha had not heard or seen or known of anything her father did.

Melanctha Herbert almost always hated her black father, but she loved very well the power in herself that came through him. And so her feeling was really closer to her black coarse father, than her feeling had ever been toward her pale yellow, sweet-appearing mother. The things she had in her of her mother never made her feel respect.

Melanctha Herbert had not loved herself in childhood. All of her youth was bitter to remember.

Melanctha had not loved her father and her mother and they had found it very troublesome to have her.

Melanctha's mother and her father had been regularly married. Melanctha's father was a big black virile negro. He only came once in a while to where Melanctha and her mother lived, but always that pleasant, sweet-appearing, pale yellow woman, mysterious and uncertain and wandering in her ways, was close in sympathy and thinking to her big black virile husband.

James Herbert was a common, decent enough, colored workman, brutal and rough to his one daughter, but then she was a most disturbing child to manage.

The young Melanctha did not love her father and her mother, and she had a break neck courage, and a tongue that could be very nasty. Then, too, Melanctha went to school and was very quick in all the learning, and she knew very well how to use this knowledge to annoy her parents who knew nothing.

Melanctha Herbert had always had a break neck courage. Melanctha always loved to be with horses; she loved to do wild things, to ride the horses and to break and tame them.

Melanctha, when she was a little girl, had had a good chance to live with horses. Near where Melanctha and her mother lived was the stable of the Bishops, a rich family who always had fine horses.

John, the Bishops' coachman, liked Melanctha very well and he always let her do anything she wanted with the horses. John was a decent, vigorous mulatto with a prosperous house and wife and children. Melanctha Herbert was older than any of his children. She was now a well grown girl of twelve and just beginning as a woman.[7]

James Herbert, Melanctha's father, knew this John, the Bishops' coachman very well.

One day James Herbert came to where his wife and daughter lived, and he was furious.

"Where's that Melanctha girl of yours," he said fiercely, "if she is to the Bishops' stables again, with that man John, I swear I kill her. Why don't you see to that girl better you, you're her mother."

James Herbert was a powerful, loose built, hard handed, black, angry negro. Herbert never was a joyous negro. Even when he drank with other men, and he did that very often, he was never really joyous. In the days when he had been most young and free and open, he had never had the wide abandoned laughter that gives the broad glow to negro sunshine.

His daughter, Melanctha Herbert, later always made a hard forced laughter. She was only strong and sweet and in her nature when she was really deep in trouble, when she was fighting so with all she

7. Entering puberty.

really had, that she did not use her laughter. This was always true of poor Melanctha who was so certain that she hated trouble. Melanctha Herbert was always seeking peace and quiet, and she could always only find new ways to get excited.

James Herbert was often a very angry negro. He was fierce and serious, and he was very certain that he often had good reason to be angry with Melanctha, who knew so well how to be nasty, and to use her learning with a father who knew nothing.

James Herbert often drank with John, the Bishops' coachman. John in his good nature sometimes tried to soften Herbert's feeling toward Melanctha. Not that Melanctha ever complained to John of her home life or her father. It was never Melanctha's way, even in the midst of her worst trouble to complain to any one of what happened to her, but nevertheless somehow every one who knew Melanctha always knew how much she suffered. It was only while one really loved Melanctha that one understood how to forgive her, that she never once complained nor looked unhappy, and was always handsome and in spirits, and yet one always knew how much she suffered.

The father, James Herbert, never told his troubles either, and he was so fierce and serious that no one ever thought of asking.

'Mis' Herbert as her neighbors called her was never heard even to speak of her husband or her daughter. She was always pleasant, sweet-appearing, mysterious and uncertain, and a little wandering in her ways.

The Herberts were a silent family with their troubles, but somehow every one who knew them always knew everything that happened.

The morning of one day when in the evening Herbert and the coachman John were to meet to drink together, Melanctha had to come to the stable joyous and in the very best of humors. Her good friend John on this morning felt very firmly how good and sweet she was and how very much she suffered.

John was a very decent colored coachman. When he thought about Melanctha it was as if she were the eldest of his children. Really he felt very strongly the power in her of a woman. John's wife always liked Melanctha and she always did all she could to make things pleasant. And Melanctha all her life loved and respected kind and good and considerate people. Melanctha always loved and wanted peace and gentleness and goodness and all her life for herself poor Melanctha could only find new ways to be in trouble.

This evening after John and Herbert had drunk awhile together, the good John began to tell the father what a fine girl he had for a daughter. Perhaps the good John had been drinking a good deal of liquor, perhaps there was a gleam of something softer than the feeling of a friendly elder in the way John then spoke of Melanctha. There had been a good deal of drinking and John certainly that very morning had felt strongly Melanctha's power as a woman. James Herbert was always a fierce, suspicious, serious negro, and drinking never made him feel more open. He looked very black and evil as he sat and listened while John grew more and more admiring as he talked half to himself, half to the father, of the virtues and the sweetness of Melanctha.

Suddenly between them there came a moment filled full with strong black curses, and then sharp razors flashed in the black hands, that held them flung backward in the negro fashion, and then for some minutes there was fierce slashing.

John was a decent, pleasant, good natured, light brown negro, but he knew how to use a razor to do bloody slashing.

When the two men were pulled apart by the other negroes who were in the room drinking, John had not been much wounded but James Herbert had gotten one good strong cut that went from his right shoulder down across the front of his whole body. Razor fighting does not wound very deeply, but it makes a cut that looks most nasty, for it is so very bloody.

Herbert was held by the other negroes until he was cleaned and plastered, and then he was put to bed to sleep off his drink and fighting.

The next day he came to where his wife and daughter lived and he was furious.

"Where's that Melanctha, of yours?" he said to his wife, when he saw her. "If she is to the Bishops' stables now with that yellow John, I swear I kill her. A nice way she is going for a decent daughter. Why don't you see to that girl better you, ain't you her mother!"

Melanctha Herbert had always been old in all her ways and she knew very early how to use her power as a woman, and yet Melanctha with all her inborn intense wisdom was really very ignorant of evil. Melanctha had not yet come to understand what they meant, the things she so often heard around her, and which were just beginning to stir strongly in her.

Now when her father began fiercely to assail her, she did not really know what it was that he was so furious to force from her. In every way that he could think of in his anger, he tried to make her say a thing she did not really know. She held out and never answered anything he asked her, for Melanctha had a breakneck courage and she just then badly hated her black father.

When the excitement was all over, Melanctha began to know her power, the power she had so often felt stirring within her and which she now knew she could use to make her stronger.

James Herbert did not win this fight with his daughter. After awhile he forgot it as he soon forgot John and the cut of his sharp razor.

Melanctha almost forgot to hate her father, in her strong interest in the power she now knew she had within her.

Melanctha did not care much now, any longer, to see John or his wife or even the fine horses. This life was too quiet and accustomed and no longer stirred her to any interest or excitement.

Melanctha now really was beginning as a woman. She was ready, and she began to search in the streets and in dark corners to discover men and to learn their natures and their various ways of working.

In these next years Melanctha learned many ways that lead to wisdom. She learned the ways, and dimly in the distance she saw wisdom. These years of learning led very straight to trouble for Melanctha, though in these years Melanctha never did or meant anything that was really wrong.

Girls who are brought up with care and watching can always find moments to escape into the world, where they may learn the ways that lead to wisdom. For a girl raised like Melanctha Herbert, such escape was always very simple. Often she was alone, sometimes she was with a fellow seeker, and she strayed and stood, sometimes by railroad yards, sometimes on the docks or around new buildings where many men were working. Then when the darkness covered everything all over, she would begin to learn to know this man or that. She would advance, they would respond, and then she would withdraw a little, dimly, and always she did not know what it was that really held her. Sometimes she would almost go over, and then the strength in her of not really knowing, would stop the average man in his endeavor. It was a strange experience of ignorance and power and desire. Melanctha did not know what it was that she so badly wanted. She was afraid, and yet she did not understand that here she really was a coward.

Boys had never meant much to Melanctha. They had always been too young to content her. Melanctha had a strong respect for any kind of successful power. It was this that always kept Melanctha nearer, in her feeling toward her virile and unendurable black father, than she ever was in her feeling for her pale yellow, sweet-appearing mother. The things she had in her of her mother, never made her feel respect.

In these young days, it was only men that for Melanctha held anything there was of knowledge and power. It was not from men however that Melanctha learned to really understand this power.

From the time that Melanctha was twelve until she was sixteen she wandered, always seeking but never more than very dimly seeing wisdom. All this time Melanctha went on with her school learning; she went to school rather longer than do most of the colored children.

Melanctha's wanderings after wisdom she always had to do in secret and by snatches, for her mother was then still living and 'Mis' Herbert always did some watching, and Melanctha with all her hard courage dreaded that there should be much telling to her father, who came now quite often to where Melanctha lived with her mother.

In these days Melanctha talked and stood and walked with many kinds of men, but she did not learn to know any of them very deeply. They all supposed her to have world knowledge and experience. They, believing that she knew all, told her nothing, and thinking that she was deciding with them, asked for nothing, and so though Melanctha wandered widely, she was really very safe with all the wandering.

It was a very wonderful experience this safety of Melanctha in these days of her attempted learning. Melanctha herself did not feel the wonder, she only knew that for her it all had no real value.

Melanctha all her life was very keen in her sense for real experience. She knew she was not getting what she so badly wanted, but with all her break neck courage Melanctha here was a coward, and so she could not learn to really understand.

Melanctha liked to wander, and to stand by the railroad yard, and watch the men and the engines and the switches and everything that was busy there, working. Railroad yards are a ceaseless fascination. They satisfy every kind of nature. For the lazy man whose blood flows very slowly, it is a steady soothing world of motion which supplies him with the sense of a strong moving power. He need not work and yet he has it very deeply; he has it even better than the man who works in it or owns it. Then for natures[8] that like to feel emotion without the trouble of having any suffering, it is very nice to get the swelling in the throat, and the fullness, and the heart beats, and all the flutter of excitement that comes as one watches the people come and go, and hears the engine pound and give a long drawn whistle. For a child watching through a hole in the fence above the yard, it is a wonder world of mystery and movement. The child loves all the noise, and then it loves the silence of the wind that comes before the full rush of the pounding train, that bursts out from the tunnel where it lost itself and all its noise in darkness, and the child loves

8. Stein, influenced by the American philosopher William James (1842–1910), believed in character types or "natures" and attempted to describe all possible American character types in *The Making of Americans* (written 1906–1911, published in 1925), constructing elaborate charts of various combinations of primary and secondary characteristics. These typologies eventually became so tortuously complicated that she abandoned them.

all the smoke, that sometimes comes in rings, and always puffs with fire and blue color.

For Melanctha the yard was full of the excitement of many men, and perhaps a free and whirling future.

Melanctha came here very often and watched the men and all the things that were so busy working. The men always had time for, "Hullo sis, do you want to sit on my engine," and, "Hullo, that's a pretty lookin' yaller[9] girl, do you want to come and see him cookin."

All the colored porters[1] liked Melanctha. They often told her exciting things that had happened; how in the West they went through big tunnels where there was no air to breathe, and then out and winding around edges of great canyons on thin high spindling trestles, and sometimes cars, and sometimes whole trains fell from the narrow bridges, and always up from the dark places death and all kinds of queer devils looked up and laughed in their faces. And then they would tell how sometimes when the train went pounding down steep slippery mountains, great rocks would racket and roll down around them, and sometimes would smash in the car and kill men; and as the porters told these stories their round, black, shining faces would grow solemn, and their color would go grey beneath the greasy black, and their eyes would roll white in the fear and wonder of the things they could scare themselves by telling.

There was one, big, serious, melancholy, light brown porter who often told Melanctha stories, for he liked the way she had of listening with intelligence and sympathetic feeling, when he told how the white men in the far South tried to kill him because he made one of them who was drunk and called him a damned nigger, and who refused to pay money for his chair to a nigger, get off the train between stations. And then this porter had to give up going to that part of the Southern country, for all the white men swore that if he ever came there again they would surely kill him.

Melanctha liked this serious, melancholy light brown negro very well, and all her life Melanctha wanted and respected gentleness and goodness, and this man always gave her good advice and serious kindness, and Melanctha felt such things very deeply, but she could never let them help her or affect her to change the ways that always made her keep herself in trouble.

Melanctha spent many of the last hours of the daylight with the porters and with other men who worked hard, but when darkness came it was always different. Then Melanctha would find herself with the, for her, gentlemanly classes. A clerk, or a young express

9. Slang for light-skinned African American.
1. Railroad attendants, mainly sleeping-car workers; these jobs were among the best available to African-American working men during this period.

agent[2] would begin to know her, and they would stand, or perhaps, walk a little while together.

Melanctha always made herself escape but often it was with an effort. She did not know what it was that she so badly wanted, but with all her courage Melanctha here was a coward, and so she could not learn to understand.

Melanctha and some man would stand in the evening and would talk together. Sometimes Melanctha would be with another girl and then it was much easier to stay or to escape, for then they could make way for themselves together, and by throwing words and laughter to each other, could keep a man from getting too strong in his attention.

But when Melanctha was alone, and she was so, very often, she would sometimes come very near to making a long step on the road that leads to wisdom. Some man would learn a good deal about her in the talk, never altogether truly, for Melanctha all her life did not know how to tell a story wholly. She always, and yet not with intention, managed to leave out big pieces which make a story very different, for when it came to what had happened and what she had said and what it was that she had really done, Melanctha never could remember right. The man would sometimes come a little nearer, would detain her, would hold her arm or make his jokes a little clearer, and then Melanctha would always make herself escape. The man thinking that she really had world wisdom would not make his meaning clear, and believing that she was deciding with him he never went so fast that he could stop her when at last she made herself escape.

And so Melanctha wandered on the edge of wisdom. "Say, Sis, why don't you when you come here stay a little longer?" they would all ask her, and they would hold her for an answer, and she would laugh, and sometimes she did stay longer, but always just in time she made herself escape.

Melanctha Herbert wanted very much to know and yet she feared the knowledge. As she grew older she often stayed a good deal longer, and sometimes it was almost a balanced struggle, but she always made herself escape.

Next to the railroad yard it was the shipping docks that Melanctha loved best when she wandered. Often she was alone, sometimes she was with some better kind of black girl, and she would stand a long time and watch the men working at unloading, and see the steamers do their coaling[3] and she would listen with full feeling to the yowling

---

2. These were also low-wage, low-status railroad workers, but they were white and had higher status than African-American porters.
3. Loading coal for fuel.

of the free swinging negroes, as they ran, with their powerful loose jointed bodies and their childish savage yelling, pushing, carrying, pulling great loads from the ships to the warehouses.

The men would call out, "Say, Sis, look out or we'll come and catch yer," or "Hi, there, you yaller girl, come here and we'll take you sailin'." And then, too, Melanctha would learn to know some of the serious foreign sailors who told her all sorts of wonders, and a cook would sometimes take her and her friends over a ship and show where he made his messes[4] and where the men slept, and where the shops were, and how everything was made by themselves, right there, on ship board.

Melanctha loved to see these dark and smelly places. She always loved to watch and talk and listen with men who worked hard. But it was never from these rougher people that Melanctha tried to learn the ways that lead to wisdom. In the daylight she always liked to talk with rough men and to listen to their lives and about their work and their various ways of doing, but when the darkness covered everything all over, Melanctha would meet, and stand, and talk with a clerk or a young shipping agent who had seen her watching, and so it was that she would try to learn to understand.

And then Melanctha was fond of watching men work on new buildings. She loved to see them hoisting, digging, sawing and stone cutting. Here, too, in the daylight, she always learned to know the common workmen. "Heh, Sis, look out or that rock will fall on you and smash you all up into little pieces. Do you think you would make a nice jelly?" And then they would all laugh and feel that their jokes were very funny. And "Say, you pretty yaller girl, would it scare you bad to stand up here on top where I be? See if you've got grit and come up here where I can hold you. All you got to do is to sit still on that there rock that they're just hoistin', and then when you get here I'll hold you tight, don't you be scared Sis."

Sometimes Melanctha would do some of these things that had much danger, and always with such men, she showed her power and her break neck courage. Once she slipped and fell from a high place. A workman caught her and so she was not killed, but her left arm was badly broken.

All the men crowded around her. They admired her boldness in doing and in bearing pain when her arm was broken. They all went along with her with great respect to the doctor, and then they took her home in triumph and all of them were bragging about her not squealing.

James Herbert was home where his wife lived, that day. He was furious when he saw the workmen and Melanctha. He drove the men

4. Meals.

away with curses so that they were all very nearly fighting, and he would not let a doctor come in to attend Melanctha. "Why don't you see to that girl better, you, you're her mother."

James Herbert did not fight things out now any more with his daughter. He feared her tongue, and her school learning, and the way she had of saying things that were very nasty to a brutal black man who knew nothing. And Melanctha just then hated him very badly in her suffering.

And so this was the way Melanctha lived the four years of her beginning as a woman. And many things happened to Melanctha, but she knew very well that none of them had led her on to the right way, that certain way that was to lead her to world wisdom.

Melanctha Herbert was sixteen when she first met Jane Harden. Jane was a negress, but she was so white that hardly any one could guess it. Jane had had a good deal of education. She had been two years at a colored college. She had had to leave because of her bad conduct. She taught Melanctha many things. She taught her how to go the ways that lead to wisdom.

Jane Harden was at this time twenty-three years old and she had had much experience. She was very much attracted by Melanctha, and Melanctha was very proud that this Jane would let her know her.

Jane Harden was not afraid to understand. Melanctha who had strong the sense for real experience, knew that here was a woman who had learned to understand.

Jane Harden had many bad habits. She drank a great deal, and she wandered widely. She was safe though now, when she wanted to be safe, in this wandering.

Melanctha Herbert soon always wandered with her. Melanctha tried the drinking and some of the other habits, but she did not find that she cared very much to do them. But every day she grew stronger in her desire to really understand.

It was now no longer, even in the daylight, the rougher men that these two learned to know in their wanderings, and for Melanctha the better classes were now a little higher. It was no longer express agents and clerks that she learned to know, but men in business, commercial travelers,[5] and even men above these, and Jane and she would talk and walk and laugh and escape from them all very often. It was still the same, the knowing of them and the always just escaping, only now for Melanctha somehow it was different, for though it was always the same thing that happened it had a different flavor, for now Melanctha was with a woman who had wisdom, and dimly she began to see what it was that she should understand.

It was not from the men that Melanctha learned her wisdom. It

5. Traveling salesmen.

was always Jane Harden herself who was making Melanctha begin
to understand.

Jane was a roughened woman. She had power and she liked to use
it, she had much white blood and that made her see clear, she liked
drinking and that made her reckless. Her white blood was strong in
her and she had grit and endurance and a vital courage. She was
always game, however much she was in trouble. She liked Melanctha
Herbert for the things that she had like her, and then Melanctha
was young, and she had sweetness, and a way of listening with intelligence and sympathetic interest, to the stories that Jane Harden
often told out of her experience.

Jane grew always fonder of Melanctha. Soon they began to wander, more to be together than to see men and learn their various
ways of working. Then they began not to wander, and Melanctha
would spend long hours with Jane in her room, sitting at her feet
and listening to her stories, and feeling her strength and the power
of her affection, and slowly she began to see clear before her one
certain way that would be sure to lead to wisdom.[6]

Before the end came, the end of the two years in which Melanctha
spent all her time when she was not at school or in her home, with
Jane Harden, before these two years were finished, Melanctha had
come to see very clear, and she had come to be very certain, what it
is that gives the world its wisdom.

Jane Harden always had a little money and she had a room in the
lower part of the town. Jane had once taught in a colored school.
She had had to leave that too on account of her bad conduct. It was
her drinking that always made all the trouble for her, for that can
never be really covered over.

Jane's drinking was always growing worse upon her. Melanctha
had tried to do the drinking but it had no real attraction for her.

In the first year, between Jane Harden and Melanctha Herbert,
Jane had been much the stronger. Jane loved Melanctha and she
found her always intelligent and brave and sweet and docile, and
Jane meant to, and before the year was over she had taught Melanctha what it is that gives many people in the world their wisdom.

Jane had many ways in which to do this teaching. She told Melanctha many things. She loved Melanctha hard and made Melanctha
feel it very deeply.[7] She would be with other people and with men
and with Melanctha, and she would make Melanctha understand
what everybody wanted, and what one did with power when one had
it.

Melanctha sat at Jane's feet for many hours in these days and felt

6. Sexually charged "wisdom" in this case has lesbian connotations.
7. This refers ambiguously to lesbian sexual experience.

Jane's wisdom. She learned to love Jane and to have this feeling very deeply. She learned a little in these days to know joy, and she was taught too how very keenly she could suffer. It was very different this suffering from that Melanctha sometimes had from her mother and from her very unendurable black father. Then she was fighting and she could be strong and valiant in her suffering, but here with Jane Harden she was longing and she bent and pleaded with her suffering.

It was a very tumultuous, very mingled year, this time for Melanctha, but she certainly did begin to really understand.

In every way she got it from Jane Harden. There was nothing good or bad in doing, feeling, thinking or in talking, that Jane spared her. Sometimes the lesson came almost too strong for Melanctha, but somehow she always managed to endure it and so slowly, but always with increasing strength and feeling, Melanctha began to really understand.

Then slowly, between them, it began to be all different. Slowly now[8] between them, it was Melanctha Herbert, who was stronger. Slowly now they began to drift apart from one another.

Melanctha Herbert never really lost her sense that it was Jane Harden who had taught her, but Jane did many things that Melanctha now no longer needed. And then, too, Melanctha never could remember right when it came to what she had done and what had happened. Melanctha now sometimes quarreled with Jane, and they no longer went about together, and sometimes Melanctha really forgot how much she owed to Jane Harden's teaching.

Melanctha began now to feel that she had always had world wisdom. She really knew of course, that it was Jane who had taught her, but all that began to be covered over by the trouble between them, that was now always getting stronger.

Jane Harden was a roughened woman. Once she had been very strong, but now she was weakened in all her kinds of strength by her drinking. Melanctha had tried the drinking but it had had no real attraction for her.

Jane's strong and roughened nature and her drinking made it always harder for her to forgive Melanctha, that now Melanctha did not really need her any longer. Now it was Melanctha who was stronger and it was Jane who was dependent on her.

Melanctha was now come to be about eighteen years old. She was a graceful, pale yellow, good looking, intelligent, attractive negress, a little mysterious sometimes in her ways, and always good and pleasant, and always ready to do things for people.

8. "Now" is the word Stein uses to signal the "continuous present"—see "Portraits and Repetition" in *Lectures in America*, (New York: Random House, 1935).

Melanctha from now on saw very little of Jane Harden. Jane did not like that very well and sometimes she abused Melanctha, but her drinking soon covered everything all over.

It was not in Melanctha's nature to really lose her sense for Jane Harden. Melanctha all her life was ready to help Jane out in any of her trouble, and later, when Jane really went to pieces, Melanctha always did all that she could to help her.

But Melanctha Herbert was ready now herself to do teaching. Melanctha could do anything now that she wanted. Melanctha knew now what everybody wanted.

Melanctha had learned how she might stay a little longer; she had learned that she must decide when she wanted really to stay longer, and she had learned how when she wanted to, she could escape.

And so Melanctha began once more to wander. It was all now for her very different. It was never rougher men now that she talked to, and she did not care much now to know white men of the, for her, very better classes.[9] It was now something realler that Melanctha wanted, something that would move her very deeply, something that would fill her fully with the wisdom that was planted now within her, and that she wanted badly, should really wholly fill her.

Melanctha these days wandered very widely. She was always alone now when she wandered. Melanctha did not need help now to know, or to stay longer, or when she wanted, to escape.

Melanctha tried a great many men, in these days before she was really suited. It was almost a year that she wandered and then she met with a young mulatto. He was a doctor who had just begun to practice. He would most likely do well in the future, but it was not this that concerned Melanctha. She found him good and strong and gentle and very intellectual, and all her life Melanctha liked and wanted good and considerate people, and then too he did not at first believe in Melanctha. He held off and did not know what it was that Melanctha wanted. Melanctha came to want him very badly. They began to know each other better. Things began to be very strong between them. Melanctha wanted him so badly that now she never wandered. She just gave herself to this experience.

Melanctha Herbert was now, all alone, in Bridgepoint. She lived now with this colored woman and now with that one, and she sewed, and sometimes she taught a little in a colored school as substitute for some teacher. Melanctha had now no home nor any regular employment. Life was just commencing for Melanctha. She had youth and had learned wisdom, and she was graceful and pale yellow and very pleasant, and always ready to do things for people, and she

9. The railroad clerks and express agents she used to "begin to know."

was mysterious in her ways and that only made belief in her more fervent.

During the year before she met Jefferson Campbell,[1] Melanctha had tried many kinds of men but they had none of them interested Melanctha very deeply. She met them, she was much with them, she left them, she would think perhaps this next time it would be more exciting, and always she found that for her it all had no real meaning. She could now do everything she wanted, she knew now everything that everybody wanted, and yet it all had no excitement for her. With these men, she knew she could learn nothing. She wanted some one that could teach her very deeply and now at last she was sure that she had found him, yes she really had it, before she had thought to look if in this man she would find it.

During this year 'Mis' Herbert as her neighbors called her, Melanctha's pale yellow mother was very sick, and in this year she died.

Melanctha's father during these last years did not come very often to the house where his wife lived and Melanctha.[2] Melanctha was not sure that her father was now any longer here in Bridgepoint. It was Melanctha who was very good now to her mother. It was always Melanctha's way to be good to any one in trouble.

Melanctha took good care of her mother. She did everything that any woman could, she tended and soothed and helped her pale yellow mother, and she worked hard in every way to take care of her, and make her dying easy. But Melanctha did not in these days like her mother any better, and her mother never cared much for this daughter who was always a hard child to manage, and who had a tongue that always could be very nasty.

Melanctha did everything that any woman could, and at last her mother died, and Melanctha had her buried. Melanctha's father was not heard from, and Melanctha in all her life after, never saw or heard or knew of anything that her father did.

It was the young doctor, Jefferson Campbell, who helped Melanctha toward the end, to take care of her sick mother. Jefferson Campbell had often before seen Melanctha Herbert, but he had never liked her very well, and he had never believed that she was any good. He had heard something about how she wandered. He knew a little too of Jane Harden, and he was sure that this Melanctha Herbert, who was her friend and who wandered, would never come to any good.

Dr. Jefferson Campbell was a serious, earnest, good young joyous

---

1. Adele in *Q.E.D.*, the character based on Stein, becomes the male African American doctor Jefferson Campbell in "Melanctha."
2. Another contradiction in the text: Melanctha does not live with her mother at this point in the chronology.

doctor. He liked to take care of everybody and he loved his own colored people. He always found life very easy did Jeff Campbell, and everybody liked to have him with them. He was so good and sympathetic, and he was so earnest and so joyous. He sang when he was happy, and he laughed, and his was the free abandoned laughter that gives the warm broad glow to negro sunshine.

Jeff Campbell had never yet in his life had real trouble. Jefferson's father was a good, kind, serious, religious man. He was a very steady, very intelligent, and very dignified, light brown, grey haired negro. He was a butler and he had worked for the Campbell family many years, and his father and his mother before him had been in the service of this family as free people.

Jefferson Campbell's father and his mother had of course been regularly married. Jefferson's mother was a sweet, little, pale brown, gentle woman who reverenced and obeyed her good husband, and who worshipped and admired and loved hard her good, earnest, cheery, hard working doctor boy who was her only child.

Jeff Campbell had been raised religious by his people but religion had never interested Jeff very much. Jefferson was very good. He loved his people and he never hurt them, and he always did everything they wanted and that he could to please them, but he really loved best science and experimenting and to learn things, and he early wanted to be a doctor, and he was always very interested in the life of the colored people.

The Campbell family had been very good to him and had helped him on with his ambition. Jefferson studied hard, he went to a colored college, and then he learnt to be a doctor.

It was now two or three years, that he had started in to practice. Everybody liked Jeff Campbell, he was so strong and kindly and cheerful and understanding, and he laughed so with pure joy, and he always liked to help all his own colored people.

Dr. Jeff knew all about Jane Harden. He had taken care of her in some of her bad trouble. He knew about Melanctha too, though until her mother was taken sick he had never met her. Then he was called in to help Melanctha to take care of her sick mother. Dr. Campbell did not like Melanctha's ways and he did not think that she would ever come to any good.

Dr. Campbell had taken care of Jane Harden in some of her bad trouble. Jane sometimes had abused Melanctha to him. What right had that Melanctha Herbert who owed everything to her, Jane Harden, what right had a girl like that to go away to other men and leave her, but Melanctha Herbert never had any sense of how to act to anybody. Melanctha had a good mind, Jane never denied her that, but she never used it to do anything decent with it. But what could you expect when Melanctha had such a brute of a black nigger father, and Melanctha was always abusing her father and yet she was just like him, and really she admired him so much and he never had any sense of what he owed to anybody, and Melanctha was just like him and she was proud of it too, and it made Jane so tired to hear Melanctha talk all the time as if she wasn't. Jane Harden hated people who had good minds and didn't use them, and Melanctha always had that weakness, and wanting to keep in with people, and never really saying that she wanted to be like her father, and it was so silly of Melanctha to abuse her father, when she was so much like him and she really liked it. No, Jane Harden had no use for Melanctha. Oh yes, Melanctha always came around to be good to her. Melanctha was always sure to do that. She never really went away and left one. She didn't use her mind enough to do things straight out like that. Melanctha Herbert had a good mind, Jane never denied that to her, but she never wanted to see or hear about Melanctha Herbert any more, and she wished Melanctha wouldn't come in any more to see her. She didn't hate her, but she didn't want to hear about her father and all that talk Melanctha always made, and that just meant nothing to her. Jane Harden was very tired of all that now. She didn't have any use now any more for Melanctha, and if Dr. Campbell saw her he better tell her Jane didn't want to see her, and she could take her talk to somebody else, who was ready to believe her. And then Jane Harden would drop away and forget Melanctha and all her life before, and then she would begin to drink and so she would cover everything all over.

Jeff Campbell heard all this very often, but it did not interest him very deeply. He felt no desire to know more of this Melanctha. He heard her, once, talking to another girl outside of the house, when he was paying a visit to Jane Harden. He did not see much in the talk that he heard her do. He did not see much in the things Jane Harden said when she abused Melanctha to him. He was more interested in Jane herself than in anything he heard about Melanctha. He knew Jane Harden had a good mind, and she had had power, and she could really have done things, and now this drinking covered everything all over. Jeff Campbell was always very sorry when he had to see it. Jane Harden was a roughened woman, and yet Jeff found a great many strong good things in her, that still made him like her.

Jeff Campbell did everything he could for Jane Harden. He did not care much to hear about Melanctha. He had no feeling, much, about her. He did not find that he took any interest in her. Jane Harden was so much a stronger woman, and Jane really had had a good mind, and she had used it to do things with it, before this drinking business had taken such a hold upon her.

Dr. Campbell was helping Melanctha Herbert to take care of her sick mother. He saw Melanctha now for long times and very often, and they sometimes talked a good deal together, but Melanctha never said anything to him about Jane Harden. She never talked to him about anything that was not just general matters, or about medicine, or to tell him funny stories. She asked him many questions and always listened very well to all he told her, and she always remembered everything she heard him say about doctoring, and she always remembered everything that she had learned from all the others.

Jeff Campbell never found that all this talk interested him very deeply. He did not find that he liked Melanctha when he saw her so much, any better. He never found that he thought much about Melanctha. He never found that he believed much in her having a good mind, like Jane Harden. He found he liked Jane Harden always better, and that he wished very much that she had never begun that bad drinking.

Melanctha Herbert's mother was now always[3] getting sicker. Melanctha really did everything that any woman could. Melanctha's mother never liked her daughter any better. She never said much, did 'Mis' Herbert, but anybody could see that she did not think much of this daughter.

Dr. Campbell now often had to stay a long time to take care of 'Mis' Herbert. One day 'Mis' Herbert was much sicker and Dr. Campbell thought that this night, she would surely die. He came back late to the house, as he had said he would, to sit up and watch 'Mis' Herbert, and to help Melanctha, if she should need anybody to be with her. Melanctha Herbert and Jeff Campbell sat up all that night together. 'Mis' Herbert did not die. The next day she was a little better.

This house where Melanctha had always lived with her mother was a little red brick, two story house. They had not much furniture to fill it and some of the windows were broken and not mended. Melanctha did not have much money to use now on the house, but with a colored woman, who was their neighbor and good natured and who had always helped them, Melanctha managed to take care of her mother and to keep the house fairly clean and neat.

Melanctha's mother was in bed in a room upstairs, and the steps from below led right up into it. There were just two rooms on this upstairs floor. Melanctha and Dr. Campbell sat down on the steps, that night they watched together, so that they could hear and see Melanctha's mother and yet the light would be shaded, and they could sit and read, if they wanted to, and talk low some, and yet not disturb 'Mis' Herbert.

Dr. Campbell was always very fond of reading. Dr. Campbell had

3. Within the Steinian continuous present, "now always" suggests steadier, more rapid change than does "now" by itself.

not brought a book with him that night. He had just forgotten it. He had meant to put something in his pocket to read, so that he could amuse himself, while he was sitting there and watching. When he was through with taking care of 'Mis' Herbert, he came and sat down on the steps just above where Melanctha was sitting. He spoke about how he had forgotten to bring his book with him. Melanctha said there were some old papers in the house, perhaps Dr. Campbell could find something in them that would help pass the time for a while for him. All right, Dr. Campbell said, that would be better than just sitting there with nothing. Dr. Campbell began to read through the old papers that Melanctha gave him. When anything amused him in them, he read it out to Melanctha. Melanctha was now pretty silent, with him. Dr. Campbell began to feel a little, about how she responded to him. Dr. Campbell began to see a little that perhaps Melanctha had a good mind. Dr. Campbell was not sure yet that she had a good mind, but he began to think a little that perhaps she might have one.

Jefferson Campbell always liked to talk to everybody about the things he worked at and about his thinking about what he could do for the colored people. Melanctha Herbert never thought about these things the way that he did. Melanctha had never said much to Dr. Campbell about what she thought about them. Melanctha did not feel the same as he did about being good and regular in life, and not having excitements all the time, which was the way that Jefferson Campbell wanted that everybody should be, so that everybody would be wise and yet be happy. Melanctha always had strong the sense for real experience. Melanctha Herbert did not think much of this way of coming to real wisdom.

Dr. Campbell soon got through with his reading, in the old newspapers, and then somehow he began to talk along about the things he was always thinking. Dr. Campbell said he wanted to work so that he could understand what troubled people, and not to just have excitements, and he believed you ought to love your father and your mother and to be regular in all your life, and not to be always wanting new things and excitements, and to always know where you were, and what you wanted, and to always tell everything just as you meant it. That's the only kind of life he knew or believed in, Jeff Campbell repeated. "No I ain't got any use for all the time being in excitements and wanting to have all kinds of experience all the time. I got plenty of experience just living regular and quiet and with my family, and doing my work, and taking care of people, and trying to understand it. I don't believe much in this running around business and I don't want to see the colored people do it. I am a colored man and I ain't sorry, and I want to see the colored people like what is good and what I want them to have, and that's to live regular and work hard and understand things, and that's enough to keep any decent man excited." Jeff Campbell spoke now with some anger. Not to'Melanctha, he did not think of her at all when he was talking. It was the life he wanted that he spoke to, and the way he wanted things to be with the colored people.[4]

But Melanctha Herbert had listened to him say all this. She knew he meant it, but it did not mean much to her, and she was sure some day he would find out, that it was not all, of real wisdom. Melanctha knew very well what it was to have real wisdom. "But how about Jane Harden?" said Melanctha to Jeff Campbell, "seems to me Dr. Campbell you find her to have something in her, and you go there very often, and you talk to her much more than you do to the nice girls that stay at home with their people, the kind you say you are really wanting. It don't seem to me Dr. Campbell, that what you say and what you do seem to have much to do with each other. And about your being so good Dr. Campbell," went on Melanctha, "You don't care about going to church much yourself, and yet you always are saying you believe so much in things like that, for people. It seems to me, Dr. Campbell you want to have a good time just like all us others, and then you just keep on saying that it's right to be good and you ought not to have excitements, and yet you really don't want to do it Dr. Campbell, no more than me or Jane Harden. No, Dr. Campbell, it certainly does seem to me you don't know very well yourself, what you mean, when you are talking."

Jefferson had been talking right along, the way he always did when he got started, and now Melanctha's answer only made him talk a little harder. He laughed a little, too, but very low, so as not to disturb 'Mis' Herbert who was sleeping very nicely, and he looked brightly at Melanctha to enjoy her, and then he settled himself down to answer.

"Yes," he began, "it certainly does sound a little like I didn't know very well what I do mean, when you put it like that to me, Miss Melanctha, but that's just because you don't understand enough about what I meant, by what I was just saying to you. I don't say, never, I don't want to know all kinds of people, Miss Melanctha, and I don't say there ain't many kinds of people, and I don't say ever, that I don't find some like Jane Harden very good to know and talk to, but it's the strong things I like in Jane Harden, not all her excitements. I don't admire the bad things she does, Miss Melanctha, but Jane Harden is a strong woman and I always respect that in her. No I know you don't believe what I say, Miss Melanctha, but I mean it, and it's all just because you don't understand it when I say it. And

4. Jeff Campbell's ideas are similar to those of Booker T. Washington (1856–1915), the highly influential author of *Up From Slavery* (1901) and founder of Tuskegee Institute, who believed that African Americans should lead irreproachable, humble lives of service.

as for religion, that just ain't my way of being good, Miss Melanctha, but it's a good way for many people to be good and regular in their way of living, and if they believe it, it helps them to be good, and if they're honest in it, I like to see them have it. No, what I don't like, Miss Melanctha, is this what I see so much with the colored people, their always wanting new things just to get excited."

Jefferson Campbell here stopped himself in this talking. Melanctha Herbert did not make any answer. They both sat there very quiet.

Jeff Campbell then began again on the old papers. He sat there on the steps just above where Melanctha was sitting, and he went on with his reading, and his head went moving up and down, and sometimes he was reading, and sometimes he was thinking about all the things he wanted to be doing, and then he would rub the back of his dark hand over his mouth, and in between he would be frowning with his thinking, and sometimes he would be rubbing his head hard to help his thinking. And Melanctha just sat still and watched the lamp burning, and sometimes she turned it down a little, when the wind caught it and it would begin to get to smoking.

And so Jeff Campbell and Melanctha Herbert sat there on the steps, very quiet, a long time, and they didn't seem to think much, that they were together. They sat there so, for about an hour, and then it came to Jefferson very slowly and as a strong feeling that he was sitting there on the steps, alone, with Melanctha. He did not know if Melanctha Herbert was feeling very much about their being there alone together. Jefferson began to wonder about it a little. Slowly he felt that surely they must both have this feeling. It was so important that he knew that she must have it. They both sat there, very quiet, a long time.

At last Jefferson began to talk about how the lamp was smelling. Jefferson began to explain what it is that makes a lamp get to smelling. Melanctha let him talk. She did not answer, and then he stopped in his talking. Soon Melanctha began to sit up straighter and then she started in to question.

"About what you was just saying Dr. Campbell about living regular and all that, I certainly don't understand what you meant by what you was just saying. You ain't a bit like good people Dr. Campbell, like the good people you are always saying are just like you. I know good people Dr. Campbell, and you ain't a bit like men who are good and got religion. You are just as free and easy as any man can be Dr. Campbell, and you always like to be with Jane Harden, and she is a pretty bad one and you don't look down on her and you never tell her she is a bad one. I know you like her just like a friend Dr. Campbell, and so I certainly don't understand just what it is you mean by all that you was just saying to me. I know you mean honest Dr. Campbell, and I am always trying to believe you, but I can't say as I see just what you mean when you say you want to be good and real pious, because I am very certain Dr. Campbell that you ain't that kind of a man at all, and you ain't never ashamed to be with queer[5] folks Dr. Campbell, and you seem to be thinking what you are doing is just like what you are always saying, and Dr. Campbell, I certainly don't just see what you mean by what you say."

Dr. Campbell almost laughed loud enough to wake 'Mis' Herbert. He did enjoy the way Melanctha said these things to him. He began to feel very strongly about it that perhaps Melanctha really had a good mind. He was very free now in his laughing, but not so as to make Melanctha angry. He was very friendly with her in his laughing, and then he made his face get serious, and he rubbed his head to help him in his thinking.

"I know Miss Melanctha" he began, "It ain't very easy for you to understand what I was meaning by what I was just saying to you, and perhaps some of the good people I like so wouldn't think very much, any more than you do, Miss Melanctha, about the ways I have to be good. But that's no matter Miss Melanctha. What I mean Miss Melanctha by what I was just saying to you is, that I don't, no, never, believe in doing things just to get excited. You see Miss Melanctha I mean the way so many of the colored people do it. Instead of just working hard and caring about their working and living regular with their families and saving up all their money, so they will have some to bring up their children better, instead of living regular and doing like that and getting all their new ways from just decent living, the colored people just keep running around and perhaps drinking and doing everything bad they can ever think of, and not just because they like all those bad things that they are always doing, but only just because they want to get excited. No Miss Melanctha, you see I am a colored man myself and I ain't sorry, and I want to see the colored people being good and careful and always honest and living always just as regular as can be, and I am sure Miss Melanctha, that that way everybody can have a good time, and be happy and keep right and be busy, and not always have to be doing bad things for new ways to get excited. Yes Miss Melanctha, I certainly do like everything to be good, and quiet, and I certainly do think that is the best way for all us colored people. No, Miss Melanctha too, I don't mean this except only just the way I say it. I ain't got any other meaning Miss Melanctha, and it's that what I mean when I am saying about being really good. It ain't Miss Melanctha to be pious and not liking every kind of people, and I don't say ever Miss Melanctha that when other kind of people come regular into your life you shouldn't want

5. This does not explicitly or exclusively mean homosexual here, though homosexuality is suggested; it describes people who do not live the respectable, routinized lives Jeff Campbell believes African Americans should live.

to know them always. What I mean Miss Melanctha by what I am always saying is, you shouldn't try to know everybody just to run around and get excited. It's that kind of way of doing that I hate so always Miss Melanctha, and that is so bad for all us colored people. I don't know as you understand now any better what I mean by what I was just saying to you. But you certainly do know now Miss Melanctha, that I always mean it what I say when I am talking."

"Yes I certainly do understand you when you talk so Dr. Campbell. I certainly do understand now what you mean by what you was always saying to me. I certainly do understand Dr. Campbell that you mean you don't believe it's right to love anybody." "Why sure no, yes I do Miss Melanctha, I certainly do believe strong in loving, and in being good to everybody, and trying to understand what they all need, to help them." "Oh I know all about that way of doing Dr. Campbell, but that certainly ain't the kind of love I mean when I am talking. I mean real, strong, hot love Dr. Campbell, that makes you do anything for somebody that loves you." "I don't know much about that kind of love yet Miss Melanctha. You see it's this way with me always Miss Melanctha. I am always so busy with my thinking about my work I am doing and so I don't have time for just fooling, and then too, you see Miss Melanctha, I really certainly don't ever like to get excited, and that kind of loving hard does seem always to mean just getting all the time excited. That certainly is what I always think from what I see of them that have it bad Miss Melanctha, and that certainly would never suit a man like me. You see Miss Melanctha I am a very quiet kind of fellow, and I believe in a quiet life for all the colored people. No Miss Melanctha I certainly never have mixed myself up in that kind of trouble."

"Yes I certainly do see that very clear Dr. Campbell," said Melanctha, "I see that's certainly what it is always made me not know right about you and that's certainly what it is that makes you really mean what you was always saying. You certainly are just too scared Dr. Campbell to really feel things way down in you. All you are always wanting Dr. Campbell, is just to talk about being good, and to play with people just to have a good time, and yet always to certainly keep yourself out of trouble. It don't seem to me Dr. Campbell that I admire that way to do things very much. It certainly ain't really to me being very good. It certainly ain't any more to me Dr. Campbell, but that you certainly are awful scared about really feeling things way down in you, and that's certainly the only way Dr. Campbell I can see that you can mean, by what it is that you are always saying to me."

"I don't know about that Miss Melanctha, I certainly don't think I can't feel things very deep in me, though I do say I certainly do like to have things nice and quiet, but I don't see harm in keeping out of danger Miss Melanctha, when a man knows he certainly don't want to get killed in it, and I don't know anything that's more awful dangerous Miss Melanctha than being strong in love with somebody. I don't mind sickness or real trouble Miss Melanctha, and I don't want to be talking about what I can do in real trouble, but you know something about that Miss Melanctha, but I certainly don't see much in mixing up just to get excited, in that awful kind of danger. No Miss Melanctha I certainly do only know just two kinds of ways of loving. One kind of loving seems to me, is like one has a good quiet feeling in a family when one does his work, and is always living good and being regular, and then the other way of loving is just like having it like any animal that's low in the streets together, and that don't seem to me very good Miss Melanctha, though I don't say ever that it's not all right when anybody likes it, and that's all the kinds of love I know Miss Melanctha, and I certainly don't care very much to get mixed up in that kind of a way just to be in trouble."

Jefferson stopped and Melanctha thought a little.

"That certainly does explain to me Dr. Campbell what I been thinking about you this long time. I certainly did wonder how you could be so live, and knowing everything, and everybody, and talking so big always about everything, and everybody always liking you so much, and you always looking as if you was thinking, and yet you really was never knowing about anybody and certainly not being really very understanding. It certainly is all Dr. Campbell because you is so afraid you will be losing being good so easy, and it certainly do seem to me Dr. Campbell that it certainly don't amount to very much that kind of goodness."

"Perhaps you are right Miss Melanctha," Jefferson answered. "I don't say never, perhaps you ain't right Miss Melanctha. Perhaps I ought to know more about such ways Miss Melanctha. Perhaps it would help me some, taking care of the colored people, Miss Melanctha. I don't say, no, never, but perhaps I could learn a whole lot about women the right way, if I had a real good teacher."

'Mis' Herbert just then stirred a little in her sleep. Melanctha went up the steps to the bed to attend her. Dr. Campbell got up too and went to help her. 'Mis' Herbert woke up and was a little better. Now it was morning and Dr. Campbell gave his directions to Melanctha, and then left her.

Melanctha Herbert all her life long, loved and wanted good, kind and considerate people. Jefferson Campbell was all the things that Melanctha had ever wanted. Jefferson was a strong, well built, good looking, cheery, intelligent and good mulatto. And then at first he had not cared to know Melanctha, and when he did begin to know her he had not liked her very well, and he had not thought that she would ever come to any good. And then Jefferson Campbell was so very gentle. Jefferson never did some things like other men, things that now were beginning to be ugly, for Melanctha. And then too Jefferson Campbell did not seem to know very well what it was that Melanctha really wanted, and all this was making Melanctha feel his power with her always getting stronger.

Dr. Campbell came in every day to see 'Mis' Herbert. 'Mis' Herbert, after that night they watched together, did get a little better, but 'Mis' Herbert was really very sick, and soon it was pretty sure that she would have to die. Melanctha certainly did everything, all the time, that any woman could. Jefferson never thought much better of Melanctha while she did it. It was not her being good, he wanted to find in her. He knew very well Jane Harden was right, when she said Melanctha was always being good to everybody but that that did not make Melanctha any better for her. Then too, 'Mis' Herbert never liked Melanctha any better, even on the last day of her living, and so Jefferson really never thought much of Melanctha's always being good to her mother.

Jefferson and Melanctha now saw each other, very often. They now always liked to be with each other, and they always now had a good time when they talked to one another. They, mostly in their talking to each other, still just talked about outside things and what they were thinking. Except just in little moments, and not those very often, they never said anything about their feeling. Sometimes Melanctha would tease Jefferson a little just to show she had not forgotten, but mostly she listened to his talking, for Jefferson still always liked to talk along about the things he believed in. Melanctha was liking Jefferson Campbell better every day, and Jefferson was beginning to know that Melanctha certainly had a good mind, and he was beginning to feel a little her real sweetness. Not in her being good to 'Mis' Herbert, that never seemed to Jefferson to mean much in her, but there was a strong kind of sweetness in Melanctha's nature that Jefferson began now to feel when he was with her.

'Mis' Herbert was now always getting sicker. One night again Dr. Campbell felt very certain that before it was morning she would surely die. Dr. Campbell said he would come back to help Melanctha watch her, and to do anything he could to make 'Mis' Herbert's dying more easy for her. Dr. Campbell came back that evening, after he was through with his other patients, and then he made 'Mis' Herbert easy, and then he came and sat down on the steps just above where Melanctha was sitting with the lamp, and looking very tired. Dr. Campbell was pretty tired too, and they both sat there very quiet.

"You look awful tired to-night, Dr. Campbell," Melanctha said at last, with her voice low and very gentle, "Don't you want to go lie down and sleep a little? You're always being much too good to everybody, Dr. Campbell. I like to have you stay here watching to-night with me, but it don't seem right you ought to stay here when you got so much always to do for everybody. You are certainly very kind to come back, Dr. Campbell, but I can certainly get along to-night without you. I can get help next door sure if I need it. You just go 'long home to bed, Dr. Campbell. You certainly do look as if you need it."

Jefferson was silent for some time, and always he was looking very gently at Melanctha.

"I certainly never did think, Miss Melanctha, I would find you to be so sweet and thinking, with me." "Dr. Campbell" said Melanctha, still more gentle, "I certainly never did think that you would ever feel it good to like me. I certainly never did think you would want to see for yourself if I had sweet ways in me."

They both sat there very tired, very gentle, very quiet, a long time. At last Melanctha in a low, even tone began to talk to Jefferson Campbell.

"You are certainly a very good man, Dr. Campbell, I certainly do feel that more every day I see you. Dr. Campbell, I sure do want to be friends with a good man like you, now I know you. You certainly, Dr. Campbell, never do things like other men, that's always ugly for me. Tell me true, Dr. Campbell, how you feel about being always friends with me. I certainly do know, Dr. Campbell, you are a good man, and if you say you will be friends with me, you certainly never will go back on me, the way so many kinds of them do to every girl they ever get to like them. Tell me for true, Dr. Campbell, will you be friends with me."

"Why, Miss Melanctha," said Campbell slowly, "why you see I just can't say that right out that way to you. Why sure you know Miss Melanctha, I will be very glad if it comes by and by that we are always friends together, but you see, Miss Melanctha, I certainly am a very slow-minded quiet kind of fellow though I do say quick things all the time to everybody, and when I certainly do want to mean it what I am saying to you, I can't say things like that right out to everybody till I know really more for certain all about you, and how I like you, and what I really mean to do better for you. You certainly do see what I mean, Miss Melanctha." "I certainly do admire you for talking honest to me, Jeff Campbell," said Melanctha. "Oh, I am always honest, Miss Melanctha. It's easy enough for me always to be honest, Miss Melanctha. All I got to do is always just to say right out what I am thinking. I certainly never have got any real reason for not saying it right out like that to anybody."

They sat together, very silent. "I certainly do wonder, Miss Melanctha," at last began Jeff Campbell, "I certainly do wonder, if we know very right, you and me, what each other is really thinking. I certainly do wonder, Miss Melanctha, if we know at all really what each other means by what we are always saying." "That certainly do

mean, by what you say, that you think I am a bad one, Jeff Campbell,"
flashed out Melanctha. "Why no, Miss Melanctha, why sure I don't
mean any thing like that at all, by what I am saying to you. You know
well as I do, Miss Melanctha, I think better of you every day I see
you, and I like to talk with you all the time now, Miss Melanctha,
and I certainly do think we both like it very well when we are
together, and it seems to me always more, you are very good and
sweet always to everybody. It only is, I am really so slow-minded in
my ways, Miss Melanctha, for all I talk so quick to everybody, and I
don't like to say to you what I don't know for very sure, and I certainly
don't know for sure I know just all what you mean by what you are
always saying to me. And you see, Miss Melanctha, that's what makes
me say what I was just saying to you when you asked me."

"I certainly do thank you again for being honest to me, Dr. Campbell," said Melanctha. "I guess I leave you now, Dr. Campbell. I think
I go in the other room and rest a little. I leave you here, so perhaps
if I ain't here you will maybe sleep and rest yourself a little. Good
night now, Dr. Campbell, I call you if I need you later to help me,
Dr. Campbell, I hope you rest well, Dr. Campbell."

Jeff Campbell, when Melanctha left him, sat there and he was
very quiet and just wondered. He did not know very well just what
Melanctha meant by what she was always saying to him. He did not
know very well how much he really knew about Melanctha Herbert.
He wondered if he should go on being so much all the time with her.
He began to think about what he should do now with her. Jefferson
Campbell was a man who liked everybody and many people liked
very much to be with him. Women liked him, he was so strong, and
good, and understanding, and innocent, and firm, and gentle. Sometimes they seemed to want very much he should be with them. When
they got so, they always had made Campbell very tired. Sometimes
he would play a little with them, but he never had had any strong
feeling for them. Now with Melanctha Herbert everything seemed
different. Jefferson was not sure that he knew here just what he
wanted. He was not sure he knew just what it was that Melanctha
wanted. He knew if it was only play, with Melanctha, that he did not
want to do it. But he remembered always how she had told him he
never knew how to feel things very deeply. He remembered how she
told him he was afraid to let himself ever know real feeling, and then
too, most of all to him, she had told him he was not very understanding. That always troubled Jefferson very keenly, he wanted very badly
to be really understanding. If Jefferson only knew better just what
Melanctha meant by what she said. Jefferson always had thought he
knew something about women. Now he found that really he knew
nothing. He did not know the least bit about Melanctha. He did not
know what it was right that he should do about it. He wondered if

it was just a little play that they were doing. If it was a play he did not want to go on playing, but if it was really that he was not very understanding, and that with Melanctha Herbert he could learn to really understand, then he was very certain he did not want to be a coward. It was very hard for him to know what he wanted. He thought and thought, and always he did not seem to know any better what he wanted. At last he gave up this thinking. He felt sure it was only play with Melanctha. "No, I certainly won't go on fooling with her any more this way," he said at last out loud to himself, when he was through with this thinking. "I certainly will stop fooling, and begin to go on with my thinking about my work and what's the matter with people like 'Mis' Herbert," and Jefferson took out his book from his pocket, and drew near to the lamp, and began with some hard scientific reading.

Jefferson sat there for about an hour reading, and he had really forgotten all about his trouble with Melanctha's meaning. Then 'Mis' Herbert had some trouble with her breathing. She woke up and was gasping. Dr. Campbell went to her and gave her something that would help her. Melanctha came out from the other room and did things as he told her. They together made 'Mis' Herbert more comfortable and easy, and soon she was again in her deep sleep.

Dr. Campbell went back to the steps where he had been sitting. Melanctha came and stood a little while beside him, and then she sat down and watched him reading. By and by they began with their talking. Jeff Campbell began to feel that perhaps it was all different. Perhaps it was not just play, with Melanctha. Anyway he liked it very well that she was with him. He began to tell her about the book he was just reading.

Melanctha was very intelligent always in her questions. Jefferson knew now very well that she had a good mind. They were having a very good time, talking there together. And then they began again to get quiet.

"It certainly was very good in you to come back and talk to me Miss Melanctha," Jefferson said at last to her, for now he was almost certain, it was no game she was playing. Melanctha really was a good woman, and she had a good mind, and she had a real, strong sweetness, and she could surely really teach him. "Oh I always like to talk to you Dr. Campbell" said Melanctha, "And then you was only just honest to me, and I always like it when a man is really honest to me." Then they were again very silent, sitting there together, with the lamp between them, that was always smoking. Melanctha began to lean a little more toward Dr. Campbell, where he was sitting, and then she took his hand between her two and pressed it hard, but she said nothing to him. She let it go then and leaned a little nearer to him. Jefferson moved a little but did not do anything in answer. At last, "Well," said Melanctha sharply to him. "I was just thinking" began Dr. Campbell slowly, "I was just wondering," he was beginning to get ready to go on with his talking. "Don't you ever stop with your thinking long enough ever to have any feeling Jeff Campbell," said Melanctha a little sadly.[6] "I don't don't know," said Jeff Campbell slowly, "I don't know Miss Melanctha much about that. No, I don't stop thinking much Miss Melanctha and if I can't ever feel without stopping thinking, I certainly am very much afraid Miss Melanctha that I never will do much with that kind of feeling. Sure you ain't worried Miss Melanctha, about my really not feeling very much all the time. I certainly do think I feel some, Miss Melanctha, even though I always do it without ever knowing how to stop with my thinking." "I am certainly afraid I don't think much of your kind of feeling Dr. Campbell." "Why I think you certainly are wrong Miss Melanctha I certainly do think I feel as much for you Miss Melanctha, as you ever feel about me, sure I do. I don't think you know me right when you talk like that to me. Tell me just straight out how much do you care about me, Miss Melanctha." "Care about you Jeff Campbell," said Melanctha slowly. "I certainly do care for you Jeff Campbell less than you are always thinking and much more than you are ever knowing."

Jeff Campbell paused on this, and he was silent with the power of Melanctha's meaning. They sat there together very silent, a long time. "Well Jeff Campbell," said Melanctha. "Oh," said Dr. Campbell and he moved himself a little, and then they were very silent a long time. "Haven't you got nothing to say to me Jeff Campbell?" said Melanctha. "Why yes, what was it we were just saying about to one another. You see Miss Melanctha I am a very quiet, slow minded kind of fellow, and I am never sure I know just exactly what you mean by all that you are always saying to me. But I do like you very much Miss Melanctha and I am very sure you got very good things in you all the time. You sure do believe what I am saying to you Miss Melanctha." "Yes I believe it when you say it to me, Jeff Campbell," said Melanctha, and then she was silent and there was much sadness in it. "I guess I go in and lie down again Dr. Campbell," said Melanctha. "Don't go leave me Miss Melanctha," said Jeff Campbell quickly. "Why not, what you want of me Jeff Campbell?" said Melanctha. "Why," said Jeff Campbell slowly, "I just want to go on talking with you. I certainly do like talking about all kinds of things with you. You certainly know that all right, Miss Melanctha." "I guess I go lie down again and leave you here with your thinking," said Melanctha gently. "I certainly am very tired to night Dr. Campbell. Good night I hope you rest well Dr. Campbell." Melanctha stooped over him, where he

6. See *Q.E.D.* page 186, where Helen, the character based on May Bookstaver, says to Adele, "Haven't you ever stopped thinking long enough to feel?"

was sitting, to say this good night, and then, very quick and sudden, she kissed him and then, very quick again, she went away and left him.

Dr. Campbell sat there very quiet, with only a little thinking and sometimes a beginning feeling, and he was alone until it began to be morning, and then he went, and Melanctha helped him, and he made 'Mis' Herbert more easy in her dying. 'Mis' Herbert lingered on till about ten o'clock the next morning, and then slowly and without much pain she died away. Jeff Campbell staid till the last moment, with Melanctha, to make her mother's dying easy for her. When it was over he sent in the colored woman from next door to help Melanctha fix things, and then he went away to take care of his other patients. He came back very soon to Melanctha. He helped her to have a funeral for her mother. Melanctha then went to live with the good natured woman, who had been her neighbor. Melanctha still saw Jeff Campbell very often. Things began to be very strong between them.

Melanctha now never wandered, unless she was with Jeff Campbell. Sometimes she and he wandered a good deal together. Jeff Campbell had not got over his way of talking to her all the time about all the things he was always thinking. Melanctha never talked much, now, when they were together. Sometimes Jeff Campbell teased her about her not talking to him. "I certainly did think Melanctha you was a great talker from the way Jane Harden and everybody said things to me, and from the way I heard you talk so much when I first met you. Tell me true Melanctha, why don't you talk more now to me, perhaps it is I talk so much I don't give you any chance to say things to me, or perhaps it is you hear me talk so much you don't think so much now of a whole lot of talking. Tell me honest Melanctha, why don't you talk more to me." "You know very well Jeff Campbell," said Melanctha "You certainly do know very well Jeff, you don't think really much, of my talking. You think a whole lot more about everything than I do Jeff, and you don't care much what I got to say about it. You know that's true what I am saying Jeff, if you want to be real honest, the way you always are when I like you so much." Jeff laughed and looked fondly at her. "I don't say ever I know, you ain't right, when you say things like that to me, Melanctha. You see you always like to be talking just what you think everybody wants to be hearing from you, and when you are like that, Melanctha, honest, I certainly don't care very much to hear you, but sometimes you say something that is what you are really thinking, and then I like a whole lot to hear you talking." Melanctha smiled, with her strong sweetness, on him, and she felt her power very deeply. "I certainly never do talk very much when I like anybody really, Jeff. You see, Jeff, it ain't much use to talk about what a woman is really feeling in her.

You see all that, Jeff, better, by and by, when you get to really feeling. You won't be so ready then always with your talking. You see, Jeff, if it don't come true what I am saying." "I don't ever say you ain't always right, Melanctha," said Jeff Campbell. "Perhaps what I call my thinking ain't really so very understanding. I don't say, no never now any more, you ain't right, Melanctha, when you really say things to me. Perhaps I see it all to be very different when I come to really see what you mean by what you are always saying to me." "You is very sweet and good to me always, Jeff Campbell," said Melanctha. " 'Deed I certainly am not good to you, Melanctha. Don't I bother you all the time with my talking, but I really do like you a whole lot, Melanctha." "And I like you, Jeff Campbell, and you certainly are mother, and father, and brother, and sister, and child and everything, always to me.[7] I can't say much about how good you been to me, Jeff Campbell, I never knew any man who was good and didn't do things ugly, before I met you to take care of me, Jeff Campbell. Good-by, Jeff, come see me to-morrow, when you get through with your work-ing." "Sure Melanctha, you know that already," said Jeff Campbell, and then he went away and left her.

These months had been an uncertain time for Jeff Campbell. He never knew how much he really knew about Melanctha. He saw her now for long times and very often. He was beginning always more and more to like her. But he did not seem to himself to know very much about her. He was beginning to feel he could almost trust the goodness in her. But then, always, really, he was not very sure about her. Melanctha always had ways that made him feel uncertain with her, and yet he was so near, in his feeling for her. He now never thought about all this in real words any more. He was always letting it fight itself out in him. He was now never taking any part in this fighting that was always going on inside him.

Jeff always loved now to be with Melanctha and yet he always hated to go to her. Somehow he was always afraid when he was to go to her, and yet he had made himself very certain that here he would not be a coward. He never felt any of this being afraid, when he was with her. Then they always were very true, and near to one another. But always when he was going to her, Jeff would like any-thing that could happen that would keep him a little longer from her.

It was a very uncertain time, all these months, for Jeff Campbell. He did not know very well what it was that he really wanted. He was very certain that he did not know very well what it was that Melanc-tha wanted. Jeff Campbell had always all his life loved to be with people, and he had loved all his life always to be thinking, but he

---

7. See *Q.E.D.* page 202, where Helen says, at leaving Adele, "I seem to be taking farewell of parents, brothers sisters my own child, everything at once."

was still only a great boy, was Jeff Campbell, and he had never before had any of this funny kind of feeling. Now, this evening, when he was free to go and see Melanctha, he talked to anybody he could find who would detain him, and so it was very late when at last he came to the house where Melanctha was waiting to receive him.

Jeff came in to where Melanctha was waiting for him, and he took off his hat and heavy coat, and then drew up a chair and sat down by the fire. It was very cold that night, and Jeff sat there, and rubbed his hands and tried to warm them. He had only said "How do you do" to Melanctha, he had not yet begun to talk to her. Melanctha sat there, by the fire, very quiet. The heat gave a pretty pink glow to her pale yellow and attractive face. Melanctha sat in a low chair, her hands, with their long, fluttering fingers, always ready to show her strong feeling, were lying quiet in her lap. Melanctha was very tired with her waiting for Jeff Campbell. She sat there very quiet and just watching. Jeff was a robust, dark, healthy, cheery negro. His hands were firm and kindly and unimpassioned. He touched women always with his big hands, like a brother. He always had a warm broad glow, like southern sunshine. He never had anything mysterious in him. He was open, he was pleasant, he was cheery, and always he wanted, as Melanctha once had wanted, always now he too wanted really to understand.

Jeff sat there this evening in his chair and was silent a long time, warming himself with the pleasant fire. He did not look at Melanctha who was watching. He sat there and just looked into the fire. At first his dark, open face was smiling, and he was rubbing the back of his black-brown hand over his mouth to help him in his smiling. Then he was thinking, and he frowned and rubbed his head hard, to help him in his thinking. Then he smiled again, but now his smiling was not very pleasant. His smile was now wavering on the edge of scorning. His smile changed more and more, and then he had a look as if he were deeply down, all disgusted. Now his face was darker, and he was bitter in his smiling, and he began, without looking from the fire, to talk to Melanctha, who was now very tense with her watching.

"Melanctha Herbert", began Jeff Campbell, "I certainly after all this time I know you, I certainly do know little, real about you. You see, Melanctha, it's like this way with me"; Jeff was frowning, with his thinking and looking very hard into the fire, "You see it's just this way, with me now, Melanctha. Sometimes you seem like one kind of a girl to me, and sometimes you are like a girl that is all different to me, and the two kinds of girls is certainly very different to each other, and I can't see any way they seem to have much to do, to be together in you. They certainly don't seem to be made much like as if they could have anything really to do with each other. Sometimes you are a girl to me I certainly never would be trusting, and you got a laugh then so hard, it just rattles, and you got ways so bad, I can't believe you mean them hardly, and yet all that I just been saying is certainly you one way I often see you, and it's what your mother and Jane Harden always found you, and it's what makes me hate so, to come near you. And then certainly sometimes, Melanctha, you certainly is all a different creature, and sometimes then there comes out in you what is certainly a thing, like a real beauty. I certainly, Melanctha, never can tell just how it is that it comes so lovely. Seems to me when it comes it's got a real sweetness, that is more wonderful than a pure flower, and a gentleness, that is more tender than the sunshine, and a kindness, that makes one feel like summer, and then a way to know, that makes everything all over, and all that, and it does certainly seem to be real for the little while it's lasting, for the little while that I can surely see it, and it gives me to feel like I certainly had got real religion. And then when I got rich with such a feeling, comes all that other girl, and then that seems more likely that that is really you what's honest, and then I certainly do get awful afraid to come to you, and I certainly never do feel I could be very trusting with you. And then I certainly don't know anything at all about you, and I certainly don't know which is a real Melanctha Herbert, and I certainly don't feel no longer, I ever want to talk to you. Tell me honest, Melanctha, which is the way that is you really, when you are alone, and real, and all honest. Tell me, Melanctha, for I certainly do want to know it."

Melanctha did not make him any answer, and Jeff, without looking at her, after a little while, went on with his talking. "And then, Melanctha, sometimes you certainly do seem sort of cruel, and not to care about people being hurt or in trouble, something so hard about you it makes me sometimes real nervous, sometimes somehow like you always, like your being, with 'Mis' Herbert. You sure did do everything that any woman could, Melanctha, I certainly never did see anybody do things any better, and yet, I don't know how to say just what I mean, Melanctha, but there was something awful hard about your feeling, so different from the way I'm always used to see good people feeling, and so it was the way Jane Harden and 'Mis' Herbert talked when they felt strong to talk about you, and yet, Melanctha, somehow I feel so really near to you, and you certainly have got an awful wonderful, strong kind of sweetness. I certainly would like to know for sure, Melanctha, whether I got really anything to be afraid for. I certainly did think once, Melanctha, I knew something about all kinds of women. I certainly know now really, how I don't know anything sure at all about you, Melanctha, though I been with you so long, and so many times for whole hours with you, and

I like so awful much to be with you, and I can always say anything I am thinking to you. I certainly do awful wish, Melanctha, I really was more understanding. I certainly do that same, Melanctha."

Jeff stopped now and looked harder than before into the fire. His face changed from his thinking back into that look that was so like as if he was all through and through him, disgusted with what he had been thinking. He sat there a long time, very quiet, and then slowly, somehow, it came strongly to him that Melanctha Herbert, there beside him, was trembling and feeling it all to be very bitter. "Why, Melanctha," cried Jeff Campbell, and he got up and put his arm around her like a brother. "I stood it just so long as I could bear it, Jeff," sobbed Melanctha, and then she gave herself away, to her misery, "I was awful ready, Jeff, to let you say anything you liked that gave you any pleasure. You could say all about me what you wanted, Jeff, and I would try to stand it, so as you would be sure to be liking it, Jeff, but you was too cruel to me. When you do that kind of seeing how much you can make a woman suffer, you ought to give her a little rest, once sometimes, Jeff. They can't any of us stand it so for always, Jeff. I certainly did stand it just as long as I could, so you would like it, but I,—oh Jeff, you went on too long to-night Jeff. I couldn't stand it not a minute longer the way you was doing of it, Jeff. When you want to be seeing how the way a woman is really made of, Jeff, you shouldn't never be so cruel, never to be thinking how much she can stand, the strong way you always do it, Jeff." "Why, Melanctha," cried Jeff Campbell, in his horror, and then he was very tender to her, and like a good, strong, gentle brother in his soothing of her, "Why Melanctha dear, I certainly don't now see what it is you mean by what you was just saying to me. Why Melanctha, you poor little girl, you certainly never did believe I ever knew I was giving you real suffering. Why, Melanctha, how could you ever like me if you thought I ever could be so like a red Indian?"[8] "I didn't just know, Jeff," and Melanctha nestled to him, "I certainly never did know just what it was you wanted to be doing with me, but I certainly wanted you should do anything you liked, you wanted, to make me more understanding for you. I tried awful hard to stand it, Jeff, so as you could do anything you wanted with me." "Good Lord and Jesus Christ, Melanctha!" cried Jeff Campbell. "I certainly never can know anything about you real, Melanctha, you poor little girl," and Jeff drew her closer to him, "But I certainly do admire and trust you a whole lot now, Melanctha. I certainly do, for I certainly never did think I was hurting you at all, Melanctha, by the things I always been saying to you, Melanctha, you poor little, sweet, trembling baby now, be good, Melanctha. I certainly can't ever tell you how awful sorry I

---

8. Ironic use by Stein of derogatory racial stereotyping.

am to hurt you so, Melanctha. I do anything I can to show you how I never did mean to hurt you, Melanctha." "I know, I know," murmured Melanctha, clinging to him. "I know you are a good man, Jeff. I always know that, no matter how much you can hurt me." "I sure don't see how you can think so, Melanctha, if you certainly did think I was trying so hard just to hurt you." "Hush, you are only a great big boy, Jeff Campbell, and you don't know nothing yet about real hurting," said Melanctha, smiling up through her crying, at him. "You see, Jeff, I never knew anybody I could know real well and yet keep on always respecting, till I came to know you real well, Jeff." "I sure don't understand that very well, Melanctha. I ain't a bit better than just lots of others of the colored people. You certainly have been unlucky with the kind you met before me, that's all, Melanctha. I certainly ain't very good, Melanctha." "Hush, Jeff, you don't know nothing at all about what you are," said Melanctha. "Perhaps you are right, Melanctha. I don't say ever any more, you ain't right, when you say things to me, Melanctha," and Jefferson sighed, and then he smiled, and then they were quiet a long time together, and then after some more kindness, it was late, and then Jeff left her.

Jeff Campbell, all these months, had never told his good mother anything about Melanctha Herbert. Somehow he always kept his seeing her so much now, to himself. Melanctha too had never had any of her other friends meet him. They always acted together, these two, as if their being so much together was a secret, but really there was no one who would have made it any harder for them. Jeff Campbell did not really know how it had happened that they were so secret. He did not know if it was what Melanctha wanted. Jeff had never spoken to her at all about it. It just seemed as if it were well understood between them that nobody should know that they were so much together. It was as if it were agreed between them, that they should be alone by themselves always, and so they would work out together what they meant by what they were always saying to each other.

Jefferson often spoke to Melanctha about his good mother. He never said anything about whether Melanctha would want to meet her. Jefferson never quite understood why all this had happened so, in secret. He never really knew what it was that Melanctha really wanted. In all these ways he just, by his nature, did, what he sort of felt Melanctha wanted. And so they continued to be alone and much together, and now it had come to be the spring time, and now they had all out-doors to wander.

They had many days now when they were very happy. Jeff every day found that he really liked Melanctha better. Now surely he was beginning to have real, deep feeling in him. And still he loved to talk himself out to Melanctha, and he loved to tell her how good it all was to him, and how he always loved to be with her, and to tell her always all about it. One day, now Jeff arranged, that Sunday they would go out and have a happy, long day in the bright fields, and they would be all day just alone together. The day before, Jeff was called in to see Jane Harden.

Jane Harden was very sick almost all day and Jeff Campbell did everything he could to make her better. After a while Jane became more easy and then she began to talk to Jeff about Melanctha. Jane did not know how much Jeff was now seeing of Melanctha. Jane these days never saw Melanctha. Jane began to talk of the time when she first knew Melanctha. Jane began to tell how in these days Melanctha had very little understanding. She was young then and she had a good mind. Jane Harden never would say Melanctha never had a good mind, but in those days Melanctha certainly had not been very understanding. Jane began to explain to Jeff Campbell how in every way, she Jane, had taught Melanctha. Jane then began to explain how eager Melanctha always had been for all that kind of learning. Jane Harden began to tell how they had wandered. Jane began to tell how Melanctha once had loved her, Jane Harden. Jane began to tell Jeff of all the bad ways Melanctha had used with her. Jane began to tell all she knew of the way Melanctha had gone on, after she had left her. Jane began to tell all about the different men, white ones and blacks, Melanctha never was particular about things like that, Jane Harden said in passing, not that Melanctha was a bad one, and she had a good mind, Jane Harden never would say that she hadn't, but Melanctha always liked to use all the understanding ways that Jane had taught her, and so she wanted to know everything, always, that they knew how to teach her.

Jane was beginning to make Jeff Campbell see much clearer. Jane Harden did not know what it was that she was really doing with all this talking. Jane did not know what Jeff was feeling. Jane was always honest when she was talking, and now it just happened she had started talking about her old times with Melanctha Herbert. Jeff understood very well that it was all true what Jane was saying. Jeff Campbell was beginning now to see very clearly. He was beginning to feel very sick inside him. He knew now many things Melanctha had not yet taught him. He felt very sick and his heart was very heavy, and Melanctha certainly did seem very ugly to him. Jeff was at last beginning to know what it was to have deep feeling. He took care a little longer of Jane Harden, and then he went to his other patients, and then he went home to his room, and he sat down and at last he had stopped thinking. He was very sick and his heart was very heavy in him. He was very tired and all the world was very dreary to him, and he knew very well now at last, he was really feeling. He knew it now from the way it hurt him. He knew very well that now at last he was beginning to really have understanding. The next day he had arranged to spend, long and happy, all alone in the spring fields with Melanctha, wandering. He wrote her a note and said he could not go, he had a sick patient and would have to stay home with him. For three days after, he made no sign to Melanctha. He was very sick all these days, and his heart was very heavy in him, and he knew very well that now at last he had learned what it was to have deep feeling.

At last one day he got a letter from Melanctha. "I certainly don't rightly understand what you are doing now to me Jeff Campbell," wrote Melanctha Herbert. "I certainly don't rightly understand Jeff Campbell why you ain't all these days been near me, but I certainly do suppose it's just another one of the queer kind of ways you have to be good, and repenting of yourself all of a sudden. I certainly don't say to you Jeff Campbell I admire very much the way you take to be good Jeff Campbell. I am sorry Dr. Campbell, but I certainly am afraid I can't stand it no more from you the way you have been just acting. I certainly can't stand it any more the way you act when you have been as if you thought I was always good enough for anybody to have with them, and then you act as if I was a bad one and you always just despise me. I certainly am afraid Dr. Campbell I can't stand it any more like that. I certainly can't stand it any more the way you are always changing. I certainly am afraid Dr. Campbell you ain't man enough to deserve to have anybody care so much to be always with you. I certainly am awful afraid Dr. Campbell I don't ever any more want to really see you. Good-by Dr. Campbell I wish you always to be real happy."

Jeff Campbell sat in his room, very quiet, a long time, after he got through reading this letter. He sat very still and first he was very angry. As if he, too, did not know very badly what it was to suffer keenly. As if he had not been very strong to stay with Melanctha when he never knew what it was that she really wanted. He knew he was very right to be angry, he knew he really had not been a coward. He knew Melanctha had done many things it was very hard for him to forgive her. He knew very well he had done his best to be kind, and to trust her, and to be loyal to her, and now;—and then Jeff suddenly remembered how one night Melanctha had been so strong to suffer, and he felt come back to him the sweetness in her, and then Jeff knew that really, he always forgave her, and that really, it all was that he was so sorry he had hurt her, and he wanted to go straight away and be a comfort to her. Jeff knew very well, that what Jane Harden had told him about Melanctha and her bad ways, had been a true story, and yet he wanted very badly to be with Melanctha. Perhaps she could teach him to really understand it better. Perhaps she could teach him how it could be all true, and yet how he could be right to believe in her and to trust her.

Jeff sat down and began his answer to her. "Dear Melanctha," Jeff wrote to her. "I certainly don't think you got it all just right in the letter, I just been reading, that you just wrote me. I certainly don't think you are just fair or very understanding to all I have to suffer to keep straight on to really always to believe in you and trust you. I certainly don't think you always are fair to remember right how hard it is for a man, who thinks like I was always thinking, not to think you do things very bad very often. I certainly don't think, Melanctha, I ain't right when I was so angry when I got your letter to me. I know very well, Melanctha, that with you, I never have been a coward. I find it very hard, and I never said it any different, it is hard to me to be understanding, and to know really what it is you wanted, and what it is you are meaning by what you are always saying to me. I don't say ever, it ain't very hard for you to be standing that I ain't very quick to be following whichever way that you are always leading. You know very well, Melanctha, it hurts me very bad and way inside me when I have to hurt you, but I always got to be real honest with you. There ain't no other way for me to be, with you, and I know very well it hurts me too, a whole lot, when I can't follow so quick as you would have me. I don't like to be a coward to you, Melanctha, and I don't like to say what I ain't meaning to you. And if you don't want me to do things honest, Melanctha, why I can't ever talk to you, and you are right when you say, you never again want to see me, but if you got any real sense of what I always been feeling with you, and if you got any right sense, Melanctha, of how hard I been trying to think and to feel right for you, I will be very glad to come and see you, and to begin again with you. I don't say anything now, Melanctha, about how bad I been this week, since I saw you, Melanctha. It don't ever do any good to talk such things over. All I know is I do my best, Melanctha, to you, and I don't say, no, never, I can do any different than just to be honest and come as fast as I think it's right for me to be going in the ways you teach me to be really understanding. So don't talk any more foolishness, Melanctha, about my always changing. I don't change, never, and I got to do what I think is right and honest to me, and I never told you any different, and you always knew it very well that I always would do just so. If you like me to come and see you to-morrow, and go out with you, I will be very glad to, Melanctha. Let me know right away, what it is you want me to be doing for you, Melanctha.

Very truly yours,
JEFFERSON CAMPBELL

"Please come to me, Jeff." Melanctha wrote back for her answer. Jeff went very slowly to Melanctha, glad as he was, still to be going to her. Melanctha came, very quick, to meet him, when she saw him from where she had been watching for him. They went into the house together. They were very glad to be together. They were very good to one another.

"I certainly did think, Melanctha, this time almost really, you never did want me to come to you at all any more to see you," said Jeff Campbell to her, when they had begun again with their talking to each other. "You certainly did make me think, perhaps really this time, Melanctha, it was all over, my being with you ever, and I was very mad, and very sorry, too, Melanctha."

"Well you certainly was very bad to me, Jeff Campbell," said Melanctha, fondly.

"I certainly never do say any more you ain't always right, Melanctha," Jeff answered and he was very ready now with cheerful laughing, "I certainly never do say that any more, Melanctha, if I know it, but still, really, Melanctha, honest, I think perhaps I wasn't real bad to you any more than you just needed from me."

Jeff held Melanctha in his arms and kissed her. He sighed then and was very silent with her. "Well, Melanctha," he said at last, with some more laughing, "well, Melanctha, any way you can't say ever it ain't, if we are ever friends good and really, you can't say, no, never, but that we certainly have worked right hard to get both of us together for it, so we shall sure deserve it then, if we can ever really get it." "We certainly have worked real hard, Jeff, I can't say that ain't all right the way you say it," said Melanctha. "I certainly never can deny it, Jeff, when I feel so worn with all the trouble you been making for me, you bad boy, Jeff," and then Melanctha smiled and then she sighed, and then she was very silent with him.

At last Jeff was to go away. They stood there on the steps for a long time trying to say good-by to each other. At last Jeff made himself really say it. At last he made himself, that he went down the steps and went away.

On the next Sunday they arranged, they were to have the long happy day of wandering that they had lost last time by Jane Harden's talking. Not that Melanctha Herbert had heard yet of Jane Harden's talking.

Jeff saw Melanctha every day now. Jeff was a little uncertain all this time inside him, for he had never yet told to Melanctha what it was that had so nearly made him really want to leave her. Jeff knew that for him, it was not right he should not tell her. He knew they could only have real peace between them when he had been honest, and had really told her. On this long Sunday Jeff was certain that he would really tell her.

They were very happy all that day in their wandering. They had taken things along to eat together. They sat in the bright fields and they were happy, they wandered in the woods and they were happy. Jeff always loved in this way to wander. Jeff always loved to watch everything as it was growing, and he loved all the colors in the trees and on the ground, and the little, new, bright colored bugs he found in the moist ground and in the grass he loved to lie on and in which he was always so busy searching. Jeff loved everything that moved and that was still, and that had color, and beauty, and real being.

Jeff loved very much this day while they were wandering. He almost forgot that he had any trouble with him still inside him. Jeff loved to be there with Melanctha Herbert. She was always so sympathetic to him for the way she listened to everything he found and told her, the way she felt his joy in all this being, the way she never said she wanted anything different from the way they had it. It was certainly a busy and a happy day, this their first long day of really wandering.

Later they were tired, and Melanctha sat down on the ground, and Jeff threw himself his full length beside her. Jeff lay there, very quiet, and then he pressed her hand and kissed it and murmured to her, "You certainly are very good to me, Melanctha." Melanctha felt it very deep and did not answer. Jeff lay there a long time, looking up above him. He was counting all the little leaves he saw above him. He was following all the little clouds with his eyes as they sailed past him. He watched all the birds that flew high beyond him, and all the time Jeff knew he must tell to Melanctha what it was he knew now, that which Jane Harden, just a week ago, had told him. He knew very well that for him it was certain that he had to say it. It was hard, but for Jeff Campbell the only way to lose it was to say it, the only way to know Melanctha really, was to tell her all the struggle he had made to know her, to tell her so she could help him to understand his trouble better, to help him so that never again he could have any way to doubt her.

Jeff lay there a long time, very quiet, always looking up above him, and yet feeling very close now to Melanctha. At last he turned a little toward her, took her hands closer in his to make him feel it stronger, and then very slowly, for the words came very hard for him, slowly he began his talk to her.

"Melanctha," began Jeff, very slowly, "Melanctha, it ain't right I shouldn't tell you why I went away last week and almost never got the chance again to see you. Jane Harden was sick, and I went in to take care of her. She began to tell everything she ever knew about you. She didn't know how well now I know you. I didn't tell her not to go on talking. I listened while she told me everything about you. I certainly found it very hard with what she told me. I know she was talking truth in everything she said about you. I knew you had been free in your ways, Melanctha, I knew you liked to get excitement the way I always hate to see the colored people take it. I didn't know, till I heard Jane Harden say it, you had done things so bad, Melanctha.

When Jane Harden told me, I got very sick, Melanctha. I couldn't bear hardly, to think, perhaps I was just another like them to you, Melanctha. I was wrong not to trust you perhaps, Melanctha, but it did make things very ugly to me. I try to be honest to you, Melanctha, the way you say you really want it from me."

Melanctha drew her hands from Jeff Campbell. She sat there, and there was deep scorn in her anger.

"If you wasn't all through just selfish and nothing else, Jeff Campbell, you would take care you wouldn't have to tell me things like this, Jeff Campbell."

Jeff was silent a little, and he waited before he gave his answer. It was not the power of Melanctha's words that held him, for, for them, he had his answer, it was the power of the mood that filled Melanctha, and for that he had no answer. At last he broke through this awe, with his slow fighting resolution, and he began to give his answer.

"I don't say ever, Melanctha," he began, "it wouldn't have been more right for me to stop Jane Harden in her talking and to come to you to have you tell me what you were when I never knew you. I don't say it, no never to you, that that would not have been the right way for me to do, Melanctha. But I certainly am without any kind of doubting, I certainly do know for sure, I had a good right to know about what you were and your ways and your trying to use your understanding, every kind of way you could to get your learning. I certainly did have a right to know things like that about you, Melanctha. I don't say it ever, Melanctha, and I say it very often, I don't say ever I shouldn't have stopped Jane Harden in her talking and come to you and asked you yourself to tell me all about it, but I guess I wanted to keep myself from how much it would hurt me more, to have you yourself say it to me. Perhaps it was I wanted to keep you from having it hurt you so much more, having you to have to tell it to me. I don't know, I don't say it was to help you from being hurt most, or to help me. Perhaps I was a coward to let Jane Harden tell me 'stead of coming straight to you, to have you tell me, but I certainly am sure, Melanctha, I certainly had a right to know such things about you. I don't say it ever, ever, Melanctha, I hadn't the just right to know those things about you." Melanctha laughed her harsh laugh. "You needn't have been under no kind of worry, Jeff Campbell, about whether you should have asked me. You could have asked, it wouldn't have hurt nothing. I certainly never would have told you nothing." "I am not so sure of that, Melanctha," said Jeff Campbell. "I certainly do think you would have told me. I certainly do think I could make you feel it right to tell me. I certainly do think all I did wrong was to let Jane Harden tell me. I certainly do know I never did wrong, to learn what she told me. I certainly know very

well, Melanctha, if I had come here to you, you would have told it
all to me, Melanctha."

He was silent, and this struggle lay there, strong, between them.
It was a struggle, sure to be going on always between them. It was a
struggle that was as sure always to be going on between them, as
their minds and hearts always were to have different ways of working.

At last Melanctha took his hand, leaned over him and kissed him.
"I sure am very fond of you, Jeff Campbell," Melanctha whispered
to him.

Now for a little time there was not any kind of trouble between
Jeff Campbell and Melanctha Herbert. They were always together
now for long times, and very often. They got much joy now, both of
them, from being all the time together.

It was summer now, and they had warm sunshine to wander. It
was summer now, and Jeff Campbell had more time to wander, for
colored people never get sick so much in summer. It was summer
now, and there was a lovely silence everywhere, and all the noises,
too, that they heard around them were lovely ones, and added to the
joy, in these warm days, they loved so much to be together.

They talked some to each other in these days, did Jeff Campbell
and Melanctha Herbert, but always in these days their talking more
and more was like it always is with real lovers. Jeff did not talk so
much now about what he before always had been thinking. Sometimes Jeff would be, as if he was just waking from himself to be
with Melanctha, and then he would find he had been really all the
long time with her, and he had really never needed to be doing any
thinking.

It was sometimes pure joy Jeff would be talking to Melanctha, in
these warm days he loved so much to wander with her. Sometimes
Jeff would lose all himself in a strong feeling. Very often now, and
always with more joy in his feeling, he would find himself, he did
not know how or what it was he had been thinking. And Melanctha
always loved very well to make him feel it. She always now laughed
a little at him, and went back a little in him to his before, always
thinking, and she teased him with his always now being so good with
her in his feeling, and then she would so well and freely, and with
her pure, strong ways of reaching, she would give him all the love
she knew now very well, how much he always wanted to be sure he
really had it.

And Jeff took it straight now, and he loved it, and he felt, strong,
the joy of all this being, and it swelled out full inside him, and he
poured it all out back to her in freedom, in tender kindness, and in
joy, and in gentle brother fondling. And Melanctha loved him for it
always, her Jeff Campbell now, who never did things ugly, for her,
like all the men she always knew before always had been doing to

her. And they loved it always, more and more, together, with this new feeling they had now, in these long summer days so warm; they, always together now, just these two so dear, more and more to each other always, and the summer evenings when they wandered, and the noises in the full streets, and the music of the organs, and the dancing, and the warm smell of the people, and of dogs and of the horses, and all the joy of the strong, sweet pungent, dirty, moist, warm negro southern summer.

Every day now, Jeff seemed to be coming nearer, to be really loving. Every day now, Melanctha poured it all out to him, with more freedom. Every day now, they seemed to be having more and more, both together, of this strong, right feeling. More and more every day now they seemed to know more really, what it was each other one was always feeling. More and more now every day now, he did not think anything in words about what he was always doing. Every day now more and more Melanctha would let out to Jeff her real, strong feeling.

One day there had been much joy between them, more than they ever yet had had with their new feeling. All the day they had lost themselves in warm wandering. Now they were lying there and resting, with a green, bright, light-flecked world around them.

What was it that now really happened to them? What was it that Melanctha did, that made everything get all ugly for them? What was it that Melanctha felt then, that made Jeff remember all the feeling he had had in him when Jane Harden told him how Melanctha had learned to be so very understanding? Jeff did not know how it was that it had happened to him. It was all green, and warm, and very lovely to him, and now Melanctha somehow had made it all so ugly for him. What was it Melanctha was now doing with him? What was it he used to be thinking was the right way for him and all the colored people to be always trying to make it right, the way they should be always living? Why was Melanctha Herbert now all so ugly for him?

Melanctha Herbert somehow had made him feel deeply just then, what very more it was that she wanted from him. Jeff Campbell now felt in him what everybody always had needed to make them really understanding, to him. Jeff felt a strong disgust inside him; not for Melanctha herself, to him, not for himself really, in him, not for what it was that everybody wanted, in them; he only had disgust because he never could know really in him, what it was he wanted, to be really right in understanding, for him, he only had disgust because he never could know really what it was really right to him to be always doing, in the things he had before believed in, the things he before had believed in for himself and for all the colored people, the living regular, and the never wanting to be always having new things, just to keep on, always being in excitements. All the old thinking now came up very strong inside him. He sort of turned away then, and threw Melanctha from him.[9]

Jeff never, even now, knew what it was that moved him. He never, even now, was ever sure, he really knew what Melanctha was, when she was real herself, and honest. He thought he knew, and then there came to him some moment, just like this one, when she really woke him up to be strong in him. Then he really knew he could know nothing. He knew then, he never could know what it was she really wanted with him. He knew then he never could know really what it was he felt inside him. It was all so mixed up inside him. All he knew was he wanted very badly Melanctha should be there beside him, and he wanted very badly, too, always to throw her from him. What was it really that Melanctha wanted with him? What was it really, he, Jeff Campbell, wanted she should give him? "I certainly did think now," Jeff Campbell groaned inside him, "I certainly did think now I really was knowing all right, what I wanted. I certainly did really think now I was knowing how to be trusting with Melanctha. I certainly did think it was like that now with me sure, after all I've been through all this time with her. And now I certainly do know I don't know anything that's very real about her. Oh the good Lord help and keep me!" and Jeff groaned hard inside him, and he buried his face deep in the green grass underneath him, and Melanctha Herbert was very silent there beside him.

Then Jeff turned to look and see her. She was lying very still there by him, and the bitter water on her face was biting.[1] Jeff was so very sorry then, all over and inside him, the way he always was when Melanctha had been deep hurt by him. "I didn't mean to be so bad again to you, Melanctha, dear one," and he was very tender to her. "I certainly didn't never mean to go to be so bad to you, Melanctha, darling. I certainly don't know, Melanctha, darling, what it is makes me act so to you sometimes, when I certainly ain't meaning anything like I want to hurt you. I certainly don't mean to be so bad, Melanctha, only it comes so quick on me before I know what I am acting to you. I certainly am all sorry, hard, to be so bad to you, Melanctha, darling." "I suppose, Jeff," said Melanctha, very low and bitter, "I suppose you are always thinking, Jeff, somebody had ought to be ashamed with us two together, and you certainly do think you don't see any way to it, Jeff, for me to be feeling that way ever, so you certainly don't see any way to it, only to do it just so often for me. That certainly is the way always with you, Jeff Campbell, if I understand you right the way you are always acting to me. That certainly

9. See *Q.E.D.* pages 207–8, for the same episode, narrated with Adele's fearful sexual disgust made much more explicit than Jeff Campbell's is here.
1. Used instead of "tears" for the purpose of stylization—"bitter" alliterates with "biting," and the entire clause, like much of the writing of *Three Lives*, particularly in "Melanctha," is noticeably poetic.

is right the way I am saying it to you now, Jeff Campbell. You certainly didn't anyway trust me now no more, did you, when you just acted so bad to me. I certainly am right the way I say it Jeff now to you. I certainly am right when I ask you for it now, to tell me what I ask you, about not trusting me more then again, Jeff, just like you never really knew me. You certainly never did trust me just then, Jeff, you hear me?" "Yes, Melanctha," Jeff answered slowly. Melanctha paused. "I guess I certainly never can forgive you this time, Jeff Campbell," she said firmly. Jeff paused too, and thought a little. "I certainly am afraid you never can no more now again, Melanctha," he said sadly.

They lay there very quiet now a long time, each one thinking very hard on their own trouble. At last Jeff began again to tell Melanctha what it was he was always thinking with her. "I certainly do know, Melanctha, you certainly now don't want any more to be hearing me just talking, but you see, Melanctha, really, it's just like this way always with me. You see, Melanctha, its like this way now all the time with me. You remember, Melanctha, what I was once telling to you, when I didn't know you very long together, about how I certainly never did know more than just two kinds of ways of loving, one way the way it is good to be in families and the other kind of way, like animals are all the time just with each other, and how I didn't ever like that last kind of way much for any of the colored people. You see Melanctha, it's like this way with me. I got a new feeling now, you been teaching to me, just like I told you once, just like a new religion to me, and I see perhaps what really loving is like, like really having everything together, new things, little pieces all different, like I always before been thinking was bad to be having, all go together like, to make one good big feeling. You see, Melanctha, it's certainly like that you make me been seeing, like I never know before any way there was of all kinds of loving to come together to make one way really truly lovely. I see that now, sometimes, the way you certainly been teaching me, Melanctha, really, and then I love you those times, Melanctha, like a real religion, and then it comes over me all sudden, I don't know anything real about you Melanctha, dear one, and then it comes over me sudden, perhaps I certainly am wrong now, thinking all this way so lovely, and not thinking now any more the old way I always before was always thinking, about what was the right way for me, to live regular and all the colored people, and then I think, perhaps, Melanctha you are really just a bad one, and I think, perhaps I certainly am doing it so because I just am too anxious to be just having all the time excitements, like I don't ever like really to be doing when I know it, and then I always get so bad to you, Melanctha, and I can't help it with myself then, never, for I want to be always right really in the ways, I have to do them. I certainly do very badly want to be right, Melanctha, the only way I know is right Melanctha really, and I don't know any way, Melanctha, to find out really, whether my old way, the way I always used to be thinking, or the new way, you make so like a real religion to me sometimes, Melanctha, which way certainly is the real right way for me to be always thinking, and then I certainly am awful good and sorry, Melanctha, I always give you so much trouble, hurting you with the bad ways I am acting. Can't you help me to any way, to make it all straight for me, Melanctha, so I know right and real what it is I should be acting. You see, Melanctha, I don't want always to be a coward with you, if I only could know certain what was the right way for me to be acting. I certainly am real sure, Melanctha, that would be the way I would be acting, if I only knew it sure for certain now, Melanctha. Can't you help me any way to find out real and true, Melanctha, dear one. I certainly do badly want to know always, the way I should be acting."

"No, Jeff, dear, I certainly can't help you much in that kind of trouble you are always having. All I can do now, Jeff, is to just keep certainly with my believing you are good always, Jeff, and though you certainly do hurt me bad, I always got strong faith in you, Jeff, more in you certainly, than you seem to be having in your acting to me, always so bad, Jeff."

"You certainly are very good to me, Melanctha, dear one," Jeff said, after a long, tender silence. "You certainly are very good to me, Melanctha, darling, and me so bad to you always, in my acting. Do you love me good, and right, Melanctha, always?" "Always and always, you be sure of that now you have me. Oh you Jeff, you always be so stupid." "I certainly never can say now you ain't right, when you say that to me so, Melanctha," Jeff answered. "Oh, Jeff dear, I love you always, you know that now, all right, for certain. If you don't know it right now, Jeff, really, I prove it to you now, for good and always." And they lay there a long time in their loving, and then Jeff began again with his happy free enjoying.

"I sure am a good boy to be learning all the time the right way you are teaching me, Melanctha, darling," began Jeff Campbell, laughing, "You can't say no, never, I ain't a good scholar for you to be teaching now, Melanctha, and I am always so ready to come to you every day, and never playing hooky ever from you. You can't say ever, Melanctha, now can you, I ain't a real good boy to be always studying to be learning to be real bright, just like my teacher. You can't say ever to me, I ain't a good boy to you now, Melanctha." "Not near so good, Jeff Campbell, as such a good, patient kind of teacher, like me, who never teaches any ways it ain't good her scholars should be knowing, ought to be really having, Jeff, you hear me? I certainly don't think I am right for you, to be forgiving always, when you are so bad, and I so patient, with all this hard teaching always." "But you do forgive me always, sure, Melanctha, always?" "Always and always, you be sure Jeff, and I certainly am afraid I never can stop with my forgiving, you always are going to be so bad to me, and I always going to have to be so good with my forgiving." "Oh! Oh!" cried Jeff Campbell, laughing, "I ain't going to be so bad for always, sure I ain't, Melanctha, my own darling. And sure you do forgive me really, and sure you love me true and really, sure, Melanctha?" "Sure, sure, Jeff, boy, sure now and always, sure now you believe me, sure you do, Jeff, always." "I sure hope I does, with all my heart, Melanctha, darling." "I sure do that same, Jeff, dear boy, now you really know what it is to be loving, and I prove it to you now so, Jeff, you never can be forgetting. You see now, Jeff, good and certain, what I always before been saying to you, Jeff, now." "Yes, Melanctha, darling," murmured Jeff, and he was very happy in it, and so the two of them now in the warm air of the sultry, southern, negro sunshine, lay there for a long time just resting.

And now for a real long time there was no open trouble any more between Jeff Campbell and Melanctha Herbert. Then it came that Jeff knew he could not say out any more, what it was he wanted, he could not say out any more, what it was, he wanted to know about, what Melanctha wanted.

Melanctha sometimes now, when she was tired with being all the time so much excited, when Jeff would talk a long time to her about what was right for them both to be always doing, would be, as if she gave way in her head, and lost herself in a bad feeling. Sometimes when they had been strong in their loving, and Jeff would have rise inside him some strange feeling, and Melanctha felt it in him as it would soon be coming, she would lose herself then in this bad feeling that made her head act as if she never knew what it was they were doing. And slowly now, Jeff soon always came to be feeling that his Melanctha would be hurt very much in her head in the ways he never liked to think of, if she would ever now again have to listen to his trouble, when he was telling about what it was he still was wanting to make things for himself really understanding.

Now Jeff began to have always a strong feeling that Melanctha could no longer stand it, with all her bad suffering, to let him fight out with himself what was right for him to be doing. Now he felt he must not, when she was there with him, keep on, with this kind of fighting that was always going on inside him. Jeff Campbell never knew yet, what he thought was the right way, for himself and for all the colored people to be living. Jeff was coming always each time closer to be really understanding, but now Melanctha was so bad in her suffering with him, that he knew she could not any longer have him with her while he was always showing that he never really yet was sure what it was, the right way, for them to be really loving.

Jeff saw now he had to go so fast, so that Melanctha never would have to wait any to get from him always all that she ever wanted. He never could be honest now, he never could be now, any more, trying to be really understanding, for always every moment now he felt it to be a strong thing in him, how very much it was Melanctha Herbert always suffered.

Jeff did not know very well these days, what it was, was really happening to him. All he knew every now and then, when they were getting strong to get excited, the way they used to when he gave his feeling out so that he could be always honest, that Melanctha somehow never seemed to hear him, she just looked at him and looked as if her head hurt with him, and then Jeff had to keep himself from being honest, and he had to go so fast, and to do everything Melanctha ever wanted from him.

Jeff did not like it very well these days, in his true feeling. He knew now very well Melanctha was not strong enough inside her to stand any more of his slow way of doing. And yet now he knew he was not honest in his feeling. Now he always had to show more to Melanctha than he was ever feeling. Now she made him go so fast, and he knew it was not real with his feeling, and yet he could not make her suffer so any more because he always was so slow with his feeling.

It was very hard for Jeff Campbell to make all this way of doing, right, inside him. If Jeff Campbell could not be straight out, and real honest, he never could be very strong inside him. Now Melanctha, with her making him feel, always, how good she was and how very much she suffered in him, made him always go so fast then, he could not be strong then, to feel things out straight then inside him. Always now when he was with her, he was being more, than he could already yet, be feeling for her. Always now, with her, he had something inside him always holding in him, always now, with her, he was far ahead of his own feeling.

Jeff Campbell never knew very well these days what it was that was going on inside him. All he knew was, he was uneasy now always to be with Melanctha. All he knew was, that he was always uneasy when he was with Melanctha, not the way he used to be from just not being very understanding, but now, because he never could be honest with her, because he was now always feeling her strong suffering, in her, because he knew now he was having a straight, good feeling with her, but she went so fast, and he was so slow to her; Jeff knew his right feeling never got a chance to show itself as strong, to her.

All this was always getting harder for Jeff Campbell. He was very proud to hold himself to be strong, was Jeff Campbell. He was very tender not to hurt Melanctha, when he knew she would be sure to feel it badly in her head a long time after, he hated that he could not now be honest with her, he wanted to stay away to work it out all alone, without her, he was afraid she would feel it to suffer, if he kept away now from her. He was uneasy always, with her, he was uneasy when he thought about her, he knew now he had a good, straight, strong feeling of right loving for her, and yet now he never could use it to be good and honest with her.

Jeff Campbell did not know, these days, anything he could do to make it better for her. He did not know anything he could do, to set himself really right in his acting and his thinking toward her. She pulled him so fast with her, and he did not dare to hurt her, and he could not come right, so fast, the way she always needed he should be doing it now, for her.

These days were not very joyful ones now any more, to Jeff Campbell, with Melanctha. He did not think it out to himself now, in words, about her. He did not know enough, what was his real trouble, with her.

Sometimes now and again with them, and with all this trouble for a little while well forgotten by him, Jeff, and Melanctha with him, would be very happy in a strong, sweet loving. Sometimes then, Jeff would find himself to be soaring very high in his true loving. Sometimes Jeff would find then, in his loving, his soul swelling out full inside him. Always Jeff felt now in himself, deep feeling.

Always now Jeff had to go so much faster than was real with his feeling. Yet always Jeff knew now he had a right, strong feeling. Always now when Jeff was wondering, it was Melanctha he was doubting, in the loving. Now he would often ask her, was she real now to him, in her loving. He would ask her often, feeling something queer about it all inside him, though yet he was never really strong in his doubting, and always Melanctha would answer to him, "Yes Jeff, sure, you know it, always," and always Jeff felt a doubt now, in her loving.

Always now Jeff felt in himself, deep loving. Always now he did not know really, if Melanctha was true in her loving.

All these days Jeff was uncertain in him, and he was uneasy about which way he should act so as not to be wrong and put them both into bad trouble. Always now he was, as if he must feel deep into Melanctha to see if it was real loving he would find she now had in her, and always he would stop himself, with her, for always he was afraid now that he might badly hurt her.

Always now he liked it better when he was detained when he had to go and see her. Always now he never liked to go to be with her, although he never wanted really, not to be always with her. Always now he never felt really at ease with her, even when they were good friends together. Always now he felt, with her, he could not be really honest to her. And Jeff never could be happy with her when he could not feel strong to tell all his feeling to her. Always now every day he found it harder to make the time pass, with her, and not let his feeling come so that he would quarrel with her.

And so one evening, late, he was to go to her. He waited a little long, before he went to her. He was afraid, in himself, to-night, he would surely hurt her. He never wanted to go when he might quarrel with her.

Melanctha sat there looking very angry, when he came in to her. Jeff took off his hat and coat and then sat down by the fire with her.

"If you come in much later to me just now, Jeff Campbell, I certainly never would have seen you no more never to speak to you, 'thout your apologising real humble to me." "Apologising Melanctha," and Jeff laughed and was scornful to her, "Apologising, Melanctha, I ain't proud that kind of way, Melanctha, I don't mind apologising to you, Melanctha, all I mind, Melanctha is to be doing of things wrong, to you." "That's easy, to say things that way, Jeff to me. But you never was very proud Jeff, to be courageous to me." "I don't know about that Melanctha. I got courage to say some things hard, when I mean them, to you." "Oh, yes, Jeff, I know all about that, Jeff, to me. But I mean real courage, to run around and not care nothing about what happens, and always to be game in any kind of trouble. That's what I mean by real courage, to me, Jeff, if you want to know it." "Oh, yes, Melanctha, I know all that kind of courage. I see plenty of it all the time with some kinds of colored men and with some girls like you Melanctha, and Jane Harden. I know all about how you are always making a fuss to be proud because you don't holler so much when you run in to where you ain't got any business to be, and so you get hurt, the way you ought to. And then, you kind of people are very brave then, sure, with all your kinds of suffering, but the way I see it, going round with all my patients, that kind of courage makes all kind of trouble, for them who ain't so noble with their courage, and then they got it, always to be bearing it, when the end comes, to be hurt the hardest. It's like running around and being game to spend all your money always, and then a man's wife and children are the ones do all the starving and they don't ever get a name for being brave, and they don't ever want to be doing all that suffering, and they got to stand it and say nothing. That's the way I see it a good deal now with all that kind of braveness in some of the colored people. They always make a lot of noise to show they are so brave not to holler, when they got so much suffering they always bring all on themselves, just by doing things they got no business to be doing. I don't say, never, Melanctha, they ain't got good courage not to holler, but I never did see much in looking for that kind of trouble just to show you ain't going to holler. No its all right being brave every day, just living regular and not having new ways all the time just to get excitements, the way I hate to see it in all the colored people. No I don't see much, Melanctha, in being brave just to get it good, where you've got no business. I ain't ashamed Melanctha, right here to tell you, I ain't ashamed ever to say I ain't got no longing to be brave, just to go around and look for trouble." "Yes that's just like you always, Jeff, you never understand things right, the way you are always feeling in you. You ain't got no way to understand right, how it depends what way somebody goes to look for new things, the way it makes it right for them to get excited." "No Melanctha, I certainly never do say I understand much anybody's got a right to think they won't have real bad trouble, if they go and look hard where they are certain sure to find it. No Melanctha, it certainly does sound very pretty all this talking about danger and being game and never hollering, and all that way of talking, but when two men are just fighting, the strong man mostly gets on top with doing good hard pounding, and the man that's getting all that pounding, he mostly never likes it so far as I have been able yet to see it, and I don't see much difference what kind of noble way they are made of when they ain't got any kind of business to get together there to be fighting. That certainly is the only way I ever see it happen right, Melanctha, whenever I happen to be anywhere I can be looking." "That's because you never can see anything that ain't just so simple, Jeff, with everybody, the way you always think it. It do make all the difference the kind of way anybody is made to do things game Jeff Campbell." "Maybe Melanctha, I certainly never say no you ain't right, Melanctha. I just been telling it to you all straight, Melanctha, the way I always see it. Perhaps if you run around where you ain't got any business, and you stand up very straight and say, I am so brave, nothing can ever ever hurt me, maybe nothing will ever hurt you then Melanctha. I never have seen it do so. I never can say truly any differently to you Melanctha, but I always am ready to be learning from you, Melanctha. And perhaps when somebody cuts into you real hard, with a brick he is throwing, perhaps you never will do any hollering then, Melanctha. I certainly don't ever say no, Melanctha to you, I only say that ain't the way yet I ever see it happen when I had a chance to be there looking."

They sat there together, quiet by the fire, and they did not seem to feel very loving.

"I certainly do wonder," Melanctha said dreamily, at last breaking into their long unloving silence. "I certainly do wonder why always it happens to me I care for anybody who ain't no ways good enough for me ever to be thinking to respect him."

Jeff looked at Melanctha. Jeff got up then and walked a little up and down the room, and then he came back, and his face was set and dark and he was very quiet to her.

"Oh dear, Jeff, sure, why you look so solemn now to me. Sure Jeff I never am meaning anything real by what I just been saying. What was I just been saying Jeff to you. I only certainly was just thinking how everything always was just happening to me."

Jeff Campbell sat very still and dark, and made no answer.

"Seems to me, Jeff you might be good to me a little to-night when my head hurts so, and I am so tired with all the hard work I have been doing, thinking, and I always got so many things to be a trouble to me, living like I do with nobody ever who can help me. Seems to me you might be good to me Jeff to-night, and not get angry, every little thing I am ever saying to you."

"I certainly would not get angry ever with you, Melanctha, just because you say things to me. But now I certainly been thinking you really mean what you have been just then saying to me." "But you say all the time to me Jeff, you ain't no ways good enough in your loving to me, you certainly say to me all the time you ain't no ways good or understanding to me." "That certainly is what I say to you always, just the way I feel it to you Melanctha always, and I got it right in me to say it, and I have got a right in me to be very strong and feel it, and to be always sure to believe it, but it ain't right for you Melanctha to feel it. When you feel it so Melanctha, it does certainly make everything all wrong with our loving. It makes it so I certainly never can bear to have it."

They sat there then a long time by the fire, very silent, and not loving, and never looking to each other for it. Melanctha was moving and twitching herself and very nervous with it. Jeff was heavy and sullen and dark and very serious in it.

"Oh why can't you forget I said it to you Jeff now, and I certainly am so tired, and my head and all now with it."

Jeff stirred, "All right Melanctha, don't you go make yourself sick now in your head, feeling so bad with it," and Jeff made himself do it, and he was a patient doctor again now with Melanctha when he felt her really having her head hurt with it. "It's all right now Melanctha darling, sure it is now I tell you. You just lie down now a little, dear one, and I sit here by the fire and just read awhile and just watch with you so I will be here ready, if you need me to give you something to help you resting." And then Jeff was a good doctor to her, and very sweet and tender with her, and Melanctha loved him to be there to help her, and then Melanctha fell asleep a little, and Jeff waited there beside her until he saw she was really sleeping, and then he went back and sat down by the fire.

And Jeff tried to begin again with his thinking, and he could not make it come clear to himself, with all his thinking, and he felt everything all thick and heavy and bad, now inside him, everything that he could not understand right, with all the hard work he made, with his thinking. And then he moved himself a little, and took a book to forget his thinking, and then as always, he loved it when he was reading, and then very soon he was deep in his reading, and so he forgot now for a little while that he never could seem to be very understanding.

And so Jeff forgot himself for awhile in his reading, and Melanctha was sleeping. And then Melanctha woke up and she was screaming. "Oh, Jeff, I thought you gone away for always from me. Oh, Jeff, never now go away no more from me. Oh, Jeff, sure, sure, always be just so good to me."

There was a weight in Jeff Campbell from now on, always with him, that he could never lift out from him, to feel easy. He always was trying not to have it in him and he always was trying not to let Melanctha feel it, with him, but it was always there inside him. Now Jeff Campbell always was serious, and dark, and heavy, and sullen, and he would often sit a long time with Melanctha without moving.

"You certainly never have forgiven to me, what I said to you that night, Jeff, now have you?" Melanctha asked him after a long silence, late one evening with him. "It ain't ever with me a question like forgiving, Melanctha, I got in me. It's just only what you are feeling for me, makes any difference to me. I ain't ever seen anything since in you, makes me think you didn't mean it right, what you said about not thinking now any more I was good, to make it right for you to be really caring so very much to love me."

"I certainly never did see no man like you, Jeff. You always wanting to have it all clear out in words² always, what everybody is always feeling. I certainly don't see a reason, why I should always be explaining to you what I mean by what I am just saying. And you ain't got no feeling ever for me, to ask me what I meant, by what I was saying when I was so tired, that night. I never know anything right I was saying." "But you don't ever tell me now, Melanctha, so I really hear you say it, you don't mean it the same way, the way you said it to me." "Oh Jeff, you so stupid always to me and always just bothering with your always asking to me. And I don't never any way remember ever anything I been saying to you, and I am always my head, so it hurts me it half kills me, and my heart jumps so, sometimes I think I die so when it hurts me, and I am so blue always, I think sometimes I take something to just kill me, and I got so much to bother thinking always and doing, and I got so much to worry, and all that, and then

---

2. In *Q.E.D.*, Adele says to Helen, just before the end of the novel, "Nothing is too good or holy for clear thinking and definite expression" (page 226). Note the shift between *Q.E.D.* and "Melanctha" in Stein's authorial relation to this moment: in the former, Adele's point of view is endorsed; in the latter, Melanctha's accusation carries some weight. The scene culminating in this remark by Melanctha is based very closely on a pivotal scene in *Q.E.D.*, in which the stalemate of Adele and Helen's relationship begins to become clear (pages 209–12).

you come and ask me what I mean by what I was just saying to you. I certainly don't know, Jeff, when you ask me. Seems to me, Jeff, sometimes you might have some kind of a right feeling to be careful to me." "You ain't got no right Melanctha Herbert," flashed out Jeff through his dark, frowning anger, "you certainly ain't got no right always to be using your being hurt and being sick, and having pain, like a weapon, so as to make me do things it ain't never right for me to be doing for you. You certainly ain't got no right to be always holding your pain out to show me." "What do you mean by them words, Jeff Campbell." "I certainly do mean them just like I am saying them, Melanctha. You act always like I been responsible all myself for all our loving one another. And if its anything anyway that ever hurts you, you act like as if it was me made you just begin it all with me. I ain't no coward, you hear me, Melanctha? I never put my trouble back on anybody, thinking that they made me. I certainly am right ready always, Melanctha, you certainly had ought to know me, to stand all my own trouble for me, but I tell you straight now, the way I think it Melanctha, I ain't going to be as if I was the reason why you wanted to be loving, and to be suffering so now with me." "But ain't you certainly ought to be feeling it so, to be right, Jeff Campbell. Did I ever do anything but just let you do everything you wanted to me. Did I ever try to make you be loving to me. Did I ever do nothing except just sit there ready to endure your loving with me. But I certainly never, Jeff Campbell, did make any kind of way as if I wanted really to be having you for me."

Jeff stared at Melanctha. "So that's the way you say it when you are thinking right about it all, Melanctha. Well I certainly ain't got a word to say ever to you any more, Melanctha, if that's the way its straight out to you now, Melanctha." And Jeff almost laughed out to her, and he turned to take his hat and coat, and go away now forever from her.

Melanctha dropped her head on her arms, and she trembled all over and inside her. Jeff stopped a little and looked very sadly at her. Jeff could not so quickly make it right for himself, to leave her.

"Oh, I certainly shall go crazy now, I certainly know that," Melanctha moaned as she sat there, all fallen and miserable and weak together.

Jeff came and took her in his arms, and held her. Jeff was very good then to her, but they neither of them felt inside all right, as they once did, to be together.

From now on, Jeff had real torment in him.

Was it true what Melanctha had said that night to him? Was it true that he was the one had made all this trouble for them? Was it true, he was the only one, who always had had wrong ways in him?

Waking or sleeping Jeff now always had this torment going on inside him.

Jeff did not know now any more, what to feel within him. He did not know how to begin thinking out this trouble that must always now be bad inside him. He just felt a confused struggle and resentment always in him, a knowing, no, Melanctha was not right in what she had said that night to him, and then a feeling, perhaps he always had been wrong in the way he never could be understanding. And then would come strong to him, a sense of the deep sweetness in Melanctha's loving and a hating the cold slow way he always had to feel things in him.

Always Jeff knew, sure, Melanctha was wrong in what she had said that night to him, but always Melanctha had had deep feeling with him, always he was poor and slow in the only way he knew how to have any feeling. Jeff knew Melanctha was wrong, and yet he always had a deep doubt in him. What could he know, who had such slow feeling in him? What could he ever know, who always had to find his way with just thinking. What could he know, who had to be taught such a long time to learn about what was really loving? Jeff now always had this torment in him.

Melanctha was now always making him feel her way, strong whenever she was with him. Did she go on to do it just to show him, did she do it so now because she was no longer loving, did she do it so because that was her way to make him be really loving. Jeff never did know how it was that it all happened so to him.

Melanctha acted now the way she had said it always had been with them. Now it was always Jeff who had to do the asking. Now it was always Jeff who had to ask when would be the next time he should come to see her. Now always she was good and patient to him, and now always she was kind and loving with him, and always Jeff felt it was, that she was good to give him anything he ever asked or wanted, but never now any more for her own sake to make her happy in him. Now she did these things, as if it was just to please her Jeff Campbell who needed she should now have kindness for him. Always now he was the beggar, with them. Always now Melanctha gave it, not of her need, but from her bounty to him. Always now Jeff found it getting harder for him.

Sometimes Jeff wanted to tear things away from before him, always now he wanted to fight things and be angry with them, and always now Melanctha was so patient to him.

Now, deep inside him, there was always a doubt with Jeff, of Melanctha's loving. It was not a doubt yet to make him really doubting, for with that, Jeff never could be really loving, but always now he knew that something, and that not in him, something was wrong with their loving. Jeff Campbell could not know any right way to think out what was inside Melanctha with her loving, he could not use any way now to reach inside her to find if she was true in her loving, but now something had gone wrong between them, and now he never felt sure in him, the way once she had made him, that now at last he really had got to be understanding.

Melanctha was too many[3] for him. He was helpless to find out the way she really felt now for him. Often Jeff would ask her, did she really love him. Always she said, "Yes Jeff, sure, you know that," and now instead of a full sweet strong love with it, Jeff only felt a patient, kind endurance in it.

Jeff did not know. If he was right in such a feeling, he certainly never any more did want to have Melanctha Herbert with him. Jeff Campbell hated badly to think Melanctha ever would give him love, just for his sake, and not because she needed it herself, to be with him. Such a way of loving would be very hard for Jeff to be enduring.

"Jeff what makes you act so funny to me. Jeff you certainly now are jealous to me. Sure Jeff, now I don't see ever why you be so foolish to look so to me." "Don't you ever think I can be jealous of anybody ever Melanctha, you hear me. It's just, you certainly don't ever understand me. It's just this way with me always now Melanctha. You love me, and I don't care anything what you do or what you ever been to anybody. You don't love me, then I don't care any more about what you ever do or what you ever be to anybody. But I never want you to be being good Melanctha to me, when it ain't your loving makes you need it. I certainly don't ever want to be having any of your kind of kindness to me. If you don't love me, I can stand it. All I never want to have is your being good to me from kindness. If you don't love me, then you and I certainly do quit right here Melanctha, all strong feeling, to be always living to each other. It certainly never is anybody I ever am thinking about when I am thinking with you Melanctha darling. That's the true way I am telling you Melanctha, always. It's only your loving me ever gives me anything to bother me Melanctha, so all you got to do, if you don't really love me, is just certainly to say so to me. I won't bother you more then than I can help to keep from it Melanctha. You certainly need never to be in any worry, never, about me Melanctha. You just tell me straight out Melanctha, real, the way you feel it. I certainly can stand it all right, I tell you true Melanctha. And I never will care to know why or nothing Melanctha. Loving is just living Melanctha to me, and if you don't really feel it now Melanctha to me, there ain't ever nothing

3. Too much. In Mark Twain's *The Adventures of Huckleberry Finn*, "too many for me" is a characteristic expression of Huck's; this may be an allusion to that novel. In *Q.E.D.*, this line, spoken by Adele and referring to what she calls Helen's "double personality," is "You certainly are one too many for me" (page 195).

between us then Melanctha, is there? That's straight and honest just
the way I always feel it to you now Melanctha. Oh Melanctha, darling, do you love me? Oh Melanctha, please, please, tell me honest,
tell me, do you really love me?"

"Oh you so stupid Jeff boy, of course I always love you. Always and
always Jeff and I always just so good to you. Oh you so stupid Jeff
and don't know when you got it good with me. Oh dear, Jeff I certainly am so tired Jeff to-night, don't you go be a bother to me. Yes
I love you Jeff, how often you want me to tell you. Oh you so stupid
Jeff, but yes I love you. Now I won't say it no more now tonight Jeff,
you hear me. You just be good Jeff now to me or else I certainly get
awful angry with you. Yes I love you, sure, Jeff, though you don't any
way deserve it from me. Yes, yes I love you. Yes Jeff I say it till I
certainly am very sleepy. Yes I love you now Jeff, and you certainly
must stop asking me to tell you. Oh you great silly boy Jeff Campbell,
sure I love you, oh you silly stupid, my own boy Jeff Campbell. Yes
I love you and I certainly never won't say it one more time to-night
Jeff, now you hear me."

Yes Jeff Campbell heard her, and he tried hard to believe her. He
did not really doubt her but somehow it was wrong now, the way
Melanctha said it. Jeff always now felt baffled with Melanctha.
Something, he knew, was not right now in her. Something in her
always now was making stronger the torment that was tearing every
minute at the joy he once always had had with her.

Always now Jeff wondered did Melanctha love him. Always now
he was wondering, was Melanctha right when she said, it was he had
made all their beginning. Was Melanctha right when she said, it was
he had the real responsibility for all the trouble they had and still
were having now between them. If she was right, what a brute he
always had been in his acting. If she was right, how good she had
been to endure the pain he had made so bad so often for her. But
no, surely she had made herself to bear it, for her own sake, not for
his to make him happy. Surely he was not so twisted in all his long
thinking. Surely he could remember right what it was had happened
every day in their long loving. Surely he was not so poor a coward as
Melanctha always seemed to be thinking. Surely, surely, and then
the torment would get worse every minute in him.

One night Jeff Campbell was lying in his bed with his thinking,
and night after night now he could not do any sleeping for his thinking. To-night suddenly he sat up in his bed, and it all came clear to
him, and he pounded his pillow with his fist, and he almost shouted
out alone there to him, "I ain't a brute the way Melanctha has been
saying. Its all wrong the way I been worried thinking. We did begin
fair, each not for the other but for ourselves, what we were wanting.
Melanctha Herbert did it just like I did it, because she liked it bad

enough to want to stand it. It's all wrong in me to think it any way except the way we really did it. I certainly don't know now whether she is now real and true in her loving. I ain't got any way ever to find out if she is real and true now always to me. All I know is I didn't ever make her to begin to be with me. Melanctha has got to stand for her own trouble, just like got to stand for my own trouble. Each man has got to do it for himself when he is in real trouble. Melanctha, she certainly don't remember right when she says I made her begin and then I made her trouble. No by God, I ain't no coward nor a brute either ever to her. I been the way I felt it honest, and that certainly is all about it now between us, and everybody always has just got to stand for their own trouble. I certainly am right this time the way I see it." And Jeff lay down now, at last in comfort, and he slept, and he was free from his long doubting torment.

"You know Melanctha," Jeff Campbell began, the next time he was alone to talk a long time to Melanctha. "You know Melanctha, sometimes I think a whole lot about what you like to say so much about being game and never doing any hollering. Seems to me Melanctha, I certainly don't understand right what you mean by not hollering. Seems to me it certainly ain't only what comes right away when one is hit, that counts to be brave to be bearing, but all that comes later from your getting sick from the shock of being hurt once in a fight, and all that, and all the being taken care of for years after, and the suffering of your family, and all that, you certainly must stand and not holler, to be certainly really brave the way I understand it." "What you mean Jeff by your talking." "I mean, seems to me really not to holler, is to be strong not to show you ever have been hurt. Seems to me, to get your head hurt from your trouble and to show it, ain't certainly no braver than to say, oh, oh, how bad you hurt me, please don't hurt me mister. It just certainly seems to me, like many people think themselves so game just to stand what we all of us always just got to be standing, and everybody stands it, and we don't certainly none of us like it, and yet we don't ever most of us think we are so much being game, just because we got to stand it."[4]

"I know what you mean now by what you are saying to me now Jeff Campbell. You make a fuss now to me, because I certainly just have stopped standing everything you like to be always doing so cruel to me. But that's just the way always with you Jeff Campbell, if you want to know it. You ain't got no kind of right feeling for all I always been forgiving to you." "I said it once for fun, Melanctha, but now I certainly do mean it, you think you got a right to go where you got no business, and you say, I am so brave nothing can hurt me, and

---

4. In *Q.E.D.*, Adele says to Helen, "People of your heroic kind consider yourselves heroes when you are doing no more than the rest of us who look upon it only as humbly submitting to inevitable necessity" (page 211).

then something, like always, it happens to hurt you, and you show your hurt always so everybody can see it, and you say, I am so brave nothing did hurt me except he certainly didn't have any right to, and see how bad I suffer, but you never hear me make a holler, though certainly anybody got any feeling, to see me suffer, would certainly never touch me except to take good care of me. Sometimes I certainly don't rightly see Melanctha, how much more game that is than just the ordinary kind of holler." "No, Jeff Campbell, and made the way you is you certainly ain't likely ever to be much more understanding." "No, Melanctha, nor you neither. You think always, you are the only one who ever can do any way to really suffer." "Well, and ain't I certainly always been the only person knows how to bear it. No, Jeff Campbell, I certainly be glad to love anybody really worthy, but I made so, I never seem to be able in this world to find him." "No, and your kind of way of thinking, you certainly Melanctha never going to any way be able to ever to be finding of him. Can't you understand Melanctha, ever, how no man certainly ever really can hold your love for long times together. You certainly Melanctha, you ain't got down deep loyal feeling, true inside you, and when you ain't just that moment quick with feeling, then you certainly ain't ever got anything more there to keep you. You see Melanctha, it certainly is this way with you, it is, that you ain't ever got any way to remember right what you been doing, or anybody else that has been feeling with you. You certainly Melanctha, never can remember right, when it comes what you have done and what you think happens to you." "It certainly is all easy for you Jeff Campbell to be talking. You remember right, because you don't remember nothing till you get home with your thinking everything all over, but I certainly don't think much ever of that kind of way of remembering right, Jeff Campbell. I certainly do call it remembering right Jeff Campbell, to remember right just when it happens to you, so you have a right kind of feeling not to act the way you always been doing to me, and then you go home Jeff Campbell, and you begin with your thinking, and then it certainly is very easy for you to be good and forgiving with it. No, that ain't to me, the way of remembering Jeff Campbell, not as I can see it not to make people always suffer, waiting for you certainly to get to do it. Seems to me like Jeff Campbell, I never could feel so like a man was low and to be scorning of him, like that day in the summer, when you threw me off just because you got one of those fits of your remembering. No, Jeff Campbell, its real feeling every moment when its needed, that certainly does seem to me like real remembering. And that way, certainly, you don't never know nothing like what should be right Jeff Campbell. No Jeff, it's me that always certainly has had to bear it with you. It's always me that certainly has had to suffer, while you go home to remember. No you certainly ain't got no sense yet Jeff, what you need to make you really feeling. No, it certainly is me Jeff Campbell, that always has got to be remembering for us both, always. That's what's the true way with us Jeff Campbell, if you want to know what it is I am always thinking." "You is certainly real modest Melanctha, when you do this kind of talking, you sure is Melanctha," said Jeff Campbell laughing. "I think sometimes Melanctha I am certainly awful conceited, when I think sometimes I am all out doors, and I think I certainly am so bright, and better than most everybody I ever got anything now to do with, but when I hear you talk this way Melanctha, I certainly do think I am a real modest kind of fellow." "Modest!" said Melanctha, angry, "Modest, that certainly is a queer thing for you Jeff to be calling yourself even when you are laughing." "Well it certainly does depend a whole lot what you are thinking with," said Jeff Campbell. "I never did use to think I was so much on being real modest Melanctha, but now I know really I am, when I hear you talking. I see all the time there are many people living just as good as I am, though they are a little different to me. Now with you Melanctha if I understand you right what you are talking, you don't think that way of no other one that you are ever knowing." "I certainly could be real modest too, Jeff Campbell," said Melanctha, "If I could meet somebody once I could keep right on respecting when I got so I was really knowing with them. But I certainly never met anybody like that yet, Jeff Campbell, if you want to know it." "No, Melanctha, and with the way you got of thinking, it certainly don't look as if you ever will Melanctha, with your never remembering anything only what you just then are feeling in you, and you not understanding what any one else is ever feeling, if they don't holler just the way you are doing. No Melanctha, I certainly don't see any ways you are likely ever to meet one, so good as you are always thinking you be."

"No, Jeff Campbell, it certainly ain't that way with me at all the way you say it. It's because I am always knowing what it is I am wanting, when I get it. I certainly don't never have to wait till I have it, and then throw away what I got in me, and then come back and say, that's a mistake I just been making, it ain't that never at all like I understood it, I want to have, bad, what I didn't think it was I wanted. It's that way of knowing right what I am wanting, makes me feel nobody can come right with me, when I am feeling things, Jeff Campbell. I certainly do say Jeff Campbell, I certainly don't think much of the way you always do it, always never knowing what it is you are ever really wanting and everybody always got to suffer. No Jeff, I don't certainly think there is much doubting which is better and the stronger with us two, Jeff Campbell."

"As you will, Melanctha Herbert," cried Jeff Campbell, and he rose up, and he thundered out a black oath, and he was fierce to leave her now forever, and then with the same movement, he took her in his arms and held her.

"What a silly goose boy you are, Jeff Campbell," Melanctha whispered to him fondly.

"Oh yes," said Jeff, very dreary. "I never could keep really mad with anybody, not when I was a little boy and playing. I used most to cry sometimes, I couldn't get real mad and keep on a long time with it, the way everybody always did it. It's certainly no use to me Melanctha, I certainly can't ever keep mad with you Melanctha, my dear one. But don't you ever be thinking it's because I think you right in what you been just saying to me. I don't Melanctha really think it that way, honest, though I certainly can't get mad the way I ought to. No Melanctha, little girl, really truly, you ain't right the way you think it. I certainly do know that Melanctha, honest. You certainly don't do me right Melanctha, the way you say you are thinking. Good-bye Melanctha, though you certainly is my own little girl for always." And then they were very good a little to each other, and then Jeff went away for that evening, from her.

Melanctha had begun now once more to wander. Melanctha did not yet always wander, but a little now she needed to begin to look for others. Now Melanctha Herbert began again to be with some of the better kind of black girls, and with them she sometimes wandered. Melanctha had not yet come again to need to be alone, when she wandered.

Jeff Campbell did not know that Melanctha had begun again to wander. All Jeff knew, was that now he could not be so often with her.

Jeff never knew how it had come to happen to him, but now he never thought to go to see Melanctha Herbert, until he had before, asked her if she could be going to have time then to have him with her. Then Melanctha would think a little, and then she would say to him, "Let me see Jeff, to-morrow, you was just saying to me. I certainly am awful busy you know Jeff just now. It certainly does seem to me this week Jeff, I can't anyways fix it. Sure I want to see you soon Jeff. I certainly Jeff got to do a little more now, I been giving so much time, when I had no business, just to be with you when you asked me. Now I guess Jeff, I certainly can't see you no more this week Jeff, the way I got to do things." "All right Melanctha," Jeff would answer and he would be very angry. "I want to come only just certainly as you want me now Melanctha." "Now Jeff you know I certainly can't be neglecting always to be with everybody just to see you. You come see me next week Tuesday Jeff, you hear me. I don't think Jeff I certainly be so busy, Tuesday." Jeff Campbell would then go away and leave her, and he would be hurt and very angry, for it was hard for a man with a great pride in himself, like Jeff Campbell, to feel himself no better than a beggar. And yet he always came as she said he should, on the day she had fixed for him, and always Jeff Campbell was not sure yet that he really understood what it was Melanctha wanted. Always Melanctha said to him, yes she loved him, sure he knew that. Always Melanctha said to him, she certainly did love him just the same as always, only sure he knew now she certainly did seem to be right busy with all she certainly now had to be doing.

Jeff never knew what Melanctha had to do now, that made her always be so busy, but Jeff Campbell never cared to ask Melanctha such a question. Besides Jeff knew Melanctha Herbert would never, in such a matter, give him any kind of a real answer. Jeff did not know whether it was that Melanctha did not know how to give a simple answer. And then how could he, Jeff, know what was important to her. Jeff Campbell always felt strongly in him, he had no right to interfere with Melanctha in any practical kind of a matter. There they had always, never asked each other any kind of question. There they had felt always in each other, not any right to take care of one another. And Jeff Campbell now felt less than he had ever, any right to claim to know what Melanctha thought it right that she should do in any of her ways of living. All Jeff felt a right in himself to question, was her loving.

Jeff learned every day now, more and more, how much it was that he could really suffer. Sometimes it hurt so in him, when he was alone, it would force some slow tears from him. But every day, now that Jeff Campbell, knew more how it could hurt him, he lost his feeling of deep awe that he once always had had for Melanctha's feeling. Suffering was not so much after all, thought Jeff Campbell, if even he could feel it so it hurt him. It hurt him bad, just the way he knew he once had hurt Melanctha, and yet he too could have it and not make any kind of a loud holler with it.

In tender hearted natures, those that mostly never feel strong passion, suffering often comes to make them harder. When these do not know in themselves what it is to suffer, suffering is then very awful to them and they badly want to help everyone who ever has to suffer, and they have a deep reverence for anybody who knows really how to always suffer. But when it comes to them to really suffer, they soon begin to lose their fear and tenderness and wonder. Why it isn't so very much to suffer, when even I can bear to do it. It isn't very pleasant to be having all the time, to stand it, but they are not so much wiser after all, all the others just because they know too how to bear it.

Passionate natures who have always made themselves, to suffer, that is all the kind of people who have emotions that come to them as sharp as a sensation, they always get more tender-hearted when they suffer, and it always does them good to suffer. Tender-hearted, unpassionate, and comfortable natures always get much harder when they suffer, for so they lose the fear and reverence and wonder they once had for everybody who ever has to suffer, for now they know themselves what it is to suffer and it is not so awful any longer to them when they know too, just as well as all the others, how to have it.

And so it came in these days to Jeff Campbell. Jeff knew now always, way inside him, what it is to really suffer, and now every day with it, he knew how to understand Melanctha better. Jeff Campbell still loved Melanctha Herbert and he still had a real trust in her and he still had a little hope that some day they would once more get together, but slowly, every day, this hope in him would keep growing always weaker. They still were a good deal of time together, but now they never any more were really trusting with each other. In the days when they used to be together, Jeff had felt he did not know much what was inside Melanctha, but he knew very well, how very deep always was his trust in her; now he knew Melanctha Herbert better, but now he never felt a deep trust in her. Now Jeff never could be really honest with her. He never doubted yet, that she was steady only to him, but somehow he could not believe much really in Melanctha's loving.

Melanctha Herbert was a little angry now when Jeff asked her, "I never give nobody before Jeff, ever more than one chance with me, and I certainly been giving you most a hundred Jeff, you hear me." "And why shouldn't you Melanctha, give me a million, if you really love me!" Jeff flashed out very angry. "I certainly don't know as you deserve that anyways from me, Jeff Campbell." "It ain't deserving, I am ever talking about to you Melanctha. Its loving, and if you are really loving to me you won't certainly never any ways call them chances." "Deed Jeff, you certainly are getting awful wise Jeff now, ain't you, to me." "No I ain't Melanctha, and I ain't jealous either to you. I just am doubting from the way you are always acting to me." "Oh yes Jeff, that's what they all say, the same way, when they certainly got jealousy all through them. You ain't got no cause to be jealous with me Jeff, and I am awful tired of all this talking now, you hear me."

Jeff Campbell never asked Melanctha any more if she loved him. Now things were always getting worse between them. Now Jeff was always very silent with Melanctha. Now Jeff never wanted to be honest to her, and now Jeff never had much to say to her.

Now when they were together, it was Melanctha always did most of the talking. Now she often had other girls there with her. Melanctha was always kind to Jeff Campbell but she never seemed to need to be alone now with him. She always treated Jeff, like her best friend, and she always spoke so to him and yet she never seemed now to very often want to see him.

Every day it was getting harder for Jeff Campbell. It was as if now, when he had learned to really love Melanctha, she did not need any more to have him. Jeff began to know this very well inside him.

Jeff Campbell did not know yet that Melanctha had begun again to wander. Jeff was not very quick to suspect Melanctha. All Jeff knew was, that he did not trust her to be now really loving to him.

Jeff was no longer now in any doubt inside him. He knew very well now he really loved Melanctha. He knew now very well she was not any more a real religion to him. Jeff Campbell knew very well too now inside him, he did not really want Melanctha, now if he could no longer trust her, though he loved her hard and really knew now what it was to suffer.

Every day Melanctha Herbert was less and less near to him. She always was very pleasant in her talk and to be with him, but somehow now it never was any comfort to him.

Melanctha Herbert now always had a lot of friends around her. Jeff Campbell never wanted to be with them. Now Melanctha began to find it, she said it often to him, always harder to arrange to be alone now with him. Sometimes she would be late for him. Then Jeff always would try to be patient in his waiting, for Jeff Campbell knew very well how to remember, and he knew it was only right that he should now endure this from her.

Then Melanctha began to manage often not to see him, and once she went away when she had promised to be there to meet him.

Then Jeff Campbell was really filled up with his anger. Now he knew he could never really want her. Now he knew he never any more could really trust her.

Jeff Campbell never knew why Melanctha had not come to meet him. Jeff had heard a little talking now, about how Melanctha Herbert had commenced once more to wander. Jeff Campbell still sometimes saw Jane Harden, who always needed a doctor to be often there to help her. Jane Harden always knew very well what happened to Melanctha. Jeff Campbell never would talk to Jane Harden anything about Melanctha. Jeff was always loyal to Melanctha. Jeff never let Jane Harden say much to him about Melanctha, though he never let her know that now he loved her. But somehow Jeff did know now about Melanctha, and he knew about some men that Melanctha met with Rose Johnson very often.

Jeff Campbell would not let himself really doubt Melanctha, but Jeff began to know now very well, he did not want her. Melanctha Herbert did not love him ever, Jeff knew it now, the way he once had thought that she could feel it. Once she had been greater for

him than he had thought he could ever know how to feel it. Now
Jeff had come to where he could understand Melanctha Herbert.
Jeff was not bitter to her because she could not really love him, he
was bitter only that he had let himself have a real illusion in him.
He was a little bitter too, that he had lost now, what he had always
felt real in the world, that had made it for him always full of beauty
and now he had not got this new religion really, and he had lost what
he before had to know what was good and had real beauty.

Jeff Campbell was so angry now in him, because he had begged
Melanctha always to be honest to him. Jeff could stand it in her not
to love him, he could not stand it in her not to be honest to him.

Jeff Campbell went home from where Melanctha had not met him,
and he was sore and full of anger in him.

Jeff Campbell could not be sure what to do, to make it right inside
him. Surely he must be strong now and cast this loving from him,
and yet, was he sure he now had real wisdom in him. Was he sure
that Melanctha Herbert never had had a real deep loving for him.
Was he sure Melanctha Herbert never had deserved a reverence
from him. Always now Jeff had this torment in him, but always now
he felt more that Melanctha never had real greatness for him.

Jeff waited to see if Melanctha would send any word to him.
Melanctha Herbert never sent a line to him.

At last Jeff wrote his letter to Melanctha. "Dear Melanctha, I certainly do know you ain't been any way sick this last week when you
never met me right the way you promised, and never sent me any
word to say why you acted a way you certainly never could think was
the right way you should do it to me. Jane Harden said she saw you
that day and you went out walking with some people you like now
to be with. Don't be misunderstanding me now any more Melanctha.
I love you now because that's my slow way to learn what you been
teaching, but I know now you certainly never had what seems to me
real kind of feeling. I don't love you Melanctha any more now like a
real religion, because now I know you are just made like all us others.
I know now no man can ever really hold you because no man can
ever be real to trust in you, because you mean right Melanctha, but
you never can remember, and so you certainly never have got any
way to be honest. So please you understand me right now Melanctha,
it never is I don't know how to love you. I do know now how to love
you, Melanctha, really. You sure do know that, Melanctha, in me.
You certainly always can trust me. And so now Melanctha, I can say
to you certainly real honest with you, I am better than you are in my
right kind of feeling. And so Melanctha, I don't never any more want
to be a trouble to you. You certainly make me see things Melanctha,
I never any other way could be knowing. You been very good and
patient to me, when I was certainly below you in my right feeling. I

certainly never have been near so good and patient to you ever any way Melanctha, I certainly know that Melanctha. But Melanctha, with me, it certainly is, always to be good together, two people certainly must be thinking each one as good as the other, to be really loving right Melanctha. And it certainly must never be any kind of feeling, of one only taking, and one only just giving, Melanctha, to me. I know you certainly don't really ever understand me now Melanctha, but that's no matter. I certainly do know what I am feeling now with you real Melanctha. And so good-bye now for good Melanctha. I say I can never ever really trust you real Melanctha, that's only just certainly from your way of not being ever equal in your feeling to anybody real, Melanctha, and your way never to know right how to remember. Many ways I really trust you deep Melanctha, and I certainly do feel deep all the good sweetness you certainly got real in you Melanctha. Its only just in your loving me Melanctha. You never can be equal to me and that way I certainly never can bear any more to have it. And so now Melanctha, I always be your friend, if you need me, and now we never see each other any more to talk to."

And then Jeff Campbell thought and thought, and he could never make any way for him now, to see it different, and so at last he sent this letter to Melanctha.

And now surely it was all over in Jeff Campbell. Surely now he never any more could know Melanctha. And yet, perhaps Melanctha really loved him. And then she would know how much it hurt him never any more, any way, to see her, and perhaps she would write a line to tell him. But that was a foolish way for Jeff ever to be thinking. Of course Melanctha never would write a word to him. It was all over now for always, everything between them, and Jeff felt it a real relief to him.

For many days now Jeff Campbell only felt it as a relief in him. Jeff was all locked up and quiet now inside him. It was all settling down heavy in him, and these days when it was sinking so deep in him, it was only the rest and quiet of not fighting that he could really feel inside him. Jeff Campbell could not think now, or feel anything else in him. He had no beauty nor any goodness to see around him. It was a dull, pleasant kind of quiet he now had inside him. Jeff almost began to love this dull quiet in him, for it was more nearly being free for him than anything he had known in him since Melanctha Herbert first had moved him. He did not find it a real rest yet for him, he had not really conquered what had been working so long in him, he had not learned to see beauty and real goodness yet in what had happened to him, but it was rest even if he was sodden now all through him. Jeff Campbell liked it very well, not to have fighting always going on inside him.

And so Jeff went on every day, and he was quiet, and he began again to watch himself in his working; and he did not see any beauty now around him, and it was dull and heavy always now inside him, and yet he was content to have gone so far in keeping steady to what he knew was the right way for him to come back to, to be regular, and see beauty in every kind of quiet way of living, the way he had always wanted it for himself and for all the colored people. He knew he had lost the sense he once had of joy all through him, but he could work, and perhaps he would bring some real belief back into him about the beauty that he could not now any more see around him.

And so Jeff Campbell went on with his working, and he staid home every evening, and he began again with his reading, and he did not do much talking, and he did not seem to himself to have any kind of feeling.

And one day Jeff thought perhaps he really was forgetting, one day he thought he could soon come back and be happy in his old way of regular and quiet living.

Jeff Campbell had never talked to any one of what had been going on inside him. Jeff Campbell liked to talk and he was honest, but it never came out from him, anything he was ever really feeling, it only came out from him, what it was that he was always thinking. Jeff Campbell always was very proud to hide what he was really feeling. Always he blushed hot to think things he had been feeling. Only to Melanctha Herbert, had it ever come to him, to tell what it was that he was feeling.

And so Jeff Campbell went on with this dull and sodden, heavy, quiet always in him, and he never seemed to be able to have any feeling. Only sometimes he shivered hot with shame when he remembered some things he once had been feeling. And then one day it all woke up, and was sharp in him.

Dr. Campbell was just then staying long times with a sick man who might soon be dying. One day the sick man was resting. Dr. Campbell went to the window to look out a little, while he was waiting. It was very early now in the southern springtime. The trees were just beginning to get the little zigzag crinkles in them, which the young buds always give them. The air was soft and moist and pleasant to them. The earth was wet and rich and smelling for them. The birds were making sharp fresh noises all around them. The wind was very gentle and yet urgent to them. And the buds and the long earthworms, and the negroes, and all the kinds of children, were coming out every minute farther into the new spring watery, southern sunshine.

Jeff Campbell too began to feel a little his old joy inside him. The sodden quiet began to break up in him. He leaned far out of the window to mix it all up with him. His heart went sharp and then it almost stopped inside him. Was it Melanctha Herbert he had just seen passing by him? Was it Melanctha, or was it just some other girl, who made him feel so bad inside him? Well, it was no matter, Melanctha was there in the world around him, he did certainly always know that in him. Melanctha Herbert was always in the same town with him, and he could never any more feel her near him. What a fool he was to throw her from him. Did he know she did not really love him. Suppose Melanctha was now suffering through him. Suppose she really would be glad to see him. And did anything else he did, really mean anything now to him? What a fool he was to cast her from him. And yet did Melanctha Herbert want him, was she honest to him, had Melanctha, ever loved him, and did Melanctha now suffer by him? Oh! Oh! Oh! and the bitter water once more rose up in him.

All that long day, with the warm moist young spring stirring in him, Jeff Campbell worked, and thought, and beat his breast, and wandered, and spoke aloud, and was silent, and was certain, and then in doubt and then keen to surely feel, and then all sodden in him; and he walked, and he sometimes ran fast to lose himself in his rushing, and he bit his nails to pain and bleeding, and he tore his hair so that he could be sure he was really feeling, and he never could know what it was right, he now should be doing. And then late that night he wrote it all out to Melanctha Herbert, and he made himself quickly send it without giving himself any time to change it.

"It has come to me strong to-day Melanctha, perhaps I am wrong the way I now am thinking. Perhaps you do want me badly to be with you. Perhaps I have hurt you once again the way I used to. I certainly Melanctha, if I ever think that really, I certainly do want bad not to be wrong now ever any more to you. If you do feel the way to-day it came to me strong may-be you are feeling, then say so Melanctha to me, and I come again to see you. If not, don't say anything any more ever to me. I don't want ever to be bad to you Melanctha, really. I never want ever to be a bother to you. I never can stand it to think I am wrong; really, thinking you don't want me to come to you. Tell me Melanctha, tell me honest to me, shall I come now any more to see you." "Yes" came the answer from Melanctha, "I be home Jeff to-night to see you."

Jeff Campbell went that evening late to see Melanctha Herbert. As Jeff came nearer to her, he doubted that he wanted really to be with her, he felt that he did not know what it was he now wanted from her. Jeff Campbell knew very well now, way inside him, that they could never talk their trouble out between them. What was it Jeff wanted now to tell Melanctha Herbert? What was it that Jeff Campbell now could tell her? Surely he never now could learn to trust her. Surely Jeff knew very well all that Melanctha always had inside her. And yet it was awful, never any more to see her.

Jeff Campbell went in to Melanctha, and he kissed her, and he held her, and then he went away from her and he stood still and looked at her. "Well Jeff!" "Yes Melanctha!" "Jeff what was it made you act so to me?" "You know very well Melanctha, it's always I am thinking you don't love me, and you are acting to me good out of kindness, and then Melanctha you certainly never did say anything to me why you never came to meet me, as you certainly did promise to me you would that day I never saw you!" "Jeff don't you really know for certain, I always love you?" "No Melanctha, deed I don't know it in me. Deed and certain sure Melanctha, if I only know that in me, I certainly never would give you any bother." "Jeff, I certainly do love you more seems to me always, you certainly had ought to feel that in you." "Sure Melanctha?" "Sure Jeff boy, you know that." "But then Melanctha why did you act so to me?" "Oh Jeff you certainly been such a bother to me. I just had to go away that day Jeff, and I certainly didn't mean not to tell you, and then that letter you wrote came to me and something happened to me. I don't know right what it was Jeff, I just kind of fainted, and what could I do Jeff, you said you certainly never any more wanted to come and see me!" "And no matter Melanctha, even if you knew, it was just killing me to act so to you, you never would have said nothing to me?" "No of course, how could I Jeff when you wrote that way to me. I know how you was feeling Jeff to me, but I certainly couldn't say nothing to you." "Well Melanctha, I certainly know I am right proud too in me, but I certainly never could act so to you Melanctha, if I ever knew any way at all you ever really loved me. No Melanctha darling, you and me certainly don't feel much the same way ever. Any way Melanctha, I certainly do love you true Melanctha." "And I love you too Jeff, even though you don't never certainly seem to believe me." "No I certainly don't any way believe you Melanctha, even when you say it to me. I don't know Melanctha how, but sure I certainly do trust you, only I don't believe now ever in your really being loving to me. I certainly do know you trust me always Melanctha, only somehow it ain't ever all right to me. I certainly don't know any way otherwise Melanctha, how I can say it to you." "Well I certainly can't help you no ways any more Jeff Campbell, though you certainly say it right when you say I trust you Jeff now always. You certainly is the best man Jeff Campbell, I ever can know, to me. I never been anyways thinking it can be ever different to me." "Well you trust me then Melanctha, and I certainly love you Melanctha, and seems like to me Melanctha, you and me had ought to be a little better than we certainly ever are doing now to be together!" You certainly do think that way, too, Melanctha to me. But may be you do really love me.

Tell me, please, real honest now Melanctha darling, tell me so I really always know it in me, do you really truly love me?" "Oh you stupid, stupid boy, Jeff Campbell. Love you, what do you think makes me always to forgive you. If I certainly didn't always love you Jeff, I certainly never would let you be always being all the time such a bother to me the way you certainly Jeff always are to me. Now don't you dass[5] ever any more say words like that ever to me. You hear me now Jeff, or I do something real bad sometime, so I really hurt you. Now Jeff you just be good to me. You know Jeff how bad I need it, now you should always be good to me!"

Jeff Campbell could not make an answer to Melanctha. What was it he should now say to her? What words could help him to make their feeling any better? Jeff Campbell knew that he had learned to love deeply, that, he always knew very well now in him, Melanctha had learned to be strong to be always trusting, that he knew too now inside him, but Melanctha did not really love him, that he felt always too strong for him. That fact always was there in him, and it always thrust itself firm, between them. And so this talk did not make things really better for them.

Jeff Campbell was never any more a torment to Melanctha, he was only silent to her. Jeff often saw Melanctha and he was very friendly with her and he never any more was a bother to her. Jeff never any more now had much chance to be loving with her. Melanctha never was alone now when he saw her.

Melanctha Herbert had just been getting thick in her trouble with Jeff Campbell, when she went to that church where she first met Rose, who later was married regularly to Sam Johnson. Rose was a good-looking, better kind of black girl, and had been brought up quite like their own child by white folks. Rose was living now with colored people. Rose was staying just then with a colored woman, who had known 'Mis' Herbert and her black husband and this girl Melanctha.

Rose soon got to like Melanctha Herbert and Melanctha now always wanted to be with Rose, whenever she could do it. Melanctha Herbert always was doing everything for Rose that she could think of that Rose ever wanted. Rose always liked to be with nice people who would do things for her. Rose had strong common sense and she was lazy. Rose liked Melanctha Herbert, she had such kind of fine ways in her. Then, too, Rose had it in her to be sorry for the subtle, sweet-natured, docile, intelligent Melanctha Herbert who always was so blue sometimes, and always had had so much trouble. Then, too, Rose could scold Melanctha, for Melanctha Herbert

5. Dialect for "dare."

never could know how to keep herself from trouble, and Rose was always strong to keep straight, with her simple selfish wisdom.

But why did the subtle, intelligent, attractive, half white girl Melanctha Herbert, with her sweetness and her power and her wisdom, demean herself to do for and to flatter and to be scolded, by this lazy, stupid, ordinary, selfish black girl. This was a queer thing in Melanctha Herbert.

And so now in these new spring days, it was with Rose that Melanctha began again to wander. Rose always knew very well in herself what was the right way to do when you wandered. Rose knew very well, she was not just any common kind of black girl, for she had been raised by white folks, and Rose always saw to it that she was engaged to him when she had any one man with whom she ever always wandered. Rose always had strong in her the sense for proper conduct. Rose always was telling the complex and less sure Melanctha, what was the right way she should do when she wandered.

Rose never knew much about Jeff Campbell with Melanctha Herbert. Rose had not known about Melanctha Herbert when she had been almost all her time with Dr. Campbell.

Jeff Campbell did not like Rose when he saw her with Melanctha. Jeff would never, when he could help it, meet her. Rose did not think much about Dr. Campbell. Melanctha never talked much about him to her. He was not important now to be with her.

Rose did not like Melanctha's old friend Jane Harden when she saw her. Jane despised Rose for an ordinary, stupid, sullen black girl. Jane could not see what Melanctha could find in that black girl, to endure her. It made Jane sick to see her. But then Melanctha had a good mind, but she certainly never did care much to really use it. Jane Harden now really never cared any more to see Melanctha, though Melanctha still always tried to be good to her. And Rose, she hated that stuck up, mean speaking, nasty, drunk thing, Jane Harden. Rose did not see how Melanctha could bear to ever see her, but Melanctha always was so good to everybody, she never would know how to act to people the way they deserved that she should do it.

Rose did not know much about Melanctha, and Jeff Campbell and Jane Harden. All Rose knew about Melanctha was her old life with her mother and her father. Rose was always glad to be good to poor Melanctha, who had had such an awful time with her mother and her father, and now she was alone and had nobody who could help her. "He was a awful black man to you Melanctha, I like to get my hands on him so he certainly could feel it. I just would Melanctha, now you hear me."

Perhaps it was this simple faith and simple anger and simple moral way of doing in Rose, that Melanctha now found such a comfort to her. Rose was selfish and was stupid and was lazy, but she was decent and knew always what was the right way she should do, and what she wanted, and she certainly did admire how bright was her friend Melanctha Herbert, and she certainly did feel how very much it was she always suffered and she scolded her to keep her from more trouble, and she never was angry when she found some of the different ways Melanctha Herbert sometimes had to do it.

And so always Rose and Melanctha were more and more together, and Jeff Campbell could now hardly ever any more be alone with Melanctha.

Once Jeff had to go away to another town to see a sick man. "When I come back Monday Melanctha, I come Monday evening to see you. You be home alone once Melanctha to see me." "Sure Jeff, I be glad to see you!"

When Jeff Campbell came to his house on Monday there was a note there from Melanctha. Could Jeff come day after to-morrow, Wednesday? Melanctha was so sorry she had to go out that evening. She was awful sorry and she hoped Jeff would not be angry.

Jeff was angry and he swore a little, and then he laughed, and then he sighed. "Poor Melanctha, she don't know any way to be real honest, but no matter, I sure do love her and I be good if only she will let me."

Jeff Campbell went Wednesday night to see Melanctha. Jeff Campbell took her in his arms and kissed her. "I certainly am awful sorry not to see you Jeff Monday, the way I promised, but I just couldn't Jeff, no way I could fix it." Jeff looked at her and then he laughed a little at her. "You want me to believe that really now Melanctha. All right I believe it if you want me to Melanctha. I certainly be good to you to-night the way you like it. I believe you certainly did want to see me Melanctha, and there was no way you could fix it." "Oh Jeff dear," said Melanctha, "I sure was wrong to act so to you. It's awful hard for me ever to say it to you, I have been wrong in my acting to you, but I certainly was bad this time Jeff to you. It do certainly come hard to me to say it Jeff, but I certainly was wrong to go away from you the way I did it. Only you always certainly been so bad Jeff, and such a bother to me, and making everything always so hard for me, and I certainly got some way to do it to make it come back sometimes to you. You bad boy Jeff, now you hear me, and this certainly is the first time Jeff I ever yet said it to anybody, I ever been wrong, Jeff, you hear me!" "All right Melanctha, I sure do forgive you, cause it's certainly the first time I ever heard you say you ever did anything wrong the way you shouldn't," and Jeff Campbell laughed and kissed her, and Melanctha laughed and loved him, and they really were happy now for a little time together.

And now they were very happy in each other and then they were silent and then they became a little sadder and then they were very quiet once more with each other.

"Yes I certainly do love you Jeff!" Melanctha said and she was very dreamy. "Sure, Melanctha." "Yes Jeff sure, but not the way you are now ever thinking. I love you more and more seems to me Jeff always, and I certainly do trust you more and more always to me when I know you. I do love you Jeff, sure yes, but not the kind of way of loving you are ever thinking it now Jeff with me. I ain't got certainly no hot passion any more now in me. You certainly have killed all that kind of feeling now Jeff in me.[6] You certainly do know that Jeff, now the way I am always, when I am loving with you. You certainly do know that Jeff, and that's the way you certainly do like it now in me. You certainly don't mind now Jeff, to hear me say this to you."

Jeff Campbell was hurt so that it almost killed him. Yes he certainly did know now what it was to have real hot love in him, and yet Melanctha certainly was right, he did not deserve she should ever give it to him. "All right Melanctha I ain't ever kicking. I always will give you certainly always everything you want that I got in me. I take anything you want now to give me. I don't say never Melanctha it don't hurt me, but I certainly don't say ever Melanctha it ought ever to be any different to me." And the bitter tears rose up in Jeff Campbell, and they came and choked his voice to be silent, and he held himself hard to keep from breaking.

"Good-night Melanctha," and Jeff was very humble to her. "Good-night Jeff, I certainly never did mean any way to hurt you. I do love you, sure Jeff every day more and more, all the time I know you." "I know Melanctha, I know, it's never nothing to me. You can't help it, anybody ever the way they are feeling. It's all right now Melanctha, you believe me, good-night now Melanctha, I got now to leave you, good-by Melanctha, sure don't look so worried to me, sure Melanctha I come again soon to see you." And then Jeff stumbled down the steps, and he went away fast to leave her.

And now the pain came hard and harder in Jeff Campbell, and he groaned, and it hurt him so, he could not bear it. And the tears came, and his heart beat, and he was hot and worn and bitter in him.

Now Jeff knew very well what it was to love Melanctha. Now Jeff Campbell knew he was really understanding. Now Jeff knew what it was to be good to Melanctha. Now Jeff was good to her always.

Slowly Jeff felt it a comfort in him to have it hurt so, and to be good to Melanctha always. Now there was no way Melanctha ever had had to bear things for him, worse than he now had it in him.

6. In *Q.E.D.*, Helen says to Adele, "I don't care for you passionately any more, I am afraid you have killed all that in me as you know," but then goes on to say, "but I never wanted you so much before and I have learned to trust you and depend upon you" (page 221). Melanctha is less duplicitous than Helen: again, Stein gives Melanctha more substance and credibility as a character than she gave Helen.

Now Jeff was strong inside him. Now with all the pain there was peace in him. Now he knew he was understanding, now he knew he had a hot love in him, and he was good always to Melanctha Herbert who was the one had made him have it. Now he knew he could be good, and not cry out for help to her to teach him how to bear it. Every day Jeff felt himself more a strong man, the way he once had thought was his real self, the way he knew it. Now Jeff Campbell had real wisdom in him, and it did not make him bitter when it hurt him, for Jeff knew now all through him that he was really strong to bear it.

And so now Jeff Campbell could see Melanctha often, and he was patient, and always very friendly to her, and every day Jeff Campbell understood Melanctha Herbert better. And always Jeff saw Melanctha could not love him the way he needed she should do it. Melanctha Herbert had no way she ever really could remember.

And now Jeff knew there was a man Melanctha met very often, and perhaps she wanted to try to have this man to be good, for her. Jeff Campbell never saw the man Melanctha Herbert perhaps now wanted. Jeff Campbell only knew very well that there was one. Then there was Rose that Melanctha now always had with her when she wandered.

Jeff Campbell was very quiet to Melanctha. He said to her, now he thought he did not want to come any more especially to see her. When they met, he always would be glad to see her, but now he never would go anywhere any more to meet her. Sure he knew she always would have a deep love in him for her. Sure she knew that. "Yes Jeff, I always trust you Jeff, I certainly do know that all right." Jeff Campbell said, all right he never could say anything to reproach her. She knew always that he really had learned all through him how to love her. "Yes, Jeff, I certainly do know that." She knew now she could always trust him. Jeff always would be loyal to her though now she never was any more to him like a religion, but he never could forget the real sweetness in her. That Jeff must remember always, though now he never can trust her to be really loving to any man for always, she never did have any way she ever could remember. If she ever needed anybody to be good to her, Jeff Campbell always would do anything he could to help her. He never can forget the things she taught him so he could be really understanding, but he never any more wants to see her. He be like a brother to her always, when she needs it, and he always will be a good friend to her. Jeff Campbell certainly was sorry never any more to see her, but it was good that they now knew each other really. "Good-by Jeff you always been very good always to me." "Good-by Melanctha you know you always can trust yourself to me." "Yes, I know, I know Jeff, really." "I certainly got to go now Melanctha, from you. I go this time, Melanctha really," and Jeff Campbell went away and this time he never looked back to her. This time Jeff Campbell just broke away and left her.

Jeff Campbell loved to think now he was strong again to be quiet, and to live regular, and to do everything the way he wanted it to be right for himself and all the colored people. Jeff went away for a little while to another town to work there, and he worked hard, and he was very sad inside him, and sometimes the tears would rise up in him, and then he would work hard, and then he would begin once more to see some beauty in the world around him. Jeff had behaved right and he had learned to have a real love in him. That was very good to have inside him.

Jeff Campbell never could forget the sweetness in Melanctha Herbert, and he was always very friendly to her, but they never any more came close to one another. More and more Jeff Campbell and Melanctha fell away from all knowing of each other, but Jeff never could forget Melanctha. Jeff never could forget the real sweetness she had in her, but Jeff never any more had the sense of a real religion for her. Jeff always had strong in him the meaning of all the new kind of beauty Melanctha Herbert once had shown him, and always more and more it helped him with his working for himself and for all the colored people.

Melanctha Herbert, now that she was all through with Jeff Campbell, was free to be with Rose and the new men she met now.

Rose was always now with Melanctha Herbert. Rose never found any way to get excited. Rose always was telling Melanctha Herbert the right way she should do, so that she could not always be in trouble. But Melanctha Herbert could not help it, always she would find new ways to get excited.

Melanctha was all ready now to find new ways to be in trouble. And yet Melanctha Herbert never wanted not to do right. Always Melanctha Herbert wanted peace and quiet, and always she could only find new ways to get excited.

"Melanctha," Rose would say to her, "Melanctha, I certainly have got to tell you, you ain't right to act so with that kind of feller. You better just had stick to black men now, Melanctha, you hear me what I tell you, just the way you always see me do it. They're real bad men, now I tell you Melanctha true, and you better had hear to me. I been raised by real nice kind of white folks, Melanctha, and I certainly knows awful well, soon as ever I can see 'em acting, what is a white man will act decent to you and the kind it ain't never no good to a colored girl to ever go with. Now you know real Melanctha how I always mean right good to you, and you ain't got no way like me Melanctha, what was raised by white folks, to know right what is the way you should be acting with men. I don't never want to see you have bad trouble come hard to you now Melanctha, and so you just hear to me now Melanctha, what I tell you, for I knows it. I don't say never certainly to you Melanctha, you never had ought to have nothing to do ever with no white men, though it ain't never to me Melanctha, the best kind of a way a colored girl can have to be acting, no I never do say to you Melanctha, you hadn't never ought to be with white men, though it ain't never the way I feel it ever real right for a decent colored girl to be always doing, but not never Melanctha, now you hear me, no not never no kind of white men like you been with always now Melanctha when I see you. You just hear to me Melanctha, you certainly had ought to hear to me Melanctha, I say it just like I knows it awful well, Melanctha, and I knows you don't know no better, Melanctha, how to act so, the ways I seen it with them kind of white fellers, them as never can know what to do right by a decent girl they have ever got to be with them. Now you hear to me Melanctha, what I tell you."

And so it was Melanctha Herbert found new ways to be in trouble. But it was not very bad this trouble, for these white men Rose never wanted she should be with, never meant very much to Melanctha. It was only that she liked it to be with them, and they knew all about fine horses, and it was just good to Melanctha, now a little, to feel real reckless with them. But mostly it was Rose and other better kind of colored girls and colored men with whom Melanctha Herbert now always wandered.

It was summer now and the colored people came out into the sunshine, full blown with the flowers. And they shone in the streets and in the fields with their warm joy, and they glistened in their black heat, and they flung themselves free in their wide abandonment of shouting laughter.

It was very pleasant in some ways, the life Melanctha Herbert now led with Rose and all the others. It was not always that Rose had to scold her.

There was not anybody of all these colored people, excepting only Rose, who ever meant much to Melanctha Herbert. But they all liked Melanctha, and the men all liked to see her do things, she was so game always to do anything anybody ever could do, and then she was good and sweet to do anything anybody ever wanted from her.

These were pleasant days then, in the hot southern negro sunshine, with many simple jokes and always wide abandonment of laughter. "Just look at that Melanctha there a running. Don't she just go like a bird when she is flying. Hey Melanctha there, I come and catch you, hey Melanctha, I put salt on your tail to catch you,"[7] and then the man would try to catch her, and he would fall full on the earth and roll in an agony of wide-mouthed shouting laughter.

7. A method for catching birds by preventing them from being able to fly; evidently, this has a sexual double meaning.

And this was the kind of way Rose always liked to have Melanctha do it, to be engaged to him, and to have a good warm nigger[8] time with colored men, not to go about with that kind of white man, never could know how to act right, to any decent kind of girl they could ever get to be with them.

Rose, always more and more, liked Melanctha Herbert better. Rose often had to scold Melanctha Herbert, but that only made her like Melanctha better. And then Melanctha always listened to her, and always acted every way she could to please her. And then Rose was so sorry for Melanctha, when she was so blue sometimes, and wanted somebody should come and kill her.

And Melanctha Herbert clung to Rose in the hope that Rose could save her. Melanctha felt the power of Rose's selfish, decent kind of nature. It was so solid, simple, certain to her. Melanctha clung to Rose, she loved to have her scold her, she always wanted to be with her. She always felt a solid safety in her. Rose always was, in her way, very good to let Melanctha be loving to her. Melanctha never had any way that she could ever get real power, to come close inside to her. Melanctha was always very humble to her. Melanctha was always ready to do anything Rose wanted from her. Melanctha needed badly to have Rose always willing to let Melanctha cling to her. Rose was a simple, sullen, selfish, black girl, but she had a solid power in her. Rose had strong the sense of decent conduct, she had strong the sense for decent comfort. Rose always knew very well what it was she wanted, and she knew very well what was the right way to do to get everything she wanted, and she never had any kind of trouble to perplex her. And so the subtle intelligent attractive half white girl Melanctha Herbert loved and did for, and demeaned herself in service to this coarse, decent, sullen, ordinary, black, childish Rose and now this unmoral promiscuous shiftless Rose was to be married to a good man of the negroes, while Melanctha Herbert with her white blood and attraction and her desire for a right position was perhaps never to be really regularly married. Sometimes the thought of how all her world was made filled the complex, desiring Melanctha with despair. She wondered often how she could go on living when she was so blue. Sometimes Melanctha thought she would just kill herself, for sometimes she thought this would be really the best thing for her to do.[9]

Rose was now to be married to a decent good man of the negroes. His name was Sam Johnson, and he worked as a deck-hand on a coasting steamer, and he was very steady, and he got good wages.

8. Rose is the only character in the novella, other than the porter who refers to a white man's insulting, racist use of the word, who uses the word "nigger." It is an ironic use of the word, because Rose intends to disparage whites and to affirm her African-American identity.
9. The novella has come full circle structurally, returning to its introduction of Melanctha on page 54.

Rose first met Sam Johnson at church, the same place where she had met Melanctha Herbert. Rose liked Sam when she saw him, she knew he was a good man and worked hard and got good wages, and Rose thought it would be very nice and very good now in her position to get really, regularly married.

Sam Johnson liked Rose very well and he always was ready to do anything she wanted. Sam was a tall, square shouldered, decent, a serious, straightforward, simple, kindly, colored workman. They got on very well together, Sam and Rose, when they were married. Rose was lazy, but not dirty, and Sam was careful but not fussy. Sam was a kindly, simple, earnest, steady workman, and Rose had good common decent sense in her, of how to live regular, and not to have excitements, and to be saving so you could be always sure to have money, so as to have everything you wanted.

It was not very long that Rose knew Sam Johnson, before they were regularly married. Sometimes Sam went into the country with all the other young church people, and then he would be a great deal with Rose and with her Melanctha Herbert. Sam did not care much about Melanctha Herbert. He liked Rose's ways of doing, always better. Melanctha's mystery had no charm for Sam ever. Sam wanted a nice little house to come to when he was tired from his working, and a little baby all his own he could be good to. Sam Johnson was ready to marry as soon as ever Rose wanted he should do it. And so Sam Johnson and Rose one day had a grand real wedding and were married. Then they furnished completely, a little red brick house and then Sam went back to his work as deck hand on a coasting steamer.

Rose had often talked to Sam about how good Melanctha was and how much she always suffered. Sam Johnson never really cared about Melanctha Herbert, but he always did almost everything Rose ever wanted, and he was a gentle, kindly creature, and so he was very good to Rose's friend Melanctha. Melanctha Herbert knew very well Sam did not like her, and so she was very quiet, and always let Rose do the talking for her. She only was very good to always help Rose, and to do anything she ever wanted from her, and to be very good and listen and be quiet whenever Sam had anything to say to her. Melanctha liked Sam Johnson, and all her life Melanctha loved and wanted good and kind and considerate people, and always Melanctha loved and wanted people to be gentle to her, and always she wanted to be regular, and to have peace and quiet in her, and always Melanctha could only find new ways to be in trouble. And Melanctha needed badly to have Rose, to believe her, and to let her cling to her. Rose was the only steady thing Melanctha had to cling to and so Melanctha demeaned herself to be like a servant, to wait on, and always to be scolded, by this ordinary, sullen, black, stupid, childish woman.

Rose was always telling Sam he must be good to poor Melanctha. "You know Sam," Rose said very often to him, "You certainly had ought to be very good to poor Melanctha, she always do have so much trouble with her. You know Sam how I told you she had such a bad time always with that father, and he was awful mean to her always that awful black man, and he never took no kind of care ever to her, and he never helped her when her mother died so hard, that poor Melanctha. Melanctha's ma you know Sam, always was just real religious. One day Melanctha was real little, and she heard her ma say to her pa, it was awful sad to her, Melanctha had not been the one the Lord had took from them stead of the little brother who was dead in the house there from fever. That hurt Melanctha awful when she heard her ma say it. She never could feel it right, and I don't no ways blame Melanctha, Sam, for not feeling better to her ma always after, though Melanctha, just like always she is, always was real good to her ma after, when she was so sick, and died so hard, and nobody never to help Melanctha do it, and she just all alone to do everything without no help come to her no way, and that ugly awful black man she have for a father never all the time come near her. But that's always the way Melanctha is just doing Sam, the way I been telling to you. She always is being just so good to everybody and nobody ever there to thank her for it. I never did see nobody ever Sam, have such bad luck, seems to me always with them, like that poor Melanctha always has it, and she always so good with it, and never no murmur in her, and never no complaining from her, and just never saying nothing with it. You be real good to her Sam, now you hear me, now you and me is married right together. He certainly was an awful black man to her Sam, that father she had, acting always just like a brute to her and she so game and never to tell anybody how it hurt her. And she so sweet and good always to do anything anybody ever can be wanting. I don't see Sam how some men can be to act so awful. I told you Sam, how once Melanctha broke her arm bad and she was so sick and it hurt her awful and he never would let no doctor come near to her and he do some things so awful to her, she don't never want to tell nobody how bad he hurt her. That's just the way Sam with Melanctha always, you never can know how bad it is, it hurts her. You hear me Sam, you always be real good to her now you and me is married right to each other."

And so Rose and Sam Johnson were regularly married, and Rose sat at home and bragged to all her friends how nice it was to be married really to a husband.

Rose did not have Melanctha to live with her, now Rose was married. Melanctha was with Rose almost as much as ever but it was a little different now their being together.

Rose Johnson never asked Melanctha to live with her in the house, now Rose was married. Rose liked to have Melanctha come all the time to help her, Rose liked Melanctha to be almost always with her, but Rose was shrewd in her simple selfish nature, she did not ever think to ask Melanctha to live with her.

Rose was hard headed, she was decent, and she always knew what it was she needed. Rose needed Melanctha to be with her, she liked to have her help her, the quick, good Melanctha to do for the slow, lazy, selfish, black girl, but Rose could have Melanctha to do for her and she did not need her to live with her.

Sam never asked Rose why she did not have her. Sam always took what Rose wanted should be done for Melanctha, as the right way he should act toward her.

It could never come to Melanctha to ask Rose to let her. It never could come to Melanctha to think that Rose would ask her. It would never ever come to Melanctha to want it, if Rose should ask her, but Melanctha would have done it for the safety she always felt when she was near her. Melanctha Herbert wanted badly to be safe now, but this living with her, that, Rose would never give her. Rose had strong the sense for decent comfort, Rose had strong the sense for proper conduct, Rose had strong the sense to get straight always what she wanted, and she always knew what was the best thing she needed, and always Rose got what she wanted.

And so Rose had Melanctha Herbert always there to help her, and she sat and was lazy and she bragged and she complained a little and she told Melanctha how she ought to do, to get good what she wanted like she Rose always did it, and always Melanctha was doing everything Rose ever needed. "Don't you bother so, doing that Melanctha, I do it or Sam when he comes home to help me. Sure you don't mind lifting it Melanctha? You is very good Melanctha to do it, and when you go out Melanctha, you stop and get some rice to bring me to-morrow when you come in. Sure you won't forget Melanctha. I never see anybody like you Melanctha to always do things so nice for me." And then Melanctha would do some more for Rose, and then very late Melanctha would go home to the colored woman where she lived now.

And so though Melanctha still was so much with Rose Johnson, she had times when she could not stay there. Melanctha now could not really cling there. Rose had Sam, and Melanctha more and more lost the hold she had had there.

Melanctha Herbert began to feel she must begin again to look and see if she could find what it was she had always wanted. Now Rose Johnson could no longer help her.

And so Melanctha Herbert began once more to wander and with men Rose never thought it was right she should be with.

One day Melanctha had been very busy with the different kinds of ways she wandered. It was a pleasant late afternoon at the end of a long summer. Melanctha was walking along, and she was free and excited. Melanctha had just parted from a white man and she had a bunch of flowers he had left with her. A young buck,[1] a mulatto, passed by and snatched them from her. "It certainly is real sweet in you sister, to be giving me them pretty flowers," he said to her.

"I don't see no way it can make them sweeter to have with you," said Melanctha. "What one man gives, another man had certainly just as much good right to be taking." "Keep your old flowers then, I certainly don't never want to have them." Melanctha Herbert laughed at him and took them. "No, I didn't nohow think you really did want to have them. Thank you kindly mister, for them. I certainly always do admire to see a man always so kind of real polite to people." The man laughed, "You ain't nobody's fool I can say for you, but you certainly are a damned pretty kind of girl, now I look at you. Want men to be polite to you? All right, I can love you, that's real polite now, want to see me try it." "I certainly ain't got no time this evening just only left to thank you. I certainly got to be real busy now, but I certainly always will admire to see you." The man tried to catch and stop her, Melanctha Herbert laughed and dodged so that he could not touch her. Melanctha went quickly down a side street near her and so the man for that time lost her.

For some days Melanctha did not see any more of her mulatto.[2] One day Melanctha was with a white man and they saw him. The white man stopped to speak to him. Afterwards Melanctha left the white man and she then soon met him. Melanctha stopped to talk to him. Melanctha Herbert soon began to like him.

Jem Richards, the new man Melanctha had begun to know now, was a dashing kind of fellow, who had to do with fine horses and with racing. Sometimes Jem Richards would be betting and would be good and lucky, and be making lots of money. Sometimes Jem would be betting badly, and then he would not be having any money.

Jem Richards was a straight man. Jem Richards always knew that by and by he would win again and pay it, and so Jem mostly did win again, and then he always paid it.

Jem Richards was a man other men always trusted. Men gave him money when he lost all his, for they all knew Jem Richards would win again, and when he did win they knew, and they were right, that he would pay it.

Melanctha Herbert all her life had always loved to be with horses. Melanctha liked it that Jem knew all about fine horses. He was a reckless man was Jem Richards. He knew how to win out, and always all her life, Melanctha Herbert loved successful power.

1. Derogatory term for a young African-American man.
2. This character faintly echoes Jeff.

Melanctha Herbert always liked Jem Richards better. Things soon began to be very strong between them.

Jem was more game even than Melanctha. Jem always had known what it was to have real wisdom. Jem had always all his life been understanding.

Jem Richards made Melanctha Herbert come fast with him. He never gave her any time with waiting. Soon Melanctha always had Jem with her. Melanctha did not want anything better. Now in Jem Richards, Melanctha found everything she had ever needed to content her.[3]

Melanctha was now less and less with Rose Johnson. Rose did not think much of the way Melanctha now was going. Jem Richards was all right, only Melanctha never had no sense of the right kind of way she should be doing. Rose often was telling Sam now, she did not like the fast way Melanctha was going. Rose told it to Sam, and to all the girls and men, when she saw them. But Rose was nothing just then to Melanctha. Melanctha Herbert now only needed Jem Richards to be with her.

And things were always getting stronger between Jem Richards and Melanctha Herbert. Jem Richards began to talk now as if he wanted to get married to her. Jem was deep in his love now for her. And as for Melanctha, Jem was all the world now to her. And so Jem gave her a ring, like white folks, to show he was engaged to her, and would by and by be married to her. And Melanctha was filled full with joy to have Jem so good to her.

Melanctha always loved to go with Jem to the races. Jem had been lucky lately with his betting, and he had a swell turnout[4] to drive in, and Melanctha looked very handsome there beside him.

Melanctha was very proud to have Jem Richards want her. Melanctha loved it the way Jem knew how to do it. Melanctha loved Jem and loved that he should want her. She loved it too, that he wanted to be married to her. Jem Richards was a straight decent man, whom other men always looked up to and trusted. Melanctha needed badly a man to content her.

Melanctha's joy made her foolish. Melanctha told everybody about how Jem Richards, that swell man who owned all those fine horses and was so game, nothing ever scared him, was engaged to be married to her, and that was the ring he gave her.

Melanctha let out her joy very often to Rose Johnson. Melanctha had begun again now to go there.

Melanctha's love for Jem made her foolish. Melanctha had to have

---

3. "Wisdom," "knowledge," and "understanding," having accumulated complex, multiple meanings in the course of the novella, are reduced exclusively to sexual meanings here.

4. Stylish, expensive carriage and horses.

some one always now to talk to and so she went often to Rose Johnson.

Melanctha put all herself into Jem Richards. She was mad and foolish in the joy she had there.

Rose never liked the way Melanctha did it. "No Sam I don't say never Melanctha ain't engaged to Jem Richards the way she always says it, and Jem he is all right for that kind of a man he is, though he do think himself so smart and like he owns the earth and everything he can get with it, and he sure gave Melanctha a ring like he really meant he should be married right soon with it, only Sam, I don't ever like it the way Melanctha is going. When she is engaged to him Sam, she ain't not right to take on so excited. That ain't no decent kind of a way a girl ever should be acting. There ain't no kind of a man going stand that, not like I knows men Sam, and I sure does know them. I knows them white and I knows them colored, for I was raised by white folks, and they don't none of them like a girl to act so. That's all right to be so when you is just only loving, but it ain't no ways right to be acting so when you is engaged to him, and when he says, all right he get really regularly married to you. You see Sam I am right like I am always and I knows it. Jem Richards, he ain't going to the last to get real married, not if I knows it right, the way Melanctha now is acting to him. Rings or anything ain't nothing to them, and they don't never do no good for them, when a girl acts foolish like Melanctha always now is acting. I certainly will be right sorry Sam, if Melanctha has real bad trouble come now to her, but I certainly don't no ways like it Sam the kind of way Melanctha is acting to him. I don't never say nothing to her Sam. I just listens to what she is saying always, and I thinks it out like I am telling to you Sam but I don't never say nothing no more now to Melanctha. Melanctha didn't say nothing to me about that Jem Richards till she was all like finished with him, and I never did like it Sam, much, the way she was acting, not coming here never when she first ran with those men and met him. And I didn't never say nothing to her, Sam, about it, and it ain't nothing ever to me, only I don't never no more want to say nothing to her, so I just listens to what she got to tell like she wants it. No Sam, I don't never want to say nothing to her. Melanctha just got to go her own way, not as I want to see her have bad trouble ever come hard to her, only it ain't in me never Sam, after Melanctha did so, ever to say nothing more to her how she should be acting. You just see Sam like I tell you, what way Jem Richards will act to her, you see Sam I just am right like I always am when I knows it."

Melanctha Herbert never thought she could ever again be in trouble. Melanctha's joy had made her foolish.

And now Jem Richards had some bad trouble with his betting. Melanctha sometimes felt now when she was with him that there was something wrong inside him. Melanctha knew he had had trouble with his betting but Melanctha never felt that that could make any difference to them.

Melanctha once had told Jem, sure he knew she always would love to be with him, if he was in jail or only just a beggar. Now Melanctha said to him, "Sure you know Jem that it don't never make any kind of difference you're having any kind of trouble, you just try me Jem and be game, don't look so worried to me. Jem sure I know you love me like I love you always, and its all I ever could be wanting Jem to me, just your wanting me always to be with you. I get married Jem to you soon ever as you can want me, if you once say it Jem to me. It ain't nothing to me ever, anything like having any money Jem, why you look so worried to me."

Melanctha Herbert's love had surely made her mad and foolish. She thrust it always deep into Jem Richards and now that he had trouble with his betting, Jem had no way that he ever wanted to be made to feel it. Jem Richards never could want to marry any girl while he had trouble. That was no way a man like him should do it. Melanctha's love had made her mad and foolish, she should be silent now and let him do it. Jem Richards was not a kind of man to want a woman to be strong to him, when he was in trouble with his betting. That was not the kind of a time when a man like him needed to have it.

Melanctha needed so badly to have it, this love which she had always wanted, she did not know what she should do to save it. Melanctha saw now, Jem Richards always had something wrong inside him. Melanctha soon dared not ask him. Jem was busy now, he had to sell things and see men to raise money. Jem could not meet Melanctha now so often.

It was lucky for Melanctha Herbert that Rose Johnson was coming now to have her baby. It had always been understood between them, Rose should come and stay then in the house where Melanctha lived with an old colored woman, so that Rose could have the Doctor from the hospital near by to help her, and Melanctha there to take care of her the way Melanctha always used to do it.

Melanctha was very good now to Rose Johnson. Melanctha did everything that any woman could, she tended Rose, and she was patient, submissive, soothing and untiring, while the sullen, childish, cowardly, black Rosie grumbled, and fussed, and howled, and made herself to be an abomination and like a simple beast.

All this time Melanctha was always being every now and then with Jem Richards. Melanctha was beginning to be stronger with Jem Richards. Melanctha was never so strong and sweet and in her nature as when she was deep in trouble, when she was fighting so with all she had, she could not do any foolish thing with her nature.

Always now Melanctha Herbert came back again to be nearer to Rose Johnson. Always now Melanctha would tell all about her troubles to Rose Johnson. Rose had begun now a little again to advise her.

Melanctha always told Rose now about the talks she had with Jem Richards, talks where they neither of them liked very well what the other one was saying. Melanctha did not know what it was Jem Richards wanted. All Melanctha knew was, he did not like it when she wanted to be good friends and get really married, and then when Melanctha would say, "all right, I never wear your ring no more Jem, we ain't not any more to meet ever like we ever going to get really regular married," then Jem did not like it either. What was it Jem Richards really wanted?

Melanctha stopped wearing Jem's ring on her finger. Poor Melanctha, she wore it on a string she tied around her neck so that she could always feel it, but Melanctha was strong now with Jem Richards, and he never saw it. And sometimes Jem seemed to be awful sorry for it, and sometimes he seemed kind of glad of it, Melanctha never could make out really what it was Jem Richards wanted.

There was no other woman yet to Jem, that Melanctha knew, and so she always trusted that Jem would come back to her, deep in his love, the way once he had had it and had made all the world like she once had never believed anybody could really make it. But Jem Richards was more game than Melanctha Herbert. He knew how to fight to win out, better. Melanctha really had already lost it, in not keeping quiet and waiting for Jem to do it.

Jem Richards was not yet having better luck in his betting. He never before had had such a long time without some good coming to him in his betting. Sometimes Jem talked as if he wanted to go off on a trip somewhere and try some other place for luck with his betting. Jem Richards never talked as if he wanted to take Melanctha with him.

And so Melanctha sometimes was really trusting, and sometimes she was all sick inside her with her doubting. What was it Jem really wanted to do with her? He did not have any other woman, in that Melanctha could be really trusting, and when she said no to him, no she never would come near him, now he did not want to have her, then Jem would change and swear, yes sure he did want her, now and always right here near him, but he never now any more said he wanted to be married soon to her. But then Jem Richards never would marry a girl, he said that very often, when he was in this kind of trouble, and now he did not see any way he could get out of his trouble. But Melanctha ought to wear his ring, sure she knew he never had loved any kind of woman like he loved her. Melanctha would wear the ring a little while, and then they would have some more trouble, and then she would say to him, no she certainly never would any more wear anything he gave her, and then she would wear it on the string so nobody could see it but she could always feel it on her.

Poor Melanctha, surely her love had made her mad and foolish.

And now Melanctha needed always more and more to be with Rose Johnson, and Rose had commenced again to advise her, but Rose could not help her. There was no way now that anybody could advise her. The time when Melanctha could have changed it with Jem Richards was now all past for her. Rose knew it, and Melanctha too, she knew it, and it almost killed her to let herself believe it.

The only comfort Melanctha ever had now was waiting on Rose till she was so tired she could hardly stand it. Always Melanctha did everything Rose ever wanted. Sam Johnson began now to be very gentle and a little tender to Melanctha. She was so good to Rose and Sam was so glad to have her there to help Rose and to do things and to be a comfort to her.

Rose had a hard time to bring her baby to its birth and Melanctha did everything that any woman could.

The baby though it was healthy after it was born did not live long. Rose Johnson was careless and negligent and selfish and when Melanctha had to leave for a few days the baby died. Rose Johnson had liked her baby well enough and perhaps she just forgot it for a while, anyway the child was dead and Rose and Sam were very sorry, but then these things came so often in the negro world in Bridgepoint that they neither of them thought about it very long. When Rose had become strong again she went back to her house with Sam.[5] And Sam Johnson was always now very gentle and kind and good to Melanctha who had been so good to Rose in her bad trouble.

Melanctha Herbert's troubles with Jem Richards were never getting any better. Jem always now had less and less time to be with her. When Jem was with Melanctha now he was good enough to her. Jem Richards was worried with his betting. Never since Jem had first begun to make a living had he ever had so much trouble for such a long time together with his betting. Jem Richards was good enough now to Melanctha but he had not much strength to give her. Melanctha could never any more now make him quarrel with her. Melanctha never now could complain of his treatment of her, for surely, he said it always by his actions to her, surely she must know how a man was

---

5. Note that this paragraph, up to this point, and the paragraph before it, repeat almost verbatim the opening of the novella. There is an inconsistency here, however: there had been no indication in the opening section that Rose had given birth to her child, and that the child had died, somewhere other than in her own home.

when he had trouble on his mind with trying to make things go a little better.

Sometimes Jem and Melanctha had long talks when they neither of them liked very well what the other one was saying, but mostly now Melanctha could not make Jem Richards quarrel with her, and more and more, Melanctha could not find any way to make it right to blame him for the trouble she now always had inside her. Jem was good to her, and she knew, for he told her, that he had trouble all the time now with his betting. Melanctha knew very well that for her it was all wrong inside Jem Richards, but Melanctha had now no way that she could really reach him.

Things between Melanctha and Jem Richards were now never getting any better. Melanctha now more and more needed to be with Rose Johnson. Rose still liked to have Melanctha come to her house and do things for her, and Rose liked to grumble to her and to scold her and to tell Melanctha what was the way Melanctha always should be doing so she could make things come out better and not always be so much in trouble. Sam Johnson in these days was always very good and gentle to Melanctha. Sam was now beginning to be very sorry for her.

Jem Richards never made things any better for Melanctha. Often Jem would talk so as to make Melanctha almost certain that he never any more wanted to have her. Then Melanctha would get very blue, and she would say to Rose, sure she would kill herself, for that certainly now was the best way she could do.

Rose Johnson never saw it the least bit that way. "I don't see Melanctha why you should talk like you would kill yourself just because you're blue. I'd never kill myself Melanctha cause I was blue. I'd maybe kill somebody else but I'd never kill myself. If I ever killed myself, Melanctha it'd be by accident and if I ever killed myself by accident, Melanctha, I'd be awful sorry. And that certainly is the way you should feel it Melanctha, now you hear me, not just talking foolish like you always do. It certainly is only your way just always being foolish makes you all that trouble to come to you always now, Melanctha, and I certainly right well knows that. You certainly never can learn no way Melanctha ever with all I certainly been telling to you, ever since I know you good, that it ain't never no way like you do always is the right way you be acting ever and talking, the way I certainly always have seen you do so Melanctha always. I certainly am right Melanctha about them ways you have to do it, and I knows it; but you certainly never can noways learn to act right Melanctha, I certainly do know that, I certainly do my best Melanctha to help you with it only you certainly never do act right Melanctha, not to nobody ever, I can see it. You never act right by me Melanctha no more than by everybody. I never say nothing to you Melanctha when you do so, for I certainly never do like it when I just got to say it to you, but you just certainly done with that Jem Richards you always say wanted real bad to be married to you, just like I always said to Sam you certainly was going to do it. And I certainly am real kind of sorry like for you Melanctha, but you certainly had ought to have come to see me to talk to you, when you first was engaged to him so I could show you, and now you got all this trouble come to you Melanctha like I certainly know you always catch it. It certainly ain't never Melanctha I ain't real sorry to see trouble come so hard to you, but I certainly can see Melanctha it all is always just the way you always be having it in you not never to do right. And now you always talk like you just kill yourself because you are so blue, that certainly never is Melanctha, no kind of a way for any decent kind of a girl to do."

Rose had begun to be strong now to so Melanctha and she was impatient very often with her, but Rose could now never any more be a help to her. Melanctha Herbert never could know now what it was right she should do. Melanctha always wanted to have Jem Richards with her and now he never seemed to want her, and what could Melanctha do. Surely she was right now when she said she would just kill herself, for that was the only way now she could do.

Sam Johnson always, more and more, was good and gentle to Melanctha. Poor Melanctha, she was so good and sweet to do anything anybody ever wanted, and Melanctha always liked it if she could have peace and quiet, and always she could only find new ways to be in trouble. Sam often said this now to Rose about Melanctha.

"I certainly don't never want Sam to say bad things about Melanctha, for she certainly always do have most awful kind of trouble come hard to her, but I never can say I like it real right Sam the way Melanctha always has to do it. Its now just the same with her like it is always she has to do it, now the way she is with that Jem Richards. He certainly now don't never want to have her but Melanctha she ain't got no right kind of spirit. No Sam I don't never like the way any more Melanctha is acting to him, and then Sam, she ain't never real right honest, the way she always should do it. She certainly just don't kind of never Sam tell right what way she is doing with it. I don't never like to say nothing Sam no more to her about the way she always has to be acting. She always say, yes all right Rose, I do the way you say it, and then Sam she don't never noways do it. She certainly is right sweet and good, Sam, is Melanctha, nobody ever can hear me say she ain't always ready to do things for everybody any way she ever can see to do it, only Sam some ways she never does act real right ever, and some ways, Sam, she ain't ever real honest with it. And Sam sometimes I hear awful kind of things she been doing, some girls know about her how she does it, and sometimes they tell me what kind of ways she has to do it, and Sam it certainly do seem to me like more and more I certainly am awful afraid Melanctha never will come to any good. And then Sam, some- times, you hear it, she always talk like she kill herself all the time she is so blue, and Sam that certainly never is no kind of way any decent girl ever had ought to do. You see Sam, how I am right like I always is when I knows it. You just be careful, Sam, now you hear me, you be careful Sam sure, I tell you, Melanctha more and more I see her I certainly do feel Melanctha no way is really honest. You be careful, Sam now, like I tell you, for I knows it, now you hear to me, Sam, what I tell you, for I certainly always is right, Sam, when I knows it."

At first Sam tried a little to defend Melanctha, and Sam always was good and gentle to her, and Sam liked the ways Melanctha had to be quiet to him, and to always listen as if she was learning, when she was there and heard him talking, and then Sam liked the sweet way she always did everything so nicely for him; but Sam never liked to fight with anybody ever, and surely Rose knew best about Melanc- tha and anyway Sam never did really care much about Melanctha. Her mystery never had had any interest for him. Sam liked it that she was sweet to him and that she always did everything Rose ever wanted that she should be doing, but Melanctha never could be important to him. All Sam ever wanted was to have a little house and to live regular and to work hard and to come home to his dinner, when he was tired with his working and by and by he wanted to have some children all his own to be good to, and so Sam was real sorry for Melanctha, she was so good and so sweet always to them, and Jem Richards was a bad man to behave so to her, but that was always the way a girl got it when she liked that kind of a fast fellow. Anyhow Melanctha was Rose's friend, and Sam never cared to have anything to do with the kind of trouble always came to women, when they wanted to have men, who never could know how to behave good and steady to their women.

And so Sam never said much to Rose about Melanctha. Sam was always very gentle to her, but now he began less and less to see her. Soon Melanctha never came any more to the house to see Rose and Sam never asked Rose anything about her.

Melanctha Herbert was beginning now to come less and less to the house to be with Rose Johnson. This was because Rose seemed always less and less now to want her, and Rose would not let Melanc- tha now do things for her. Melanctha was always humble to her and Melanctha always wanted in every way she could to do things for her. Rose said no, she guessed she do that herself like she likes to have it better. Melanctha is real good to stay so long to help her, but Rose guessed perhaps Melanctha better go home now, Rose don't need nobody to help her now, she is feeling real strong, not like just after she had all that trouble with the baby, and then Sam, when he comes home for his dinner he likes it when Rose is all alone there just to give him his dinner. Sam always is so tired now, like he always is in the summer, so many people always on the steamer, and they make so much work so Sam is real tired now, and he likes just to eat his dinner and never have people in the house to be a trouble to him.

Each day Rose treated Melanctha more and more as if she never wanted Melanctha any more to come there to the house to see her. Melanctha dared not ask Rose why she acted in this way to her. Melanctha badly needed to have Rose always there to save her. Melanctha wanted badly to cling to her and Rose had always been so solid for her. Melanctha did not dare to ask Rose if she now no longer wanted her to come and see her.

Melanctha now never any more had Sam to be gentle to her. Rose always sent Melanctha away from her before it was time for Sam to come home to her. One day Melanctha had stayed a little longer, for Rose that day had been good to let Melanctha begin to do things for her. Melanctha then left her and Melanctha met Sam Johnson who stopped a minute to speak kindly to her.

The next day Rose Johnson would not let Melanctha come in to her. Rose stood on the steps, and there she told Melanctha what she thought now of her.

"I guess Melanctha it certainly ain't no ways right for you to come here no more just to see me. I certainly don't Melanctha no ways like to be a trouble to you. I certainly think Melanctha I get along better now when I don't have nobody like you are, always here to help me, and Sam he do so good now with his working, he pay a little girl something to come every day to help me. I certainly do think Melanctha I don't never want you no more to come here just to see me." "Why Rose, what I ever done to you, I certainly don't think you is right Rose to be so bad now to me." "I certainly don't no ways Melanctha Herbert think you got any right ever to be complaining the way I been acting to you. I certainly never do think Melanctha Herbert, you hear to me, nobody ever been more patient to you than I always been to like you, only Melanctha, I hear more things now so awful bad about you, everybody always is telling to me what kind of a way you always have been doing so much, and me always so good to you, and you never no ways, knowing how to be honest to me. No Melanctha it ain't ever in me, not to want you to have good luck come to you, and I like it real well Melanctha when you some time learn how to act the way it is decent and right for a girl to be doing, but I don't no ways ever like it the kind of things everybody tell me now about you. No Melanctha, I can't never any more trust you. I certainly am real sorry to have never any more to see you, but there ain't no other way, I ever can be acting to you. That's all I ever got any more to say to you now Melanctha." "But Rose, deed; I certainly don't know, no more than the dead, nothing I ever done to make you act so to me. Anybody say anything bad about me Rose, to you, they just a pack of liars to you, they certainly is Rose, I tell you true. I certainly never done nothing I ever been ashamed to tell you. Why you act so bad to me Rose. Sam he certainly don't think ever like you do, and Rose I always do everything I can, you ever want me to do for you." "It ain't never no use standing there talking, Melanctha Herbert. I just can tell it to you, and Sam, he don't know nothing about women ever the way they can be acting. I certainly am very sorry Melanctha, to have to act so now to you, but I certainly can't do no other way with you, when you do things always so bad, and everybody is talking so about you. It ain't no use to you to stand there and say it different to me Melanctha. I certainly am always right Melanctha Herbert, the way I certainly always have been when I knows it, to you. No Melanctha, it just is, you never can have no kind of a way to act right, the way a decent girl has to do, and I done my best always to be telling it to you Melanctha Herbert, but it don't never do no good to tell nobody how to act right; they certainly never can learn when they ain't got no sense right to know it, and you never have no sense right Melanctha to be honest, and I ain't never wishing no harm to you ever Melanctha Herbert, only I don't never want any more to see you come here. I just say to you now, like I always been saying to you, you don't know never the right way, any kind of decent girl has to be acting, and so Melanctha Herbert, me and Sam, we don't never any more want you to be setting your foot in my house here Melanctha Herbert, I just tell you. And so you just go along now, Melanctha Herbert, you hear me, and I don't never wish no harm to come to you."

Rose Johnson went into her house and closed the door behind her. Melanctha stood like one dazed, she did not know how to bear this blow that almost killed her. Slowly then Melanctha went away without even turning to look behind her.

Melanctha Herbert was all sore and bruised inside her. Melanctha had needed Rose always to believe her, Melanctha needed Rose always to let her cling to her, Melanctha wanted badly to have somebody who could make her always feel a little safe inside her, and now Rose had sent her from her. Melanctha wanted Rose more than she had ever wanted all the others. Rose always was so simple, solid, decent, for her. And now Rose had cast her from her. Melanctha was lost, and all the world went whirling in a mad weary dance around her.

Melanctha Herbert never had any strength alone ever to feel safe inside her. And now Rose Johnson had cast her from her, and

Melanctha could never any more be near her. Melanctha Herbert knew now, way inside her, that she was lost, and nothing any more could ever help her.

Melanctha went that night to meet Jem Richards who had promised to be at the old place to meet her. Jem Richards was absent in his manner to her. By and by he began to talk to her, about the trip he was going to take soon, to see if he could get some luck back in his betting. Melanctha trembled, was Jem too now going to leave her. Jem Richards talked some more then to her, about the bad luck he always had now, and how he needed to go away to see if he could make it come out any better.

Then Jem stopped, and then he looked straight at Melanctha.

"Tell me Melanctha right and true, you don't care really nothing more about me now Melanctha," he said to her.

"Why you ask me that, Jem Richards," said Melanctha.

"Why I ask you that Melanctha, God Almighty, because I just don't give a damn now for you any more Melanctha. That the reason I was asking."

Melanctha never could have for this an answer. Jem Richards waited and then he went away and left her.

Melanctha Herbert never again saw Jem Richards. Melanctha never again saw Rose Johnson, and it was hard to Melanctha never any more to see her. Rose Johnson had worked in to be the deepest of all Melanctha's emotions.

"No, I don't never see Melanctha Herbert no more now," Rose would say to anybody who asked her about Melanctha. "No, Melanctha she never comes here no more now, after we had all that trouble with her acting so bad with them kind of men she liked so much to be with. She don't never come to no good Melanctha Herbert don't, and me and Sam don't want no more to see her. She didn't do right ever the way I told her. Melanctha just wouldn't, and I always said it to her, if she don't be more kind of careful, the way she always had to be acting, I never did want no more she should come here in my house no more to see me. I ain't no ways ever against any girl having any kind of a way, to have a good time like she wants it, but not that kind of a way Melanctha always had to do it. I expect some day Melanctha kill herself, when she act so bad like she do always, and then she get so awful blue. Melanctha always says that's the only way she ever can think it a easy way for her to do. No, I always am real sorry for Melanctha, she never was no just common kind of nigger, but she don't never know not with all the time I always was telling it to her, no she never no way could learn, what was the right way she should do. I certainly don't never want no kind of harm to come bad to Melanctha, but I certainly do think she will most kill herself some time, the way she always say it would be easy way for her to do. I never see nobody ever could be so awful blue."

But Melanctha Herbert never really killed herself because she was so blue, though often she thought this would be really the best way for her to do. Melanctha never killed herself, she only got a bad fever and went into the hospital where they took good care of her and cured her.

When Melanctha was well again, she took a place and began to work and to live regular. Then Melanctha got very sick again, she began to cough and sweat and be so weak she could not stand to do her work.

Melanctha went back to the hospital, and there the Doctor told her she had the consumption,[6] and before long she would surely die. They sent her where she would be taken care of, a home for poor consumptives, and there Melanctha stayed until she died.

---

6. Tuberculosis, generally incurable at this time, especially for the poor.

The Gentle Lena[1]

LENA WAS patient, gentle, sweet and german. She had been a servant for four years and had liked it very well.

Lena had been brought from Germany to Bridgepoint by a cousin and had been in the same place there for four years.

This place Lena had found very good. There was a pleasant, unexacting mistress and her children, and they all liked Lena very well.

There was a cook there who scolded Lena a great deal but Lena's german patience held no suffering and the good incessant woman really only scolded so for Lena's good.[2]

Lena's german voice when she knocked and called the family in the morning was as awakening, as soothing, and as appealing, as a delicate soft breeze in midday, summer. She stood in the hallway every morning a long time in her unexpectant and unsuffering german patience calling to the young ones to get up. She would call and wait a long time and then call again, always even, gentle, patient, while the young ones fell back often into that precious, tense, last bit of sleeping that gives a strength of joyous vigor in the young, over them that have come to the readiness of middle age, in their awakening.

Lena had good hard work all morning, and on the pleasant, sunny afternoons she was sent out into the park to sit and watch the little two year old girl baby of the family.

The other girls, all them that make the pleasant, lazy crowd, that watch the children in the sunny afternoons out in the park, all liked the simple;[3] gentle, german Lena very well. They all, too, liked very well to tease her, for it was so easy to make her mixed and troubled, and all helpless, for she could never learn to know just what the other quicker[4] girls meant by the queer things they said.[5]

The two or three of these girls, the ones that Lena always sat with, always worked together to confuse her. Still it was pleasant, all this life for Lena.

1. Lena gets her name, but not her character traits, from Stein's Baltimore servant, Lena Lebender.
2. This cook echoes Anna in "The Good Anna."
3. Indicates lacking in intelligence as well as straightforward, uncomplicated; measurement of intelligence was a major preoccupation at the turn of the last century.
4. More intelligent.
5. Incomprehensible to Lena; see the following paragraph.

The little girl fell down sometimes and cried, and then Lena had to soothe her. When the little girl would drop her hat, Lena had to pick it up and hold it. When the little girl was bad and threw away her playthings, Lena told her she could not have them and took them from her to hold until the little girl should need them.

It was all a peaceful life for Lena, almost as peaceful as a pleasant leisure. The other girls, of course, did tease her, but then that only made a gentle stir within her.

Lena was a brown and pleasant creature, brown as blonde races often have them brown, brown, not with the yellow or the red or the chocolate brown of sun burned countries, but brown with the clear color laid flat on the light toned skin beneath, the plain, spare brown that makes it right to have been made with hazel eyes, and not too abundant straight, brown hair, hair that only later deepens itself into brown[6] from the straw yellow of a german childhood.

Lena had the flat chest, straight back and forward falling shoulders of the patient and enduring working woman, though her body was now still in its milder girlhood and work had not yet made these lines too clear.

The rarer feeling[7] that there was with Lena, showed in all the even quiet of her body movements, but in all it was the strongest in the patient, old-world ignorance, and earth made pureness of her brown, flat, soft featured face. Lena had eyebrows that were a wondrous thickness. They were black, and spread, and very cool, with their dark color and their beauty, and beneath them were her hazel eyes, simple and human, with the earth patience[8] of the working, gentle, german woman.

Yes it was all a peaceful life for Lena. The other girls, of course, did tease her, but then that only made a gentle stir within her.

"What you got on your finger Lena," Mary, one of the girls she always sat with, one day asked her. Mary was good natured, quick, intelligent and Irish.[9]

Lena had just picked up the fancy paper made accordion that the little girl had dropped beside her, and was making it squeak sadly as she pulled it with her brown, strong, awkward finger.

"Why, what is it, Mary, paint?" said Lena, putting her finger to her mouth to taste the dirt spot.

6. The repetition of "brown" does not indicate mixed race, but does anticipate the racialized non-normative sexuality of Melanctha.
7. Something that raises Lena above the ordinary emotionally and makes her a finer person despite her intellectual limitation.
8. The repetition of "earth" emphasizes Lena's peasant origins and is the same kind of stereotype Stein simultaneously uses and works against in "Melanctha."
9. "Irish" is capitalized here the way "Bohemian" is in "The Good Anna": it is used as a negative epithet for an immigrant group of lower status at this time.

"That's awful poison Lena, don't you know?" said Mary, "that green paint that you just tasted."

Lena had sucked a good deal of the green paint from her finger. She stopped and looked hard at the finger. She did not know just how much Mary meant by what she said.

"Ain't it poison, Nellie, that green paint, that Lena sucked just now," said Mary. "Sure it is Lena, its real poison, I ain't foolin' this time anyhow."

Lena was a little troubled. She looked hard at her finger where the paint was, and she wondered if she had really sucked it.

It was still a little wet on the edges and she rubbed it off a long time on the inside of her dress, and in between she wondered and looked at the finger and thought, was it really poison that she had just tasted.

"Ain't it too bad, Nellie, Lena should have sucked that," Mary said.

Nellie smiled and did not answer. Nellie was dark and thin, and looked Italian. She had a big mass of black hair that she wore high up on her head, and that made her face look very fine.

Nellie always smiled and did not say much, and then she would look at Lena to perplex her.

And so they all three sat with their little charges in the pleasant sunshine a long time. And Lena would often look at her finger and wonder if it was really poison that she had just tasted and then she would rub her finger on her dress a little harder.[1]

Mary laughed at her and teased her and Nellie smiled a little and looked queerly at her.

Then it came time, for it was growing cooler, for them to drag together the little ones, who had begun to wander, and to take each one back to its own mother. And Lena never knew for certain whether it was really poison, that green stuff that she had tasted.

During these four years of service, Lena always spent her Sundays out at the house of her aunt, who had brought her four years before to Bridgepoint.

This aunt, who had brought Lena, four years before, to Bridgepoint, was a hard, ambitious, well meaning, german woman. Her husband was a grocer in the town, and they were very well to do. Mrs. Haydon, Lena's aunt, had two daughters who were just beginning as young ladies, and she had a little boy who was not honest and who was very hard to manage.

Mrs. Haydon was a short, stout, hard built, german woman. She always hit the ground very firmly and compactly as she walked. Mrs. Haydon was all a compact and well hardened mass, even to her face,

---

1. This episode demonstrates Lena's subnormal intelligence, her passivity, and her tolerance.

reddish and darkened from its early blonde, with its hearty, shiny, cheeks, and doubled chin well covered over with the up-roll from her short, square neck.

The two daughters, who were fourteen and fifteen, looked like unkneaded, unformed mounds of flesh beside her.

The elder girl, Mathilda,[2] was blonde, and slow, and simple, and quite fat. The younger, Bertha, who was almost as tall as her sister, was dark, and quicker, and she was heavy, too, but not really fat.

These two girls the mother had brought up very firmly. They were well taught for their position. They were always both well dressed, in the same kinds of hats and dresses, as is becoming in two german sisters. The mother liked to have them dressed in red. Their best clothes were red dresses, made of good heavy cloth, and strongly trimmed with braid of a glistening black. They had stiff, red felt hats, trimmed with black velvet ribbon, and a bird. The mother dressed matronly, in a bonnet and in black, always sat between her two big daughters, firm, directing, and repressed.

The only weak spot in this good german woman's conduct was the way she spoiled her boy, who was not honest and who was very hard to manage.

The father of this family was a decent, quiet, heavy, and uninterfering german man. He tried to cure the boy of his bad ways, and make him honest, but the mother could not make herself let the father manage, and so the boy was brought up very badly.

Mrs. Haydon's girls were now only just beginning as young ladies, and so to get her niece, Lena, married, was just then the most important thing that Mrs. Haydon had to do.

Mrs. Haydon had four years before gone to Germany to see her parents, and had taken the girls with her. This visit had been for Mrs. Haydon most successful, though her children had not liked it very well.

Mrs. Haydon was a good and generous woman, and she patronized her parents grandly, and all the cousins who came from all about to see her. Mrs. Haydon's people were of the middling class of farmers. They were not peasants, and they lived in a town of some pretension, but it all seemed very poor and smelly to Mrs. Haydon's american born daughters.

Mrs. Haydon liked it all. It was familiar, and then here she was so wealthy and important. She listened and decided, and advised all of her relations how to do things better. She arranged their present and their future for them, and showed them how in the past they had been wrong in all their methods.

2. Another ironic name switch: this derogatory character description echoes that of Miss Mary Wadsmith in "The Good Anna," but Stein gives her the name of the character in "The Good Anna," Miss Mathilda, based on Stein herself.

Mrs. Haydon's only trouble was with her two daughters, whom she could not make behave well to her parents. The two girls were very nasty to all their numerous relations. Their mother could hardly make them kiss their grandparents, and every day the girls would get a scolding. But then Mrs. Haydon was so very busy that she did not have time to really manage her stubborn daughters.

These hard working, earth-rough german cousins were to these american born children, ugly and dirty, and as far below them as were italian or negro[3] workmen, and they could not see how their mother could ever bear to touch them, and then all the women dressed so funny, and were worked all rough and different.[4]

The two girls stuck up their noses at them all, and always talked in English to each other about how they hated all these people and how they wished their mother would not do so. The girls could talk some German, but they never chose to use it.

It was her eldest brother's family that most interested Mrs. Haydon. Here there were eight children, and out of the eight, five of them were girls.

Mrs. Haydon thought it would be a fine thing to take one of these girls back with her to Bridgepoint and get her well started. Everybody liked that she should do so, and they were all willing that it should be Lena.

Lena was the second girl in her large family. She was at this time just seventeen years old. Lena was not an important daughter in the family. She was always sort of dreamy and not there.[5] She worked hard and went very regularly at it, but even good work never seemed to bring her near.

Lena's age just suited Mrs. Haydon's purpose. Lena could first go out to service, and learn how to do things, and then, when she was a little older, Mrs. Haydon could get her a good husband. And then Lena was so still and docile, she would never want to do things her own way. And then, too, Mrs. Haydon, with all her hardness had wisdom, and she could feel the rarer strain there was in Lena.

Lena was willing to go with Mrs. Haydon. Lena did not like her german life very well. It was not the hard work but the roughness that disturbed her. The people were not gentle, and the men when they were glad were very boisterous, and would lay hold of her and roughly tease her. They were good people enough around her, but it was all harsh and dreary for her.

Lena did not really know that she did not like it. She did not know

3. Note the use of lower case for "american," "italian," and "negro," comparable to "german," all neutral descriptive adjectives.
4. This sudden shift to the girls' point of view is characteristic of Stein's style throughout *Three Lives*.
5. Lena's dreaminess connects to her "rarer feeling" as well as to her passivity and absence from her own life ("not there").

that she was always dreamy and not there. She did not think whether it would be different for her away off there in Bridgepoint. Mrs. Haydon took her and got her different kinds of dresses, and then took her with them to the steamer. Lena did not really know what it was that had happened to her.

Mrs. Haydon, and her daughters, and Lena traveled second class on the steamer. Mrs. Haydon's daughters hated that their mother should take Lena. They hated to have a cousin, who was to them, little better than a nigger[6] and then everybody on the steamer there would see her. Mrs. Haydon's daughters said things like this to their mother, but she never stopped to hear them, and the girls did not dare to make their meaning very clear. And so they could only go on hating Lena hard, together. They could not stop her from going back with them to Bridgepoint.

Lena was very sick on the voyage. She thought, surely before it was over that she would die. She was so sick she could not even wish that she had not started. She could not eat, she could not moan, she was just blank and scared, and sure that every minute she would die. She could not hold herself in, nor help herself in her trouble. She just staid where she had been put, pale, and scared, and weak, and sick, and sure that she was going to die.

Mathilda and Bertha Haydon had no trouble from having Lena for a cousin on the voyage, until the last day that they were on the ship, and by that time they had made their friends and could explain.

Mrs. Haydon went down every day to Lena, gave her things to make her better, held her head when it was needful, and generally was good and did her duty by her.

Poor Lena had no power to be strong in such trouble. She did not know how to yield to her sickness nor endure. She lost all her little sense of being[7] in her suffering. She was so scared, and then at her best, Lena, who was patient, sweet and quiet, had not self-control, nor any active courage.

Poor Lena was so scared and weak, and every minute she was sure that she would die.

After Lena was on land again a little while, she forgot all her bad suffering. Mrs. Haydon got her the good place, with the pleasant unexacting mistress, and her children, and Lena began to learn some English and soon was very happy and content.

All her Sundays out Lena spent at Mrs. Haydon's house. Lena would have liked much better to spend her Sundays with the girls she always sat with, and who often asked her, and who teased her and made a gentle stir within her, but it never came to Lena's unexpectant and unsuffering german nature to do something different

6. Again Stein ascribes this word to unsympathetic characters, as she does in "Melanctha."
7. Her already very small sense of herself as a substantial or significant human being.

from what was expected of her, just because she would like it that way better. Mrs. Haydon had said that Lena was to come to her house every other Sunday, and so Lena always went there.

Mrs. Haydon was the only one of her family who took any interest in Lena. Mr. Haydon did not think much of her. She was his wife's cousin and he was good to her, but she was for him stupid, and a little simple, and very dull, and sure some day to need help and to be in trouble. All young poor relations, who were brought from Germany to Bridgepoint were sure, before long, to need help and to be in trouble.

The little Haydon boy was always very nasty to her. He was a hard child for any one to manage, and his mother spoiled him very badly. Mrs. Haydon's daughters as they grew older did not learn to like Lena any better. Lena never knew that she did not like them either. She did not know that she was only happy with the other quicker girls, she always sat with in the park, and who laughed at her and always teased her.

Mathilda Haydon, the simple, fat, blonde, older daughter felt very badly that she had to say that this was her cousin Lena, this Lena who was little better for her than a nigger. Mathilda was an overgrown, slow, flabby, blonde, stupid, fat girl, just beginning as a woman; thick in her speech and dull and simple in her mind, and very jealous of all her family and of other girls, and proud that she could have good dresses and new hats and learn music, and hating very badly to have a cousin who was a common servant. And then Mathilda remembered very strongly that dirty nasty place that Lena came from and that Mathilda had so turned up her nose at, and where she had been made so angry because her mother scolded her and liked all those rough cow-smelly people.

Then, too, Mathilda would get very mad when her mother had Lena at their parties, and when she talked about how good Lena was, to certain german mothers in whose sons, perhaps, Mrs. Haydon might find Lena a good husband. All this would make the dull, blonde, fat Mathilda very angry. Sometimes she would get so angry that she would, in her thick, slow way, and with jealous anger blazing in her light blue eyes, tell her mother that she did not see how she could like that nasty Lena; and then her mother would scold Mathilda, and tell her that she knew her cousin Lena was poor and Mathilda must be good to poor people.

Mathilda Haydon did not like relations to be poor. She told all her girl friends what she thought of Lena, and so the girls would never talk to Lena at Mrs. Haydon's parties. But Lena in her unsuffering and unexpectant patience never really knew that she was slighted. When Mathilda was with her girls in the street or in the park and would see Lena, she always turned up her nose and barely nodded to her, and then she would tell her friends how funny her mother was to take care of people like that Lena, and how, back in Germany, all Lena's people lived just like pigs.

The younger daughter, the dark, large, but not fat, Bertha Haydon, who was very quick in her mind, and in her ways, and who was the favorite with her father, did not like Lena, either. She did not like her because for her Lena was a fool and so stupid, and she would let those Irish and Italian girls laugh at her and tease her, and everybody always made fun of Lena, and Lena never got mad, or even had sense enough to know that they were all making an awful fool of her.

Bertha Haydon hated people to be fools. Her father, too, thought Lena was a fool, and so neither the father nor the daughter ever paid any attention to Lena, although she came to their house every other Sunday.

Lena did not know how all the Haydons felt. She came to her aunt's house all her Sunday afternoons that she had out, because Mrs. Haydon had told her she must do so. In the same way Lena always saved all of her wages. She never thought of any way to spend it. The german cook, the good woman who always scolded Lena, helped her to put it in the bank each month, as soon as she got it. Sometimes before it got into the bank to be taken care of, somebody would ask Lena for it. The little Haydon boy sometimes asked and would get it, and sometimes some of the girls, the ones Lena always sat with, needed some more money; but the german cook, who always scolded Lena, saw to it that this did not happen very often. When it did happen she would scold Lena very sharply, and for the next few months she would not let Lena touch her wages, but put it in the bank for her on the same day that Lena got it.

So Lena always saved her wages, for she never thought to spend them, and she always went to her aunt's house for her Sundays because she did not know that she could do anything different.

Mrs. Haydon felt more and more every year that she had done right to bring Lena, back with her, for it was all coming out just as she had expected. Lena was good and never wanted her own way, she was learning English, and saving all her wages, and soon Mrs. Haydon would get her a good husband.

All these four years Mrs. Haydon was busy looking around among all the german people that she knew for the right man to be Lena's husband, and now at last she was quite decided.

The man Mrs. Haydon wanted for Lena was a young german-american tailor, who worked with his father. He was good and all the family were very saving, and Mrs. Haydon was sure that this would be just right for Lena, and then too, this young tailor always did whatever his father and his mother wanted.

This old german tailor and his wife, the father and the mother

Herman Kreder, who was to marry Lena Mainz, were very thrifty, careful people. Herman was the only child they had left with them, and he always did everything they wanted. Herman was now twenty-eight years old, but he had never stopped being scolded and directed by his father and his mother. And now they wanted to see him married.

Herman Kreder did not care much to get married. He was a gentle soul and a little fearful. He had a sullen temper, too. He was obedient to his father and his mother. He always did his work well. He often went out on Saturday nights and on Sundays, with other men. He liked it with them but he never became really joyous. He liked to be with men and he hated to have women with them.[8] He was obedient to his mother, but he did not care much to get married.

Mrs. Haydon and the elder Kreders had often talked the marriage over. They all three liked it very well. Lena would do anything that Mrs. Haydon wanted, and Herman was always obedient in everything to his father and his mother. Both Lena and Herman were saving and good workers and neither of them ever wanted their own way.

The elder Kreders, everybody knew, had saved up all their money, and they were hard, good german people, and Mrs. Haydon was sure that with these people Lena would never be in any trouble. Mr. Haydon would not say anything about it. He knew old Kreder had a lot of money and owned some good houses, and he did not care what his wife did with that simple, stupid Lena, so long as she would be sure never to need help or to be in trouble.

Lena did not care much to get married. She liked her life very well where she was working. She did not think much about Herman Kreder. She thought he was a good man and she always found him very quiet. Neither of them ever spoke much to the other. Lena did not care much just then about getting married.

Mrs. Haydon spoke to Lena about it very often. Lena never answered anything at all. Mrs. Haydon thought, perhaps Lena did not like Herman Kreder. Mrs. Haydon could not believe that any girl not even Lena, really had no feeling about getting married.

Mrs. Haydon spoke to Lena very often about Herman. Mrs. Haydon sometimes got very angry with Lena. She was afraid that Lena, for once, was going to be stubborn, now when it was all fixed right for her to be married.

"Why you stand there so stupid, why don't you answer, Lena," said Mrs. Haydon one Sunday, at the end of a long talking that she was giving Lena about Herman Kreder, and about Lena's getting married to him.

"Yes ma'am," said Lena, and then Mrs. Haydon was furious with

8. Note that Herman prefers to be with men, just as Lena prefers to be with women: Stein suggests homosociality at least, and probably also homoeroticism.

this stupid Lena. "Why don't you answer with some sense, Lena, when I ask you if you don't like Herman Kreder. You stand there so stupid and don't answer just like you ain't heard a word what I been saying to you. I never see anybody like you, Lena. If you going to burst out at all, why don't you burst out sudden instead of standing there so silly and don't answer. And here I am so good to you, and find you a good husband so you can have a place to live in all your own. Answer me, Lena, don't you like Herman Kreder? He is a fine young fellow, almost too good for you, Lena, when you stand there so stupid and don't make no answer. There ain't many poor girls that get the chance you got now to get married."

"Why, I do anything you say, Aunt Mathilda. Yes, I like him. He don't say much to me, but I guess he is a good man, and I do anything you say for me to do."

"Well then Lena, why you stand there so silly all the time and not answer when I asked you."

"I didn't hear you say you wanted I should say anything to you. I didn't know you wanted me to say nothing. I do whatever you tell me it's right for me to do. I marry Herman Kreder, if you want me."

And so for Lena Mainz the match was made.

Old Mrs. Kreder did not discuss the matter with her Herman. She never thought that she needed to talk such things over with him. She just told him about getting married to Lena Mainz who was a good worker and very saving and never wanted her own way, and Herman made his usual little grunt in answer to her.

Mrs. Kreder and Mrs. Haydon fixed the day and made all the arrangements for the wedding and invited everybody who ought to be there to see them married.

In three months Lena Mainz and Herman Kreder were to be married.

Mrs. Haydon attended to Lena's getting all the things that she needed. Lena had to help a good deal with the sewing. Lena did not sew very well. Mrs. Haydon scolded because Lena did not do it better, but then she was very good to Lena, and she hired a girl to come and help her. Lena still stayed on with her pleasant mistress, but she spent all her evenings and her Sundays with her aunt and all the sewing.

Mrs. Haydon got Lena some nice dresses. Lena liked that very well. Lena liked having new hats even better, and Mrs. Haydon had some made for her by a real milliner who made them very pretty.

Lena was nervous these days, but she did not think much about getting married. She did not know really what it was, that, which was always coming nearer.

Lena liked the place where she was with the pleasant mistress and the good cook, who always scolded, and she liked the girls she always sat with. She did not ask if she would like being married any better. She always did whatever her aunt said and expected, but she was always nervous when she saw the Kreders with their Herman. She was excited and she liked her new hats, and everybody teased her and every day her marrying was coming nearer, and yet she did not really know what it was, this that was about to happen to her.

Herman Kreder knew more what it meant to be married and he did not like it very well. He did not like to see girls and he did not want to have to have one always near him. Herman always did everything that his father and his mother wanted and now they wanted that he should be married.

Herman had a sullen temper; he was gentle and he never said much. He liked to go out with other men, but he never wanted that there should be any women with them. The men all teased him about getting married. Herman did not mind the teasing but he did not like very well the getting married and having a girl always with him.

Three days before the wedding day, Herman went away to the country to be gone over Sunday. He and Lena were to be married Tuesday afternoon. When the day came Herman had not been seen or heard from.

The old Kreder couple had not worried much about it. Herman always did everything they wanted and he would surely come back in time to get married. But when Monday night came, and there was no Herman, they went to Mrs. Haydon to tell her what had happened.

Mrs. Haydon got very much excited. It was hard enough to work so as to get everything all ready, and then to have that silly Herman go off that way, so no one could tell what was going to happen. Here was Lena and everything all ready, and now they would have to make the wedding later so that they would know that Herman would be sure to be there.

Mrs. Haydon was very much excited, and then she could not say much to the old Kreder couple. She did not want to make them angry, for she wanted very badly now that Lena should be married to their Herman.

At last it was decided that the wedding should be put off a week longer. Old Mr. Kreder would go to New York to find Herman, for it was very likely that Herman had gone there to his married sister.

Mrs. Haydon sent word around, about waiting until a week from that Tuesday, to everybody that had been invited, and then Tuesday morning she sent for Lena to come down to see her.

Mrs. Haydon was very angry with poor Lena when she saw her. She scolded her hard because she was so foolish, and now Herman had gone off and nobody could tell where he had gone to, and all because Lena always was so dumb and silly. And Mrs. Haydon was just like a mother to her, and Lena always stood there so stupid and did not answer what anybody asked her, and Herman was so silly too, and now his father had to go and find him. Mrs. Haydon did not think that any old people should be good to their children. Their children always were so thankless, and never paid any attention, and older people were always doing things for their good. Did Lena think it gave Mrs. Haydon any pleasure, to work so hard to make Lena happy, and get her a good husband, and then Lena was so thankless and never did anything that anybody wanted. It was a lesson to poor Mrs. Haydon not to do things any more for anybody. Let everybody take care of themselves and never come to her with any troubles; she knew better now than to meddle to make other people happy. It just made trouble for her and her husband did not like it. He always said she was too good, and nobody ever thanked her for it, and there Lena was always standing stupid and not answering anything anybody wanted. Lena could always talk enough to those silly girls she liked so much, and always sat with, but who never did anything for her except to take away her money, and here was her aunt who tried so hard and was so good to her and treated her just like one of her own children and Lena stood there, and never made any answer and never tried to please her aunt, or to do anything that her aunt wanted. "No, it ain't no use your standin' there and cryin', now, Lena. Its too late now to care about that Herman. You should have cared some before, and then you wouldn't have to stand and cry now, and be a disappointment to me, and then I get scolded by my husband for taking care of everybody, and nobody ever thankful. I am glad you got the sense to feel sorry now, Lena, anyway, and I try to do what I can to help you out in your trouble, only you don't deserve to have anybody take any trouble for you. But perhaps you know better next time. You go home now and take care you don't spoil your clothes and that new hat, you had no business to be wearin' that this morning, but you ain't got no sense at all, Lena. I never in my life see anybody be so stupid."

Mrs. Haydon stopped and poor Lena stood there in her hat, all trimmed with pretty flowers, and the tears coming out of her eyes, and Lena did not know what it was that she had done, only she was not going to be married and it was a disgrace for a girl to be left by a man on the very day she was to be married.

Lena went home all alone, and cried in the street car.

Poor Lena cried very hard all alone in the street car. She almost spoiled her new hat with her hitting it against the window in her crying. Then she remembered that she must not do so.

The conductor was a kind man and he was very sorry when he saw her crying. "Don't feel so bad, you get another feller, you are such a nice girl," he said to make her cheerful. "But Aunt Mathilda said now, I never get married," poor Lena sobbed out for her answer. "Why you really got trouble like that," said the conductor, "I just said that now to josh you. I didn't ever think you really was left by a feller. He must be a stupid feller. But don't you worry, he wasn't much good if he could go away and leave you, lookin' to be such a nice girl. You just tell all your trouble to me, and I help you." The car was empty and the conductor sat down beside her to put his arm around her, and to be a comfort to her. Lena suddenly remembered where she was, and if she did things like that her aunt would scold her. She moved away from the man into the corner. He laughed, "Don't be scared." he said, "I wasn't going to hurt you. But you just keep up your spirit. You are a real nice girl, and you'll be sure to get a real good husband. Don't you let nobody fool you. You're all right and I don't want to scare you."

The conductor went back to his platform to help a passenger get on the car. All the time Lena stayed in the street car, he would come in every little while and reassure her, about her not to feel so bad about a man who hadn't no more sense than to go away and leave her. She'd be sure yet to get a good man, she needn't be so worried, he frequently assured her.

He chatted with the other passenger who had just come in, a very well dressed old man, and then with another who came in later, a good sort of a working man, and then another who came in, a nice lady, and he told them all about Lena's having trouble, and it was too bad there were men who treated a poor girl so badly. And everybody in the car was sorry for poor Lena and the workman tried to cheer her, and the old man looked sharply at her, and said she looked like a good girl, but she ought to be more careful and not to be so careless, and things like that would not happen to her, and the nice lady went and sat beside her and Lena liked it, though she shrank away from being near her.

So Lena was feeling a little better when she got off the car, and the conductor helped her, and he called out to her, "You be sure you keep up a good heart now. He wasn't no good that feller and you were lucky for to lose him. You'll get a real man yet, one that will be better for you. Don't you be worried, you're a real nice girl as I ever see in such trouble," and the conductor shook his head and went back into his car to talk it over with the other passengers he had there.

The german cook, who always scolded Lena, was very angry when she heard the story. She never did think Mrs. Haydon would do so much for Lena, though she was always talking so grand about what she could do for everybody. The good german cook always had been a little distrustful of her. People who always thought they were so much never did really do things right for anybody. Not that Mrs.

Haydon wasn't a good woman. Mrs. Haydon was real, good, german woman, and she did really mean to do well by her niece Lena. The cook knew that very well, and she had always said so, and she always had liked and respected Mrs. Haydon, who always acted very proper to her, and Lena was so backward, when there was a man to talk to, Mrs. Haydon did have hard work when she tried to marry Lena. Mrs. Haydon was a good woman, only she did talk sometimes too grand. Perhaps this trouble would make her see it wasn't always so easy to do, to make everybody do everything just like she wanted. The cook was very sorry now for Mrs. Haydon. All this must be such a disappointment, and such a worry to her, and she really had always been very good to Lena. But Lena had better go and put on her other clothes and stop with all that crying. That wouldn't do nothing now to help her, and if Lena would be a good girl, and just be real patient, her aunt would make it all come out right yet for her. "I just tell Mrs. Aldrich, Lena, you stay here yet a little longer. You know she is always so good to you, Lena, and I know she let you, and I tell her all about that stupid Herman Kreder. I got no patience, Lena, with anybody who can be so stupid. You just stop now with your crying, Lena, and take off them good clothes and put them away so you don't spoil them when you need them, and you can help me with the dishes and everything will come off better for you. You see if I ain't right by what I tell you. You just stop crying now Lena quick, or else I scold you."

Lena still choked a little and was very miserable inside her but she did everything just as the cook told her.

The girls Lena always sat with were very sorry to see her look so sad with her trouble. Mary the Irish girl sometimes got very angry with her. Mary was always very hot when she talked of Lena's aunt Mathilda, who thought she was so grand, and had such stupid, stuck up daughters. Mary wouldn't be a fat fool like that ugly tempered Mathilda Haydon, not for anything anybody could ever give her. How Lena could keep on going there so much when they all always acted as if she was just dirt to them, Mary never could see. But Lena never had any sense of how she should make people stand round for her, and that was always all the trouble with her. And poor Lena, she was so stupid to be sorry for losing that gawky fool who didn't ever know what he wanted and just said "ja" to his mamma and his papa, like a baby, and was scared to look at a girl straight, and then sneaked away the last day like as if somebody was going to do something to him. Disgrace, Lena talking about disgrace! It was a disgrace for a girl to be seen with the likes of him, let alone to be married to him. But that poor Lena, she never did know how to show herself off for what she was really. Disgrace to have him go away and leave her. Mary would just like to get a chance to show him. If Lena wasn't worth fifteen like Herman Kreder, Mary would just eat her own head all up. It was a good riddance Lena had of that Herman Kreder and his stingy, dirty parents, and if Lena didn't stop crying about it,— Mary would just naturally despise her.[9]

Poor Lena, she knew very well how Mary meant it all, this she was always saying to her. But Lena was very miserable inside her. She felt the disgrace it was for a decent german girl that a man should go away and leave her. Lena knew very well that her aunt was right when she said the way Herman had acted to her was a disgrace to everyone that knew her. Mary and Nellie and the other girls she always sat with were always very good to Lena but that did not make her trouble any better. It was a disgrace the way Lena had been left, to any decent family, and that could never be made any different to her.

And so the slow days wore on, and Lena never saw her Aunt Mathilda. At last on Sunday she got word by a boy to go and see her aunt Mathilda. Lena's heart beat quick for she was very nervous now with all this that had happened to her. She went just as quickly as she could to see her Aunt Mathilda.

Mrs. Haydon quick, as soon as she saw Lena, began to scold her for keeping her aunt waiting so long for her, and for not coming in all the week to see her, to see if her aunt should need her, and so her aunt had to send a boy to tell her. But it was easy; even for Lena, to see that her aunt was not really angry with her. It wasn't Lena's fault, went on Mrs. Haydon, that everything was going to happen all right for her. Mrs. Haydon was very tired taking all this trouble for her, and when Lena couldn't even take trouble to come and see her aunt, to see if she needed anything to tell her. But Mrs. Haydon really never minded things like that when she could do things for anybody. She was tired now, all the trouble she had been taking to make things right for Lena, but perhaps now Lena heard it she would learn a little to be thankful to her. "You get all ready to be married Tuesday, Lena, you hear me," said Mrs. Haydon to her. "You come here Tuesday morning and I have everything all ready for you. You wear your new dress I got you, and your hat with all them flowers on it, and you be very careful coming you don't get your things all dirty, you so careless all the time, Lena, and not thinking, and you act sometimes you never got no head at all on you. You go home now, and you tell your Mrs. Aldrich that you leave her Tuesday. Don't you go forgetting now, Lena, anything I ever told you what you should do to be careful. You be a good girl, now Lena. You get married Tuesday to Herman Kreder." And that was all Lena ever knew of what had happened all this week to Herman Kreder. Lena forgot there was anything to know about it. She was really to be married

9. Note the difference in tone, rhythm, and vocabulary in Stein's representation of this Irish voice.

Tuesday, and her Aunt Mathilda said she was a good girl, and now there was no disgrace left upon her.

Lena now fell back into the way she always had of being always dreamy and not there, the way she always had been, except for the few days she was so excited, because she had been left by a man the very day she was to have been married. Lena was a little nervous all these last days, but she did not think much about what it meant for her to be married.

Herman Kreder was not so content about it. He was quiet and was sullen and he knew he could not help it. He knew now he just had to let himself get married. It was not that Herman did not like Lena Mainz. She was as good as any other girl could be for him.[1] She was a little better perhaps than other girls he saw, she was so very quiet, but Herman did not like to always have to have a girl around him. Herman had always done everything that his mother and his father wanted. His father had found him in New York, where Herman had gone to be with his married sister.

Herman's father when he had found him coaxed Herman a long time and went on whole days with his complaining to him, always troubled but gentle and quite patient with him, and always he was worrying to Herman about what was the right way his boy Herman should always do, always whatever it was his mother ever wanted from him, and always Herman never made him any answer.

Old Mr. Kreder kept on saying to him, he did not see how Herman could think now, it could be any different. When you make a bargain you just got to stick right to it, that was the only way old Mr. Kreder could ever see it, and saying you would get married to a girl and she got everything all ready, that was a bargain just like one you make in business and Herman he had made it, and now Herman he would just have to do it, old Mr. Kreder didn't see there was any other way a good boy like his Herman had, to do it. And then too that Lena Mainz was such a nice girl and Herman hadn't ought to really give his father so much trouble and make him pay out all that money, to come all the way to New York just to find him, and they both lose all that time from their working, when all Herman had to do was just to stand up, for an hour, and then he would be all right married, and it would be all over for him, and then everything at home would never be any different to him.

And his father went on; there was his poor mother saying always how her Herman always did everything before she ever wanted, and now just because he got notions in him, and wanted to show people how he could be stubborn, he was making all this trouble for her, and making them pay all that money just to run around and find him.

1. This is the closest Stein comes to overtly stating that Herman is homosexual.

"You got no idea Herman, how bad mama is feeling about the way you been acting Herman," said old Mr. Kreder to him. "She says she never can understand how you can be so thankless Herman. It hurts her very much you been so stubborn, and she find you such a nice girl for you, like Lena Mainz who is always just so quiet and always saves up all her wages, and she never wanting her own way at all like some girls are always all the time to have it, and your mama trying so hard, just so you could be comfortable Herman to be married, and then you act so stubborn Herman. You like all young people Herman, you think only about yourself, and what you are just wanting, and your mama she is thinking only what is good for you to have, for you in the future. Do you think your mama wants to have a girl around to be a bother, for herself, Herman. Its just for you Herman she is always thinking, and she talks always about how happy she will be, when she sees her Herman married to a nice girl, and then when she fixed it all up so good for you, so it never would be any bother to you, just the way she wanted you should like it, and you say yes all right, I do it, and then you go away like this and act stubborn, and make all this trouble everybody to take for you, and we spend money, and I got to travel all round to find you. You come home now with me Herman and get married, and I tell your mama she better not say anything to you about how much it cost me to come all the way to look for you—Hey Herman," said his father coaxing, "Hey, you come home now and get married. All you got to do Herman is just to stand up for an hour Herman, and then you don't never to have any more bother to it—Hey Herman!—you come home with me to-morrow and get married. Hey Herman."

Herman's married sister liked her brother Herman, and she had always tried to help him, when there was anything she knew he wanted. She liked it that he was so good and always did everything that their father and their mother wanted, but still she wished it could be that he could have more his own way, if there was anything he ever wanted.

But now she thought Herman with his girl was very funny. She wanted that Herman should be married. She thought it would do him lots of good to get married. She laughed at Herman when she heard the story. Until his father came to find him, she did not know why it was Herman had come just then to New York to see her. When she heard the story she laughed a good deal at her brother Herman and teased him a good deal about his running away, because he didn't want to have a girl to be all the time around him.

Herman's married sister liked her brother Herman, and she did not want him not to like to be with women. He was good, her brother Herman, and it would surely do him good to get married. It would make him stand up for himself stronger. Herman's sister always laughed at him and always she would try to reassure him. "Such a nice man as my brother Herman acting like as if he was afraid of women. Why the girls all like a man like you Herman, if you didn't always run away when you saw them. It do you good really Herman to get married, and then you got somebody you can boss around when you want to. It do you good Herman to get married, you see if you don't like it, when you really done it. You go along home now with papa, Herman and get married to that Lena. You don't know how nice you like it Herman when you try once how you can do it. You just don't be afraid of nothing, Herman. You good enough for any girl to marry, Herman. Any girl be glad to have a man like you to be always with them Herman. You just go along home with papa and try it what I say, Herman. Oh you so funny Herman, when you sit there, and then run away and leave your girl behind you. I know she is crying like anything Herman for to lose you. Don't be bad to her Herman. You go along home with papa now and get married Herman. I'd be awful ashamed Herman, to really have a brother didn't have spirit enough to get married, when a girl is just dying for to have him. You always like me to be with you Herman. I don't see why you say you don't want a girl to be all the time around you. You always been good to me Herman, and I know you always be good to that Lena, and you soon feel just like as if she had always been there with you. Don't act like as if you wasn't a nice strong man, Herman. Really I laugh at you Herman, but you know I like awful well to see you real happy. You go home and get married to that Lena, Herman. She is a real pretty girl and real nice and good and quiet and she make my brother Herman very happy. You just stop your fussing now with Herman, papa. He go with you to-morrow papa, and you see he like it so much to be married, he make everybody laugh just to see him be so happy. Really truly, that's the way it will be with you Herman. You just listen to me what I tell you Herman." And so his sister laughed at him and reassured him, and his father kept on telling what the mother always said about her Herman, and he coaxed him and Herman never said anything in answer, and his sister packed his things up and was very cheerful with him, and she kissed him, and then she laughed and then she kissed him, and his father went and bought the tickets for the train, and at last late on Sunday he brought Herman back to Bridgepoint with him.

It was always very hard to keep Mrs. Kreder from saying what she thought, to her Herman, but her daughter had written her a letter, so as to warn her not to say anything about what he had been doing, to him, and her husband came in with Herman and said, "Here we are come home mama, Herman and me, and we are very tired it was so crowded coming," and then he whispered to her. "You be good to Herman, mama, he didn't mean to make us so much trouble," and so old Mrs. Kreder, held in what she felt was so strong in her to say to her Herman. She just said very stiffly to him, "I'm glad to see you come home to-day, Herman." Then she went to arrange it all with Mrs. Haydon.

Herman was now again just like he always had been, sullen and very good, and very quiet, and always ready to do whatever his mother and his father wanted. Tuesday morning came, Herman got his new clothes on and went with his father and his mother to stand up for an hour and get married. Lena was there in her new dress, and her hat with all the pretty flowers, and she was very nervous for now she knew she was really very soon to be married. Mrs. Haydon had everything all ready. Everybody was there just as they should be and very soon Herman Kreder and Lena Mainz were married.

When everything was really over, they went back to the Kreder house together. They were all now to live together, Lena and Herman and the old father and the old mother, in the house where Mr. Kreder had worked so many years as a tailor, with his son Herman always there to help him.

Irish Mary had often said to Lena she never did see how Lena could ever want to have anything to do with Herman Kreder and his dirty stingy parents. The old Kreders were to an Irish nature, a stingy dirty couple. They had not the free-hearted, thoughtless, fighting, mud bespattered, ragged, peat-smoked cabin dirt that irish[2] Mary knew and could forgive and love. Theirs was the german dirt of saving, of being dowdy and loose and foul in your clothes so as to save them and yourself in washing, having your hair greasy to save it in the soap and drying, having your clothes dirty, not in freedom, but because so it was cheaper, keeping the house close and smelly because so it cost less to get it heated, living so poorly not only so as to save money but so they should never even know themselves that they had it, working all the time not only because from their nature they just had to and because it made them money but also that they never could be put in any way to make them spend their money.

This was the place Lena now had forher home and to her it was very different than it could be for an irish Mary. She too was german and was thrifty, though she was always so dreamy and not there. Lena was always careful with things and she always saved her money, for that was the only way she knew how to do it. She never had taken care of her own money and she never had thought how to use it.

Lena Mainz had been, before she was Mrs. Herman Kreder, always clean and decent in her clothes and in her person, but it was not because she ever thought about it or really needed so to have it, it

2. The lower case indicates that "irish" functions here as a descriptive adjective rather than a negative epithet.

was the way her people did in the german country where she came
from, and her Aunt Mathilda and the good german cook who always
scolded, had kept her on and made her, with their scoldings, always
more careful to keep clean and to wash real often. But there was no
deep need in all this for Lena and so, though Lena did not like the
old Kreders, though she really did not know that, she did not think
about their being stingy dirty people.

Herman Kreder was cleaner than the old people, just because it
was his nature to keep cleaner, but he was used to his mother and
his father, and he never thought that they should keep things
cleaner. And Herman too always saved all his money, except for that
little beer he drank when he went out with other men of an evening
the way he always liked to do it, and he never thought of any other
way to spend it. His father had always kept all the money for them
and he always was doing business with it. And then too Herman
really had no money, for he always had worked for his father, and
his father had never thought to pay him.[3]

And so they began all four to live in the Kreder house together,
and Lena began soon with it to look careless and a little dirty, and
to be more lifeless with it, and nobody ever noticed much what Lena
wanted, and she never really knew herself what she needed.

The only real trouble that came to Lena with their living all four
there together, was the way old Mrs. Kreder scolded. Lena had
always been used to being scolded, but this scolding of old Mrs.
Kreder was very different from the way she ever before had had to
endure it.

Herman, now he was married to her, really liked Lena very well.
He did not care very much about her but she never was a bother to
him being there around him, only when his mother worried and was
nasty to them because Lena was so careless, and did not know how
to save things right for them with their eating, and all the other ways
with money, that the old woman had to save it.

Herman Kreder had always done everything his mother and his
father wanted but he did not really love his parents very deeply. With
Herman it was always only that he hated to have any struggle. It was
all always all right with him when he could just go along and do the
same thing over every day with his working, and not to hear things,
and not to have people make him listen to their anger. And now his
marriage, and he just knew it would, was making trouble for him. It
made him hear more what his mother was always saying, with her
scolding. He had to really hear it now because Lena was there, and
she was so scared and dull always when she heard it. Herman knew
very well with his mother, it was all right if one ate very little and

3. Herman is horribly exploited by his parents, just as Lena will be.

worked hard all day and did not hear her when she scolded, the way Herman always had done before they were so foolish about his getting married and having a girl there to be all the time around him, and now he had to help her so the girl could learn too, not to hear it when his mother scolded, and not to look so scared, and not to eat much, and always to be sure to save it.

Herman really did not know very well what he could do to help Lena to understand it. He could never answer his mother back to help Lena, that never would make things any better for her, and he never could feel in himself any way to comfort Lena, to make her strong not to hear his mother, in all the awful ways she always scolded. It just worried Herman to have it like that all the time around him. Herman did not know much about how a man could make a struggle with a mother, to do much to keep her quiet, and indeed Herman never knew much how to make a struggle against anyone who really wanted to have anything very badly. Herman all his life never wanted anything so badly, that he would really make a struggle against any one to get it. Herman all his life only wanted to live regular and quiet, and not talk much and to do the same way every day like every other with his working. And now his mother had made him get married to this Lena and now with his mother making all that scolding, he had all this trouble and this worry always on him.

Mrs. Haydon did not see Lena now very often. She had not lost her interest in her niece Lena, but Lena could not come much to her house to see her, it would not be right, now Lena was a married woman. And then too Mrs. Haydon had her hands full just then with her two daughters, for she was getting them ready to find them good husbands, and then too her own husband now worried her very often about her always spoiling that boy of hers, so he would be sure to turn out no good and be a disgrace to a german family, and all because his mother always spoiled him. All these things were very worrying now to Mrs. Haydon, but still she wanted to be good to Lena, though she could not see her very often. She only saw her when Mrs. Haydon went to call on Mrs. Kreder or when Mrs. Kreder came to see Mrs. Haydon, and that never could be very often. Then too these days Mrs. Haydon could not scold Lena, Mrs. Kreder was always there with her, and it would not be right to scold Lena when Mrs. Kreder was there, who had now the real right to do it. And so her aunt always said nice things now to Lena, and though Mrs. Haydon sometimes was a little worried when she saw Lena looking sad and not careful, she did not have time just then to really worry much about it.

Lena now never any more saw the girls she always used to sit with. She had no way now to see them and it was not in Lena's nature to

search out ways to see them, nor did she now ever think much of
the days when she had been used to see them. They never any of
them had come to the Kreder house to see her. Not even Irish Mary[4]
had ever thought to come to see her. Lena had been soon forgotten
by them. They had soon passed away from Lena and now Lena never
thought any more that she had ever known them.

The only one of her old friends who tried to know what Lena liked
and what she needed, and who always made Lena come to see her,
was the good german cook who had always scolded. She now scolded
Lena hard for letting herself go so, and going out when she was
looking so untidy. "I know you going to have a baby Lena, but that's
no way for you to be looking. I am ashamed most to see you come
and sit here in my kitchen, looking so sloppy and like you never used
to Lena. I never see anybody like you Lena. Herman is very good to
you, you always say so, and he don't treat you bad ever though you
don't deserve to have anybody good to you, you so careless all the
time, Lena, letting yourself go like you never had anybody tell you
what was the right way you should know how to be looking. No,
Lena, I don't see no reason you should let yourself go so and look so
untidy Lena, so I am ashamed to see you sit there looking so ugly,
Lena. No Lena that ain't no way ever I see a woman make things
come out better, letting herself go so every way and crying all the
time[5] like as if you had real trouble. I never wanted to see you marry
Herman Kreder, Lena, I knew what you got to stand with that old
woman always, and that old man, he is so stingy too and he don't
say things out but he ain't any better in his heart than his wife with
her bad ways, I know that Lena, I know they don't hardly give you
enough to eat, Lena, I am real sorry for you Lena, you know that
Lena, but that ain't any way to be going round so untidy Lena, even
if you have got all that trouble. You never see me do like that Lena,
though sometimes I got a headache so I can't see to stand to be
working hardly,[6] and nothing comes right with all my cooking, but I
always see Lena, I look decent. That's the only way a german girl can
make things come out right Lena. You hear me what I am saying to
you Lena. Now you eat something nice Lena, I got it all ready for
you, and you wash up and be careful Lena and the baby will come
all right to you, and then I make your Aunt Mathilda see that you
live in a house soon, all alone with Herman and your baby, and then
everything go better for you. You hear me what I say you Lena.
Now don't let me ever see you come looking like this any more Lena,

4. Mary becomes "Irish," rather than "irish," when the narrative casts her in a negative light.
5. This is the first time we hear that Lena cries continuously, because the narration is from
   the point of view of the cook, one of only two characters in the story wholly sympathetic
   to Lena; the other is the streetcar conductor, who also notices Lena crying and tries to
   comfort her.
6. Again, the cook echoes Anna.

and you just stop with that always crying. You ain't got no reason to be sitting there now with all that crying, I never see anybody have trouble it did them any good to do the way you are doing, Lena. You hear me Lena. You go home now and you be good the way I tell you Lena, and I see what I can do. I make your Aunt Mathilda make old Mrs. Kreder let you be till you get your baby all right. Now don't you be scared and so silly Lena. I don't like to see you act so Lena when really you got a nice man and so many things really any girl should be grateful to be having. Now you go home Lena to-day and you do the way I say, to you, and I see what I can do to help you."

"Yes Mrs. Aldrich" said the good german woman to her mistress later, "Yes Mrs. Aldrich that's the way it is with them girls when they want so to get married. They don't know when they got it good Mrs. Aldrich. They never know what it is they're really wanting when they got it, Mrs. Aldrich. There's that poor Lena, she just been here crying and looking so careless so I scold her, but that was no good that marrying for that poor Lena, Mrs. Aldrich. She do look so pale and sad now Mrs. Aldrich, it just break my heart to see her. She was a good girl was Lena, Mrs. Aldrich, and I never had no trouble with her like I got with so many young girls nowadays, Mrs. Aldrich, and I never see any girl any better to work right than our Lena, and now she got to stand it all the time with that old woman Mrs. Kreder. My! Mrs. Aldrich, she is a bad old woman to her. I never see Mrs. Aldrich how old people can be so bad to young girls and not have no kind of patience with them. If Lena could only live with her Herman, he ain't so bad the way men are, Mrs. Aldrich, but he is just the way always his mother wants him, he ain't got no spirit in him, and so I don't really see no help for that poor Lena. I know her aunt, Mrs. Haydon, meant it all right for her Mrs. Aldrich, but poor Lena, it would be better for her if her Herman had stayed there in New York that time he went away to leave her. I don't like it the way Lena is looking now, Mrs. Aldrich. She looks like as if she don't have no life left in her hardly, Mrs. Aldrich, she just drags around and looks so dirty and after all the pains I always took to teach her and to keep her nice in her ways and looking. It don't do no good to them, for them girls to get married Mrs. Aldrich, they are much better when they only know it, to stay in a good place when they got it, and keep on regular with their working. I don't like it the way Lena looks now Mrs. Aldrich. I wish I knew some way to help that poor Lena, Mrs. Aldrich, but she is a bad old woman, that old Mrs. Kreder, Herman's mother. I speak to Mrs. Haydon real soon, Mrs. Aldrich, I see what we can do now to help that poor Lena."

These were really bad days for poor Lena. Herman always was real good to her and now he even sometimes tried to stop his mother from scolding Lena. "She ain't well now mama, you let her be now

you hear me. You tell me what it is you want she should be doing, I
tell her. I see she does it right just the way you want it mama. You
let be, I say now mama, with that always scolding Lena. You let be,
I say now, you wait till she is feeling better." Herman was getting
really strong to struggle, for he could see that Lena with that baby
working hard inside her, really could not stand it any longer with his
mother and the awful ways she always scolded.

It was a new feeling Herman now had inside him that made him
feel he was strong to make a struggle. It was new for Herman Kreder
really to be wanting something, but Herman wanted strongly now to
be a father, and he wanted badly that his baby should be a boy and
healthy. Herman never had cared really very much about his father
and his mother, though always, all his life, he had done everything
just as they wanted, and he had never really cared much about his
wife, Lena, though he always had been very good to her, and had
always tried to keep his mother off her, with the awful way she always
scolded, but to be really a father of a little baby, that feeling took
hold of Herman very deeply. He was almost ready, so as to save his
baby from all trouble, to really make a strong struggle with his mother
and with his father, too, if he would not help him to control his
mother.

Sometimes Herman even went to Mrs. Haydon to talk all this
trouble over. They decided then together, it was better to wait there
all four together for the baby, and Herman could make Mrs. Kreder
stop a little with her scolding, and then when Lena was a little
stronger, Herman should have his own house for her, next door to
his father, so he could always be there to help him in his working,
but so they could eat and sleep in a house where the old woman
could not control them and they could not hear her awful scolding.

And so things went on, the same way, a little longer. Poor Lena
was not feeling any joy to have a baby. She was scared the way she
had been when she was so sick on the water. She was scared now
every time when anything would hurt her. She was scared and still
and lifeless, and sure that every minute she would die. Lena had no
power to be strong in this kind of trouble, she could only sit still and
be scared, and dull, and lifeless, and sure that every minute she
would die.

Before very long, Lena had her baby. He was a good, healthy little
boy, the baby. Herman cared very much to have the baby. When
Lena was a little stronger he took a house next door to the old couple,
so he and his own family could eat and sleep and do the way they
wanted. This did not seem to make much change now for Lena. She
was just the same as when she was waiting with her baby. She just
dragged around and was careless with her clothes and all lifeless,
and she acted always and lived on just as if she had no feeling. She

always did everything regular with the work, the way she always had
had to do it, but she never got back any spirit in her. Herman was
always good and kind, and always helped her with her working. He
did everything he knew to help her. He always did all the active new
things in the house and for the baby. Lena did what she had to do
the way she always had been taught it. She always just kept going
now with her working, and she was always careless, and dirty, and a
little dazed, and lifeless. Lena never got any better in herself of this
way of being that she had had ever since she had been married.

Mrs. Haydon never saw any more of her niece, Lena. Mrs. Haydon
had now so much trouble with her own house, and her daughters
getting married, and her boy, who was growing up, and who always
was getting so much worse to manage. She knew she had done right
by Lena. Herman Kreder was a good man, she would be glad to get
one so good, sometimes, for her own daughters, and now they had
a home to live in together, separate from the old people, who had
made their trouble for them. Mrs. Haydon felt she had done very
well by her niece, Lena, and she never thought now she needed any
more to go and see her. Lena would do very well now without her
aunt to trouble herself any more about her.

The good german cook who had always scolded, still tried to do
her duty like a mother to poor Lena. It was very hard now to do right
by Lena. Lena never seemed to hear now what anyone was saying to
her. Herman was always doing everything he could to help her. Herman always, when he was home, took good care of the baby. Herman
loved to take care of his baby. Lena never thought to take him out
or to do anything she didn't have to.

The good cook sometimes made Lena come to see her. Lena would
come with her baby and sit there in the kitchen, and watch the good
woman cooking, and listen to her sometimes a little, the way she
used to, while the good german woman scolded her for going around
looking so careless when now she had no trouble, and sitting there
so dull, and always being just so thankless. Sometimes Lena would
wake up a little and get back into her face her old, gentle, patient,
and unsuffering sweetness, but mostly Lena did not seem to hear
much when the good german woman scolded. Lena always liked it
when Mrs. Aldrich her good mistress spoke to her kindly, and then
Lena would seem to go back and feel herself to be like she was when
she had been in service. But mostly Lena just lived along and was
careless in her clothes, and dull, and lifeless.

By and by Lena had two more little babies. Lena was not so much
scared now when she had the babies. She did not seem to notice
very much when they hurt her, and she never seemed to feel very
much now about anything that happened to her.

They were very nice babies, all these three that Lena had, and

Herman took good care of them always. Herman never really cared much about his wife, Lena. The only things Herman ever really cared for were his babies. Herman always was very good to his children. He always had a gentle, tender way when he held them. He learned to be very handy with them. He spent all the time he was not working, with them. By and by he began to work all day in his own home so that he could have his children always in the same room with him.

Lena always was more and more lifeless and Herman now mostly never thought about her. He more and more took all the care of their three children. He saw to their eating right and their washing, and he dressed them every morning, and he taught them the right way to do things, and he put them to their sleeping, and he was now always every minute with them. Then there was to come to them, a fourth baby. Lena went to the hospital near by to have the baby. Lena seemed to be going to have much trouble with it. When the baby was come out at last, it was like its mother lifeless.[7] While it was coming, Lena had grown very pale and sicker. When it was all over Lena had died, too, and nobody knew just how it had happened to her.

The good german cook who had always scolded Lena, and had always to the last day tried to help her, was the only one who ever missed her. She remembered how nice Lena had looked all the time she was in service with her, and how her voice had been so gentle and sweet-sounding, and how she always was a good girl, and how she never had to have any trouble with her, the way she always had with all the other girls who had been taken into the house to help her. The good cook sometimes spoke so of Lena when she had time to have a talk with Mrs. Aldrich, and this was all the remembering there now ever was of Lena.

Herman Kreder now always lived very happy, very gentle, very quiet, very well content alone with his three children. He never had a woman any more to be all the time around him. He always did all his own work in his house, when he was through every day with the work he was always doing for his father. Herman always was alone, and he always worked alone, until his little ones were big enough to help him. Herman Kreder was very well content now and he always lived very regular and peaceful, and with every day just like the next one, always alone now with his three good, gentle[8] children.

FINIS

---

7. Both Lena and her fourth baby die in childbirth, a fate very common at this time, and one with which Stein was familiar from the Baltimore clinic where she worked as a medical student.
8. This word is heavily ironic here.

Q.E.D.[1]

PHEBE: Good shepherd, tell this youth what 'tis to love.

SILVIUS: It is to be all made of sighs and tears;
And so am I for Phebe.

PHEBE: And I for Ganymede.

ORLANDO: And I for Rosalind.

ROSALIND: And I for no woman.

SILVIUS: It is to be all made of faith and service;
And so am I for Phebe.

PHEBE: And I for Ganymede.

ORLANDO: And I for Rosalind.

ROSALIND: And I for no woman.

SILVIUS: It is to be all made of fantasy,
All made of passion, and all made of wishes;
All adoration, duty, and observance,
All humbleness, all patience, and impatience,
All purity, all trial, all deservings;
And so am I for Phebe.

PHEBE: And so am I for Ganymede.

ORLANDO: And so am I for Rosalind.

ROSALIND: And so am I for no woman.

PHEBE: If this be so, why blame you me to love you?

SILVIUS: If this be so, why blame you me to love you?

ORLANDO: If this be so, why blame you me to love you?

ROSALIND: Who do you speak to, 'Why blame you me to love you?'

ORLANDO: To her that is not here, nor doth not hear.

ROSALIND: Pray you, no more of this: 'tis like the howling of Irish
wolves against the moon.

AS YOU LIKE IT 5:2[2]

2. Shakespeare's comedy of 1599–1600. This passage has multifaceted and ironic relevance
to *Q.E.D.*: its repetitive, circular structure invokes the triangle of the novella's plot; the
content of Silvius's lines constitutes an ironic reference to the fantasy quality and the
shallowness of Helen's feeling toward Adele and also to Adele's distressing passion for
Helen; and Rosalind's lines offer a veiled reference to gender-crossing: she is disguised as
a young man (a "youth") during this scene.

Book 1:

Adele[3]

THE LAST MONTH of Adele's life in Baltimore had been such a succession of wearing experiences that she rather regretted that she was not to have the steamer[4] all to herself. It was very easy to think of the rest of the passengers as mere wooden objects; they were all sure to be of some abjectly familiar type that one knew so well that there would be no need of recognising their existence, but these two people who would be equally familiar if they were equally little known would as the acquaintance progressed, undoubtedly expose large tracts of unexplored and unknown qualities, filled with new and strange excitements. A little knowledge is not a dangerous thing,[5] on the contrary it gives the most cheerful sense of completeness and content.

"Oh yes" Adele said to a friend the morning of her sailing[6] "I would rather be alone just now but I dare say they will be amusing enough. Mabel Neathe[7] of course I know pretty well; that is we haven't any very vital relations but we have drunk much tea together and sentimentalised[8] over it in a fashion more or less interesting. As for Helen Thomas I don't know her at all although we have met a number of times. Her talk is fairly amusing and she tells very good stories, but she isn't my kind much. Still I don't think it will be utterly hopeless. Heigho it's an awful grind; new countries, new people and new experiences all to see, to know and to understand; old countries, old friends and old experiences to keep on seeing, knowing and understanding."

They had been several days on the ship and had learned to make themselves very comfortable. Their favorite situation had some disadvantages; it was directly over the screw[9] and they felt the jar every time that it left the water, but then the weather was not very rough and so that did not happen very frequently.

All three of them were college bred American women of the wealthier class but with that all resemblance between them ended.

3. Adele is based directly on Gertrude Stein; this is an autobiographical work with few details changed.
4. Steamship.
5. Ironic reversal of the cliché "a little knowledge is a dangerous thing," which is probably based on Part 2, stanza 2, line 1 of Alexander Pope's *An Essay on Criticism* (1711): "A little learning is a dangerous thing."
6. Adele is on a steamship, but the standard term for the departure of the ship was still "sailing."
7. Character based on Mabel Haynes: Stein does not bother to, or chooses not to, change her first name.
8. Expressed shallow, obvious sentiments or opinions.
9. The steamship's propeller.

Their appearance, their attitudes and their talk both as to manner and to matter showed the influence of different localities, different forebears and different family ideals. They were distinctly American but each one at the same time bore definitely the stamp of one of the older civilisations, incomplete and frustrated in this American version but still always insistent.

The upright figure was that of Helen Thomas.[1] She was the American version of the English handsome girl. In her ideal completeness she would have been unaggressively determined, a trifle brutal and entirely impersonal; a woman of passions but not of emotions, capable of long sustained action, incapable of regrets. In this American edition it amounted at its best to no more than a brave bluff. In the strength of her youth Helen still thought of herself as the unfrustrated ideal; she had as yet no suspicion of her weakness, she had never admitted to herself her defeats.

As Mabel Neathe lay on the deck with her head in Helen's lap, her attitude of awkward discomfort and the tension of her long angular body sufficiently betrayed her New England origin. It is one of the peculiarities of American womanhood that the body of a coquette often encloses the soul of a prude and the angular form of a spinster is possessed by a nature of the tropics. Mabel Neathe had the angular body of a spinster but the face told a different story. It was pale yellow brown in complexion and thin in the temples and forehead; heavy about the mouth, not with the weight of flesh but with the drag of unidealised passion, continually sated and continually craving. The long formless chin accentuated the lack of moral significance. If the contour had been a little firmer the face would have been baleful. It was a face that in its ideal completeness would have belonged to the decadent days of Italian greatness. It would never now express completely a nature that could hate subtly and poison deftly. In the American woman the aristocracy had become vulgarised and the power weakened. Having gained nothing moral, weakened by lack of adequate development of its strongest instincts, this nature expressed itself in a face no longer dangerous but only unillumined and unmoral, but yet with enough suggestion of the older aristocratic use to keep it from being merely contemptibly dishonest.

The third member of the group had thrown herself prone on the deck with the freedom of movement and the simple instinct for comfort that suggested a land of laziness and sunshine. She nestled close to the bare boards as if accustomed to make the hard earth soft by loving it. She made just a few wriggling movements to adapt her large curves to the projecting boards of the deck, gave a sigh of satisfaction and murmured "How good it is in the sun."

1. Based on May Bookstaver.

They all breathed in the comfort of it for a little time and then
Adele raising herself on her arm continued the interrupted talk. "Of
course I am not logical," she said "logic is all foolishness. The whole
duty of man consists in being reasonable and just. I know Mabel that
you don't consider that an exact portrait of me but nevertheless it is
true. I am reasonable because I know the difference between understanding and not understanding and I am just because I have no
opinion about things I don't understand."

"That sounds very well indeed" broke in Helen "but somehow I
don't feel that your words really express you. Mabel tells me that you
consider yourself a typical middle-class person, that you admire
above all things the middle-class ideals and yet you certainly don't
seem one in thoughts or opinions. When you show such a degree of
inconsistency how can you expect to be believed?"

"The contradiction isn't in me," Adele said sitting up to the occasion and illustrating her argument by vigorous gestures, "it is in your
perverted ideas. You have a foolish notion that to be middle-class is
to be vulgar, that to cherish the ideals of respectability and decency
is to be commonplace and that to be the mother of children is to be
low. You tell me that I am not middle-class and that I can believe in
none of these things because I am not vulgar, commonplace and
low, but it is just there where you make your mistake. You don't
realise the important fact that virtue and vice have it in common that
they are vulgar when not passionately given. You think that they carry
within them a different power. Yes they do because they have different world-values, but as for their relation to vulgarity, it is as true
of vice as of virtue that you can't sell what should be passionately
given without forcing yourself into many acts of vulgarity and the
chances are that in endeavoring to escape the vulgarity of virtue, you
will find yourselves engulfed in the vulgarity of vice. Good gracious!
here I am at it again. I never seem to know how to keep still, but you
both know already that I have the failing of my tribe. I believe in the
sacred rites of conversation even when it is a monologue."

"Oh don't stop yourself," Mabel said quietly, "it is entertaining and
we know you don't believe it." "Alright" retorted Adele "you think
that I have no principles because I take everything as it comes but
that is where you are wrong. I say bend again and again but retain
your capacity for regaining an upright position, but you will have to
learn it in your own way, I am going to play with the sunshine." And
then there was a long silence.

They remained there quietly in the warm sunshine looking at the
bluest of blue oceans, with the wind moulding itself on their faces
in great soft warm chunks. At last Mabel sat up with a groan. "No,"
she declared, "I cannot any longer make believe to myself that I am
comfortable. I haven't really believed it any of the time and the jar

of that screw is unbearable. I am going back to my steamer chair."
Thereupon ensued between Helen and Mabel the inevitable and
interminable offer and rejection of companionship that politeness
demands and the elaborate discussion and explanation that always
ensues when neither offer nor rejection are sincere. At last Adele
broke in with an impatient "I always did thank God I wasn't born a
woman,"[2] whereupon Mabel hastily bundled her wraps and disappeared down the companion-way.

The two who were left settled down again quietly but somehow
the silence now subtly suggested the significance of their being
alone together. This consciousness was so little expected by either
of them that each was uncertain of the other's recognition of it.
Finally Adele lifted her head and rested it on her elbow. After another
interval of silence she began to talk very gently without looking at
her companion.

"One hears so much of the immensity of the ocean but that isn't
at all the feeling that it gives me," she began. "My quarrel with it is
that it is the most confined space in the world. A room just big
enough to turn around in is immensely bigger. Being on the ocean
is like being placed under a nice clean white inverted saucer. All the
boundaries are so clear and hard. There is no escape from the knowledge of the limits of your prison. Doesn't it give you too a sensation
of intolerable confinement?" She glanced up at her companion who
was looking intently at her but evidently had not been hearing her
words. After a minute Helen continued the former conversation as
if there had been no interruption. "Tell me" she said "what do you
really mean by calling yourself middle-class? From the little that I
have seen of you I think that you are quite right when you say that
you are reasonable and just but surely to understand others and even
to understand oneself is the last thing a middle-class person cares
to do." "I never claimed to be middle-class in my intellect and in
truth" and Adele smiled brightly. "I probably have the experience of
all apostles, I am rejected by the class whose cause I preach but that
has nothing to do with the case. I simply contend that the middle-
class ideal which demands that people be affectionate, respectable,
honest and content, that they avoid excitements and cultivate serenity is the ideal that appeals to me, it is in short the ideal of affectionate family life, of honorable business methods."[3]

"But that means cutting passion quite out of your scheme of
things!"

2. Reference to lesbian gender indeterminacy; also, ironic reference to the Hebrew prayer
said every morning by traditional Jewish men in which they thank God for not making
them women; women pray for the strength to bear their lot in life.
3. Adele's credo here is also that of Dr. Jefferson Campbell in "Melanctha."

"Not simple moral passions, they are distinctly of it, but really my chief point is a protest against this tendency of so many of you to go in for things simply for the sake of an experience. I believe strongly that one should do things either for the sake of the thing done or because of definite future power which is the legitimate result of all education. Experience for the paltry purpose of having had it is to me both trivial and immoral. As for passion" she added with increasing earnestness "you see I don't understand much about that. It has no reality for me except as two varieties, affectionate comradeship on the one hand and physical passion in greater or less complexity on the other and against the cultivation of that latter I have an almost puritanic horror and that includes an objection to the cultivation of it in any of its many disguised forms. I have a sort of notion that to be capable of anything more worth while one must have the power of idealising another and I don't seem to have any of that."

After a pause Helen explained it. "That is what makes it possible for a face as thoughtful and strongly built as yours to be almost annoyingly unlived and youthful and to be almost foolishly happy and content." There was another silence and then Adele said with conviction "I could undertake to be an efficient pupil if it were possible to find an efficient teacher," and then they left it there between them.

In the long idle days that followed an affectionate relation gradually grew between these two. In the chilly evenings as Adele lay at her side on the deck, Helen would protect her from the wind and would allow her hand to rest gently on her face and her fingers to flutter vaguely near her lips. At such times Adele would have dimly a sense of inward resistance, a feeling that if she were not so sluggish she would try to decide whether she should yield or resist but she felt too tired to think, to yield or to resist and so she lay there quite quiet, quite dulled.

These relations formed themselves so gradually and gently that only the nicest observer could have noted any change in the relations of the three. Their intercourse was apparently very much what it had been. There were long conversations in which Adele vehemently and with much picturesque vividness explained her views and theories of manners, people and things, in all of which she was steadily opposed by Helen who differed fundamentally in all her convictions, aspirations and illusions.

Mabel would listen always with immense enjoyment as if it were a play and enacted for her benefit and queerly enough although the disputants were much in earnest in their talk and in their oppositions, it was a play and enacted for her benefit.

One afternoon Adele was lying in her steamer chair yielding herself to a sense of physical weariness and to the disillusionment of recent failures.[4] Looking up she saw Helen looking down at her. Adele's expression changed. "I beg your pardon" she said "I didn't know any one was near. Forgive the indecency of my having allowed the dregs of my soul to appear on the surface." "It is I who ought to apologise for having observed you" Helen answered gravely. Adele gave her a long look of unimpassioned observation. "I certainly never expected to find you one of the most gentle and considerate of human kind," she commented quietly and then Helen made it clearer. "I certainly did not expect that you would find me so," she answered.

This unemphasised interchange still left them as before quite untouched. It was an impartial statement from each one, a simple observation on an event. Time passed and still no charged words, glances or movements passed between them, they gave no recognition of each other's consciousness.

One evening lying there in the darkness yielding to a suggestion rather than to an impulse Adele pressed the fluttering fingers to her lips. The act was to herself quite without emphasis and without meaning.

The next night as she lay down in her berth,[5] she suddenly awakened out of her long emotional apathy. For the first time she recognised the existence of Helen's consciousness and realised how completely ignorant she was both as to its extent and its meaning. She meditated a long time. Finally she began to explain to herself. "No I don't understand it at all," she said. "There are so many possibilities and then there is Mabel," and she dropped into another meditation. Finally it took form. "Of course Helen may be just drifting as I was, or else she may be interested in seeing how far I will go before my principles get in my way or whether they will get in my way at all, and then again it's barely possible that she may really care for me and again she may be playing some entirely different game.— And then there is Mabel.—Apparently she is not to know, but is that real; does it make any difference; does Helen really care or is she only doing it secretly for the sense of mystery. Surely she is right. I am very ignorant. Here after ten days of steady companionship I haven't the vaguest conception of her, I haven't the slightest clue to her or her meanings. Surely I must be very stupid" and she shook her head disconsolately "and to-morrow is our last day together and I am not likely to find out then. I would so much like to know" she

4. Probably a reference to Stein's waning of both interest and level of performance in medical school.
5. Bed.

continued "but I can see no way to it, none at all except," and she smiled to herself "except by asking her and then I have no means of knowing whether she is telling me the truth. Surely all is vanity for I once thought I knew something about women," and with a long sigh of mystification she composed herself to sleep.

The next afternoon leaving Mabel comfortable with a book, Adele, with a mind attuned to experiment wandered back with Helen to their favorite outlook. It was a sparkling day and Adele threw herself on the deck joyous with the sunshine and the blue. She looked up at Helen for a minute and then began to laugh, her eyes bright with amusement. "Now what?" asked Helen. "Oh nothing much, I was just thinking of the general foolishness, Mabel and you and I. Don't you think it's pretty foolish?" There was nothing mocking in her face nothing but simple amusement.

Helen's face gave no response and made no comment but soon she hit directly with words. "I am afraid" she said "that after all you haven't a nature much above passionettes. You are so afraid of losing your moral sense that you are not willing to take it through anything more dangerous than a mud-puddle."

Adele took it frankly, her smile changed to meditation. "Yes there is something in what you say," she returned "but after all if one has a moral sense there is no necessity in being foolhardy with it. I grant you it ought to be good for a swim of a mile or two, but surely it would be certain death to let it loose in mid-ocean. It's not a heroic point of view I admit, but then I never wanted to be a hero, but on the other hand," she added "I am not anxious to cultivate cowardice. I wonder—" and then she paused. Helen gave her a little while and then left her.

Adele continued a long time to look out on the water. "I wonder" she said to herself again. Finally it came more definitely. "Yes I wonder. There isn't much use in wondering about Helen. I know no more now than I did last night and I am not likely to be much wiser. She gives me no means of taking hold and the key of the lock is surely not in me. It can't be that she really cares enough to count, no that's impossible," and she relapsed once more into silence.

Her meditations again took form. "As for me is it another little indulgence of my superficial emotions or is there any possibility of my really learning to realise stronger feelings. If it's the first I will call a halt promptly and at once. If it's the second I won't back out, no not for any amount of moral sense," and she smiled to herself. "Certainly it is very difficult to tell. The probabilities are that this is only another one of the many and so I suppose I had better quit and leave it. It's the last day together and so to be honorable I must quit at once." She then dismissed it all and for some time longer found it very pleasant there playing with the brightness. At last she went forward and joined the others. She sat down by Helen's side and promptly changed her mind. It was really quite different, her moral sense had lost its importance.

Helen was very silent that evening all through the tedious table d'hôte dinner. The burden of the entertainment rested on Adele and she supported it vigorously. After dinner they all went back to their old station. It was a glorious night that last one on the ship. They lay on the deck the stars bright overhead and the wine-colored sea following fast behind the ploughing screw. Helen continued silent, and Adele all through her long discourse on the superior quality of California starlight and the incidents of her childhood with which she was regaling Mabel, all through this talk she still wondered if Helen really cared.

"Was I brutal this afternoon?" she thought it in definite words "and does she really care? If she does it would be only decent of me to give some sign of contrition for if she does care I am most woefully ashamed of my levity, but if she doesn't and is just playing with me then I don't want to apologise." Her mind slowly alternated between these two possibilities. She was beginning to decide in favor of the more generous one, when she felt Helen's hand pressing gently over her eyes. At once the baser interpretation left her mind quite completely. She felt convinced of Helen's rare intensity and generosity of feeling. It was the first recognition of mutual dependence.

Steadily the night grew colder clearer and more beautiful. Finally Mabel left them. They drew closer together and in a little while Adele began to question. "You were very generous," she said "tell me how much do you care for me." "Care for you my dear" Helen answered "more than you know and less than you think." She then began again with some abruptness "Adele you seem to me capable of very genuine friendship. You are at once dispassionate in your judgments and loyal in your feelings; tell me will we be friends?" Adele took it very thoughtfully. "One usually knows very definitely when there is no chance of an acquaintance becoming a friendship but on the other hand it is impossible to tell in a given case whether there is. I really don't know," she said. Helen answered her with fervor. "I honor you for being honest." "Oh honest," returned Adele lightly. "Honesty is a selfish virtue. Yes I am honest enough." After a long pause she began again meditatively, "I wonder if either of us has the slightest idea what is going on in the other's head." "That means that you think me very wicked?" Helen asked. "Oh no" Adele responded "I really don't know enough about you to know whether you are wicked or not. Forgive me I don't mean to be brutal" she added earnestly "but I really don't know."

There was a long silence and Adele looked observingly at the stars. Suddenly she felt herself intensely kissed on the eyes and on the lips. She felt vaguely that she was apathetically unresponsive. There was another silence. Helen looked steadily down at her. "Well!" she brought out at last. "Oh" began Adele slowly "I was just thinking." "Haven't you ever stopped thinking long enough to feel?" Helen questioned gravely. Adele shook her head in slow negation. "Why I suppose if one can't think at the same time I will never accomplish the feat of feeling. I always think. I don't see how one can stop it. Thinking is a pretty continuous process" she continued "sometimes it's more active than at others but it's always pretty much there." "In that case I had better leave you to your thoughts" Helen decided. "Ah! don't go," exclaimed Adele. "I don't want to stir." "Why not?" demanded Helen. "Well" Adele put it tentatively "I suppose it's simply inertia." "I really must go" repeated Helen gently, there was no abruptness in her voice or movement. Adele sat up, Helen bent down, kissed her warmly and left.

Adele sat for a while in a dazed fashion. At last she shook her head dubiously and murmured, "I wonder if it was inertia." She sat some time longer among the tossed rugs and finally with another dubious head-shake said with mock sadness, "I asked the unavailing stars and they replied not, I am afraid it's too big for me" and then she stopped thinking. She kept quiet some time longer watching the pleasant night. At last she gathered the rugs together and started to go below. Suddenly she stopped and dropped heavily on a bench. "Why" she said in a tone of intense interest, "it's like a bit of mathematics. Suddenly it does itself and you begin to see," and then she laughed. "I am afraid Helen wouldn't think much of that if it's only seeing. However I never even thought I saw before and I really do think I begin to see. Yes it's very strange but surely I do begin to see."

All during the summer Adele did not lose the sense of having seen, but on the other hand her insight did not deepen. She meditated abundantly on this problem and it always ended with a childlike pride in the refrain "I did see a little, I certainly did catch a glimpse."

She thought of it as she and her brother lay in the evenings on the hill-side at Tangiers[6] feeling entirely at home with the Moors[7] who in their white garments were rising up and down in the grass like so many ghostly rabbits. As they lay there agreeing and disagreeing in

6. In Morocco.
7. Archaic word for dark-skinned Arabs.

endless discussion with an intensity of interest that long familiarity had in no way diminished, varied by indulgence in elaborate foolishness and reminiscent jokes, she enjoyed to the full the sense of family friendship. She felt that her glimpse had nothing to do with all this. It belonged to another less pleasant and more incomplete emotional world. It didn't illuminate this one and as yet it was not very alluring in itself but as she remarked to herself at the end of one of her unenlightening discussions on this topic, "It is something one ought to know. It seems almost a duty."

Sitting in the court of the Alhambra watching the swallows fly in and out of the crevices of the walls, bathing in the soft air filled with the fragrance of myrtle and oleander and letting the hot sun burn her face and the palms of her hands, losing herself thus in sensuous delight she would murmur again and again. "No it isn't just this, it's something more, something different. I haven't really felt it but I have caught a glimpse."

One day she was sitting on a hill-side looking down at Granada desolate in the noon-day sun. A young Spanish girl carrying a heavy bag was climbing up the dry, brown hill. As she came nearer they smiled at each other and exchanged greetings. The child sat down beside her. She was one of those motherly little women found so often in her class, full of gentle dignity and womanly responsibility.

They sat there side by side with a feeling of complete companionship, looking at each other with perfect comprehension, their intercourse saved from the interchange of common-places by their ignorance of each other's language. For some time they sat there, finally they arose and walked on together. They parted as quiet friends part, and as long as they remained in sight of each other they turned again and again and signed a gentle farewell.

After her comrade had disappeared Adele returned to her insistent thought. "A simple experience like this is very perfect, can my new insight give me realler joys?" she questioned. "I doubt it very much" she said. "It doesn't deepen such experiences in fact it rather annoyingly gets in my way and disturbs my happy serenity. Heavens what an egotist I am!" she exclaimed and then she devoted herself to the sunshine on the hills.

Later on she was lying on the ground reading again Dante's *Vita Nuova*. She lost herself completely in the tale of Dante and Beatrice. She read it with absorbed interest for it seemed now divinely illuminated. She rejoiced abundantly in her new understanding and exclaimed triumphantly "At last I begin to see what Dante is talking about and so there is something in my glimpse and it's alright and worth while" and she felt within herself a great content.

Book 2:

Mabel Neathe

1

MABEL NEATHE'S ROOM fully met the habit of many hours of unaggressive lounging. She had command of an exceptional talent for atmosphere. The room with its very good shape, dark walls but mediocre furnishings and decorations was more than successfully unobtrusive, it had perfect quality. It had always just the amount of light necessary to make mutual observation pleasant and yet to leave the decorations in obscurity or rather to inspire a faith in their being good.

It is true of rooms as of human beings that they are bound to have one good feature and as a Frenchwoman dresses to that feature in such fashion that the observer must see that and notice nothing else, so Mabel Neathe had arranged her room so that one enjoyed one's companions and observed consciously only the pleasant fire-place.

But the important element in the success of the room as atmosphere consisted in Mabel's personality. The average guest expressed it in the simple comment that she was a perfect hostess, but the more sympathetic observers put it that it was not that she had the manners of a perfect hostess but the more unobtrusive good manners of a gentleman.

The chosen and they were a few individuals rather than a set found this statement inadequate although it was abundantly difficult for them to explain their feeling. Such an Italian type frustrated by its setting in an unimpassioned and moral community was of necessity misinterpreted although its charm was valued. Mabel's ancestry did not supply any explanation of her character. Her kinship with decadent Italy was purely spiritual.

The capacity for composing herself with her room in unaccented and perfect values was the most complete attribute of that kinship that her modern environment had developed. As for the rest it after all amounted to failure, failure as power, failure as an individual. Her passions in spite of their intensity failed to take effective hold on the objects of her desire. The subtlety and impersonality of her atmosphere which in a position of recognised power would have had compelling attraction, here in a community of equals where there could be no mystery as the seeker had complete liberty in seeking she lacked the vital force necessary to win. Although she was unscrupulous the weapons she used were too brittle, they could always be broken in pieces by a vigorous guard.

Modern situations never endure for a long enough time to allow

subtle and elaborate methods to succeed. By the time they are beginning to bring about results the incident is forgotten. Subtlety moreover in order to command efficient power must be realised as
dangerous and the modern world is a difficult place in which to be
subtly dangerous, the risks are too great. Mabel might now compel
by inspiring pity, she could never in her world compel by inspiring
fear.

Adele had been for some time one of Mabel's selected few. Her
enjoyment of ease and her habit of infinite leisure, combined with
her vigorous personality and a capacity for endless and picturesque
analysis of all things human had established a claim which her
instinct for intimacy without familiarity and her ready adjustment to
the necessary impersonality which a relation with Mabel demanded,
had confirmed.

"It's more or less of a bore getting back for we are all agreed that
Baltimore isn't much of a town to live in, but this old habit is certainly very pleasant" she remarked as she stretched herself comfortably on the couch "and after all, it is much more possible to cultivate
such joys when a town isn't wildly exciting. No my tea isn't quite
right" she continued. "It's worth while making a fuss you know when
there is a possibility of obtaining perfection, otherwise any old tea is
good enough. Anyhow what's the use of anything as long as it isn't
Spain? You must really go there some time." They continued to make
the most of their recent experiences in this their first meeting.

"Did you stay long in New York after you landed?" Mabel finally
asked. "Only a few days" Adele replied "I suppose Helen wrote you
that I saw her for a little while. We lunched together before I took
my train," she added with a consciousness of the embarrassment that
that meeting had caused her. "You didn't expect to like her so much,
did you?" Mabel suggested. "I remember you used to say that she
impressed you as almost coarse and rather decadent and that you
didn't even find her interesting. And you know" she added "how
much you dislike decadence."

Adele met her with frank bravado. "Of course I said that and as
yet I don't retract it. I am far from sure that she is not both coarse
and decadent and I don't approve of either of those qualities. I do
grant you however that she is interesting, at least as a character, her
talk interests me no more than it ever did" and then facing the game
more boldly, she continued "but you know I really know very little
about her except that she dislikes her parents and goes in for society
a good deal. What else is there?"

Mabel drew a very unpleasant picture of that parentage. Her
description of the father a successful lawyer and judge, and an exces-
sively brutal and at the same time small-minded man who exercised
great ingenuity in making himself unpleasant was not alluring, nor

that of the mother who was very religious and spent most of her time mourning that it was not Helen that had been taken instead of the others a girl and boy whom she remembered as sweet gentle children.

One day when Helen was a young girl she heard her mother say to the father "Isn't it sad that Helen should have been the one to be left."

Mabel described their attempts to break Helen's spirit and their anger at their lack of success. "And now" Mabel went on "they object to everything that she does, to her friends and to everything she is interested in. Mrs. T. always sides with her husband. Of course they are proud of her good looks, her cleverness and social success but she won't get married and she doesn't care to please the people her mother wants her to belong to. They don't dare to say anything to her now because she is so much better able to say things that hurt than they are."

"I suppose there is very little doubt that Helen can be uncommonly nasty when she wants to be," laughed Adele, "and if she isn't sensitive to other people's pain, a talent for being successful in bitter repartee might become a habit that would make her a most uncomfortable daughter. I believe I might condole with the elders if they were to confide their sorrows to me. By the way doesn't Helen address them the way children commonly do their parents, she always speaks of them as Mr. and Mrs. T." "Oh yes" Mabel explained, "they observe the usual forms."

"It's a queer game," Adele commented, "coming as I do from a community where all no matter how much they may quarrel and disagree have strong family affection and great respect for the ties of blood, I find it difficult to realise." "Yes there you come in with your middle-class ideals again" retorted Mabel.

She then lauded Helen's courage and daring. "Whenever there is any difficulty with the horses or anything dangerous to be done they always call in Helen.[1] Her father is also very small-minded in money matters. He gives her so little and whenever anything happens to the carriage if she is out in it, he makes her pay and she has to get the money as best she can. Her courage never fails and that is what makes her father so bitter, that she never gives any sign of yielding and if she decides to do a thing she is perfectly reckless, nothing stops her."

"That sounds very awful" mocked Adele "not being myself of an heroic breed, I don't somehow realise that type much outside of story-books. That sort of person in real life doesn't seem very real, but I guess it's alright. Helen has courage I don't doubt that."

Mabel then described Helen's remarkable endurance of pain. She

---

1. Melanctha has the same courage and skill with horses.

fell from a haystack one day and broke her arm. After she got home, her father was so angry that he wouldn't for some time have it attended to and she faced him boldly to the end. "She never winces or complains no matter how much she is hurt," Mabel concluded.[2] "Yes I can believe that" Adele answered thoughtfully.

Throughout the whole of Mabel's talk of Helen, there was an implication of ownership that Adele found singularly irritating. She supposed that Mabel had a right to it but in that thought she found little comfort.

As the winter advanced, Adele took frequent trips to New York. She always spent some of her time with Helen. For some undefined reason a convention of secrecy governed their relations. They seemed in this way to emphasise their intention of working the thing out completely between them. To Adele's consciousness the necessity of this secrecy was only apparent when they were together. She felt no obligation to conceal this relation from her friends.

They arranged their meetings in the museums or in the park and sometimes they varied it by lunching together and taking interminable walks in the long straight streets. Adele was always staying with relatives and friends and although there was no reason why Helen should not have come to see her there, something seemed somehow to serve as one. As for Helen's house it seemed tacitly agreed between them that they should not complicate the situation by any relations with Helen's family and so they continued their homeless wanderings.

Adele spent much of their time together in announcing with great interest the result of her endless meditations. She would criticise and examine herself and her ideas with tireless interest. "Helen," she said one day, "I always had an impression that you talked a great deal but apparently you are a most silent being. What is it? Do I talk so hopelessly much that you get discouraged with it as a habit?" "No," answered Helen, "although I admit one might look upon you in the light of a warning, but really I am very silent when I know people well. I only talk when I am with superficial acquaintances." Adele laughed. "I am tempted to say for the sake of picturesque effect, that in that respect I am your complete opposite, but honesty compels me to admit in myself an admirable consistency. I don't know that the quantity is much affected by any conditions in which I find myself, but really Helen why don't you talk more to me?" "Because you know well enough that you are not interested in my ideas, in fact that they bore you. It's always been very evident. You know" Helen continued affectionately, "that you haven't much talent for

2. The broken arm episode reappears in "Melanctha."

concealing your feelings and impressions." Adele smiled, "Yes you are certainly right about most of your talk, it does bore me," she admitted. "But that is because it's about stuff that you are not really interested in. You don't really care about general ideas and art values and musical development and surgical operations and Heaven knows what all and naturally your talk about those things doesn't interest me. No talking is interesting that one hasn't hammered out oneself. I know I always bore myself unutterably when I talk the thoughts that I hammered out some time ago and that are no longer meaningful to me, for quoting even oneself lacks a flavor of reality, but you, you always make me feel that at no period did you ever have the thoughts that you converse with. Surely one has to hit you awfully hard to shake your realler things to the surface."

These meetings soon became impossible. It was getting cold and unpleasant and it obviously wouldn't do to continue in that fashion and yet neither of them undertook to break the convention of silence which they had so completely adopted concerning the conditions of their relation.

One day after they had been lunching together they both felt strongly that restaurants had ceased to be amusing. They didn't want to stay there any longer but outside there was an unpleasant wet snow-storm, it was dark and gloomy and the streets were slushy. Helen had a sudden inspiration. "Let us go and see Jane Fairfield," she said, "you don't know her of course but that makes no difference. She is queer and will interest you and you are queer and will interest her. Oh! I don't want to listen to your protests, you are queer and interesting even if you don't know it and you like queer and interesting people even if you think you don't and you are not a bit bashful in spite of your convictions to the contrary, so come along." Adele laughed and agreed.[3]

They wandered up to the very top of an interminable New York apartment house. It was one of the variety made up apparently of an endless number of unfinished boxes of all sizes piled up in a great oblong leaving an elevator shaft in the centre. There is a strange effect of bare wood and uncovered nails about these houses and no amount of upholstery really seems to cover their hollow nakedness.

Jane Fairfield was not at home but the elevator boy trustingly let them in to wait. They looked out of the windows at the city all gloomy and wet and white stretching down to the river, and they watched the long tracks of the elevated making such wonderful perspective that it never really seemed to disappear, it just infinitely met.

3. See Jane Harden in "Melanctha," based on Jane Fairfield; note, also, the ambiguous use of the word "queer," more explicitly implying homosexual here than in "Melanctha," but carrying that connotation in both texts.

Finally they sat down on the couch to give their hostess just another quarter of an hour in which to return, and then for the first time in Adele's experience something happened in which she had no definite consciousness of beginnings. She found herself at the end of a passionate embrace.

Some weeks after when Adele came again to New York they agreed to meet at Helen's house. It had been arranged quite as a matter of course as if no objection to such a proceeding had ever been entertained. Adele laughed to herself as she thought of it. "Why we didn't before and why we do now are to me equally mysterious" she said shrugging her shoulders. "Great is Allah, Mohammed is no Shodah![4] though I dimly suspect that sometimes he is."

When the time came for keeping her engagement Adele for some time delayed going and remained lying on her friend's couch begging to be detained. She realised that her certain hold on her own frank joyousness and happy serenity was weakened. She almost longed to back out, she did so dread emotional complexities. "Oh for peace and a quiet life!" she groaned as she rang Helen's door-bell.

In Helen's room she found a note explaining that being worried as it was so much past the hour of appointment, she had gone to the Museum as Adele had perhaps misunderstood the arrangement. If she came in she was to wait. "It was very bad of me to fool around so long" Adele said to herself gravely and then sat down very peacefully to read.

"I am awfully sorry" Adele greeted Helen as she came into the room somewhat intensely, "it never occurred to me that you would be bothered, it was just dilatoriness on my part," and then they sat down. After a while Helen came and sat on the arm of Adele's chair. She took her head between tense arms and sent deep into her eyes a long straight look of concentrated question. "Haven't you anything to say to me?" she asked at last. "Why no, nothing in particular," Adele answered slowly. She met Helen's glance for a moment, returned it with simple friendliness and then withdrew from it.

"You are very chivalrous," Helen said with sad self-defiance. "You realise that there ought to be shame somewhere between us and as I have none, you generously undertake it all." "No I am not chivalrous" Adele answered, "but I realise my deficiencies. I know that I always take an everlasting time to arrive anywhere really and that the rapidity of my superficial observation keeps it from being realised. It is certainly all my fault. I am so very deceptive. I arouse false expectations. You see," she continued meeting her again with pleasant

4. Fool; Muslims might well find this disrespectful, joking transformation of the Muslim prayer "Great is Allah, and Mohammed is his prophet" offensively sacrilegious.

friendliness, "you haven't yet learned that I am at once impetuous and slow-minded."

Time passed and they renewed their habit of desultory meetings at public places, but these were not the same as before. There was between them now a consciousness of strain, a sense of new adjust-ments, of uncertain standards and of changing values.

Helen was patient but occasionally moved to trenchant criticism, Adele was irritable and discursive but always ended with a frank almost bald apology for her inadequacy.

In the course of time they again arranged to meet in Helen's room. It was a wet rainy, sleety day and Adele felt chilly and unresponsive. Throwing off her hat and coat, she sat down after a cursory greeting and looked meditatively into the fire. "How completely we exemplify entirely different types" she began at last without looking at her com-panion. "You are a blooming Anglo-Saxon. You know what you want and you go and get it without spending your days and nights chang-ing backwards and forwards from yes to no. If you want to stick a knife into a man you just naturally go and stick straight and hard. You would probably kill him but it would soon be over while I, I would have so many compunctions and considerations that I would cut up all his surface anatomy and make it a long drawn agony but unless he should bleed to death quite by accident, I wouldn't do him any serious injury. No you are the very brave man,[5] passionate but not emotional, capable of great sacrifice but not tender-hearted.

"And then you really want things badly enough to go out and get them and that seems to me very strange. I want things too but only in order to understand them and I never go and get them. I am a hopeless coward, I hate to risk hurting myself or anybody else. All I want to do is to meditate endlessly and think and talk. I know you object because you believe it necessary to feel something to think about and you contend that I don't give myself time to find it. I recognise the justice of that criticism and I am doing my best these days to let it come."

She relapsed into silence and sat there smiling ironically into the fire. The silence grew longer and her smile turned into a look almost of disgust. Finally she wearily drew breath, shook her head and got up. "Ah! don't go," came from Helen in quick appeal. Adele answered the words. "No I am not going. I just want to look at these books." She wandered about a little. Finally she stopped by Helen's side and stood looking down at her with a gentle irony that wavered on the edge of scorn.

"Do you know" she began in her usual tone of dispassionate

5. Again, an ironic reference to lesbian gender indeterminacy.

inquiry "you are a wonderful example of double personality. The you that I used to know and didn't like, and the occasional you that when I do catch a glimpse of it seems to me so very wonderful, haven't any possible connection with each other. It isn't as if my conception of you had gradually changed because it hasn't. I realise always one whole you consisting of a laugh so hard that it rattles, a voice that suggests a certain brutal coarseness and a point of view that is aggressively unsympathetic, and all that is one whole you and it alternates with another you that possesses a purity and intensity of feeling that leaves me quite awestruck and a gentleness of voice and manner and an infinitely tender patience that entirely overmasters me. Now the question is which is really you because these two don't seem to have any connections. Perhaps when I really know something about you, the whole will come together but at present it is always either the one or the other and I haven't the least idea which is reallest. You certainly are one too many for me." She shrugged her shoulders, threw out her hands helplessly and sat down again before the fire. She roused at last and became conscious that Helen was trembling bitterly. All hesitations were swept away by Adele's instant passionate sympathy for a creature obviously in pain and she took her into her arms with pure maternal tenderness. Helen gave way utterly. "I tried to be adequate to your experiments" she said at last "but you had no mercy. You were not content until you had dissected out every nerve in my body and left it quite exposed and it was too much, too much. You should give your subjects occasional respite even in the ardor of research." She said it without bitterness. "Good God" cried Adele utterly dumbfounded "did you think that I was deliberately making you suffer in order to study results? Heavens and earth what do you take me for! Do you suppose that I for a moment realised that you were in pain. No! no! it is only my cursed habit of being concerned only with my own thoughts, and then you know I never for a moment believed that you really cared about me, that is one of the things that with all my conceit I never can believe. Helen how could you have had any use for me if you thought me capable of such wanton cruelty?" "I didn't know," she answered "I was willing that you should do what you liked if it interested you and I would stand it as well as I could." "Oh! Oh!" groaned Adele yearning over her with remorseful sympathy "surely dear you believe that I had no idea of your pain and that my brutality was due to ignorance and not intention." "Yes! yes! I know" whispered Helen, nestling to her. After a while she went on, "You know dear you mean so very much to me for with all your inveterate egotism you are the only person with whom I have ever come into close contact, whom I could continue to respect." "Faith" said Adele ruefully "I confess I can't see why. After all even at my best I am only tolerably decent. There are plenty of others, your experience has been unfortunate that's all, and then you know you are always shut yourself off by that fatal illusion of yours that you could stand completely alone." And then she chanted with tender mockery, "And the very strong man Kwasind[6] and he was a very strong man" she went on "even if being an unconquerable solitary wasn't entirely a success."

2

All through the winter Helen at intervals spent a few days with Mabel Neathe in Baltimore. Adele was always more or less with them on these occasions. On the surface they preserved the same relations as had existed on the steamer. The only evidence that Mabel gave of a realisation of a difference was in never if she could avoid it leaving them alone together.

It was tacitly understood between them that on these rare occasions they should give each other no sign. As the time drew near when Adele was once more to leave for Europe this time for an extended absence, the tension of this self-imposed inhibition became unendurable and they as tacitly ceased to respect it.

Some weeks before her intended departure Adele was one afternoon as usual taking tea with Mabel. "You have never met Mr. and Mrs. T. have you?" Mabel asked quite out of the air. They had never definitely avoided talking of Helen but they had not spoken of her unnecessarily. "No" Adele answered, "I haven't wanted to. I don't like perfunctory civilities and I know that I belong to the number of Helen's friends of whom they do not approve." "You would not be burdened by their civility, they never take the trouble to be as amiable as that." "Are your experiences so very unpleasant when you are stopping there? I shouldn't think that you would care to do it often." "Sometimes I feel as if it couldn't be endured but if I didn't, Helen would leave them and I think she would regret that and so I don't want her to do it. I have only to say the word and she would leave them at once and sometimes I think she will do it anyway. If she once makes up her mind she won't reconsider it. Of course I wouldn't say such things to any one but you, you know." "I can quite believe that," said Adele rather grimly, "isn't there anything else that you would like to tell me just because I am I. If so don't let me get in your way." "I have never told you about our early relations," Mabel continued. "You know Helen cared for me long before I knew anything about it. We used to be together a great deal at College and every now and then she would disappear for a long time into the country and it wasn't until long afterwards that I found out the rea-

6. From Henry Wadsworth Longfellow's epic poem *Hiawatha* (1855); Kwasind, the hero Hiawatha's close friend, is a "very strong man."

son of it. You know Helen never gives way. You have no idea how wonderful she is. I have been so worried lately" she went on "lest she should think it necessary to leave home for my sake because it is so uncomfortable for me in the summer when I spend a month with her." "Well then why don't you make a noble sacrifice and stay away? Apparently Helen's heroism is great enough to carry her through the ordeal." Adele felt herself to be quite satisfactorily vulgar. Mabel accepted it literally. "Do you really advise it?" she asked. "Oh yes" said Adele "there is nothing so good for the soul as self-imposed periods of total abstinence." "Well, I will think about it" Mabel answered "it is such a comfort that you understand everything and one can speak to you openly about it all." "That's where you are entirely mistaken" Adele said decisively, "I understand nothing. But after all" she added, "it isn't any of my business anyway. Adios," and she left.

When she got home she saw a letter of Helen's on the table. She felt no impulse to read it. She put it well away. "Not that it is any of my business whether she is bound and if so how," she said to herself. "That is entirely for her to work out with her own conscience. For me it is only a question of what exists between us two. I owe Mabel nothing"; and she resolutely relegated it all quite to the background of her mind.

Mabel however did not allow the subject to rest. At the very next opportunity she again asked Adele for advice. "Oh hang it all" Adele broke out "what do I know about it? I understand nothing of the nature of the bond between you." "Don't you really?" Mabel was seriously incredulous. "No I don't." Adele answered with decision, and the subject dropped.

Adele communed with herself dismally. "I was strong-minded to put it out of my head once, but this time apparently it has come to stay. I can't deny that I do badly want to know and I know well enough that if I continue to want to know the only decent thing for me to do is to ask the information of Helen. But I do so hate to do that. Why? well I suppose because it would hurt so to hear her admit that she was bound. It would be infinitely pleasanter to have Mabel explain it but it certainly would be very contemptible of me to get it from her. Helen is right, it's not easy this business of really caring about people. I seem to be pretty deeply in it" and she smiled to herself "because now I don't regret the bother and the pain. I wonder if I am really beginning to care" and she lost herself in a revery.

Mabel's room was now for Adele always filled with the atmosphere of the unasked question. She could dismiss it when alone but Mabel was clothed with it as with a garment although nothing concerning it passed between them.

Adele now received a letter from Helen asking why she had not written, whether it was that faith had again failed her. Adele at first found it impossible to answer; finally she wrote a note at once ambiguous and bitter.

At last the tension snapped. "Tell me then" Adele said to Mabel abruptly one evening. Mabel made no attempt to misunderstand but she did attempt to delay. "Oh well if you want to go through the farce of a refusal and an insistence, why help yourself," Adele broke out harshly, "but supposing all that done, I say again tell me." Mabel was dismayed by Adele's hot directness and she vaguely fluttered about as if to escape. "Drop your intricate delicacy" Adele said sternly "you wanted to tell, now tell." Mabel was cowed. She sat down and explained.

The room grew large and portentous and to Mabel's eyes Adele's figure grew almost dreadful in its concentrated repulsion. There was a long silence that seemed to roar and menace and Mabel grew afraid. "Good-night" said Adele and left her.

Adele had now at last learned to stop thinking. She went home and lay motionless a long time. At last she got up and sat at her desk. "I guess I must really care a good deal about Helen" she said at last, "but oh Lord," she groaned and it was very bitter pain. Finally she roused herself. "Poor Mabel" she said "I could almost find it in my heart to be sorry for her. I must have looked very dreadful."

On the next few occasions nothing was said. Finally Mabel began again. "I really supposed Adele that you knew, or else I wouldn't have said anything about it at all and after I once mentioned it, you know you made me tell." "Oh yes I made you tell." Adele could admit it quite cheerfully; Mabel seemed so trivial. "And then you know," Mabel continued "I never would have mentioned it if I had not been so fond of you." Adele laughed, "Yes it's wonderful what an amount of devotion to me there is lying around the universe; but what will Helen think of the results of this devotion of yours?" "That is what worries me" Mabel admitted "I must tell her that I have told you and I am afraid she won't like it." "I rather suspect she won't" and Adele laughed again "but there is nothing like seizing an opportunity before your courage has a chance to ooze. Helen will be down next week, you know, and that will give you your chance but I guess now there has been enough said," and she definitely dismissed the matter.

Adele found it impossible to write to Helen, she felt too sore and bitter but even in spite of her intense revulsion of feeling, she realised that she did still believe in that other Helen that she had attempted once to describe to her. In spite of all evidence she was convinced that something real existed there, something that she was bound to reverence.

She spent a painful week struggling between revulsion and respect. Finally two days before Helen's visit, she heard from her. "I am afraid I can bear it no longer" Helen wrote. "As long as I believed there was a chance of your learning to be something more than your petty complacent self, I could willingly endure everything, but now you remind me of an ignorant mob. You trample everything ruthlessly under your feet without considering whether or not you kill something precious and without being changed or influenced by what you so brutally destroy. I am like Diogenes in quest of an honest man; I want so badly to find some one I can respect and I find them all worthy of nothing but contempt. You have done your best. I am sorry."

For some time Adele was wholly possessed by hot anger, but that changed to intense sympathy for Helen's pain. She realised the torment she might be enduring and so sat down at once to answer. "Perhaps though she really no longer cares" she thought to herself and hesitated. "Well whether she does or not makes no difference I will at least do my part."

"I can make no defense" she wrote "except only that in spite of all my variations there has grown within me steadily an increasing respect and devotion to you. I am not surprised at your bitterness but your conclusions from it are not justified. It is hardly to be expected that such a changed estimate of values, such a complete departure from established convictions as I have lately undergone could take place without many revulsions. That you have been very patient I fully realise but on the other hand you should recognise that I too have done my best and your word to the contrary notwithstanding that best has not been contemptible. So don't talk any more nonsense about mobs. If your endurance is not equal to this task, why admit it and have done with it; if it is I will try to be adequate."

Adele knew that Helen would receive her letter but there would not be time to answer it as she was to arrive in Baltimore the following evening. They were all three to meet at the opera that night so for a whole day Adele would be uncertain of Helen's feeling toward her. She spent all her strength throughout the day in endeavoring to prepare herself to find that Helen still held her in contempt. It had always been her habit to force herself to realise the worst that was likely to befall her and to submit herself before the event. She was never content with simply thinking that the worst might happen and having said it to still expect the best, but she had always accustomed herself to bring her mind again and again to this worst possibility until she had really mastered herself to bear it. She did this because she always doubted her own courage and distrusted her capacity to meet a difficulty if she had not inured herself to it beforehand.

All through this day she struggled for her accustomed definite resignation and the tremendous difficulty of accomplishment made her keenly realise how much she valued Helen's regard.

She did not arrive at the opera until after it had commenced. She knew how little command she had of her expression when deeply moved and she preferred that the first greeting should take place in the dark. She came in quietly to her place. Helen leaned across Mabel and greeted her. There was nothing in her manner to indicate anything and Adele realised by her sensation of sick disappointment that she had really not prepared herself at all. Now that the necessity was more imperative she struggled again for resignation and by the time the act was over she had pretty well gained it. She had at least mastered herself enough to entertain Mabel with elaborate discussion of music and knife fights. She avoided noticing Helen but that was comparatively simple as Mabel sat between them.

Carmen[7] that night was to her at once the longest and the shortest performance that she had ever sat through. It was short because the end brought her nearer to hopeless certainty. It was long because she could only fill it with suspense.

The opera was at last or already over, Adele was uncertain which phrase expressed her feeling most accurately, and then they went for a little while to Mabel's room. Adele was by this time convinced that all her relation with Helen was at an end.

"You look very tired to-night, what's the matter?" Mabel asked her. "Oh!" she explained "there's been a lot of packing and arranging and good-bys to say and farewell lunches and dinners to eat. How I hate baked shad,[8] it's a particular delicacy now and I have lunched and dined on it for three days running so I think it's quite reasonable for me to be worn out. Good-by no don't come downstairs with me. Hullo Helen has started down already to do the honors. Good-by I will see you again to-morrow." Mabel went back to her room and Helen was already lost in the darkness of the lower hall. Adele slowly descended the stairs impressing herself with the necessity of self-restraint.

"Can you forgive me?" and Helen held her close. "I haven't anything to forgive if you still care," Adele answered. They were silent together a long time. "We will certainly have earned our friendship when it is finally accomplished," Adele said at last.

"Well good-by," Mabel began as the next day Adele was leaving for good. "Oh! before you go I want to tell you that it's alright. Helen was angry but it's alright now. You will be in New York for a few days

---

7. 1875 opera by Georges Bizet, also based on a tragic love triangle.
8. American freshwater fish.

before you sail" she continued. "I know you won't be gone for a whole year, you will be certain to come back to us before long. I will think of your advice" she concluded. "You know it carries so much weight coming from you." "Oh of course" answered Adele and thought to herself, "What sort of a fool does Mabel take me for anyway."

Adele was in Helen's room the eve of her departure. They had been together a long time. Adele was sitting on the floor her head resting against Helen's knee. She looked up at Helen and then broke the silence with some effort. "Before I go" she said "I want to tell you myself what I suppose you know already, that Mabel has told me of the relations existing between you." Helen's arms dropped away. "No I didn't know." She was very still. "Mabel didn't tell you then?" Adele asked. "No" replied Helen. There was a sombre silence. "If you were not wholly selfish, you would have exercised self-restraint enough to spare me this," Helen said. Adele hardly heard the words, but the power of the mood that possessed Helen awed her. She broke through it at last and began with slow resolution.

"I do not admit" she said, "that I was wrong in wanting to know. I suppose one might in a spirit of quixotic[9] generosity deny oneself such a right but as a reasonable being, I feel that I had a right to know. I realise perfectly that it was hopelessly wrong to learn it from Mabel instead of from you. I admit I was a coward, I was simply afraid to ask you." Helen laughed harshly. "You need not have been," she said "I would have told you nothing." "I think you are wrong, I am quite sure that you would have told me and I wanted to spare myself that pain, perhaps spare you it too, I don't know. I repeat I cannot believe that I was wrong in wanting to know."

They remained there together in an unyielding silence. When an irresistible force meets an immovable body what happens? Nothing. The shadow of a long struggle inevitable as their different natures lay drearily upon them. This incident however decided was only the beginning. All that had gone before was only a preliminary. They had just gotten into position.

The silence was not oppressive but it lasted a long time. "I am very fond of you Adele" Helen said at last with a deep embrace.

It was an hour later when Adele drew a deep breath of resolution, "What foolish people those poets are who say that parting is such sweet sorrow.[1] Although it isn't for ever I can't find a bit of sweetness in it not one tiny little speck. Helen I don't like at all this business

9. Idealistic and noble but in an unrealistic, impractical, self-deluded way; based on the central characteristics of the hero of Miguel Cervantes's *Don Quixote* (Part I, 1605; Part II, 1615).

1. Quotation from Shakespeare's *Romeo and Juliet* (Act II, scene ii, line 185) so famous that it has become a cliché about the paradoxically pleasurable promise of reuniting contained within the sadness of parting.

of leaving you." "And I" Helen exclaimed "when in you I seem to be taking farewell of parents, brothers sisters my own child, everything at once. No dear you are quite right there is nothing pleasant in it."

"Then why do they put it into the books?" Adele asked with dismal petulance. "Oh dear! but at least it's some comfort to have found out that they are wrong. It's one fact discovered anyway. Dear we are neither of us sorry that we know enough to find it out, are we?" "No," Helen answered "we are neither of us sorry."

On the steamer Adele received a note of farewell from Mabel in which she again explained that nothing but her great regard for Adele would have made it possible for her to speak as she had done. Adele lost her temper. "I am willing to fight in any way that Mabel likes" she said to herself "underhand or overhand, in the dark, or in the light, in a room or out of doors but at this I protest. She unquestionably did that for a purpose even if the game was not successful. I don't blame her for the game, a weak man must fight with such weapons as he can hold but I don't owe it to her to endure the hypocrisy of a special affection. I can't under the circumstances be very straight but I'll not be unnecessarily crooked. I'll make it clear to her but I'll complicate it in the fashion that she loves."

"My dear Mabel" she wrote, "either you are duller than I would like to think you or you give me credit for more good-natured stupidity than I possess. If the first supposition is correct then you have nothing to say and I need say nothing; if the second then nothing that you would say would carry weight so it is equally unnecessary for you to say anything. If you don't understand what I am talking about then I am talking about nothing and it makes no difference, if you do then there's enough said." Mabel did not answer for several months and then began again to write friendly letters.

It seemed incredible to Adele this summer that it was only one year ago that she had seemed to herself so simple and all morality so easily reducible to formula. In these long lazy Italian days she did not discuss these matters with herself. She realised that at present morally and mentally she was too complex, and that complexity too much astir. It would take much time and strength to make it all settle again. It might, she thought, be eventually understood, it might even in a great deal of time again become simple but at present it gave little promise.

She poured herself out fully and freely to Helen in their ardent correspondence. At first she had had some hesitation about this. She knew that Helen and Mabel were to be together the greater part of the summer and she thought it possible that both the quantity and the matter of the correspondence, if it should come to Mabel's notice would give Helen a great deal of bother. She hesitated a long time whether to suggest this to Helen and to let her decide as to the expediency of being more guarded.

There were many reasons for not mentioning the matter. She realised that not alone Helen but that she herself was still uncertain as to the fidelity of her own feeling. She could not as yet trust herself and hesitated to leave herself alone with a possible relapse.

"After all," she said to herself, "it is Helen's affair and not mine. I have undertaken to follow her lead even into very devious and underground ways but I don't know that it is necessary for me to warn her. She knows Mabel as well as I do. Perhaps she really won't be sorry if the thing is brought to a head."

She remembered the reluctance that Helen always showed to taking precautions or to making any explicit statement of conditions. She seemed to satisfy her conscience and keep herself from all sense of wrong-doing by never allowing herself to expect a difficulty. When it actually arrived the active necessity of using whatever deception was necessary to cover it, drowned her conscience in the violence of action. Adele did not as yet realise this quality definitely but she was vaguely aware that Helen would shut her mind to any explicit statement of probabilities, that she would take no precautions and would thus avoid all sense of guilt. In this fashion she could safeguard herself from her own conscience.

Adele recognised all this dimly. She did not formulate it but it aided to keep her from making any statement to Helen.

She herself could not so avoid her conscience, she simply had to admit a change in moral basis. She knew what she was doing, she realised what was likely to happen and the way in which the new developments would have to be met.

She acknowledged to herself that her own defence lay simply in the fact that she thought the game was worth the candle. "After all" she concluded, "there is still the most important reason for saying nothing. The stopping of the correspondence would make me very sad and lonely. In other words I simply don't want to stop it and so I guess I won't."

For several months the correspondence continued with vigor and ardour on both sides. Then there came a three weeks' interval and no word from Helen then a simple friendly letter and then another long silence.

Adele lying on the green earth on a sunny English hillside communed with herself on these matters day after day. She had no real misgiving but she was deeply unhappy. Her unhappiness was the unhappiness of loneliness not of doubt. She saved herself from intense misery only by realising that the sky was still so blue and the country-side so green and beautiful. The pain of passionate longing was very hard to bear. Again and again she would bury her face in the cool grass to recover the sense of life in the midst of her sick despondency.

"There are many possibilities but to me only one probability," she said to herself. "I am not a trustful person in spite of an optimistic temperament but I am absolutely certain in the face of all the facts that Helen is unchanged. Unquestionably there has been some complication. Mabel has gotten hold of some letters and there has been trouble. I can't blame Mabel much. The point of honor would be a difficult one to decide between the three of us."

As time passed she did not doubt Helen but she began to be much troubled about her responsibility in the matter. She felt uncertain as to the attitude she should take.

"As for Mabel" she said to herself "I admit quite completely that I simply don't care. I owe her nothing. She wanted me when it was pleasant to have me and so we are quits. She entered the fight and must be ready to bear the results. We were never bound to each other, we never trusted each other and so there has been no breach of faith. She would show me no mercy and I need grant her none, particularly as she would wholly misunderstand it. It is very strange how very different one's morality and one's temper are when one wants something really badly. Here I, who have always been hopelessly soft-hearted and good-natured and who have always really preferred letting the other man win, find myself quite cold-blooded and relentless. It's a lovely morality that in which we believe even in serious matters when we are not deeply stirred, it's so delightfully noble and gentle." She sighed and then laughed. "Well, I hope some day to find a morality that can stand the wear and tear of real desire to take the place of the nice one that I have lost, but morality or no morality the fact remains that I have no compunctions on the score of Mabel.

"About Helen that's a very different matter. I unquestionably do owe her a great deal but just how to pay it is the difficult point to discover. I can't forget that to me she can never be the first consideration as she is to Mabel for I have other claims that I would always recognise as more important. I have neither the inclination or the power to take Mabel's place and I feel therefore that I have no right to step in between them. On the other hand morally and mentally she is in urgent need of a strong comrade and such in spite of all evidence I believe myself to be. Some day if we continue she will in spite of herself be compelled to choose between us and what have I to offer? Nothing but an elevating influence.

"Bah! what is the use of an elevating influence if one hasn't bread and butter. Her possible want of butter if not of bread, considering her dubious relations with her family must be kept in mind. Mabel could and would always supply them and I neither can nor will. Alas for an unbuttered influence say I. What a grovelling human I am anyway. But I do have occasional sparkling glimpses of faith and those when they come I truly believe to be worth much bread and butter. Perhaps Helen also finds them more delectable. Well I will state the case to her and abide by her decision."

She timed her letter to arrive when Helen would be once more at home alone. "I can say to you now" she wrote "what I found impossible in the early summer. I am now convinced and I think you are too that my feeling for you is genuine and loyal and whatever may be our future difficulties we are now at least on a basis of understanding and trust. I know therefore that you will not misunderstand when I beg you to consider carefully whether on the whole you had not better give me up. I can really amount to so little for you and yet will inevitably cause you so much trouble. That I dread your giving me up I do not deny but I dread more being the cause of serious annoyance to you. Please believe that this statement is sincere and is to be taken quite literally."

"Hush little one" Helen answered "oh you stupid child, don't you realise that you are the only thing in the world that makes anything seem real or worth while to me. I have had a dreadful time this summer. Mabel read a letter of mine to you and it upset her completely. She said that she found it but I can hardly believe that. She asked me if you cared for me and I told her that I didn't know and I really don't dearest. She did not ask me if I cared for you. The thing upset her completely and she was jealous of my every thought and I could not find a moment even to feel alone with you. But don't please don't say any more about giving you up. You are not any trouble to me if you will only not leave me. It's alright now with Mabel, she says that she will never be jealous again." "Oh Lord!" groaned Adele "well if she isn't she would be a hopeless fool. Anyhow I said I would abide by Helen's decision and I certainly will but how so proud a woman can permit such control is more than I can understand."

Book 3:

Helen

1

THERE IS NO PASSION more dominant and instinctive in the human spirit than the need of the country to which one belongs. One often speaks of homesickness as if in its intense form it were the peculiar property of Swiss mountaineers, Scandinavians, Frenchmen and those other nations that too have a poetic background, but poetry is no element in the case. It is simply a vital need for the particular air that is native, whether it is the used up atmosphere of London, the clean-cut cold of America or the rarefied air of Swiss mountains. The time comes when nothing in the world is so important as a breath of one's own particular climate. If it were one's last penny it would be used for that return passage.

An American in the winter fogs of London can realise this passionate need, this desperate longing in all its completeness. The dead weight of that fog and smoke laden air, the sky that never suggests for a moment the clean blue distance that has been the accustomed daily comrade, the dreary sun, moon and stars that look like painted imitations on the ceiling of a smoke-filled room, the soggy, damp, miserable streets, and the women with bedraggled, frayed-out skirts, their faces swollen and pimply with sordid dirt ground into them until it has become a natural part of their ugly surface all become day after day a more dreary weight of hopeless oppression.[1]

A hopeful spirit resists. It feels that it must be better soon, it cannot last so forever; this afternoon, to-morrow this dead weight must lift, one must soon again realise a breath of clean air, but day after day the whole weight of fog, smoke and low brutal humanity rests a weary load on the head and back and one loses the power of straightening the body to actively bear the burden, it becomes simply a despairing endurance.

Just escaped from this oppression, Adele stood in the saloon of an ocean steamer looking at the white snow line of New York harbor. A little girl one of a family who had also fled from England after a six months trial, stood next to her. They stayed side by side their faces close to the glass. A government ship passed flying the flag. The little girl looked deeply at it and then with slow intensity said quite to herself, "There is the American flag, it looks good." Adele echoed it, there was all America and it looked good; the clean sky and the white snow and the straight plain ungainly buildings all in a cold and brilliant air without spot or stain.

Adele's return had been unexpected and she landed quite alone. "No it wasn't to see you much as I wanted you," she explained to Helen long afterwards, "it was just plain America. I landed quite alone as I had not had time to let any of my friends know of my arrival but I really wasn't in a hurry to go to them much as I had longed for them all. I simply rejoiced in the New York streets, in the long spindling legs of the elevated, in the straight high undecorated houses, in the empty upper air and in the white surface of the snow. It was such a joy to realise that the whole thing was without mystery and without complexity, that it was clean and straight and meagre

1. Stein was extremely depressed during her stay in London in 1902; here she projects that depression onto London itself.

and hard and white and high. Much as I wanted you I was not eager for after all you meant to me a turgid and complex world, difficult yet necessary to understand and for the moment I wanted to escape all that, I longed only for obvious, superficial, clean simplicity."

Obeying this need Adele after a week of New York went to Boston. She steeped herself in the very essence of clear eyed Americanism. For days she wandered about the Boston streets rejoicing in the passionless intelligence of the faces. She revelled in the American streetcar crowd with its ready intercourse, free comments and airy persiflage all without double meanings which created an atmosphere that never suggested for a moment the need to be on guard.

It was a cleanliness that began far inside of these people and was kept persistently washed by a constant current of clean cold water. Perhaps the weight of stains necessary to the deepest understanding might be washed away, it might well be that it was not earthy enough to be completely satisfying, but it was a delicious draught to a throat choked with soot and fog.

For a month Adele bathed herself in this cleanliness and then she returned to New York eager again for a world of greater complexity.

For some time after her return a certain estrangement existed between Helen and herself. Helen had been much hurt at her long voluntary absence and Adele as yet did not sufficiently understand her own motives to be able to explain. It had seemed to her only that she rather dreaded losing herself again with Helen.

This feeling between them gradually disappeared. In their long sessions in Helen's room, Adele now too cultivated the habit of silent intimacy. As time went on her fear of Helen and of herself gradually died away and she yielded herself to the complete joy of simply being together.

One day they agreed between them that they were very near the state of perfect happiness. "Yes I guess it's alright" Adele said with a fond laugh "and when it's alright it certainly is very good. Am I not a promising pupil?" she asked. "Not nearly so good a pupil as so excellent a teacher as I am deserves" Helen replied. "Oh! Oh!" cried Adele, "I never realised it before but compared with you I am a model of humility. There is nothing like meeting with real arrogance. It makes one recognise a hitherto hidden virtue," and then they once more lost themselves in happiness.

It was a very real oblivion. Adele was aroused from it by a kiss that seemed to scale the very walls of chastity. She flung away on the instant filled with battle and revulsion. Utterly regardless of Helen she lay her face buried in her hands. "I never dreamed that after all that has come I was still such a virgin soul" she said to herself, "and that like Parsifal a kiss could make me frantic with realisation" and then she lost herself in the full tide of her fierce disgust.

She lay long in this new oblivion. At last she turned. Helen lay very still but on her face were bitter tears. Adele with her usual reaction of repentance tried to comfort. "Forgive me!" she said "I don't know what possessed me. No you didn't do anything it was all my fault." "And we were so happy" Helen said. After a long silence she asked "Was it that you felt your old distrust of me again?" "Yes," replied Adele briefly. "I am afraid I can't forgive this," Helen said. "I didn't suppose that you could," Adele replied.

They continued to meet but each one was filled with her own struggle. Adele finally reopened the subject. "You see" she explained "my whole trouble lies in the fact that I don't know on what ground I am objecting, whether it is morality or a meaingless instinct. You know I have always had a conviction that no amount of reasoning will help in deciding what is right and possible for one to do. If you don't begin with some theory of obligation, anything is possible and no rule of right and wrong holds. One must either accept some theory or else believe one's instinct or follow the world's opinion.

"Now I have no theory and much as I would like to, I can't really regard the world's opinion. As for my instincts they have always been opposed to the indulgence of any feeling of passion. I suppose that is due to the Calvinistic influence that dominates American training and has interfered with my natural temperament. Somehow you have made me realise that my attitude in the matter was degrading and material, instead of moral and spiritual but in spite of you my puritan instincts again and again say no and I get into a horrible mess. I am beginning to distrust my instincts and I am about convinced that my objection was not a deeply moral one. I suppose after all it was a good deal cowardice. Anyhow" she concluded, "I guess I haven't any moral objection any more and now if I have lost my instincts it will be alright and we can begin a new deal." "I am afraid I can't help you much" Helen answered "I can only hold by the fact that whatever you do and however much you hurt me I seem to have faith in you, in spite of yourself." Adele groaned. "How hopelessly inadequate I am," she said.

This completeness of revulsion never occurred again, but a new opposition gradually arose between them. Adele realised that Helen demanded of her a response and always before that response was ready. Their pulses were differently timed.[2] She could not go so fast and Helen's exhausted nerves could no longer wait. Adele found herself constantly forced on by Helen's pain. She went farther than she could in honesty because she was unable to refuse anything to one who had given all. It was a false position. All reactions had now to

2. This is both an explicit sexual reference and also a more general comment about the temperamental incompatibility of the two women.

be concealed as it was evident that Helen could no longer support that struggle. Their old openness was no longer possible and Adele ceased to express herself freely.

She realised that her attitude was misunderstood and that Helen interpreted her slowness as essential deficiency. This was the inevitable result of a situation in which she was forced constantly ahead of herself. She was sore and uneasy and the greater her affection for Helen became the more irritable became her discontent.

One evening they had agreed to meet at a restaurant and dine before going to Helen's room. Adele arriving a half hour late found Helen in a state of great excitement. "Why what's the matter?" Adele asked. "Matter" Helen repeated "you kept me waiting for you and a man came in and spoke to me and it's the first time that I have ever been so insulted." Adele gazed at her in astonishment. "Great guns!" she exclaimed "what do you expect if you go out alone at night. You must be willing to accept the consequences. The men are quite within their rights." "Their rights! They have no right to insult me." Adele shook her head in slow wonderment. "Will we ever understand each other's point of view," she said. "A thing that seems to unworldly, unheroic me so simple and inevitable and which I face quietly a score of times seems to utterly unnerve you while on the other hand,—but then we won't go into that, have something to eat and you will feel more cheerful."

"If you had been much later," Helen said as they were walking home, "I would have left and never have had anything farther to do with you until you apologised." "Bah!" exclaimed Adele. "I haven't any objection to apologising, the only thing I object to is being in the wrong. You are quite like a storybook" she continued, "you still believe in the divine right of heroics and of ladies. You think there is some higher power that makes the lower world tremble, when you say, 'Man how dare you!' That's all very well when the other man wants to be scared but when he doesn't it's the strongest man that wins."

They had been together for some time in the room, when Helen broke the silence. "I wonder," she said, "why I am doomed always to care for people who are so hopelessly inadequate." Adele looked at her a few moments and then wandered about the room. She returned to her seat, her face very still and set. "Oh! I didn't mean anything" said Helen, "I was only thinking about it all." Adele made no reply. "I think you might be patient with me when I am nervous and tired" Helen continued petulantly "and not be angry at everything I say." "I could be patient enough if I didn't think that you really meant what you have said," Adele answered. "I don't care what you say, the trouble is that you do believe it." "But you have said it yourself again and again" Helen complained. "That is perfectly true" returned

Adele "but it is right for me to say it and to believe it too, but not for you. If you believe it, it puts a different face on the whole matter. It makes the situation intolerable." They were silent, Helen nervous and uneasy, and Adele rigid and quiet. "Oh why can't you forget it?" Helen cried at last. Adele roused herself. "It's alright" she said "don't bother. You are all tired out, come lie down and go to sleep." She remained with her a little while and then went into another room to read. She was roused from an unpleasant revery by Helen's sudden entrance. "I had such a horrible dream" she said "I thought that you were angry and had left me never to come back. Don't go away, please stay with me."

"You haven't forgiven me yet?" Helen asked the next morning as Adele was about to leave her. "It isn't a question of forgiveness, it's a question of your feeling," Adele replied steadily. "You have given no indication as yet that you did not believe what you said last night." "I don't know what I said," Helen evaded "I am worried and pestered and bothered and you just make everything harder for me and then accuse me of saying things that I shouldn't. Well perhaps I shouldn't have said it." "But nevertheless you believe it," Adele returned stubbornly. "Oh I don't know what I believe. I am so torn and bothered, can't you leave me alone?" "You have no right to constantly use your pain as a weapon!" Adele flashed out angrily. "What do you mean by that?" Helen demanded. "I mean that you force me on by your pain and then hold me responsible for the whole business. I am willing to stand for my own trouble but I will not endure the whole responsibility of yours." "Well aren't you responsible?" asked Helen, "have I done anything but be passive while you did as you pleased? I have been willing to endure it all, but I have not taken one step to hold you." Adele stared at her. "So that's your version of the situation is it? Oh well then there is no use in saying another word." She started to go and then stood irresolutely by the door. Helen dropped her head on her arms. Adele returned and remained looking down at her stubborn and unhappy. "Oh I shall go mad," Helen moaned. Adele stood motionless. Helen's hand dropped and Adele kneeling beside her took her into her arms with intense fondness, but they both realised that neither of them had yielded.

They were each too fond of the other ever to venture on an ultimatum for they realised that they would not be constant to it. The question of relative values and responsibilities was not again openly discussed between them. Subtly perhaps unconsciously but nevertheless persistently Helen now threw the burden of choice upon Adele. Just how it came about she never quite realised but inevitably now it was always Adele that had to begin and had to ask for the next meeting. Helen's attitude became that of one anxious to give all but unfortunately prevented by time and circumstances. Adele was sure that it was not that Helen had ceased to care but that intentionally or not she was nevertheless taking full advantage of the fact that Adele now cared equally as much.

Adele chafed under this new dispensation but nevertheless realised that it was no more than justice. In fact her submission went deeper. On the night of their quarrel she had realised for the first time Helen's understanding of what their relations had been and she now spent many weary nights in endeavoring to decide whether that interpretation was just and if she really was to that degree responsible. As time went on she became hopelessly confused and unhappy about the whole matter.

One night she was lying on her bed gloomy and disconsolate. Suddenly she burst out, "No I am not a cad. Helen has come very near to persuading me that I am but I really am not. We both went into this with our eyes open, and Helen fully as deliberately as myself. I never intentionally made her suffer however much she may think I did. No if one goes in, one must be willing to stand for the whole game and take the full responsibility of their own share."

"You know I don't understand your attitude at all," Adele said to Helen the next day. "I am thinking of your indignation at those men speaking to you that night when we had the quarrel. It seems to me one must be prepared to stand not only the actual results of one's acts but also all the implications of them. People of your heroic kind consider yourselves heroes when you are doing no more than the rest of us who look upon it only as humbly submitting to inevitable necessity." "What do you mean?" asked Helen. "Why simply that when one goes out of bounds one has no claim to righteous indignation if one is caught." "That depends somewhat on the method of going," answered Helen, "one can go out of bounds in such a manner that one's right must be respected." "One's right to do wrong?" Adele asked. "No for when it is done so it isn't wrong. You have not yet learned that things are not separated by such hard and fast lines, but I understand your meaning. You object because I have stopped enduring everything from you. You have no understanding of all that I have forgiven." "I have said it in fun and now I say it in earnest," Adele answered angrily "you are too hopelessly arrogant. Are you the only one that has had to endure and forgive?" "Oh yes I suppose that you think that you too have made serious sacrifices but I tell you that I never realised what complete scorn I was capable of feeling as that night when I kissed you and you flung me off in that fashion because you didn't know what it was that you wanted." "You are intolerable" Adele answered fiercely, "I at least realise that I am not always in the right, but you, you are incapable of understanding anything except your own point of view, or realising even distantly the value of a humility which acknowledges an error." "Humility" Helen repeated, "that is a strange claim for you to make for yourself." "May be," Adele answered "all things are relative. I never realised my virtue until it was brought out by contrast." "Oh I could be humble too," Helen retorted "if I could see any one who had made good a superior claim, but that hasn't come yet." "No, and with your native blindness it isn't likely that it ever will, that's quite true." "No it isn't blindness, it's because I understand values before I act on them. Oh yes I know you are generous enough after you have gone home and have had time to think it over, but it's the generosity of instinctive acts that counts and as to that I don't think there is much doubt as to who is the better man." "As you will!" cried Adele bursting violently from her chair with a thundering imprecation and then with the same movement and a feeling of infinite tenderness and sorrow she took Helen into her arms and kissed her. "What a great goose you are," said Helen fondly. "Oh yes I know it" Adele answered drearily, "but it's no use I can't remain angry even for one long moment. Repentance comes too swiftly but nevertheless I have a hopelessly persistent mind and after the pressure is removed I return to the old refrain. Dear don't forget, you really are in the wrong."

In spite of this outburst of reconciliation, things did not really improve between them. Helen still pursued her method of granting in inverse ratio to the strength of Adele's desire, and Adele's unhappiness and inward resistance grew steadily with the increase of her affection.

Before long the old problem of Mabel's claims further complicated the situation. "I am going abroad this summer again with Mabel," Helen said one day. Adele made no comment but the question "At whose expense?" was insistently in her mind.

In spite of the conviction that she owed Mabel nothing, she had had an uneasy sense concerning her during the whole winter. She had avoided going to Boston again as she did not wish to see her. She realised a sense of shame at the thought of meeting her. In spite of the clearness of her reasoning, she could not get rid of the feeling that she had stolen the property of another.

On the few occasions when the matter was spoken of between them, Helen while claiming her right to act as she pleased, admitted the validity of Mabel's claim. She declared repeatedly that in the extreme case if she had to give up some one it would be Adele and not Mabel, as Mabel would be unable to endure it, and Adele and herself were strong enough to support such a trial.

Just how Helen reconciled these conflicting convictions, Adele did not understand but as her own reconcilements were far from convincing to herself, she could ask for no explanations of the other's conscience. This statement of a foreign trip, probably at Mabel's expense made her once more face the situation. She had a strong sense of the sanctity of money obligations. She recognised as paramount the necessary return for value received in all cash considerations. Perhaps Helen had her own money but of this Adele was exceedingly doubtful.[3] She wanted badly to know but she admitted to herself that this question she dared not ask.

The recognition of Helen's willingness to accept this of Mabel brought her some comfort. She lost her own sense of shame toward Mabel. "After all" she thought, "I haven't really robbed her of anything. She will win out eventually so I can meet her with a clearer conscience." She then told Helen that she intended going to Boston for a week before her return to Europe. Helen said nothing but it was evident that she did not wish her to go.

In this last month together there was less openness and confidence between them than at any time in their whole relation. Helen seemed content and indifferent but yet persisted always in answer to any statement of doubt from Adele that she was quite unchanged. Adele felt that her own distrust, stubbornness and affection were all steadily increasing. She deeply resented Helen's present attitude which was that of one granting all and more than all to a discontented petitioner. She felt Helen's continued statement of the sacrifices that she was making and even then the impossibility of satisfying her as both untruthful and insulting, but the conditions between them had become such that no explanations were possible.

Helen's attitude was now a triumph of passivity. Adele was forced to accept it with what grace she might. Her only consolation lay in the satisfaction to her pride in realising Helen's inadequacy in a real trial of generosity. When together now they seemed quite to have changed places. Helen was irritating and unsatisfying, Adele patient and forbearing.

"I wonder if we will see each other in Italy" Adele said one day. "I certainly very much hope so" answered Helen. "It is only a little over a week and then I go to Boston and then I will be in New York only a few days before I sail," continued Adele, "when will I see you?" "On Monday evening" suggested Helen. "Good" agreed Adele.

On Monday morning Adele received a note from Helen explaining that the arrival of a friend made it impossible for her to see her alone before the end of the week but she would be glad if she would join them at lunch. Adele was deeply hurt and filled with bitter resentment. She understood Helen's intention whether conscious or not

3. The clear implication here is that Helen stays with Mabel because Mabel is supporting her financially, or "keeping" her.

in this delay. The realisation that in order to accomplish her ends Helen would not hesitate to cause her any amount of pain gave her a sense of sick despondency. She wrote a brief note saying that she did not think her presence at this lunch would tend greatly to the gayety of nations but that she would be at home in the evening if Helen cared to come. She got a hurried reply full of urgent protest but still holding to the original plan. "I guess this is the end of the story," Adele said to herself.

"The situation seems utterly hopeless" she wrote, "we are more completely unsympathetic and understand each other less than at any time in our whole acquaintance. It may be my fault but nevertheless I find your attitude intolerable. You need feel no uneasiness about my going to Boston. I will not cause any trouble and as for the past I realise that as a matter of fact I have in no way interfered as you both still have all that is really vital to you."

"I guess that settles it," she said drearily as she dropped the letter into the mail-box. Helen made no sign. The days passed very quickly for Adele. All her actual consciousness found the definite ending of the situation a great relief. As long as one is firmly grasping the nettles there is no sting. The bitter pain begins when the hold begins to relax. At the actual moment of a calamity the undercurrents of pain, repentance and vain regret are buried deep under the ruins of the falling buildings and it is only when the whole mass begins to settle that they begin to well up here and there and at last rush out in an overwhelming flood of bitter pain. Adele in these first days that passed so quickly was peaceful and almost content. It was almost the end of the week when walking down town one day she saw Helen in the distance. It gave her a sudden shock and at first she was dazed but not moved by it, but gradually she became entirely possessed by the passion of her own longing and the pity of Helen's possible pain. Without giving herself time for consideration she wrote to her and told her that having seen her she had realised the intensity of her own affection but that she did not feel that she had been in the wrong either in feeling or expressing resentment but that if Helen cared to come, she would be at home in the morning to see her. "Certainly I will come," Helen answered.

When they met they tried to cover their embarrassment with commonplaces. Suddenly Adele frankly gave it up and went to the window and stared bravely out at the trees. Helen left standing in the room fought it out, finally she yielded and came to the window.

There was no ardor in their reconciliation, they had both wandered too far. Gradually they came together more freely but even then there was no openness of explanation between them. "As long as you have a soreness within that you don't express, nothing can be right between us," Helen said but to this appeal Adele could not make an open answer. There were things in her mind which she knew absolutely that Helen would not endure to hear spoken and so they could meet in mutual fondness but not in mutual honesty.

"Your letter upset me rather badly," Helen said some hours later. "In fact I am rather afraid I fainted." "But you would not have said a word to me, no matter how much you knew I longed for it?" Adele asked. "No" answered Helen "how could I?" "We are both proud women," Adele said "but mine doesn't take that form. As long as I thought there was a possibility of your caring, no amount of pain or humiliation would keep me from coming to you. But you do realise don't you," she asked earnestly "that however badly I may behave or whatever I may say or do my devotion and loyalty to you are absolute?" "Yes" answered Helen "I know it. I have learned my lesson too and I do trust you always." They both realised this clearly, Adele had learned to love and Helen to trust but still there was no real peace between them.

"Don't worry about me, I won't get into any trouble in Boston" Adele said cheerily as they parted. "You come back on Sunday?" Helen asked. "Yes and will see you Sunday evening and then only a few days and then I will be on the ocean. Unless we Marconi to each other we will then for some little time be unable to get into difficulties."

From Boston Adele wrote a letter to Helen full of nonsense and affection. She received just before her return a curt and distant answer.

"Well now what's gone wrong" she said impatiently, "will there never be any peace?"

When she arrived at Helen's room Sunday evening, Helen had not yet returned. She sat down and waited impatiently. Helen came in after a while radiant and cordial but very unfamiliar. Adele quietly watched her. Helen moved about and talked constantly. Adele was unresponsive and looked at her quite stolidly. At last Helen became quiet. Adele looked at her some time longer and then laughed. "Aren't you ashamed of yourself?" she asked. Helen made an effort to be heroic but failed. "Yes I am" she admitted "but your letter was so cocky and you had caused me so much trouble that I couldn't resist that temptation. There yes I am ashamed but it comes hard for me to say it." Adele laughed joyously. "Well it's the first and probably the last time in your history that you have ever realised your wrong-doing so let's celebrate" and there was peace between them.

It was not however a peace of long duration for soon it had all come back. Helen was once more inscrutable and Adele resentful and unhappy.

Adele was to sail on the next day and they were spending this last morning together. Adele was bitterly unhappy at the uncertainty of it all and Helen quite peaceful and content. Adele to conceal her feelings wandered up to a bookcase and began to read. She stuck to it resolutely until Helen, annoyed, came up to her. "Pshaw" she said "why do you spend our last morning together in this fashion?" "Because I am considerably unhappy," Adele replied. "Well you had better do as I do, wait to be unhappy until after you are gone," Helen answered. Adele remembered their parting a year ago when Helen's point of view had been different. "I might reply" she began, "but then I guess I won't" she added. "That I won't be unhappy even then, were you going to say?" Helen asked. "No I wasn't going to be quite as obvious as that," Adele answered and then wandered disconsolately about the room. She came back finally and sat on the arm of Helen's chair but held herself drearily aloof. "Why do you draw away from me, when you are unhappy?" Helen finally burst out. "Don't you trust me at all?"

A little later Adele was about to leave. They were standing at the door looking intently at each other. "Do you really care for me any more?" Adele asked at last. Helen was angry and her arms dropped. "You are impossible" she answered. "I have never before in my life ever given anybody more than one chance, and you, you have had seventy times seven and are no better than at first." She kissed her resignedly. "You have succeeded in killing me" she said drearily, "and now you are doing your best to kill yourself. Good-by I will come to see you this evening for a little while."

In the evening they began to discuss a possible meeting in Italy. "If I meet you there" Adele explained "I must do it deliberately for in the natural course of things I would be in France as my brother does not intend going South this summer. It's a question that you absolutely must decide. There is no reason why I should not come except only as it would please or displease you. As for Mabel she knows that I am fond of you and so it isn't necessary for me to conceal my emotions. It is only a question of you and your desires. You can't leave it to me" she concluded, "for you know, I have no power of resisting temptation, but I am strong enough to do as you say, so you must settle it." "I can certainly conceal my emotions so it would be perfectly safe even if you can't," answered Helen. "I am afraid though I haven't any more power of resisting temptation than you but I will think it over." Just as they parted Helen decided. "I think dear that you had better come" she said. "Alright" answered Adele.

2

There was nothing to distinguish Mabel Neathe and Helen Thomas from the average American woman tourist as they walked down the

Via Nazionale.[4] Their shirt-waists[5] trimly pinned down, their veils depending in graceless folds from their hats, the little bags with the steel chain firmly grasped in the left hand, the straightness of their backs and the determination of their observation all marked them an integral part of that national sisterhood which shows a more uncompromising family likeness than a continental group of sisters with all their dresses made exactly alike.

This general American sisterhood has a deeper conformity than the specific European, because in the American it is a conformity from within out. They all look alike not because they want to or because they are forced to do it, but simply because they lack individual imagination.

The European sisterhood conform to a common standard for economy or because it is a tradition to which they must submit but there is always the pathetic attempt to assert individual feeling in the difference of embroidery on a collar, or in a variation in tying of a bow and sometimes in the very daring by a different flower in the hat.

These two Americans then were like all the others. There was the same want of abundant life, the same inwardly compelled restrained movement, which kept them aloof from the life about them and the same intensely serious but unenthusiastic interest in the things to be observed. It was the walking of a dutiful purpose full of the necessity of observing many things among an alien mass of earthy spontaneity whose ideal expression is enthusiasm.

Behind them out of a side street came a young woman, the cut of whose shirt-waist alone betrayed her American origin. Large, abundant, full-busted and joyous, she seemed a part of the rich Roman life. She moved happily along, her white Panama hat well back on her head and an answering smile on her face as she caught the amused glances that fell upon her. Seeing the two in front she broke into a run, clapped them on the shoulder and as they turned with a start, she gave the national greeting "Hullo."

"Why Adele" exclaimed Helen, "where did you come from? You look as brown and white and clean as if you had just sprung out of the sea." With that they all walked on together. Adele kept up a lively talk with Mabel until they came to the pilgrimage church of the Santa Maria Maggiore. In the shelter of that great friendly hall she exchanged a word with Helen. "How are things going?" she asked. "Very badly" Helen replied.

They wandered about all together for a while and then they agreed to take a drive out into the Campagna.[6] They were all keenly con-

---

4. Fashionable street in Rome, in the Piazza di Spagna—the "Spanish Steps."
5. Blouses; a particularly American fashion for women.
6. Countryside near Rome.

scious of the fact that this combination of themselves all together was most undesirable but this feeling was covered by an enthusiastic and almost convincing friendly spontaneity, and indeed the spontaneity and the friendliness were not forced or hypocritical for if it had not been that they all wanted something else so much more they would have had great enjoyment in what they had. As it was the friendliness was almost enough to give a substantial basis to many moments of their companionship.

They spent that day together and then the next and by that time the tension of this false position began to tell on all of them.

The burden of constant entertainment and continual peace-keeping began to exhaust Adele's good-nature, and she was beginning to occasionally show signs of impatient boredom. Mabel at first accepted eagerly enough all the entertainment offered her by Adele but gradually there came a change. Helen was constantly depressed and silent and Adele wishing to give her time to recover devoted herself constantly to Mabel's amusement. This seemed to suggest to Mabel for the first time that Adele's devotion was not only accepted but fully returned. This realisation grew steadily in her mind. She now ceased to observe Adele and instead kept constant and insistent watch on Helen. She grew irritable and almost insolent. She had never before in their triple intercourse resented Adele's presence but she began now very definitely to do so.

On the evening of their second day together Helen and Adele had a half hour's stroll alone. "Things do seem to be going badly, what's the trouble?" Adele asked. "I don't know exactly why but this summer Mabel is more jealous than ever before. It isn't only you" she hastened to explain, "it is the same with everybody in whom I am ever so slightly interested. As for you nothing can induce her to believe that you came here simply because you had never been here before and wanted to see Rome. She positively refused to read your letter to me which I wanted to show her." Adele laughed. "How you do keep it up!" she said. "What do you expect? Mabel would be a fool if she believed anything but the truth for after all I could have struggled along without Rome for another year." After a while Adele began again. "I don't want you to have me at all on your mind. I am fully able to take care of myself. If you think it will be better if I clear out I will go." "No" said Helen wearily "that would not help matters now." "I owe you so much for all that you have taught me," Adele went on earnestly "and my faith in you is now absolute. As long as you give me that nothing else counts." "You are very generous" murmured Helen. "No it's not generosity" Adele insisted "it's nothing but justice for really you do mean very much to me. You do believe that." "Yes I believe it," Helen answered.

Adele fulfilled very well the duty that devolved upon her that of keeping the whole thing moving but it was a severe strain to be always enlivening and yet always on guard. One morning she began one of her old time lively disputes with Helen who soon became roused and interested. In the midst Mabel got up and markedly left them. Helen stopped her talk. "This won't do," she said "we must be more careful," and for the rest of the day she exerted herself to cajole, flatter and soothe Mabel back to quiescence.

"Why in the name of all that is wonderful should we both be toadying to Mabel in this fashion?" Adele said to herself disgustedly. "What is it anyway that Helen wants? If it's the convenience of owning Mabel, Jupiter,[7] she comes high. Helen doesn't love her and if she were actuated by pure kindness and duty and she really wanted to spare her she would tell me to leave. And as for Mabel it is increasing all her native hypocrisy and underhand hatreds and selfishness and surely she is already overly endowed with these qualities. As for me the case is simple enough. I owe Mabel nothing but I want Helen and Helen wants me to do this. It certainly does come high." She was disgusted and exasperated and kept aloof from them for a while. Helen upon this grew restless. She instinctively endeavored to re-stimulate Adele by accidental momentary contacts, by inflections of voice and shades of manner, by all delicate charged signs such as had for some time been definitely banished between them.

"What a condemned little prostitute it is," Adele said to herself between a laugh and a groan. "I know there is no use in asking for an explanation. Like Kate Croy[8] she would tell me 'I shall sacrifice nothing and nobody' and that's just her situation, she wants and will try for everything, and hang it all, I am so fond of her and do somehow so much believe in her that I am willing to help as far as within me lies. Besides I certainly get very much interested in the mere working of the machinery. Bah! it would be hopelessly unpleasant if it didn't have so many compensations."

The next morning she found herself in very low spirits. "I suppose the trouble with me is that I am sad with longing and sick with desire," she said to herself drearily and then went out to meet the others.

Helen on that day seemed even more than ever worn and tired and she even admitted to not feeling very well. Adele in spite of all her efforts continued irritable and depressed. Mabel made no comments but was evidently observant. Adele's mood reacted on Helen whose eyes followed her about wearily and anxiously. "Helen" said Adele hurriedly in the shadow of a church corner. "Don't look at me

7. Supreme deity of ancient Rome; expletive in keeping with the Italian setting.
8. Selfish, hypocritical character in Henry James's novel *The Wings of the Dove* (1902), which is set in Venice rather than Rome. Stein denied being influenced by Henry James, but it is clear that she was; she did not deny the enormous influence of his brother William, with whom she studied at Harvard.

like that, you utterly unnerve me and I won't be able to keep it up. I am alright, just take care of yourself."

"I wonder whether Helen has lost her old power of control or whether the difference lies in me" she said to herself later. "Perhaps it is that I have learned to read more clearly the small variations in her looks and manner. I am afraid though it isn't that. I think she is really becoming worn out. There would be no use in my going away now for then Mabel would be equally incessant as she was last summer. Now at least I can manage Helen a little time to herself by employing Mabel. Good Heavens she is certainly paying a big price for her whistle."

The situation did not improve. Helen became constantly more and more depressed and Adele found it always more and more difficult to keep it all going. She yearned over Helen with passionate tenderness but dared not express it. She recognised that nothing would be more complete evidence for Mabel than such signs of Helen's dependence, so she was compelled to content herself with brief passionate statements of love, sympathy and trust in those very occasional moments when they were alone. Helen had lost the power of quickly recovering and so even these rare moments could only be sparingly used.

One afternoon they were all three lounging in Helen's and Mabel's room taking the usual afternoon siesta. Adele was lying on the bed looking vacantly out of the window at the blue sky filled with warm sunshine. Mabel was on a couch in a darkened corner and Helen was near her sitting at a table. Adele's eyes after a while came back into the room. Helen was sitting quietly but unconsciously her eyes turned toward Adele as if looking for help and comfort.

Adele saw Mabel's eyes grow large and absorbent. They took in all of Helen's weariness, her look of longing and all the meanings of it all. The drama of the eyes was so complete that for the moment Adele lost herself in the spectacle.

Helen was not conscious that there had been any betrayal and Adele did not enlighten her. She realised that such consciousness would still farther weaken her power of control.

On the next day Mabel decided that they should leave Rome the following day and on that evening Helen and Adele managed a farewell talk.

"I suppose it would be better if we did not meet again" Adele said "but somehow I don't like the thought of that. Well anyhow I must be in Florence and in Sienna as that is the arrangement that I have made with Hortense Block, and I will let you know full particulars, and then we will let it work itself out." "Yes it's all very unhappy" answered Helen "but I suppose I would rather see you than not." Adele laughed drearily and then stood looking at her and her mind filled as always with its eternal doubt. "But you do care for me?" she broke out abruptly; "you know" she added "somehow I never can believe that since I have learned to care for you." "I don't care for you passionately any more, I am afraid you have killed all that in me as you know, but I never wanted you so much before and I have learned to trust you and depend upon you." Adele was silent, this statement hurt her more keenly than she cared to show. "Alright" she said at last "I must accept what you are able to give and even then I am hopelessly in your debt." After a while she began again almost timidly. "Must you really do for Mabel all that you are doing?" she asked. "Must you submit yourself so? I hate to speak of it to you but it does seem such a hopeless evil for you both." Helen made no reply. "I do love you very much" Adele said at last. "I know it" murmured Helen.

In the week that Adele now spent wandering alone about Rome, in spite of the insistent pain of the recent separation, she was possessed of a great serenity. She felt that now at last she and Helen had met as equals. She was no longer in the position, that she had so long resented, that of an unworthy recipient receiving a great bounty. She had proved herself capable of patience, endurance and forbearance. She had shown herself strong enough to realise power and yet be generous and all this gave her a sense of peace and contentment in the very midst of her keen sorrow and hopeless perplexity.

She abandoned herself now completely to the ugly, barren sunburned desolation of mid-summer Rome. Her mood of loneliness and bitter sorrow mingled with a sense of recovered dignity and strength found deep contentment in the big desert spaces, in the huge ugly dignified buildings and in the great friendly church halls.

It was several weeks before they met again and in that time the exaltation of her Roman mood had worn itself out and Adele found herself restless and unhappy. She had endeavored to lose her melancholy and perplexity by endless tramping over the Luccan[9] hills but had succeeded only in becoming more lonely sick and feverish.

Before leaving Rome she had written a note stating exactly at what time she was to be in Florence and in Sienna so that if Mabel desired and Helen were willing they might avoid her.

She came to Florence and while waiting for a friend with whom she was to walk to Sienna, she wandered disconsolately about the streets endeavoring to propitiate the gods by forcing herself to expect the worst but finding it difficult to discover what that worst would be whether a meeting or an absence.

One day she was as usual indulging in this dismal self-mockery.

9. Lucca province, in Tuscany, Italy, is a fertile river valley surrounded by hills.

She went into a restaurant for lunch and there unexpectedly found Mabel and Helen. Adele gave a curt "Hullo, where did you come from?" and then sat weary and disconsolate. The others gave no sign of surprise. "Why you look badly, what's the matter with you?" Mabel asked. "Oh I am sick and I've got fever and malaise that's all. I suppose I caught a cold in the Luccan hills," Adele answered indifferently, and then she relapsed into a blank silence. They parted after lunch. "When will we see you again?" Mabel asked. "Oh I'll come around this evening after dinner for a while," answered Adele and left them.

"It's no joke," she said dismally to herself "I am a whole lot sick, and as for Helen she seems less successfully than ever to support the strain, while Mabel is apparently taking command of the situation. Well the game begins again tonight" and she went home to gather strength for it.

That evening there was neither more nor less constraint among them than before but it was evident that in this interval the relative positions had somewhat changed. Helen had less control than ever of the situation. Adele's domination was on the wane and Mabel was becoming the controlling power.

When Adele left Helen accompanied her downstairs. She realised as Helen kissed her that they had not been as discreet as usual in their choice of position for they stood just under a bright electric light. She said nothing to Helen but as she was going home she reflected that if Mabel had the courage to attack she would this evening from her window have seen this and be able to urge it as a legitimate grievance.

All the next day Adele avoided them but in the evening she again went to their room as had been agreed.

Mabel was now quite completely in possession and Helen as completely in abeyance. Adele disregarded them both and devoted herself to the delivery of a monologue on the disadvantages of foreign residence. As she arose to leave, Helen made no movement. "The fat is on the fire sure enough," she said to herself as she left.

The next day they met in a gallery and lunched together. Mabel was insistently domineering, Helen subservient and Adele disgusted and irritable. "Isn't Helen wonderfully good-natured" Mabel said to Adele as Helen returned from obeying one of her petulant commands. Adele looked at Helen and laughed. "That isn't exactly the word I should use," she said with open scorn.

Later in the day Helen found a moment to say to Adele, "Mabel saw us the other night and we had an awful scene. She said it was quite accidentally but I don't see how that can be." "What is the use of keeping up that farce, of course I knew all about it," Adele answered without looking at her.

The situation did not change. On the next day Helen showed an elaborate piece of antique jewelry that Mabel had just given her. Adele's eyes rested a moment on Helen and then she turned away filled with utter scorn and disgust. "Oh it's simply prostitution" she said to herself bitterly. "How a proud woman and Helen is a proud woman can yield such degrading submission and tell such abject lies for the sake of luxuries beats me. Seems to me I would rather starve or at least work for a living. Still one can't tell if one were hard driven. It's easy talking when you have everything you want and independence thrown in. I don't know if I were hard pressed I too might do it for a competence but it certainly comes high."

From now on Adele began to experience still lower depths of unhappiness. Her previous revulsions and perplexities were gentle compared to those that she now endured. Helen was growing more anxious as she saw Adele's sickness and depression increase but she dared not make any sign for Mabel was carrying things with a high hand.

On the afternoon of Adele's last day in Florence, Mabel and Helen came over to her room and while they were there Mabel left the room for a minute. Adele took Helen's hand and kissed it. "I am afraid I do still care for you" she said mournfully. "I know you do but I cannot understand why," Helen answered. "No more do I" and Adele smiled drearily, "but I simply don't seem to be able to help it. Not that I would even if I could" she hastened to add. "I am sorry I can't do more for you" Helen said, "but I find it impossible." "Oh you have no right to say that to me" Adele exclaimed angrily. "I have made no complaint and I have asked you for nothing and I want nothing of you except what you give me of your need and not because of mine," and she impatiently paced the room. Before anything further could be added Mabel had returned. Helen now looked so pale and faint that Mabel urged her to lie down and rest. Adele roused herself and suggested an errand to Mabel in such fashion that a refusal would have been an open confession of espionage and this Mabel was not willing to admit and so she departed.

Adele soothed Helen and after a bit they both wandered to the window and stood staring blankly into the street. "Yes" said Adele gravely and steadily "in spite of it all I still do believe in you and do still tremendously care for you." "I don't understand how you manage it" Helen answered. "Oh I don't mean that I find it possible to reconcile some of the things that you do even though I remember constantly that it is easy for those who have everything to condemn the errors of the less fortunate." "I don't blame your doubts" said Helen "I find it difficult to reconcile myself to my own actions, but how is it that you don't resent more the pain I am causing you?" "Dearest" Adele broke out vehemently "don't you see that that is why I used to be so angry with you because of your making so much of your endurance. There is no question of forgiveness. Pain doesn't count. Oh it's unpleasant enough and Heaven knows I hate and dread it but it isn't a thing to be remembered. It is only the loss of faith, the loss of joy that count."

In that succeeding week of steady tramping, glorious sunshine, free talk and simple comradeship, Adele felt all the cobwebs blow out of her heart and brain. While winding joyously up and down the beautiful Tuscan hills and swinging along the hot dusty roads all foulness and bitterness were burned away. She became once more the embodiment of joyous content. She realised that when Mabel and Helen arrived at Sienna it would all begin again and she resolved to take advantage of this clean interval to set herself in order. She tried to put the whole matter clearly and dispassionately before her mind.

It occurred to her now that it was perhaps some past money obligation which bound Helen to endure everything rather than force honesty into her relations with Mabel. She remembered that when she first began to know Helen she had heard something about a debt for a considerable sum of money which Helen had contracted. She remembered also that one day in Rome in answer to a statement of hers Helen had admitted that she knew Mabel was constantly growing more hypocritical and selfish but that she herself had never felt it for toward her in every respect Mabel had always been most generous.

Adele longed to ask Helen definitely whether this was the real cause of her submission but now as always she felt that Helen would not tolerate an open discussion of a practical matter.

To Adele this excuse was the only one that seemed valid for Helen's submission. For any reason except love or a debt contracted in the past such conduct was surely indefensible. There was no hope of finding out for Adele realised that she had not the courage to ask the question but in this possible explanation she found much comfort.

In the course of time Mabel and Helen arrived in Sienna and Adele found herself torn from the peaceful contemplation of old accomplishment to encounter the turgid complexity of present difficulties. She soon lost the health and joyousness of her week of peace and sunshine and became again restless and unhappy. The situation was absolutely unchanged. Mabel was still insolent in her power and Helen still humbly obedient. Adele found this spectacle too much for patient endurance and she resolved to attempt once more to speak to Helen about it.

The arranging of reasonably long periods of privacy was now comparatively easy as it was a party of four instead of a party of three.

One evening all four went out for a walk and soon this separation was effected. "You looked pretty well when we came but now you are all worn out again" Helen said as they stood looking over the walls of the fortress at the distant lights. Adele laughed. "What do you expect under the stimulation of your society?" she said. "But you know you used to object to my disagreeably youthful contentment. You ought to be satisfied now and you certainly don't look very blooming yourself.—No things haven't improved" Adele went on with visible effort, and then it came with a burst. "Dear don't you realise what a degrading situation you are putting both yourself and Mabel in by persisting in your present course? Can't you manage to get on some sort of an honest footing? Every day you are increasing her vices and creating new ones of your own." "I don't think that's quite true" Helen said coldly "I don't think your statement is quite fair." "I think it is," Adele answered curtly. They walked home together in silence. They arrived in the room before the others. Helen came up to Adele for a minute and then broke away. "Oh if she would only be happy" she moaned. "You are wrong, you are hideously wrong!" Adele burst out furiously and left her.

For some days Adele avoided her for she could not find it in her heart to endure this last episode. The cry "if she would only be happy" rang constantly in her ears. It expressed a recognition of Mabel's preeminent claim which Adele found it impossible to tolerate. It made plain to her that after all in the supreme moment Mabel was Helen's first thought and on such a basis she found herself unwilling to carry on the situation.

Finally Helen sought her out and a partial reconciliation took place between them.

From now on it was comparatively easy for them to be alone together for as the constraint between them grew, so Mabel's civility and generosity returned. Their intercourse in these interviews consisted in impersonal talk with long intervals of oppressive silences. "Won't you speak to me?" Adele exclaimed, crushed under the weight of one of these periods. "But I cannot think of anything to say," Helen answered gently.

"It is evident enough what happened that evening in Florence" Adele said to herself after a long succession of these uncomfortable interviews. "Helen not only denied loving me but she also promised in the future not to show me any affection and now when she does and when she doesn't she is equally ashamed, so this already hopeless situation is becoming well-nigh intolerable."

Things progressed in this fashion of steadily continuous discomfort. Helen preserved a persistent silence and Adele developed an increasing resentment toward that silence. Mabel grew always more civil and considerate and trustful. The day before their final parting Adele and Helen went together for a long walk. Their intercourse as was usual now consisted in a succession of oppressive silences.

Just as they were returning to the town Adele stopped abruptly and faced Helen. "Tell me" she said "do you really care for me any more?" "Do you suppose I would have stayed on here in Sienna if I didn't?" Helen answered angrily. "Won't you ever learn that it is facts that tell?" Adele laughed ruefully. "But you forget," she said, "that there are many facts and it isn't easy to know just what they tell." They walked on for a while and then Adele continued judicially, "No you are wrong in your theory of the whole duty of silence. I admit that I have talked too much but you on the other hand have not talked enough. You hide yourself behind your silences. I know you hate conclusions but that isn't a just attitude. Nothing is too good or holy for clear thinking and definite expression. You hate conclusions because you may be compelled to change them. You stultify yourself to any extent rather than admit that you too have been in the wrong."

"It doesn't really matter" Helen said that night of their final separation, "in what mood we part for sooner or later I know we are bound to feel together again." "I suppose so," answered Adele joylessly. Their last word was characteristic. "Good-by" said Adele "I do love you very much." "And I you" answered Helen "although I don't say so much about it."

For many weeks now there was no communication between them and Adele fought it out with her conscience her pain and her desire.

"I really hardly know what to say to you" she wrote at last. "I don't dare say what I think because I am afraid you might find that an impertinence and on the other hand I feel rather too bitterly toward you to write a simple friendly letter."

"Oh you know well enough what I want. I don't want you ever again to deny that you care for me. The thought of your doing it again takes all the sunshine out of the sky for me. Dear I almost wish sometimes that you did not trust me so completely because then I might have some influence with you for now as you know you have my faith quite absolutely and as that is to you abundantly satisfying I lose all power of coming near you."

Helen answered begging her not to destroy the effect of her patient endurance all the summer and assuring her that such conditions could not again arise.

Adele read the letter impatiently. "Hasn't she yet learned that things do happen and she isn't big enough to stave them off" she exclaimed. "Can't she see things as they are and not as she would make them if she were strong enough as she plainly isn't.

"I am afraid it comes very near being a dead-lock," she groaned dropping her head on her arms.

FINIS

Oct. 24, 1903

CONTEXTS

Biography

LINDA WAGNER-MARTIN

[Writing the Early Novels]†

Any separation between avant-garde art and literature in Paris early in the twentieth century is artificial. Friendships among the artists Picasso, Georges Braque, André Derain and writers Paul Fort, Paul Claudel, Pierre Mac Orlan, Alfred Jarry, André Salmon, Guillaume Apollinaire, Max Jacob, Paul Moréas, Maurice Cremnitz, Maurice Raynal, Blaise Cendrars, and others are evidence of the great reciprocity that existed between innovative painting and writing. In 1905 the advance man for the new arts, Guillaume Apollinaire, began publishing art criticism in *La Plume* and *Je Dis Tout* (he also wrote a gossip column, "La Vie anecdotique," for *Le Mercure de France*). Until his death from influenza in 1918, he was a clearinghouse of information for the worlds of both art and literature. Given his "Rabelasian" personality,[1] provocative and often comic, whether he was urging people to see exhibits or writing pornography, Apollinaire enacted in life the same kind of "surprise" he demanded[2] for art.

During 1903, after the demise of the literary magazine *Revue Blanche, La Plume* sponsored weekly poetry gatherings[3] to which came Apollinaire, Max Jacob, André Salmon, Alfred Jarry, Pierre Reverdy, Charles Vildrac, Georges Duhamel, and others. The Montmartre café Lapin Agile (the Dancing Rabbit) became the headquarters for these artists who shared admiration for Rimbaud and other symbolist poets, a blatant anticlericalism, and beliefs in occult powers. Maurice de Vlaminck and André Derain, former athletes, brought a less elite group of Parisians to another vortex of activity,

† From *"Favored Strangers:" Gertrude Stein and Her Family* (Piscataway: Rutgers UP, 1995), pp. 74–80, 282–83. Copyright © 1995 by Linda Wagner-Martin. Reprinted by permission of Rutgers University Press.
1. Cecily Mackworth, *Guillaume Apollinaire and the Cubist Life* (London: John Murray, 1961), 76.
2. Roger Shattuck, *The Banquet Years: The Arts in France, 1885–1918* (New York: Harcourt, Brace, 1958), p. 262; [Guillaume Apollinaire: French experimental poet who was a close friend of Stein's. He also used the word *abruptness* in *Selected Writings of Guillaume Apollinaire*, trans. Roger Shattuck (New York: New Directions, 1971), p. 237—Editor.]
3. Shattuck, 201–202.

Paul Fort's Tuesday night soirees at the Closerie des Lilas.[4] Fort believed in living life to the full; he planned special evenings to honor artists, and when the cafe closed at 2 A.M., he and Apollinaire, Picasso, Jacob, and others "nactambulised" through the streets till dawn. These forays—marked by sexual encounters of various kinds, drugs and alcohol, and fortune telling—resembled the adventures of the younger "Picasso gang." Fernande Olivier described these younger men as "frequently drunk, shouting and declaiming."[5] Noting that Picasso "always carried a Browning," she reported that his waking up the neighbors with revolver shots was not uncommon.

Once a week the artists—fascinated with the possibilities of moving images—went to the local cinema; other nights were spent at the circus, the Cirque Medrano. Friends with the clowns Footit and Chocolat and other performers, the men were attracted by the unconventional lifestyles and the mixture of daring and sorrow in the clowns' performances. The Steins sometimes went along. Gertrude recalled, "The clowns had commenced dressing up in misfit clothes instead of the old classic costume and these clothes later so well known on Charlie Chaplin were the delight of Picasso and all his friends."[6] As part of this attention to costuming, Picasso and Max Jacob searched Paris for what would appear to be laborers' clothes, buying sweaters in one of the city's most expensive wool shops. Leo and Gertrude's brown corduroy and strap sandals were also seen as costume.[7]

Picasso brought many of these artists and writers to Leo and Gertrude's salon; by early 1906 Gertrude knew them and liked their aesthetics, motivated as they were by the desire for fame rather than money.[8] However, seeing them in the cafés and entertaining them in the salon led the Steins to adopt distancing techniques: intimacy with people so bent on the unconventional could be dangerous. Issues of class also surfaced. As Matisse asked, when the Steins introduced him to Picasso, what did Gertrude, a woman of quality, have in common with such a man?[9] The sedate atmosphere of Sally and Mike's salon, which ended with late tea, was meant to curb guests' possible high spirits. In contrast, Gertrude, undisturbed by rowdiness, listed Picasso, Max Jacob, and Apollinaire as her favorites. She wrote about the last, "Nobody but Guillaume . . . could make fun of his hosts, make fun of their guests, make fun of their

4. Mackworth, 96.
5. Quoted in Nigel Gosling, *Paris 1900–1914: The Miraculous Years* (London: Weidenfeld and Nicolson, 1978), 72.
6. Stein, *The Autobiography of Alice B. Toklas* (New York: Random House, 1933), 51.
7. Guillaume Apollinaire, *Apollinaire on Art: Essays and Reviews, 1902–1918*, trans. Susan Suleiman, ed. Leroy G. Breunig (New York: Viking, 1960), 29.
8. Gosling, 80.
9. Stein, 65.

food and spur them to always greater and greater effort."[1] She also wrote Mabel Dodge that Apollinaire "is so suave you can never tell what he is doing."[2]

As for Max Jacob, he had an appealing history, something like Gertrude's own. He had first prepared for a career in foreign service and then finished a law degree without ever practicing law. Brilliantly interested in language and its function in society, he was "a compulsive punster,"[3] managing to introduce a surreal dimension into every conversation. One of his hobbies was classifying people into his own thirty-six astrologically defined categories, complete with files of detailed histories about them. Gertrude liked his manipulation of language, his sense of fun, and his irreverence for custom. She also liked his rapport with Picasso, who had been his best friend since 1903 when Picasso had drawn Max a comic strip in eight parts, "The Plain and Simple Story of Max Jacob and His Glory, or, Virtue's Reward."[4]

When Gertrude posed for a painting by Felix Vallotton in 1906, she added to the knowledge she had gained from posing for Picasso. She saw that the painters were working like their writer friends to incorporate fragments of modern life into art, hoping to create effects that evoked the mysterious "fourth dimension."[5] Apollinaire, who coined the literary use of that phrase, explored new techniques in the poems he wrote from early in the century.[6] One of the first changes in the new spirit of literature was to use street speech in poems; as Apollinaire wrote in "Palace": "Lady of my thoughts with ass of fine pearl / Neither pearl nor ass can the Orient rival."[7] Mixing vulgarity with lyricism was meant to create both humor and sensuality. Words were also intended to be suggestive; at times the literal meaning of lines was intentionally obscured. From the same poem, the image of the rose merges with that of the body and the sun: "Flogged flesh or roses from the rose garden. . . . / And the sun mirror of roses is broken." The poem also juxtaposes unexpected and unpleasant images: "We entered the dining room nostrils / Sniffed an odor of grease and burnt fat phlegm / We had twenty soups three were color of urine / And the king had two poached eggs in bouillon."

In his search for new sources of imagery, Apollinaire turned to the

1. Stein, 99.
2. Gertrude Stein to Mabel Dodge, Yale American Literature Collection; reprinted in Mabel Dodge Luhan, *Movers and Shakers*, Vol. 3 (1936; reprint, Albuquerque: U of New Mexico P, 1985), 29–30.
3. Moishe Black, introduction to Max Jacob, *Hesitant Fire: Selected Prose of Max Jacob*, trans. and ed. Moishe Black and Maria Green (Lincoln: U of Nebraska P, 1991), xiii–xvi.
4. Rosamond Bernier, *Matisse, Picasso, Miró As I Knew Them* (New York: Knopf, 1991), 109.
5. Mackworth, 86.
6. Published in Guillaume Apollinaire, *Alcools*, trans. Anne Hyde Greet (Berkeley: U of California P, 1965).
7. Scott Bates, *Guillaume Apollinaire* (Boston: Twayne, 1967).

symbolists. Foreshadowing surrealism, he laced his work with dream imagery, insisting that the real drew from both observable life and an often-hidden interior life. The subjects of Apollinaire's poems were similar to those of Picasso's Blue Period paintings: drawn from the common, the bent and wizened figures, wasted by hard work and poverty, nevertheless suggested transcendence. Picasso and Apollinaire also saw themselves as Nietzschean supermen, able to excel through a combination of artistic genius and sheer physical strength. They agreed to create at least one new work each day and by means of this series production to transform the existing art world.

Gertrude's writing also became a daily event, and it, too, drew on both extended consciousness and reality. As she described her life with Leo: "We were settled in Paris together and we were always together and I was writing. . . . I was writing."[8] In 1905 she wrote friends that she was "working tremendously."[9] The steadiness of her writing paralleled the production of the painters; Matisse, she noted reverently, was always working.[1] (As Henry Peyre explained, Matisse believed in "constant labor in order to reach spontaneousness"—the goal of the avant garde.[2])

After Gertrude had finished Q.E.D., she started two other novels. *The Making of Americans* in its first comparatively short version is the story of Julia Dehning's life shaped by her poor marital choice. Like Henry James's *The Wings of the Dove*, Gertrude's fiction showed the ways society disenfranchised unmarried women. Ironically, this first version of what was to become a monumental work seemed to be a complex response to what she saw as Bryn Mawr cynicism and May's unfaithfulness: the text stated repeatedly that being "middle class" is good, "the only thing always healthy, human, vital and from which has always sprung the best the world can know."[3] Stressing that a "normal" family life is strengthening, Gertrude implies that sexual deviance is dangerous and tempers her praise of individuality by warning that it must be governed by "conventional respectability."

Fernhurst [1902], the second novella she completed, retold the true story of Alfred Hodder, a brilliant Harvard philosopher who took a post at Bryn Mawr and once there began an affair with Mary Gwinn, an English professor. Gwinn was already involved with Helen Carey Thomas, soon to be president of the college. In real life, Hodder and Gwinn eloped; in *Fernhurst*, he leaves the college for a dis-

8. Stein, *Everybody's Autobiography* (New York: Random House, 1937), 58.
9. John Malcolm Brinnin, *The Third Rose: Gertrude Stein and Her World* (Boston: Little, Brown, 1959), 75.
1. Stein, *The Autobiography of Alice B. Toklas*, 39.
2. Henri Peyre, "The Lesson of Matisse," in *Homage to Matisse, The Yale Literary Magazine* 123, Fall 1955: 7–10.
3. Stein, "The Making of Americans," in *Fernhurst, Q.E.D., and Other Early Writings*, ed. Leon Katz (New York: Liveright, 1971), 145.

appointing career, without Gwinn, who resumes her liaison with Thomas. Gertrude's version of the narrative further probed the theme of sexual betrayal though the introduction of a new character, Hodder's wife, Nancy, to make what she called an "interesting quartet" of people.[4] Like Gertrude, Nancy is an "eager, anxious and moral" Westerner.[5] She consistently denies her husband's adultery; only when Helen Thomas confronts her with the affair does she admit its existence. Stein describes Nancy as bound by "her straight Western morality," terribly hurt by her husband's infidelity.

In case readers missed the sympathy with which Nancy was drawn, Gertrude as author announced that *Fernhurst* was an American story and that American values differed from French: "It is the French habit to consider that in the usual grouping of two and an extra . . . it is the two . . . who are of importance."[6] She pointed out that, in contrast, the American reader finds morality more important than ecstasy and the lonely extra of more value than the happy two." While her implied defense of lesbian love might seem contrived, Stein's emphasis on the power of sincere caring—and its frequent betrayal—was stated almost too didactically.

By 1906, steeped in naturalist novels and with these works of her own behind her, Gertrude began writing about common people. The subjects of her next writings—"The Good Anna," "The Gentle Lena," and "Melanctha," composed in that order for their inclusion in *Three Lives*—differ appreciably from the educated, white middle-class characters of *Q.E.D.* and *Fernhurst*. The radical aspect of these early fictions was her exploration of sexual power, both heterosexual and lesbian, though the latter was not shocking in Paris, where "discreet homosexuality was fashionable for both sexes."[7] The radicalism in *Three Lives* was Gertrude's choice of inarticulate, lower-class characters as protagonists and the harshly objective style she used to present them.

Critics have cited as important influences on *Three Lives* the painting of Mme Cézanne hanging above Gertrude as she wrote and her reading—and planning to translate—Flaubert's lyric story about the servant Félicité, "Un Coeur simple" from his *Trois Contes*.[8] The unhappiness of the three women characters in Stein's portraits also echoed the author's life in 1905, still shadowed by her love for May Bookstaver. About this time, Emma Lootz Erving had written her that May was reading aloud at dinner parties excerpts from

4. Stein, *Fernhurst*, in *Fernhurst, Q.E.D., and Other Early Writings*, 43.
5. Ibid., 39.
6. Ibid., 38.
7. Gosling, 36.
8. Brinnin, 56–64; James R. Mellow, *Charmed Circle: Gertrude Stein and Company* (New York: Praeger, 1974), 71–77; Janet Hobhouse, *Everybody Who Was Anybody* (Bookthrift Co., 1978), 70–73.

Gertrude's letters to her; Emma warned her not to write anything she did not want others to hear.[9] Chagrined, Gertrude accepted the fact that her relationship with May was over.

Using her art to disguise her continuing pain, Stein observed her subjects scientifically. Her choice of Anna Federner, the German house servant, as protagonist distanced her from her own life. To draw the good-hearted martyr, she used a vocabulary so repetitious it seemed simple: the reader knew Anna through her "arduous and troubled life,"[1] her "strong, strained, worn-out body,"[2] and her lesbian love for Mrs. Lehntman, her "only romance."[3]

As Anna's name suggests, the character was based on Lena Lebender, the woman who ran Gertrude and Leo's household in Baltimore. In Stein's telling, however, Anna became complex, partly through the emphasis on her love for women. Her aim in life was—supposedly—to serve, but the text showed that Anna was happy only when she controlled the people for whom she worked. Dedicated to wiping out sensual pleasure in life, Anna exhausted herself into an early grave. Gertrude's ironic emphasis on Anna's "good" life, with its core of self-abnegating service, was the beginning of her characteristic double meaning in fiction. Contrasted with Anna's tight-lipped insistence on propriety was the relaxed acceptance of Miss Mathilda, her slovenly but generous mistress, a humorous self-portrait of Gertrude.

In the second story of *Three Lives*, that of the victimized Lena Mainz, Gertrude focused on wider social and gender issues. When Lena, a naive, uneducated German immigrant, is brought to the States by her aunt, the powerful Mrs. Haydon, she becomes a puppet. Her aunt finds work for her and decides whom and when (as well as whether) she will marry. The debacle of Lena's marriage ends with her death during her fourth childbirth. The story is an admonitory narrative about power within marriage, the power of heterosexual culture (the fact that Mrs. Haydon is always referred to by her title as married woman underscores the values of the culture). The implications of Lena's story are frightening: that women deserve to make their own choices about sexuality, marriage, and motherhood and that when those choices are taken away, the will to live may also vanish.

The last of the three lives was that of the inscrutable Melanctha, a young mulatto whose chief occupation is "wandering,"[4] expressing her passionate, uncalculating nature through liaisons of various kinds. Melanctha, in Gertrude's words, "always loved too hard and

---

9. E. L. Erving to Stein, Yale American Literature Collection, 1906.
1. Stein, Gertrude. *Three Lives*. New York: Grafton Press, 1909), 82.
2. Ibid., p. 82.
3. Ibid., 52.
4. Ibid., 97.

much too often."[5] Influenced in part by her Paris friends' fascination with African art, Stein moved from her portraits of German women—led through their ineffectual modesty and their culture's mandates to miserable deaths—to that of a black woman. If "Negro" art was fashionable, she felt that no one knew black culture better than she. During her teen years in Oakland, California, she had listened to and watched blacks in Fruitvale; during her practical training at medical school, she had known black women as patients in Baltimore.[6]

Melanctha Herbert's understanding, Gertrude suggested, stemmed from her bisexuality. In adolescence, Melanctha explored heterosexual relationships with dockworkers, but later she became intimate with Jane Harden. Stein says clearly, "It was not from the men that Melanctha learned her wisdom."[7] The two years of their relationship pass quietly, with no "wandering" for either of them; Melanctha spends "long hours with Jane in her room,"[8] a description that echoes scenes from *Q.E.D.* Melanctha's later liaison with Rose, the narrative of which opens the novella, adds to the lesbian strand of the story.

After thirty-five pages of Melanctha's bisexual history, Gertrude introduces Jeff Campbell, the black doctor who grows to love Melanctha while he attends her dying mother. The story then becomes an extended dialogue between the arbitrarily rational Campbell and the purposefully inarticulate Melanctha, a tour de force of voiced dialogue unlike anything in literature of the time. During the lengthy Jeff-Melanctha interchanges, Stein draws Jeff as the rational speaker who wants permanence, exclusivity, security. His polemical insistence is shown to be absurd when contrasted with Melanctha's silences. She loves through action; she gives Jeff what she has to give and does not talk about it. While he accepts her love, he verbalizes all parts of their relationship and forces her into language that becomes destructive. Whatever she says, he argues against. By the end of the dialogue, the reader sees that Gertrude has constructed a classic philosophical discourse between reason and emotion.

Her fiction continued what was becoming her life process, melding the knowledge she had acquired from her studies of philosophy, psychology, and medicine with the new insights gained from literature and painting. Gertrude's main interest was presenting the person: her fascination with the portrait was a culmination of years of

5. Ibid., 89.
6. Ralph Church, "A Rose is a Rose is a Rose" (memoir) (Bancroft Library, U of California, Berkeley).
7. Stein, *Three Lives*, 104.
8. Ibid., 105.

formal study as well as the result of the contemporary artistic excitement over portraiture. Some of Cézanne's best paintings are portraits; Picasso's work is largely portraiture; Matisse's most effective distortions are of representations of the human figure and face. In "Melanctha" Gertrude created a double portrait—or, rather, the fictional portrait of the author as deeply divided person. Although the dialogue between Jeff and Melanctha has been described as typical of conversations between Gertrude and May Bookstaver, with Stein represented by Jeff Campbell and Bookstaver by Melanctha, Gertrude portrayed herself, too, in the character of Melanctha.[9] Born of very different—and irreconcilable—parents, isolated from family and friends, the maturing Melanctha—like Gertrude—tried to escape her feelings of difference and looked to sexual love for self-knowledge. Jeff and Melanctha's impasse mirrors Gertrude's sense of her conflicted emotional loyalties to both self and beloved.

In 1905, at thirty-one, Gertrude remained confused about what direction her life should take. Still toying with more than friendship with May, Etta Cone, and Dolene Guggenheimer, she saw no way to align emotional and sexual understanding with intellect. The affair with Jeff is only one segment of Melanctha's portrait; Melanctha as protagonist exists past her involvement with Campbell and loses her will to live more because of her failed relationship with Rose than from the disappointment of other lost loves. But her death in *Three Lives* parallels the deaths of Anna and Lena, all three women victims in some way of prescriptive heterosexual culture.

Gertrude's identification with the character of Melanctha mitigates what seems to be racism in the text. In her notebooks, she repeated that her own sensual nature was "dirty"[1]: "the Rabelaisian, nigger abandonment . . . daddy side. bitter taste fond of it." She may have been reacting to Leo's comment that "mysticism and sexual abandonment have it in common that they deny the intellect,"[2] and, in that context, Jeff Campbell's rationality may mirror Leo's attitudes as well as those of Gertrude as intellectual. But here locating herself in the camp of the sensual, she used the stereotype of the sexual black woman (and of Melanctha's black father) as a kind of self-portrait. When she used the phrase "the simple, promiscuous unmorality of the black people,"[3] she was writing about herself: *she* wanted a simple erotic relationship, but her society censured that pleasure, calling *her* relationship promiscuous and "unmoral." In some ways, the language of "Melanctha" works to create the same effect that the ironic stereotyping of the good Anna and the sadly

9. Mabel Weeks to Gertrude Stein (1908), quoted in Mellow, *Charmed Circle*, 127.
1. Stein, Notebooks D13–47, Yale American Literature Collection.
2. Ibid., 41.
3. Stein, *Three Lives*, 60.

gentle Lena does. The reader of Gertrude's *Three Lives* comes to understand that, in any society that imposes its rule over women's lives, misreading and misunderstanding can result.

Stein first gave her narratives of women's lives—titled "Three Histories" at this time—to her sister-in-law to read. After Sally approved the stories, Etta Cone typed the manuscript, and Gertrude then sent it to Hutch Hapgood in New York.[4] Though he warned her that some readers might think her writing "superficially irritating and difficult,"[5] he wrote that he found the stories "extremely good—full of reality, truth, unconventionality. I am struck with their deep humanity, and with the really remarkable way you have of getting deep into human psychology. . . . The Negro story seemed to me wonderfully strong and true." Most important, Hapgood sent the stories on to Pitts Duffield, a prospective publisher. Gertrude, relieved that someone as well-read as Hutch liked her work, said little about her project to Leo, whose criticism about anything she wrote was consistent— and all too predictable. But after having put *Q.E.D.* and *Fernhurst* away and questioning whether she could indeed write a major novel, she was excited to know that somewhere in New York City her recent work was being read.

4. Stein, *The Autobiography of Alice B. Toklas*, 51–52.
5. Yale American Literature Collection; reprinted in Donald Gallup, ed., *The Flowers of Friendship: Letters Written to Gertrude Stein* (New York: Knopf, 1953), 31–32.

Intellectual Backgrounds

WILLIAM JAMES

The Sense of Time†

The sensible present has duration. Let anyone try, I will not say to arrest, but to notice or attend to, the *present* moment of time. One of the most baffling experiences occurs. Where is it, this present? It has melted in our grasp, fled ere we could touch it, gone in the instant of becoming. As a poet, quoted by Mr. Hodgson, says, "Le moment où je parle est déjà loin de moi," and it is only as entering into the living and moving organization of a much wider tract of time that the strict present is apprehended at all. It is, in fact, an altogether ideal abstraction, not only never realized in sense, but probably never even conceived of by those unaccustomed to philosophic meditation. Reflection leads us to the conclusion that it *must* exist, but that it *does* exist can never be a fact of our immediate experience. The only fact of our immediate experience is what has been well called 'the specious' present, a sort of saddle-back of time with a certain length of its own, on which we sit perched, and from which we look in two directions into time. The unit of composition of our perception of time is a *duration*, with a bow and a stern, as it were—a rearward- and a forward-looking end. It is only as parts of this *duration-block* that the relation of *succession* of one end to the other is perceived. We do not first feel one end and then feel the other after it, and from the perception of the succession infer an interval of time between, but we seem to feel the interval of time as a whole, with its two ends embedded in it. The experience is from the outset a synthetic datum, not a simple one; and to sensible perception its elements are inseparable, although attention looking back may easily decompose the experience, and distinguish its beginning from its end.

The moment we pass beyond a very few seconds our consciousness

† From *Psychology: Briefer Course* Frederick Burkhardt, Gen. Ed., Fredson Bowers, Textual Ed. (Cambridge: Harvard UP, 1984), pp. 245–50. Copyright © 1984 by the President and Fellows of Harvard College. Reprinted by permission of the publisher. The American philosopher William James (1842–1910), who taught Stein philosophy while at Radcliffe College (1893–97), profoundly influenced Stein's career.

of duration ceases to be an immediate perception and becomes a construction more or less symbolic. To realize even an hour, we must count 'now! now! now! now!' indefinitely. Each 'now' is the feeling of a separate *bit* of time, and the exact sum of the bits never makes a clear impression on our mind. The *longest bit of duration* which we can apprehend at once so as to discriminate it from longer and shorter bits of time would seem (from experiments made for another purpose in Wundt's laboratory[1]) to be about 12 seconds. *The shortest interval* which we can feel as time at all would seem to be ⅟₅₀₀ of a second. That is, Exner recognized two electric sparks to be successive when the second followed the first at that interval.

We have no sense for empty time. Let one sit with closed eyes and, abstracting entirely from the outer world, attend exclusively to the passage of time, like one who wakes, as the poet says, "to hear time flowing in the middle of the night, and all things creeping to a day of doom."[2] There seems under such circumstances as these no variety in the material content of our thought, and what we notice appears, if anything, to be the pure series of durations budding, as it were, and growing beneath our indrawn gaze. Is this really so or not? The question is important; for, if the experience be what it roughly seems, we have a sort of special sense for pure time—a sense to which empty duration is an adequate stimulus; while if it be an illusion, it must be that our perception of time's flight, in the experiences quoted, is due to the *filling* of the time, and to our *memory* of a content which it had a moment previous, and which we feel to agree or disagree with its content now.

It takes but a small exertion of introspection to show that the latter alternative is the true one, and that *we can no more perceive a duration than we can perceive an extension, devoid of all sensible content*. Just as with closed eyes we see a dark visual field in which a curdling play of obscurest luminosity is always going on; so, be we never so abstracted from distinct outward impressions, we are always inwardly immersed in what Wundt has somewhere called the twilight of our general consciousness. Our heart-beats, our breathing, the pulses of our attention, fragments of words or sentences that pass through our imagination, are what people this dim habitat. Now, all these processes are rhythmical, and are apprehended by us, as they occur, in their totality; the breathing and pulses of attention, as

---

1. Wilhelm Wundt (1832–1920), German philosopher, established the world's first laboratory devoted to psychological experimentation.
2. From the poem "The Mystic" by Alfred Lord Tennyson (1809–1892):

> He often lying broad awake, and yet
> Remaining from the body, and apart
> In intellect and power and will, hath heard
> Time flowing in the middle of the night,
> And all things creeping to a day of doom.

coherent successions, each with its rise and fall; the heart-beats similarly, only relatively far more brief; the words not separately, but in
connected groups. In short, empty our minds as we may, some form
of *changing process* remains for us to feel, and cannot be expelled.
And along with the sense of the process and its rhythm goes the
sense of the length of time it lasts. Awareness of *change* is thus the
condition on which our perception of time's flow depends; but there
exists no reason to suppose that empty time's own changes are sufficient for the awareness of change to be aroused. The change must
be of some concrete sort.

Appreciation of Longer Durations.—In the experience of watching empty time flow—'empty' to be taken hereafter in the relative
sense just set forth—we tell it off in pulses. We say 'now! now! now!'
or we count 'more! more! more!' as we feel it bud. This composition
out of units of duration is called the law of time's *discrete flow*. The
discreteness is, however, merely due to the fact that our successive
acts of *recognition* or *apperception* of *what* it is are discrete. The
sensation is as continuous as any sensation can be. All continuous
sensations are *named* in beats. We notice that a certain finite 'more'
of them is passing or already past. To adopt Hodgson's image, the
sensation is the measuring-tape, the perception the dividing-engine
which stamps its length. As we listen to a steady sound, we *take it
in* in discrete pulses of recognition, calling it successively 'the same!
the same! the same!' The case stands no otherwise with time.

After a small number of beats our impression of the amount we
have told off becomes quite vague. Our only way of knowing it accurately is by counting, or noticing the clock, or through some other
symbolic conception. When the times exceed hours or days, the conception is absolutely symbolic. We think of the amount we mean
either solely as a *name*, or by running over a few salient *dates* therein,
with no pretence of imagining the full durations that lie between
them. No one has anything like a *perception* of the greater length of
the time between now and the first century than of that between
now and the tenth. To an historian, it is true, the longer interval will
suggest a host of additional dates and events, and so appear a more
multitudinous thing. And for the same reason most people will think
they directly perceive the length of the past fortnight to exceed that
of the past week. But there is properly no comparative time-*intuition*
in these cases at all. It is but dates and events representing time,
their abundance symbolizing its length. I am sure that this is so, even
where the times compared are no more than an hour or so in length.
It is the same with spaces of many miles, which we always compare
with each other by the numbers that measure them.

From this we pass naturally to speak of certain familiar variations
in our estimation of lengths of time. *In general, a time filled with*

varied and interesting experiences seems short in passing, but long as we look back. On the other hand, a tract of time empty of experiences seems long in passing, but in retrospect short. A week of travel and sight-seeing may subtend an angle more like three weeks in the memory; and a month of sickness yields hardly more memories than a day. The length in retrospect depends obviously on the multitudinousness of the memories which the time affords. Many objects, events, changes, many subdivisions, immediately widen the view as we look back. Emptiness, monotony, familiarity, make it shrivel up.

The same space of time seems shorter as we grow older—that is, the days, the months, and the years do so; whether the hours do so is doubtful, and the minutes and seconds to all appearance remain about the same. An old man probably does not *feel* his past life to be any longer than he did when he was a boy, though it may be a dozen times as long. In most men all the events of manhood's years are of such familiar *sorts* that the individual impressions do not last. At the same time more and more of the earlier events get forgotten, the result being that no greater multitude of distinct objects remains in the memory.

So much for the apparent shortening of tracts of time in *retrospect*. They shorten *in passing* whenever we are so fully occupied with their content as not to note the actual time itself. A day full of excitement, with no pause, is said to pass 'ere we know it.' On the contrary, a day full of waiting, of unsatisfied desire for change, will seem a small eternity. *Tædium, ennui, Langweile, boredom,* are words for which, probably, every language known to man has its equivalent. It comes about whenever, from the relative emptiness of content of a tract of time, we grow attentive to the passage of the time itself. Expecting, and being ready for, a new impression to succeed; when it fails to come, we get an empty time instead of it; and such experiences, ceaselessly renewed, make us most formidably aware of the extent of the mere time itself. Close your eyes and simply wait to hear somebody tell you that a minute has elapsed, and the full length of your leisure with it seems incredible. You engulf yourself into its bowels as into those of that interminable first week of an ocean voyage, and find yourself wondering that history can have overcome many such periods in its course. All because you attend so closely to the mere feeling of the time *per se*, and because your attention to that is susceptible of such fine-grained successive subdivision. The *odiousness* of the whole experience comes from its insipidity; for *stimulation* is the indispensable requisite for pleasure in an experience, and the feeling of bare time is the least stimulating experience we can have. The sensation of tedium is a *protest*, says Volkmann, against the entire present.

The feeling of past time is a present feeling. In reflecting on the *modus operandi* of our consciousness of time, we are at first tempted to suppose it the easiest thing in the world to understand. Our inner states succeed each other. They know themselves as they are; then of course, we say, they must know their own succession. But this philosophy is too crude; for between the mind's own changes *being* successive, and *knowing their own succession*, lies as broad a chasm as between the object and subject of any case of cognition in the world. *A succession of feelings, in and of itself, is not a feeling of succession. And since, to our successive feelings, a feeling of their succession is added, that must be treated as an additional fact requiring its own special elucidation*, which this talk about the feelings knowing their time-relations as a matter of course leaves all untouched.

If we represent the actual time-stream of our thinking by an horizontal line, the thought *of* the stream or of any segment of its length, past, present, or to come, might be figured in a perpendicular raised upon the horizontal at a certain point. The length of this perpendicular stands for a certain object or content, which in this case is the time thought of at the actual moment of the stream upon which the perpendicular is raised.

There is thus a sort of *perspective projection* of past objects upon present consciousness, similar to that of wide landscapes upon a camera-screen.

And since we saw a while ago that our maximum distinct *perception* of duration hardly covers more than a dozen seconds (while our maximum vague perception is probably not more than that of a minute or so), we must suppose that *this amount of duration is pictured fairly steadily in each passing instant of consciousness* by virtue of some fairly constant feature in the brain-process to which the consciousness is tied. *This feature of the brain-process, whatever it be, must be the cause of our perceiving the fact of time at all.* The duration thus steadily perceived is hardly more than the 'specious present,' as it was called a few pages back. Its *content* is in a constant flux, events dawning into its forward end as fast as they fade out of its rearward one, and each of them changing its time-coefficient from 'not yet,' or 'not quite yet,' to 'just gone,' or 'gone,' as it passes by. Meanwhile, the specious present, the intuited duration, stands permanent, like the rainbow on the waterfall, with its own quality unchanged by the events that stream through it. Each of these, as it slips out, retains the power of being reproduced; and when reproduced, is reproduced with the duration and neighbors which it originally had. Please observe, however, that the reproduction of an event, *after* it has once completely dropped out of the rearward end of the specious present, is an entirely different psychic fact from its direct perception in the specious present as a thing immediately past. A creature might be entirely devoid of *reproductive* memory, and yet have the time-sense; but the latter would be limited, in his case, to the few seconds immediately passing by. * * *

OTTO WEININGER

Emancipated Women†

As an immediate application of the attempt to establish the principle of intermediate sexual forms by means of a differential psychology, we must now come to the question which it is the special object of this book to answer, theoretically and practically, I mean the woman question, theoretically so far as it is not a matter of ethnology and national economics, and practically in so far as it is not merely a matter of law and domestic economy, that is to say, of social science in the widest sense. The answer which this chapter is about to give must not be considered as final or as exhaustive. It is rather a necessary preliminary investigation, and does not go beyond deductions from the principles that I have established. It will deal with the exploration of individual cases and will not attempt to found on these any laws of general significance. The practical indications that it will give are not moral maxims that could or would guide the future; they are no more than technical rules abstracted from past cases. The idea of male and female types will not be discussed here; that is reserved for the second part of my book. This preliminary investigation will deal with only those charactero-logical conclusions from the principle of sexually intermediate forms that are of significance in the woman question.

The general direction of the investigation is easy to understand from what has already been stated. A woman's demand for emancipation and her qualification for it are in direct proportion to the amount of maleness in her. The idea of emancipation, however, is many-sided, and its indefiniteness is increased by its association with many practical customs which have nothing to do with the theory of emancipation. By the term emancipation of a woman, I imply neither her mastery at home nor her subjection of her husband. I have not in mind the courage which enables her to go freely by night or by day unaccompanied in public places, or the disregard of social rules which prohibit bachelor women from receiving visits from men, or discussing or listening to discussions of sexual matters. I exclude

† From *Sex & Character* (London: William Heinemann, 1906), pp. 64–75.

from my view the desire for economic independence, the becoming fit for positions in technical schools, universities and conservatoires or teachers' institutes. And there may be many other similar movements associated with the word emancipation which I do not intend to deal with. Emancipation, as I mean to discuss it, is not the wish for an outward equality with man, but what is of real importance in the woman question, the deep-seated craving to acquire man's character, to attain his mental and moral freedom, to reach his real interests and his creative power. I maintain that the real female element has neither the desire nor the capacity for emancipation in this sense. All those who are striving for this real emancipation, all women who are truly famous and and are of conspicuous mental ability, to the first glance of an expert reveal some of the anatomical characters of the male, some external bodily resemblance to a man. Those so-called "women" who have been held up to admiration in the past and present, by the advocates of woman's rights, as examples of what women can do, have almost invariably been what I have described as sexually intermediate forms. The very first of the historical examples, Sappho herself, has been handed down to us as an example of the sexual invert, and from her name has been derived the accepted terms for perverted sexual relations between women. The contents of the second and third chapter thus at once become important with regard to the woman question. The characterological material at our disposal with regard to celebrated and emancipated women is too vague to serve as the foundation of any satisfactory theory. What is wanted is some principle which would enable us to determine at what point between male and female such individuals were placed. My law of sexual affinity is such a principle. Its application to the facts of homo-sexuality showed that the woman who attracts and is attracted by other women is herself half male. Interpreting the historical evidence at our disposal in the light of this principle, we find that the degree of emancipation and the proportion of maleness in the composition of a woman are practically identical. Sappho was only the forerunner of a long line of famous women who were either homo-sexually or bisexually inclined. Classical scholars have defended Sappho warmly against the implication that there was anything more than mere friendship in her relations with her own sex, as if the accusation were necessarily degrading. In the second part of my book, however, I shall show reasons in favour of the possibility that homo-sexuality is a higher form than hetero-sexuality. For the present, it is enough to say that homo-sexuality in a woman is the outcome of her masculinity and presupposes a higher degree of development. Catherine II of Russia, and Queen Christina of Sweden, the highly gifted although deaf, dumb and blind, Laura Bridgman,[1] George Sand,[2] and a very large number of highly gifted women and girls concerning whom I myself have been able to collect information, were partly bisexual, partly homo-sexual.

I shall now turn to other indications in the case of the large number of emancipated women regarding whom there is no evidence as to homo-sexuality, and I shall show that my attribution of maleness is no caprice, no egotistical wish of a man to associate all the higher manifestations of intelligence with the male sex. Just as homo-sexual or bisexual women reveal their maleness by their preference either for women or for womanish men, so hetero-sexual women display maleness in their choice of a male partner who is not preponderatingly male. * * *

---

1. Laura Bridgman (1829–1889) was the first blind deaf-mute known to be successfully educated. In the 1840s, Charles Dickens popularized her in a romantic account of her life. [*Editor's note.*]
2. Pseudonym of Amandine Aurore Lucie Dupin, baronne Dudevant (1804–1876), reform-minded French novelist. [*Editor's note.*]

CRITICISM

Contemporary Reception

"Three Lives"

Three Lives by Gertrude Stein is a rather peculiar exposition of the art of character delineation, in which is shown the constant repetition of ideas in minds of low caliber and meager cultivation, the three lives depicted being those of three servant women, one of whom is a mulatto. The thing is novel in that it departs of traditional lines, the method of the great masters in this respect being one of summing up, or statement of ultimate and fixed condition, rather than a detailed showing of the repeated thoughts in the brain by which such conditions are arrived at. Of course, it must be admitted that such repetition does occur, even in cultivated and brilliant minds, but it is a question if the mind-working of such persons as Miss Stein has chosen could be made interesting by any process whatsoever. If she should attempt the same things with minds of a higher caliber, the result might be more entertaining.

    —*Washington (D.C.) Herald*, December 12, 1909

"Fiction, But Not Novels"

Three Lives by Gertrude Stein is fiction which no one who reads it can ever forget, but a book for a strictly limited audience. The three lives are "The Good Anna," "The Gentle Lena," and "Melanctha." The good Anna was Miss Mathilda's housekeeper. The gentle Lena, when she had been in this country long enough to know the English, married the good son of German parents. Melanctha is a colored girl, her lover the very best type evolved in the race, a young physician. In this remarkable book one watches humanity groping in the mists of existence. As character study one can speak of it only in superlatives. The originality of its narrative form is as notable. As these humble human lives are groping in bewilderment so does the story telling itself. Not written in the vernacular, it yet gives that impression. At first one fancies the author using repetition as a refrain is used in poetry. But it is something more subtle still; something involved, something turning back, for a new beginning, for a lost strand in the spinning. It makes of the book a very masterpiece of realism, for the reader never escapes from the atmosphere of those lives, so subtly is the incantation wrought into these seeming simple pages. Here is a literary artist of such originality that it is not easy to conjecture what special influences have gone into the making of her. But the indwelling spirit of it all is a sweet enlightened sympathy, an unsleeping sense of humor, and an exquisite carefulness in detail. But it is tautology to praise Miss Stein's work for this quality or that. Enough has surely been said to call the attention of those who will value her work to this new and original artist to come into the field of fiction.

—*Kansas City Star*, December 18, 1909

"Notable Piece of Realism"

Three Lives is in some respects a remarkable piece of realism. The author, Gertrude Stein, has given expression to her own temperament, to her own way of seeing the world. The style is somewhat unusual; at times it is a little difficult to follow, and sometimes it becomes prosy. It is only when one has read the book slowly—not as a story, but as a serious picture of life—that one grasps the author's conception of her humble characters, their thought and their tragedies.

—*Boston Evening Globe*, December 18, 1909

"*Three Lives*. By Gertrude Stein"

These stories of the Good Anna, Melanctha, and the Gentle Lena have a quite extraordinary vitality conveyed in a most eccentric and difficult form. The half-articulated phrases follow unrelentingly the blind mental and temperamental gropings of three humble souls wittingly or unwittingly at odds with life. Whoever can adjust himself to the repetitions, false starts, and general circularity of the manner will find himself very near real people. Too near, possibly. The present writer had an uncomfortable sense of being immured with a girl wife, a spinster, and a woman who is neither, between imprisoning walls which echoed exactly all thoughts and feelings. These stories utterly lack construction and focus but give that sense of urgent life which one gets more commonly in Russian literature than elsewhere. How the Good Anna spent herself barely for everybody in reach, the Gentle Lena for the notion of motherhood, while the mulattress Melanctha perished partly of her own excess of temperament, but more from contact with a life-diminishing prig and emotionally inert surroundings, readers who are willing to pay a stiff entrance fee in patient attention may learn for themselves. From Miss Stein, if she can consent to clarify her method, much may be expected. As it is, she writes quite as a Browning escaped from the bonds of verse might wallow in fiction, only without his antiseptic whimsicality.

—*The Nation*, January 20, 1910

"Curious Fiction Study"

It is probable that for every reader who accepts Gertrude Stein's first published book, *Three Lives*, there will be many who reject it. The broken rhythm of the prose, the commonness of the wording will probably be so repellant that the reader will not linger long enough to permit these qualities to produce their rightful effect and swing him into the imaginative understanding of the simple, mystic, humble lives of the women of whom the author writes.

It is hard to discuss the book without quoting the style, and it is impossible to quote unless whole pages be quoted. But it can be said that the slow, broken rhythm of the prose corresponds to the rhythm of the "lives" and to the reader's rhythmic comprehension; and that by this very token it is artistically justified, crudely inartistic as it may at first seem.

The subjects of the three tales Miss Stein tells are Anna and Lena, both servants, one good, the other gentle, one always managing the people about her, the other molded passively and almost uncomprehendingly by the people around her, and finally Melanctha, a colored girl, wandering and experiencing and learning, but never well utilizing what she has learned.

Nothing could be concretely more unlike the work of Henry James than is this work of Miss Stein's, and yet there is one most interesting relationship. James is the great master of conversation because his conversations are not patched up like mosaics out of separate people's remarks, but are themselves living, moving "situations" which must be understood as wholes if the words are to have real meaning. And James presents us the world he knows largely through these conversations.

Now, Miss Stein has no such tense, active, intellectual world to show us as James. She presents obscure, humble, vague, flowing, undefined life; but she presents us by an analogous method. She gives us no mosaics of life bits, but the living mass as it flows. Her murmuring people are as truly shown as are James' people who not only talk but live while they talk.

The place of such work as this is always obscure when first examined. It is certainly worth considering as a curiosity; doubtless also as an artist's story; possibly as much more than this.

—*Chicago Record Herald*, January 22, 1910

"A Futurist Novel"

Style is a matter of little importance when a certain effect is sought. Gertrude Stein knows this well when she merely sketches her *Three*

Lives. There is a spirit in the method with which she tells us of the lives of three simple souls, and by this spirit, which comes from an instinctive feeling toward her subjects, Miss Stein accomplishes more than she could by any rhetorical or academic "style." Take, for example, this passage:

"It was very hard for Jeff Campbell to make all this way of doing, right, inside him. If Jeff Campbell could not be straight out, and real honest, he never could be very strong inside him. Now, Melanctha, with her making him feel, always, how good she was and how very much she suffered in him, made him always go so fast then, he could not be strong then, to feel things out straight then inside him."

If we try to analyze this from the point of view of "good English" construction it would seem incomprehensible. But analyze it from the view point of effectiveness, character picture and feeling, and there can be no doubt of the end accomplished. There is a picture of an emotional situation before us which arouses a deeper understanding and interest than could be done by the very best of conventional English.

To the willing reader of *Three Lives* each sketch means the acquaintance of an intimate life, its passions, emotions, feelings and happenings. We go through all the intimacies of "Good Anna's" soul. Physically and spiritually she stands before us unmasked. We see all her struggles with other humans. Her simple life passes on undramatically, with no events of worldwide importance to give us "thrills." We pass with her through the changes which life brings, and finally sit with her in the hospital in her last illness. And we weep when that simple soul is no more. We have known "Good Anna" in all her human weakness, and we have loved her as Miss Stein loved her.

For "Melanctha" and the "Gentle Lena," Miss Stein's other sketches, we can say as much. We are never burdened with a mass of detail, but when these lives are over—as all lives must be over some day—we have learned to understand passion, feelings and thought which we seldom recognize in ourselves, much less in others.

We cannot read these lives without thinking and sensitive minds. We must study the lines, the colors, the directions and, above all else, the spirit of the author. The mind must be keen and alert. For the blur which this futurist in writing at first creates cannot be cleared until we are willing to bring the thought and intelligence to its interpretation which we needed when examining *The Nude Descending the Stairs.*[1] Let us welcome the new art, if it brings such wealth of simplicity and effectiveness as Miss Stein has shown in these sketches.

—*Philadelphia Public Ledger*, April 10, 1915

1. Cubist painting (1912) by the French-born American painter Marcel Duchamp (1887–1968).

WILLIAM CARLOS WILLIAMS

The Work of Gertrude Stein†

Stein's theme is writing. But in such a way as to be writing envisioned as the first concern of the moment, dragging behind it a dead weight of logical burdens, among them a dead criticism which broken through might be a gap by which endless other enterprises of the understanding should issue—for refreshment.

It is a revolution of some proportions that is contemplated, the exact nature of which may be no more than sketched here but whose basis is humanity in a relationship with literature hitherto little contemplated.

And at the same time it is a general attack on the scholastic viewpoint, that mediæval remnant, with whose effects from generation to generation literature has been infested to its lasting detriment. It is a break away from that paralyzing vulgarity of logic for which the habits of science and philosophy coming over into literature (where they do not belong) are to blame.

It is this logicality as a basis for literary action which in Stein's case, for better or worse, has been wholly transcended.

She explains her own development in connection with *Tender Buttons* (1914), "It was my first conscious struggle with the problem of correlating sight, sound and sense, and eliminating rhythm;—now I am trying grammar and eliminating sight and sound (*transition* No. 14, Fall, 1928).

Having taken the words to her choice, to emphasize further what she has in mind she has completely unlinked them (in her most recent work) from their former relationships in the sentence. This was absolutely essential and unescapable. Each under the new arrangement has a quality of its own, but not conjoined to carry the burden science, philosophy and every higgledy piggledy figment of law and order have been laying upon them in the past. They are like a crowd at Coney Island, let us say, seen from an airplane.

Whatever the value of Miss Stein's work may turn out finally to be, she has at least accomplished her purpose of getting down on paper this much that is decipherable. She has placed writing on a plane where it may deal unhampered with its own affairs, unburdened with scientific and philosophic lumber.

For after all, science and philosophy are today, in their effect upon the mind, little more than fetishes of unspeakable abhorrence. And

† From *Selected Essays* (New York: Random House, 1954). Reprinted in *Imaginations* (New York: New Directions, 1970). Copyright © 1970 by Florence H. Williams. Reprinted by permission of New Directions Publishing Corp.

it is through a subversion of the art of writing that their grip upon us has assumed its steel-like temper.

What are philosophers, scientists, religionists; they that have filled up literature with their pap? Writers, of a kind. Stein simply erases their stories, turns them off and does without them, their logic (founded merely on the limits of the perceptions) which is supposed to transcend the words, along with them. Stein denies it. The words, in writing, she discloses, transcend everything.

Movement (for which in a petty way logic is taken) the so-called search for truth and beauty is for us the effect of a breakdown of the attention. But movement must not be confused with what we attach to it but, for the rescuing of the intelligence, must always be considered aimless; without progress.

This is the essence of all knowledge.

Bach might be an illustration of movement not suborned by a freight of purposed design, loaded upon it as in almost all later musical works; statement unmusical and unnecessary. Stein's "They lived very gay then" has much of the same quality of movement to be found in Bach—the composition of the words determining not the logic, not the "story," not the theme even, but the movement itself. As it happens, "They were both gay there" is as good as some of Bach's shorter fugues.

* * *

Writing, like everything else is much a question of refreshed interest. It is directed, not idly, but as most often happens (though not necessarily so), toward that point not to be predetermined where movement is blocked (by the end of logic perhaps). It is about these parts, if I am not mistaken, that Gertrude Stein will be found.

There remains to be explained the bewildering volume of what Miss Stein has written, the quantity of her work, its very apparent repetitiousness, its iteration, what I prefer to call its extension, the final clue to her meaning.

It is, of course, a progression (not a progress) beginning, conveniently, with "Melanctha" (from *Three Lives*), and coming up to today.

How in a democracy, such as the United States, can writing, which has to compete with excellence elsewhere and in other times, remain in the field and be at once objective (true to fact) intellectually searching, subtle and instinct with powerful additions to our lives? It is impossible, without invention of some sort, for the very good reason that observations about us engenders the very opposite of what we seek: triviality, crassness, and intellectual bankruptcy. And yet what we do see can in no way be excluded. Satire and flight are two possibilities but Miss Stein has chosen otherwise.

But if one remain in a place and reject satire, what then? To be democratic, local (in the sense of being attached with integrity to actual experience) Stein, or any other artist, must for subtlety ascend to a plane of almost abstract design to keep alive. To writing, then, as an art in itself. Yet what actually impinges on the senses must be rendered as it appears, by use of which, only, and under which, untouched, the significance has to be disclosed. It is one of the major problems of the artist.

"Melanctha" is a thrilling clinical record of the life of a colored woman in the present day United States, told with directness and truth. It is without question one of the best bits of characterization produced in America. It is universally admired. This is where Stein began.

But for Stein to tell a story of that sort, even with the utmost genius, was not enough under the conditions in which we live, since by the very nature of its composition such a story does violence to the larger scene which would be portrayed.

True, a certain way of delineating the scene is to take an individual like Melanctha and draw her carefully. But this is what happens. The more carefully the drawing is made, the greater the genius involved and the greater the interest that attaches, therefore, to the character as an individual, the more exceptional that character becomes in the mind of the reader and the less typical of the scene.

It was no use for Stein to go on with *Three Lives*. There that phase of the work had to end. See *Useful Knowledge* [1928], the parts on the U.S.A. Stein's pages have become like the United States viewed from an airplane—the same senseless repetitions, the endless multiplications of toneless words, with these she had to work.

No use for Stein to fly to Paris and *forget* it. The thing, the United States, the unmitigated stupidity, the drab tediousness of the democracy, the overwhelming number of the offensively ignorant, the dull of nerve—is *there* in the artist's mind and cannot be escaped by taking a ship. She must resolve it if she can, if she is to *be*. That must be the artist's articulation with existence.

Truly, the world is full of emotion—more or less—but it is caught in bewilderment to a far more important degree. And the purpose of art, so far as it has any, is not at least to copy that, but lies in the resolution of difficulties to its own comprehensive organization of materials. And by so doing, in this case, rather than by copying, it takes its place as *most* human.

To deal with Melanctha, with characters of whomever it may be, the modern Dickens, is *not* therefore human. To write like that is not, in the artist, to be human at all, since nothing is resolved, nothing is done to resolve the bewilderment which makes of emotion an inanity. That, is to overlook the gross instigation and with all subtlety to examine the object minutely for "the truth"—which if there is anything more commonly practised or more stupid, I have yet to come upon it.

To be most useful to humanity, or to anything else for that matter, an art, writing, must stay art, not seeking to be science, philosophy, history, the humanities, or anything else it has been made to carry in the past. It is this enforcement which underlies Gertrude Stein's extension and progression to date.

CARL VAN VECHTEN

A Stein Song†

Gertrude Stein rings bells, loves baskets, and wears handsome waist-coats. She has a tenderness for green glass and buttons have a tenderness for her. In the matter of fans you can only compare her with a motion-picture star in Hollywood and three generations of young writers have sat at her feet. She has influenced without coddling them. In her own time she is a legend and in her own country she is with honor. Keys to sacred doors have been presented to her and she understands how to open them. She writes books for children, plays for actors, and librettos for operas. Each one of them is one. For her a rose is a rose and how!

I composed this strictly factual account of Miss Stein and her activities for a catalogue of the Gotham Book Mart in 1940, but all that I said then seems to be truer than ever today. Gertrude Stein currently is not merely a legend, but also a whole folklore, a subject for an epic poem, and the young GIs who crowded into her Paris apartment on the rue Christine during and after the Greater War have augmented the number of her fans until their count is as hard to reckon as that of the grains of sand on the shore by the sea. During the war I frequently received letters from soldiers and sailors who, with only two days' furlough at their disposal and a long way to travel, sometimes by jeep, spent all of their free hours in Paris with the author of *Tender Buttons*. Other GIs bore her away on a flying tour of Germany and still others carried her by automobile to Belgium to speak to their comrades there. In Paris she gave public talks to groups of them too large to fit into her apartment. *Life* and the *New York Times Magazine* contracted for articles from her pen. Her play of existence in occupied France, *Yes Is for a Very Young Man* [published 1946], was presently produced at the Community Playhouse

† From *Selected Writings of Gertrude Stein*, ed. Carl Van Vechten (New York: Random House, 1946), pp. xviii–xxiv. Copyright © 1946 by Random House, Inc. Used by permission of Random House, Inc.

in Pasadena, California. Some of these tributes, naturally, were due to her personality and charm, but most of them stem directly from the library shelves which hold her collected works. Furthermore, as she once categorically informed Alfred Harcourt, it is to her so-called "difficult" works that she owes her world-wide celebrity.

There is more direct testimony regarding her experiences with the GIs in her letters to me. On November 26, 1944, after the coming of the Americans, an event excitingly described in this Collection, she cabled me: "Joyous Days. Endless Love." In 1945, she wrote, "How we love the American army we never do stop loving the American army one single minute." If you will recall Alexandre Dumas's motto, *J'aime qui m'aime,*[1] you will be certain they loved her too. Still later she wrote me: "Enclosed is a description of a talk I gave them which did excite them, they walked me home fifty strong after the lecture was over and in the narrow streets of the quarter they made all the automobiles take side streets, the police looked and followed a bit but gave it up." Captain Edmund Geisler, her escort on the Belgian excursion, said to me, "Wherever she spoke she was frank and even belligerent. She made the GIs awfully mad, but she also made them think and many ended in agreement with her."

II

In *Everybody's Autobiography* [published 1937], Gertrude Stein confesses: "It always did bother me that the American public were more interested in me than in my work." Perhaps this statement may be affirmed justifiably of the anonymous masses, but it would be incorrect to apply it generally to the critics, novelists, and reviewers who frequently have considered her writings worth discussing seriously. It has occurred to me that a brief summary of the opinions of a few of these distinguished gentlemen might serve to reassure the reading world at large and Miss Stein herself on this controversial point.

André Maurois, for example, says of her: "In the universal confusion (the war years and after) she remains intelligent: she has kept her poetic sense and even her sense of humor." Of *Wars I Have Seen* [published 1945] he writes: "The originality of the ideas, the deliberate fantasy of the comparisons, the naïveté of the tone, combined with the profundity of the thought, the repetitions, the absence of punctuation, all that first irritates the reader finally convinces him so that more orthodox styles appear insipid to him. Gertrude Stein is believed to be a difficult writer. This is false. There is not a single phrase in this book that cannot be comprehended by a schoolgirl of sixteen years."

1. "I am those who love me."

Here is Ben Ray Redman's testimony: "Few writers have ever dared to be, or have ever been able to be, as simple as she, as simple as a child, pointing straight, going straight to the heart of a subject, to its roots; pointing straight, when and where adults would take a fancier way than pointing because they have learned not to point. . . . In the past, perhaps wilfully, she has often failed to communicate, and it was either her misfortune or her fun, depending on her intention."

Or perhaps you would prefer Virgil Thomson's capsule definition: "To have become a Founding Father of her century is her own reward for having long ago, and completely, dominated her language."

An earlier, sympathetic, and highly descriptive view is that of Sherwood Anderson: "She is laying word against word, relating sound to sound, feeling for the taste, the smell, the rhythm of the individual word. She is attempting to do something for the writers of our English speech that may be better understood after a time, *and she is not in a hurry.* . . . There is a thing one might call 'the extension of the province of his art' one wants to achieve. One works with words and one would like words that have a taste on the lips, that have a perfume to the nostrils, rattling words one can throw into a box and shake, making a sharp jingling sound, words that, when seen on the printed page, have a distinct arresting effect upon the eye, words that when they jump out from under the pen one may feel with the fingers as one might caress the cheeks of his beloved. And what I think is that these books of Gertrude Stein do in a very real sense recreate life in words."

William Carlos Williams's opinion is correlated to the above: "Having taken the words to her choice, to emphasize further what she has in mind she has completely unlinked them (in her most recent work: 1930) from their former relationships to the sentence. This was absolutely essential and unescapable. Each under the new arrangement has a quality of its own, but not conjoined to carry the burden science, philosophy, and every higgledy-piggledy figment of law and order have been laying upon them in the past. They are like a crowd at Coney Island, let us say, seen from an airplane. . . . She has placed writing on a plane where it may deal unhampered with its own affairs, unburdened with scientific and philosophic lumber."

Edmund Wilson feels compelled to admit: "Whenever we pick up her writings, however unintelligible we may find them, we are aware of a literary personality of unmistakable originality and distinction."

Julian Sawyer contends: "If the name of anything or everything is dead, as Miss Stein has always rightly contested, the only thing to do to keep it alive is to rename it. And that is what Miss Stein did and does."

Pursuing these commentators, I fall upon Thornton Wilder who asserts: "There have been too many books that attempted to flatter or woo or persuade or coerce the reader. Miss Stein's theory of the audience insists on the fact that the richest rewards for the reader have come from those works in which the authors admitted no consideration of an audience into their creating mind."

And as a coda, allow me to permit Joseph Alsop, Jr., to speak: "Miss Stein is no out-pensioner upon Parnassus; no crank; no seeker after personal publicity; no fool. She is a remarkably shrewd woman, with an intelligence both sensitive and tough, and a single one of her books, *Three Lives*, is her sufficient ticket of admission to the small company of authors who have had something to say and have known how to say it."

III

If Picasso is applauded for painting pictures which do not represent anything he has hitherto seen, if Schoenberg can pen a score that sounds entirely new even to ears accustomed to listen to modern music, why should an employer of English words be required to form sentences which are familiar in meaning, shape, and sound to any casual reader? Miss Stein herself implies somewhere that where there is communication (or identification) there can be no question of creation. This is solid ground, walked on realistically, as anyone who has been exposed to performances of music by Reger, for example, can readily testify. However, it must be borne in mind that composers and painters are not always inspired to *absolute* creation: Schoenberg wrote music for *Pelléas et Mélisande* and the tuneful *Verklaerte Nacht*, while Picasso had his rose and blue and classic periods which are representational. Like the composer and painter Miss Stein has her easier moments (*The Autobiography of Alice B. Toklas*, for instance, is written in imitation of Miss Toklas's own manner) and even in her more "difficult" pages there are variations, some of which are in the nature of experiment: One of the earliest of her inventions was her use of repetition which she describes as "insistence." "Once started expressing this thing, expressing anything there can be no repetition because the essence of that expression is insistence, and if you insist you must each time use emphasis and if you use emphasis it is not possible while anybody is alive that they should use exactly the same emphasis. . . . It is exactly like a frog hopping he cannot ever hop exactly the same distance or the same way of hopping at every hop. A bird's singing is perhaps the nearest thing to repetition but if you listen they too vary their insistence." Then she began to find new names for things, names which were not nouns, if possible, and, renaming things, became so enchanted sometimes with her own talent and the music of the words as they dropped that she became enamored of the magic of the mere sounds,

but quickly she sensed this was an impasse and began more and more
to strive to express her exact meaning with pronouns, conjunctions,
and participial clauses. After a while she came back to nouns, realizing that nouns, the names of things, make poetry, "When I said, A
rose is a rose is a rose, and then later made that into a ring, I made
poetry and what did I do I caressed completely caressed and
addressed a noun." She had another period of exciting discovery
when she found that paragraphs are emotional and sentences are
not. Finally, it came to her that she could condense and concentrate
her meaning into one word at a time, "even if there were always one
after the other." "I found," she has told us, "that any kind of book if
you read with glasses and somebody is cutting your hair and so you
cannot keep the glasses on and you use your glasses as a magnifying
glass and so read word by word reading word by word makes the
writing that is not anything be something. . . . So that shows to you
that a whole thing is not interesting because as a whole well as a
whole there has to be remembering and forgetting, but one at a time,
oh one at a time is something oh yes definitely something." But do
not get the idea that her essential appeal is to the ear or the subconscious. "It is her eyes and mind that are important and concerned in
choosing." Perhaps the most concrete explanation of her work that
she has ever given us is the following (from *The Autobiography of
Alice B. Toklas*): "Gertrude Stein, in her work, has always been possessed by the intellectual passion for exactitude in the description of
inner and outer reality. She has produced a simplification by this
concentration, and as a result the destruction of associational emotion in poetry and prose. She knows that beauty, music, decoration,
the result of emotion should never be the cause, even events should
not be the cause of emotion nor should emotion itself be the cause
of poetry or prose. They should consist of an exact reproduction of
either an outer or inner reality." She says again, this time in *What
Are Masterpieces* [1936], "If you do not remember while you are
writing, it may seem confused to others but actually it is clear and
eventually that clarity will be clear that is what a masterpiece is, but
if you remember while you are writing it will seem clear at the time
to any one but the clarity will go out of it that is what a masterpiece
is not."

In whatever style it pleases Miss Stein to write, however, it is her
custom to deal almost exclusively with "actualities," portraits of people she *knows*, descriptions of places, objects, and events which sur-
round her and with which she is immediately concerned. This
quality, true of almost all of her writing since *Three Lives* and *The
Making of Americans*, her perpetual good humor, and her sense of
fun, which leads her occasionally into intentional obscurantism, all
assist in keeping part of her prospective audience at a little distance

behind her. There is, for instance, in *Four Saints* at the close of the celebrated *Pigeons on the Grass* air (an air the meaning of which has been elucidated both by Miss Stein and Julian Sawyer) a passage which runs *Lucy Lily Lily Lucy*, etc., beautifully effective as sung to the music in Virgil Thomson's score. Those who believe this to be meaningless embroidery, like *Hey, nonny nonny* in an Elizabethan ballad, are perfectly sane. Miss Stein enjoyed the sound of the words, *but* the words did not come to her out of thin air, as is evidenced by a discovery I made recently. Lucy Lily Lamont is a girl who lives on page 35 of *Wars I Have Seen* and from the context one might gather that Miss Stein knew her a long time ago. Another example of this bewildering kind of reference is the "October 15" paragraph in *As a Wife Has a Cow* [1923] in the current collection. In my note to that idyl I have referred the reader to the probable origin of this passage. The books of this artist are indeed full of these sly references to matters unknown to their readers and only someone completely familiar with the routine, and roundabout, ways of Miss Stein's daily life would be able to explain every line of her prose, but without even mentioning Joyce's *Ulysses* or Eliot's *The Waste Land*, could not the same thing be said truthfully of Shakespeare's Sonnets?

No wonder Miss Stein exclaims pleasurably somewhere or other: "Also there is why is it that in this epoch the only real literary thinking has been done by a woman."

DONALD SUTHERLAND

[*Three Lives*]†

To make roughly an anatomy of *Three Lives*, from the broadest elements down, and beginning with narrative structure. Not only does *Three Lives* make a profitable exercise in literary anatomy but it contains already many principles which will stay for the later work of Gertrude Stein.

Simple narrative structure is when events are shown as leading from one to the other in temporal and causal succession until some conclusion such as death, marriage, riches, success, failure, or just arriving or going away is reached. The comparison of narrative structure to architecture is right, insofar as both a story and a building make an arrangement or an enclosed place for living, a field of presence for the mind, by which everything outside of it can be dismissed from concern. It functions like the frame of a picture, to isolate what

† From *Gertrude Stein: A Biography of Her Work* (New Haven: Yale University Press, 1951), pp. 22–52. Reprinted by permission of the publisher.

goes on inside it for complete attention and realization. Or it can be like the flat surface of a picture, to which everything presented is referred for realization. Of course the plane of action in writing like the plane of flat space in painting is treated differently, multiplied or broken or scattered or tilted or even destroyed by certain writers in certain historical periods.

But history aside, why is it that anyone likes and accepts a simple consecutive story as the plane of reference for presenting life to the mind? Regardless of interest and suspense and conflict and surprise and so on, and quite regardless of folk tales and fairy tales being genito-urinary metaphors or something, why is it all so often done in narrative? One reason is that events following each other continuously and coming to a conclusion flatter or confirm our sense of causing and controlling and possessing what we do and of being really the object of what happens to us. No matter how awful what happens is, in a story it happens to somebody and somebody makes it happen and these agents and sufferers get a very concrete and solid meaning from the events, which we may not feel continuously that we have in our lives. Another reason could be that most of our physical activities, eating, walking, working, and making love, do go on in a continuous series of movements until a conclusion of some sort is reached. So narrative may be an objectification and so a stabilizing and a reassurance of this natural way of doing anything.

But if narrative is natural and likable and it is, why is it often so difficult and sometimes a falsification to use it? Just as the Doric temple could not contain the Roman or Romanesque or Gothic or Renaissance religious life, so a simple narrative structure often cannot contain the life, whether religious or secular. It is a nice game to match architectural and narrative styles, as Marivaux with the Trianon, or Proust with Palladio and the reflections and reverberations of the Venetian palaces which make a use of classicism, or even Gertrude Stein with Louis Sullivan, who established the theory as well as the fact of the skyscraper; but I wish to account for *Three Lives* historically awhile, more than to describe it by comparisons.

Happily the situation in narrative to Gertrude Stein when she began can be shown by "Un Coeur Simple," the story by Flaubert which she was translating when she began writing *Three Lives*, in particular the first of the stories "The Good Anna."

Flaubert if one likes was a naturalist, which means that his art was a mortification or resolution or reduction of romanticism, which in turn has a very clear relation to simple narrative, so we may begin there. If classicism is integrated by the equivalence of the inner life to the outer event, or by the feeling that they both exist in a closely interdependent relevance, romanticism can be taken to be the collapse of that unity. In romanticism the inner life proceeds in incoherence or syncopation with outer events. From their state of incoherence with present events, the romantics do look away to the past or future or just to foreign civilizations where the classical equivalence was or is or might be. The romantic is not an adventurer but an exile and a wanderer. Complete immediate narrative cannot be written because the main reality is away and what exists in the present is purely emotion and reflection or dreaming. Romanticism produces no architecture, not even revivals, but it does use the ruins of other styles to dream in. When the romantics write narrative it has to go on elsewhere, that is, to be real it has to be separate and exotic. Chateaubriand cannot write his autobiography without supposing himself already dead.

Flaubert intermittently came out of romanticism. The change was in ceasing to look away at a distant coherence and in looking at a present incoherence steadily. Flaubert naturally had no illusions about his bourgeois present, and it was perhaps more terrible to him than anything the romantics had to put up with, because he kept his attention more and more obsessively fixed upon it, but it was reality, the reality. And it was incoherent, or split. Flaubert, in *Madame Bovary*, synchronized or made contrapuntal, so to speak, the two separate parts of present reality, much as Cervantes had done it in *Don Quijote*. Just as the chivalric world of Don Quijote is as present and real as that of Sancho Panza, so the romantic world of Emma Bovary is as real as that of Homais. It is their incoherent coexistence in the present which makes the whole orientation or thesis for the work of art. In "Un Coeur Simple," the dying Félicité, who is a simpler or nutshell Bovary, identifies her beloved stuffed parrot with the dove of the Holy Ghost, and this confrontation is a variant of the windmill which is a giant to Don Quijote. It is grotesque, but precisely the grotesque is for these writers the first quality of the full reality. As early as 1838 Flaubert had invented a separate god of the grotesque, Yuk, and declared him to be as universal as death. The standard form for the representation of the final grotesque is tragicomedy, and the manner is irony, whether grim or gentle or desperate or resigned or whatever. It is within this range that "Un Coeur Simple" and then *Three Lives* were written.

Before going into the consequences of this orientation to form, one may here ask the question: Why Flaubert? Why his reputation in America? At the least his reputation has been for using *le mot juste* and having the perfect style. We used to like formal exactitude and perfection as we used to like it in motors. We also used to think that the actual was our business and realism of some sort our native method. Even our most elaborate myths started at Nantucket and Brooklyn Bridge. This prejudice no doubt had its influence on Gertrude Stein, but more immediately her studies under William James

who was going to invent pragmatism, and her anatomical studies at
Johns Hopkins, would have inclined her to the exhaustive precisions
of Flaubert. And it was not Zola.[1] There was no room in Zola for
anything like the pragmatist proposition that truth is what you make
it. Truth for Zola was simply and finally scientific causality, whether
biological or social. For all his enormous energy, his moral courage,
his easy way with solids and masses, he was intellectually gross. He
was not a philosopher or a psychologist nor as a scientist more than
an enthusiast. All of which may be nothing against his art, but it
would very much keep him from influencing a young woman of Gertrude Stein's training, while the generally more professional mind
and sensibility of Flaubert—within realism or naturalism—would
attract her. She says in *Paris France* [published 1940] that she was
very early interested in Zola as a realist but more interested in the
Russian realists,[2] no doubt because the Russians eminently were
dramatists of the incommensurability between the inner and the
outer life.

At any rate, the difficulties of simple narrative structure under the
strain of ambivalence or two bearings are well enough shown by the
trouble between the main story and the interpolated stories of *Don
Quijote*. The major theme, Quijote-Sancho, can never be brought to
the certain progress and simple outlines of the interpolated
romances. The irrelevance of the external events to the inner life
they contain is exploited by Flaubert in the account of the route of
the fiacre containing Emma and her lover, or the medical details of
her death, or in the wanderings of Félicité about Le Havre. His
famous technique of "dissociation"—as with the interweaving of the
public speech with the conversation of Emma and Rodolphe—is
exactly and obviously this thing. The technique, instead of "dissociation," is really the association of incompatibles.

The plan for presenting this dual or incoherent reality becomes
naturally a simple series of confrontations of a person taken as the
vehicle of the inner life, with people or situations representing the
outer events. The confrontations or episodes can be more or less
resolved or simply abandoned one by one, but the sequence of events
has no meaning in itself except as an accumulation of demonstrations. Thus there is only an episodic structure concluded by the
death of the subject—Don Quijote, Emma Bovary, Félicité, the
Good Anna.

An episodic structure was made disreputable as early as Aristotle,
who was all for unity of external action, and the inner life except as
ethics did not concern him. But if unity in terms of external events

1. Émile Zola (1840–1902), French novelist and advocate for social reform, founder of naturalism in fiction. [*Editor's note.*]
2. *Paris France* (B. T. Batsford, 1940), p. 7.

no longer accounts adequately for the full reality, what sort of unity or completion can there be? There are many answers to that, but one answer was the life of one person. Biography had already found that an adequate unity often enough, and the biographical convention had been useful in the novel since Marivaux and Richardson at least, but the life told about had had meaning as adventure, as an example of some virtue or vice, or simply as a figure as real and elaborate as a living person known for a long time. In the scientific climate of the 19th century the single life took on the meaning of a case history, or the natural and inevitable performance of any instance of a species. If man is the species the interest is less in the rare cases and sports than in the average and ordinary. The literary record of an ordinary life is not a documentation of the single case for its own sake or for the sake of adding to our knowledge of single cases, but a demonstration of how the single case expresses the essentials of the whole species or subspecies. To the naturalists the species man was above all the maladjusted animal, or, to avoid misunderstanding perhaps, the unadjustable animal. The subtitle of *Madame Bovary* is *Moeurs de Province*, or *Provincial Behavior*, and this does not mean that it is a documentation of the French provinces—which had come, mixed with other intentions, with Balzac, and was to come again with the vulgarization by Zola—but that it is a demonstration by a specific instance of the characteristic provincialism of the species man. Not being God, he is always in some province or other, whether he is restless or contented in it. The view is fatalistic and can be ironical. The epigraph to *Three Lives* is the flat observation of Jules Laforgue,[3] "Donc je suis un malheureux et ce n'est ni ma faute ni celle de la vie." And when that has been settled, the intelligence is free from guilt and grievance, to go on and describe the behavior of the species. This really does not need any justification, but in these days of responsibilities and imperatives it is just as well to say that Homer and Shakespeare and Cervantes wrote from that same attitude, and that while a social purpose and reform and revolution do very well in their way, the virtue of art consists in seeing farther than that and more than that, whether the prospect glows or darkens.

It so happens, however, that the naturalists, with *Three Lives* in their wake, had among their significances an obvious social one. Flaubert was ferociously political, with a particular hatred for the middle class. His complaint against them was in the main their abject fear of being alive and the ineffable clumsiness of their behavior. His values were aristocratic. Gertrude Stein could naturally not take up a French political attitude. The American middle class if one can

3. Her bow to Laforgue, though it covers his fatalism, evidently cannot indicate any sympathy with his liking for von Hartmann's philosophy of the unconscious.

distinguish such a thing still had its health, and the remains of what
might be called the New England aristocracy had nothing promising
for the national life, either in the way of values or of impulse. She
had settled the New England type rather brutally in her classifications at Radcliffe. And so soon after the Civil War the southern
aristocracy could not be taken seriously. At all events the early work
of Gertrude Stein accepts and loves the middle class as being the
vital class in America. Very much later she had wicked things to say
about our lower middle class,[4] but as late as *The Making of Americans*
she said passionately, against other claims, that anything worth while
had always come from the middle class. Even if that is not entirely
so, the attitude is far from foolish.

In *Three Lives* she deals with the poor, whom she had known as
servants and patients in Baltimore, but there is very little if any political meaning to it. They are primarily human and not social types.
She had what was then not a sentimental or programmatic but a
natural democratic feeling that any human being was important just
as that, as a human being. This feeling was no doubt reinforced and
made confident by her philosophical and medical training, but it was,
to start with, a native and direct curiosity about everybody. Later, as
I will show, this basic democratic feeling in her developed not into
political theory but into a sort of secular saintliness.

So "the good Anna" is first of all a human type, living and dying
as that type does. She is presented first not as a child or a young girl
but in her full development, in a situation which gives full expression
to her typical kind of force, which is incessant managing will. The
first chapter gives her as the type of that, the second chapter gives
her life, and the third chapter her death. It is a curious kind of construction, which derives from "Un Coeur Simple." Flaubert begins:
"Pendant un demi-siècle, les bourgeois de Pont-L'Evêque envièrent
à Mme Aubain sa servante Félicité. Pour cent francs par an, elle
faisait la cuisine et le ménage, cousait, lavait, repassait, savait brider
un cheval, engraisser les volailles, battre le beurre, et resta fidèle à
sa maitresse,—qui cependant n'était pas une personne agréable."[5]
After this summary presentation Flaubert goes on to recount
assorted episodes demonstrating Félicité's courage, loyalty, generosity, affection, etc. "Elle avait eu, comme une autre, son histoire
d'amour."[6] "The Good Anna" begins: "The tradesmen of Bridgepoint
learned to dread the sound of 'Miss Mathilda,' for with that name

---

4. See *Wars I Have Seen* (Random House, 1945), p. 27.
5. For half a century, the bourgeoisie of Pont-L'Evêque envied Madame Aubin for her servant
   Félicité. For a hundred francs a year, she cooked and kept house, she washed, ironed and
   sewed, she knew how to bridle a horse, fatten the poultry, and churn the butter, and she
   remained faithful to her mistress, who, however, was not a likable person. [*Editor's note.*]
6. She had had, like everyone else, her own love story. [*Editor's note.*]

the good Anna always conquered." And later: "The widow Mrs. Lehntman was the romance in Anna's life."

Now while the situations and episodes in "The Good Anna" are chosen and arranged to show the character of the subject in various relationships, the qualities of the character are not primarily moral. The word "good," which is repeated as constantly as a Homeric epithet before the name Anna, does not indicate an evaluation of the character or a conclusion about it but the constantly present essence of the character which is there as a fact and not as a value. Like the word "poor" which is used of Anna, Melanctha, and Lena, it gives a rather perfunctory general shape to the character, like the terribly simple shape of a Cézanne head or apple. Both the epithet and the shape of the apple look awkward and crude from the point of view of more graceful and less serious art, say that of Whistler or Pater, but these raw simplicities are necessary to hold down or stabilize an extreme complexity of interrelationship. It is like the melodrama of Henry James. Not to press these parallels too far, but as the Cézanne apple has weight and existence not by its shape or by perspective but by an equilibrium of relationships within the space of the picture, so the good Anna gets weight and existence, almost as a physical consistency, from her relationships within the account.

> Anna found her place with large, abundant women, for such were always lazy, careless or all helpless, and so the burden of their lives could fall on Anna, and give her just content. Anna's superiors must be always these large helpless women, or be men, for none others could give themselves to be made so comfortable and free.
>
> Anna had no strong natural feeling to love children, as she had to love cats and dogs, and a large mistress. She never became deeply fond of Edgar and Jane Wadsmith. She naturally preferred the boy, for boys love always better to be done for and made comfortable and full of eating, while in the little girl she had to meet the feminine, the subtle opposition, showing so early always in a young girl's nature.[7]
>
> Miss Mary was sitting in a large armchair by the fire. All the nooks and crannies of the chair were filled full of her soft and spreading body. She was dressed in a black satin morning gown, the sleeves, great monster things, were heavy with the mass of her soft flesh. She sat there always, large, helpless, gentle. She had a fair, soft, regular, good-looking face, with pleasant, empty, grey-blue eyes, and heavy sleepy lids.
>
> Behind Miss Mary was the little Jane, nervous and jerky with excitement as she saw Anna come into the room.

7. *Three Lives* (Modern Library, 1933), p. 25.

"Miss Mary," Anna began. She had stopped just within the door, her body and her face stiff with repression, her teeth closed hard and the white lights flashing sharply in the pale, clean blue of her eyes. Her bearing was full of the strange coquetry of anger and of fear, the stiffness, the bridling, the suggestive movement underneath the rigidity of forced control, all the queer ways the passions have to show themselves all one.

"Miss Mary," the words came slowly with thick utterance and with jerks, but always firm and strong. "Miss Mary, I can't stand it any more like this. When you tell me anything to do, I do it. I do everything I can and you know I work myself sick for you. The blue dressings in your room makes too much work to have for summer. Miss Jane don't know what work is. If you want to do things like that I go away."

Anna stopped still. Her words had not the strength of meaning they were meant to have, but the power in the mood of Anna's soul frightened and awed Miss Mary through and through.

Like in all large and helpless women, Miss Mary's heart beat weakly in the soft and helpless mass it had to govern. Little Jane's excitements had already tried her strength. Now she grew pale and fainted quite away.[8]

This last scene is as an event no more than a slapstick episode. It comes from a gift Gertrude Stein had and never lost, for extremely broad and reckless farce. In this same story she distinguishes two varieties or gradations of it.

"Her freakish humor now first showed itself, her sense of fun in the queer ways that people had, that made her later find delight in brutish servile Katy, in Sally's silly ways and in the badness of Peter and of Rags."[9]

"Anna always had a humorous sense from this old Katy's twisted peasant english, from the roughness on her tongue of buzzing s's and from the queer ways of her servile brutish humor."[1]

As the passions are all one the humor is all one through its gradations, and very much continuous with Gertrude Stein. She had an extraordinary mimetic faculty that allowed her not only to take on the full nature of her subject—in this case to the point of composing her episode in the manner of her characters—but to follow the gradations of a theme or feeling into its farthest and faintest developments. For example the character of dogs becomes quite comparable to the character of people, and this not sentimentally or meta-

8. *Ibid.*, pp. 28–29.
9. *Ibid.*, pp. 37–38.
1. *Ibid.*, p. 17.

phorically but as the brain of a dog can be studied with the human brain and is not very different.

> And then Peter never strayed away, and he looked out of his nice eyes and he liked it when you rubbed him down, and he forgot you when you went away, and he barked whenever there was any noise.
>
> When he was a little pup he had one night been put into the yard and that was all of his origin she knew. The good Anna loved him well and spoiled him as a good german mother always does her son.
>
> Little Rags was very different in his nature. He was a lively creature made out of ends of things, all fluffy and dust color, and he was always bounding up into the air and darting all about over and then under silly Peter and often straight into solemn fat, blind, sleepy Baby, and then in a wild rush after some stray cat.
>
> Rags was a pleasant, jolly little fellow. The good Anna liked him very well, but never with her strength as she loved her good looking coward, foolish young man, Peter.
>
> Baby was the dog of her past life and she held Anna with old ties of past affection. Peter was the spoiled, good looking young man, of her middle age, and Rags was always something of a toy. She liked him but he never struck in very deep.[2]

Gertrude Stein is here dealing with broad classifications or types of character and relationship, minutely distinguished and identified. The scientific accuracy or the accuracy of intuition very consciously overrides the inaccuracies of common sense which would say one's feelings about a dog have little or no relation to one's feelings about a person. The humor of this kind of paradox, a rather broad sympathetic irony, is, as I suggested, the pervading tone of this work. The same irony carries the scene with Miss Mary, where the event is broad to the point of vulgarity, but where the feelings involved are distinguished and identified with great finesse. This intricate and accurate elaboration of the broad, the normal, the commonplace, is a method she used all her life. It is at once American and classical, as I will try to show much later.

She was trained to a very sharp scalpel and there is a medical neatness about how Miss Mary fills her chair and Anna's being just inside the door. It is a somewhat forced neatness of contour as one finds it in Cézanne and in Flaubert, in Juan Gris. With Gertrude Stein it is, among other things, a sort of feminine daintiness that can become a fussiness now and then, and that can work either as an irritation or a personal charm on the reader. But here it makes very

2. *Ibid.*, p. 68.

clear the constant definition of Anna's character by the description of its functions in a variety of relationships. For closer and closer definition and distinction the terms naturally have to be very simple, if it is all going to be clear. The terms of the definition or expression are used in as absolute a sense as may be. In the sentence "The tradesmen of Bridgepoint learned to dread the sound of 'Miss Mathilda,' for with that name the good Anna always conquered" the word "conquered" is used absolutely. It is *le mot juste* with a vengeance. It does not depend, for the expression of the present subject, on connotations of Alexander the Great or Cortez. It is used in its essential or axiomatic meaning of succeeding and dominating in an enterprise against resistance. It is used without historical resonance and suggestion, without, so to speak, the conventional perspective of literary language. To some extent, in this early work, it may play *against* conventional perspective, as the relational depth in Cézanne seems to play paradoxically against traditional perspective, but that paradox is a secondary interest. As with Cézanne, the new usage stands by itself as solid and accurate, without reference to what it contradicts. The verbal irony here, such as it may be, is only a minor distraction, at most an incidental reflection of the larger and more serious irony at the heart of the work. At any rate, she relied less and less on the rather cosmetic interest of verbal irony, and made no apologies for absolute and categorical meaning. This was directly against another contemporary movement, of composition by the multiplication of resonances and ambiguities.

If the character then is defined by its relationships and its consistency of force, there is the question of presentation. The narrative becomes episodic, as I have explained, and there are plenty of flat statements, generalities, and discourses. That is, the *presentation* does still rely on demonstration and even on explanation. But the really extraordinary thing about the good Anna is that the character is thought of also as a musical continuity. Already in Radcliffe Gertrude Stein had described the conflict between the conscious and the automatic parts of her subjects in experiments as being like two themes going on together in music, one and the other dominating alternately. This and the opera may have been the beginning of the idea. Solomons noted that her attention was mainly auditory,[3] and she herself speaks of doing a great deal of listening then, not to what was being said so much as to the way it was being said, the rise and fall, and the characteristic variety of emphasis. She used to call this "the rhythm of a personality." The phrase sounds now like a rather fancy affectation, but it had an exact and responsible meaning within what was being thought about human psychology at the time. It was

3. *Psychological Review*, III (1896), No. 5, 500.

not rhythm for pleasure in rhythm but a thing existing in the living personality that could be accurately registered and described. The means for registering this was inevitably the language as spoken or as written. In *Three Lives* this is conveyed clearly enough in the dialogue parts. There is a handsome example of this projection by rhythm in dialogue in a scene between the good Anna and Mrs. Lehntman.

> "I know you was careless, Mrs. Lehntman, but I didn't think that you could do this so. No, Mrs. Lehntman, it ain't your duty to take up with no others, when you got two children of your own, that got to get along just any way they can, and you know you ain't got any too much money all the time, and you are all so careless here and spend it all the time, and Julia and Willie growin' big. It ain't right, Mrs. Lehntman, to do so."
>
> This was as bad as it could be. Anna had never spoken her mind so to her friend before. . . . And then too Mrs. Lehntman could not really take in harsh ideas. She was too well diffused to catch the feel of any sharp firm edge.
>
> Now she managed to understand all this in a way that made it easy for her to say, "Why, Anna, I think you feel too bad about seeing what the children are doing every minute in the day. Julia and Willie are real good, and they play with all the nicest children in the square. . . . No indeed Anna, it's easy enough to say I should send this poor, cute little boy to a'sylum when I could keep him here so nice, but you know Anna, you wouldn't like to do it yourself, now you really know you wouldn't, Anna, though you talk to me so hard.—My, it's hot to-day, what you doin' with that ice tea in there Julia, when Miss Annie is waiting all this time for her drink?"
>
> Julia brought in the ice tea. . . .
>
> "Here Miss Annie," Julia said, "Here, Miss Annie, is your glass of tea, I know you like it good and strong."
>
> "No, Julia, I don't want no ice tea here. Your mamma ain't able to afford now using her money upon ice tea for her friends. It ain't right she should now any more. . . ."
>
> "My, Miss Annie is real mad now," Julia said, as the house shook, as the good Anna shut the outside door with a concentrated shattering slam.[4]

In this passage the hard rage of Anna, the bland diffusion of Mrs. Lehntman, and the nasty silliness of Julia are conveyed by the rhythm of the talk I think very well. But in prose, since there can be no explicit indication of staccato or legato or speed or *dolce*, the exact phrasing can easily be lost by the reader. Gertrude Stein supplies some direction, not only from the natural assumptions of the scene

4. *Three Lives*, pp. 44–45.

but by such words as sharp, firm, hard, and then for Mrs. Lehntman, diffused, easy. With these directions one can so to speak interpret the piece fairly accurately. But the rhythm involves much more than the matters of beat and phrasing and metrics. The physical verbal rhythm is in itself relatively simple and heavy, like the vocabulary. It would correspond to say a simple ¾ time in comparison to the elaborate syncopations and runs and glides and suspensions of late 19th century prose, or poetry—or to the palette of Cézanne as against an infinitely graduated impressionist palette, say that of Monet. But as with the vocabulary, the simplification of the rhythm is there to carry and clarify something complicated. Very much as, in the experiment I quoted at length in the first chapter, a metronome controlled the succession of meaningless syllables, as a condition for the functioning of the attention in memorizing, so here the functioning of the attention of the characters in speech (which would be according to Gertrude Stein's early definition a reflex of their total character) goes on against a simplified verbal rhythm. It has to be simple to disengage the special personal emphasis and to carry a rhythm of ideas. By a rhythm of ideas I mean only that as anyone goes on talking, or as we say expressing himself, there is in the sequence and force of the things said a very definite rate of change and a pattern of recurrence. The rate of change is largely a matter of the duration of interest, or as we would say the attention span, or as they said at Radcliffe a pulse beat of consciousness, quickened or sluggish. This is much more natural than it sounds. In the 19th century novel the thing said expresses the character insofar as it shows an attitude or, in Aristotle's word, a predilection. What a man has to say about his mother, about foreigners, about the new wing to the rectory expresses his character. We get not the essence of the character in process so much as little incidents or lights about the character. After an accumulation of them one can feel the character is all there and alive, that one knows what to expect of him in any little action. The patter passages of Jane Austen, Trollope, and Dickens do go beyond this, to presenting the mind of the character in process directly, but it all tends to be crippled by the conventions of current grammar and literary style or dialect, or obstructed by material furthering the plot or the atmosphere or the philosophy.

In the passage quoted above and in the scene with Miss Mary quoted earlier, the ideas expressed have hardly any personal idiosyncrasy, they are in themselves the bleakest commonplaces, and this neutrality serves as a foil to make clear the extremely delicate sequence and emphasis of the ideas as they come out of the character in accordance with the vital intensity and frequency of that character. The ideas of the enraged Anna come with a steady insistence as well as abrupt change. Consider how the pressure that has to be put not only on the metric but on the meaning of the phrase "to do so" expresses the violence in Anna more directly than external description or greater eloquence of vocabulary and idea. The repetition of the name Mrs. Lehntman is Anna's way of making the woman stay there and hold still under the pounding reproaches. The use of the word "here" in the phrase "and you are all so careless here and spend it all the the time" is again a way of arresting the household for the attack. The repetition of the phrase "all the time" is again a way of enveloping their behavior for total condemnation. In contrast the charming "easy" maundering expostulation of Mrs. Lehntman dwells softly on irrelevances until the final incoherence of calling for the ice tea. Gertrude Stein says earlier, "It was wonderful how Mrs. Lehntman could listen and not hear, could answer and yet not decide, could say and do what she was asked and yet leave things as they were before."[5]

This differs from the method of Proust. With him the peculiarities of speech, the curious idiom of vocabulary, both verbal and ideal, all project the precise social or historical coloring of the character. Not that drama and an expressive rhythm are not in it, but they are not disengaged from an extremely complex harmonics in every phrase uttered by Françoise or Charlus, for example. Gertrude Stein reduces the tonality, the pedal, and disengages the pure melody and rhythm. We are out of Wagner say into Satie. This is one part of what she called the destruction of associational emotion.

In "The Good Anna" she tries numerous other methods for presenting the characters alive, besides direct dialogue. One attempt is to run Anna's abrupt rhythm across the dialogue into the narrative: " 'Peter!,'—her voice rose higher,—'Peter!,'—Peter was the youngest and the favorite dog,—'Peter if you don't leave Baby alone,'—Baby was an old, blind terrier that Anna had loved for many years,—'Peter if you don't leave Baby alone, I take a rawhide to you, you bad dog.' "[6] The consistency corresponding to the rhythm is given in physical descriptions: "At this time Anna, about twenty-seven years of age, was not yet all thin and worn. The sharp bony edges and corners of her head and face were still rounded out with flesh, but already the temper and the humor showed sharply in her clean blue eyes, and the thinning was begun about the lower jaw, that was so often strained with the upward pressure of resolve."[7] The quality of incessant strain and pressure, Anna's particular quality, pervades nearly everything in the story, from the structure and transitions to the least

5. *Ibid.*, p. 39.
6. *Ibid.*, p. 12.
7. *Ibid.*, p. 28.

matters of style. It is, like the work of Flaubert, exhaustively coordinated. It seems all to be written on the signature as it were of one of the earliest sentences: "Anna led an arduous and troubled life."

Whatever this analysis may make it look like, "The Good Anna" is not merely an exercise in technique, though certainly very brilliant as an exercise. The story comes really from a simple animal necessity to express something living. It is more a matter of feeling than philosophy that decides that remarks about people or the story of what happened to them does not adequately or directly express them living. It takes a very vivid, even rank sense of life and a great intellectual vitality not to sacrifice the intuition of the living to the inadequate but accepted form, and then to use all available means and inventions to express that living as truly as one can. "The Good Anna" is an effort to do so.

But the impact and influence of *Three Lives* were mainly by its verbal novelty. It destroyed the extenuated rhetoric of the late 19th century. Wordsworth and the romantics had broken up the late classical rhetoric and regulated the written language on the natural idiom or on personal impulse. Language, like people, put off the perruque and wore an open collar. But the complex and ineffable longings of the natural life became standardized into attitudes, Byronic and others, and the language settled into as perfunctory a rhetoric as the classical. It wound up as art for art. And people did their hair correspondingly, making necessary the antimacassar. Then Gertrude Stein inevitably came to the crew cut.

Three Lives, more radically than any other work of the time in English, brought the language back to life. Not the life of the peasantry or the emotions or the proletariat but life as it was lived by anybody living in the century, the average or normal life as the naturalists had seen it. Gertrude Stein in this work tried to coordinate the composition of the language with the process of consciousness, which, we have seen, was to her a close reflex of the total living personality. If this was to be done at least two serious things had to happen to the language:

First the word had to have not its romantic or literary meaning but the immediate meaning it had to the contemporary using it, a literal axiomatic meaning confined to the simple situations of the average life. The heroines of *Three Lives*, two German women and a Negress, have no connection whatever with the literary past of the language. The words are not used either as the authentic dialect of Baltimore Germans or Negroes; rather the perfunctory dialect convention serves as a pretext for liberating the language from literary convention.

The second necessity was to destroy 19th century syntax and word order, which could not follow the movement of a consciousness moving naturally, this movement being, in the early 20th century, of the utmost importance. Gertrude Stein had read a great deal of Elizabethan prose and poetry, in particular the prose of Robert Greene, and to that extent had a precedent and model for an extremely loose syntax which could follow the immediate interest and impulse of the consciousness, whether lively and extravagant or simply ruminant. The prose of Greene is normally full of the rather swaggering rapid movement and brutal emphasis of his person.[8] The prose and construction of "The Good Anna" are based on something of the same quality in the character of the heroine.

As Whitman for example had destroyed 19th century metrics and verse forms, Gertrude Stein destroyed 19th century syntax and word order. Her work at this is comparable to what G. M. Hopkins was doing with syntax in his poetry, but there is a very great difference between them. Hopkins had as a Jesuit a casuist training in very fine distinctions of idea, a training corresponding considerably to the medical and philosophical training of Gertrude Stein. But, and I believe this is important, Hopkins was a straight baroque poet. The baroque style[9] is equivalent to the Jesuit style, none too roughly, and they are both creations of the Counter Reformation, motivated by a desire to keep an escaping thing under. Under authority or under a formula or under the intellect or under the eye, it does not much matter. The baroque means, as a conquest, to bring everything under a closed system and within reach of the authorities. ("Glory be to God for dappled things.") The tension of the baroque is simply that struggle, heroic or sometimes just frantic. In the time of Hopkins the religious motive happened to coincide with a similar motive on the part of 19th century science and also the British Empire. All in all it leads to a closed and finished art, the stuffing of something inside something else, even if it wrenches the container considerably. Joyce, in the 20th century, went on with this, cramming everything into the scheme of the *Odyssey* or cyclic time, so that one may say that he was the last hypertrophy of the 19th century and destroyed it by overdoing it.

The early work of Gertrude Stein is still rather haunted by the pretention to universal inclusion, not of Catholicism of course but

8. Greene, in his tract on Coney-catching, claimed a propriety (even τὸ πρέπον) in using a plain style for a low subject. This fact is historically curious but entirely unimportant. His appeal to a classical theory in fashion is a casual justification of a much more important thing, his perfectly direct undecorated literal vision of the subject. Gertrude Stein always admired this tradition, through Defoe and Trollope.

9. "The baroque" can of course be more generally defined as the collision of the romantic with the classical, their struggle or their embrace on about equal terms. I do not think it should be carried beyond that to mean any mixture, however unequal, of the classic and romantic, because that would ultimately include everything. In any event, I use the term here in its ordinary sense, to mean the baroque par excellence, that of the 16th and 17th centuries, and later styles organized on virtually the same grounds.

of naturalistic or evolutionary science. *The Making of Americans* is a universal history of human types and *Three Lives* has the paradigmatic force of naturalist writing. But the form and method and intent differ greatly from the insular Catholic product. The virtue of that product is to re-create the corporeal presence of everything within its little room, but the art of Gertrude Stein, being not insular but continental, is, even so early, generalized and disembodied, representing rather than including the totality of cases by single simple axioms. The form itself makes an enclosure, but this, as a reflection of a theory of consciousness, does not stand as a receptacle but as a field of activity, "a space of time that is filled always filled with moving."[1] Otherwise her work, like that of Whitman, is all wide open spaces. It is absolutely not institutional or sectarian, it cannot be cathartic or tragic or salvationist, it is not out to justify or condemn or set things right. She had, to a startling degree, no sense of alienation from the universe but took it as a miraculously given thing. She speaks somewhere of the daily miracle that happens to the artist. The religious parallel to this very secular art would be not doctrine or ritual or institution but arbitrarily the state of grace. She teased everyone by calling this her being a genius. She was, I have no doubt, but the importance of that for the reader is not in the value but in the orientation it gives her work.

"The Good Anna," as pioneer work, does have its uncertainties and imperfections. I do not see how, for example, it is not a mistake to use the word "nay," or to mention the Struldbrugs, or to speak of "the dust which settles with the ages." But if these are errors they are errors with a meaning. They take up the prophetic tone of voice used loudly enough by Whitman, Melville, and later Hart Crane and Wolfe, to carry over the wide open spaces. In the case of Gertrude Stein it is the first appearance of the sibylline manner[2] that is found in a great deal of her later work, where it perfectly belongs.

The third story of *Three Lives*, "The Gentle Lena," contains no great novelty beyond "The Good Anna." It is in a way a pendant to the first story in that Lena is a study of a soft and fluid and even absent consciousness and character as against the emphatic and hard presence of Anna. "Lena was patient, gentle, sweet and german." It is a delicious little story and prettily turned. It at least shows that Gertrude Stein was even this early capable of grace and easy elegance in the midst of her revolution. Further, it has a simple tenderness within complete clarity which so far as I know is unique

1. *Lectures in America* (Random House, 1935), p. 161.
2. Barring of course the daily themes she wrote at Radcliffe. The magniloquence of many passages in the themes is a combination of George Eliot's influence, youth, and very likely a deliberate flouting of New England reticence.

in our literature. The nearest thing to it would be Sherwood Anderson.

But according to the general agreement the big thing in *Three Lives* is the middle story, "Melanctha." It is a tragic love story ending in death from consumption, so that it is available to the traditional literary taste and the educated emotions. Furthermore it is, as Carl Van Vechten says, "perhaps the first American story in which the Negro is regarded as a human being and not as an object for condescending compassion or derision."[3] It is a good deal to have attained that clarity and equilibrium of feeling in a difficult question, but "Melanctha" as a piece of literature does much more.

Where "The Good Anna" and "The Gentle Lena" are composed as the presentation of a single type in illustrative incidents, Melanctha is composed on the dramatic trajectory of a passion. If "The Good Anna" roughly corresponds to "Un Coeur Simple," "Melanctha" corresponds roughly to *Madame Bovary*. Very roughly, and there is most likely no direct influence, but it makes an illuminating comparison.

Madame Bovary and the course of her passion are presented in an elaborate series of incidents, situations, landscapes, interiors, extraneous issues; in short they are measured and realized against a thick objective context as the things in the context are measured against her desire. Strangely enough this desire is never directly presented. It is measured somewhat by its casual source in her romantic reading—as Don Quijote is casually accounted for by his reading of the romances of chivalry—and it is known later by its various objects such as travel in far lands, luxuries, poetry written to her, and so on. As a blind desire, and probably as a death wish, it is symbolized by the awful blind beggar who is as it were Emma's *Doppelgänger* and who is finally put out of the way by Homais, the type of cheap rationalism. Emma's power is measured again by her being too much for Charles, for Léon, and even for Rodolphe, and by the pathetic infatuation of the boy Justin. She has certainly a variety of states of mind, wild desire, remorse, boredom, religiosity, fear, and so on, but they are a succession of distinct states, presented as complete and not as in process. In brief, Flaubert's art was spatial and intensely pictorial, not temporal and musical. Expressing directly and exactly the immediate movement, pulse, and process of a thing simply was not his business. But it was in this early period Gertrude Stein's business, and in "Melanctha" she did express at length the process of a passion.

She did not yet disengage the essential vitality entirely from its natural context. There are some few descriptions of railroad yards, docks, country scenes, houses, yards, rooms, windows, but these are

3. Preface, *Three Lives*, p. x.

reduced to a telling minimum. There is also some accounting for the
complex forces in the heroine's character by the brutality of her
father and the sweet indifference of her mother. She is described at
the beginning of the story by contrast and association with Rose
Johnson, her hard-headed decent friend, and again by the same contrast enlarged at the end of the story, when Rose casts her off. But
the real demonstration of the story is the dialogue between Melanctha and her lover Jeff Campbell. In this long dialogue, which is like
a duel or duet, the traditional incoherence between the inner and
the outer life has been replaced by an incoherence between two
subjectivities. It is conceived of as a difference in tempo, the slow
Jeff against the quick Melanctha.[4] Also there is already very much
present in this story the difference, the radical and final difference
in people, defined in *The Making of Americans* as the attacking and
the resisting kinds or types. It is not quite the difference between
active and passive, as both kinds are based on a persistence in being
or in living, and they are further complicated by a deviousness and
modulation in function. For example, how does a naturally attacking
kind resist and how does a naturally resisting kind get provoked to
attack? All this is elaborately and dramatically worked out in the long
dialogue. "It was a struggle, sure to be going on always between them.
It was a struggle that was as sure always to be going on between
them, as their minds and hearts always were to have different ways
of working."[5] Their differences, shade by shade, and their gradual
reconciliations are presented through the whole course of the affair
from indifference to gradual fascination to the struggle for domination by a variety of means, to the decline into brotherly and sisterly
affection, and finally to the final break.

Gertrude Stein had already, in a story written in 1903 and called
Quod Erat Demonstrandum [*Q.E.D.*] but not published until 1950
and under the title *Things as They Are*,[6] worked out a very similar
dialectic of a passion. It is very interesting as a preliminary exercise
for "Melanctha." As its first title suggests, it is an intensive and
exhaustive study of relations in a triangle. In its way it is a Jamesian
study or demonstration, and its heroine mentions and quotes the
heroine and/or villainess of James' novel *The Wings of the Dove*, Kate
Croy. But *Things as They Are* bears a more striking resemblance to
the *Adolphe* of Benjamin Constant, it has the same merciless direct-

---

4. This conception, of tempo of character as the cardinal difficulty in a love story, is already
   distinct if not developed in her Radcliffe theme of December 29, 1894. (See Rosalind S.
   Miller, *Gertrude Stein: Form and Intelligibility* [Exposition Press, 1949], p. 124.) This
   theme, entitled "The Great Enigma," is no doubt drawn from a real episode, and the
   conception of character probably rose directly out of experience, not out of other literature
   or the psychological laboratory, though this last surely verified and developed the idea.
5. *Three Lives*, p. 153.
6. Banyan Press, 1950.

ness and concentration, and though Gertrude Stein had probably not read *Adolphe* in 1903 this earliest work belongs to the tradition of *Adolphe* and of *La Princesse de Clèves*. It has the same unwavering intellectual clarity applied to the perpetually shifting relationships of a passion throughout its course. That much is already mastered in this first work, but the handling tends more to commentary than to presentation and has not the sure grasp of the personal cadences of a character's thought and feeling that makes the analyses in "Melanctha" a direct expression of character in movement. This is partly the fault of the characters themselves in *Things as They Are*. They are white American college women, whose speech and thought are bound to be at odds with their feeling. Gertrude Stein treats this difficulty handsomely enough as subject matter, but the expressive power of the prose is limited by its very propriety to the subject matter. It is very pure, immensely intelligent, and astonishing for a first work in 1903, but it is polite, cultivated, educated, literary. Compare with the passage from "Melanctha," quoted above, the following from *Things as They Are*:

"Time passed and they renewed their habit of desultory meetings at public places, but these were not the same as before. There was between them now a consciousness of strain, a sense of new adjustments, of uncertain standards and of changing values."[7]

"Melanctha," in which the characters are Negroes, has thereby the advantage of "uneducated" speech, and of a direct relationship between feeling and word, a more fundamental or universal drama. It is a measure of her strength that in making the most of the advantage Gertrude Stein abandoned polite or cultivated writing completely and forever, so completely that the press where she had *Three Lives* printed sent to inquire if she really knew English.

At all events, "Melanctha" is, as I said the work of Henry James was, a time continuum less of events than of considerations of their meaning. The events considered in "Melanctha" are mostly the movements of the passion, how Jeff and Melanctha feel differently toward each other from moment to moment.

Like the characters of James, Melanctha and Jeff are preternaturally articulate about their feelings, but where James keeps the plausibilities by using highly cultivated characters to express the complicated meaning in an endless delicacy of phrasing, Gertrude Stein uses the simplest possible words, the common words used by everybody, and a version of the most popular phrasing, to express the very complicated thing. It is true and exciting that James often used the simplest possible word for his complicated meaning, but he had a tendency to isolate it to the attention, to force it to carry its

7. *Things as They Are*, p. 30.

full weight by printing it in italics or putting it in quotes, or dislo-
cating it from its more usual place in the word order, or repeating
it. Gertrude Stein uses repetition and dislocation to make the word
bear all the meaning it has, but actually one has to give her work
word by word the deliberate attention one gives to something written
in italics. It has been said that her work means more when one reads
it in proof or very slowly, and that is certainly true, the work has to
be read word by word, as a succession of single meanings accumu-
lating into a larger meaning, as for example the words in the stanza
of a song being sung. Unhappily all our training and most of our
reasons for reading are against this. Very likely the desire for simplicity in style is most often a desire that the words and ideas along
the way to the formulated conclusion, the point, be perfectly negligible and that we have no anxious feeling we are missing anything
as we rush by. But as an example of how Gertrude Stein forces the
simplest negligible words to stay there in a full meaning:

> "Can't you understand Melanctha, ever, how no man certainly
> ever really can hold your love for long times together. You cer-
> tainly Melanctha, you ain't got down deep loyal feeling, true
> inside you, and when you ain't just that moment quick with
> feeling, then you certainly ain't ever got anything more there to
> keep you. You see Melanctha, it certainly is this way with you,
> it is, that you ain't ever got any way to remember right what you
> been doing, or anybody else that has been feeling with you. You
> certainly Melanctha, never can remember right, when it comes
> what you have done and what you think happens to you." "It
> certainly is all easy for you Jeff Campbell to be talking. You
> remember right, because you don't remember nothing till you
> get home with your thinking everything all over, but I certainly
> don't think much ever of that kind of way of remembering right,
> Jeff Campbell. I certainly do call it remembering right Jeff
> Campbell, to remember right just when it happens to you, so
> you have a right kind of feeling not to act the way you always
> been doing to me, and then you go home Jeff Campbell, and
> you begin with your thinking, and then it certainly is very easy
> for you to be good and forgiving with it. No, that ain't to me,
> the way of remembering Jeff Campbell, not as I can see it not
> to make people always suffer, waiting for you certainly to get to
> do it. . . ."[8]

The passage is, if one likes, about the synchronization of feeling
upon the present activity. Anyone can see what is meant by the argument if the feeling discussed is understood to be sexual feeling. But

8. *Three Lives*, pp. 180–181.

the thing which makes this passage absolutely accurate and not euphemistic is that the subject is literally feeling, all feeling, inasmuch as all the passions are one. In brief, making abstraction of objects and situations, sexual feeling behaves no differently from other feelings. The readiness, slowness, concentration or absentmindedness, domination or dependence in sexual feeling are about the same as in all the other activities of a character. So that we have here a perfect propriety and fullness of diction.

The relatively simple dislocations of "you ain't got down deep loyal feeling, true inside you," from the more commonplace order "you have no true feeling of loyalty deep down inside you," not only jar the words awake into their full meaning but follow with much greater exactitude the slow, passionate, clumsy emphasis of Jeff Campbell's feeling.

The phrase "remembering right" could be replaced by a more familiar cliché, "profiting aptly by past experience," or by scientific gabble like "the coordination of habitual reflexes upon the present object," but the advantage of the simpler new phrase is that it expresses the matter in terms of the fundamental and final activities and categories of the mind. It is part of the "impulse to elemental abstraction," the description in terms of the final and generic as against description by context and association. It is like the generically round and sitting apple of Cézanne as against a delicately compromised and contextuated and reverberating apple of the impressionists. The propriety of the simple popular abstraction used in "Melanctha" is in this, that the two subjectivities at odds are seen, and so to be described, directly—directly from common knowledge, and not, as with *Madame Bovary*, seen refracted and described indirectly through an exterior context embodying considerable special knowledge. The immediate terms of *Madame Bovary* are saturated with French history, the immediate terms of "Melanctha" are the final categories of mental process—to know, to see, to hear, to wish, to remember, to suffer, and the like.

However, "Melanctha" is more than an exact chart of the passions. The conjugation or play of the abstractions proceeds according to the vital rhythm or tempo of the characters. In this way the essential quality of the characters is not only described but presented immediately. As Emma Bovary is *seen* against the rake Rodolphe and then against the pusillanimous Léon, and is thereby defined, so Melanctha is, in her quick tempo, *played* against the slow Jeff Campbell and then against the very fast "dashing" Jem Richards.

Gertrude Stein later made some remarks about *Three Lives* in the light of her later problems of expression. In *Composition as Explanation* she said:

> In beginning writing I wrote a book called *Three Lives* this was written in 1905. I wrote a negro story called *Melanctha*. In that there was a constant recurring and beginning there was a marked direction in the direction of being in the present although naturally I had been accustomed to past present and future, and why, because the composition forming around me was a prolonged present. A composition of a prolonged present is a natural composition in the world as it has been these thirty years [1926] it was more and more a prolonged present. I created then a prolonged present naturally I knew nothing of a continuous present but it came naturally to me to make one, it was simple it was clear to me and nobody knew why it was done like that, I did not myself although naturally to me it was natural. . . .
>
> In the first book [*Three Lives*] there was a groping for a continuous present and for using everything by beginning again and again.[9]

The difference between a prolonged and a continuous present may be defined as this, that a prolonged present assumes a situation or a theme and dwells on it and develops it or keeps it recurring, as in much opera, and Bach, for example. The continuous present would take each successive moment or passage as a completely new thing essentially, as with Mozart or Scarlatti or, later, Satie. This Gertrude Stein calls beginning again. But the problem is really one of the dimensions of the present as much as of the artist's way with it. The "specious" present which occupied William James is an arbitrary distinction between past and future as they flow together in time. But for purposes of action and art it has to be assumed as an operable space of time. For the composer this space of time can be the measure, or whatever unit can be made to express something without dependence on succession as the condition of its interest. For the writer it can be the sentence or the paragraph or the chapter or the scene or the page or the stanza or whatever. Gertrude Stein experimented with all these units in the course of her work, but in the early work the struggle was mainly with the sentence and the paragraph.

9. *Composition as Explanation* (Hogarth Press, 1926), pp. 16–17, 18.

RICHARD BRIDGMAN

[*Q.E.D.* and "Melanctha"]†

"I do not wish to imply that there is any remedy for any defect."
—"If You Had Three Husbands"

For as good a book as it is, *Q.E.D.* (or *Things As They Are*,[1] as its editors entitled it) has had a minimal reputation. During the first thirty years of its existence it would seem that only Leo Stein knew about it. Then, according to the story told in *The Autobiography of Alice B. Toklas*,[2] Gertrude Stein came upon the manuscript accidentally and, with some hesitation, gave it to Louis Bromfield to read. He thought it "vastly interesting" and mentioned to her the possibility of having it published, in spite of the "great difficulties" that might present (Gallup, *Flowers*, 249–50).[3] But when the *Yale Catalogue* of Gertrude Stein's writing was compiled in 1941, she denied permission to include the novel. (Haas, "Gertrude Stein Talking," 5).[4] Admirers finally printed it after her death, but in an edition of only five hundred and sixteen copies. Although the book has since been received with respect by the few who have read it, it is now out of print and virtually unobtainable. This is regrettable, for the book is an indispensable link in the development of Gertrude Stein's prose.

The subject of the book was a dangerous one in 1903—three young women in a passionate stalemate. It was based upon Gertrude Stein's frustrated romance with May Bookstaver, a Baltimore friend. In writing the book, she drew upon letters she had retained from the long affair, letters which Alice Toklas claimed to have destroyed in 1932 "in a passion."[5] Although one may conclude that the book had to be written, it is doubtful that any reputable publisher of the time would have accepted it.

Her original title for the novel was the classical signature to a geometric proof. It stood for the presence of a fixed relationship among the three female characters, a relationship "proved" by the

---

† From *Gertrude Stein in Pieces* (New York: Oxford UP, 1970), pp. 40–58. Copyright © 1971 by Richard Bridgman. Used by permission of Oxford University Press.

1. Stein, *Things As They Are* (Pawlet, Vermont: The Banyan Press, 1950).
2. Stein, *The Autobiography of Alice B. Toklas* (New York: Random House, 1933).
3. Donald Gallup, ed., *The Flowers of Friendship: Letters Written to Gertrude Stein* (New York: Knopf, 1953). Hereafter referred to as Gallup.
4. Robert Bartlett Haas, "Gertrude Stein Talking—A Transatlantic Interview" (1945), published in the *Uclan Review* VIII, Summer 1962: 3–11; IX, Spring 1963: 40–48; IX, Winter 1964: 44–48). Hereafter referred to as Haas.
5. It is probable that the distractions of this affair were largely responsible for Gertrude Stein's poor record in her fourth year at medical school. But the facts are still insufficiently clear to permit a definitive judgment in the matter.

logic of the novel. At Harvard, Gertrude Stein had counselled resignation before implacable fate. "You must submit sooner or later to
be ground in the same mill with your fellows . . . Be still, it is inevitable" (*RAD*, 122).[6] Although she remembered herself as "very full
of convictions" in her youth and possessed by a strong missionary
impulse that drove her to try to change people and to get them to
"change themselves," she also had a strong fatalistic streak (*LIA*,
136).[7] But if one could not alter one's fundamental nature, at least
one could learn to understand it.

Things As They Are, the title Alice Toklas and Carl Van Vechten
gave to the book, expresses the mingled ambition and resignation of
its ending. It is drawn from the next to the last sentence of the book.
"Can't she see things as they are," asks the young heroine, "and not
as she would make them if she were strong enough as she plainly
isn't" (87). The sentence elevates clear vision over all else. Whatever
reality is, that must be accepted. Gertrude Stein felt this strongly
enough to repeat the sentiment in the early pages of *The Making of
Americans*:[8] ". . . now it had come to her, to see, as dying men are
said to see, clearly and freely things as they are and not as she wished
them to be for her" (33).

The prospect of understanding brought a measure of relief. It
might stabilize the life that swirled uncontrollably around her. Yet,
mechanistic certainty in human intercourse is as distressing as
chaos. The cost paid for understanding in *Things As They Are* was
painful and generated only pessimistic conclusions. The three
women had no way out of their impasse. Or, virtually no way out.
The thinnest fissure of possible escape was visible in the concluding
sentence. " 'I am afraid it comes very near being a dead-lock,' she
groaned dropping her head on her arms" (88).

Things As They Are continues Gertrude Stein's study of a spirited
young woman who tries to deal honestly with feelings that happen
to be forbidden by society. The book is no less candid than her naïvely confessional themes submitted at Harvard. Here was Hortense
Sänger undergoing a fresh temptation, except that after the passage
of ten years, Gertrude Stein had given up melodrama. Humor, compassion, objectivity—these now govern the portrait of her heroine.

Adele is a hearty young woman, given to exclaiming "Great guns!,"
"Jupiter!" and "Hang it all" (58, 75). Upon taking her leave, she cries,
"Adios" (53). She is associated with freedom and easy informality,
with the sun and the western starlight. But the very first sentence of
Things As They Are tells us that she has just undergone "a succession

6. RAD refers to Stein, Radcliffe Manuscripts, Yale American Literature Collection (YALC).
7. LIA refers to Stein, *Lectures in America* (New York: Random House, 1935).
8. Stein, *The Making of Americans* (Dijon: Contact Editions, Maurice Darantière, 1925).
    Hereafter referred to as *MOA*.

of wearing experiences." A few pages later, she yields herself "to a sense of physical weariness and to the disillusionment of recent failures" (3, 10). As she descends into a vortex of misery, this attractive girl with some medical experience displays a wry, unflinching candor and a calm resolve.

Adele is obliged to endure an assault upon her emotions from a quarter not only unexpected but also socially prohibited. Coming into the orbit of a pair of women, the gravity of her presence rearranges all the lines of force. The woman to whom Adele is attracted is Helen Thomas, an "American version of the English handsome girl" (4). Over the course of the story, Helen's character changes from what seems to be a wise, maternal tenderness into a passively suffering endurance. She is being kept by one Sophie Neathe. Late in the book, when Sophie gives Helen a piece of antique jewelry, Adele exclaims, "Oh it's simply prostitution" (81). Sophie is the decadent rich girl, the aristocrat, "vulgarized and the power weakened . . . unillumined and unmoral" (5). Heavy about the mouth from "the drag of unidealized passion," Sophie possesses crafty power. Insofar as anyone does, it is she who prevails in the end.

The story is told in three parts, each devoted to one person in the triangle. In summary, the plot is as follows. The three women are on shipboard apparently travelling to Europe. With naïve pride Adele expands upon her "almost puritanic horror" of cultivating the physical passions (9). Even at that moment she is being drawn closer to Helen. After an increasingly intense series of embraces, she spends a summer in Tangiers and Spain, reflecting upon the meaning of her experience.

Later, the trio is found back in the United States, Sophie in Baltimore, Helen in New York, and Adele visiting both. Adele and Helen have some random meetings that culminate in a tryst, a winter night's embrace, and declarations of love. But Sophie, her suspicions aroused, informs Adele of her proprietary rights to Helen. This counterattack leads to an estrangement of the lovers, followed by a reconciliation.

The remainder of the story is a psychological study of the maneuverings necessitated by the fixed character of each woman. The resolutions, failures, readjustments, misunderstandings, pressures, quarrels, fresh beginnings, subtle changes, and predictable consistencies in behavior all conclude in an exhausted stalemate.

While remorseless in exposing the self-deception of her chief character, Gertrude Stein manages it without the slightest taint of self-hatred or cynicism. The pompousness of her heroine is even peculiarly winning. Adele characterizes herself as "a hopeless coward. I hate to risk hurting myself or anybody else. All I want to do is to meditate endlessly and think and talk" (31). She compliments

Helen on her ability to stab, straight and hard. She herself has "so many compunctions and considerations" that she would merely scarify the victim's surface anatomy, so that "unless he should bleed to death quite by accident, I wouldn't do him any serious injury" (31). This is the portrait of a Henry James innocent, one capable of devastating her more sophisticated acquaintances quite inadvertently. To protect herself from the reality of her being, Adele leads an abstract, verbal existence. She has yet to mature, to have the opportunity to sin and fall. It takes the fires of illicit passion to melt the armor of moral rhetoric she wears at the beginning of the book.

If *Things As They Are* lacks the guilt-laden atmosphere expected in a confessional work, that is a tribute to Gertrude Stein's ironic objectivity. That is not to say, however, that she was not dramatizing issues of passionate concern to her. The book centers on the clash between Adele's principles and her desires. Its ending is no cautionary instance of sentimentality, no lugubrious lament for the loss of high idealism. Nor is it a brutalized celebration of sensation's triumph over ethics. The integrity of the body is accepted on less than elevated aspirations.

At the beginning of the novel, Adele confidently recognizes only two varieties of feeling—"affectionate comradeship" and "physical passion" (9). The latter she rejects with horror. "As for my instincts they have always been opposed to the indulgence of any feeling of passion" (57). Adele therefore defiantly appoints herself champion of the maligned middle class. As presented, Adele's allegiance is partly the exaggerated posturing of a young intellectual. But her role was not an unnatural one for Gertrude Stein, who in spite of her literary practices consistently opted for normality over eccentricity.

When challenged that she does not seem middle-class, Adele happily takes up the gauntlet. "You have a foolish notion that to be middle-class is to be vulgar . . . commonplace . . . low" (6). Although she admits that she is "rejected by the class whose cause I preach," she contends that "the middle-class ideal which demands that people be affectionate, respectable, honest and content, that they avoid excitements and cultivate serenity is the ideal that appeals to me . . ." (8).

A similar young woman had counselled stoic calm when she was at Harvard. Her arguments would reappear in "Melanctha," this time expressed by the young Negro doctor who despairs of his race's predilection for excitement rather than "regular living." In *The Making of Americans* Gertrude Stein speaks directly to the reader in defense of the middle class, for although she knows "one can find no one among you all to belong to it," she insists that it is "always human, vital and worthy" (34).

This strong commitment to bourgeois decency is dramatically

challenged in *Things As They Are*. Helen accuses Adele of being a "passionette," a girl who thinks a lot about love, and flirts with it, but lacks the courage to follow out its consequences. "You are so afraid of losing your moral sense that you are not willing to take it through anything more dangerous than a mud-puddle" (12). This attack is not presented as the sophistry of a seducer. Adele acknowledges the possible justice of the accusation. " 'I never wanted to be a hero, but on the other hand,' she added 'I am not anxious to cultivate cowardice. I wonder—' " (13). When Adele finally yields to an embrace "that seemed to scale the very walls of chastity," she does not lapse into self-recrimination (56). She undertakes the affair in full consciousness of what she is doing and remains observant of her reactions throughout its duration. The combination is an unusual one, for her analysis is neither cold-blooded nor emotionally indulgent. The book's expression of feeling is genuine, but maturely controlled. As the passionately confused young woman of the Radcliffe themes joins the scientific observer of Johns Hopkins, the several parts of Gertrude Stein come together in a drama of learning just what things, in fact, are.

Although there is some stylistic awkwardness in *Things As They Are*, it is nothing like her disastrously uneven college work. On the whole, the book has a forceful economy that is not easily imitable. At times the prose displays evidence of a strained rhetoric and there are moments of uncertain and even neglected punctuation as well as idiomatic imbalance. These traits, along with her admirable clarity, are evident in the following passage, which describes the affair near the end of the book.

> Their intercourse in these interviews consisted in impersonal talk with long intervals of oppressive silences. "Won't you speak to me" Adele exclaimed crushed under the weight of one of these periods. "But I cannot think of anything to say," Helen answered gently. (85)

The excellence of *Things As They Are* is that, without forcing a conclusion, it was able to express the subtlety of human behavior within a controlled framework. The story ends neither in triumph nor defeat, but in a painful human stand-off. Gertrude Stein had not scanted the suffering but had reproduced and accepted it. And yet the absolutism of her proof was unsatisfactory. Her vision exceeded her answer. So, changing her terms, she began again. She was now thirty years old and still only an apprentice in her chosen field.

From the fall of 1903 when she completed *Things As They Are* until the spring of 1905 when she began *Three Lives*,[9] Gertrude Stein was

9. Stein, *Three Lives* (New York: Grafton Press, 1909).

still shaken by her wrecked love affair. Recording it had been insufficient therapy. Withdrawn, despairing, and cynical, she worked at
two projects during this period. Both would eventually be fitted into
The Making of Americans. One was the story of the unhappy marriage of her cousin Bird Stein, begun in New York, the other was the
so-called "Hodder episode." Both were imaginative alternatives to
the stalemate of *Things As They Are*.[1]

"The Hodder episode" originated in a complicated scandal that
involved both people and institutions familiar to the Steins. In brief,
the episode concerned a married professor who fell in love with a
woman who also taught at his college, and who lived with the female
dean of the college. The professor and the dean compete for the
affections of the woman. In the course of the contest, the professor
leaves his bewildered wife. She returns to her father, and after a short
time, her husband dies.

The two academic women are new versions of Sophie and Helen
in *Things As They Are*. Dean Hannah Charles is the somewhat sinister avatar of Sophie Neathe. Described as one of those "vigorous
egotistic sensual natures" with "general unmoral desires . . . and
unmoral ways of calling them into realisation," she "in common with
many of her generation believed wholly in the essential sameness of
sex and . . . had devoted her life to the development of this doctrine"
(434, 463, 462). Her companion, Cora Dounor, was "possessed of a
sort of transfigured innocence." But she desired "to experience the
extreme forms of sensuous life and to make even immoral experiences of her own" (435). "In this shy abstracted learned creature
there was a desire for sordid life" (437–8).

With the abused wife, these two women constitute the basic trio
dominating Gertrude Stein's imagination: a strong, clever sensualist
possessed of power; a handsome girl of refined intelligence who is
hypnotized by the flesh; and a naïve, rather plain moralist with deep
affectionate needs running below the surface. Now though, the
Adele figure was on the sidelines, suffering and baffled. While her
husband and the dean carry on their war, she is left in her misery.
"It was a long agony, she never became wiser or more indifferent,
she struggled on always in the same dazed eager way" (434).

After completing this bleak episode, Gertrude Stein put her projected "family novel" to one side and ruminated on other possibilities.
Several titles occurred to her. "The Making of an Author being a
History of one woman and many others" was one example. As an
alternative, she tried, "The Progress of Jane Sands, being a His-

---

1. For an understanding of Gertrude Stein's preliminary drafts of *The Making of Americans*.
I have relied upon Leon Katz's invaluable dissertation, "The First Making of *The Making
of Americans*," which is based upon an analysis of Gertrude Stein's unpublished notebooks,
drafts of the novel, and extensive interviews with her contemporaries.

tory . . ." etc. Even in these titles, the conceptual problems on Gertrude Stein's mind are evident. She hesitated between taking herself as representative of all mankind and creating a universal history. And first she saw herself shaped by the forces around her, then as moving purposefully forward, making progress. Behind these titles, the implicit questions were, am I at bottom the same as everyone else, or am I unique? And, am I the inevitable product of many forces, or am I what I make myself?

She fixed on the title "*Three Histories* by Jane Sands."[2] That title remained on the ensuing manuscript until 1909 when her publisher prevailed upon her to change it to *Three Lives*. He thought her title "much too formal" and moreover, he did not wish to have her book confused with his firm's "real historical publications" (Frederick H. Hitchcock to GS, 9 April 1909, YCAL). Even though she was paying the printing costs of the book and had resisted all other suggested modifications, she inexplicably accepted the revised title.

Flaubert was the source for the original title of *Three Histories*. In a series of retrospective meditations, Gertrude Stein developed a spotty history of her evolution as a writer. *The Making of Americans* was usually the starting-point, but occasionally her theorizing reached back to *Three Lives*. To account for it, she invoked the names of Flaubert and Cézanne. For anyone then seriously concerned with literature, the respectful mention of Flaubert was mandatory. He was a tutelary presence, the artist dedicated at once to a remorseless realism and to the aesthetic restoration of his craft. Leo Stein's enthusiasm for Flaubert induced his sister to read him and even to attempt a translation of the *Trois Contes*. Félicité, the servant woman of "Un Coeur Simple," reminded Gertrude Stein of her own Baltimore housekeeper, Lena Lebender. Félicité's parrot even makes an appearance in "The Good Anna." However, "Anna never really loved the parrot and so she gave it to the Drehten girls to keep" (62). Other than giving *Three Lives* its original impetus, Flaubert was of minimal significance for Gertrude Stein. For a time his example caused her to put her personal concerns to one side. Shortly though they returned to the center of her consciousness.

As for Cézanne, she and Leo had begun collecting his paintings late in 1904. Two things about Cézanne's art impressed her: his skillfully crude depiction of elemental subjects; and his attentiveness to all the details of his composition. Until Cézanne, she said years later, a painting was composed around a central idea. All other ele-

2. The name "Sands" had some deep significance for her. At this time she made a list of possible noms de plume. "Jane Sandys, Pauline Manders, Pauline Sandys and Jane Sandys" (Katz, 73). Twenty years later in a personal letter, she rejected "Sands" as being "for some psychological reasons which I have never fathomed" unacceptable "for names for nom de plumes for almost anything and it should always be refused" (letter to Ellen Daniel, 5? June? 1929, YCAL).

ments were subordinated to it. But Cézanne "conceived the idea that in composition one thing was as important as another thing." So strongly did this conception strike her, she went on, that she began to write *Three Lives* (Haas, 8).

Cézanne was one of her brother's enthusiasms, about whom he was then articulating his ideas. In one of his long, didactic letters to Mabel Weeks, Leo wrote that Cézanne always displayed "this remorseless intensity, this endless, unending, gripping of the form, the unceasing effort to force it to reveal its absolute self-existing quality of mass." Cézanne approached the canvas as a plane surface on which his art would be realized. The realization would be a made object, not an attempt at representation. Leo also pointed out that the work of the painters in whom he and Gertrude first interested themselves—Monet, Renoir, Degas, and Cézanne—was "all non-dramatic. When figures are composed in a group their relations are merely spatial. At most they are relations of movement concurrent or opposite".[3]

Gertrude Stein had already intuitively employed such spatial relationships in her Radcliffe themes and in *Things As They Are*. Lacking a narrative imagination, she concentrated on building her characters with substantial psychological detail. Sometimes she sketched her subject in a summary moment—the man calmly standing in the mud puddle after missing his trolley to Cambridge, or Hortense, throwing her books down in the library. Or she placed two contrasting persons in one another's company—Adele with Helen, Helen with Sophie. By changing a person's location, she revealed new facets of his personality. There was an Adele one, an Adele two, an Adele three, according to where and with whom she found herself. Similarly, the progressive accumulation of experience produced an Adele A, an Adele B, and an Adele C.

With her interest in the analysis of character, Gertrude Stein was naturally drawn to the idea of regarding human relations as a composition. Her affinity for Cézanne arose then from sources deeper than the fact that she lived with Leo. Portraiture and composition attracted her long before she listened to her brother's monologues on aesthetic theory.

The pessimism with which *Things As They Are* concluded recurred in the epigraph to *Three Lives*: "So, I'm unhappy and neither I nor life is responsible for it."[4]

3. Leo Stein, *Journey into the Self*, ed. Edmund Fuller (New York: Crown, 1950).
4. "Donc je suis un malheureux et ce n'est ni ma faute ni celle de la vie." Ascribed to Jules Laforgue, the quotation sounds as if it came from *Moralités Légendaires*, but I have not been able to locate it.

Three Lives centers on Baltimore's poor, mainly German immigrant women and Negroes. In it, whether hard-working or indigent, moral or loose-living, all are quietly victimized by fate. The three central characters die before their time: Anna of exhaustion following a "hard" operation; Lena while having her fourth baby; and Melanctha in a state of consumptive despair. In spite of its frequent cheerfulness, the over-all impression *Three Lives* makes is of decent people beleaguered by busybodies, disagreeable children, and plain bad luck until at last they succumb out of sheer weariness.

Situations familiar to Gertrude Stein arise obsessively over and over in *Three Lives*. There are parental outcries against their children's willfulness. People are abandoned by their friends and lovers. More specifically, the Bridgepoint where the stories are laid is Baltimore. The unsuccessful and sometimes illicit practice of medicine is in the background. Anna keeps house at one point for a physician, and one of her friends is a midwife whose clientele is principally unwed mothers. Anna's employer, Miss Mathilda, is a silhouette of Gertrude Stein herself. A large and knowledgeable woman who enjoys long "tramps" in the country, she is an art patron who in the summer travels "across the ocean" until at last she leaves permanently for a "new country" (15, 21, 22, 17, 64, 76).

"The Good Anna," first of the *Three Lives* to be written, opens on a sentimental note. It describes the scoldings and mutterings of a loyal servant who is clearly intended to be endearing. A good deal of archness is expended on pet dogs too. But gradually Gertrude Stein begins to build a portrait of a conscience-ridden German-Catholic housekeeper who drives herself and those under her remorselessly, at the cost of recurrent headaches. In particular, she enjoys a maternal badgering of the men for whom she works. In time though, her irritable, "strained worn-out" body gives way. Her last words to the author express her enduring affection. "Miss Annie died easy, Miss Mathilda, and sent you her love" (82).

Gertrude Stein experimented with her style in "The Good Anna." Flaubert's example in "Un Coeur Simple" had suggested new ways of presenting a working-class woman. It is worth noting here that, although the prose of "Melanctha" differs from that of "The Good Anna," the reason for the change is not that "Melanctha" concerns Negroes. Racial distinctions cannot account for the change observable in these two sentences:

> "Mrs. Lehntman, I don't see what business it is for you to take another baby for your own, when you can't do right by Julia and Willie you got here already" (43, Anna speaking).

"I don't see Melanctha why you should talk like you would kill yourself just because you're blue" (87, Rose, a black girl, speaking).

The important stylistic innovations of "Melanctha" have nothing to do with the Negro, even though some readers have suggested that the story's notable attenuation is due to Gertrude Stein's trying to express the slow, languid life of the Negro. Rather, Gertrude Stein's style evolved as she composed *Three Lives*. In the beginning, with "The Good Anna," she found an entrance to a style of her own through a faintly foreign idiom appropriate to her immigrant heroine. Her own stylistic infelicities were absorbed into the discordant language of the immigrant working-class.

It was easy to blacken all the Drehtens, their poverty, the husband's drinking, the four big sons carrying on and always lazy, the awkward, ugly daughters dressing up with Anna's help and trying to look so fine, and the poor, weak, hard-working sickly mother, so easy to degrade with large dosings of contemptuous pity. (50).

At times the narrative voice addresses the reader directly, as if the story were being told by a reflective neighbor—"You see that Anna led an arduous and troubled life" (13). But it is impossible to assign a single, consistent identity to this voice that will satisfactorily account for its sound. Many odd and discordant phrases turn up in it, some the result of trying to render reality, some the result of forcing the prose surface. One old German woman's English is marked by "the roughness on her tongue of buzzing s's" (17). A rebuke is delivered "to his own good" instead of "for" (37). Such faintly off-kilter usage is common in "The Good Anna." "Then they did the operation" (82). The foreign idiom is audible in "Doctor got married now very soon" (57).

In addition to immigrant speech, there is also the self-conscious college graduate—"a dog that's old . . . is like a dreary, deathless Struldbrug, the dreary dragger on of death through life" (74). And the sophisticated experimenter—"Her half brother never left her out of his festive raisined bread giving progresses" (79). And the philosopher—"In friendship, power always has its downward curve" (54).

The writing preserved Gertrude Stein's several moods. This early in her career she made no attempt to unify the style in revision. Rather she accepted the vagaries of her sensibility. The result was undeniably peculiar. The mixture of patches of normal prose, awkward locutions, cultivated eccentricities, and reflections of servant mentality produced a crazy quilt of a style.

In great part, the irresolution of her prose was caused by the self-education to which she was submitting in the very act of composition. Her vision was lucid enough, but she lacked the means to express it adequately. Sooner than lose her perception of the tangle of life through the pruning of revision, she accepted the mess of her prose. Honesty was her ethic; art, her education; improvisation, her method. As an energetic, clever, fervent, and haphazardly educated young woman, she was gambling that she could turn her very handicaps to creative ends.

Although it was placed last in the book, "The Gentle Lena" was the second written and the shortest of the *Three Lives*. It describes a simple creature who desires only the kindness of others. She is manipulated, notably by an aunt who makes a marriage match for her. Two very fine scenes follow. One concerns Lena, who after having been left at the altar and scolded for it, cries in a street-car on her way home. The other describes her fiancé, who is cajoled by his father to return from New York where he fled to avoid the marriage and to fulfill his obligations. Had Gertrude Stein been willing to cultivate her talent for sympathetic realism, she might have become a superior novelist as that term is customarily understood. But she was far more interested in the inner workings of the mind than in the observable behavior of others. Epistemology consumed her, so that she concentrated upon her own sensibility and its relationship to the world around her.

After Lena and her fiancé marry, they have a reasonably contented relationship, until she dies in childbirth. "When the baby was come out at last, it was like its mother lifeless. While it was coming, Lena had grown very pale and sicker. When it was all over Lena had died too, and nobody knew just how it had happened to her" (279).

No one—Dreiser, Willa Cather, Steinbeck—has written any better in that vein about mild, put-upon people than Gertrude Stein did in "The Gentle Lena."[5]

But the working-class milieu did not centrally engage Gertrude Stein. She had happened into it through the suggestive examples of Flaubert and Cézanne. But she was more interested in style as a carrier of knowledge than she was in investigating the lives of common people. Therefore, excellent as the story is, the emphasis here will be upon its stylistic distinctiveness.

"The Gentle Lena" possesses a more consistent voice than does "The Good Anna." The prose surface is much less patchy. In part this is because she wrote several very long paragraphs of monologue

5. Its original title was "Maggie" (Katz, 71, n. 2). Stephen Crane's *Maggie*, published privately in 1893, was not generally circulated until 1896. Leon Katz, "The First Making of *The Making of Americans*: A Study Based on Gertrude Stein's Notebooks and Early Versions of Her Novel (1902–08)," Ph.D. dissertation, Columbia University, 1963.

and of indirect discourse. She was drawn to those slowly revolving speeches in which a person takes a few basic concepts which he then states and restates with slight variations.

> . . . and your mama trying so hard, just so you could be comfortable Herman to be married, and then you act so stubborn Herman. You like all young people Herman, you think only about yourself, and what you are just wanting, and your mama she is thinking only what is good for you to have, for you in the future. (264)

Although such speeches sound authentic, what counted for Gertrude Stein in them was not their mimetic success, but the revelation they provided of human psychology. Such revolving discourse (the speech continues in the same vein for another fifteen lines) represented her initial venture into what she would later call the "prolonged present." By this she meant the stretching-out of discourse, pulling it until at last it became the "continuous present," that circular, infinitely slow movement, like taffy in the making, always there, always complete. Stylized extensions of the monologue just quoted dominated her writing around 1910. For example:

> Sound coming out of her comes out of her and is expressing sound coming out of her. Expressing sound coming out of her is something sound coming out of her is doing. Sound coming out of her is something. Sound is coming out of her.[6]

While the differences between this passage and the one from "The Gentle Lena" are striking, it is clear that the source of its circularity is human speech. Stripping away the narrative line and depersonalizing the references was a job that Gertrude Stein had yet to do, but her stylistic revolution was underway.

Reference to "Melanctha," the longest of the *Three Lives*, is the grudging tribute most critics pay to the endurance of Gertrude Stein's reputation. They regard it not as a curiosity like *Tender Buttons*, nor trivial like the autobiographies of the thirties. It appears to be a work of social naturalism, and better still, it treats the Negro not only sympathetically, but as if he were white.

These are mistaken assessments of "Melanctha." They misrepresent Gertrude Stein's achievement, for "Melanctha" was only an early way-station on her road to artistic maturity. Furthermore, in spite of the general appreciation of her skill at rendering the "primitive mentality," Gertrude Stein's treatment of the Negro is both condescending and false. The principals of the story are not black at all,

---

6. Gertrude Stein, *TWO: Gertrude Stein and Her Brother* (New Haven: Yale UP, 1951).

but only new, revised versions of the characters Gertrude Stein had described in *Things As They Are*. As for the background of "Melanctha," it swarms with clichés about the happy, promiscuous, razor-fighting, church-going darky.[7]

Equally strange, sensible critics have accepted verbatim Gertrude Stein's claim in *The Autobiography of Alice B. Toklas* that, because she was posing for Picasso at the time she wrote "Melanctha," she wove into the story those "poignant incidents" that she observed as she walked down the hill from Montmartre to Montparnasse.[8] It is impossible to imagine what incidents she had in mind, especially since the story has very little action, but rather progresses slowly through a series of psychological encounters.

In fact, "Melanctha" picks up the situation Gertrude Stein had treated in *Things As They Are,* and which she had left there in a stalemate. The frustrated trio is reduced to two persons in a standoff. This permitted Gertrude Stein to show in greater schematic detail how people in love are inevitably attracted to one another, then equally inevitably, separated. Calm seeks passion, conventionality seeks liberation, while conversely turmoil seeks peace and looseness yearns for control. But having located their opposites, these forces are then repelled. Calm finds tumult too unsettling and tumult cannot abide the monotony of calm.

Provided names, the forces are Jeff Campbell, a Negro physician who while attending a sick woman, falls in love with that woman's daughter, Melanctha. Their earlier names were Adele and Helen, and previous to that at Radcliffe, Gertrude Stein had presented the antithetical pair of Sally, the "fiery and impetuous" girl, and her irritatingly passive and nameless lover. The discovery of these "perfect antipodes" first took place in Gertrude Stein's imagination, was then played out in some form in her actual life, then re-entered her imagination for a retrospective analysis. Ideas that she first conceived in the Psychological Laboratory about the essential nature of human beings were fusing, deep in her consciousness. In "Cultivated Motor Automatism," Gertrude Stein had divided her subjects into two types, the first nervous and easily aroused, the second anemic and phlegmatic. She held persistently to this basic duality throughout her early career as she moved towards an ambitious study of men

7. Haldeen Braddy's article "The Primitive in Gertrude Stein's 'Melanctha' " is a representative assessment of the story. Braddy is sometimes a shrewd reader, but his sociological views are less than satisfactory, as when he comments: "As a study of primal natures, 'Melanctha' is almost wholly preoccupied with the subject of sex, perhaps an inevitable concern for simple people with little else to think about" (360). Even were this a tenable human proposition, it would be contradicted by the fact that Melanctha was sufficiently educated to serve as a substitute teacher, and her main affair was carried on with a bourgeois physician.

8. P. 60.

and women. At the same time she was fashioning a style capable of embodying her understanding of how people presented themselves to her consciousness. The one problem was inseparable from the other.

Sophie, the third member of the *Things As They Are* triangle, still exists in the person of the selfish Rose with whom Melanctha lives for a time. But her pragmatic hardness never centrally engages Gertrude Stein's attention. The duller aspects of Adele are now represented by Jeff. Like her, he objects to people who do things simply for the sake of experience. In his case, such people are the bulk of his race. Like Adele too, he defends the virtues of middle-class prudence. Unlike her though, he is priggish rather than independent. His compunctions seem skittish and shallow rather than morally anguished. Furthermore, Jeff lacks the good humor and wry self-knowledge that Adele possesses. Although he suffers as she did, he does so blindly, without wisdom.

The compelling fascination of the story centers in its heroine, "Darkflower." Whether black or not, she is the mysterious woman of deep feeling and irregular behavior rising in all her complexity out of the blonde pallor of America. Melanctha elaborates the contradictory depths of Helen Thomas and in the process, her character expands to absorb into itself the character of Gertrude Stein. Jeff's impoverishment is the result. He yields the positive aspects of Adele to enrich Melanctha. She is moody, but tender, frightened but brave, maternal yet sexually desirable, aggressive yet masochistic. As had Helen, she once overheard her mother and father express their disappointment in her rebellious existence. They remembered their other children—now dead—as quieter, more obedient. Like their creator, Helen and Melanctha both have impatient, suspicious fathers and sweet-appearing, vague mothers. Both fictional girls suffer broken arms in a display of reckless courage, an injury that infuriates their respective fathers. In Melanctha's case, the violence of her father's reaction and the context of precocious exploration in which the broken arm occurs, suggest the conclusion that the arm's fracture is a surrogate for initial sexual experience.[9] Finally, after the strain of a protracted and indecisive romance, both Helen and Melanctha exhibit increasing passivity. But whereas Helen was obliged to hold up her angle of the deterministic triangle of *Things As They Are*, Melanctha lapses into a decline that ends in death.

"Melanctha" then gathers together Gertrude Stein's main preoccupations: the rejected child, the sexual torment of the impetuous girl, the proddings of conscience, ill-fated relationships, and ultimately, abandonment.

9. I have discussed this point at greater length in "Melanctha," *American Literature*, XXXIII (November 1961), 350–59.

A subject newly raised by the story concerns the distortions of memory. One of the issues over which Jeff and Melanctha quarrel is that she cannot "remember right." The accusation is verified early in the story. When recounting an incident, Melanctha is said to "leave out big pieces," although not deliberately (100). This creates a disparity between what she claimed to have done and what she actually did. Yet this flaw is ultimately provided a serious and eloquent defense.

Gertrude Stein's argument on behalf of one kind of "remembering" occurs during a protracted dispute between Jeff and Melanctha. He again accuses her of living only for the moment. Her life lacks the continuity that a systematic and accurate memory can provide. "When you ain't just that moment quick with feeling, then you certainly ain't ever got anything more there to keep you" (180–81). Melanctha's challenge to this interpretation is that "You don't remember nothing till you get home with your thinking everything all over." Rather than displaying appropriate spontaneous reactions, he behaves cruelly and clumsily, which in retrospect he regrets. "You go home Jeff Campbell, and you begin with your thinking, and then it certainly is very easy for you to be good and forgiving." Melanctha speaks on behalf of immediacy. Her name for it is "remembering right." For her, the human way to live is "to remember right just when it happens to you, so you have a right kind of feeling. . . . real feeling every moment when its [*sic*] needed" (181).

Gertrude Stein poured a reserve of conviction into this defense of behavior which is intuitively sanctioned rather than the result of post-mortem rectitude. Throughout her career the antinomian warred with the scientist. Her conflict originated in her dissatisfaction with any ethic then available to her. She was too puritanic to accept unrestrained hedonism, and yet circumstance was denying her the expression of her considerable passions in conventional ways. She tried to solve her dilemma by understanding it. After the narratives of *Three Lives*, she turned to increasingly detailed analyses of character. But, finding herself perpetually frustrated in her attempts to provide a full, satisfactory description of any one or any thing, she eventually found herself driven to rely upon her own subjective response, expressed in whatever words emerged at the moment of concentration. As in Melanctha's defense here, she came to justify spontaneous composition as living in the present at the front edge of time. It seemed to her superior to living in historical memory, feeding on the aftermath of an existence of which one was never more than partially aware.

In "Melanctha," Gertrude Stein had not yet quite chosen sides. As she had in *Things As They Are*, she presented the debate between a morality of constraint and loyalty to primal feeling, without openly judging the ultimate validity of either position. Jeff's reflective mind attempting to analyze his experience in order to construct a code of behavior is presented almost as sympathetically as Melanctha's breakneck emotional existence the purity of which is derived from the directness of its response to life. "Melanctha" therefore emphasizes the doubleness of human nature. Its protagonists are antithetical, and Melanctha's own duality is remarked upon by Jeff. She seemed two different girls to him: one, whom he would never trust, has "a laugh then so hard, it just rattles;" the other, whom he worships, possesses "a real sweetness, that is more wonderful than a pure flower" (138).

The final point to make about "Melanctha" is that it is by far the most stylistically experimental of the *Three Lives*. Not just eccentric, or careless, or inept, but openly experimental. It is the mental processes imputed to the people the story describes that shape its prose. The story contains a large number of sexual euphemisms. Melanctha's puberty is referred to as "her beginning as a woman" (103). Men respond to her nubile presence with crude double entendres. "Hullo, sis, do you want to sit on my engine." "Do you want to come and see him cookin." "Hi there, you yaller girl, come here and we'll take you sailin." "Do you think you would make a nice jelly?" (98, 101, 102). Her first major trauma of breaking her arm follows her responding to a dare to mount to "a high place." "Come up here where I can hold you . . . when you get here I'll hold you tight, don't you be scared Sis" (102). Melanctha's subsequent relationship with Jane Harden has sexual overtones too. She "wanders" with this woman of "much experience" who teaches her "wisdom" and makes her feel "the power of her affection" (103–5).

These examples could be multiplied. Euphemisms and other kinds of verbal substitution eventually became an important feature of Gertrude Stein's style. Although in time she would provide this activity with an aesthetic rationale, it began as a form of evasiveness. It is true that such euphemisms in part reflected the verbally puritanic milieu about which she was writing in *Three Lives*. But it was also personally useful for Gertrude Stein, since it permitted the broaching of taboo subjects. It may give some perspective to recall that Theodore Dreiser, writing at exactly the same time as Gertrude Stein, was obliged to endure obloquy, censorship and prosecution for what were considerably more genteel and conventionally moralistic statements made in *Sister Carrie* and in *The Genius*.

In "The Good Anna," the narrator observed that a doctor "got into trouble doing things that were not right to do" (64). The context suggests this is an example of society's indirection in referring to an abortionist. But the construction of the reference intrigued Gertrude Stein. It provided a means of making a statement without exposing

herself. Rather than say, "Leo hurt my feelings by ridiculing my writing," she could say, "Leo did to me what he shouldn't have done."
By selecting general nouns and verbs, and replacing nouns with pronouns that lacked distinct referents and if possible, gender—"one"
and "some"—she moved steadily towards abstraction. In miniature,
her evolution looked this way:

> Martha was really not telling any one very much in her young
> living the feeling she had in her about anything . . . (*MOA*, 413)

> Two knowing each other all their living might tell each other
> sometime what each one of them thought the other one had
> been . . . (*MOA*, 746)

> He was not in any way one of the two of them. He was one. He
> was the one who was the one who was the one. (*TWO*, 99)

These sentences seek to stabilize a chaotic world by progressively
elevating particular cases of isolation and estrangement to more general categories. Stated at a sufficiently high level of abstraction, individual problems appear to become universal dicta. Gertrude Stein's
slow apprehension of this encouraged in her the ambition of pre-
paring a history of all mankind, by which she did not mean a chronological narrative, but a perpetually valid description.

The prose of "Melanctha" reflected not only the euphemistic
nature of popular speech, but also its erratic and repetitive qualities.
Statements in it are rough-hewn and approximate. "Jem Richards
made Melanctha Herbert come fast with him. He never gave her any
time with waiting" (218). Meaning leaps gaps, indifferent to normal
transitions. "Jem Richards, that swell man who owned all those fine
horses and was so game, nothing ever scared him, was engaged to
be married to her, and that was the ring he gave her" (219). Identical
ideas are reiterated in succeeding paragraphs with only the slightest
variation. "Melanctha's joy made her foolish..," "Melanctha's love for
Jem had made her foolish..," "She was mad and foolish in the joy
she had there" (219).

While such examples are still tied to the story, it is not difficult to
see how they could easily lead to a preoccupation with the prose
surface itself, at the expense of the imagined reality she was attempting to create. The dialogues of "Melanctha" might more properly be
called duets. The voices sing across one another, following an independent melody, yet influenced by one another's music. One long
interchange begins:

> Jeff what makes you act so funny to me. Jeff you certainly now
> are jealous to me. Sure Jeff, now I don't see ever why you be so
> foolish to look so to me.

He answers:

> Don't you ever think I can be jealous of anybody ever Melanc-
> tha, you hear me. It's just, you certainly don't ever understand
> me. It's just this way with me always now Melanctha. (176)

In time, Gertrude Stein minimized the colloquial awkwardness
and emphasized the patterning. She abandoned any pretense of imitating different people. Rather, all her prose emerged from a single
sensibility. This did not mean that the results were invariably unified,
for they were not. But it did mean that the stylistic variants emanated
from the directing intelligence alone.

Gertrude Stein had some success in trying to render other people
in her early work. But she had more compelling problems to solve
in her own life than could be handled by polishing the techniques
of verisimilitude, were she capable of it. The technical possibilities
she had glimpsed in the mottled prose surface of *Three Lives* tanta-
lized her. Her next work was a major and decisive effort at liberation.

CARL WOOD

Continuity of Romantic Irony: Stein's Homage to Laforgue in *Three Lives*†

ABSTRACT

"Donc je suis un malheureux, et ce n'est ni ma faute, ni celle de la
vie." This paradoxical epigraph attributed to Laforgue in Stein's
Three Lives is the basis for a subtle development which interrelates
the three stories thematically. Each story involves an unhappy protagonist, but in drawing out the implications of the epigraph, Stein
prevents the reader from blaming either her characters' personalities
or life itself for their predicaments. The ironic tension between personality and life runs through all of *Three Lives* and is never resolved.
This ironic tension determines the book's structure and makes *Three
Lives* part of a modern literary tradition derived from the Romantics
and illustrated also in works by Mann, Gide, and Joyce.

The epigraph at the beginning of Gertrude Stein's first published
book may be considered archetypical of the utterances of Jules
Laforgue, the short-lived, post-Baudelairean poet whom Warren
Ramsey has called "the greatest of French Romantic ironists"[1]:

† From *Comparative Literature Studies* 12 (1975): 147–58.
1. Warren Ramsey, *Jules Laforgue and the Ironic Inheritance* (New York, 1953), p. 139.

"Donc je suis un malheureux, et ce n'est ni ma faute, ni celle de la vie" ("I'm unhappy of course, and it's neither my fault nor life's").[2] The major hallmarks of the mature Laforguean style and attitude are clearly present here: the peculiar combination of pessimism and light-heartedness; the intentionally ineloquent, conversational style; and the ironic joining of the "dissenting voices of instinct and judgment" (Ramsey, p. 238). But Stein seems to be indulging in a little of her own irony here, for Laforgue never wrote these lines.[3] As she was to do with many other individuals, Stein seems here to have studied and distilled Laforgue's thought and style into a statement peculiarly adapted to her own artistic purposes. The inventive manipulation involved in Stein's re-creation of Laforgue here, as well as the paradoxical, suggestively ambivalent content of the fictional epigraph, are part of the continuation in *Three Lives* of the tradition of Romantic irony, perhaps the most important aspect of Romantic literature that has survived into the twentieth century.

Ramsey's tribute to Laforgue as a Romantic ironist is made during a discussion of the poem "Soirs de Fête" from *Les Fleurs de Bonne l'olonté*. The structure and content of this poem, like those of Heinrich Heine's[4] often cited "Seegespenst" from *Die Nordsee*, typify what are perhaps the two basic features of Romantic irony: the artist writes with a divided consciousness, committed simultaneously to two contradictory feelings or perceptions, and he self-consciously and paradoxically manipulates the work's form to express this divided commitment in a way that places the reader in a similar dilemma as he attempts to interpret the work. In Laforgue's poem, as in Heine's, an elaborate picture is drawn, creating a distinct impression, which is then sharply modified at the end of the poem by a sudden shift in perspective. Most of Laforgue's poem describes the figure of the alienated poet juxtaposed to a "foolish crowd" ("foule sotte") which remains utterly oblivious of his presence after his late arrival at a party. At the end of the poem, as he is about to depart for presumably high adventure denied to the crowd, he pauses to utter a curse: "Et je maudis la nuit et la gloire! / Et ce coeur qui veut qu'on me dédaigne!" ("And I execrate nighttime and glory, / And this heart that desires to be scorned!").[5] This sudden turn at the end of the poem, as Laforgue acknowledges that the scorn he encounters is actually

---

2. Gertrude Stein, *Three Lives* (New York, 1933), p. 5. All citations from this book are taken from this edition. *Three Lives* was originally published in 1909.

3. It seems a safe assumption that Stein invented the epigraph since these lines do not occur in the 1922 Mercure de France edition of Laforgue's works, a considerably more inclusive edition than Stein had access to, and since no one has suggested that Stein saw any unpublished writings of Laforgue, who died sixteen years before her first trip to France as an adult.

4. German poet and social critic (1797–1856). [*Editor's note.*]

5. Jules Laforgue, *Oeuvres complètes de Jules Laforgue*, ed. Mercure de France (Paris 1922), II, 70. The translation is Ramsey's (p. 159).

not contrary to his own desires, puts the self-pitying and haughty Byronic stance of the rest of the poem in a new perspective and demonstrates, as Ramsey points out, "Laforgue's ability to see around his own position" (p. 159) and view it ironically.

The irony at the end of this poem is, however, additive or cumulative rather than corrective. It supplements the impression created in the first part of the poem and results in an ambivalent, overlapping perspective that does not negate the value that Laforgue has put on his estrangement. Rather, in this poem, Laforgue ironically expresses genuine feelings and judgments by viewing them simultaneously from an outside perspective and thus leaves the reader without a clearly resolved final estimate of the validity of the poet's alienated demeanor. A similar effect is created in Heine's "Seegespenst," where the beautiful and longing description of the sea-traveller's vision of his beloved and her city in the depths leaves the reader wondering at the end of the poem whether it is good or bad that at the last moment the boorish sea captain prevents the traveller from casting himself into the ocean to join his long-lost darling.

As these examples suggest, Romantic irony is far more complex and subtle in its effect than the corrective irony used by such eighteenth-century wits as Voltaire and Swift to expose the absurdity of Panglossian philosophy or contemporary English mores. The Romantic ironist finds himself in an emotional state similar to Byron's symbolic suspension between the prison and the palace, the heavens and the waters, on the Venetian Bridge of Sighs in Canto IV of *Childe Harold's Pilgrimage*. The ironist cannot escape from the tension of conflicting commitments in his divided consciousness. What he *can* do, however, is acknowledge his plight and simultaneously transcend it to some extent through the perfect, beautifully ambivalent form of his art. One of Friedrich Schlegel's literary fragments states, in substance, that "complete submergence in either feeling [Sentimentalität] or inventiveness [Fantasie] may lead to Romanticism of a sort, but only with the highest degree of both will there be created that tension of opposites which is absolute Romanticism or Romantic Irony."[6] And D.C. Muecke, in one of the finest modern discussions of Romantic irony, has written that "what tended to impress . . . the Romantics was the superior reality and power of the creative mind over anything it might create. . . . The theory of Romantic irony . . . recognized that implicit even in the artist's awareness and acceptance of his limitations there lay the possibility, through the self-irony of art, of transcending his predicament, not actually yet intellectually and imaginatively" (pp. 171, 215).

Although the ideality which the early German theorists of Roman-

6. Lyceums-Fragment 108 as paraphrased in translation by Douglas Colin Muecke in *The Compass of Irony* (London, 1969), p. 195.

tic irony balanced against their perception of actuality was of a more optimistic order than that of most modern writers, the Romantics' equally excruciating mental agony was derived from dilemmas of divided consciousness markedly similar to those of, for example, a Tonio Kröger[7] or his creator. A review of the uses of irony in modern literature would seem to confirm Muecke's assertion that Schlegel, in his theory of Romantic irony, had an "astonishing ability to see in Romanticism the seeds of modernism" (p. 184). While illustrating Romantic irony in literature, Muecke draws his examples principally from the twentieth century. He notes that "the Romantic Ironists regarded [the novel] as the literary form with the greatest potential" (p. 195) and demonstrates that "Romantic Irony is a basic element in modern literature as a whole" with "the best . . . , most thorough-going, almost programmatic examples [being] the novels of Thomas Mann" (pp. 185–86). It is my contention that Gertrude Stein's *Three Lives* belongs to this modern ironic tradition derived from the Romantics, and that it is thus most appropriate that Stein should begin her book by paying homage to the nineteenth-century Romantic ironist with whose work she was most familiar as an exile in Paris.[8] By noting how Stein develops her fictitious Laforguean theme and uses it as the foundation for her book's subtle thematic development, we can ascertain the relationship of *Three Lives* to twentieth-century Romantic irony.

It would hardly be an original contribution to Gertrude Stein criticism to note the importance of repetition in the style of the woman who wrote the famous sentence about the rose. Yet repetition is not

7. Eponymous protagonist of the 1903 novella by Thomas Mann (1875–1955), Nobel Prize–winning German author. [*Editor's note*.]

8. Although there is no detailed direct evidence of Stein's familiarity with Laforgue's work, there is an abundance of indirect evidence in addition to her bow to him in her book's epigraph and the implications of the structure of *Three Lives* as discussed in this essay. According to John Malcolm Brinnin in *The Third Rose* (Boston, 1959), through Picasso, whom she met in 1905, "Stein had come to know many of his Bateau Lavoir friends and neighbors" including writers, painters, and musicians, who often collaborated together and were fond of "praising . . . Baudelaire, Mallarmé and Rimbaud . . . ' (pp. 85–86). It would have been very strange if Laforgue, as an important writer closely associated with these poets, had not come in for his share of discussion and praise in this fecund artistic atmosphere during an epoch in which, according to René Taupin, "[l']influence de Laforgue est assez général . . . en France" (*L'Influence du symbolisme français sur la poesie américaine de 1910 à 1920* [Paris, 1929], p. 225). (Note also Ramsey's remark that "in France . . . the presence of Laforgue has been one of the most vital since 1887" [p. 179].) One of the Bateau Lavoir poets whom Stein grew to know well at this time was Guillaume Apollinaire, whom Roger Shattuck places directly in the poetic line of Laforgue (*The Banquet Years* [Garden City, N.Y., 1961], p. 317). Apollinaire's part in bringing Stein into contact with the literary currents of the time is suggested in *The Autobiography of Alice B. Toklas* (New York, 1933) when Toklas and Stein visit his apartment and find him surrounded by young French poets (p. 77). Finally most of Stein's biographers assume Laforgue's influence on her (see, e.g., Donald Sutherland, *Gertrude Stein: a Biography of her Work* [New Haven, 1951], p. 28; James R. Mellow, *Charmed Circle: Gertrude Stein and Company* [New York, 1974], p. 71), and Edmund Wilson, in *Axel's Castle* (New York, 1931), even regards Stein as a late continuer of the Symbolist movement which Laforgue helped to form (pp. 243, 96).

only basic to the style of Stein's first book, but also functions within the structure of *Three Lives* to interconnect and contrast the stories in a way that illuminates the irony of the book's epigraph. In Part I of Stein's first story, "The Good Anna," the repetition so character-istic of her work is used on the level of language and plot with sharp ironic effect.

Stein uses plenty of simple, corrective irony in her portrait of Anna. The middle-aged, sharp-tongued, immigrant housekeeper with whom we are confronted at the beginning of the story is clearly a petty and incorrigible domestic tyrant. Her sharp eyes and scolding tongue are constantly in action to assure that all within her purview act in accordance with "the right way . . . to do" (p. 18). She insists, for example, that her dogs maintain her "high ideals for canine chas-tity and discipline" (p. 12), even during their frequent "periods of evil thinking" (p. 13). If Anna disciplines her dogs so firmly, one can imagine how the underservants fare. Anna rules the social life of Sallie, the most docile of them, exactly like that of the dogs. One of Anna's favorite tests of the animals' moral training is to leave the room and then sneak back to surprise them a few moments later. When, in spite of Anna's scolding, Sallie continues to see the butcher boy secretly on the housekeeper's days off, Anna applies the tech-nique she has used successfully on her dogs. Entering the house silently, she creeps back to open the kitchen door: "At the sound of her hand upon the knob there was a wild scramble and a bang, and then Sallie sitting there alone . . . but, alas, the butcher boy forgot his overcoat in his escape" (p. 12). Thus, the repetition between the two scenes of Anna's discipline ironically underlines her cruel dis-respect for others when she is enforcing "the right way . . . to do."

The verbal repetition in this part of "The Good Anna" centers upon the thrice stated judgment, "Anna led an arduous and troubled life" (pp. 11, 13, 21). When this statement first appears, after Anna's shrewd and belligerent dealings with the tradesmen at the beginning of the story, the words already seem somewhat excessive. The cor-rective irony of the statement is plain when these words next occur after Anna is shown enforcing "canine chastity." When the statement appears for the final time, after her confrontation with the butcher boy, the words emphasize the parallels between the two scenes of discipline, thoroughly condemning Anna's repressive character.

Judging from what we see of Anna in the first part of her story, her life could be called arduous and troubled only from her own point of view. Appropriately, therefore, the story's first part is told almost exclusively from Anna's subjective standpoint as this tyrannical bus-ybody is shown imposing arduousness and trouble upon the lives of those around her. As the story progresses, however, a new contra-dictory view of Anna is revealed, introducing the kind of overlapping perspective and paradoxical tension one encounters in the poems of Laforgue and Heine. The first part of this story makes it very plain that, in addition to her repression of Sally and the dogs, Anna also thoroughly manages and interferes with her employer's life. This part of Anna's story closes, however, with the statement that Miss Mathilda would often have to save Anna from the housekeeper's own friends (p. 23). This introduces a new point of view on Anna's character and implies that there may be more to her "arduous and troubled life" than the reader has yet been allowed to see. The second part of Anna's story presents a wider perspective on this life and raises the book's wit to the level of Romantic irony.

Before one has read past the first page of Part II, it is apparent that Anna applies her rigid view of "the right way . . . to do" to herself as well as to others. It is also immediately clear that she, too, suffers the usual unfortunate consequences of this view. For example, she leaves her job in Germany because of her inflexible views on the proper place of her class, and even though she is sickened by the smell in the freshly painted kitchen in Miss Mathilda's house, she refuses to move out even for one evening into the empty parlour (p. 24). Examples of Anna's native generosity and forgiveness are multiplied in Part II. It soon becomes apparent, as Anna is shown lending out her money unwisely to the poor (pp. 54, 65, 66), why Miss Mathilda believes that she needs to "save" her housekeeper.

The major new element here which calls into question our earlier judgment of Anna is her experience with the widow Mrs. Lehntman. In Mrs. Lehntman, Anna meets someone whom she cannot bend to her will, partly because of the widow's amiably unreliable and indomitable character, but also because "Mrs. Lehntman was the romance in Anna's life," as we are informed in nearly identical words no fewer than six times (pp. 30, 34, 52, 55, 70). This phrase seems ironic enough when it is first introduced immediately after the first major triumph of Anna's will in America. By the end of the story of Anna's relationship with her closest friend, however, these words have taken on quite a different connotation. When Anna first is attracted to Mrs. Lehntman, the widow is an attractive, generous individual who uses her influence on Anna for the housekeeper's own good. As the friendship develops, however, Anna slowly comes under the other woman's power. Then, after Anna has become thoroughly dependent on her, Mrs. Lehntman fails her by taking up with a mysterious doctor of doubtful reputation.

Earlier, the repeated statement about the women's romance was followed by the explanation that "romance is the ideal in one's life and it is very lonely living with it lost" (p. 55). This is the unhappy situation in which Anna finds herself when Mrs. Lehntman deserts her. Trying to forget, she immerses herself in her new job, which happens to be in the household of Miss Mathilda. This is the time at which Part I occurred, and the reader now has quite a different perspective on Anna's actions in that part of her story. From this new point of view, she appears no less tyrannical, but we now know that her insistent management of others is part of her struggle to get over the collapse of her life's great romance. Moreover, it soon becomes apparent that this period of happiness in Anna's life is also temporary, for the time of Anna's happy employment at Miss Mathilda's is ending and the housekeeper has nothing to look forward to: "The good Anna could not talk as if this thing were real, it was too weary to be left with strangers" (p. 75). In retrospect, the irony of the refrain in Part I about Anna's arduous and troubled life seems double-edged.

Part III continues the narrative, chronicling Anna's brief holding action against the final attacks of fate while the effect of the loss of those closest to her slowly makes itself felt. Finally, Anna's deteriorating health forces her to undergo an operation, and she dies. Her last thoughts are of her dogs and of the departed stranger, Miss Mathilda.

Thus, through Stein's use of the narrative manipulations and shifting perspectives of Romantic irony she has created one of our most moving and believable literary portraits of a lower-class American woman. The reader's discovery in Part II that he has condemned Anna on incomplete evidence makes him even more sympathetic toward her as he sees the end of her romance and her pitiable death. Nevertheless, one cannot so soon forget the quite accurate initial portrayal of her oppressive effect on Miss Mathilda's household. Stein has presented the reader with conflicting views of Anna which cannot be resolved to form a neat, coherent estimate of her character. At the end of the story we are forced to the paradoxical awareness that Anna is both the triumphant domestic tyrant of Part I and a pitiful, basically unhappy individual, perhaps not unlike the person described in the book's epigraph.[9] While Anna is surely a "malheureuse," however, the application of the last part of the epigraph is less clear at this point. One must read the following story of a similar unhappy woman before the large ironic implications of the epigraph begin to become clear and before one can see how such unhappiness can be considered as neither one's own fault nor that of life.

9. No critic has noted the important role that the epigraph plays in the structure of *Three Lives*. Mellow's unelucidated remark that "the point of view of the book reflects the epigraph" (p. 71) appears to mean no more than Brinnin's suggestion that the Laforgue quotation functions mainly to establish the atmosphere for Stein's "gray proletarian stories" (p. 67) or Sutherland's statement that the epigraph is simply a flat Naturalist observation which sets "the intelligence . . . free from guilt and grievance, to go on and describe the behavior of the species" (p. 28). Elizabeth Sprigge, in *Gertrude Stein: Her Life and Work* (New York, 1957), mentions the epigraph only in connecting the spirit of "sweetness and sadness" in *Three Lives* with Picasso's harlequins (p. 64).

The paradoxical overlapping perspective of Stein's Romantic irony in the story "Melanctha" appears first in the portrayal of this black woman's frustrating and unfulfilling romance with a young doctor, Jeff Campbell. The very intellectual Jeff is from the black middle class and has not pursued the kind of "wandering" in search of "the ways that lead to wisdom" that the lower-class Melanctha Herbert has experienced during her vaguely but delightfully described "beginning as a woman" (pp. 95–97). Therefore, despite their attraction to each other and their interminable conversations and arguments, they find it impossible to communicate at a deep level, and it early becomes apparent that the relationship is doomed to failure in advance. Much of their verbal interaction consists of blaming each other for the deterioration of their romance, and since this process is chronicled exclusively from Jeff's point of view as he suffers and struggles to learn to understand and love Melanctha, her changeableness and complaints seem mainly responsible for the couple's unhappiness. By the time Jeff has convinced himself of his enduring love for Melanctha, however, we see that what had appeared to be selfish and fickle amorous maneuvers in Melanctha were genuinely painful emotional struggles and that they have taken their toll on her sensibility. She has lost her respect for Jeff[1] along with any hope that he could face his emotions honestly, and she has begun to wander in search of a new object for her affections. In retrospect we see that the romance has been described from the distorted emotional perspective of a repressed individual who has been trying unsuccessfully to fit Melanctha's complex and powerful emotions into his naively conventional moral and sociological categories. Nevertheless, one can ignore neither the admirable qualities of this sincere, intelligent, well-intentioned young doctor nor the role of Melanctha's impatience and nagging in the failure of her life's great romance. The question throughout their arguments as to which of them is principally at fault for their mutual unhappiness remains unresolved.

Melanctha sustains permanent psychological damage from her agonizingly extended relationship with Jeff, and she never really recovers from its collapse. She is so eager to make something come of a later romance that she ruins the relationship (p. 221);[2] and no

---

1. Oscar Cargill, in *Intellectual America* (New York, 1949), seems not to have noticed the process of disillusionment which begins with Melanctha's scornful anger and "harsh laugh" after the lovers' first reconciliation (pp. 151–52) and later culminates in her remark, "I certainly do wonder why always it happens to me I care for anybody who ain't no ways good enough for me ever to be thinking to respect him" (p. 169). Cargill mistakenly believes that at the end of the relationship Melanctha still respects Jeff (Cargill, p. 315).

2. The relationship is not ruined because Melanctha "insists on marriage," however, as is asserted by Cargill (p. 316). She only insists on her enduring love for her new man: "Melanctha Herbert's love had surely made her mad and foolish. She thrust it always deep into Jem Richards and now that he had trouble with his betting, Jem had no way that he ever wanted to be made to feel it" (p. 211).

longer able to maintain her emotional balance by herself, she now always feels the need of a stronger, steadier individual to rely on. Melanctha's story, like Anna's, has begun *in medias res*[3] with a description of Melanctha's submissive role in a friendship with a woman clearly inferior to her, and the question is immediately raised, "Why did the subtle, intelligent, attractive half white girl Melanctha Herbert love and do for and demean herself in service to this coarse, decent, sullen, ordinary black childish Rose . . . ?" (p. 86). When this question is repeated after the retrospective description of Melanctha's unsuccessful romance with Jeff and its aftermath, the now-obvious answer is given: "Melanctha needed badly to have Rose always willing to let Melanctha cling to her. Rose was a simple, sullen, selfish, black girl, but she had a solid power in her. . . . And so the subtle intelligent attractive half white girl Melanctha Herbert loved and did for, and demeaned herself in service to this coarse, decent, sullen, ordinary, black, childish Rose . . ." (p. 210).

Partially concealed in these adjective series about the simple, solid Rose are her important negative qualities of sullenness and selfishness. In case the reader has overlooked or forgotten the earlier illustrations of these facts, Stein kindly repeats verbatim three passages from the beginning of the story, underlining Rose's defective character. Here she is shown "making herself an abomination and like a simple beast" during childbirth (pp. 85, 222), making light of Melanctha's thoughts of suicide (pp. 87, 226), and allowing her own baby to die because "she just forgot it for awhile" (pp. 85, 225). Finally, when she mistakenly senses that her husband might be attracted to Melanctha, Rose abruptly breaks off her friendship with the sensitive young woman. Now that even Rose has deserted her, Melanctha is "all sore and bruised inside her" (p. 233). For a brief time she tries to carry on somehow, but soon the emotional sores and bruises inside her are complemented by the physical deterioration of consumption, and Melanctha dies.

At the end of Melanctha's story the meaning of the book's epigraph and Stein's use of Romantic irony in *Three Lives* as a whole begin to become apparent. Life mainly affects Melanctha, as it had Anna, through other people. However, while none of the individuals who

3. The importance of this relatively common method of beginning a story is blown out of proportion by the heavy implications which two critics attach to it. Sutherland believes that this technique at the beginning of "The Good Anna" indicates how closely Stein was imitating Flaubert's "Un Coeur Simple" (pp. 29–30). The first part of "The Good Anna," however, gives many more details about the middle portion of the heroine's life and with a far different effect from that of the simple opening passage of the Flaubert story. On the other hand, Gilbert Weinstein, in *Gertrude Stein and the Literature of the Modern Consciousness* (New York, 1970), stretches the significance of the *in medias res* opening of "Melanctha" in order to lay the groundwork for a theory which applies primarily to *The Making of Americans* and later Stein productions: "By giving the reader significant character information out of linear sequence the reader is forced to weigh all incoming information *equally*" (p. 18).

play principal roles in these two lives is without defects, there is nothing really evil about any of these secondary characters, and they intend no harm to the protagonists. In fact, the people who hurt the protagonists most—Mrs. Lehntman, Jeff, and Rose—have the best intentions toward them and initially do them more good than any of the other characters. The fault for the protagonists' unhappiness, therefore, cannot be fairly assigned to life as it affects them through these secondary characters, each of whom is searching with no great success for a satisfying life. However, the protagonists' unhappiness is not really their own fault, either. The frequently repeated phrase "Melanctha did everything that any woman could" (pp. 85, 110, 125, 139, 222, 224) would apply equally as well to Anna. Each of the protagonists struggles according to her own lights as hard as she can, for happiness.

The reader who is stimulated by the epigraph to try to assign blame for the protagonists' unhappiness is forced continually to direct his attention first to defects in the main characters' personalities, and then to the cruelty of life as they encounter it. In the last analysis, however, the reader cannot assign the blame entirely to either their characters or their experiences any more than one can fully approve or condemn Laforgue's painful but desired alienation in his poem. Caught in the dilemma that Stein has set up, one might tentatively conclude that her main characters' unhappiness can best be blamed, neither on themselves nor on life, but on the tragic interaction of both these elements. Like the protagonists of such other early twentieth-century works as Mann's "Tonio Kröger" and Lawrence's *Sons and Lovers*, Anna and Melanctha simply cannot fit into life as it presents itself to them. As a large portion of modern literature attests, many people around the turn of the century were painfully aware that their abilities and desires did not match the demands of their times. The content and implications of "The Good Anna" and "Melanctha" suggest that Stein used the book's epigraph to refer ironically to this feeling, pervasive among Romantics and moderns alike, of the individual's tragic mismatching with life as he finds it. However, *Three Lives* is not to be interpreted as a Naturalistic record of women crushed between the predictable forces of heredity and environment. The structure of the book turns it rather into something of a very late Romantic rejoinder to the Naturalists since, although the lower-class protagonists and their adverse fates involve typically Naturalistic subject matter, Stein refuses to imply any definitive, objective explanation for their unhappiness. The paradoxical Romantic irony in the book's epigraph sets up a tension which runs through all of *Three Lives* and is never resolved.

It is easy to refer to Anna and Melanctha together in discussing the implications of Stein's book, because there are so many repeated features in their parallel characters and lives. Each is an ethnic out-sider, struggling unsuccessfully for peace and happiness in the same Southern town. Religion plays an important negative role in their lives,[4] and although each woman appears for a time to dominate others (pp. 11–30, 198–205), she is in fact desperately trying to con-trol her own life and find happiness. Most importantly, each woman experiences an intense romance which ends slowly and agonizingly, leaving the partners "good friends" (pp. 71, 206) but insuring the protagonist's demise. These parallels in the women's characters and experiences closely interconnect their two lives and represent the largest-scale repetition in the book's style.[5] At this point in *Three Lives*, however, Stein has not yet completed working out the impli-cations of her epigraph.

There are similar repeated elements in "The Gentle Lena," the book's third story about an unhappy, short-lived, ethnic outsider.[6] Several principal features in Lena's character contrast it to the earlier lives presented, however, and the third story's relative brevity—40 pages after the 150-page narration of Melanctha's life—gives "The Gentle Lena" the appearance of a fictional postscript to the book that further elucidates the epigraph. Because of the basically strong characters of the first two protagonists and because they struggle so hard for happiness, it might well appear, in spite of what has already been pointed out, that life is somehow mainly at fault for their ine-luctable adverse fates. However, life provides Stein's third protago-nist with every traditional good thing it can offer a woman—a husband, children, and security—yet Lena still ends up unhappy. This seems to result mainly from her dull, passive, and nearly sub-human nature, but her unhappiness is also attributable to the demands that life makes on her. Lena, as opposed to Anna and Melanctha, would feel perfectly satisfied and fulfilled without a romance in her life. She is happiest when she is working as a gov-erness and letting her life be run by her domineering aunt. This woman is determined that Lena should have the good things of life, however, and arranges for Lena's wedding to a man whose initial clear unwillingness to marry her adds to the girl's insecurity and, combined with her unfitness for the responsibilities of motherhood,

4. Melanctha first meets her unreliable friend Rose in church (p. 87), and Stein implies that both Anna's overstrict devotion to duty and her somewhat superficial morality are con-nected with her devout German Catholicism (pp. 62–63).
5. Other parallels interconnecting the two stories include the mention of the Bishop family in each story (pp. 44, 91), the fact that each woman lives for a time in a red brick two-story house (pp. 11, 115) and dies at an early age in a hospital (pp. 82, 236), and such stylistic features as repeated phrases, verbal rhythm, and the manipulation of point of view.
6. Another resident of Bridgepoint who dies young in a hospital (p. 279), Lena resembles Anna because of her German background and because she, too, readily and unwisely gives out her hard-earned money (p. 250). Like Melanctha, Lena is accused by a benefactor of being unworthy of help (p. 256, cf. p. 232).

assures her unhappiness. This story, therefore, seems to emphasize the suggestion in *Three Lives* that the unhappiness of a personality mismatched with its experience can neither be fully blamed on the individual nor on life.

The third story, then, shows the overgenerosity of life to an individual who is incapable of enjoying the advantages that were tragically absent from Anna's and Melanctha's lives, and thus "The Gentle Lena" completes Stein's book thematically by ironically illustrating the obverse of the epigraph's character-versus-life equation. It is no accident that Stein should have chosen to pay Laforgue ironic homage by attributing this observation to him. Although the poet had been dead sixteen years before Stein first came to France as an adult, the two writers were kindred spirits, and the American must have felt this when she read Laforgue. Both were anti-traditional, self-exiled authors of experimental prose tales and had a "natural impulse to probe surgically into the passions of the eternal masculine and feminine." Both also captured "the beauty of the commonplace" in non-Naturalist styles, were fascinated by theories of the Unconscious, and shared a "gentle humor" and a "passion for verbal invention . . . [and] linguistic innovations" (Ramsey, pp. 10, 12, 242, 138–139).

Despite his nineteenth-century life span, Laforgue was a kindred spirit to a large number of abused and alienated individuals at the beginning of our century. Representing the residue of Romanticism in the thought of the late nineteenth and early twentieth centuries, Laforgue has been called "symbolic of man's modern condition" (Ramsey, p. 235). Laforgue clearly felt trapped between the conflicting demands of his personality and his time, and one of his main artistic refuges, as with such major modernists as Mann, Gide, Joyce, and Stein herself, was in the paradoxes and shifting perspectives of Romantic irony. Laforgue, however, died before he could fully analyze his dilemma and articulate his response. In his late poem "Avertissement," Laforgue summed up his character: "je vivotte, vivotte, / Bonne girouette aux trent'-six saisons, / Trop nombreaux pour dire oui ou non . . . / —Jeunes gens! que je vous serv' d'Ilote!" ("I struggle and veer / Like a weathercock with the winds that blow, / Too various to say yes or no . . . / Young men! There's a moral here!")[7] It is Stein's achievement in the first of her great experiments in the analysis of human character to have noted the paradoxical moral of the poet's life, to have expressed it in a more succinct Laforguean statement than he ever made himself, and to have illustrated it through three stylistically experimental life histories which epitomize the dilemma of the modern age.

7. Laforgue, II, 7. The translation is Ramsey's (p. 134).

314

CATHARINE R. STIMPSON

[Lesbianism in *Q.E.D.* and "Melanctha"]†

* * * A passage in *The Making of Americans* condenses that shift from some solidarity with women, particularly of her class, to aloofness from nearly all of them. Within two sentences, Stein goes from thinking about women as a sex she knows to thinking about women as a sex that may only be easier to know than men:

> I like to tell it better in a woman the kind of nature a certain kind of men and women have in living, I like to tell about it better in a woman because it is clearer in her and I know it better, a little, not very much better. One can see it in her sooner, a little, not very much sooner, one can see it as simpler.

However, Stein's self-images are more than appropriations of a male identity and masculine interests. Several of them are irrelevant to categories of sex and gender. In part, Stein is an obsessive psychologist, a Euclid of behavior, searching for "bottom natures," the substratum of individuality. She also tries to diagram psychic genotypes, patterns into which all individuals might fit. Although she plays with femaleness/maleness as categories, she also investigates an opposition of impetuousness and passivity, fire and phlegm; a variety of regional and national types; and the dualism of the "independent dependent," who tends to attack, and the "dependent independent," who tends to resist. In part, as she puzzles her way towards knowing and understanding, she presents herself as engaged in aural and oral acts, listening and hearing before speaking and telling. That sense of perception as *physical* also emerges in a passage in which she, as perceiver/describer, first incorporates and then linguistically discharges the world: "Mostly always when I am filled up with it I tell it, sometimes I have to tell it, sometimes I like to tell it, sometimes I keep on with telling it."

If the presentation of self, as person and writer, varies, the dramatization of homosexuality is paradoxical. During the decade of choice, Stein both stopped resisting her sexual impulses and found domestic pleasure in them. However, during the same period, if often before the meeting with Toklas, she takes certain lesbian or quasi-lesbian experiences and progressively disguises and encodes them in a series of books. I would speculate that she does so for several reasons. Some of them are aesthetic: the need to avoid imitating one's self; the desire to transform apprentice materials into

† From, "The Mind, The Body, and Gertrude Stein" in *Critical Inquiry* 3.3 (1977): 489–506. Reprinted by permission of the University of Chicago Press and the author.

richer, more satisfying verbal worlds. Other reasons are psychological: the need to write out hidden impulses; the wish to speak to friends without having others overhear; the desire to evade and to confound strangers, aliens, and enemies.

Whatever the motive, the literary encoding does what Morse Code does: it transmits messages in a different form which initiates may translate back into the original. However, it also distances the representation of homosexuality from its enactment in life. Curiously, the books written under the immediate influence of the May Bookstaver relationship are refreshingly free from *The Well of Loneliness* syndrome: the conviction that lesbianism is a disease, no less sinful for being fatal. Stein finds the will towards domination, ignorance, and corrupt character more immoral than homosexuality. But, during the process of encoding, what were lesbian experiences become, if possible, sadder and sadder. Accompanying this is a subtheme of *Three Lives* and *The Making of Americans*, the pathetic frustrations of women's feelings for each other: Good Anna for her employer, Miss Matilda, a character based on Stein; Good Anna for her "romance," Mrs. Lehntman; Gentle Lena for other servant girls; Melanctha Herbert for Rose Johnson; Mrs. Fanny Hersland for a governess, Madeleine Wyman.

One process of encoding takes place in the shift from *Q.E.D.* to "Melanctha," the second and most complex section of *Three Lives.* Both proven fact and inference suggest that *Q.E.D.* more or less transcribes the Stein/Bookstaver/Haynes history. The figure of Adele is surrogate for Stein; Helen Thomas for May Bookstaver; Mabel Neathe for Mabel Haynes. In *Q.E.D.* the affair between Adele and Helen symbolizes a conflict between the person who believes in control, reason, and middle-class virtues and the person who believes in action, passion, and experience. During its course, Adele abandons easy moral and intellectual formulae and grows into moral and erotic knowledge. The affair ends because the lovers' physical and emotional appeals to each other are not synchronized. As one advances, the other resists or retreats. Mabel, behind a pose of decorum and friendship for Adele, also fights to keep Helen. She is devious, brittle, jealous, and successful. That she has some money and Helen has little helps her. *Q.E.D.*'s last scene shows an isolated Adele, wondering "impatiently" why Helen refuses to "see things as they are . . .": " 'I am afraid it comes very near being a deadlock,' she groaned dropping her head on her arms."

"Melanctha" rewrites the affair between Helen and Adele in a racial context. Helen becomes Melanctha Herbert; Adele, Dr. Jefferson Campbell. Although Stein no longer explores the psychology of the rigid triangle that must break, she has several figures serve as Jeff's rivals: a black woman, Jane Harden (Stein wrote, but did not publish, *Three Lives* under the name of Jane Sands); a black man, Jem Richards; anonymous men, white and black, among whom Melanctha wanders. If the final words of *Q.E.D.* are about Adele, lonely but alive, those of "Melanctha" poignantly show Melanctha lonely and dead: "Melanctha went back to the hospital, and there the Doctor told her she had the consumption, and before long she would surely die. They sent her where she would be taken care of, a home for poor consumptives, and there Melanctha stayed until she died." It might be tempting to suggest that Stein, as she revised her experience, exorcised it through the death of the surrogate of her difficult lover. However, the pattern of *Three Lives* as a whole, which each of the three stories reduplicates, is the movement of life's guilt-less, unfortunate victims from a moment of happiness to death.

"Melanctha" does reveal two clear kinds of coding. First, female homosexuality is masculinized. Stein/Adele becomes Jeff. Wish ful-fillment or irony, Jeff is the medical doctor Stein refused to become. Next, problematic passion among whites is transferred to blacks, as if they might embody that which the dominant culture feared. The facts that Stein disliked raw racial injustice and that a black author, Richard Wright, praised "Melanctha" itself must be balanced against the fact that racial stereotypes help to print out the narrative. Not only does white blood breed finely-boned blacks, but the primitive darker race, especially in the South, embodies sensuality: ". . . wide abandoned laughter . . . makes the warm broad flow of negro sun-shine."

Though Stein did not abandon the dramatic materials of *Q.E.D.*, she ostensibly hid the manuscript. Stein has Toklas artlessly give out the public version of the manuscript's history in *The Autobiography of Alice B. Toklas*, which Stein wrote about thirty years after *Q.E.D.*

> The funny thing about this short novel is that she [Stein] com-pletely forgot about it for many years. She remembered herself beginning a little later writing The Three Lives but this first piece of writing was completely forgotten, she had never men-tioned it to me, even when I first knew her. She must have forgotten about it almost immediately. This spring just two days before our leaving for the country she was looking for some manuscript of The Making of Americans that she wanted to show to Bernard Faÿ and she came across these two carefully written volumes of this completely forgotten first novel. She was very bashful and hesitant about it, did not really want to read it. Louis Bromfield was at the house that evening and she handed him the manuscript and said to him, you read it.

Even after the manuscript was "discovered," it was not listed in the 1941 Yale catalogue of Stein's published and unpublished work, with which she helped. Finally, in 1950, under Toklas' copyright, *Q.E.D.* was published by the small Banyan Press as *Things As They Are*. A few textual emendations (for example, Adele's brother becomes her cousin) made the book slightly less autobiographical.

Stein's motives, I believe, were less to suppress public knowledge of her own homosexuality than to protect her private relationship with Toklas. Toklas was sensitive enough, as late as 1932, to burn Bookstaver's letters to Stein. In 1947, Toklas, in a letter, said about *Q.E.D.*: "It is a subject I haven't known how to handle nor known from what point to act upon. It was something I knew I'd have to meet some day and not too long hence and to cover my cowardice I kept saying—well when everything else is accomplished." She adds that she would not want *Q.E.D.* read while she was alive. "Gertrude would have understood this perfectly though of course it was never mentioned." Despite such silences, May Bookstaver retained at least a peripheral relationship with the novel. After five commercial publishers had turned *Three Lives* down, a vanity press, Grafton, issued it in 1909. Among the people who acted as Stein's agents in the transactions was Bookstaver, who had married Charles Knoblauch in 1906 and who continued for years to serve as a medium between Stein and potential readers. * * *

MARIANNE DEKOVEN

[Anti-patriarchal Writing and *Three Lives*]†

The notion of psychic repression allows us to posit the equivalence of logocentrism and phallogocentrism, or patriarchy. In spite of the fact that we—both genders—begin to acquire symbolic language well before the resolution of the Oedipal crisis, the conclusive repression of presymbolic language is coincident with the Oedipal phase, which in turn is coincident with full mastery of the use of symbolic language. Symbolic language is simply language as we commonly conceive it: primarily a way to make and order communicable, coherent meaning. It is dominated by the signified. The signifier becomes a more or less transparent communicator of meaning. We are accustomed either to forget or to ignore, except in the restricted areas of learning theory and developmental psychology, the presymbolic state of language we all experience as infants. (Kristeva also calls this language "semiotic," a term I find much less helpful, and more confusing, than the term "presymbolic.") In this presymbolic

† From *A Different Language: Gertrude Stein's Experimental Language* (Madison: The University of Wisconsin Press, 1983), pp. 20–45. Reprinted by permission of the publisher.

state, language reaches us as repetition, sound association, intonation: the signifier. What for Derrida is a suppressed cultural/historical past of nonlinear writing can also be seen as a repressed psychological past, in the individual, of presymbolic language. Presymbolic language shares with much experimental writing this ascendency of the signifier: the play of intonation, rhythm, repetition, sound association. Symbolic language is similar to conventional, grammatical, logocentric writing: they both encompass the ascendency of hierarchical order, sense, reason, the signified.

Crucially, we can link the acquisition of symbolic language in the individual with the Freudian acquisition of culture, which takes place at the resolution of the Oedipal crisis by means of capitulation to the dominant, protecting Father-as-cultural-principle. The acquisition of culture, in human society as we know it, *is* the institution of what Jacques Lacan calls the "Rule of the Father," or patriarchy (as anthropologists agree, all existing societies are patriarchal). In Freudian-Lacanian theory, to enter or acquire culture is to embrace simultaneously and exclusively the symbolic order of language and the "Rule of the Father." The two are inseparable, and both come at the cost of repressing, again simultaneously, presymbolic language and the infant's omnipotent, magical unity of the self with the outer world, of which presymbolic language is the expression. The symbolic language of the Father, of patriarchy, is in fact a compensation for that lost omnipotent unity: a means of dominating and controlling the newly alienated outer world.[1] In Lacan's theory, the repression concomitant with acquisition of symbolic language, which he sees as the repression of the ascendant signifier, creates and wholly constitutes the unconscious: the exclusive content of the unconscious is the "autonomous" or "supreme" signifier.[2]

Kristeva and other French feminist theorists of female *"différence"* (as in *"vive la différence"*) extend this formulation, correcting Lacan's (since Freud's) valorization of the phallus. For them, the content of the unconscious, repressed by the institution of the Rule of the Father (patriarchy, phallogocentrism) is what they call the female Other: the pre-Oedipal hegemony of the mother—the *"jouissance* of the mother's body"—which is concomitant with presymbolic language. Irigaray and Cixous, most closely associated with the polemic for female *différence*, argue for the restoration of the repressed female Other, a restoration which would *be*, in Lacan's analysis, the Freudian goal of "making conscious the unconscious." The means for achieving this restoration would be a new women's language, yet

1. See also D. W. Winnicott, *Playing and Reality* (New York: Basic Books, 1971).
2. See particularly "The Agency of the letter in the unconscious or reason since Freud," and "The signification of the phallus," in *Écrits: A Selection*, trans. Alan Sheridan (New York: Norton, 1977), 146–178, 281–291.

to be, or in the process now of being, invented, which develops pre-symbolic modes of signification.

However, though it is not a specifically female language, written for a female audience, experimental writing is certainly anti-patriarchal according to Kristeva's Lacanian-Derridean construct. To the extent that it relies heavily on aural signification—on the signifier itself—experimental writing is presymbolic, an expression of the pre-Oedipal union with the mother's body, a gesture, against the repression of the Rule of the Father, toward releasing into written culture the power of the Mother. Much or most of Stein's writing is heavily aural, some of it primarily so:

> Not so dots large dressed dots, big sizes, less laced, less laced diamonds, diamonds white, diamonds bright, diamonds in the in the light, diamonds light diamonds door diamonds hanging to be four, two four; all before, this bean, lessly, all most, a best, willow, vest, a green guest, guest, go go go go go go, go. Go go. Not guessed. Go go.[3]

Julia Kristeva sees that all features of experimental writing—pluridimensional, irresolvable multiplicity as well as the dominance of the signifier—are anti-patriarchal:

> For at least a century, the literary avant-garde (from Mallarmé and Lautréamont to Joyce and Artaud) has been introducing ruptures, blank spaces, and holes into language. . . . All of the modifications in the linguistic fabric are the sign of a force that has not been grasped by the linguistic or ideological system. This signification renewed, "infinitized" by the rhythm in a text, this precisely is (sexual) pleasure (*la jouissance*).
>
> However, in a culture where the speaking subjects are conceived of as masters of their speech, they have what is called a "phallic" position. The fragmentation of language in a text calls into question the very posture of this mastery. The writing that we have been discussing confronts this phallic position either to traverse it or to deny it.[4]

Although its presymbolic foregrounding of the signifier is its only positive connection to the pre-Oedipal mother, hence to the repressed female Other, experimental writing opposes in every way the foundations of patriarchal symbolic language. Experimental writing is only partly explicitly female, of the mother; it is entirely anti-patriarchal. While patriarchal, symbolic language is sensible, orderly, unitary, dominated by anterior meaning, experimental writing is a

---

3. Gertrude Stein, "Preciosilla," in *Selected Writings*, 550–551.
4. Julia Kristeva, "Oscillation du 'pouvoir' au 'refus,' " interview by Xavière Gauthier in *Tel Quel* (Summer 1974), trans. Marilyn A. August as "Oscillation between Power and Denial," *New French Feminism*, 165.

"pre-sentence-making disposition to rhythm, intonation, nonsense; makes nonsense abound within sense: makes him laugh."[5] Experimental writing "displaces, condenses, distributes. It retains all that's repressed by the Word [patriarchal logos]: by sign, by sense, by communication, by symbolic order, whatever is legislating, restrictive, paternal."[6]

Experimental writing can liberate, for both genders, the non-linearity, pluridimensionality, free play of the signifier, the continuity of the order of things with the order of symbols—in sum, our pre-Oedipal experience of language—an experience which is repressed by the institutions of patriarchy (phallogocentrism, the Rule of the Father). But patriarchy is responsible for reason, clarity, and justice as well as impersonality, hierarchy, and tyranny. Without patriarchal language, this entirely conventional study of anti-patriarchal language would not be possible. Surely we do not want to liberate the repressed at the expense of destroying the good which repression was instituted to enable. What are the limits of experimental writing?

The first or most obvious limit is of course that it need not replace, or even threaten, conventional writing. Making conscious the unconscious need not destroy the already-conscious; rather, the area of the conscious can be both enlarged and restored to wholeness. One has in mind the kind of balance Kristeva describes in *About Chinese Women*, in her vision of ancient Chinese matrilinear culture. In that culture, neither sexual order had ascendency over the other, neither was repressed or suppressed, and therefore both were equally available, in a "constant alternation between time and its 'truth,' identity and its loss, history and the timeless, signless, extra-phenomenal things that produce it. An impossible dialectic: a permanent alternation: never the one without the other."[7]

This ideal of permanent alternation or dialectic of gender modes, rather than dominance of either, is not merely an afterthought for Kristeva, designed to quell the fears of the male audience. It is central to the project of proposing an alternative to patriarchal language. Indeed, women—as "location" of an alternative to patriarchy—must

5. Julia Kristeva, *About Chinese Women*, trans. Anita Barrows (London: Marion Boyars, 1977), 29–30. For a hard look at Kristeva's evidence and argument in *About Chinese Women* and in her *Tel Quel* writing, see Gayatri Chakravorty Spivak, "French Feminism in an International Frame," *Yale French Studies* 62 (1981), 154–184, especially 157–164. While I agree with Spivak's critique of Kristeva's anthropological evidence, and of the overall rigor of her demonstrations, I do not agree that we should therefore dismiss Kristeva's conclusions. Those conclusions are based on ideas which one can reject, as one can reject Marx or Freud, but which are nonetheless powerful theoretical models of culture, and do not depend for their legitimacy on the rigor of any one writer's presentation of them. For more of Kristeva's psychology of language, see *Desire in Language* (New York: Columbia University Press, 1980), and *Polylogue* (Paris: Seuil, 1977).
6. Kristeva, *About Chinese Women*, 40.
7. Kristeva, ibid., 38.

"refuse all roles, in order, on the contrary, to summon this timeless 'truth'—formless, neither true nor false, echo of our *jouissance*, of our madness, of our pregnancies—into the order of speech and social symbolism."[8] But at the same time we must not "lock ourselves up inside" our female identity after an "initial phase" of "searching for" it;[9] we must "know that an ostensibly masculine, paternal (because supportive of time and symbol) identification is necessary in order to have some voice in the record of politics and history."[1] In this "impossible dialectic" the "paternal identification" (symbolic language, conventional writing) would *coexist* with the "maternal identification" (presymbolic language, experimental writing).[2]

Beyond that crucial but perhaps not obvious qualification, it is also necessary to postulate a related limit *within* experimental writing, a limit implied by the differentiation of "incoherent" from "unintelligible," of "semi-grammatical" from "ungrammatical." Simply successful experimental writing generally requires the presence of articulated meaning in the text. Again, to repudiate coherent meaning is not to repudiate meaning altogether. Meaning can be present and available in the text in multiple, undermined fragmented form. But without some concerted articulation of meaning, most experimental texts are unreadable.[3]

The apparent contradiction in experimental writing between its destruction of sense and its retention of a "paternal identification" (what Barthes calls, in *The Pleasure of the Text,* the "shadow of the text" of bliss)—the felt presence of articulated meaning—parallels a contradiction in Stein's own esthetic theory. In her lectures and essays, Stein elaborates two central, contradictory threads of argument: literature must be absolutely pure (serve "god" rather than "mammon," in Stein's terminology), but at the same time it must express and create its time, its "composition."[4] It must both renounce the world and embody the deepest nature, the essence, of its cultural moment.

In her extensive elaboration of the notion of artistic autonomy or purity, it is clear that Stein considers communicated content irrelevant to value in art. Artistic merit is exclusively a matter of imagination and perfection of form within a particular medium. Great

---

8. Ibid.
9. Ibid., 14.
1. Ibid., 37–38.
2. Again, experimental writing represents an actual "maternal identification" only to the extent that it employs presymbolic modes of signification. Otherwise, experimental writing is "maternal" only in that it *opposes* the language of patriarchy.
3. I qualify this assertion ("*most* experimental texts") because some purely aural modes of Stein's are quite successful.
4. The most important of these are "Composition as Explanation," *Lectures in America, The Geographical History of America, Narration,* "How Writing Is Written," "What Are Masterpieces," and *Picasso.*

literature is recognizable by qualities independent of its content: by "its complete solidity, its complete imagination, its complete existence."[5] The subject of a masterpiece might be steeped in contingency, but the work itself must be free of it:

> After all any woman in any village or men either if you like or even children know as much of human psychology as any writer that ever lived. After all there are things you do know each one in his or her way knows all of them and it is not this knowledge that makes master-pieces. . . . Those who recognize master-pieces say that is the reason but it is not. It is not the way Hamlet reacts to his father's ghost that makes the master-piece, he might have reacted according to Shakespeare in a dozen other ways and everybody would have been as much impressed by the psychology of it. . . . master-pieces . . . exist because they came to be as something that is an end in itself and in that respect it is opposed to the business of living which is relation and necessity. That is what a master-piece is not although it may easily be what a master-piece talks about. ("What Are Master-pieces," 149, 151)

However, this pure work of art is, paradoxically, both characteristic and constitutive of its time; for Stein, the "modern composition":

> People really do not change from one generation to another, . . . nothing changes from one generation to another except the things seen and the things seen make that generation, that is to say nothing changes in people from one generation to another except the way of seeing and being seen, the streets change, the way of being driven in the streets change, the buildings change, the comforts in the houses change, but the people from one generation to another do not change. The creator in the arts is like all the rest of the people living, he is sensitive to the changes in the way of living and his art is inevitably influenced by the way each generation is living, . . . Really the composition of this war, 1914–1918, was not the composition of all previous wars, the composition was not a composition in which there was one man in the centre surrounded by a lot of other men but a composition that had neither a beginning nor an end, a composition of which one corner was as important as another corner, in fact the composition of cubism. (*Picasso*, 10–11)

> One must never forget that the reality of the twentieth century is not the reality of the nineteenth century, not at all and Picasso was the only one in painting who felt it, the only one. More and

5. Gertrude Stein, "What is English Literature," *Lectures in America*, 16.

more the struggle to express it intensified. Matisse and all the others saw the twentieth century with their eyes but they saw the reality of the nineteenth century, Picasso was the only one in painting who saw the twentieth century with his eyes and saw its reality and consequently his struggle was terrifying, terrifying for himself and for the others, because he had nothing to help him, the past did not help him, nor the present, he had to do it all alone . . . *Picasso*, 21–22)

Stein's reiteration of "the only one *in painting*" implies that she is thinking of her own terrifying, solitary struggle. But what is the nature of that struggle? To realize the modern composition, as she indicates here, or to free her work from all forms of contingency?

Stein's thought offers no synthesis, no answer to that question. Her unwitting theoretical alternation between the norms of artistic purity and of expressing/creating the modern composition in fact resembles the ideal cultural alternation, the permanent dialectic, which Kristeva proposes between the modes of the Mother and the Father. It is not necessary, therefore, to try to resolve this contradiction at the theoretical level, as long as it is resolved in practice: as long as Stein's writing is incoherent rather than unintelligible, semi-grammatical rather than ungrammatical; as long as she articulates lexical meanings in a way that allows us to read.

Three Lives

> Gertrude Stein had written the story of Melanctha . . . which was the first definite step away from the nineteenth century and into the twentieth century in literature. (*The Autobiography of Alice B. Toklas*, 54)

Stein composed *Three Lives* while she stared at Cézanne's portrait of his wife and while she sat for Picasso's portrait of herself. It represents her first concerted break with conventional modes of writing. It is crucial to her experimental career, both as the source of her subsequent stylistic techniques and as a clue to the source of her rebellion against patriarchal linguistic structures.

Stein's break with literary convention in *Three Lives* is generally described as stylization of the prose surface in order to render directly the essence of a character's identity, which Stein calls the pulse of personality, and the critic Norman Weinstein calls the unique "rhythm, density, continuity, speed, quantity" of consciousness.[6] Stein also manipulates the prose surface in *Three Lives* in order to render directly what she calls a "continuous present": a notion of time, derived from William James and akin to that of Henri

---

6. Weinstein, *Gertrude Stein and the Literature of Modern Consciousness*.

Bergson, as a continuous process or succession of steadily shifting present moments rather than a linear progress or march from past through present to future. This stylization of the prose surface is seen by many critics as the beginning of Stein's progress toward an abstract, self-contained, plastic, autonomous literature, whose only concern is its articulation of formal features of language. As Richard Bridgman says, "While such examples [of dialogue from *Melanctha*] are still tied to the story, it is not difficult to see how they could easily lead to a preoccupation with the prose surface itself, at the expense of the imagined reality she was attempting to create."[7] Michael Hoffman makes a similar, even clearer statement:

> How does Stein move within just a few years from a stylized Jamesian realism to both a fragmented narrative structure and a ritualized style, and then, within less than a decade, turn to a use of language in which words cease to be purveyors of conventional meaning and become plastic counters to be manipulated purely in obedience to the artist's expressive will, just as painters manipulate nonsemantic line and color?[8]

Such judgments proceed from a concept of literary meaning borrowed from painting, where meaning must be either referential or abstract. Meaning in experimental writing need be neither: it often has no anterior, referential, thematic content, yet it has readable meaning—it is not abstract. Bridgman is certainly correct that Stein begins, with *Melanctha*, to abandon "the imagined reality she was attempting to create." But the "preoccupation with the prose surface" which leads her to do so is not, as Hoffman has it, a retreat from meaning into pure form. Rather it is the beginning of a shift from conventional, patriarchal to experimental, anti-patriarchal modes of articulating meaning.

The origins of this shift are clearest in the *overt* stylistic innovations of *Melanctha*, but they are also embedded in some of the more familiar modernist or impressionist features of all three novellas. Like a good deal of early modern fiction, *Three Lives* employs the device of obtuse or unreliable narration.[9] Generally, obtuse narration is a function of subjectivity: the narrator's psychology and involvement in the story determine her or his version of it. By allowing for this subjective structuring, we are able simultaneously to chart the limits of the narrator's perception and to see beyond them (this process is often facilitated by multiple narration, as in Conrad's *Nostromo*, Woolf's *To The Lighthouse*, etc.). In *Three Lives*, the narration

---

7. Bridgman, *Gertrude Stein in Pieces*, 57.
8. Michael Hoffman, *Gertrude Stein, Twayne's United States Authors Series*, ed. Sylvia E. Bowman (Boston: Twayne, 1976), 21.
9. Conrad's Marlow, Ford's Dowell, Faulkner's Quentin, Fitzgerald's Nick Carraway, etc.

is "omniscient third," yet nonetheless obtuse: there is a discrepancy, sometimes to the point of contradiction, between the tone of the narrative voice and the content of the narrative. Some such discrepancy is, as we know, characteristic of fiction, where irony, understatement, or a conflict of conscious and unconscious creation so often generates a complex vision. But in *Three Lives*, the discrepancy is so extreme that the narrator seems at times entirely blind to the import of what she narrates.

While the narrative voice of *Three Lives* is consistently innocent, straightforward, mildly jolly, and approving, the content is often grotesque, sinister, ridiculous. The gulf between what the narrator tells us and what we see is most vivid in some of the brilliant brief portraits, such as this one of Mrs. Haydon, Lena's aunt:

> This aunt, who had brought Lena, four years before, to Bridgepoint, was a hard, ambitious, well meaning, german woman. . . . Mrs. Haydon was a short, stout, hard built, german woman. She always hit the ground very firmly and compactly as she walked. Mrs. Haydon was all a compact and well hardened mass, even to her face, reddish and darkened from its early blonde, with its hearty, shiny cheeks, and doubled chin well covered over with the uproll from her short, square neck.[1]

The avuncular simplicity, the cheerful straightforwardness of the narrator's tone, the words "well meaning" and "hearty," muffle the frightening, repulsive discord of the "hardened mass" and the "doubled chin well covered over with the uproll from her short, square neck." If we visualize Mrs. Haydon from this description, we see a monster, which is precisely what she becomes in the course of the story.

One of the best brief portraits is of Anna's half brother, the baker:

> Her half brother, the fat baker, was a queer kind of a man. He was a huge, unwieldy creature, all puffed out all over, and no longer able to walk much, with his enormous body and the big, swollen, bursted veins in his great legs. He did not try to walk much now. He sat around his place, leaning on his great thick stick, and watching his workmen at their work.
>
> On holidays, and sometimes of a Sunday, he went out in his bakery wagon. He went then to each customer he had and gave them each a large, sweet, raisined loaf of caky bread. At every house with many groans and gasps he would descend his heavy weight out of the wagon, his good featured, black haired, flat, good natured face shining with oily perspiration, with pride in labor and with generous kindness. Up each stoop he hobbled

1. Gertrude Stein, *Three Lives* (1909; rpt. New York: Random House, 1936), 242–243.

> with the help of his big stick, and into the nearest chair in the kitchen or in the parlour, as the fashion of the house demanded, and there he sat and puffed, and then presented to the mistress or the cook the raisined german loaf his boy supplied him. (*Three Lives*, 48)

The incongruity in this portrait of the baker is summarized in the "good featured, black haired, flat, good natured face shining with oily perspiration, with pride in labor and with generous kindness." The negative "oily perspiration" is included casually, as if it conveyed the same message as the more positive "good features," "good nature," "pride in labor," and "generous kindness."

The narrative voice in *Three Lives* is not only straightforward, factual, reassuring; it is also childish, whimsical, consciously naive: the baker is "a queer kind of a man," "all puffed out all over," who "sits and puffs" in the kitchens of his customers. The diction and tone could be those of a children's story. This childish language heightens the discrepancy between narrative voice and content, here and elsewhere by means of its implied innocence concerning what seems a sexually charged disgust, and more generally in the novellas by masking the sophisticated complexity and somber implications of Stein's "imagined reality."

The three women's lives of the title all end in defeated, lonely death, a fact one would never surmise from the narrative tone. Anna, a generous, hardworking, stubborn, managing German immigrant (based on one of Stein's Baltimore servants), works herself to death for a series of selfish employers and friends who take all she offers, allow her to run their lives (the only repayment she exacts), then desert her when she has outlived her usefulness or when they are tired of her rigid control. She dies poor, of an unnamed disease, alone except for the one friend (Mrs. Drehten, the long-suffering, passive victim of poverty and a tyrannical husband) whose society represents no hope whatever of improving Anna's lot.

As "the good Anna" dies of her goodness, "the gentle Lena" dies of her gentleness. She is passive, dreamy, absent, slow-witted, out of touch with her feelings. She is forced into marriage by her aunt, the monstrous ("well meaning," "hearty") Mrs. Haydon, with the equally passive yet reluctant Herman Kreder. Herman comes into his own by triumphing over his fairytale witch of a mother—something his marriage has given him the strength to do—and his children give purpose and vitality to his life. Lena, unable to assert or even to know her will, steadily fades into near nonexistence, and dies giving birth to the fourth child.

Melanctha, who has no summarizing fatal female virtue, has a more complex death than Anna or Lena. Melanctha's story had been told before by Stein, in her first novel, originally entitled *Q.E.D.* (1903–5).[2] *Q.E.D.* is a straightforward account of Stein's first lesbian affair with May Bookstaver, whom, she met while at Johns Hopkins Medical School. May was attached to a third woman whom she would not give up. The affair ended, in stalemate, with Stein's expatriation to Paris.[3] The triangle, origin of the title *Q.E.D.*, is absent in *Melanctha*, which focuses on the temperamental differences between Jeff Campbell, Stein's surrogate, and Melanctha, a transformation of May. Jeff's involvement with Melanctha—his painful growth and final disappointment—is the center of the story, but only one episode in Melanctha's life. Melanctha, an intelligent, reckless black woman, is a much more complicated heroine/victim than Anna or Lena (Stein calls her the "complex desiring Melanctha"). Where Anna is defeated simply by her goodness and Lena by her gentleness, Melanctha is defeated by what is emerging as the fatal flaw *par excellence* of heroines in women's fiction: a divided self.[4] At crucial times in her life, including the moment when she finally has the full and passionate love she needs from Jeff, she acts against her own best interests, destroying the relationships she has worked hard to build. "Melanctha Herbert was always seeking rest and quiet, and always she could only find new ways to be in trouble" (89). From Jeff she moves on to Jem Richards, an unreliable gambler, and to the shallow, selfish Rose Johnson. She loses Jem by pressing him when he's down, and finally she loses her last hope for safety, Rose Johnson, by being too kind to Rose's husband Sam. She dies of consumption, alone, in a sanatorium for the poor.

These plot summaries are accurate and yet misleading. The bitter implications, the powerful feminist morals of these stories (the "good" woman who dies of service to others, the "gentle" woman who dies in unwanted childbirth, the "complex, desiring" woman who dies of self-defeating complexity and unsatisfied desire) are concealed or overruled not only by the narrator's tone and diction but also by narrative emphasis and temporal structure. While Stein's uses of obtuse narration to distance language ironically from content and to avoid forcing on the reader any judgment of the story seem intentional (she was translating Flaubert's *Un Coeur Simple* when she began *Three Lives*), her use of narrative tone and temporal

2. Gertrude Stein, *Q.E.D.*, in *Fernhurst, Q.E.D., and Other Early Writings* (New York: Liveright, 1971). The similarity between *Q.E.D.* and *Melanctha* has been demonstrated and discussed by Bridgman in *Gertrude Stein in Pieces* (52–54); Leon Katz, in his introduction to *Fernhurst, Q.E.D., and Other Early Writings* (ix–xx); and Catharine Stimpson in "The Mind, the Body and Gertrude Stein," 499–502.
3. For a full account of this affair and of its fictionalization in *Q.E.D.*, see Katz's introduction to *Fernhurst, Q.E.D, and Other Early Writings*.
4. See particularly Elaine Showalter, *A Literature of Their Own* (Princeton: Princeton University Press, 1977), and Sandra M. Gilbert and Susan Gubar, *The Madwoman in the Attic* (New Haven: Yale University Press, 1979).

structure as a defense against her own anger and despair appears unconscious. Throughout the novellas, Stein seems primarily interested in the comic manifestations of her heroines' psychologies, or in the inverse relation, among friends and lovers, between power and need, or in clashes resulting from the attraction of opposite temperaments. One has no sense that Stein recognizes what is clear in each plot: the defeat of a woman by dominant personality traits which are culturally defined as female. The three deaths of this trilogy are achieved in quick closing sections, almost appended as afterthought or postscript (only *The Good Anna* is divided into parts; "Part III, The Death of the Good Anna" takes up six of the story's seventy-one pages, Melanctha dies in half a page, Lena in half a paragraph).

Our attention is also diverted from the thematic implications of the plots by the characteristically impressionist temporal structure of *Three Lives*. Impressionist narrative generally begins on the eve of an important event or time, without letting the reader know that it has any particular significance. The story then "flashes back" to the events or times in the protagonist's life which build to this crucial moment, constructing the whole picture through an accretion of episodes, until the reader has a full sense of the import of that initial moment. Both *The Good Anna* and *The Gentle Lena* begin during the short time of the heroine's happiness (in service to a congenial mistress) which just precedes the reversal of her fortunes; the greater part of each story is a flashback to the life that led to that pinnacle. *Melanctha* begins with the death of Rose Johnson's baby, an episode which, despite its casual cruelty, seems at first to have no negative implications for Melanctha. Since we do not know that these initial moments immediately precede the heroine's defeated death, each novella seems to be progressing not toward death but toward a happy, or at least promising time in the character's life. (Stein in fact holds out false hope for Melanctha in the beginning of her story: "Melanctha Herbert had not *yet* been really married" [85; italics added].) It is this structure which gives the deaths of the heroines the quality of afterthought or postscript, distracting us from their actual thematic centrality.

Temporal structure works against thematic structure on other levels within *Three Lives*. The morals of these three tales depend on linear causality: Anna can be said to die of her goodness only insofar as we can see her becoming worn out and sick *because* she works too hard, eats too little, gives all her money to her friends. But linear causality in *Three Lives* is counteracted or counterbalanced by two conflicting temporal models, one which Stein calls the "continuous present," and the other which we might call "spatial form," or simply stasis.[5] To the extent that the time of the narrative is a "continuous present," the chronological events in each heroine's life are not linked casually. Instead, they are seen as a process of continual change, where one condition or state of being persists for a time and then is either suddenly transformed or gradually shifted into a different (often opposite) condition. But whether change is sudden or gradual, it is part of the natural process of life and not dependent on the will of a character or the logic of other events in the narrative. Change is often sudden: "And so Jeff Campbell went on with this dull and sodden, heavy, quiet always in him, and he never seemed to be able to have any feeling. Only sometimes he shivered hot with shame when he remembered some things he once had been feeling. And then one day it all woke up, and was sharp in him" (*Melanctha*, 194).

For gradual change, which is most characteristic of the "continuous present," Stein uses the word "now":

> Jeff Campbell never asked Melanctha any more if she loved him. Now things were always getting worse between them. Now Jeff was always very silent with Melanctha. Now Jeff never wanted to be honest to her, and now Jeff never had much to say to her.
>
> Now when they were together, it was Melanctha always did most of the talking. Now she often had other girls there with her. . . .
>
> Every day it was getting harder for Jeff Campbell. It was as if now, when he had learned to really love Melanctha, she did not need any more to have him. Jeff began to know this very well inside him. . . .
>
> Every day Melanctha Herbert was less and less near to him. She always was very pleasant in her talk and to be with him, but somehow now it never was any comfort to him.
>
> Melanctha Herbert now always had a lot of friends around her. Jeff Campbell never wanted to be with them. Now Melanctha began to find it, she said it often to him, always harder to arrange to be alone now with him. (*Melanctha*, 188–189)

With each "now," the situation is slightly worse. Stein captures a process which takes place over a period of time without isolating a past time from the "continuous present" of the narrative.

Though the kinetic model of time (life as constant change) dominates the narrative structure, the static, anti-developmental tem-

5. This term was invented by Joseph Frank in his famous essay "Spatial Form in Modern Literature," *Sewanee Review* (1945). See also Sharon Spencer, *Space, Time and Structure in the Modern Novel* (Chicago: Swallow Press, 1971), and Patricia Tobin, *Time and the Novel: The Genealogical Imperative* (Princeton: Princeton University Press, 1978).

poral model is reflected in the circularity (minus death) of each
novella, as well as in the internal structure of many vignettes. Lena
sits in the park with the other servant girls, her friends, who always
tease her. One day she is playing with a green paper accordion that
her young charge has dropped. One of her friends, Mary, suddenly
asks her what she has on her finger.

> "Why, what is it, Mary, paint?" said Lena, putting her finger to
> her mouth to taste the dirt spot.
> "That's awful poison Lena, don't you know?" said Mary, "that
> green paint that you just tasted."
> Lena had sucked a good deal of the green paint from her
> finger. She stopped and looked hard at the finger. She did not
> know just how much Mary meant by what she said.
> "Ain't it poison, Nellie, that green paint, that Lena sucked
> just now," said Mary. "Sure it is Lena, its real poison, I ain't
> foolin' this time anyhow."
> Lena was a little troubled. She looked hard at her finger where
> the paint was, and she wondered if she had really sucked it.
> It was still a little wet on the edges and she rubbed it off a
> long time on the inside of her dress, and in between she won-
> dered and looked at the finger and thought, was it really poison
> that she had just tasted.
> "Ain't it too bad, Nellie, Lena should have sucked that," Mary
> said. . . .
> And so they all three sat with their little charges in the pleas-
> ant sunshine a long time. And Lena would often look at her
> finger and wonder if it was really poison that she had just tasted
> and then she would rub her finger on her dress a little harder.
> (*The Gentle Lena*, 241–42)

There is no climax, no denouement: just a simple, static event, with
all the participants acting in characteristic ways. Crucially, development is replaced by repetition, as each character reveals her
essence by repeating the actions (Mary's teasing, Lena's dumb,
comic sucking, staring, and worrying) which Stein uses to identify
or symbolize it.

As in much impressionist and modernist fiction, narrative tone and
temporal structure are at odds in *Three Lives* with the thematic content deducible from close reading and a reconstruction of linear causality. The tone and emphasis are noncommittal, cheerful, naive, at
most mildly mocking; the thematic content is bitter, angry, implying
a sophisticated social-political awareness and judgment. Temporal
structure is preponderantly either a "continuous present" or static,
yet each novella plots a classic trajectory of rise and fall. Nothing
better epitomizes the contradictions of *Three Lives* than its epigraph,
a quotation from Jules Laforgue: "Donc je suis un malheureux et ce

/ n'est ni ma faute ni celle de la vie." These lines certainly belie the narrator's cheerful innocence, but they equally belie the conclusions we can draw with excellent justification from all three novellas that a cruel "life," at least, is very much to blame for the mistreatment and death of these women.

We need no longer speculate about the psychological reasons for Stein's diverting attention, both her own and the reader's, from her anger and sadness. Richard Bridgman and Catharine Stimpson have shown with great clarity that Stein simultaneously concealed and encoded in her literary work troublesome feelings about herself as a woman, about women's helplessness, and particularly about lesbianism, still very much considered by society a "pollutant," as Stimpson puts it, during most of Stein's life.[6] But Stein did not merely stifle or deny her anger, her sense that she did not fit and that the deficiency was not hers but rather that of the structure which excluded her. In effect, Stein's rebellion was channeled from content to linguistic structure itself.[7] A rebellion in language is much easier to ignore or misconstrue, but its attack, particularly in literature, penetrates far deeper, to the very structures which determine, within a particular culture, what can be thought.

Stein's anti-patriarchal rebellion was not conscious or intentional, as her denial of her own bitterness and anger in *Three Lives* suggests. But for her, as perhaps for Virginia Woolf, there is an extra dimension to the view of experimental writing as anti-patriarchal, because both writers defined themselves in opposition to the notions of women which patriarchy provides.

Stein's attitude toward her gender offers further material for speculation. When this material becomes particularly relevant to Stein's writing, her female self-hatred was such that she was psychologically compelled to identify herself as a man in order to be a happy, sexually active person and a functioning writer. While she lived with her brother Leo, she was a frequently depressed, subservient sister; when Leo left and Alice Toklas moved in, she became a generally happy, very productive husband. This male identification did not shift until the late twenties, when there is evidence that Stein began to feel better about her female identity. Throughout her radically experimental period, therefore, she essentially thought of herself as a man (there is direct evidence of this identification in the notebooks, where Stein says "Pablo & Matisse have a maleness that belongs to

6. Stimpson, "The Mind, the Body and Gertrude Stein," 493.
7. Stein mentions her rebellion, using the word "revolt," several times (p. 29 of the notebook numbered "2" by Professor Katz) in the notebooks; i.e., "Leon like me in ideas and revolt." (Leon is Leon Solomons, her close friend and coworker in William James's laboratory at Harvard, on whom the character of David Hersland in *The Making of Americans* is partly based.)

genius. Moi aussi, perhaps").[8] We might posit a speculative connection between this male identification, and the concomitant suppression of her female identity, with the shift of the rebellious impulse from thematic content to linguistic structure, where the subversive implications of the writing are at once more powerful and more abstruse.

In relying totally on language itself to effect the transformation of the world, Stein is also very squarely within what Richard Poirier has identified as the American literary tradition in which rebellious imaginers use style to create an alternative "world elsewhere." Writers in this tradition.

> resist within their pages the forces of environment that otherwise dominate the world. Their styles have an eccentricity of defiance . . . they [try] to create an environment of "freedom," though as writers their efforts must be wholly in language. American books are often written as if historical forces cannot possibly provide such an environment, as if history can give no life to "freedom," and as if only language can create the liberated place.[9]

Within *Three Lives*, narrative tone and temporal structure serve to detach the text from its (at least formally) more traditional elements of thematic content and causative sequence, but to no significantly greater extent than do the impressionist structures and obtuse or multiple narrations of many other early modern novels.[1] However, impressionist structure and obtuse narration have a different significance in this early work of Stein's than they have for Conrad or even Faulkner. For Stein, the detachment of writing from coherent thematic content is the beginning of leaving such content behind altogether, of attempting to create "the liberated place" entirely through language. In *Three Lives*, in addition to these impressionist forms, we begin to see some of the experimental stylistic techniques Stein will sue to develop anti-patriarchal modes of literary signification, independent of coherent, referential, unitary meaning, hierarchical order, and the dominant signified.

Much has been made of the way Stein uses voice in *Three Lives* to abstract the essence of personality or consciousness of each character—what Donald Sutherland calls "the extremely delicate sequence and emphasis of the ideas as they come out of the character in accordance with the vital intensity and frequency of that character,"[2] and Norman Weinstein labels the character's "density,

8. This remark appears in a late notebook: p. 21 of the notebook labeled "C" by Stein.
9. Richard Poirier, *A World Elsewhere* (New York: Oxford University Press, 1966), 5.
1. See Tobin, *Time and the Novel*.
2. Sutherland, *Gertrude Stein*, 38 (see p. 274).

continuity, speed and quantity" of consciousness. Stein simply calls it the rhythm or pulse of personality, which she tries to re-create in language.

One might question whether this re-creation is essentially differ-ent from the handling of speech in other writing. Certainly, great writers of all periods, and in all genres and styles—from Shakespeare through Dickens and Browning to Joyce and Faulkner—have found ways to differentiate and animate their characters' voices. However, there is a difference between achieving a vivid, full, unique charac-terization through voice, and translating the abstract essence of a character's consciousness into patterns of language. Whereas Dick-ens uses voice to reveal a character's eccentricity, or Joyce pours out the contents of a character's consciousness in an appropriate flood of words, Stein establishes an equivalence between abstract qualities of consciousness and formal qualities of language: a particular "pulse" ("density, continuity, speed, quantity") of consciousness becomes a particular kind of syntax, phrasing, rhythm, diction, tone. Character is translated into, rather than revealed by, speech. As in all artistic stylization, this translation creates (or reveals) a distance between the work of art and its subject or referential content; a dis-tance which it is the purpose of realistic art (art of verisimilitude) to deny or conceal. For Stein, this distance is another origin of the full separation of writing from coherent thematic content which char-acterizes her later work.

The stylization in Stein's voice-portraiture—her transformation of psychological essences into patterns of speech—appears from the outset in *Three Lives*, in *The Good Anna*. The difference in diction, phrasing, rhythm and syntax between Anna's tense, direct, abrupt, staccato voice and Mrs. Lehntman's soft, vague, diffuse, conciliatory voice has frequently been noted.

> As always with Anna when a thing had to come it came very short and sharp. She found it hard to breathe just now, and every word came with a jerk.
>
> "Mrs. Lehntman, it ain't true what Julia said about your tak-ing that Lily's boy to keep. I told Julia when she told me she was crazy to talk so."
>
> Anna's real excitements stopped her breath, and made her words come sharp and with a jerk. Mrs. Lehntman's feeling spread her breath, and made her words come slow, but more pleasant and more easy even than before.
>
> "Why Anna," she began, "don't you see Lily couldn't keep her boy for she is working at the Bishops' now, and he is such a cute dear little chap, and you know how fond I am of little fellers, and I thought it would be nice for Julia and for Willie to have a little brother." (*The Good Anna*, 43)

The simplicity of language in this passage masks the complexity of its construction: Stein controls prose style very carefully to render the pulse of each personality.

The prose of *The Good Anna* and *The Gentle Lena* is still well within the bounds of conventionality. However, it is more rhythmic and poetic than most conventional prose, with an unusual frequency of iambic sequences, alliteration and internal rhyme: "But they could mourn together for the world these two worn, working german women, for its sadness and its wicked ways of doing. Mrs. Drehten knew so well what one could suffer" (*The Good Anna*, 69). The rhythmic quality of the prose is linked, as we shall see more clearly in *Melanctha*, to its repetitiveness:

> Lena was a brown and pleasant creature, brown as blonde races often have them brown, brown, not with the yellow or the red or the chocolate brown of sun burned countries, but brown with the clear color laid flat on the light toned skin beneath, the plain, spare brown that makes it right to have been made with hazel eyes, and not too abundant straight, brown hair, hair that only later deepens itself into brown from the straw yellow of a german childhood. (*The Gentle Lena*, 240)

With so much repetition, and with a vocabulary so carefully limited to simple, commonplace words, Stein achieves surprisingly compact and nuanced description in this early prose, particularly in her portraiture:

> Herman Kreder did not care much to get married. He was a gentle soul and a little fearful. He had a sullen temper, too. He was obedient to his father and his mother. He always did his work well. He often went out on Saturday nights and on Sundays, with other men. He liked it with them but he never became really joyous. He liked to be with men and he hated to have women with them. He was obedient to his mother, but he did not care much to get married. (*The Gentle Lena*, 251)

Diction and word order are already somewhat unconventional in *The Good Anna* and *The Gentle Lena*, giving the prose a quality of strangeness and surprise:

> She would call and wait a long time and then call again, always even, gentle, patient, while the young ones fell back often into that precious, tense, last bit of sleeping that gives a strength of joyous vigor in the young, over them that have come to the readiness of middle age, in their awakening. (*The Gentle Lena*, 239)

Finally, Stein repeats key phrases throughout *The Good Anna* and *The Gentle Lena* which, like operatic motifs, both identify and represent her characters: "Mrs. Lehntman was the one romance in Anna's life," "Anna led an arduous and trouble life," "Lena was patient, gentle, sweet and german."

The iambic rhythms and other poetic devices call attention to the prose in a conventional way, and are not particularly important for Stein's later experimental writing. However, the limitation of vocabulary, the condensation, the repetition, the surprising diction and the unconventional word order are crucial discoveries for Stein. They are points of departure, from which many characteristic features of her experimental styles evolve.

The most noticeable feature of Stein's writing between 1906 and 1911 is its repetitiveness. It is undoubtedly safe to assert that no other writer has ever used repetition as extensively as Stein did in this period. In his book *Telling It Again and Again*, Bruce Kawin sees repetition, including Stein's, as isolating and in effect bracketing the unadulterated present moment, and therefore coming as close as writing can to a positive version of "silence" (a mystical, super-verbal, transcendent, absolute truth).[3] Stein herself considered repetition the truth about time, consciousness, personality, knowing; for her it needed no further justification. Other analyses of literary repetition emphasize, as I will, its incantatory, hypnotic effect on the reader.[4]

Repetition is a complex, overdetermined phenomenon in *Three Lives*. Partly, its purpose is mimetic: it gives a truer representation than standard writing of the raw process of consciousness. Characters and narrator in *Three Lives* all speak as their minds work, expressing the sequence of their contradictory, ambivalent thoughts and feelings, coming to no conclusions, using language both to reveal the process of consciousness and to grope toward a connection with its inchoate contents. Like a fixated, blocked mind struggling to free itself by going over and over the terms of its fixation until it has mastered them, Stein's narrator ruminates over Jeff's feelings and the dynamic of his relationship with Melanctha, pushing the story slowly forward, gradually achieving a full statement of her vision. Jeff makes a parallel struggle toward understanding himself and mastering the terms of his fixation on Melanctha. Each time the narrator rethinks the situation, she both re-covers the same ground and adds a little new territory, so that the picture slowly becomes both larger and clearer. Jeff struggles to understand, and the narrator struggles to understand Jeff's struggle:

> Then it came that Jeff knew he could not say out any more, what it was he wanted, he could not say out any more, what it was, he wanted to know about, what Melanctha wanted. . . .

3. Bruce Kawin, *Telling It Again and Again* (Ithaca: Cornell University Press, 1972).
4. See for example Edward D. Synder, *Hypnotic Poetry* (1930; rpt. New York: Octagon Books, 1971).

And slowly now, Jeff soon always came to be feeling that his
Melanctha would be hurt very much in her head in the ways he
never liked to think of, if she would ever now again have to listen
to his trouble, when he was telling about what it was he still was
wanting to make things for himself really understanding.

Now Jeff began to have always a strong feeling that Melanctha
could no longer stand it, with all her bad suffering, to let him
fight out with himself what was right for him to be doing. . . .
He never could be honest now, he never could be now, any
more, trying to be really understanding, for always every
moment now he felt it to be a strong thing in him, how very
much it was Melanctha Herbert always suffered. . . .

Jeff did not like it very well these days, in his true feeling. He
knew now very well Melanctha was not strong enough inside
her to stand any more of his slow way of doing. And yet now he
knew he was not honest in his feeling. Now he always had to
show more to Melanctha than he was ever feeling. Now she
made him go so fast, and he knew it was not real with his feeling,
and yet he could not make her suffer so any more because he
always was so slow with his feeling.

It was very hard for Jeff Campbell to make all this way of
doing, right, inside him. If Jeff Campbell could not be straight
out, and real honest, he never could be very strong inside
him. . . .

Jeff Campbell never knew very well these days what it was
that was going on inside him. All he knew was, he was uneasy
now always to be with Melanctha . . . not the way he used to be
from just not being very understanding, but . . . because he
knew now he was having a straight good feeling with her, but
she went so fast, and he was so slow to her; Jeff knew his right
feeling never got a chance to show itself as strong, to her.

All this was always getting harder for Jeff Campbell. He was
very proud to hold himself to be strong. . . . He was very tender
not to hurt Melanctha,. . . . he hated that he could not now be
honest with her, he wanted to stay away to work it out all alone,
without her, he was afraid she would feel it to suffer, if he kept
away now from her. He was uneasy always, with her, . . . he
knew now he had a good, straight, strong feeling of right loving
for her, and yet now he never could use it to be good and honest
with her. (*Melanctha*, 161–164)

It would be almost impossible to paraphrase this passage, comprised
as it is of continually shifting shades of meaning. Although we can
scarcely pinpoint the moment when a new idea or new information
is introduced, we feel by the end of the passage that we know much
more than we did at the beginning. We feel as if we are living through
an experience rather than reading about it; we come away with a

feeling of deep familiarity with or rootedness in the dimensions of
the situation unextended to a coherent intellectual grasp of them.
Melanctha is a significant step away from writing which invites thematic synthesis.

The repetition so noticeable in this writing is closely related to the
other innovative stylistic features of *Melanctha* that were so fruitful
for Stein's later work: the present participles, gerunds, progressive
verb forms—"-ing words" for convenience's sake—the incantatory
rhythm, the rhyming, the superfluous words and punctuation, the
abstract vocabulary and the emblematic use of certain key words.
The compact, evenly stressed rhythms of *The Good Anna* and *The
Gentle Lena* are transformed by repetition in *Melanctha* into a wavelike cadence with phrases or measures emphasized by rhymes. Contrast these two passages, the first from *The Good Anna* and the
second from *Melanctha*:

> Old Katy was a heavy, ugly, short and rough old german woman,
> with a strange distorted german-english all her own. Anna was
> worn out now with her attempt to make the younger generation
> do all that it should and rough old Katy never answered back,
> and never wanted her own way. No scolding or abuse could
> make its mark on her uncouth and aged peasant hide. She said
> her "Yes, Miss Annie," when an answer had to come, and that
> was always all that she could say. (*The Good Anna*, 17)

> Now when her father began fiercely to assail her, she did not
> really know what it was that he was so furious to force from her.
> In every way that he could think of in his anger, he tried to make
> her say a thing she did not really know. She held out and never
> answered anything he asked her, for Melanctha had a breakneck
> courage and she just then badly hated her black father.
>
> When the excitement was all over, Melanctha began to know
> her power, the power she had so often felt stirring within her
> and which she now knew she could use to make her stronger.
>
> James Herbert did not win this fight with his daughter. After
> awhile he forgot it as he soon forgot John and the cut of his
> sharp razor. (*Melanctha*, 95)

The first passage beats steadily, tightly along while the second rushes
forward freely and then halts at each "-er" rhyme. The rhymes at the
end of each clause support the rhythm, and the rhythm enhances
the overall incantatory, hypnotic effect of the repetition.

Related to the repetition and incantatory rhythm, and also to the
slightly unconventional word order of *The Good Anna* and *The Gentle Lena*, are the superfluous words (unnecessary for establishing
meaning) and commas, very unconventional diction and syntax,
introduced in *Melanctha*:

> It was very hard for Jeff Campbell to make all his way of doing,
> right, inside him. If Jeff Campbell could not be straight out, and
> real honest, he never could be very strong inside him. Now
> Melanctha, with her making him feel, always, how good she was
> and how very much she suffered in him, made him always go
> so fast then, he could not be strong then, to feel things out
> straight then inside him. Always now when he was with her, . . .
> he had something inside him always holding in him, always now,
> with her, he was far ahead of his own feeling. (*Melanctha*, 163)

Stein seems to be carried along by rhythm, hypnotized by her incantation, to the point where her language begins to detach itself from what it says. This detachment of language from referential meaning, embryonic in *Melanctha*, is the beginning of Stein's journey into experimental writing.

The relationship between writing and meaning is transformed in *Melanctha* in another way: the ordinary, simple vocabulary, even more reduced than in the earlier novellas, is often used so elastically, to cover so many meanings, and at the same time so indeterminately, that certain words become emblematic, invoking large, open-ended complexes of feeling and association, as well as meaning, each time they appear. These complexes of feeling, association, and meaning remain vague, inchoate; strongly felt by the reader but never clearly articulated by the narrator. Each word or phrase increases in significance as it passes through successive contexts; as its familiar, everyday meanings are gradually replaced by a large complex or cluster of undefined meanings. There are many such key emblematic words in *Melanctha*: "wisdom," "understanding," "experience," "excitement," being "quiet together." "Wisdom" becomes an emblem of everything in life that is desirable but difficult to attain; "excitement" of everything that is alluring but dangerous. We begin to lose our linguistic moorings, the illusion of stability, clarity, firmness of symbolic language which allows us the mastery required by our everyday lives in patriarchal culture.

Stein's very success in rendering in language a unique core of personality leads her away from recognizable depiction of character. In *Melanctha*, it is the wavelike cadence and the repetition of a reduced, strangely resonant and at the same time simple, childlike vocabulary that hold our attention most forcefully as we read, beyond our recognition of character, anticipation of plot, or reflection upon theme. Stein's impulse to alter conventional language in the service of realizing the essence of her subject leads her to abandon coherent thematic treatment of that subject in preference for the possibility of reinventing the structure of thought itself.

JAYNE L. WALKER

Three Lives: The Realism of the Composition†

In *The Autobiography of Alice B. Toklas*[1] Stein recalled that she wrote *Three Lives* while "looking and looking" at Cézanne's *Portrait of Mme Cézanne* (ABT, 34). Before she began these stories in 1905, she had written three narratives: *Q.E.D.*, a semiautobiographical account of a lesbian triangle; *Fernhurst*; and five chapters of a family chronicle, which later served as the beginning of *The Making of Americans*. Compared to *Three Lives* and the texts that followed, these are conventional narratives, except for the theme of lesbianism that appears in *Q.E.D. Three Lives*, and especially the story "Melanctha," which recasts *Q.E.D.* in a different social and racial milieu and a new idiom, reveals how radically Stein transformed her style in response to her initial confrontation with modernist painting.

Flaubert's "Un Coeur simple" was the literary point of departure for her first attempt to create a mode of realism analogous to Cézanne's in her own medium. In 1905 she began translating "Un Coeur simple" into English. She soon abandoned this project to write "The Good Anna," her own story of the life of a simple servant woman. After completing it, she went on to write "The Gentle Lena" and "Melanctha" and named the collection of stories *Three Lives* (originally *Three Histories*, in deliberate homage to Flaubert's *Trois Contes*).[2]

"Un Coeur simple" provided Stein with both a subject and a structural model for "The Good Anna," the first story in which she began to explore this new principle of composition. Stein's Anna, like Flaubert's Félicité, is a hardworking servant, totally devoted to her employers; her own quiet existence, like Félicité's, is shaped by events in other people's lives. Flaubert's story narrates Félicité's uneventful life from her adolescence to her death. Its episodic narrative structure demonstrates a high degree of temporal and logical discontinuity. "The Good Anna" is an equally discontinuous episodic narrative, which recounts the life span of its heroine from childhood to death. Flaubert's unemphatic narrative unfolds the repeated pattern of Félicité's ardent loves and losses—her lover, her mistress's daughter, her own nephew, and, finally, her beloved parrot—which

---

† From *The Making of a Modernist: Gertrude Stein, From* Three Lives *to* Tender Buttons (Amherst: The University of Massachusetts Press, 1984), pp. 19–41. Reprinted by permission of the author.
1. New York: Harcourt Brace, 1933.
2. In *Gertrude Stein in Pieces*, Richard Bridgman notes that Stein retained the title *Three Histories* until 1909, when her publisher persuaded her to change it to avoid confusion with his line of "real historical publications" (p. 46). The edition referenced here is New York: Random House, 1936 (see p. 291).

culminates in her epiphanic deathbed vision of the parrot as the Holy
Ghost. "The Good Anna" lacks this kind of unifying pattern, but
Stein's story makes deliberate use of some of the other narrative
strategies Flaubert employed in "Un Coeur simple." His text frequently juxtaposes short, even one-sentence paragraphs to create a
slight discontinuity of action:

> Elle eut envie de se mettre dans les demoiselles de la Vierge.
> Mme Aubain l'en dissuada.
> Un événement considérable surgit: le mariage de Paul.[3]

> [She wanted to join the ladies of the Virgin. Mme Aubain
> talked her out of it.
> An important event suddenly emerged: the marriage of Paul.]

The "événement considérable" is merely reported in passing, not
described. Stein makes similar use of short, unemphatic paragraphs
to recount the events in Anna's life:

> The wedding day grew always nearer. At last it came and went.
> (TL, 33)

The wedding of her mistress's daughter changes Anna's life, forcing
her to find a new employer; like the marriage in "Un Coeur simple,"
it is merely noted in a short paragraph. For both of these servant
women, the kinds of major events that shape the plots of conventional novels take place only in other people's lives, yet they have
considerable effects on their own situations. Character is emphati-
cally not destiny for these women. Because of their social position,
the course of their lives is the by-product of the actions of others.
Appropriately, their stories lack the strong sense of narrative causality that shapes traditional fiction.

Stein's Anna is a far more voluble character than Flaubert's Félicité. This difference indicates a major divergence between Stein's
project and the literary model that served as her point of departure.
While Félicité's speech is never quoted and only rarely reported,
Stein eagerly embraced the challenge of creating speeches for characters whose command of standard English is limited. Both Anna
and the characters in "The Gentle Lena," the second story she wrote
for *Three Lives*, are German immigrants. "Melanctha," the third
story, is set in a southern black community.

Paradoxically, the more accurately dialectal speech is rendered in
fiction, the more insistently it calls attention to itself as linguistic
artifice. The more radically language deviates from the norms of conventional narrative discourse to reproduce actual dialect features,

---

3. *Oeuvres complètes de Gustave Flaubert* (Paris: Club de l'Honêtte Homme, 1972), 4:22.

the more insistently it resists the normal tendency of prose to "dissolve" easily into meaning. In *Three Lives* Stein avoided phonetic approximations of dialectal pronunciation, but she systematically used syntactical deformation and repetition to create stylized models of the dialectal speech patterns of her characters. In the first story Anna's speeches are frequently introduced by descriptions that call attention to their abrupt, jerky rhythms:

> "Miss Mary," Anna began. She had stopped just within the door, her body and her face stiff with repression, her teeth closed hard and the white lights flashing sharply in the pale, clean blue of her eyes. Her bearing was full of the strange coquetry of anger and of fear, the stiffness, the bridling, the suggestive movement underneath the rigidness of forced control, all the queer ways the passions have to show themselves all one.
>
> "Miss Mary," the words came slowly with thick utterance and with jerks, but always firm and strong. "Miss Mary, I can't stand it any more like this. When you tell me anything to do, I do it. I do everything I can and you know I work myself sick for you. The blue dressings in your room makes too much work to have for summer. Miss Jane don't know what work is. If you want to do things like that I go away."
>
> Anna stopped still. Her words had not the strength of meaning they were meant to have, but the power in the mood of Anna's soul frightened and awed Miss Mary through and through. (29)

Her short, simple sentences, filled with grammatical errors, "had not the strength of meaning they were meant to have." Consequently, in this passage and elsewhere in the story, the narrator surrounds Anna's quoted speech with descriptions and interpretations of her body language, which emphasize the inadequacy of her language to her emotions. In contrast to Anna, Mrs. Lehntman, who is called upon to help Anna speak to her mistress in this scene, speaks "slowly" and more fluently than her friend (43). The rhythm of her long polysyndetic sentences is markedly different from Anna's "sharp and short" utterances in the preceding passage:

> "Miss Wadsmith, Anna feels how good and kind you are, and she talks about it all the time, and what you do for her in every way you can, and she is very grateful and never would want to go away from you, only she thinks it would be better now that Mrs. Goldthwaite has this big new house and will want to manage it in her own way, she thinks perhaps it would be better if Mrs. Goldthwaite had all new servants with her to begin with,

and not a girl like Anna who knew her when she was a little girl." (35)

This story simply presents Anna's difficulty with language as a naturalistic character trait. The next two stories Stein wrote explore more extensively the role of language in shaping the thoughts and the lives of characters whose imperfect command of English makes self-expression an arduous labor. By dramatizing these linguistic struggles, the stories in *Three Lives* foreground the material reality of language as an arbitrary and problematic system, far from a transparent medium of communication.

In *The Colloquial Style in America*, Richard Bridgman has observed that in nineteenth-century American fiction dialectal speech was generally confined to a "special arena fenced in by quotation marks," sharply contrasting with the normative narrative voice, except in a few first-person narratives like the *Adventures of Huckleberry Finn*.[4] In *Three Lives* the use of immigrant characters motivates the syntactical deformation that breaks their speech into unusual and assertive rhythmic patterns, but these stylistic effects overflow the restricted area bounded by quotation marks to pervade the entire narrative. Dorrit Cohn uses the rather infelicitous term "stylistic contagion," borrowed from Leo Spitzer, to describe the encroachment of a character's speech style into the surrounding discourse; Hugh Kenner, in *Joyce's Voices*, more jocularly calls it the "Uncle Charles principle."[5] The style of "The Good Anna" is strangely mixed. It frequently approaches the simple diction and awkward syntax of the characters, but it also incorporates words like "coquetry" and "repression" (in the passage cited above) that are far removed from their lexicon and, consequently, from their mental horizons as well. In the subsequent stories Stein wrote for *Three Lives*, she sharply limited her lexicon to create a narrative idiom that closely approximates the speech of the characters. This assertive, evenly textured verbal surface is analogous to the surfaces of Cézanne's canvases, with their dense patterning of brushstrokes that unite objects and background in a tapestry of color patches of equal value.

Again, Flaubert can be seen as a literary model for compositional principles similar to those suggested by Cézanne's painting. Proust described reading Flaubert as undertaking a "continuous, monstrous, dreary, indefinite march" on the "great moving sidewalk" of his prose. For Proust, the beauty of Flaubert's style, which he greatly

4. Richard Bridgman, *The Colloquial Style in America* (New York: Oxford University Press, 1966), p. 46.
5. Dorrit Cohn, *Transparent Minds: Narrative Modes for Presenting Consciousness in Fiction* (Princeton, N.J.: Princeton University Press, 1978), pp. 33. Hugh Kenner, *Joyce's Voices* (Berkeley: University of California Press, 1978), pp. 15–38.

admired, was grammatical; it derived, in part, from the powerful and original rhythms created by his "deforming syntax" (*syntaxe déformante*).[6] One of Flaubert's most striking innovations, which often motivates his peculiar manipulation of syntax, is the use of free indirect discourse that pervades most of his texts. This third-person, past-tense rendering of speech or thought which approaches the verbal style of a character allows for almost imperceptible shifts in and out of a character's point of view. It creates an even stylistic surface that approaches the structure of oral speech while it remains a distinctly "written" style. For Flaubert, the *mot juste* can be the word or phrase that is slightly wrong—flat or awkward, according to correct literary usage, but exactly the right word to approximate the sensibility of his characters.

Henry James provides an American model for a narrative discourse that incorporates traces of the rhythms of colloquial speech and thought. Although Stein always claimed not to have read James seriously until much later in her career, *Q.E.D.*, one of her earliest narratives, suggests a recent and thoughtful reading of James. It is a limited third-person narrative, with a heroine who functions as a Jamesian central intelligence. Bridgman has argued that Stein's style in this early text owes much to James's example, especially in its use of repetition to create the effect of colloquial speech.[7] James's dislocations of syntax render the fastidious mental discriminations and reevaluations of his eminently conscious characters. But *Q.E.D.* demonstrates nothing of James's technical virtuosity in registering subtle movements of consciousness through rapid alternations of psychonarrative, narrated monologue, and direct quotation of interior speech.[8] Stein did not begin the use of syntactical deformation to model the process of thought until she wrote *Three Lives*.

While James generally preferred to focus on highly articulate characters with finely tuned moral sensibilities, Flaubert was fascinated by stupidity. In the *Dictionnaire des idées reçues* and in many of his narratives as well, he lovingly and ruthlessly exposed the linguistic and mental limitations of commonplace minds, the products of middle-class culture. In "Un Coeur simple," however, he protects the simple Félicité from the corrosive effects of his irony by denying her a voice.[9] In *Three Lives*, Stein extends the narrative strategies of

---

6. Proust, "A propos du 'style' de Flaubert," pp. 73–74, 81. Cf. Alfred Thibaudet's splendid chapter "Le style de Flaubert," in *Gustave Flaubert* (Paris: Librairie Plon, 1922), especially pp. 277–82, 304–17.

7. Bridgman, *Colloquial Style in America*, pp. 169–74. *Q.E.D.*'s reference to "Kate Croy" (*sic*) clearly indicates that Stein had read at least *The Wings of the Dove* before 1903.

8. These terms are taken from Dorrit Cohn's *Transparent Minds*. This excellent study establishes a well-defined (and much-needed) critical vocabulary for analyzing fictional representations of consciousness.

9. In *Flaubert: The Uses of Uncertainty* (London: Paul Elek, 1974), Jonathan Culler observes that Félicité is one of Flaubert's characters who "have no language which they could claim

Flaubert and James into a territory they shrank from exploring—the narrowly restricted linguistic universe that confines the speech and thoughts of simple uneducated characters. In "The Gentle Lena" and "Melanctha," to a far greater degree than in the first story, the characters' speeches dominate the narratives, while anecdotal actions and circumstantial details, such as physical descriptions of characters and settings, are reduced to a minimum. In "The Gentle Lena," Stein began to combine direct quotation with extensive use of narrated monologue, Flaubert's favorite device for blurring the distinction between the characters' speech and the narrative voice. In the second and third stories of *Three Lives*, there is no escape from the linguistic and conceptual boundaries that restrict the characters' expression and their thought.

In "The Gentle Lena," the central character suffers as a result of her linguistic inadequacy. A recent immigrant from Germany with a limited command of English, she lacks the resources to defend herself adequately against the verbal barrages to which she is constantly subjected. Consequently, she becomes the passive victim of the desires, and the discourse, of others. Her aunt arranges a marriage for her, which neither she nor the prospective husband desires, but Lena can never voice her feelings: "Mrs. Haydon spoke to Lena about it very often. Lena never answered anything at all" (252). When Mrs. Haydon finally forces her to speak, her words reveal her linguistic helplessness, her total subjugation to the discourse that dominates her:

> "Why, I do anything you say, Aunt Mathilda. Yes, I like him. He don't say much to me, but I guess he is a good man, and I do anything you say for me to do."
> "Well then Lena, why you stand there so silly all the time and not answer when I asked you?"
> "I didn't hear you say you wanted I should say anything to you. I didn't know you wanted me to say nothing. I do whatever you tell me it's right for me to do. I marry Herman Kreder, if you want me." (253)

Mrs. Haydon, the German cook, and Lena's friend Mary all scold her repeatedly and at length, and the reluctant bridegroom's family subject him to similar verbal assaults. In this masterful series of long harangues, which combine narrated monologue with quoted speech, these characters unconsciously reveal the self-absorption that motivates their manipulation of Lena and Herman:

---

captures their existence, and this is what protects them, for as soon as the critic speaks of them he begins muttering clichés about the purity of simple folk, the joys of unalienated consciousness. . . . When she does speak to others the very banality of her discourse, its blatant exposure to irony, works to save it from any effective irony" (pp. 208–9).

Did Lena think it gave Mrs. Haydon any pleasure, to work so hard to make Lena happy, and get her a good husband, and then Lena was so thankless and never did anything that anybody wanted. It was a lesson to poor Mrs. Haydon not to do things any more for anybody. Let everybody take care of themselves and never come to her with any troubles; she knew better now than to meddle to make other people happy. It just made trouble for her and her husband did not like it. He always said she was too good, and nobody ever thanked her for it, and there Lena was always standing stupid and not answering anything anybody wanted. Lena could always talk enough to those silly girls she liked so much, and always sat with, but who never did anything for her except to take away her money, and here was her aunt who tried so hard and was so good to her and treated her just like one of her own children and Lena stood there, and never made any answer and never tried to please her aunt, or to do anything that her aunt wanted. "No, it ain't no use your standin' there and cryin', now, Lena. Its too late now to care about that Herman. You should have cared some before, and then you wouldn't have to stand and cry now, and be a disappointment to me, and then I get scolded by my husband for taking care of everybody, and nobody ever thankful." (256)

Mrs. Haydon herself is unaware of the persistent contradictions between her professed concern for her niece's happiness and her outrage at the girl's passive resistance to her own plans. Her syntax, which loosely strings together short phrases with a plethora of coordinating conjunctions, clearly reveals to the reader the tenuous logic of her thought processes. The syntax and movement of this passage typify the way these voluble characters entangle themselves in webs of contradictions each time they berate the young people. Their repetition of the same judgmental words heightens the reader's awareness of language as an instrument of culture, enforcing the dominant values of a community. Both Lena and Herman tacitly reject the conventional wisdom that marriage always leads to happiness, but both are unable to articulate their reasons for opposing this social norm. Lena's only defense is silence, while Herman finally takes action by running away. After this, Mrs. Haydon calls Lena "stupid" to have lost him; the cook says it is Herman who is "stupid," and, on the following page, Mary calls Lena "stupid to be sorry" to have lost him (257, 259, 260). "Stupid," "disgrace" and other judgmental words are the blunt instruments of culture which, with their repeated blows, finally force the couple to submit to marriage.

After their capitulation, Herman adapts better to marriage than Lena does. For her, marriage and children only increase her isolation and alienation. As she silently succumbs to total passivity, "gentle," the adjective used repeatedly to characterize her earlier in the story, is replaced by "lifeless." Finally Lena dies in childbirth:

> When the baby was come out at last, it was like its mother lifeless. While it was coming, Lena had grown very pale and sicker. When it was all over Lena had died, too, and nobody knew just how it had happened to her. (279)

The discourse effectively blurs the moment of passage from figurative to literal lifelessness. This bitter play on words is an appropriate conclusion for this powerful story of victimization by language and the social conventions it enforces.

When Samuel Beckett staked out "impotence, ignorance" as his artistic terrain, in contrast to Joyce's exuberant linguistic virtuosity, he believed he was the first to embrace that project: "I don't think impotence has been exploited in the past."[1] Apparently he was not acquainted with *Three Lives*, in which Stein used the verbal impotence of her characters, combined with a similarly restricted narrative idiom, to create a poetics of impotence, of antieloquence. More systematically than the first two stories she wrote for *Three Lives*, "Melanctha" probes the ways in which the confines of her characters' language shape and, finally, impede their understanding. The central incident in "Melanctha" recasts her 1903 novella *Q.E.D.*, a story of "college bred American women of the wealthier class," in the vastly different social and linguistic world of a southern black community (QED, 54). Stein considered "Melanctha" the "quintessence" of the new compositional principles she developed in response to the work of Flaubert and Cézanne (TI, 15).[2] A comparison of these two texts, written only three years apart, reveals how consciously she reevaluated the resources of her medium and how radically she transformed her narrative strategies in response to the twin challenges posed by the work of Cézanne and Flaubert.

The longest and most polished of the three works Stein wrote before *Three Lives*, *Q.E.D.* retraces the course of her own passionate and ultimately painful involvement with May Bookstaver, a fellow student at Johns Hopkins, from its tentative beginnings to her final realization of its hopelessness. Apparently Stein wrote *Q.E.D.* purely for herself, as an effort to understand her own recent and painful experience. Adele, its heroine, is a resolutely rational character, committed to verbal "analysis" and "dissection" of her experience (QED,

---

1. Quoted in Hugh Kenner, *Samuel Beckett*, rev. ed. (Berkeley: University of California Press, 1968), p. 33.
2. "TI" is "A Transatlantic Interview 1946."

72, 82). Her first speech announces this fundamental personality trait: "I am reasonable because I know the difference between understanding and not understanding and I am just because I have no opinion about things I don't understand" (56). Her intense attraction to Helen soon threatens the placidity of her "reasonableness" and forces her to deal with things she doesn't understand. Challenging her naïve faith that "all morality [is] so easily reducible to formula," her passion for Helen forces her to confront not only the question of lesbianism but also the problem of Helen's prior involvement with Mabel (93). Her gradual realization that Mabel is supporting Helen further intensifies the moral complexity of her situation.

Q.E.D. focuses on Adele's successive efforts to control her moral and emotional confusion by analyzing it in dialogues, letters, and interior monologues. According to Adele, the major obstacle that ultimately separates her from Helen is not Mabel but irreconcilable differences of temperament. "Their pulses were differently timed" (104); Helen's "courage," her emotional spontaneity, is out of sync with the slower, more "cowardly" nature of Adele's responses, which stems from her need for intellectual and moral clarity. These differences make the "long struggle" between them as "inevitable as their separate natures" (92). Her lover, who resents being subjected to Adele's constant verbal analysis, perceives her resolute rationality as a barrier to emotional intensity: "Haven't you ever stopped thinking long enough to feel?" (66). The force of her passions temporarily overrides her habitual rational controls, and she lets herself feel and accept her love for Helen, with all its painful moral ambiguities. But by this time it is too late; their different rhythms of response have thwarted the possibility of union. Before the end of the novel, Adele has regained her habitual intellectual detachment, which allows her to enjoy observing the "working of the machinery" of their schematically opposed personalities as it grinds inexorably to the final impasse (121).

"Melanctha" transforms this narrative material into the story of a heterosexual love affair set in a black community, retaining not only the fundamental personality traits of the two lovers and the course of their passions but the specific content of many passages of dialogue and meditation as well. Adele becomes Jeff Campbell, a "negro" doctor, and Helen is re-created as Melanctha, a mulatto woman. The role of Mabel is split among three characters. Jane Harden initiates Melanctha into the "wisdom" of sexual passion and later reveals Melanctha's prior sexual experience to Jeff. After her affair with Jeff is over, Melanctha's affections are dominated by Jem Richards, her lover, and Rose Johnson, her friend. Leon Katz regards Stein's transformation of *Q.E.D.*'s thinly disguised autobiographical materials into "Melanctha" as a "mode of concealment . . . done originally for psychological rather than aesthetic reasons."[3] Indeed, recasting Adele as a male character displaces the issue of lesbianism, taboo as a literary subject during Stein's lifetime, from the center of the narrative, although a trace of it still survives in Melanctha's relationship with Jane. But the other major differences between the two texts, especially the crucial change in social milieu that justifies the radical transformation of language in "Melanctha," clearly reveal the predominance of the new aesthetic concerns Stein had begun to explore in the first two stories of *Three Lives*. In conformity with the episodic narrative structures of "The Good Anna" and "The Gentle Lena," in "Melanctha" the material adapted from *Q.E.D.* becomes the central incident in a story that expands to encompass the heroine's life span from childhood to her early death. In the earlier text, the three women leave New York to travel around Europe. "Melanctha" eliminates these geographical movements, which are largely irrelevant to the dramatic interactions among the characters, and, with them, the kind of concrete descriptive details that create an illusion of circumstantial realism in *Q.E.D.* The realism of the later text inheres in the speeches and thoughts that constitute the essential action of the story.

Recasting *Q.E.D.* in the "negro" community of "Bridgeport" posed the challenge of creating a character who, like Adele and originally Stein herself, needs to "have it all clear out in words always, what everybody is always feeling," but lacks the verbal and conceptual resources provided by their class and educational background (TL, 171). Adele's mind works incessantly to impose rational order on her experiences by formulating them "in definite words" (QED, 64). "All I want to do is to meditate endlessly and think and talk," she confesses to Helen (80). Adele regards language as an infallible instrument for clarifying complex emotional and moral issues. For the characters in "Melanctha," language is, itself, part of the problem. Both Jeff and Melanctha are painfully aware of the inadequacy of their language. During one of their first conversations, Melanctha accuses Jeff, "You don't know very well yourself, what you mean, when you are talking" (TL, 118). Jeff feels the same uncertainty about the efficacy of their communication: "I certainly do wonder, Miss Melanctha, if we know at all really what each other means by what we are always saying" (128).

This sense of the limitations of language is already present as an undercurrent of irony in *Q.E.D.*, which pits Adele's garrulous nature against Helen's silences. From the beginning of their relationship, Adele's words reverberate hollowly out of emotional depths that can-

---

3. Katz, "The First Making of *The Making of Americans*," p. 57.

not—or dare not—be named. At the first stirring of these new feelings, "somehow the silence now subtly suggested the significance of their being alone together" (58). Silence, subtle suggestions, a significance that remains forever unarticulated—these are the necessary conditions of the passions Stein explores in *Q.E.D.*, written long before lesbian love entered the accepted discourse of our culture. Immersed in a relationship necessarily governed by a "convention of silence," Adele uses her verbal arsenal to evade or deny her most profound emotions (77). By the time she finally succumbs to her deepest feelings and "learn[s] to stop thinking," she has already lost Helen (86). The last interview between them shows Adele once more in complete command of her verbal resources—and, ironically, in full retreat from the significance of the emotional experiences she has undergone during the course of the narrative. She accuses Helen of hiding behind her silences, while the force of the text, for the reader, has been to reveal how much is hidden by her own customary verbosity. And her ringing affirmation, "Nothing is too good or too holy for clear thinking and definite expression," utterly denies the validity of her unspeakable—yet utterly real—emotional engagement with Helen (132).[4]

Thematically, *Q.E.D.* marks the beginning of Stein's long career of testing the limits of language, but its narrative discourse is still cast entirely in the rational, analytical language of its central character, which it ironizes and punctuates with silences but does not otherwise surpass. "Melanctha" is the first of many texts in which Stein challenges the dominant cultural discourse stylistically as well as thematically. Even more deliberately than in the other stories in *Three Lives*, in "Melanctha" the characters' distance from mainstream American culture is used to motivate a systematic stylistic demonstration of the limits of rational discourse as a medium for interpersonal communication.

In *Q.E.D.*, Adele's linguistic and conceptual system provides her with pat labels to classify her experience. She relies heavily on abstract nouns arranged in sets of binary oppositions: virtues and vices, cowardice and heroism, humility and arrogance. In "Melanctha," Jeff shares Adele's need for conceptual order, but his more restricted lexicon does not include the abstract conceptual terms that dominate Adele's discourse. His speeches consistently translate Adele's abstract nouns into gerundial forms: "heroism" becomes "being game and not hollering"; "passion" is translated into "getting excited"; "living regular" replaces "the middle-class ideal." These

4. The previous discussion of silence in *Q.E.D.* is indebted to an unpublished paper written by one of my students, Susan Abbott's "An Absence So Strange, a Presence So Vital: Issues of Lesbian Representation in Woolf, Stein, and Wittig." This paper, combined with a suggestion from Leon Katz, forced me to rethink my previous approach to the issue of irony in this text.

changes involve more than a shift to a more colloquial level of diction; Jeff's terms, derived from active verbs, suggest a closer connection to his immediate experience than Adele's abstract nouns convey. Adele can dispose of the bewildering contradictions in her lover's behavior by categorizing her as a "wonderful example of double personality" (QED, 81). Jeff, who does not have this kind of terminology at his disposal, has to work harder to come to terms with the same phenomenon in Melanctha:

> "Melanctha Herbert," began Jeff Campbell, "I certainly after all this time I know you, I certainly do know little, real about you. You see, Melanctha, it's like this way with me[.] . . . You see it's just this way, with me now, Melanctha. Sometimes you seem like one kind of a girl to me, and sometimes you are like a girl that is all different to me, and the two kinds of girls is certainly very different to each other, and I can't see any way they seem to have much to do, to be together in you. They certainly don't seem to be made much like as if they could have anything really to do with each other." (TL, 138)

Jeff's hesitations, his new beginnings, his repetitions, concretely embody the slow revolutions of his mind as he tries to define his contradictory feelings about Melanctha. His distortions of syntax ("much to do, to be together," "much like as if") function as linguistic symptoms of his inability to make a logical connection between the two extremes of Melanctha's personality. Later in the passage, which closely follows the sequence of Adele's speech in *Q.E.D.*, Jeff's language fails him completely. Adele reports her observation of Helen's "infinitely tender patience that entirely overmasters" her (81). Attempting to describe the same aspect of Melanctha's personality, Jeff is so overwhelmed that he completely loses control of his syntax: "and a kindness, that makes one feel like summer, and then a way to know, that makes everything all over, and all that" (TL, 138).

Throughout the central section of "Melanctha," Adele's succinct formulations are translated into a more limited lexicon and greatly expanded to dramatize the process of Jeff's efforts to comprehend Melanctha and his own experiences. Adele's speeches and interior monologues use abstract nouns in well-formed sentences simply to report the conclusions of her thought; they do not enact the confused, uncertain process of thinking. In "Melanctha," deformations of syntax and repetitions of words and syntactical structures radically foreground the materiality of language as an unwieldy medium the characters must work with, and against, in their efforts to resolve complex moral and emotional issues. Like a Cézanne canvas, the assertive surface of this text resists easy comprehension and forces the reader to participate in its rhythmic patterning. In a Cézanne painting, the artfully patterned surface models the process of perceiving physical objects; in "Melanctha," it embodies the slowly revolving thought processes of the characters as they take shape in language.

Jeff's struggle to understand Melanctha and his own awakening passion dramatizes the extent to which his language shapes and confines his thought. Like Adele, he begins with a moral framework that provides simple binary categories for classifying his experience: "living regular" is "good" and "getting excited" is "bad." When Jeff is introduced into the story, the narrator uses the words "good" and "bad" as if they were reliable, univocal labels, in apparent complicity with Jeff's system of moral judgment. Jeff is "good"; his father is "good"; Melanctha is "good now to her mother" (TL, 110). But in the early part of the story, which presents Melanctha's initiation into sexual and emotional maturity as a "wandering after wisdom," the rich polyvalency of the repeated words "wandering" and "wisdom" eludes moral categorization. In sharp contrast, Jeff confronts Melanctha with a rigid set of moral labels. At first he has her safely categorized: "he did not think that she would ever come to any good" (112); he refuses even to acknowledge that she had a "good mind" (116). As he comes to know her somewhat better, he reverses his initial judgment: "Melanctha really was a good woman, and she had a good mind" (131).

Beginning with their first conversation, Melanctha directly challenges Jeff's conventional notions of goodness:

> You certainly are just too scared Dr. Campbell to really feel things way down in you. All you are always wanting Dr. Campbell, is just to talk about being good, and to play with people just to have a good time, and yet always to certainly keep yourself out of trouble. It don't seem to me Dr. Campbell that I admire that way to do things very much. It certainly ain't really to me being very good. (123)

This episode begins the disintegration of the linguistic and conceptual grid through which Jeff has habitually processed his experience, which begins to break down as his passion for Melanctha strains against its rigid structures. Like Adele's in *Q.E.D.*, Jeff's passion plunges him into a moral dilemma. But Jeff's scruples seem much more narrowly moralistic than Adele's, because both the social taboo of lesbianism and the question of Helen's "prostitution" have been eliminated from this story. Brought up to believe that "real, strong, hot love" is the worst form of "getting excited," bad for himself and his people, he is afraid of sexual passion. When he learns of Melanctha's previous sexual experiences, he judges them unequivocally "bad," but the increasing strength of his feelings for her do not allow him to dismiss her so easily (151). He roughly rejects her first direct sexual advances as "ugly" (155). Although he later accepts them, the ambivalence remains: "It was all so mixed up inside him. All he knew was he wanted very badly Melanctha should be there beside him, and he wanted very badly, too, always to throw her from him" (156). The more desperately he attempts to decide who, and what, is "good" and "bad," the more obviously these words fail to provide a stable framework for moral judgments. His attempts to verbalize his feelings poignantly illustrate the insufficiency of the labels he had previously used so confidently to order his experiences.

As he constantly repeats the words "certainly" and "really" in his increasingly desperate efforts to discover what is "certain" and "real" about his experience, these verbal props signal his actual uncertainty and provide a constant ironic counterpoint to his struggles:[5]

> "I *certainly* am *wrong* now, thinking all this way so lovely, and not thinking now any more the old way I always before was always thinking, about what was the *right* way for me, . . . and then I think, perhaps, Melanctha you are really just a *bad* one, . . . and then I always get so *bad* to you, Melanctha, and I can't help it with myself then, never, for I want to be always *right really* in the ways, I have to do them. I *certainly* do very *badly* want to be *right*, Melanctha, the only way I know is *right* Melanctha *really*, and I don't know any way, Melanctha, to find out *really*, . . . which way *certainly* is the *real right* way . . . and then I *certainly* am awful *good* and sorry, Melanctha, I always give you so much trouble, hurting you with the *bad* ways I am acting. Can't you help me to any way, to make it all straight for me, Melanctha, so I know *right* and *real* what it is I should be acting. . . . I *certainly* do *badly* want to know always, the way I should be acting."
>
> "No, Jeff, dear, . . . [a]ll I can do now, Jeff, is to just keep *certainly* with my believing you are *good* always, Jeff, and though you *certainly* do hurt me *bad*, I always got strong faith in you, Jeff, more in you *certainly*, than you seem to be having in your acting to me, always so *bad*, Jeff."
>
> "You *certainly* are very *good* to me, Melanctha, . . . and me so *bad* to you always, in my acting. Do you love me *good*, and *right*, Melanctha, always?" (159–60; my emphases)

In *Q.E.D.*, Adele describes a similar conflict in terms of an opposition between "passion" and "Calvinistic influence" or "puritan instincts" (103). In the passage above and elsewhere in "Melanctha," intensive repetition of the simpler words "good" and "bad," frequently in combination with "right" and "wrong," dramatize more

5. Bridgman notes the ironic effect of the repetition of the word "certainly" (*Colloquial Style in America*, pp. 181–82).

directly the impasse these characters have talked themselves into.
Jeff and Melanctha call themselves and each other "good" and "bad."
In this dense verbal interplay, the repeated words dominate the discourse, not only as adjectives but in other syntactical functions as
well. "Bad(ly)" appears twice as an intensifying adverb, in connection
with the adjectives "good" and "right," both of which are also brought
into play as adverbs as the passage progresses. These shifts of grammatical categories augment the reader's sense of the slippery imprecision of these words. As their repetitions echo throughout the
passage, these words are gradually emptied of any univocal meaning,
while "really" and "certainly" ironically signal the characters' increasing linguistic helplessness and the impossibility of their ever achieving moral certainty through the unwieldy, ambiguous medium of
their language.

Jeff's struggles with language are more intense than Melanctha's.
Far from sharing his faith in the power of rational thought to clarify
emotional experience, she sees it as an impediment that restricts his
understanding: "you never can see anything that ain't just so simple,
Jeff, with everybody, the way you always think it" (TL, 168). The
conflict between her spontaneous, intuitive nature and Jeff's "cold
slow way . . . to feel things in him" (174) re-creates the fundamental
opposition between Helen and Adele in Q.E.D. Melanctha is a more
eloquent and sympathetic character than Helen, however, and her
challenge to Jeff's habits of mind is correspondingly more serious.
Accused of being incapable of love because she refuses to "remember
right," she strongly defends the greater value of "real feeling every
moment when its needed":

> "I certainly do call it remembering right Jeff Campbell, to
> remember right just when it happens to you, so you have a right
> kind of feeling not to act the way you always been doing to me,
> and then you go home Jeff Campbell, and you begin with your
> thinking, and then it certainly is very easy for you to be good
> and forgiving with it. No, that ain't to me, the way of remem-
> bering Jeff Campbell, not as I can see it not to make people
> always suffer, waiting for you certainly to get to do it. Seems to
> me like Jeff Campbell, I never could feel so like a man was low
> and to be scorning of him, like that day in the summer, when
> you threw me off just because you got one of those fits of your
> remembering. No, Jeff Campbell, its real feeling every moment
> when its needed, that certainly does seem to me like real remem-
> bering." (181)

In "Melanctha," these contrasting rhythms of personality are more
directly related to the question of the relationship between language
and emotional experience. Jeff is "slow" because his experience is

always mediated by rational reflection in language; his responses are always belated. Melanctha distrusts this form of mediation so strongly that she refuses to take responsibility for words she uttered in the past: "You always wanting to have it all clear out in words always, what everybody is always feeling. I certainly don't see a reason, why I should always be explaining to you what I mean by what I am just saying. . . . I never know anything right I was saying" (171). For her, "it ain't much use to talk about what a woman is really feeling in her" (135). Like Helen in *Q.E.D.*, she sees a fundamental incompatibility between "thinking" and "feeling" (132), but because she is both a more sympathetic and a more articulate character than Helen, her position has a more powerful presence in "Melanctha" than Helen's has in the earlier text.

This opposition between rational analysis and emotional immediacy was one of Stein's central preoccupations during the early years of her career, beginning with her ironic re-creation of her own painful conflict with May Bookstaver in *Q.E.D.* and culminating in *Tender Buttons*. "Melanctha," widely praised for its "colloquial realism," was a crucial step in the process that would lead Stein far beyond the boundaries of conventional realism. Melanctha's articulated opposition to Jeff's habits of mind is only one of the many ways in which this text undermines the supreme value Adele (and, presumably, once Stein herself) invested in rational thought and expression. Time and again, its forceful demonstrations of how coercively the characters' language controls—and impedes—their perceptions and judgments prefigure the radical iconoclasm of *Tender Buttons*.

Jeff learns more from his experience than Adele ever does. Gradually his speeches demonstrate to him, as well as to the reader, how inadequate his language and the conceptual framework it dictates are to the moral and emotional complexity of his experience. Through his verbal struggles with Melanctha and with his own passions, Jeff gradually comes to doubt his own habitual intellectual stance: "Perhaps what I call my thinking ain't really so very understanding" (135). As he abandons his efforts to rationalize his experiences and allows himself simply to feel them, he begins to achieve for himself the "real wisdom" of passionate life that Melanctha already possesses. When he begins to sense the loss of her love, he asks for verbal assurances, but he can no longer be comforted by her repeated declarations that she loves him. Aware now of the gap between language and the reality of emotional experience, he "could not make an answer to Melanctha. What was it he should now say to her? What words could help him to make their feeling any better?" (198). At the end of *Q.E.D.* Adele reverts to her habits of abstract categorization as a means of distancing and controlling her pain;

she dismisses Helen by labeling her a "prostitute" (121, 127). Jeff, with more wisdom, cannot use such words to deny his feelings. Even after he has lost Melanctha, he "always had strong in him the meaning of all the new kind of beauty Melanctha Herbert once had shown him, and always more and more it helped him with his working for himself and for all the colored people" (TL, 207).

Jeff's gradual attainment of this wisdom that transcends moral categories is ironically framed by Melanctha's involvement with Rose Johnson, who represents the unreflective, formulaic morality that initially governed Jeff's habits of thought. The text begins and ends with Melanctha's fatal emotional dependence on Rose, who "had strong the sense of proper conduct" (88). Ignoring Melanctha's years of faithful friendship and service, Rose harshly condemns her dealings with men as unequivocally "bad" and banishes Melanctha from her house with absolute self-righteousness. Rose mindlessly repeats the words "good" and "bad," "right" and "wrong," which were demonstrated to be so problematic in Jeff's struggles to achieve "wisdom." As Melanctha is bludgeoned by these repetitions in a rejection that finally breaks her spirit and leads to her early death, the text offers its final, ironic demonstration of the terrible power of these words both to shape and to impede judgment, by restricting thought to the categories they create.

Repetition is central to the mode of realism Stein created in "Melanctha," a densely patterned textual surface that models the process by which thoughts take shape in language. Although it makes use of some syntactical features common to nonstandard dialects, the language of "Melanctha" is not a literal transcription of Black English but a stylization of the speech and thought patterns of characters whose language is inadequate to their experience. Although the simple words the characters use are shown to be slippery, unstable instruments, their patterning forcefully enacts the play of passions, the frustrating processes of thought and communication. Wordsworth, a century before Stein, discovered the power of repetition to imitate the "craving in the mind" to bridge the gap between intense emotion and inadequate means of expression:

> There is a numerous class of readers who imagine that the same words cannot be repeated without tautology: this is a great error: virtual tautology is much oftener produced by using different words when the meaning is exactly the same. Words, a Poet's words, more particularly, ought to be weighed in the balance of feeling, and not measured by the space which they occupy upon paper. For the Reader cannot be too often reminded that Poetry is passion: it is the history or science of feelings; now every man

must know that an attempt is rarely made to communicate
impassioned feelings without something of an accompanying
consciousness of the inadequateness of our own powers, or the
deficiencies of language. During such efforts there will be a
craving in the mind, and as long as it is unsatisfied the Speaker
will cling to the same words, or words of the same character.
There are also various other reasons why repetition and apparent tautology are frequently beauties of the highest kind. Among
the chief of these reasons is the interest which the mind attaches to words, not only as symbols of the passion, but as *things*,
active and efficient, which are of themselves part of the passion.[6]

Wordsworth's project, like Stein's, was to explore the motions of the
human mind in the medium of language. In poems like "The Thorn,"
the occasion for these reflections, he created personae with limited
powers of expression, whose verbal repetitions function mimetically,
to dramatize their struggles to formulate their experiences in language. As Wordsworth observed, repetition foregrounds the materiality of language, of words "not only as symbols of the passion, but
as *things*, active and efficient, which are of themselves part of the
passion." Far more radically than Wordsworth, Stein used repetition
in "Melanctha" to undermine the functioning of words as univocal
"symbols of the passion" while emphasizing their irreducible power
to shape the process of thought.

But for Stein, as for Wordsworth, repetition has other uses as well.
Repetition of words, sound, and syntactical patterns plays a major
role in structuring poetic language. In "Melanctha," the characters'
speeches have their own "beauties" of sound and rhythm, even as
they demonstrate the speakers' linguistic inadequacy. Passages of
direct narration use the same verbal texture and rhythm to create a
rich evocation of simple, elemental patterns of action. In the following passage, repetition reveals not linguistic helplessness but poetic
power:

From the time that Melanctha *was* twelve until she *was* sixteen
she *wandered*, always seeking but never more than very dimly
seeing *wisdom*. . . .
Melanctha's *wanderings* after *wisdom* she always had to do in
secret and by snatches, for her mother *was* then still living and
'Mis' Herbert always did some *watching*. . . .

6. Note to "The Thorn" (1800), in *Poetical Works of William Wordsworth*, ed. Ernest de
Selincourt and Helen Darbishire (Oxford: Clarendon Press, 1940–49), 2:513. Frances
Ferguson's discussion of Wordsworth's writings about language in chapter 1 of *Wordsworth: Language as Counter-Spirit* (New Haven: Yale University Press, 1977) brought this
passage to my attention (pp. 11–16).

In these days Melanctha talked and stood and *walked* *w*ith many kinds of men. . . . They all supposed her to have *world* knowledge and experience. They, believing that she knew all, told her nothing, and thinking that she *w*as deciding *w*ith them, asked for nothing, and so though Melanctha *wandered widely*, she *w*as really very safe *w*ith all the *wandering*.

It *w*as a very *wonderful* experience this safety of Melanctha. . . . Melanctha herself did not feel the *wonder*. . . .

She knew she *w*as not getting *w*hat she so badly *wanted*. . . .

Melanctha liked to *wander*, and to stand by the railroad yard, and *watch* the men and the engines and the *s*witches and everything that *w*as busy there, *working*. . . . For a child *watching* through a hole in the fence above the yard, it is a *wonder world* of mystery and movement. (TL, 97–98; my emphases)

The lush surface texture flaunts its poetic play of alliteration, rhyme, and repetition of words. The repeated alliteration of *w* and *m*, the major sound motifs of the passage, contrasts with the repetition of sibilants and hard *k* sounds. Participial endings create a network of rhyme. Throughout the passage, sound creates a network of connections independent of syntax, which has a powerful semantic function. As the pattern of words beginning with *w* gradually unfolds, "wandered" and "wisdom" establish the theme and set in motion the associative chain that follows. Wandering, wanting, walking, watching, the men working—forms of these verbs recur, echoing through this passage and the pages that follow. The nouns "wonder," "world," and "wisdom" entwine themselves in this network of sound associations. A second alliterative chain links Melanctha first to her mother and then to the "mystery and movement" of the world of men. At the beginning, Melanctha's mother is watching her; by the end, Melanctha herself is watching the men working. Finally, several pages later, the words "woman" and "wife" appear to complete the sequence (103). As it gradually unfolds in the linear movement of the passage, this interplay of phonemic repetition and difference creates a rhythmic sound pattern that powerfully reinforces the life pattern of emerging sexual awareness that is the theme of the passage.

This long passage is the only section of "Melanctha" that makes systematic use of repetition to embody the rhythm of a life process. This text demonstrates the impotence of repetition, in the speeches and thoughts of its characters, more systematically than its power. In both cases, repetition is used to model the rhythm of a temporal process, and the realism inheres in the material patterning of language, foregrounded to create an iconic figuration of the object it models. After completing *Three Lives*, Stein soon lost interest in the problem of representing the speech and thought patterns of characters whose command of the language is limited and concentrated on exploring the power of repetition to render her own synoptic vision of characters and life processes.

SONIA SALDÍVAR-HULL

[Racism in "Melanctha"]†

The reader can approach Gertrude Stein's *Three Lives* in the spirit of re-discovery. Imagine the secure comfort of a naive student who "discovers" an allegedly suppressed literary mother. It was in this spirit that I began the first "life," "The Good Anna."

At first, the pathetic character of a German immigrant, Anna seems to be representative of one stereotypical version of an older woman: bitter and alone. As Stein develops her character, however, Anna's attitudes about class and gender become the narrator's assumptions of traits possessed by all "lower-class" servants. The question of whether the good Anna is really "good" becomes irrelevant as statements that I wanted to accept as ironic became suspiciously stated as facts: "Anna had always a firm old world sense of what was the right way for a girl to do,"[1] as well as the distinction Anna made between the class of "maid" and that of "servant." Anna's penchant for controlling her employers' lives seemed to be presented as a model of how "good help" should behave. The good Anna would never allow herself to sit down with her superior, Miss Mathilda: "A girl was a girl and should always act like a girl, both as to giving all respect and as to what she had to eat"(24).

At this point in the story, the naive reader could still believe that Stein presented the good Anna's servant credo as idiosyncratic to the unique character in a fiction. Stein's tone is ironic, the reader can argue. Surely Stein is being consciously ambiguous so the reader can see for herself that these are class issues that must be subverted. When we were undergraduates, our professors warned us about the intentional fallacy; as sophisticated readers we are supposed to understand that Anna's situation is a result of her own peculiarities. Readers can comfort themselves with the belief that Stein was creating a portrait of a woman who manipulates those around her by

† From *Women's Writing in Exile*, eds. Mary Lynn Broe and Angela Ingram (Chapel Hill: University of North Carolina Press, 1989), pp. 186–95. Reprinted by permission of the publisher.
1. *Three Lives*, p. 24. All references to *Three Lives* in this piece are to the 1909 Vintage Books edition.

sacrificing her own life for them.[2] Anna is the consummate martyr figure who uses self-sacrifice to gain power over people. Surely that is all Stein is saying.

This naive reader, however, was becoming more uneasy. Was it possible that Gertrude Stein, the writer I was supposed to admire, could not see the obvious class issues that contribute to Anna's character? I began to question phrases like "obedient, happy servant" and "by nature slatternly and careless," which Stein used to describe other working-class women. By now I was being forced to question whether I could ever again read for character and plot and literary technique and ignore more pressing political issues.

"Melanctha," the next "life," had promised to be an avant-garde portrait of a black woman who searches intensely for self-knowledge and seeks an outlet for her sexuality. But for the readers who are of the working class and/or are women of color, the betrayal soon is unmistakable. The more this naive reader read, the more obvious it became that Stein *believed* in the basic "unmorality of the black people," that she *believed* that the "negroes" have a simplicity which is exhibited in their "joyous, earth born, boundless joy" (86).

Clearly, the next step for the naive reader to take is to search the academic sages for published support for a growing disgust with the narrow, prejudiced portrayals of the women in *Three Lives*. We find blindness instead of insight. Issues that seemed to provide the very reasons to undermine Stein's portrayals are hailed by some critics as the reasons to study and include Stein in canon formation.

In his 1973 biography of Stein,[3] Howard Greenfeld discusses intellectual influences on her, the most important one being her relationship with William James, who first introduced the young Stein to the use of language "under unusual circumstances" (13). Her published psychological experiments are relevant to her presentation of the "lower-class" German immigrants and the "half white mulatto girl" in *Three Lives*.[4] But Greenfeld's analysis of the characters' speech in the stories is most disturbing:

> These tales, especially *Melanctha*, are somewhat unconventional in language and style. Gertrude tried to re-create the actual sounds and rhythms of her characters using colloquial speech and a kind of sing song repetition. Her overall desire was

2. See Wendy Steiner, *Exact Resemblance to Exact Resemblance: The Literary Portraiture of Gertrude Stein* (New Haven: Yale UP, 1978), and Marianne DeKoven, "Gertrude Stein and Modern Painting: Beyond Literary Cubism" (*Contemporary Literature* 22 [Winter 1981], pp. 81–95), for discussions of Stein as a cubist writer.
3. *Gertrude Stein: A Biography* (New York: Crown, 1973).
4. See John Malcolm Brinnin, *The Third Rose: Gertrude Stein and Her World* (Boston: Atlantic Monthly Press, 1959) for a thorough discussion of Stein's undergraduate psychology experiments.

to create what she felt Cezanne had created in his paintings, works in which each element was as important as the entire work itself. . . . The author herself never intrudes—the people in these stories speak for themselves, in their own voices. (Greenfeld, 42)

For Greenfeld to claim that these characters speak "in their own voices" is incomprehensible. If we accept his statement, we must ignore the always present, powerful, controlling narrative voice that is Stein. Greenfeld, however, can be explained away as a symptom of the phallocentric disease. His aestheticist, ahistorical, non-class-conscious analysis is typical of the critical approach of many scholars of his school, New Criticism.

Unfortunately, even the poststructuralist feminist critic Marianne DeKoven is not immune to using such an approach. DeKoven is one of those contemporary critics who sidesteps issues of race and class in awarding Stein a place in the feminist canon as an experimental writer whose style is emblematic of antipatriarchal writing. DeKoven claims that she cannot deconstruct Stein's work because it is already deconstructed: "It is the indeterminate, anti-patriarchal (anti-logocentric, anti-phallogocentric, presymbolic pluridimensional) writing which deconstruction, alias Jacques Derrida, proposes as an antidote to patriarchy" (xvii). Although DeKoven admits that Stein never intended for her writing to be anti-patriarchal, she insists that there is "specifically feminist content" in *Three Lives* (xviii). The feminist content, however, is obscured by more disturbing issues.

DeKoven defeats her own thesis by concentrating on purely patriarchal, theoretical concerns. She addresses only the linguistic structures in Stein's works. DeKoven also forgets the perhaps mundane concerns of the "objects" that Stein portrays in her three studies: the working class, women, and people of color. DeKoven's work is an example of the flaws of deconstruction without the mediation of either class or race analysis.

Undoubtedly it is easier for such a critic to deal with "signifiers" and forget that real people, races, and classes are affected by the stereotypes she never challenges. When DeKoven places Stein's work in opposition to patriarchal linguistic structure because of Stein's "linguistic radicalism," the critic forgets that linguistics are part of a totality—the content, the plot, the theme.

For a deconstructionist like DeKoven to look at the totality of *Three Lives*, particularly "Melanctha," would be to subvert her own thesis, which is, "in theory," valid. She claims to focus her "current French feminist, post-structuralist, and psychoanalytic criticism" on the "interplay of language and culture," yet she accepts the most insidious forms of class and race bias. Liberal feminist critics must address this bias. Her brief analysis of "Melanctha" exposes her ties to the patriarchy as much as it unwittingly unveils Stein's own prejudices. Melanctha is defeated by a "divided self," DeKoven claims (31). In the short novel, "wisdom becomes an emblem of everything in life that is desirable but difficult to attain; excitement, of everything that is alluring but dangerous" (44). DeKoven goes on to assert that "Stein's very success in rendering in language a unique core of personality leads her away from recognizable depiction of character. In *Melanctha*, it is the wavelike cadence and the repetition of a reduced, strangely resonant and at the same time simple, childlike vocabulary that hold our attention most forcefully as we read, beyond our recognition of character, anticipation of plot, or reflection upon theme" (44–45).

When we as feminist critics accept blatant slurs like the claim that black people speak with a "childlike vocabulary," when we do not question Steinian images of "negro sunshine" or assumptions of the "simple promiscuous unmorality of the black people," we are lulled and mesmerized by Stein's cadence and repetitions. Perhaps this is Stein's political agenda. The reader loses consciousness of the racism and classism because s/he is encouraged to think only of an aesthetic category, urged to remember that Stein wrote at a specific time, in a particular culture. But these embarrassments that feminist scholars do not discuss at any depth are at the center of "Melanctha." It is a story that appeals primarily to intellectuals who assume that everyone who reads Stein will accept the slurs in the spirit of linguistic authenticity, of authorial irony, of Stein's exotic depiction of the "primitive." These are the tactics of ruling-class ideology; these are the methods the ruling class employs to retain power over the dominated.

In a more sensitive essay on Stein, Catharine Stimpson discusses the author's disregard for displaying class bias.[5] Stimpson also explores how Stein's need to mask her lesbianism forced her to devise tactics that would allow her to live as a "possibly tainted anomaly." Indeed, Stimpson does address Stein's racism in her treatment of black people as strongly sexual creatures. She points out that "problematic passion among whites is transferred to blacks, as if they might embody that which the dominant culture feared" (501). But

---

5. See Catharine R. Stimpson, "The Mind, the Body, and Gertrude Stein" (*Critical Inquiry* 3 [Spring 1977], pp. 489–506) for a complete analysis of Stein's acceptance of pseudo-scientist Otto Weininger's anti-Semitic, misogynistic ideology in his 1909 *Sex and Character*. Stimpson posits that Weininger provided some hope for Stein when he claimed that "the homosexual woman is better than the rest of her sex. Actively partaking of male elements, she may aspire to those aesthetic and intellectual pursuits that are otherwise a male province" (497). Another important essay is Richard Bridgman's "Melanctha" (1961). I was surprised and further disillusioned with contemporary feminist Stein scholars when I discovered in this essay similar points as mine on the racism in "Melanctha."

she does not seem to believe that the racial issue is of prime importance as she glosses over the unpleasantness of Stein's bigotry: "The
facts that Stein disliked raw racial injustice and that a black author,
Richard Wright, praised 'Melanctha' in itself must be balanced
against the fact that racial stereotypes help to print out the narrative"
(501).

I find it disturbing that even a leading feminist like Stimpson turns
to Wright, a misogynistic writer, to exhibit her spirit of egalitarianism. Why does Stimpson need to defer to Wright's authority in her
attempt to deal with the embarrassing problem of Stein's perhaps
unintentional bigotry? Stimpson seems to believe that though she
sees the blatant racism in "Melanctha," a simple footnote stating that
white intellectuals in Stein's time overlooked it as a matter of course
says enough about the race issue.[6]

In contrast, though Stimpson is content to accept Wright's evaluation as evidence of an Afro-American consensus, John Brinnin
includes Claude McKay's response to "Melanctha": "In the telling of
the story I found nothing striking and informative about Negro life.
Melanctha, the mulattress, might have been a Jewess. And the
mulatto Jeff Campbell—he is not typical of mulattoes I have known
anywhere. He reminds me more of a type of white lover described
by a colored woman" (quoted in Brinnin, 121).

In her essay on the Afro-American female literary tradition[7] Lorraine Bethel reminds us that "Black women writers have consistently
rejected the falsification of their Black/female experience, thereby

6. This opens up the debate on the appropriation of Afro-American experience by white
feminists, an issue I cannot adequately address in this essay. For further elaboration, see
Bell Hooks in *Ain't I a Woman: Black Women and Feminism* (Boston: South End Press,
1981), especially her critique of Stimpson's " 'Thy Neighbor's Wife, Thy Neighbor's Servants' Women's Liberation and Black Civil Rights" (in *Women in Sexist Society: Studies
in Power and Powerlessness*, eds. Vivian Gornick and Barbara K. Moran [New York: Basic
Books, 1971], pp. 622–57). Richard Wright's position on Stein's representation of the
Afro-American dialect was part of another debate among the writers in the Harlem Renaissance. For a discussion of these issues see Wahneema Lubiano's chapter "The Harlem
Renaissance and the Roots of Afro-American Literary Modernism," in "Messing with the
Machine: Four Afro-American Novels and the Nexus of Vernacular, Historical Constraint,
and Narrative Strategy" (Ph.D. diss., Stanford U., 1987). Brinnin cites the Wright quotation, which appeared in a review by Wright of Stein's "Wars I Have Seen," first published
in *PM Magazine* March 11, 1945. Wright states: "Miss Stein's struggling words made the
speech of the people around me vivid. From that moment on, in my attempts at writing,
I was able to tap at will the vast pool of living words that swirled around me." In spite of
Wright's own political affiliations, the social and political position of Afro-Americans as
an internal colony in 1945 are revealed in his implication that it took reading a story
written by a white person to make him suddenly value black English. See his 1937 review
of Zora Neale Hurston's *Their Eyes Were Watching God* ("Between Laughter and Tears"
in *New Masses* 5 [October 1937], pp. 25–26) for an example of his misogynism. It is ironic
that he in effect destroyed Hurston's literary career when he critiqued her novel yet he
admired Stein's depiction of the Afro-American experience.

7. " 'This Infinity of Conscious Pain': Zora Neale Hurston and the Black Female Literary
Tradition," in *All the Women Are White, All the Blacks Are Men: But Some of Us Are Brave*,
eds. Gloria T. Hull, Patricia Bell Scott, and Barbara Smith (Old Westbury, N.Y.: Feminist
Press, 1982), pp. 176–88.

avoiding the negative stereotypes such falsification has often created in the white American female and Black male literary traditions" (177). She cites Wright's *Native Son* as an example of "how the falsification of the Black experience for the purpose of political protest can result in characters that reinforce racist stereotypes" (187).

From the first page of "Melanctha," the racial slurs obscure any sympathetic portrayal of a character in Stein's story. The stereotype begins immediately as two women are introduced. Melanctha Herbert is "patient, submissive, soothing, and untiring"; Rose Johnson is "sullen, childish, cowardly, black Rose," who "grumbled and fussed and howled and made herself to be an abomination and like a simple beast" (*Three Lives*, 85). Stein's always controlling narrator casts Rose into literary infamy as a "careless and negligent and selfish" woman whose baby dies from her neglect, although she had "liked the baby well enough and perhaps she just forgot it for awhile, anyway the child was dead and Rose and Sam her husband were very sorry but then these things came so often in the negro world in Bridgepoint, that they neither of them thought about it very long" (85).

Although Stein's assumption that poor black people care less, feel less pain about a baby's death can be explained away as a sociological reality viewed by the author when she was a Johns Hopkins medical student, the portrait is not just of one black couple who lost a child and soon forgot. It is an indictment of the "negro world in Bridgepoint" and, by association, of the "negro" world in general.

The hierarchical scale that Stein presents is as obvious as it is vicious. Of course, "white" is the privileged center. Stein takes for granted that her reader will assume that the white race is superior, so she places her characters in opposition, privileging white over black, good over bad, intelligent over simple-minded, sophisticated over childlike vocabulary. Since the world she portrays is the "other" world of black people, the gradations she makes are within the context of an already flawed black world.

Stein wants her reader to remember which "girl" is "good" and which is "bad." Since Melanctha and Rose belong to this alien, primitive race, perhaps Stein feared that her bourgeois readers would not be able to tell them apart so her technique is the "badder" the "girl," the "blacker" the skin. At one end of the spectrum is Rose, a "real black, tall, well built, sullen, stupid, childlike, good looking negress," who was "never joyous with the earth born, boundless joy of negroes," but was instead a "careless and lazy woman brought up by white folks" (85–86). Even Stein cannot decide how ultimately to place the black people in her story. She wants them all to conform to her vision of this foreign race, but she keeps undermining her own project by making exceptions. She stresses that Rose has not taken advantage of her white patrons' kindness when they raised her as their own child but, in the instinctual way of the "lower" orders, has "drifted from her white folks back to the colored people." She is unable to become part of the higher order not only because of skin color but because of the innate depravity of her black soul: "She needed decent comfort. Her white training had only made for habits, not for nature" (86).

Stein is not content to portray the "real black" Rose as inferior because of her unique psychic makeup. The implication is that Rose is deficient because of her genetic composition as well as her skin color. For Stein, color is fate in the same way that character is fate. "Rose had the simple promiscuous unmorality of the black people," the Stein narrator proclaims. The degree of the characters' sexuality is equivalent to the degree of their depravity.[8]

Tied to Rose in a kinship of dark sexuality is Melanctha's father, James. "Melanctha's father was a big black virile negro" (90). As Angela Davis suggests, the stereotype of the hypersexuality of black men seems to fascinate Stein.[9] She describes Melanctha's mother's attraction to this man solely in terms of this myth: "He only came once in a while to where Melanctha and her mother lived, but always that pleasant, sweet appearing, pale yellow woman, mysterious and uncertain and wandering in her ways, was close to sympathy and thinking to her big black virile husband" (90). James is not within the realm of the "nicer colored folk." On the contrary, this evil presence is described as a "powerful, loose built, hard handed, black angry negro. Herbert was never a joyous negro." Like the black Rose, "he never had the wide abandoned laughter that gives the broad glow to negro sunshine" (92).

Melanctha, on the other hand, "was a graceful; pale yellow, intelligent, attractive negress. She had not been raised like Rose by white folks but then she had been made with real white blood" (86). The reader should be properly impressed and should learn more about this curious specimen, a "mulatto girl," who is half white and half the product of a very black, virile James: "Melanctha was pale yellow and mysterious and a little pleasant like her mother, but the real power in Melanctha's nature came through her robust and unpleas-

8. See Stimpson, "The Mind," 497, on Stein's interest in Weininger's pseudo-scientific work. Stein still believed Weininger's claims when she wrote *Three Lives*.

9. See Davis, "Rape, Racism, and the Myth of the Black Rapist" (in *Women, Race, and Class* [New York: Vintage, 1983], pp. 172–201). Davis cites Stein's *Three Lives* in her examination of the sexual abuse of black women by white men. She states: "Such assaults have been ideologically sanctioned by politicians, scholars and journalists, and by literary artists who have often portrayed Black women as promiscuous and immoral. Even the outstanding writer Gertrude Stein described one of her Black women characters as possessing 'the simple, promiscuous unmorality of the black people' " (176).

ant and very unendurable black father. . . . Melanctha Herbert almost always hated her black father, but she loved very well the power in herself that came through him" (90).

Melanctha's mystery lies in her search for "wisdom" and in her "wandering" in quest for that self-knowledge. But Stein has already informed the reader that even "with her white blood and attraction and her desire for a right position," Melanctha is sexually active but has "not yet really been married" (86). The assumption that black people have a typically "promiscuous unmorality" has been made. The reader is to understand, then, that Melanctha's secret yearning for knowledge is inextricably tied to her sexuality, but only in a negative context: that of a deviant, savage "unmorality" found in its natural state in the inferior races. After all, these are the "colored folks," those childlike creatures Stein likes to compare fondly to nature in her acclaimed "experimental" style: "And the buds and the long earthworms, and the negroes, and all the kinds of children, were coming out every minute farther into the new spring, watery, southern sunshine" (195). The reader who has been mesmerized by Stein's radical writing style may overlook the "negro" next to the earthworm in Stein's great chain of being.[1]

Even in a scene that is supposed to show her heroine's education as a wanderer, Stein cannot resist stereotype as she caricatures the railroad porters from whom Melanctha is to "learn": "As the porters told these stories their round, black, shining faces would grow solemn, and their color would go grey beneath the greasy black, and their eyes would roll white in the fear and wonder of things they could scare themselves by telling" (99).

Stein's class prejudice further intrudes on the Melanctha persona when the wandering girl befriends black dockworkers in the daytime but turns to "upper class" black men for her real lessons. Stein depends upon this same class distinction when she portrays Melanctha's relationship with Jane Hardin, "a roughened woman," who "had much white blood and that made her see clear, she liked drinking and that made her reckless" (104). Jane initiates Melanctha into active sexuality; Stein implies a lesbian relationship along with sex with white men. Significantly, some of the most believable exchanges are between these two women who obviously care about each other as people. Stein needs to mask and code her own lesbianism, but she allows the reader a glimpse of herself as a woman-identified woman whose story might have worked if she had not needed to mask

1. For an analysis of the construct of the "mulatta" figure, see Hortense J. Spillers, "Notes on an Alternative Model: Neither/Nor," in *The Year Left 2: Toward a Rainbow Socialism*, eds. Mike Davis, Manning Marable, Fred Pfeil, and Michael Sprinker (London: Verso, 1987), pp. 176–94.

her sexuality and transfer it to an aberrant "other."[2] Jane and Melanctha's sexual wandering is more credible and described less patronizingly, but both these women have white blood and therefore Stein can deal with them more sympathetically than she does the other black characters.

When Melanctha's major love interest is introduced into the story, it becomes clear that Stein's overt racism frames the central story of Melanctha and Dr. Jefferson Campbell. As Catharine Stimpson states, this love story is a coded autobiographical version of Stein's love affair with May Bookstaver (495–501). Stein suddenly drops the racial generalizations in this subplot that makes up the major part of "Melanctha." Perhaps when Stein was being "personal," she was able to suspend racist ideology.

Unfortunately, once the racism all but disappears, blatant class bias takes its place. Jeff becomes the Stein persona who espouses a bootstrap mentality. He states that his "colored" people do "bad" things because they "want to get excited" (*Three Lives*, 121). As a mouthpiece for Stein, this character has no social or political awareness. Campbell's repressed sexuality emerges in his confused philosophy of correct behavior: "I certainly do only know just two ways of loving. One kind of loving seems to me, is like one has a good quiet feeling in a family when one does his work . . . and then the other way of loving is just like having it like any animal that's low in the streets together, and that don't seem to me very good (124).

Once this love story section is over, Stein returns to her racist frame. She concludes that Melanctha is too much a product of her "very black virile father" to settle for a bland, mulatto, bourgeois domesticity with Dr. Jeff. She drives him away and turns instead to a "lower class" man, a "young buck" who eventually discards the complex Melanctha.

Stein brings her narrative full circle when she returns to the story of Rose and Melanctha and the baby's death and Sam's sympathy for Melanctha in her troubles. With the repetition and the celebrated run-on sentences, Stein drills in racist stereotypical characterizations of these inhabitants of the Afro-American world. The narrator reminds the reader that Rose's baby dies because of her negligence and again that neither Rose nor her husband thinks about it very long. Black Rose begins to feel jealous of her husband's passing attentions to Melanctha, and in a brutal scene, the always "careless, negligent selfish" Rose severs the friendship with the victimized heroine.

2. For further elaboration of Stein's revision of the autobiographical *Q.E.D.* into the coded "Melanctha," see Stimpson, "The Mind," 498–502; also Lisa Ruddick, " 'Melanctha' and the Psychology of William James," in *Modern Fiction Studies* 28 (Winter 1982–83), pp. 543–56. (See pp. 314–17 for Stimpson.)

Melanctha's deterioration proceeds rapidly. She has driven Jeff away and is now betrayed by Rose. Stein then finishes the job by giving her previously healthy though melancholy heroine a disease, putting her in a home for "poor consumptives," and killing her off with a swift stroke of the pen in one sentence. We are to understand that since "these things [come] so often in the negro world" (85), neither Stein nor her seduced feminist readers think about issues of race and class for very long.

As a woman of color, I will reply to Benstock's question on the direction that feminist criticism is now to take. I cannot presume to be able to answer the opposition between aesthetics and content that writers such as Gertrude Stein force us to confront, but we do need to continue challenging the authority of those who forget that there are differences within the feminist project. We know what can happen when women begin to question their allies. The Chicana writers who are compelled to write what they know sometimes write passionate poetry of wife beating, of rape, of betrayal by their men and culture. These women risk the label of "vendida," sellout.

The poet Lorna Dee Cervantes writes: "Consider the power of wrestling your ally. His will is to kill you. He has nothing against you."[3] We are killing Chicana and Italian-American women's writing when we leave it out of our breakthrough *Norton Anthology of Literature by Women*. We are killing the dignity of women of color and working-class women when we continue to promote authors like Gertrude Stein without acknowledging their race and class prejudice. What are we to conclude when the editors of *NALW* include "The Gentle Lena" portion of *Three Lives* but leave out the more blatantly racist and class-biased "Melanctha" and "The Good Anna"? We must consider the power that we hold when we choose to exile some literatures and canonize others. The women exiled from the pages of feminist journals, anthologies, and course syllabi are indeed "alien and critical" as we make ourselves subjects in feminist literary analysis.

3. *Emplumada* (Pittsburgh: U of Pittsburgh P, 1981).

LISA RUDDICK

[Gender and Consciousness in "Melanctha"]†

Gertrude Stein thought of herself as having spent her life escaping from the nineteenth century into which she had been born. This chapter is about the ambivalent beginnings of that escape. With the story"Melanctha," Stein made her first leap into modernist modes of representation; she herself described the story (immodestly but plausibly) as "the first definite step away from the nineteenth century and into the twentieth century in literature."[1] Yet the text looks backward at the same time.

"Melanctha" carries on a private conversation with William James, Stein's college mentor and the central figure in the early drama of her self-definition as a modernist. Along one of its axes, Stein's story reads as a tribute to James's psychological theories—theories that despite their well-known continuities with modernist aesthetics are nineteenth-century in their ethics. Yet at the margins of the story, other material shows Stein already beginning to define herself against James.

The love plot of "Melanctha" borrows heavily from James's psychology; indeed, Stein's debt to James is much deeper than has been supposed. But like all intellectual precursors, James was a burden as well as an inspiration, and as early as "Melanctha" Stein began struggling to free herself from him. James's psychology had appealed to her in college for its heartening vision of moral and practical success, which helped her to overcome some of her own self-doubts and inhibitions; in "Melanctha," this ideology of success permeates her characterization of Jeff Campbell, who in fact is her idealized self-portrait through the lens of James. But Jeff and his success plot are already too limiting for Stein, and details at the fringes of the story signal alien ethical and artistic commitments that will soon move into the foreground as Stein wages war more consciously on her teacher.

Among the themes in "Melanctha" that stand in tension with the Jamesian plot of mental success is the notion of a wisdom superior to instrumental thinking, a wisdom grounded in the body. Technically, the story violates James's values by indulging in a kind of aimless play; more than that, it transcribes irrational process, forming itself according to a principle of motivated repetition that is contin-

---

† From *Reading Gertrude Stein: Body, Text, Gnosis* (Ithaca: Cornell University Press, 1990) 12–54. Reprinted by permission of the publisher.
1. Gertrude Stein, *The Autobiography of Alice B. Toklas* (New York: Harcourt, Brace, 1933), p. 66.

uous not with James's ideas but with the psychoanalytic view of mental life that will soon dislodge James's presence in Stein's work. Finally, "Melanctha" has a latent feminism, which places on trial the individualistic and (in Stein's mind) ultimately male value system absorbed from James, which she still honors in the characterization of Jeff Campbell.

The two lovers in the story, Melanctha and Jeff, are the products of Stein's imaginative self-splitting. As she experimented artistically with the different ethical systems that attracted her, she bifurcated herself into a manly Jamesian example and a mysterious woman who became a magnet for her conflicts. Melanctha is the locus of ambiguity in the story. As the focus of this chapter shifts, toward and then away from James, the character Melanctha assumes the appearance, first, of a mere failure in the evolutionary struggle, then of a priestess of the body, and finally of a victim of patriarchal relations.

"Melanctha" and the Psychology of William James

It is a commonplace of Stein criticism that her stylistic experimentation owes something to James's psychological theories, to which she was exposed in college. Michael J. Hoffman, Donald Sutherland, Richard Bridgman, Wendy Steiner, and others have traced features of Stein's various literary styles to James's idea of the "stream of consciousness."[2] But the content as well as the style of Stein's early fiction bears the heavy imprint of James.[3] Once his stamp on this work is evident, James is recognizable as Stein's one intellectual father, the person who contributed most to her first expressions of artistic power but who then became part of the nineteenth century that she had to escape. Her aggression against him would finally become conscious in the period of *The Making of Americans*, but

2. See Michael J. Hoffman, *The Development of Abstractionism in the Writings of Gertrude Stein* (Philadelphia: University of Pennsylvania Press, 1965), pp. 52, 86–87, 213; Hoffman, "Gertrude Stein and William James," *Personalist* 47 (1966): 226–33; Donald Sutherland, *Gertrude Stein: A Biography of Her Work* (New Haven: Yale University Press, 1951), pp. 6–8; Ronald Levinson, "Gertrude Stein, William James, and Grammar," *American Journal of Psychology* 54 (1941): 124–28; Richard Bridgman, *Gertrude Stein in Pieces* (New York: Oxford University Press, 1970), pp. 102, 133–34; Carl Van Vechten, "How to Read Gertrude Stein," in Linda Simon, ed., *Gertrude Stein: A Composite Portrait* (New York: Avon, 1974), p. 51; Edith Sitwell, from *Taken Care Of*, anthologized in Simon, p. 111; Wendy Steiner, *Exact Resemblance to Exact Resemblance: The Literary Portraiture of Gertrude Stein* (New Haven: Yale University Press, 1978), p. 46; Jayne Walker, *The Making of a Modernist: Gertrude Stein from "Three Lives" to "Tender Buttons"* (Amherst: University of Massachusetts Press, 1984), pp. 14–15.

3. Bridgman (p. 75) moves beyond the stylistic features to note something Jamesian in the "crude opposites" portrayed in *The Making of Americans*; Hoffman associates with James what he takes to be a practice in Stein of "character definition by verbalization" (*Development of Abstractionism*, p. 51); and Steiner convincingly compares James's concept of identity and Stein's manner of approaching the subjects of her literary portraits (pp. 29–30).

even in "Melanctha," where she is closest to his thinking, she embraces his ideas in one zone of her text but besieges them in another.

Stein met William James in 1893, when she took his introductory philosophy course at Harvard. James shared the lecturing with two other professors; he led the unit on psychology, assigning a newly condensed version of his *Principles of Psychology*. Before graduating, Stein enrolled in seven more psychology courses, two of them taught by James. Later she went to medical school at James's urging, with a view toward a career in psychology. Although she ultimately dropped out of medical school, Stein and her mentor remained irregularly in touch even after her expatriation. She entertained him in Paris, and in 1910, shortly before his death, James warmly acknowledged the copy of *Three Lives* she had sent him.[4]

Many years later, Stein referred to an intellectual debt to James, describing him as "the important person in [her] Radcliffe life" and one of "the strongest scientific influences that I had."[5] James's science pervades her early writing. "Melanctha," in particular, is so close, in its characterizations, to James's theory of the mind as to approach psychological allegory.

This story, generally recognized as Stein's first work of distinction, is set off from her previous literary endeavors (including, incidentally, the two other stories in *Three Lives*) by a psychological deepening, a sensitivity to the mixed tones of life. "Melanctha" reworks material from *Q.E.D.*, the very early novelette in which Stein had given a minimally disguised account of her first love affair, with May Bookstaver.[6] *Q.E.D.*, however, lacks texture; it describes the romance in a baldly schematic way. The two main characters have few features beyond those that figure in a controlling opposition: Helen, the seducer, is passionate and daring, while Adele, the character modeled on Stein, is sexually inhibited and devoted to bourgeois values. The two women argue and cause each other pain, but do not otherwise affect each other. The story ends in a situation of romantic "dead-lock."[7]

When Stein went back to this material in 1905 and reworked it as "Melanctha," she turned it into a meditation on conflicting ways of knowing. What happened was that twelve years after studying psychology in college, she began to use that training for her creative

4. See Donald Gallup, ed., *The Flowers of Friendship: Letters Written to Gertrude Stein* (New York: Knopf, 1953), p. 50; Bridgman, p. 22.
5. Stein, *The Autobiography of Alice B. Toklas*, p. 96; Stein, *Wars I Have Seen* (New York: Random House, 1945), p. 63.
6. See Leon Katz, Introduction to *Fernhurst, Q.E.D., and Other Early Writings by Gertrude Stein* (New York: Liveright, 1971), pp. xi–xvii.
7. *Q.E.D.*, in *Fernhurst*, p. 133.

work. In "Melanctha," a fusion suddenly took place between her artistic practice and her early studies with William James.

The lovers of "Melanctha" are opposed not simply in their sexual attitudes, like the couple in *Q.E.D.*, but also in their manner of focusing on the world. The battle of wills Stein had depicted in *Q.E.D.* becomes, in the characters of Melanctha Herbert and Jeff Campbell, a battle of rival modes of perception. Thus reconceived, the characters are in a position to learn from each other. The new perceptual issues, which are traceable to James, receive a delicate treatment; they enter the story not as a theoretical debate between the lovers but as a half-articulated source of strain and attraction between them.

Stein commented, many years later, on what she had learned as a psychology student at Harvard:

> I became more interested in psychology, and one of the things I did was testing reactions of the average college student. . . . [S]oon I found . . . that I was enormously interested in the types of their characters. . . . I expressed [my] results as follows:
> In these descriptions it will be readily observed that *habits of attention are reflexes of the complete character of the individual.*[8]

The experimental outcomes reflect what she had learned in James's course. In the text for that course, James had written that "what is called our 'experience' is almost entirely determined by our habits of attention."[9]

What are "habits of attention"? James describes immediate experience as presenting a barrage of sensory impressions, teeming and confused. If a person is to accomplish anything beyond "star[ing] vacantly" (*P* 223) at this array of phenomena—indeed, if he or she is to begin the business of survival—selections must be made. Our practical nature compels us to remain inattentive to all but those objects that bear upon our individual needs. As a result, he says, "we actually *ignore* most of the things before us" (*P* 37). "We are all seeing flies, moths, and beetles by the thousand," for example, but for most of us, for all "save an entomologist," these things are "nonexistent" (*P* 39). They fail to enter our experience. Our ability to bring into focus only those objects that suit our practical needs, and to

8. Stein, "The Gradual Making of The Making of Americans," in *Lectures in America* (New York: Random House, 1935), pp. 137–38 (emphasis added). Hugo Münsterberg directed the experimental work described here, but there is little evidence that he was an influence; Stein had learned her psychology from James. See *The Autobiography of Alice B. Toklas,* in which Stein gives Münsterberg a brief mention but continues: "The important person in Gertrude Stein's Radcliffe life was William James" (p. 96).

9. William James, *Psychology: The Briefer Course,* ed. Gordon Allport (New York: Harper and Row, 1961), p. 39, hereafter abbreviated as *P,* and cited in the text.

ignore the rest, James calls "selective attention"—or "habits of attention" (P 37, 39).

Some individuals, James speculates, are more fixed in their perceptual habits than others; adults, for example, are more likely than children to approach the world with inflexible patterns of attention. "In mature age," writes James, "we have generally selected those stimuli which are connected with one or more so-called permanent interests, and our attention has grown irresponsive to the rest." "Childhood," on the other hand, "has few organized interests by which to meet new impressions and decide whether they are worthy of notice or not" (P 88). The result is an extreme "sensitiveness" in youth "to immediately exciting sensorial stimuli"—particularly to stimuli of "a directly exciting quality," "intense, voluminous, or sudden"—and to "strange things, moving things, . . . etc." (P 88). The child is captivated by sensory impressions not because they serve as "means to a remote end"—not because they bear upon some personal interest—but because they are "exciting or interesting *per se*" (P 90).

Here we begin to see filaments of connection with "Melanctha." Stein describes her heroine as "always wanting new things just to get excited."[1] In James's phrase, Melanctha likes what is "exciting or interesting *per se*." This habit of attention distinguishes her from her lover, Jeff Campbell, whose perceptions are formed by specific needs. Jeff "wanted to work so that he could understand what troubled people, and not to just have excitements" (116). As happens with the adults James describes, his contact with the world always forms itself about a practical end. Jeff—who believes in "always know[ing] . . . what you wanted" from experience (117)—stands as a model for the selective mind that elevates to notice only those objects that bear upon well-formulated goals. A question endlessly debated by Jeff and Melanctha is whether life is to consist of "excitements" cultivated for their own sake or whether it should be directed toward broader ends.

For James, the attraction to what is "exciting . . . *per se*" typifies childhood. But he adds that this "sensitiveness to immediately exciting sensorial stimuli," although usually outgrown, "is never overcome in some people, whose work, to the end of life, gets done in the interstices of their mind-wandering" (P 88, 89). For these people, perceptual life continues to consist of immediate, aimless sensation; "so-called permanent interests" fail to become prominent and screen out the welter of impressions.

This description fits the case of Stein's Melanctha. James uses the term *mind-wandering*, or *wandering attention* (P 95), to describe

1. Stein, "Melanctha," in *Three Lives* (New York: Random House, 1936), p. 119, hereafter cited in the text.

such a receptiveness to sensation—and *wandering* is also Stein's word for her heroine. The references in "Melanctha" to the heroine's many "wanderings" have rightly been considered part of a sustained euphemism for sex, but one might as easily reverse the emphasis and say that sex itself stands in the story as a metaphor for a certain type of mental activity. Melanctha's promiscuity is part of an experiential promiscuity, an inability or unwillingness to approach the world selectively. Her sexual wanderings are part of a "wandering attention" that takes in experience without mediation.

The earlier novelette, *Q.E.D.*, used little indirection or euphemism. Although scenes involving anything more intimate than a "passionate embrace" were decorously skipped, it was clear what the words describing the lovers' experiences meant; there was none of the vagueness that seems to pervade "Melanctha." The "wanderings" that happen to occur in *Q.E.D.* are the quite literal wanderings of two young women through New York in search of a trysting place.[2] But in "Melanctha," sexual wanderings become "wanderings after wisdom," after "world knowledge," after "real experience" (97). "And so Melanctha wandered on the edge of wisdom," searching for "something realer" (101, 108). If this is euphemism, it is euphemism of an elaborate sort that brings to mind issues of wisdom, knowledge, and experience, as well as the romantic events described.

Melanctha and Jeff represent mental poles. James describes the apparatus of selective attention, which in Stein's story Jeff exercises and Melanctha does not, as strengthened by words and concepts, to which we "grow more and more enslaved" with the years (*P* 195). Objects that fail to conform to our semantic "pigeonholes" are "simply not taken account of at all."[3] These words and stock concepts, besides determining what objects we will select for notice, distort our perceptions of those objects that we do observe. For "whilst part of what we perceive comes through our senses from the object before us, another part (*and it may be the larger part*) always comes out of our own mind" (*P* 196).

For most people, that is, sensation is modified by ideas. We rarely perceive a datum in its "sensational nudity" (*P* 181); what James calls preperception almost always obscures the object with anterior associations. This issue enters "Melanctha" in the form of an opposition between "thinking" and "feeling." Melanctha charges Jeff with an inability to feel because of his incessant thinking. "Don't you ever stop with your thinking long enough ever to have any feeling Jeff Campbell," she asks—and he answers, "No" (132). Because she herself takes in impressions without adapting them to conventional

2. See *Q.E.D.*, in *Fernhurst*, pp. 75–80.
3. James, "The Hidden Self," in *A William James Reader*, ed. Gay Wilson Allen (Boston: Houghton Mifflin, 1971), p. 93; see, too, *P* 192, 195.

ideas or labels, every experience is new for her (119). She has what James in a fanciful moment labels genius—"the faculty of perceiving in an unhabitual way" (P 195).

James says that "thinking in words" is the most deeply ingrained method of distilling impressions (P 213). Stein's character Jeff tends (at first) to "think . . . in words" (155). Maybe this propensity has some connection to his "talking . . . all the time" (134). Melanctha, for her part, "never talked much" (134). "When you get to really feeling," she senses, "you won't be so ready then always with your talking" (135). Jeff, moreover, knows how to "remember right," whereas Melanctha "never could remember right"—the subject of a long squabble between the two (178, 100). Memory is another euphemism, this time for romantic fidelity. "No man can ever really hold you," Jeff tells Melanctha, "because . . . you never can remember" (191). But here again the sexual theme is conflated with the perceptual. Memory is part of the machinery of preperception. James writes that the associations a particular experience arouses in a person will naturally depend on his or her memories—and the more memories involved, the less fresh the experience itself will be (P 143, 193). Thus Melanctha's pathological forgetfulness is of a piece with her mind-wandering. Jeff charges her with "never remembering anything only what you just then are feeling in you" (182).

It is customary to view "Melanctha" as a story of two people who reach a romantic standoff because their natures are hopelessly "antithetical."[4] Yet there is something positive in the bond between the lovers, in spite of—or just because of—their characterological opposition. Melanctha and Jeff are not only contrasting character types but also personifications of warring principles that exist *in every mind*. According to James, every mind synthesizes the tendency to impose stock categories and the instinct for new and alien impressions. "There is an everlasting struggle in every mind between the tendency to keep unchanged, and the tendency to renovate, its ideas. Our education is a ceaseless compromise between the conservative and the progressive factors," or between the attachment to fixed categories and the "progressive" reaching after unfamiliar impressions (P 194).

The two faculties coexist in an "everlasting struggle." The relationship of the lovers in "Melanctha" is itself described as a struggle: "It was a struggle, sure to be going on always between them," and "a struggle that was as sure always to be going on between them, as their minds and hearts always were to have different ways of working" (153). The dynamic of struggle and compromise that unites the divergent energies of the mind as James describes it is a prototype

4. Bridgman, pp. 53, 56. (See p. 297, p. 300.)

for the complex pairings, partings, and mental adjustments of the lovers of "Melanctha."

The conservative and the progressive elements described by James are mutually dependent. The difficulty of being exclusively "conservative" has already been suggested. To the mind hardened in its conceptual patterns, much of the world is simply lost. The progressive factor, the impulse to seek out fresh impressions, brings such a mind back into contact with the tang of things as they are.

Some such need for novel perceptions attracts Jeff Campbell to Melanctha. He sees her as a "teacher" who can instruct him in "new feeling" and "wisdom" (125, 158, 205). He needs a kind of mental renovation: his conservatism requires the aid of the progressive tendency if it is to recover a sharp sensational focus. But Melanctha has needs, too, which draw her to Jeff, for as James says, "if we lost our stock of labels, we should be intellectually lost in the midst of the world" (P 103). Among other things, our very bodies depend upon our having stable mental categories for food, shelter, danger, and help (P 103).

Unselective perception may be exciting, but it is also impractical and ultimately life-threatening. James conceives of the issue in evolutionary terms: "Its own body . . . MUST be [a] supremely interesting [object] for each human mind. . . . I might conceivably be as much fascinated . . . by the care of my neighbor's body as by the care of my own. . . . The only check to such exuberant non-egoistic interests in natural selection, which would weed out such as were very harmful to the individual" (P 61–62). Melanctha has just these "exuberant non-egoistic interests." Not knowing what she wants, lacking selfish pursuits of any sort, she "wander[s] on the edge of wisdom" (101) without attending to her personal safety. She has a "reckless" quality—an extension of the perceptual recklessness that induces her to seek new experiences at any cost (208).

In uncanny repetition of James's formulation, the nonegoistic Melanctha is as much interested in "the care of [her] neighbor's body" as in "the care of [her] own." The only work she ever seems to do is to tend the ill, the confined, and the newborn. She stands in sharp contrast to her "selfish" friend Rose Johnson (214), who pursues her own advantage while neglecting others—the ailing Melanctha, whom she turns away at the end of the story, and her own infant, who dies because she forgets about him. In Rose one finds a projection, in caricature, of the features that receive a more complex treatment when they appear in the character of Jeff.

"Selfishness" is James's own term for the selection we exercise in the interest of survival (P 61). Rose (although in Darwinian terms her obliviousness to her offspring is problematic) is at once the supremely self-centered character of "Melanctha" and the consummate mental conservative, who knows "what she want[s]" from experience, who "never found any way to get excited," and who speaks in the voice of "strong common sense," which never proceeds beyond bland prejudgments and stock ideas (201, 207, 199). Melanctha, then, would profit from some of the conservatism or selfishness that marks Rose and, to a lesser extent, Jeff. Her perceptual life, stimulating as it is, is dangerous. She achieves knowledge through a series of close escapes, and she is only "in her nature" when "deep in trouble" (92).

Melanctha is drawn to Jeff—and finally to Rose—precisely because these characters lead lives of "solid safety" (210). "Melanctha Herbert never had any strength alone ever to feel safe inside her" (233), so she clings to those whose mental stability complements the fluidity of her own mind. "And Melanctha Herbert clung to Rose in the hope that Rose could save her. Melanctha felt the power of Rose's selfish . . . nature. . . . She always felt a solid safety in her" (210).

In the persons of Melanctha and Jeff, opposing mental tendencies draw together from mutual need. The "struggle" in which the two engage is necessary for both; it is a version of the struggle that must take place between the conservative and the progressive factors in each mind if cognition is to proceed with suppleness. And finally, it is a struggle that subtly changes the lovers. This point is missed by the reading that finds in the relationship two people "in a standoff."[5]

Jeff slowly gets the perceptual renovation he expects from Melanctha. His ability to accept change is one thing that distinguishes him from the drastically limited Rose Johnson. At first he "held off" (109); as happens when any sort of habit is changed, "the material" (to use a description of James's) opposes "a certain resistance to the modifying cause" (P 2). Jeff is for some time "too scared" (in Melanctha's view) "to really feel things" (123); he recoils from the rush of alien sensation, which, in James's phrase, is a "threatening violator or burster of our well-known series of concepts" (P 195). But he is not so fixed as to remain completely a conservative mind. Gradually he begins "to feel a little." He ceases to be "sure . . . just what he wanted"; he stops thinking "in words"; he begins to "wander"; and before long he can "lose all himself in a strong feeling" (116, 129, 155, 149, 154). His transformation is complete when "at last he had stopped thinking"—"he knew very well now at last, he was really feeling" (144).

Then he commits himself to a long phase of "wandering" with Melanctha, which gives him a new perspective on the phenomena of the immediate universe:

5. Bridgman, p. 53. (See p. 297.)

Jeff always loved in this way to wander. Jeff always loved to watch everything as it was growing, and he loved all the colors in the trees and on the ground, and the little, new, bright colored bugs he found in the moist ground and in the grass he loved to lie on and in which he was always so busy searching. Jeff loved everything that moved and that was still, and that had color, and beauty, and real being. (149)

It is a change for Jeff, who was initially repelled by "new things" altogether (119), to be interested in such sharp, individual minutiae as "little, new, bright colored bugs." This is purposeless and unselective attention at its height. The little "bugs" that now appeal to Jeff may even be Stein's way of remembering one of James's own illustrations: "We are all seeing flies, moths, and beetles by the thousand, but to whom, save an entomologist, do they say anything distinct?" (P 39). To Jeff, now that selective attention has relaxed, such trivial and unserviceable objects do enter consciousness in their particularity. Bugs are elevated to importance as vessels of "real being."

"You see Melanctha," Jeff remarks, "I got a new feeling now, you been teaching to me, . . . and I see perhaps what really loving is like, like really having everything together, new things, little pieces all different, like I always before been thinking was bad to be having" (158). "Little pieces all different": the uniqueness of each object comes into focus as the generalizations and preconceptions fade. As Stein was later fond of remarking, "what is strange is this": every phenomenon, if perceived naïvely, appears in its distinctness from all other phenomena.[6] Stein shares James's own fondness for "that quality *sui generis* which each moment of immediate experience possesses for itself."[7]

In the two sentences describing Jeff's wandering phase, the word *and* appears nine times.[8] Such a passage, in which *and* links a variety of perceptions in what seems a single moment, reflects Stein's technique of parataxis, whereby multiple phenomena are shown "all . . . equally and simultaneously existing in perceptual fact."[9] Again, attention is a submerged issue. James comments that, as a result of selective attention, "accentuation and emphasis" are ubiquitous in perception (P 37). It is virtually impossible for the normal adult to attend uniformly to a number of simultaneous impressions. Only God or a hopeless sluggard can survey all parts of the universe "at

6. Quoted in Robert Bartlett Haas, ed., *A Primer for the Gradual Understanding of Gertrude Stein* (Los Angeles: Black Sparrow Press, 1971), p. 150.
7. Ralph Barton Perry, *In the Spirit of William James* (New Haven: Yale University Press, 1938), p. 80.
8. See Stein's "Poetry and Grammar," in *Lectures in America*, p. 213; Levinson, p. 126.
9. Donald Sutherland, "Gertrude Stein and the Twentieth Century," in Haas, ed., *A Primer*, p. 149.

once and without emphasis" (*P* 223). But in Jeff, as "little pieces all different" come before consciousness connected by the equalizing *and*, this condition of dispersed attention prevails. He is learning from Melanctha how not to select.

"The sodden quiet began to break up in him" (195). But Jeff proceeds carefully, in cycles of direct feeling followed by recuperation and quiet. He "held off" (109) at the right moments. These phrases describe the risks of love, but the pain Jeff experiences is also that of incoming "wisdom" (205), of new experience, what James calls the "threatening violator or burster of our well-known series of concepts" (*P* 195). Every unfamiliar impression tears a bit at the fabric of the mind.

Jeff's periods of suffering are followed by healing and reflection. In these periods he assimilates new knowledge. "Now Jeff was strong inside him. Now with all the pain there was peace in him. . . . Now Jeff Campbell had real wisdom in him, and it did not make him bitter when it hurt him, for Jeff knew now all through him that he was really strong to bear it" (204–5). Finally, his new insights contribute to his instrumental goals as a doctor: "Jeff always had strong in him the meaning of all the new kind of beauty Melanctha Herbert once had shown him, and always more and more it helped him with his working for himself and for all the colored people" (207). He returns to "regular" living (193) in the realm of convention and practical interests, but with a formulation of the world enriched by contact with direct experience.

This, for James, is the pattern of all learning, the end toward which the tension in every mind between "the conservative and the progressive factors" draws (*P* 195). Jeff is a model of mental growth, conceived in Jamesian terms. His encounter with Melanctha, far from "destroy[ing] his life,"[1] preserves him from intellectual death by forcing a fusion between competing tendencies in his own mind.

Jeff as Stein's Self-Portrait

One way to bring out William James's importance for Stein is to place Jeff, her purest Jamesian creation, against his prototypes in her earlier writings. In Jeff, Stein was able to envision a character who resolved and benefited from internal struggle. For her earlier characters, however, self-division had assured impotence. These characters were paralyzed by the tension between promiscuous and conservative impulses. In the portrait of Jeff Campbell, Stein reconceived this self-division in positive terms, terms that had been suggested to her a decade before by James.

1. Rosalind S. Miller, *Gertrude Stein: Form and Intelligibility* (New York: Exposition Press, 1949), p. 31.

Her very early, painfully divided characters are often versions of herself, and they suggest why James's ideas might have appealed to her in the first place. Stein's attraction to James in college had much to do with his giving her a language to apply to conflicts she perceived in herself. Her obliquely autobiographical college essays, known now as the "Radcliffe Themes," shed light on her emotional life during the period in which she encountered James.[2] These pieces dwell on the figure of a young woman in whom a strongly sensual nature competes with a need for self-mastery.

"In the Red Deeps," for example, is a self-portrait of a girl frightened by her own sadomasochistic fantasy life. She recalls a period during childhood when she experimented with various sorts of self-inflicted pain and fantasized about tortures she might devise for others. But she has an attack of conscience, characterized by a "haunting fear of loss of self-control" (108). The sexual component of the forbidden impulses is underscored by the title, borrowed from the chapter in *The Mill on the Floss* about romantic secrecy and guilt.

"The Temptation" again sets illicit pleasures against self-reproach. The heroine, an indistinct surrogate for Stein, is in church one day when a strange man leans heavily against her. She enjoys the "sensuous impressions," but again has a "quick revulsion," and asks herself, "Have you no sense of shame?" Yet still "she did not move." The conflict leaves her immobilized; she vaguely indulges herself, but only passively (154–55). Later her lapse stigmatizes her; her companions, who have seen everything, upbraid her, and she becomes "one apart" (151).

When the characters Stein writes about in these college compositions are not oppressed by conscious fears of impropriety, they have vague inhibitions that are no less paralyzing. Stein writes a theme about a boy who is both frightened and interested when a pretty girl asks him to help her across a brook. Once again, "he . . . could not move" (146). Finally he accommodates her, only to flee in alarm. These characters never pass beyond the faintest stimulation; they prefer loneliness to the risk of losing control.

Although none of the characters in these early pieces is a lesbian, Stein's emerging sexual orientation must have exacerbated her sense of being "one apart," or (as a kind of self-punishing translation) secretly too sexual. Whether or not she yet defined herself as a lesbian, the pressures she was feeling, in some preliminary way, were those of the closet. Her characters in these essays do not dare to let anyone in on their sexual feelings. Stein's own romantic experience in college was limited to a mildly flirtatious friendship with her

---

2. The "Radcliffe Themes," written for a composition course in Stein's junior year, are anthologized in Miller. Hereafter they are cited in the text. I use "The Temptation" to refer both to the piece of that name and to its earlier, untitled version.

psychology teammate Leon Solomons—a friendship that, as she recalled in a later notebook, was "Platonic because neither care [*sic*] to do more."[3] The relationship was close and pleasant, but to the extent that it bordered on flirtation it ironically made her feel asexual and freakish.[4] In the meantime, as her college compositions intimate, she experienced intense longings and loneliness.

Stein's preoccupation during her late teens with conflicts such as those in the "Themes" helps to account for her interest in James's psychology, and explains why of all her professors she singled James out for a sort of hero-worship.[5] James too sees a duality in human nature, one that traps a person between eagerness and self-control. But in his view, the self-division signifies not deviance but mental health. Every mind, by his account, has a promiscuous and a repressive element. In normal perceptual life, part of us is welcoming and indiscriminate, but another part excludes data from awareness. These are the two impulses that Stein later plays against each other in Jeff Campbell.

James's theories doubtless helped to alleviate Stein's guilt about what seemed threatening appetites and, at the same time, suggested a means of forgiving herself her inhibitions. The mind James describes naturally has its thirsty or revolutionary dimension, a menace but also a source of life: we would stagnate if we lost the taste for raw sensation. Stein evidently welcomed the parallel. The unruly libidos of the Radcliffe heroines are refigured in "Melanctha" as a form of perceptual openness: Melanctha Herbert is at once sexually and perceptually promiscuous, and she helps Jeff by introducing him to "excitements" both romantic and more broadly experiential. Stein later validates her inhibitions too, by associating them with selective attention. Jeff is romantically cautious and also incapable of focusing his senses on "new things"; these qualities make him attractive to the heroine of the story. Indeed, the very struggle between yielding and self-control that immobilizes the characters of the "Radcliffe Themes" comes, with an infusion of James's psychology, to seem a creative part of consciousness.

One way to think of Jeff is as Stein's self-idealization through the filter of James. He is, after all, a version of Adele in *Q.E.D.*, who herself was a virtually unaltered Stein. But he is a transformed Adele,

---

3. P. 17 of notebook 11 in the *Making of Americans* notebooks, Gertrude Stein Collection, Yale Collection of American Literature (hereafter YCAL). Hereafter references to these notebooks will appear as *NB*, followed by the number or letter of the notebook in question, and (for convenience) the page number in Leon Katz's useful transcription of the notebooks. For example, *NB* A.12. In rare instances in which a notebook transcribed by Katz was unavailable in the original, I have relied on Katz's transcription.

4. See Bridgman's discussion (p. 29) of Stein's composition "A Modern Sonnet to His Mistress's Eyebrows," which he sees as hinting at "the idea of an amorous attachment" but also as joking about the idea.

5. See "Radcliffe Themes," p. 146.

robust and successful. Adele, incidentally—or Stein, in the intermediate phase of Q.E.D.—had fallen in love but still experienced all
the internal pressures of her earlier personae in the "Radcliffe
Themes." Like the Radcliffe heroines, Adele-Stein is torn between
her sexual curiosity and her inhibitions; the tension freezes her, making her an "unresponsive" lover (66). Ideologically, too, Adele feels
caught, as her author did, between the lesbianism that marks her as
"queer" and a bourgeois ideology that makes her wish to "avoid
excitements" and become "the mother of children."[6]

But in Jeff Campbell, Stein transforms the tension in herself
between sexual needs and conservative values into a source of
strength. Jeff's competing impulses make him a more sensitive person and a better doctor. His one excursion into forbidden "excitements" only helps him to know himself better and to do more for
others. James's ideas helped Stein to create an idealized self, conceived in terms of psychic vigor.

On the other hand, "Melanctha" also contains an image of failure
to thrive. The heroine of the story does not fare so well as her lover.
She never achieves mental balance, and she dies. In portraying
Melanctha, Stein slips outside the Jamesian framework and the self-
idealization attached to it.

Melanctha and the Wisdom of the Body

Melanctha herself, by William James's standards, is weak. One way
to account for her presence—were we to remain within the limits of
the Jamesian paradigm—would be to see her as an example of the
high costs, in Darwinian terms, of mind-wandering. Melanctha is
not ultimately changed by her affair with Jeff. Whereas he assimilates the new mode of perception Melanctha has given him, she fails
to be impressed by his "solidity," his conceptual grip on the world.
She tries to adapt to him for a time, but ends by reverting to her
former "excited," "reckless," wandering ways (219, 208).

Rose Johnson, who might have served as a replacement, then
rejects her, and the desertion "almost killed her" (233). This might
seem an extreme reaction, but in Rose, Melanctha has lost her last
point of contact with the "solid safety" of the conservative temperament (210, 233). "Melanctha needed Rose always to let her cling
to her. . . . Rose always was so simple, solid, decent, for her. And
now Rose had cast her from her. Melanctha was lost, and all the
world went whirling in a mad weary dance around her" (233).
Melanctha is "lost":as James said, without mental conservatism, "we
should be intellectually lost in the midst of the world" (P 103).

6. Q.E.D., in Fernhurst, pp. 77, 56, 59. I take the word "queer," applied to Adele, to refer to
   her lesbianism.

Melanctha loses touch with the "solid" tendency, and "all the world went whirling in a mad weary dance around her." This is a fair description of what would happen to a mind severed from all perceptual habit and banished to the flux of unfamiliar sensation. Melanctha virtually drowns in the continuum of the world.

Her physiological death, some paragraphs later, seems to follow as a matter of course. Critics have seen in the stories of *Three Lives*, each of which ends with a heroine's death, shades of naturalism. This reading assumes a special force in light of the Jamesian or Darwinian psychological drama of "Melanctha." In Stein's heroine one observes a character unfit for the world who is weeded out by a brand of natural selection. In James's psychology the person who has no mechanism of selective attention is ill suited for the business of self-preservation. The survival of the fittest militates against those "exuberant non-egoistic" individuals who, careless of their own personal safety, diffuse their attention equally over experience. But Melanctha has persisted in wandering on the perilous "edge of wisdom" (101), suppressing personal interests in the name of "excitement." In the end, "tired with being all the time so much excited" (161), she succumbs to the social and bodily suicide that, as James makes plain, would be the outcome of any life of wholly unselfish or unselective perception (P 60–61).

The case of Melanctha, if one reads it, then, in the light of James, is an admonition. Yet Melanctha's failure by James's standards could lead one as easily to question James's values as to take a critical view of the heroine. I have sketched a reading of Melanctha's story as a negative example, but it could just as well be thought of as a protest against the entire notion of mental success represented by Jeff. For in the moral universe of "Melanctha," self-preservation is not clearly the highest good. Part of the story pulls away from the psychological framework supplied by William James and from the Darwinian gospel of success attached to it.

"Melanctha" is Stein's most deeply Jamesian text, but it comes belatedly, at a point when its author is just beginning to strain against James. Within a few years her notebooks show her explicitly defining herself against him. In "Melanctha," her early ambivalence creates a kind of ethical polyphony. The story hovers somewhere between the ideas and views Stein shared with James and quite different, still indistinct values that would soon propel her in new directions.

James's psychology is shot through with Darwinism; the important thing, in his view, is to thrive. Stein's attachment to this perspective is evident in her sympathetic portrait of Jeff Campbell, the good doctor who does his work and moves ahead professionally. But Melanctha, who has no instinct for survival, is of course portrayed at least as sympathetically herself. She receives a much more positive treatment than her antecedent in *Q.E.D.*, the thoughtless seducer Helen. In the move from *Q.E.D.* to "Melanctha," the moral center of the story has shifted toward the promiscuous member of the couple, whose model was not Stein herself but her former lover May Bookstaver.

Melanctha, far from being merely an object of pitying diagnosis, has qualities that elevate her above a mere survivor like Rose. Her imperfect instinct for self-preservation is the cost of her superior "wisdom," which the story sets against instrumental knowledge as embodied by Jeff and as preached by James. Against the background of James's theories, the word *wisdom* in "Melanctha" can be thought of as referring to the heroine's reckless immersion in the senses, but the word has a spiritual resonance as well. Jeff seems to be pointing to a mysterious power in Melanctha when he speaks of a "new feeling" she has given him, "just like a new religion to me" (158). The world she opens up for him is a world of "real being" (149). This spiritual quality of hers is never explained, but it pushes her beyond the ethical boundaries defined by James's *Psychology* and, for that matter, by James's own more spiritually oriented writings.[7] Part of Stein's story is about a "way to know" that has no bearing on practical life but is more elevated than mere sensory abundance.

At the risk of trying to define precisely something the text leaves vague and suggestive, I want to approach Melanctha's wisdom by setting it alongside some other details in her story, which seem to have nothing to do with the framework of Jamesian psychology. Stein's heroine has a special intimacy with the mysteries of the body. Melanctha is close to the upheavals of birth, death, and puberty. She watches over her dying mother; this seems to be the most important thing she has ever done for or with her mother. She tends Rose Johnson as Rose gives birth, acting as a sort of midwife, even to the extent of moving Rose away from her husband for the last part of the pregnancy. ("When Rose had become strong again [after the delivery and the baby's death] she went back to her house with Sam" [225]). Melanctha's story is bounded by her own puberty, the time in her twelfth year when she is "just beginning as a woman" (91), and by her death.

These details—the death of the mother, the birth of the baby, Melanctha's puberty, and her death—were superimposed on the original plot of *Q.E.D.*, and they signal changes in Stein's thinking. The details involving birth and death—which, along with the setting in the black community, were inspired by Stein's clinical experiences

---

7. James does not associate spirituality with sexuality. See, for example, "A Suggestion about Mysticism" and "A Pluralistic Mystic," in *Essays in Philosophy*, in *Works of William James*, ed. Frederick Burkhardt, Fredson Bowers, and Ignas Skrupskelis (Cambridge: Harvard University Press, 1978).

at Johns Hopkins Medical School[8]—bear no obvious relation to the primary story of the romance with Jeff Campbell, and they give the narrative of "Melanctha" a wandering quality. Although they are never digested into the main plot, the narrative pulls back to these events, often out of sequence. The story begins, for example, not where one would expect it to begin but with the delivery of Rose's baby, which, we will later find out, actually *follows* the entire love affair of Melanctha and Jeff: "Rose Johnson made it very hard to bring her baby to its birth. Melanctha Herbert who was Rose Johnson's friend, did everything that any woman could" (85). I associate Melanctha's hazily defined wisdom with her quality of presiding at moments of bodily change or upheaval. The text makes no such connection explicitly, but these fragmentary data embedded in "Melanctha" will begin to form a more cohesive picture in Stein's later work.

Within a few years Stein will depart from James altogether by grounding her idea of consciousness in what might be called the rhythms of the body. She will develop a notion of wisdom as a kind of thought that knows its ties to the body. As her spirituality comes to the surface, an emphasis on bodily experience, as sacred and taboo, marks the difference from James's own brand of spirituality. To quote from the dense text of *Tender Buttons*, the most extraordinary thing Stein wrote in the teens, "*out of an eye* comes research" (11, emphasis added); knowledge emanates *from* the eye, like tears. Or (to use a more opaque passage) spiritual knowing or "in-sight" is continuous with anatomical functions like giving milk or sucking: "MILK. Climb up in sight climb in the whole utter" (47). *Tender Buttons* stages bodily upheavals great and small, from eating to giving birth and dying. An early hint of these preoccupations appears in the liminal Melanctha, stationed at the crises of the body.

Significantly, William James's psychology would not account in an interesting way for Melanctha's intimacy with the body. Compared to a near contemporary like Freud, James seems to keep the body out of focus, except in its role as a machine absorbing data and maintaining itself in existence. Nor would Melanctha's sexuality be something James would illuminate. Melanctha's involvements in birth, death, and sensual experience give her a kind of wisdom distinct from James's instrumental knowledge. To describe the notion of bodily consciousness that develops in Stein's subsequent work, it will be necessary to use a vocabulary closer to psychoanalysis than to the theories of James.

Stein's notebooks and subsequent works suggest to me that in her characterization of the embodied Melanctha, she was depicting something she saw in herself, for all her simultaneous identification

8. See *The Autobiography of Alice B. Toklas*, p. 100.

with (and self-projection in) the more controlled and rational Jeff Campbell. In one of the notebooks for *The Making of Americans*, Stein identified a side of herself she called "the Rabelaisian, nigger abandonment, Vollard [the art dealer], daddy side" (*NB* DB.47). That she associates her bodily gusto, or everything Rabelaisian in herself, with something she calls "nigger abandonment" suggests that the extreme racism she expresses in "Melanctha"—for example, in depicting blacks as carefree and promiscuous—served (among other things) her own need to distance a part of herself about which she was ambivalent. She had her own sensuous side, which she projected in racial terms perhaps so she could simultaneously idealize and depreciate it; and by playing to the racism of her audience, she partially disguised the dimension of self-exploration in the story.

The Style of "Melanctha": Stein's Resistance to James

The various themes that point away from James are disconnected and half-hidden; one might hardly notice them if it were not for their intimations of the direction Stein's work was soon to take. But the formal techniques of the story are a step ahead of its themes. Here a tension with James's thinking becomes obvious.

Stein divides her manner of narration between two "ways of knowing." One is linear and progressive; the other is circular and rhythmic, and has something in common with the wandering quality of Melanctha's mind. Although in its overt ethics, "Melanctha" does not decide between Jeff's and Melanctha's forms of knowledge, structurally the story succumbs to wandering. The experimental style signals a departure from the values Stein had learned from James, which her story still enshrined (thematically) in the portrait of Jeff Campbell.

Like the other stories of *Three Lives*, "Melanctha" has an obtuse narrator, one who cannot quite get a grasp on the material. The narrator seems to wish to point the story in particular directions, but keeps losing the thread. The character Jeff Campbell is instrumentally oriented; because he has practical interests, he knows where to focus his attention, knows what he wants. To the extent that it makes sense to compare a narrator's and a character's ways of thinking, the narrator of the story, by contrast, lacks a guiding conception of what he or she wants. William James would not approve of such a person or of such a way of putting a narrative together.

An "instrumental" narrator—to sustain for a moment this somewhat artificial analogy—would have pronounced emphases and an ability to tell how particular details bore on the story as a whole. Of course, all stories slip past their tellers in one way or another, but a story may be narrated in a more or less single-minded way. Stein's narrator fails to build up a theme. Periodically, he or she seems to try to form the narrative as an answer to a single question: why did Melanctha fail in life? "Why was this unmoral, promiscuous, shiftless Rose married, and that's not so common either, to a good man of the negroes, while Melanctha with her white blood and attraction and her desire for a right position had not yet been really married" (86). Yet the question, although repeated in various forms, never receives an answer. The narrator gives the impression of being accustomed to generalizing, often (as here) on the basis of racist stereotypes, but of becoming unhinged by the case of Melanctha: "But why did the subtle, intelligent, attractive, half white girl Melanctha Herbert, with her sweetness and her power and her wisdom, demean herself to do for and to flatter and to be scolded, by this lazy, stupid, ordinary, selfish black girl. This was a queer thing in Melanctha Herbert" (200).

Each time, the question why Melanctha's life has the shape it does is no sooner asked than it becomes diffused, for among other things, the heroine eludes the racist formulas through which the narrator tries to make sense of her case. The narration, as it actually evolves, lacks linear causality—an absence that Marianne DeKoven associates with a form of literary impressionism.[9] The narrative structure depends neither on an internal logic directed at accounting for Melanctha nor, in the absence of this, on the simple sequence of events in fictional time. For it begins almost at its chronological end, with the birth of Rose's baby, then slips all the way back to Melanctha's twelfth year. From there it makes its way up to her affair with Jeff Campbell, whereupon the focus unaccountably intensifies. No attempt is made to suggest what relation this material bears to the rest of Melanctha's life.

The narrator's formal sense is rather like that of the heroine, who "did not know how to tell a story wholly" (100). In fact, the lack of linearity becomes most pronounced in the portions of the narrative devoted exclusively to Melanctha. It is as if the mind-wandering heroine caused wandering disturbances in the way her own story is told. Jeff's story, considered in isolation, not only focuses on an instance of mental progress but also has itself a progressive form. In his case, the facts do appear in their proper temporal sequence. By the end, moreover, we can give a fair account of what his experiences have meant: we know that his affair has hurt him but has deepened him personally and professionally. Only Melanctha's experience comes to us in a confused order, and fails to build toward a conclusion. It ends with a nonconclusion; surprisingly, she gets sick, seems to get

9. See DeKoven, pp. 32–33. See also DeKoven's insightful discussion (pp. 30–32) of the obtuse narrative voice of *Three Lives*. (See pp. 326–28.)

better, and dies. William James would have a terminology to apply to this confusion, but as a moral matter he would have no patience with a story that succumbed to this kind of shapelessness.

Another form of wandering that Stein's narrator shares with the heroine is a reluctance or inability to tag some data as more important than others—a collapse of emphasis. The earlier version of "Melanctha," *Q.E.D.*, moved firmly and easily to its crises. By comparison, all the stories of *Three Lives* curiously fail to advance or to build to a pitch. The dramatic outlines are flattened. The obtuse narrators resist (or are incapable of) theatrical moments, beginnings, and summations, failing to take proper hold even of genuine crises. The deaths of the heroines are reduced to casual data: "They sent [Melanctha] where she would be taken care of, a home for poor consumptives, and there Melanctha stayed until she died" (236). "While [the baby] was coming, Lena had grown very pale and sicker. When it was all over Lena had died, too, and nobody knew just how it had happened to her" (279).

A parallel absence of emphasis *within* sentences in "Melanctha" often creates a look of confusion. The narrator has, for example, three or four strong impressions of Rose Johnson, which have nothing in particular to do with one another. Rose is good-looking; she is dark-skinned; she is moody; she is selfish. Rather than subordinate any one of these thoughts to another, the narrator lists them all together: "Rose Johnson was a real black, tall, well built, sullen, stupid, childlike, good looking negress" (85).

Both the absence of linearity and the lack of emphasis are part of what a genuine Jamesian disciple would denounce as a failure of selective attention. The narrators of *Three Lives* lack clear "interests" that would keep them on a single track. Yet, as we already know, James does make a place for aimlessness. He suggests the importance of relaxing one's emphases from time to time; in this respect it is possible to see a continuity between his ideas and Stein's characterization of the reckless Melanctha. For this reason too one *might* think of the unfocused style and structure of "Melanctha" as continuous with Stein's early interest in *The Principles of Psychology*.

Such a view would run as follows. James claims that we coarsen experience by our emphases and designs; each act of selection has its cost in lost perceptual abundance. Stein, in embracing aimlessness, undoes selective attention; she makes a copious record of existence without exalting special objects to dominance. She gives a sense of the quality our perceptions have before we limit and rearrange them to suit our customary interests.

Although the stories of *Three Lives* are not so indiscriminate in focus as to constitute what we would now call stream-of-consciousness narratives, they do approach what James himself meant by the term he coined. James's chapter on "The Stream of Thought" (retitled "The Stream of Consciousness" for the abridged *Psychology*) is a reply to associationist psychology, which pictured sensations and ideas as discrete links in a chain. James claims that it is artificial to think of consciousness as atomized; our psychic life looks like a clean succession of thoughts only when we limit our account of it to those mental states that we inwardly name and fix our attention on. Between these sharp focuses, there is a "free water of consciousness," an indistinct mass of associations and connections that occupies us between one halting place and the next and suffuses even our clearest perceptions (*P* 32). We notice these in disinterested moments, when selective attention is relaxed. Consciousness "is nothing jointed; it flows" (*P* 26). Each thought casts ripples before and after, and we always have at least a "dawning sense of whither it is to lead" (*P* 33).

These ideas, then, might with some justice be viewed as containing a prophecy of Gertrude Stein's style. If Stein seems to let her focus wander, it is because she has no thought of moving forward as if life fell in segments. She strains against habits of attention that select and divide, and (by her own later account) against literary habits that parcel experience into "a beginning and a middle and an end."[1] I mean to say something more precise than that Stein's style resonates with James in the same way that all experimental modern narrative does. The special sense of "stream of consciousness" is retained here; the repetitive style of "Melanctha" replaces the expected peaks or halting places with a continuous flow of fading and beckoning—or overlapping—thoughts.

In *Q.E.D.* ideas were expressed singly: " 'You are wrong, you are hideously wrong!' Adele burst out furiously."[2] "Melanctha" shows how a thought like this can dissolve into a succession of thoughts, each suffused with echoes from the last: " 'Oh Jeff dear,' said Melanctha, *I sure was wrong* to act so to you. *It's awful hard* for me ever to say it to you, *I have been wrong* in my acting to you, but I certainly was bad this time Jeff to you. *It do certainly come hard to me* to say it Jeff, but *I certainly was wrong* to go away from you the way I did it' " (202, emphases added). In spite of the repetitive content, no two of these phrases are identical. As in all the repetitive paragraphs of *Three Lives*, each pulse of thinking brings a configuration not quite the image of what preceded it. For as James notes, when one dips into the stream of mental life one finds perpetual difference. Habitually we think of a particular object or sensation as identical each time we encounter it; the task of attention is to recognize. But a liberated or innocent eye sees that the mass of periph-

1. Stein, *The Geographical History of America* (New York: Random House, 1936), p. 218.
2. *Q.E.D.*, in *Fernhurst*, p. 131.

eral thoughts endlessly changes, conspiring with an unstable context to produce a different constellation of experience each time an object is encountered. "When the identical fact recurs, we *must* think of it in a fresh manner, see it under a somewhat different angle, apprehend it in different relations from those in which it last appeared" (*P* 23).For Stein to allow herself *exact* repetition would be to falsify the small mutations of consciousness.

Others have speculated in similar ways about possible connections between Stein's technique and James's idea of the stream of consciousness.[3] Yet—to return to my larger point—whatever Stein's style might owe to James, she deviates from his values. It is a mistake to think of James's thoughts on the stream of consciousness as offering an implicit model for a diffuse or wandering literary style. That is to confuse his descriptive and his prescriptive aims.

James's chapter on the stream of thought is meant to describe an overlooked dimension of mental experience, not to champion it; he urges a theoretical attention to the fluid periphery of consciousness, not immersion in it at the expense of one's rational grip on things. The last thing he would recommend (in a text or in life) would be to suspend habits of conception in favor of the flux of momentary impressions. No writer who had read the *Psychology* with unmixed sympathy would be led by it to a style like Stein's. In James's scheme of things, wandering is the meanest possible use of the mind. It is a species of rest—something that occupies us between one focus and the next, or overcomes us in moments of fatigue. Whoever declines to rise from it is the moral equivalent of an infant or a brute. From the vantage point of James's psychology, Melanctha's mind is deficient because it does nothing but drift.

James himself, significantly, was repelled by "wandering" literature, as we know from his letters and elsewhere. "Literature," he writes, "has no character when full of slack and wandering and superfluity. Neither does life. *Character* everywhere demands the stern and sacrificial mood as one of its factors. *The price must be paid.*"[4] The crises and essential moments of consciousness fall precisely where aimlessness terminates and attention finds its object. These are the instants that produce all action. "Attention and effort" are indeed "two names for the same psychic fact" (*P* 16). Nor is there any value in a life that never finds its focus in volition and action—in the "manly concrete deed" (*P* 15). James's ethics is opposed to an art that never seems to announce its point. Thus, if we think of Stein's style as affected by her exposure to his theories, we must

3. See, for example, Hoffman, "Gertrude Stein and William James," pp. 226–33; Sutherland, pp. 6–8; and Bridgman, p. 102.
4. William James, "Is Life Worth Living?" Quoted in Ralph Barton Perry, *The Thought and Character of William James*, 2 vols. (Boston: Little, Brown, 1935), 2:271.

recognize that she has altered the focus by emphasizing a part of consciousness that he views as secondary and, when exercised exclusively, debased.

This gap is part of a tension between James's Victorianism and Stein's modernism. Our association of the idea of the stream of consciousness both with James's psychology and with techniques of modern fiction might contribute to a mistaken image of him as a sort of prophet of modernism. But James as the advocate of the "manly deed" is closer to Carlyle and Emerson, whom he revered, than to most of the artists we associate with modernism. James stands after all between two periods; aesthetically, therefore, he may present the appearance of either a strategist for the modernism Stein embodies or a member of the very generation she was distancing herself from when she wrote that she spent her life escaping from the nineteenth century.

He was both: Stein used James to hurtle herself into a modernist practice that was more modern than James. As an instance of this paradox, James's psychology indirectly contributed to a breakdown of moral contours in Stein's fiction. We saw that in the process of assimilating James, Stein found a way beyond the paralyzing self-scrutiny of the "Radcliffe Themes." In those compositions, and in Q.E.D., she struggled tediously with her own moralism, unable to write about her sexual yearnings without revulsion. Her first work using James's thought, on the other hand, shifts the focus to less charged perceptual themes, freeing her to consider various types of experience without so much displaced self-reproach. In *Three Lives,* Mrs. Lehntman and Melanctha Herbert are sexual wanderers, but their lack of self-restraint largely escapes judgment because it is a symptom of their indiscriminate attention.

The paradox is that James himself was an unembarrassed moralist, who would not have approved of being used in this way. Stein applied his ideas in a skewed form, with the effect of making her work relativistic, far more relativistic than James.

The collapse of ethical definition, one result of her use of James, of course contributes to the modern quality of *Three Lives*. "Melanctha," unlike the earlier Q.E.D., is unmistakably a product of the twentieth century, in no small measure because of the dim-sighted, innocent narrator who fails to bring things to an ethical focus. Q.E.D. written before Stein's Jamesian period (though after her studies with him), has a strident ethics: it is about lapses from innocence and problems of conduct. Even its title promises some sort of proof or absolute certainty. *Three Lives* (with its non-judgmental, descriptive title) offers us conformists and troublemakers but does not finally decide that one form of existence is finer than another.

It would not be too paradoxical to say that Stein, the moment she began to use James for her art, became more purely psychological than he. James's account of experience never isolates issues of perception from ethical questions. Even in the largely descriptive *Psychology,* he does not hesitate to advance certain values. His popular chapter "Habit," for example, is vocally prescriptive. It offers this sort of "practical maxim": *"Keep the faculty of effort alive in you by a little gratuitous exercise every day. That is, be systematically ascetic or heroic in little unnecessary points" (P* 16).

Not surprisingly, James's own tastes in literature favored works with implicit moral applications.[5] It is understandable (if ironic, for all the same reasons) that when Stein sent him a copy of *Three Lives,* in certain respects her purest Jamesian narrative, he lost interest after forty pages or so.[6] Stein's ethical blankness is the result of careful experimentation. The "Radcliffe Themes," her earliest preserved pieces, had been charged with ideals—among them, James's ideals of effort and heroism. A brief tribute to James himself captures her characteristic tone in these college years: "Is life worth living? Yes, a thousand times yes when the world still holds such spirits as Prof. James. . . . He stands firmly, nobly for the dignity of man. His faith is . . . that . . . of a strong man willing to fight, to suffer and endure" (146).

This is Gertrude Stein in a vein unfamiliar to most of us. She is trying out, at this point, whatever postures come to hand. *Three Lives* is the first sign of dislocation; here, moral absolutes give way to the more impartial norms of psychology, and Stein abandons questions of virtue and vice to ask whether a character is interesting or perceptually alive. Hence, she shifts the sympathetic center of the story from the scrupulous Adele of *Q.E.D.* (who becomes Jeff Campbell) toward the less moralistic, and more exciting, Melanctha Herbert.

The style and structure of "Melanctha," then, record a troubled debt to James. James uses the term *mind-wandering* to disparage a relaxed attention. Stein's story, on the other hand, is an unabashed experiment in a kind of mind-wandering; it unsettles expectations of linearity, dramatic emphasis, and moral definition.

Unconscious Pressures on the Narrative

What I want finally to suggest is that "Melanctha," in spite of its lack of linearity, does have a wholeness that transcends the term *mind-wandering.* The story coheres, in ways that demand another sort of vocabulary than James's. Although it seems aimless from one perspective, the story in its way is motivated—not by what James would

5. See Perry, *Thought and Character* 2:259–60.
6. Gallup, p. 50. James warmly acknowledges receipt of *Three Lives* but admits having put it down after a brief sitting.

call "interests" on the part of the author or narrator but by unconscious process.

"Melanctha" has a shape, which it gets not from logic or chronology, as *Q.E.D.* did, but from a tissue of associations resembling what
psychoanalysis terms primary process. I have described the narrator's
unfocused quality as a function of a relaxed attention. According to
James, a lapse of selective attention has the effect of letting *any*
impression or association enter consciousness. But though this formulation might describe Dorothy Richardson's rendition (often) of
the associative process, it does not square with Stein's "Melanctha."
Her narrator puts together events and images that are symbolically
cognate.

What secretly preoccupies the narrator of "Melanctha" is a pair of
events that keeps repeating itself: a woman fails to mother; a man
harms a woman sexually. The two events that ultimately destroy
Melanctha are her expulsion by Rose Johnson, on whom she has
depended for protection, and her sexual exploitation by Jem Richards. This sequence is anticipated by the two episodes that open the
story, similar instances of failed mothering and sexualized male
aggression. The first sentences describe Rose Johnson's unwillingness to give birth and her subsequent failure to keep her baby alive:
"Rose Johnson made it very hard to bring her baby to its birth . . .
Rose Johnson was careless and negligent and selfish, and when
Melanctha had to leave for a few days, the baby died" (85). Then the
narrator's mind digresses to Melanctha's twelfth year, when she
became the object of inappropriate attention from a coachman and
consequently of quasi-sexual violence from her father. "Now when
her father began fiercely to assail her, she did not really know what
it was that he was so furious to force from her" (95).

The opening details—the death of the baby and the sexual attentions in Melanctha's twelfth year—appear to be digressions, but they
fix a motif for the rest of the story. The narrator places these details
alongside the subsequent betrayals by Rose and Jem, but without
announcing a logical connection. Perhaps the repetitions unconsciously supply an answer to the question, why did Melanctha fail?
Women, that is, did not give her maternal protection; men (with the
important exception of Jeff) abused her. This generalization fits not
only the two opening details and the final brutalities of Rose and Jem
but also the events of Melanctha's very early life, presided over by a
weak, unprotective mother and a rough, possessive father.

But the pattern, if it exists in the back of the narrator's mind, never
coalesces into a generalization. Instead of explicitly condemning
those who repeatedly fail Melanctha, the narrator expresses a vague
pity for her that seems almost to locate the blame with her: "poor
Melanctha could only find new ways to be in trouble" (93). The only

sign of an impulse to extend blame to others is the repeated deviation of the narrator's mind from the expected chronology to characters and events that repeat the betrayal. What superficially looks like mind-wandering is a mix of obsessive reiteration and displacement.

Anger is deflected once more in the account of Melanctha's death. Again, those who should be caring for her fail to do so; the narrator, however, rather than make a charge of negligence, gives a bland juxtaposition of facts. "They sent her where she would be taken care of, a home for poor consumptives, and there Melanctha stayed until she died" (236). The sentence would be emotionally intelligible if it read, "*but* there she died." The narrator doubly muffles the death, by consigning it to an adverbial clause: "until she died."

Suppressed anger, then, is a possible cause for the narrator's associative manner. In any case, the affect that might have accompanied the account of Melanctha's ruin is displaced into a series of analogies. The telling of the story is at once eerily repetitive and superficially cold. Thus the story, though aimless compared to something like *Q.E.D.*, is shaped by an unconscious logic—a logic of displacement. If the text seems modern in its wandering style, it also seems so in its associative logic. Nineteenth-century fiction, of course, often has a dream logic, but subordinated to another logic. *Jane Eyre,* for example, is arguably itself about a series of failed or lost mothers and male aggressors, but that narrative follows not the paths of the narrator's associations but (with rare exceptions) the sequence of events in time. Although Jane Eyre as a narrator has anger she wishes to control, we do not often sense the tug of repressed feelings on the *direction* of her story. By way of contrast, "Melanctha," like much other experimental fiction of the modern period, foregrounds primary process as a shaping principle.

William James sees each person's conceptual framework as besieged by a disorganized mass of impressions and associations, not by a rival, unconscious logic. Stein's story has what we might call an irrational form, a phrase James would have considered an oxymoron. It was, of course, Freud who at just this time was giving such a phrase meaning—to the mystification, incidentally, of William James, who wrote of his younger colleague in Vienna, "I can make nothing in my own case with his dream theories, and obviously 'symbolism' is a dangerous method."[7]

Stein is not (yet) articulating an *idea* of the unconscious, but her formal experiment in "Melanctha" points away from the concept of the stream of consciousness as articulated by William James. The

7. *The Letters of William James*, ed. Henry James, 2 vols. (Boston: Atlantic Monthly Press, 1920), 2:327–28. In spite of his methodological doubts, however, James admired Freud's efforts and thought that something useful would come of them. See Perry, *Thought and Character* 2:122.

story is structured according to a principle of motivated repetition, a logic of the unconscious. Motivated repetition, as we will see, is just what will overrun and finally destroy sequential narrative in Stein's next major work, *The Making of Americans*.

The unconscious patterning of "Melanctha" owes nothing to Freud. Stein knew (or would soon know) quite a bit about Freud, but like some of her fellow modernists—I think particularly of Joyce, Woolf, and Faulkner—she made "discoveries" in fiction that suggestively paralleled Freud's theoretical discoveries without being due to them. Like these other novelists, she would come to view with ambivalent interest Freud's excavation of what seemed a similar psychic turf. Her writing, however, develops the look of unconscious process unusually early. Of the three writers I have named, only Joyce had by this time begun to do significant work, and beside Stein's story his *Dubliners*, however innovative in its symbolism and its forms of indirection, looks conventionally linear.

What was happening intellectually to Stein to stimulate or assist in the formal experiments of "Melanctha"? I think her shift toward something like primary process was—oddly—a secondary consequence of her involvement with modern art. The innovations of "Melanctha" reflect the intellectual atmosphere of Stein's first years amid the Parisian avant-garde. She had expatriated in 1903 and was living with her brother Leo, who himself was deeply involved in the business of "expounding L'Art Moderne."[8] A point that emerges clearly from the excellent and abundant scholarship on Stein's relationship to postimpressionist and cubist art is the importance of Cézanne to her first literary experiments.[9] Stein herself said in a famous interview that Cézanne (whose portrait of his wife she continually scrutinized while working on *Three Lives*) gave her a "new feeling about composition," for he did not subordinate the elements on his canvas to a "central idea." Instead, she said, he "conceived the idea that in composition one thing was as important as another thing. Each part is as important as the whole, and that impressed me enormously."[1]

We have seen a kind of prose transliteration of this dispersal of emphasis in the wandering style of "Melanctha"—the story to which Stein herself pointed as exemplifying the strategies she had evolved under Cézanne's influence.[2] So what art historians call Cézanne's

8. Letter of Leo Stein to Mabel Weeks, quoted in James R. Mellow, *Charmed Circle: Gertrude Stein and Company* (New York: Avon, 1974), p. 84.
9. See Marjorie Perloff, "Poetry as Word-System: The Art of Gertrude Stein," in *The Poetics of Indeterminacy* (Princeton: Princeton University Press, 1981), p. 91; Walker, esp. pp. 1–13.
1. Robert Bartlett Haas, "Gertrude Stein Talking: A Transatlantic Interview," in Haas, ed., *A Primer*, p. 15.
2. Ibid.

"flatness"[3] furnishes not only an analogue but also an important inspiration for the kinds of stylistic flatness to be observed in "Melanctha."

Something else comes out in Stein's story: a kind of motivated repetition suggestive of veiled and displaced preoccupations. This second innovation is original to Stein; nothing in her artistic or literary environment prepares us for it. How did it evolve? As Stein, under the stimulus of Cézanne, began to develop a wandering style, the relaxation of emphasis freed up material from her own unconscious. The repetitive brooding that goes on in the margins of her story is her own brooding.

My reason for suggesting as much is that the pair of events that covertly structures her story (failed mothering and male sexual bullying) will recur in her subsequent work and then will resolve itself in various directions. In *The Making of Americans,* Stein revives the disappointing parents of "Melanctha," this time (as we will see) consciously making them portraits of her own mother and father. But there she comes to terms with the figure of her father, unleashing her now explicit rage and at the same time stealing back some good things from him. In *G.M.P.* and *Tender Buttons,* she goes on to revise and redeem the figure of the weak and remote mother.

I am saying that these texts performed psychological work, of a sort not unlike that which Virginia Woolf said *To the Lighthouse* performed for her.[4] "Melanctha" contains the faintest beginning of that work, as Stein raises parental specters to give them a preliminary inspection. But her anger and disappointment are still expressing themselves in various displacements.

The Feminism of "Melanctha"

I have been describing the narrative of "Melanctha" as driven by an unconscious logic; the narrator, instead of directly reacting to Melanctha's betrayal, displaces anger by multiplying scenes of violation without affect. A different reading might view the anger of the story as feminist anger, which is not so much repressed as camouflaged. The suppression of affect could be rhetorical rather than pathological, reflecting ideological rather than emotional conflict. The repetitive content may enable the narrator—or the author—to make some points about a woman's victimization without risking a straightforward polemic.

Marianne DeKoven has posited that the stories of *Three Lives* mask their own "powerful feminist morals."[5] This seems to me a

3. See Richard Shiff, "Seeing Cézanne," *Critical Inquiry* 4 (1978): 781.
4. See Virginia Woolf, *A Writer's Diary,* ed. Leonard Woolf (London: Hogarth Press, 1969), pp. 101–2, 136.
5. DeKoven, p. 32. (See p. 327.)

plausible and very suggestive idea, particularly since Stein in an earlier phase of her life had openly entertained feminist ideas, which
seem to have gone underground during or after her time in medical
school.[6] I have been considering scenes of maternal failure and sexual violation at the margins of the love plot. Structurally, these
scenes have the effect of undermining linear narrative. Their content—to consider it for a moment in isolation—is potentially feminist, in the sense of highlighting the situations of exploited or
overlooked women. This content alone might account for the placement of this material at the margins.

In the context of James's psychology, Melanctha seems a defective
member of the species, who never develops the practical interests
that would save her. The story also gives a competing picture of her
as the embodiment of a superior, disinterested wisdom. But a third
possible view of her is neither as a failure nor as a wise woman but
as a victim. The acts of violation that fill the background of the love
plot are violations to which women, in the universe of "Melanctha,"
are peculiarly vulnerable.

Melanctha does not find an adequate mother; Rose, the hoped-
for protector, repeats the rejecting behavior of Melanctha's own
mother, who had "never cared much for this daughter" (110). Men
for their part—Jem Richards and Melanctha's father—treat her with
a sexualized brutality. This pattern can be reconceived as follows:
the women about Melanctha are too weak or uncaring to protect her
from the damaging advances of men. If Rose had provided shelter
and comfort, Melanctha would have avoided the ruinous affair with
Jem. Again, if Melanctha's mother had been loving and attentive,
she would have served as a buffer against the "unendurable" father
who, about the time of the girl's puberty, begins to hover about her
threateningly (90, 97). The father actually uses the mother's indifference to justify his own invasiveness: "A nice way she is going for
a decent daughter. Why don't you see to that girl better you, ain't
you her mother!" (94). His interest in his daughter, which flourishes
just as she reaches puberty, seems incestuous; there is a disturbing
vagueness in Rose's statement that Melanctha's father has done
"some things so awful to her, she don't never want to tell nobody
how bad he hurt her" (214). Her mother does nothing to protect
Melanctha from his attacks.

One could see Melanctha's subsequent victimizations as issuing

6. During her first year in medical school, Stein gave a speech, "The Value of College Education for Women," modeled closely on ideas in Charlotte Perkins Gilman's *Women and
Economics.* There is a copy of the speech in YCAL. But Elyse Blankley has shown that
Stein did not ally herself wholeheartedly with women's causes. See "Beyond the 'Talent
of Knowing': Gertrude Stein and the New Woman," in Michael J. Hoffman, ed., *Critical
Essays on Gertrude Stein* (Boston: G. K. Hall, 1986), pp. 196–209. Catharine Stimpson
discusses Stein's use of Gilman's ideas, in "The Mind, the Body, and Gertrude Stein,"
Critical Inquiry 3 (1977): 490.

from her own pathology, for she chooses friends and lovers who reproduce her parents' damaging behavior. Rose Johnson is so patently self-centered that Melanctha is foolish to "cling to her" (233); Jem Richards is a bad choice too, for he makes no pretense of being anything but "fast" and mean (230). Melanctha seems masochistically to seek situations that recreate her early pain. At least once, in Jeff Campbell, she meets a kind man who is nothing like her father and who even has a warmly maternal side; he addresses her protectively as a "poor little girl," a "poor little, sweet, trembling baby" (141).[7] But she does not stay in this relationship, which might have ended the cycle of rejection and domination. Her next serious affair is with the destructive Jem.

Yet if Melanctha is masochistic, so, arguably, are the other heroines of *Three Lives*—which is to say that the sickness may be cultural.[8] The servant whose story is told in "The Good Anna" is so devoted to her subordinate role that she works herself to death. "She worked away her appetite, her health and strength, and always for the sake of those who begged her not to work so hard." Finally her "worn" body cannot withstand an operation, and she dies (32). Lena, of the final story, is passively good: she represses her own desires entirely, placing herself in the hands of people who put her in frightening and alienating positions. Ultimately she numbs herself fatally, forgetting her fear of childbirth. "Lena was not so much scared now when she had the babies. She did not seem to notice very much when they hurt her, and she never seemed to feel very much now about anything that happened to her" (278). She becomes pregnant with a fourth child and dies giving birth.

Either *Three Lives* portrays three masochistic pathologies, or—not an entirely inconsistent idea—the book gives a picture of a world that prompts self-punishing behavior in women. For the stories implicitly criticize a culture that does not always value women enough to teach them self-protection. All three stories contain instances of people (often women) who value boys more than girls. Anna, when she has two children in her charge, "naturally preferred the boy" (25); in general, she "loved to work for men" (37).[9] In "The Gentle Lena," the heroine's aunt "spoiled her boy" (243); later, Lena's husband "wanted badly that his baby should be a boy" (275). Lena herself is overlooked, for obscure but associated reasons, by her own parents, who willingly part with her since "Lena was not an important daughter in the family" (245).

This motif, besides having something in common with Stein's own

7. There is something unsettling, however, about the context of Jeff's pity for Melanctha: he has caused her pain.

8. "What is clear in each plot [is] the defeat of a woman by dominant personality traits which are culturally defined as female." DeKoven, p. 32.

9. The reason she gives in both instances is that males are a pleasure to feed (pp. 25, 37).

sense of having been insufficiently valued by her parents, sheds light
on her heroine's self-destructive behavior. Melanctha's mother has
always devalued Melanctha in favor of a brother who died young.
"One day," Rose relates, "Melanctha was real little, and she heard
her ma say to her pa, it was awful sad to her, Melanctha had not
been the one the Lord had took from them stead of the little brother.
. . . That hurt Melanctha awful" (213). I connect this rejection in
favor of the brother with the remark that "Melanctha Herbert had
not loved herself in childhood" (90).

In the context of William James, Melanctha seems the model of
the "exuberant non-egoistic individual" who fails to take care of herself because she lacks a selective attention. But the marginal material
about her family suggests a different source for her lack of egoism—
that she was not valued enough as a child to feel worthy of care. Her
response to this rejection is to devalue her own femininity. She not
only ceases to love her mother—we hear that as a child "Melanctha
had not liked her mother very well" (90)—but also traces her own
insufficiency to her mother. She grows up wishing to be like her
"virile" father, rather than to inherit her mother's passive, feminine
traits: "Melanctha had a strong respect for any kind of successful
power. It was this that always kept Melanctha nearer, in her feeling
toward her virile and unendurable black father, than she ever was in
her feeling for her pale yellow, sweet-appearing mother. The things
she had in her of her mother, never made her feel respect" (96). This
situation doubly explains the lack of a bond between Melanctha and
her mother. The mother, simply, prefers a son, and the daughter
reacts both by wishing to grow up to be manly and by feeling repelled
by the mother's own feminine qualities. The lack of a maternal presence in Melanctha's childhood is due to familial values that favor
males and make women repugnant to each other. This is the family
scenario Freud naturalized as the female response to "castration."[1]

The two final crises repeat the pattern, this time outside the family.
Rose fails to be an adequate friend partly because of the new primacy
of a man in her thoughts: she considers Melanctha's presence a threat
to her hold on her new husband, so she exiles her friend (231).
Melanctha's response to this rejection is, again, to seek out a source of
virile energy; Jem Richards, to whom she now turns, has the same
"successful power" that Melanctha respected in her father (217).

But the irony is that by identifying with strong men, Melanctha,
far from absorbing their power, only makes herself vulnerable to it.
Her father is no kinder to her for her identification with him; perhaps

1. Sigmund Freud, "Some Psychical Consequences of the Anatomical Distinction between
the Sexes," in *The Standard Edition of the Complete Psychological Works of Sigmund
Freud*, trans. James Strachey (London: Hogarth Press, 1953–74), 19:253–54, hereafter
cited as SE.

her very admiration confirms his sense of his own superiority and thus his contempt for her. When she later turns to Jem, his toughness, according to the same paradox, is just what defeats her: "Jem . . . knew how to fight to win out, better. Melanctha really had already lost it" (223). For Jem's lasting ties are with men. He is "a man other men always trusted," "a straight man," who, in the exclusively male world of gambling and exchange, pays back what he owes (217). When he detaches himself from Melanctha, it is because he places his standing as a gambler above his relationship with any woman: "Jem Richards was not a kind of man to want a woman to be strong to him, when he was in trouble with his betting" (221).

Where male power commands exclusive respect, women's bonds among themselves, and their relationships with men, are troubled. The stories of *Three Lives* are feminist to the extent that the portraits of three overlooked and self-defeating women form a generalization about women's damaged self-image in a world of male privilege.

Yet the feminism is muffled, never articulated in such a generalization. In fact, some attention is required to notice issues of gender at all. The narrator of the stories either is innocent of critique or sees a pernicious social arrangement but resists taking an explicit stand on it, relying instead on the rhetorical effect of a bland accumulation of facts. The narrator—or perhaps Stein herself, as De-Koven suggests[2]—is passive to the status quo. Like the character Lena, the teller of these stories has an "unexpectant and unsuffering . . . patience" (239). One might call the stories near-feminist. But they fix the themes for Stein's later work, which is politically charged and precise. Between *Three Lives* in 1906 and the work of the teens Stein will develop a deeper understanding of the mechanism by which sexual arrangements are constructed, and will therefore be able to envision change.

The failure of maternal alliances is just what *Tender Buttons* and the other works of the teens will redeem. *Tender Buttons* not only portrays male privilege but also suggests how it perpetuates itself, and points to a means of subversion. The beginning of change, as envisioned in that text, is to reconstruct female bonds, the bonds that in *Three Lives* are shown in a damaged form. *Tender Buttons* explores the possibility of loving a "sister" who is "not a mister" (65) and of recovering, through her, a lost and degraded mother.

I have been talking about a number of features of "Melanctha" that stand outside the central love plot and complicate the relationship of Stein's thinking to the psychology of William James. But the tension between this last feature, Stein's latent feminism, and James's psychology needs some clarification. Nothing in that psy-

2. DeKoven, p. 32. (See p. 327.)

chology *logically* stands in the way of a feminist politics, but the radical form Stein's feminism took, as the next chapters suggest, led her directly away from the things she had most valued in James.

Three Lives shows a Jamesian voice in dialogue for the first time with a feminist voice. The Jamesian romantic plot of "Melanctha" and the near-feminist material at the margins of the story point to antithetical views of mental and social life. Stein's story simultaneously encourages two ways of understanding the heroine and the world in which she struggles. The first notion is that success in life is a matter of individual will—that people thrive by "knowing what they want." According to this view, which is also James's view, a character like Jeff Campbell has a more active will or attention than Melanctha, and therefore is able to focus on things in a more productive way. Melanctha, seen from this perspective, is a sensualist who fashions her own doom by refusing to decide "what she wants," despite Jeff's attempts to persuade her to be more self-interested.

But the story is also susceptible to the view that the ability or inability to thrive is socially determined. Melanctha, viewed within her social context, seems to suffer not because of a feeble will but because of values within and beyond her family that minimize her as a woman and prompt a cycle of self-defeating behavior. The same ambiguity is apparent in the other two women's tales in *Three Lives*; and for the whole volume Stein chose an epigraph from Laforgue that perfectly suspends the question of blame: "Donc je suis un malheureux et ce n'est *ni* ma faute *ni* celle de la vie."[3] The two views of Melanctha—the Jamesian and the feminist views—are not absolutely contradictory. Quite plausibly, Melanctha, within a male-dominated culture, is orphaned emotionally and *hence* does not value herself enough to decide to thrive. But one's view of her own role in her failure changes as one moves from the debates with Jeff on the Jamesian theme of "knowing what one wants" to the account of her early brutalization by her family.

Stein's work of the next few years brings into sharper relief the tension between a Jamesian and a feminist ethics. The difference between the two is the difference between liberal or individualist values and radical critique. To speak more biographically, it is also the difference between a male and a female identification on Stein's part. To call James a "male" theorist would involve problems of definition, but in Stein's mind James was synonymous with an ideal of rugged masculinity. She referred to him as "a strong man willing to fight, to suffer and endure."[4] His is a psychology of the strong man; at the low end of the moral spectrum he sees the "weakling," and at

3. "Therefore I am an unhappy person and it is *neither* my fault *nor* that of life" (emphases added).
4. "Radcliffe Themes," p. 146.

the high end lies the ideal of the *"kräftige Seele,"* which expresses itself in the "manly concrete deed."[5]

In "Melanctha," Stein reenvisioned herself according to that model—and as a man. Yet even as Stein made Jeff male, she dislodged him from the center of the story, and projected another part of herself onto a female character. Jeff was her self-idealization according to William James, but Melanctha absorbed features of her author's history as a self-alienated woman in a male culture. Stein bifurcated herself, that is, into a Jamesian male and a victimized woman. (At the same time, her story included but marginalized a further, crucial part of herself, her lesbianism: Melanctha has a homoerotic relationship with Jane Harden, but as an incidental episode on the way to her heterosexual self-discovery. Later, Stein will look past this heterosexist narrative.)

After "Melanctha," Stein's work never again places the manly and the female self-images in such precise counterpoint. "Melanctha" is the last and fullest expression of her bond with James and the first product of her incipient feminism. A male identification had pervaded her earlier writings: Stein had projected herself either into male protagonists or into women characters who disowned their gender, like Adele of *Q.E.D.* who was capable of the remark, "I always did thank God I wasn't born a woman" (58). After *Three Lives*, a female identification will move into view. Even in this later phase, Stein tends to think of herself as variously male and female; in her erotic relationship with Alice Toklas, for example, she pictures herself alternately as "sister" and "husband," and even as "king."[6] But once James fades as a presence, the texts never again have an ethics of manliness.

I have been describing the stories of *Three Lives* as near-feminist. With seven years, Stein's writing will have an overt feminism, not in the sense of announcing its ideology—in fact the writing style suddenly becomes opaque—but in the sense of containing a coded account of what patriarchy is and how it works. In her poetry of the early teens, Stein brings out the strain of protest that is deflected and compromised in "Melanctha." More than that, she develops a view of female possibilities that is not only angry but also rhapsodic and freeing. She comes to envision women not simply as objects of pity but also as powerful agents of subversion. In order to begin to think in these terms, Stein must move beyond an unconscious equation of women with impotence and death, putting behind her the specter of the weak and victimized mother.

5. Letter quoted in Perry, *Thought and Character* 2:272. James is saying in this context that we are all "weakling[s]" except insofar as we "escape" from that state, moment by moment, through heroic acts that express (and earn us) a *kräftige Seele*. The reference to the "manly concrete deed" is from *P* 15.

6. *TB* 29; Stein, "Lifting Belly," in *The Yale Gertrude Stein*, ed. Richard Kostelanetz (New Haven: Yale University Press, 1980), pp. 16, 49, 21.

First, however, she makes a circuit, itself difficult and freeing, through the father. *The Making of Americans* is a labor of brave self-analysis, in which Stein identifies some of her fears about her social and artistic roles and works past them toward new forms of self-trust.

MARIANNE DeKOVEN

[Race, Sexuality, and Form in "Melanctha"]†

Dr. Jefferson Campbell, the transformation in "Melanctha" of the Gertrude Stein character in the autobiographical *Q.E.D.*, might say just the same thing (though in different language) of his ambivalent feeling toward Melanctha. The position of race in the configuration of ambivalence in "Melanctha" is in many ways very different from that in *The Nigger of the "Narcissus"*[1]—the characters in "Melanctha" are all black. However, the visibility of the characters' race disappears and reappears throughout the text. In long sequences, particularly in the central movement of the novella that treats the love affair of Jeff and Melanctha, racial specificity (except in the speech rhythms) is suspended—we enter into what Conrad might call the truth of the characters, independent of racial stereotype or antistereotype, as we do into the truth of Jimmy's dying.

Nonetheless, it is clear that the race of Stein's characters enables her, as Wait's blackness enables Conrad, simultaneously to undo her own naturalist narrative and to explore dangerous thematic possibilities. Stein uses American racial stereotyping both in the service of, and against the grain of, her ostensible naturalist story. As Conrad does in *The Nigger of the "Narcissus,"* she incorporates race into this fiction chaotically, undecidably.

Repeated passages of crude, profoundly offensive racial stereotyping should not be, but almost always are, overlooked by Stein critics.[2] I would guess that sequences such as the following, which comes right at the beginning of the novella, have kept "Melanctha" off numerous syllabi:

> Rose Johnson was a real black, tall, well built, sullen, stupid, childlike, good looking negress. She laughed when she was happy and grumbled and was sullen with everything that troubled. . . .

---

† From *Rich and Strange: Gender, History, Modernism* (Princeton: Princeton University Press, 1991), pp. 71–79. Reprinted by permission of the publisher.
1. Novel by Joseph Conrad (1857–1924), published in 1897.
2. I am guilty of that oversight in *A Different Language: Gertrude Stein's Experimental Writing* (Madison: University of Wisconsin Press, 1983). In my case, and I suspect in many others, it is a result of mortified denial rather than indifference.

Rose laughed when she was happy but she had not the wide, abandoned laughter that makes the warm broad glow of negro sunshine. Rose was never joyous with the earth-born, boundless joy of negroes. Hers was just ordinary, any sort of woman laughter.

Rose Johnson was careless and was lazy, but she had been brought up by white folks and she needed decent comfort. Her white training had only made for habits, not for nature. Rose had the simple, promiscuous unmorality of the black people. (85–86)

The attributes of this repellent racial stereotyping that were liberating for Stein are apparent here: "*abandoned* laughter," "*earth-born, boundless* joy," "*promiscuous* unmorality."[3] Stein carefully distinguishes the "yellow," partly white, "complex and intelligent" Melanctha from the lazy, stupid, sullen, careless, black Rose, but it is Melanctha's "negro" qualities—her abandonment, her promiscuity, and her connection to the boundless joy of the earth (quite obviously, post-Cixous and Irigaray, maternal jouissance)—that excite Stein, quite literally, and unleash her new writing. It is Melanctha's "wandering," which summarizes and encodes the "negro" element of her racial identity, that necessitates the self-justifications that simultaneously confirm the naturalist narrative and carry Stein past the point of no return in acknowledging the excitement those "negro" qualities make her feel.

Racial stereotypes and counterstereotypes function in complex, undecidable concatenations throughout the text. It is worth noting that the only character conceived as a noncontradictory racial stereotype, the gambler Jem Richards (Melanctha's desperate last attempt to save herself through heterosexual involvement), is the least vividly realized character in the text. The rest of the characters simultaneously embody and contradict racial stereotypes. We have already seen that Rose Johnson is in a sense a classic stereotype, but Stein carefully counters that stereotype by making her an orphan who was raised by whites and who therefore "needed decent comfort." Also, having been raised by whites, she never laughed with the "wide, abandoned laughter that makes the warm broad glow of negro sunshine."

Rose's foil is Jane Harden, Melanctha's first (erotically cathected) woman ally and mentor (Rose is her last). Jane is, schematically, Rose's opposite: intelligent where Rose is stupid, reckless and generous where Rose is careful and shrewdly selfish. Again, Stein simultaneously employs and undercuts racist stereotype. Jane, like Melanctha, is intelligent and light-skinned, and the two qualities are

---

3. New York: Vintage-Random House, 1936. This projection of repressed sexuality onto blacks is a staple of racism. The difference in "Melanctha," as in *The Nigger of the "Narcissus,"* is that Stein and Conrad enter into the subjectivity of their racially other characters.

linked: "Jane was a negress, but she was so white that hardly any one could guess it. Jane had had a good deal of education" (103). But, in spite of her "white" qualities, Jane is "bad" in a racially stereotyped way: "Jane Harden had many bad habits. She drank a great deal and she wandered widely" (104). The light-skinned, well-educated, intelligent woman suffers and dies from the "promiscuous unmorality of the black people," while the "sullen, stupid, childlike" black woman carefully marries and ensconces herself within a safe, bourgeois life.

Jeff Campbell is the most bourgeois, moralistic character in the novella; he has devoted his life to redeeming blacks from their "carelessness" and "simple promiscuous unmorality," or, as he would tellingly put it, their constant need for new "excitements." Before he becomes involved with and educated by Melanctha, he leads a life of narrow predictability and timidity. Stein assigns to him her own problem, as she had diagnosed it in Q.E.D., of excessive intellection and concomitant blockage of emotion ("thinking rather than feeling"): evidently, sexual inhibition. But he is dark-skinned, more strongly identified with "the race" than Melanctha, both by the narrative and by his own concept of his mission in life (to save black people from themselves). Furthermore, he is described more frequently than any other character as laughing with the "wide, abandoned laughter that makes the warm broad glow of negro sunshine."

Melanctha herself constitutes the novella's most complex deployment of racist stereotype. The text makes it clear that her intelligence and general appeal are attributable to her light skin, the predominance of her "white blood": "Melanctha Herbert was a graceful, pale yellow, intelligent, attractive negress. She had not been raised like Rose by white folks but then she had been half made with real white blood" (86). However, the key characteristics that distinguish her from Jeff, and generate plot, are not her "white" intelligence, grace, and attractiveness but her need to "wander," which Jeff links to the need of "the negros" continually to seek new "excitements." Stein takes Melanctha's "wandering" much more seriously than either she or Jeff takes "negro excitements"—the former is at least in part an earnest desire for a deeper knowledge of life, while the latter is mere restless self-indulgence. Nonetheless, it is apparent that Melanctha's crucial "wandering," which thematizes the formal "wandering" of the text, at least partly falls into the category of, or looks like, the "simple promiscuous unmorality of the black people." The portion of the text devoted to viewing Melanctha's troubles from her own point of view constructs, as I have said, a persuasive rationalization of, or justification for, what Jeff Campbell considers her untrustworthy, shameful, "wandering" behavior, a justification that makes him the guilty party in his ungenerous inability to trust Melanctha: "I certainly am right the way I say it Jeff now to you. I certainly am right when I ask

you for it now, to tell me what I ask you, about not trusting me more
then again, Jeff, just like you never really knew me. You certainly
never did trust me just then, Jeff, you hear me?" (157–58).

Melanctha is also characterized as strong and determined, with a
"break-neck courage" and proud stoicism in the face of pain. She
derives these positive attributes from her father, a very negative,
harsh, violent character, whose blackness is always emphasized
whenever he is mentioned: "Melanctha was pale yellow and mysterious and a little pleasant like her mother, but the real power in
Melanctha's nature came through her robust and unpleasant and
very unendurable black father. . . . Melanctha's father was a big
black virile negro. . . . James Herbert was a common, decent enough,
colored workman, brutal and rough to his one daughter" (90–91).
James Herbert is another repellent racist stereotype, "big black virile"
and also working class, who brutalizes his wife and daughter and has
a knife fight in a bar. But he is the source of "the real power in
Melanctha's nature," which encompasses a great deal more than
courage, determination, and stoicism—it is an existential power, a
force of being, much like James Wait's.

Class is a less overtly visible issue in "Melanctha" than it is in *The
Nigger of the "Narcissus,"* but it functions undecidably along with race
in Stein's dislocation of conventional naturalist narrative. The class
status of each character is carefully, though unobtrusively, established. Melanctha, through her father, is working class; her association with the middle-class doctor Jeff Campbell is an important
upward move for her. The educated Jane Harden provides Melanctha's initial access to middle-class possibilities. Rose offers a less
upwardly mobile but stable version of bourgeois domesticity, though
Melanctha's association with her is clearly a last step downward, just
as much because her husband Sam is working class as because Rose
herself is unworthy of Melanctha. Melanctha's last lover, Jem Richards, is a member of the quasi-criminal (non)class of reckless, root-
less gamblers. Her move toward him abandons the class ladder in a
gesture not of subversion but rather of hopelessness—upward mobility might not offer much, but it is the only game in town.

In this account, the class status of the characters accords with the
naturalist antibildungsroman protagonist's trajectory of rise and fall
through the class system (see, for example, *Sister Carrie*[4]). But,
again, the energizing, positively valued "wandering" that radicalizes
this text, the source of its subversive power as an early modernist
work, is just as much associated with lower-class status as it is with
blackness. This empowered subversiveness disrupts the naturalist
class trajectory. Jane Harden's positively valued "wandering," which

4. 1900 novel by American author Theodore Dreiser (1871–1945).

gives her the "wisdom" that she imparts to Melanctha, is at odds with her middle-class educational attainments; in fact, it leads directly to her expulsion from college. Similarly, it is Melanctha's "wandering" that makes her relationship with Jeff, her move to the middle class, impossible, while, in the meantime, his contact with Melanctha's "wandering" broadens and deepens him. Her move downward here is not an inevitable outcome of the great impersonal social machine grinding down the helpless individual; it is rather the outcome of her magnetic "power," which is like (and is originally ignited by) Jane Harden's.

Similarly, it is not Rose Johnson's stupidity or laziness that hurts Melanctha, finally, but rather Rose's narrow bourgeois selfishness (her tenacity in clinging to her domestic security) that pushes Melanctha down the final step toward her ignominious death. And it is Melanctha's working-class black father, again, who gives her the strength of her nature without which there would be no story. In both of these instances, conventional assumptions about the impact of class status overtly endorsed by the text are overthrown.

*   *   *

* * * "Melanctha" opens with a childbirth episode. Like Conrad's, it emphasizes difficulty, torment, and life-death liminality. These are the opening paragraphs of "Melanctha":

> Rose Johnson made it very hard to bring her baby to its birth.
> Melanctha Herbert who was Rose Johnson's friend, did everything that any woman could. She tended Rose, and she was patient, submissive, soothing, and untiring, while the sullen, childish, cowardly, black Rosie grumbled and fussed and howled and made herself to be an abomination and like a simple beast.
> The child though it was healthy after it was born, did not live long. Rose Johnson was careless and negligent and selfish, and when Melanctha had to leave for a few days, the baby died. Rose Johnson had liked the baby well enough and perhaps she just forgot it for awhile, anyway the child was dead and Rose and Sam her husband were very sorry but then these things came so often in the negro world in Bridgepoint, that they neither of them thought about it very long. (85)

The shocking aspects of this episode, particularly given its position as entry into the text, have been almost universally overlooked. The adjectival racism in the description of Rose is overshadowed by the blanket condemnation of "the negro world in Bridgepoint," in which the death of a baby is no big deal. And to open a novella so casually and nonjudgmentally with what amounts to infanticide, then to move on quickly to other matters as if it had not happened, is a drastic textual strategy indeed. There is something nightmarish in that quiet "perhaps she just forgot it for awhile." It introduces a world of unthinkable deprivation of nurturance and echoes the indifference of Melanctha's own mother toward her—Melanctha had, as a child, overheard her mother say that she wished Melanctha, the difficult daughter, had died instead of Melanctha's brother, the beloved son.

The painful, difficult birth-into-death of the black Johnson baby parallels James Wait's birth and death. Both are intimately implicated in the disruption of traditional narrative. Again, it is the "promiscuous unmorality of the black people" associated with the working-class Rose Johnson that constitutes the subversive force of "wandering," both thematically and, as we will see, formally in this novella. As in *The Nigger of the "Narcissus,"* the maternal in "Melanctha" is the locus of those powerful, dark forces that are just as compelling, and potentially liberating, as they are damned. The word Stein chooses to describe Melanctha's subversiveness, "wandering," suggests the classical notion that hysteria, the prime manifestation of thwarted female rebellion, is a "wandering womb": that dark cave that modernism partly brings to light. The new story is being born— the birth is painful and the progeny cannot yet live, but the process, as embedded in form, is irreversible. * * *

CORINNE E. BLACKMER

[African Masks and Passing in Stein and Larsen]†

> To this day camouflage terrorizes me.
>
> The pattern of skin which makes a being invisible against its habitat.
>
> And—yes—this camouflage exists for its protection. I am not what I seem to be . . .
>
> The onlooker may be startled to recognize the visible being. The onlooker may react with disbelief: sometimes, with recognition.
> [MICHELLE CLIFF, "PASSING,"
> IN *The Land of Look Behind*, 1985]

On February 1, 1929, Nella Larsen,[1] then an emerging figure on the Harlem Renaissance literary scene, enclosed a copy of her recently

† From the *Journal of the History of Sexuality* 4.2 (1993). Copyright © by The University of Chicago. All rights reserved. Reprinted by permission of the author.
1. American novelist and short-story writer (1891–1964). [*Editor's note.*]

issued first novel, *Quicksand*, with a letter of introduction to Gertrude Stein:

> I have often talked with our friend Carl Van Vechten about you. Particularly about you and Melanctha, which I have read many times. And always I get from it some new thing—a truly great story. I never cease to wonder how you came to write it and just why you and not some one of us should so accurately have caught the spirit of this race of mine.
>
> Carl asked me to send you my poor first book, and I am doing so. Please don't think me too presumptuous. I hope some day to have the great good fortune of seeing and talking with you.[2]

Although Larsen briefly met the older expatriate writer in Paris the following year, her auspicious literary career ended soon after the publication of her second novel, *Passing*, which she wrote during the same period as this letter to Stein.[3] On her part, Stein received this communication as welcome evidence that her long period of artistic isolation had finally closed and that "Melanctha," one of her best known if still least understood works, had at last found an appreciative and discerning reader.[4] Carl Van Vechten, the literary agent and close friend of both writers, not only served as the conduit of communication between the two women, but he also strove to break down the barriers of aesthetic convention and racial prejudice that made audiences reluctant and, in many cases, unable to receive their innovative writings and challenging perspectives.[5] Although scholars

---

2. Donald Gallup, ed., *The Flowers of Friendship: Letters Written to Gertrude Stein* (New York, 1953), p. 216.

3. Mary Helen Washington, "Nella Larsen: Mystery Woman of the Harlem Renaissance," *Ms*, December 1980, pp. 44–50.

4. Stein reported to Carl Van Vechten that receiving the letter from Larsen "touched [her] a lot." Van Vechten had earlier told Stein that Larsen had found "Melanctha" "the best Negro story she has ever read (she is Negro herself)" (*Letters of Gertrude Stein and Carl Van Vechten: 1913–1946*, ed. Edward Burns, 2 vols. [New York, 1986], 1:192, 147). This exchange of letters took place during the time when Stein was reissuing *Three Lives* and when her opera, *Four Saints in Three Acts*, with an all-black cast, had been performed successfully in the United States. Stein nevertheless continued to face great difficulty getting her experimental writings into print. It was not until 1935, when Stein was fifty-nine and, as Richard Kostelanetz notes, "one of the most respected writers in the English language," that "any major American publishing firm invest[ed] its own name and money in a book of hers" (Gertrude Stein, *The Yale Gertrude Stein*, edited and with an introduction by Richard Kostelanetz [New Haven, CT, 1980], p. xxix).

5. Some African American critics understandably have found Van Vechten (the author of the notoriously, if ironically, entitled 1926 novel *Nigger Heaven*) problematic in his public, paternalistic role as the white literary patron of the Harlem Renaissance. When his own self-protective mask of heterosexuality is removed, however, it becomes clear that Van Vechten, himself a gay man, was actually endeavoring to promote an interracial gay and lesbian sensibility, to give support and encouragement, and to channel funds and publicity to African American artists. As Eric Garber notes, many of the leading figures of the Harlem Renaissance—for example, Bruce Nugent, Langston Hughes, Wallace Thurman, Countee Cullen, Claude McKay, Alain Locke, Bessie Smith, Gertrude "Ma" Rainey, Ethel

acknowledge that Stein influenced such male authors as Sherwood Anderson, William Faulkner, Ernest Hemingway, Thornton Wilder, and Richard Wright, the complex lines of influence between "Melanctha" and *Passing*, which have thus far received no critical attention, belie the commonly received notion that Stein exerted little or no "visible influence upon subsequent women writers."[6]

That the closely related concerns of both of these authors' works with representing the intersections of gender, race, and sexuality through tropes of masking and passing have heretofore gone unnoticed not only indicates that earlier commentators found these topics unspeakable, but also that exclusive focus on one category of difference tends to inhibit analysis of how overlapping differences operate in syncopation. In addition, because Larsen did not imitate Stein's distinctive "cubist" style of repetition and simple oral diction, the similarities between these two works have not been apparent to those who have focused almost exclusively on the formal aspects of Stein's linguistic innovations. Nonetheless, the themes and central characters of *Passing* suggest that Larsen interpreted the "complex and desiring" Melanctha Herbert, Stein's protagonist who "wanders" in search of "wisdom," as an embodiment of the acute invisibility and vulnerability of those who belong to many worlds and whose inability to discover a "right position" results from the failure of others to perceive and, therefore, to "read" them competently.

In *Passing*, Larsen reconfigures the predicament and character of Melanctha Herbert in her portrayal of Clare Kendry, who, like Stein's bisexual mulatta protagonist, oscillates between the separate realms of black and white culture and heterosexual and lesbian desire. Furthermore, the ironies inherent in the conflict between the bohemian Clare and her bourgeois friend Irene Redfield become emblematic of the social and artistic conundrums Larsen herself experienced as an African American woman writer attempting to break from the polemics of nineteenth-century "racial uplift" fiction. In much the same manner, the conflicts Stein explores in "Melanctha" reveal her own attempt to create narrative structures that transgress the representations of character, race, and sexuality that informed conventional Victorian fiction.

Waters, Josephine Baker, Alberta Hunter, and Gladys Bentley—were gay, lesbian, or bisexual (Eric Garber, "A Spectacle in Color: The Lesbian and Gay Subculture of Jazz Age Harlem," in *Hidden from History: Reclaiming the Gay and Lesbian Past*, ed. Martin Bauml Duberman, Martha Vicinus, and George Chauncey, Jr. [New York, 1989], pp. 318–31). White gays and lesbians frequented the homosexual underworld because they found social acceptance there and identified with other outcasts from American life. Garber suggests that "this identification and feeling of kinship . . . may have been the beginnings of homosexual 'minority consciousness' " (p. 329).

6. Kostelanetz, ed., p. xxxi.

Both "Melanctha" and *Passing* explore the central role that racial visibility and invisibility play in establishing gender roles and sexual identities for black and white women alike. Both works, moreover, employ the mask as a mediating metaphor of concealment and revelation, which permits both the authors and their central characters to articulate their desires subversively and thus to "pass" undetected through worlds marked by oppositional boundary lines of race, sexuality, and gender. However, in light of Leo Stein's proclamation that "Melanctha" had "nothing to do with Negroes" but was a racially encoded reworking of his sister's unpublished autobiographical novel *Q.E.D.*, some critics have interpreted the novella's racial text solely in terms of its palimpsestic lesbian subtext.[7] Conversely, critics until recently have overlooked issues of same-sex desire and have interpreted *Passing* as a text concerned solely with heterosexual jealousy and issues of racial identity and solidarity.[8] In her 1989 introduction to the reissue of *Passing*, however, Deborah E. McDowell argues convincingly that Larsen employed the then-conventional narrative of racial passing to camouflage the more dangerous story of the "unnamed and unacknowledged desire" between the two female protagonists.[9] Nonetheless, interpreting either text in such a manner that either racial difference or same-sex desire merely substitutes for and thereby erases or essentializes the other perpetuates a pattern of opposition and exclusion that both authors seek to disrupt. For Stein and Larsen, racial and sexual taboos inevitably intersect and function to contain the desires of nonconformist and independent women to define themselves.

7. Leo Stein, *Journey into the Self: Being the Letters, Papers, and Journals of Leo Stein*, ed. Edmund Fuller (New York, 1950), p. 137. Leo, who was resentful of his sister after he was displaced by her lover, Alice B. Toklas, is neither a reliable character witness nor a particularly insightful reader of her fiction. In a letter to Mabel Weeks, written when his sister had achieved fame with *The Autobiography of Alice B. Toklas*, Leo says: "I read that first novel [*Q.E.D.*] which she says she had completely forgotten, and though the stuff was interesting . . . the writing was impossible. There was no objectification. This brings to mind the fact that a very intelligent Negro writer—Eric Walrond—said to me once that Gertrude was the only white person who had given real Negro psychology. I laughed and said, of course, the book was really not about Negroes and had only Negro local color, and as the psychology of whites and Negroes of the same cultural grade is essentially the same, the extra psychology will give Negro psychology, provided he understands that cultural group" (p. 137). For examples of readings that, following Leo Stein's example, attempt to explain—and, indeed, apologize for—the putative racism of "Melanctha" by positing that the text is actually concerned with lesbianism, see Catharine R. Stimpson, "The Mind, the Body, and Gertrude Stein," *Critical Inquiry* 3 (1977): 491–506; Lisa Ruddick, " 'Melanctha' and the Psychology of William James," *Modern Fiction Studies* 28 (1982–83): 543–56; and Jane Rule, *Lesbian Images* (Trumansburg, NY, 1982), pp. 62–73.

8. See Mary Youman, "Nella Larsen's *Passing*: A Study in Irony," *College Language Association Journal* 18 (1974): 235–41; Cheryl A. Wall, "Passing for What? Aspects of Identity in Nella Larsen's Novels," *Black American Literature Forum* 26 (1986): 97–111; and Nella Larsen, *Passing*, with an introduction by Hoyt Fuller (New York, 1971).

9. Nella Larsen, *Quicksand and Passing*, edited and with an introduction by Deborah E. McDowell (New Brunswick, NJ, 1989), p. xxx.

Racial Veils and Sexual "Deadlocks": Q.E.D. and Quicksand

Earlier efforts on the part of both authors to break down dualisms of perception, history, and narrative form, however, end intentionally in deadlocks. Both Q.E.D. and Quicksand might be seen as anti-bildungsromans, in which the principal characters discover that the forms of experience they have inherited from their parent culture and their education are limiting and self-defeating because they cannot accommodate their sexuality. If the autobiographical backdrop of Q.E.D. is the Johns Hopkins University School of Medicine, where Stein had an unsuccessful stint as a medical student, then that of Quicksand is Larsen's unsatisfactory experience as a nurse at Tuskegee Institute, which Booker T. Washington had founded to "uplift" uneducated rural blacks, and which Larsen renames "Naxos" in her text.[1] Although both these institutions are ostensibly dedicated to the betterment of humanity, they seek to "reform" blacks and women by promulgating systems of belief in Christian morality and biological science that deny the inherent worth and value of both groups.

Quicksand, the novel that Larsen sent to Stein, opens with the main protagonist, Helga Crane, feeling torn between the ideals of self-sacrifice for her race and sex and her own desire to flee from the conformist and puritanical ethos of Naxos. The reductive rhetoric of racial uplift transforms the school into a regimented, machine-like communal "showplace" that represses joyousness, spontaneity, and autonomous learning, and thus hardly encourages the independent spirit of students or teachers:

> This great community, she thought, was no longer a school. It had grown into a machine. It was now a showplace in the black belt, exemplification of the white man's magnanimity, refutation of the black man's inefficiency. Life had died out of it. It was, Helga decided, now only a big knife with cruelly sharp edges, ruthlessly cutting all to a pattern, the white man's pattern. Teachers as well as students were subjected to the paring process, for it tolerated no innovations, no individualisms. Ideas it rejected . . . Enthusiasm, spontaneity, if not actually suppressed, were at least openly regretted as unladylike or ungentlemanly qualities. [p. 39][2]

1. "Naxos," which is both an allusion to Greek mythology and an anagram of "Saxon," may be a conscious attempt on Larsen's part to suggest that Naxos, like Tuskegee Institute itself, merely inversely reflects the values and ideals of Anglo-Saxon culture and society.
2. Unless otherwise stated, the texts of Nella Larsen's Quicksand and Passing are quoted from McDowell, ed. (n. 8 above); that of "Melanctha" from Gertrude Stein, Three Lives (New York, 1936); and that of Q.E.D. from Gertrude Stein, Fernhurst, Q.E.D., and Other Early Writings, ed. Leon Katz (New York, 1971).

Helga does not wish to be made over in the image of the white race, but her sense of racial integrity conflicts with prescribed notions of proper ladyhood, which deny or degrade female sexuality. Thus Helga must confront the historical impact of the nineteenth-century "cult of true womanhood," which constructed white female sexuality as "purifying" and that of black women as "degrading."[3] Helga feels simultaneously ashamed and proud of her race and her sexual appeal. This paradox is manifested in her relationship with her fiancé and fellow teacher, James Vayle, whose name alludes to "the Veil," the central metaphor in W. E. B. Du Bois's *The Souls of Black Folk*.[4] Helga flees from Naxos and James Vayle when she realizes that only "that nameless . . . shameless impulse" (p. 18) of sexual desire keeps James bound in devotion to her. But her flight proves ineffective, and the remainder of the novel shows how the "Veil" of racial and sexual self-division that both covers Helga and exposes her to shame pursues her. The novel closes with Helga resolutely planning her next escape, although the anticipated birth of her fifth baby indicates that death will soon literally engulf her. Larsen demonstrates that the unrestrained expression of sexuality within marriage poses a greater threat to women than repressed desire, but she offers no alternative vision in this novel to the tragic divisions caused by the internalization of the "Veil."

Q.E.D., the barely fictionalized recounting of the triangulated lesbian relationship in which Stein became involved while studying medicine at Johns Hopkins University, likewise ends in a deadlock, with the central protagonist humiliated by her rejection by the woman whose advances she had long resisted. Although never directly alluded to in *Q.E.D.*, the fact that Stein became involved with May Bookstaver at the same time that her coursework exposed her to theories of medical sexology and eugenics exacerbated her emotional dilemma and precipitated a collision at the intersection of nineteenth-century female romantic friendship and twentieth-century lesbianism—much as *Quicksand* dramatizes a collision between nineteenth-century propriety and racial uplift and twentieth-century urban progress and personal freedom. In both

---

3. Hazel V. Carby, *Reconstructing Womanhood: The Emergence of the Afro-American Woman Novelist* (New York, 1987), pp. 80–82.

4. Larsen is clearly thinking of W. E. B. Du Bois's famous criticism of Booker T. Washington for "that curious double movement," or duplicity, whereby "real progress may be negative and actual advance be relative retrogression" (W. E. B. Du Bois, *The Souls of Black Folk* [1903; rpt. New York, 1990], p. 39). The "Veil" refers to the color line, enforced through de jure segregation by the U.S. Supreme Court's "separate but equal" interpretation of the Fourteenth Amendment in *Plessy v. Ferguson* (1896), which separates the races from one another, prevents the dominant white race from perceiving the humanity of other races, and makes black people themselves prey to inner division and conflicting (that is, assimilationist versus separatist) aims.

cases the conflicts center on navigating the opposing forces of bourgeois "propriety," bohemian "liberty," and lower-class "license."

Based largely on working-class women confined in prisons or asy-
lums, the case studies in sexology and eugenics that Stein read at
Johns Hopkins linked sexually "deviant" behaviors such as prostitution and perversion to social and racial "degeneracy."[5] According to
this model, lesbians and prostitutes were genetic victims of uncon-
trollable aberrant behaviors. Since heterosexual orientation was
regarded as normative, "deviants" from this pattern were involuntary
transgressors who had no claim to legitimate choice or social protection. These dualistic social perceptions of homosexuality placed
Stein in a classic double bind. On the one hand, the scientific belief
that lesbianism was pathologically determined indicated that those
"afflicted" with this "disease" were passive victims, yet societal fears
that sexual behavior, in fact, was voluntarily chosen resulted in the
stigmatization of homosexuals as "social outlaws." The fact that society viewed "deviants" both as hapless victims and willful perpetrators
of sexual "perversity" informed the protracted debate between Stein
and Bookstaver—and their fictional counterparts, Adele and Helen
Thomas—over the relative value of intuition and direct experience,
on the one hand, and conscious reason and speculative deliberation
on the other.

In *Q.E.D.*, Adele confesses to Helen that although she does not
consider herself "born a woman" (p. 58) and thus is not confined to
the "biological destiny" of matrimony and motherhood, she nonetheless feels imprisoned by her beliefs regarding proper social and
sexual decorum:

> I believe strongly that one should do things either for the sake
> of the thing done or because of definite future power which is
> the legitimate result of all education. Experience for the paltry
> purpose of having had it is to me both trivial and immoral. As
> for passion . . . it has no reality for me except as two varieties,
> affectionate comradeship on the one hand and physical passion
> in greater or less complexity on the other and against the cul-
> tivation of that latter I have an almost puritanical horror and
> that includes an objection to the cultivation of it in any of its
> many disguised forms. [p. 59]

Ironically, in pressing the distinction between "affectionate comradeship" and "physical passion," Adele cultivates one of the concealed forms of passion that she claims horrify her. She cannot
ignore the disturbing sexual undercurrents in her ostensibly innoc-
uous romantic friendship with Helen. Since Adele knows that unex-

5. Lillian Faderman, *Odd Girls and Twilight Lovers: A History of Lesbian Life in Twentieth-
Century America* (New York, 1989), pp. 37–61.

amined personal experience leads to powerlessness, her conscious avoidance of sexuality replicates the snare of passive womanhood she seeks to escape. Thus, just as Helga travels to escape or to discover some method of rending the "Veil," Adele spends much of the remainder of *Q.E.D.* in an exhaustive series of discussions with Helen, attempting to understand the nature of her feelings and searching for appropriate means to actualize them.

When Mabel, Helen's longtime lover, feels her power over Helen slipping away, she discloses to her rival Adele the "scandal" that constitutes knowledge of homosexual identity within closeted communities and tells her the "sordid" details of her sexual and financial affairs with Helen. Adele oscillates between moral nausea over the revelation that Helen has "prostituted" herself and sympathy for her helpless economic dependency. Feeling herself increasingly compromised by her ambivalent position within this romantic triangle, Adele embarks on yet another round of obsessive questioning regarding the nature and meaning of human relationships. By the time Adele has resolved to dispense with her conflicts, Helen claims she has come to absolutely trust Adele but cannot break from her dependent relationship with Mabel. Moreover, Helen trusts Adele because her endless dithering has vitiated the passion she once felt for her. *Q.E.D.* thus ends with Adele, thrust back into the role of the romantic friend and rejected by Helen, recognizing that the dynamics of the relationship are "very near being a dead-lock" (p. 133). As does Helga Crane in *Quicksand*, Adele finds herself a victim of her internalized propriety, which leaves her a divided and powerless spectator in the drama of human passion.

Character Typology and "Bottom Rhythms"

The title *Q.E.D.*, the scientific abbreviation for *quod erat demonstrandum* ("that which was to be proven"), shows Stein's preoccupation with a scientific approach to human behavior and relationships. According to Stein, the failure of her relationship with May Bookstaver stemmed from an internal mechanism that governed their acts and responses and made their timing and rhythms mismatched. The incompatibility of her fictional characters reflects this premise:

> Adele realised that Helen demanded of her a response and always before that response was ready. Their pulses were differently timed. . . . It was a false position. . . . She realised that her attitude was misunderstood and that Helen interpreted her slowness as essential deficiency. This was the inevitable result of a situation in which she was forced constantly ahead of herself. She was sore and uneasy and the greater her affection for

Helen became the more irritable became her discontent. [p. 104]

This analysis indicates that Stein applied the premises of psychological experiments she had conducted as an undergraduate at Radcliffe in an effort to understand the failure of her relationship with May. In "Cultivated Motor Automatism: A Study of Character in Relation to Attention," Stein examined how different individuals imbricated meaning and experience in producing automatic writing on repeated occasions. The repetition would permit them to "cultivate" their automatic writing and provide evidence of recurring patterns in the writing that made it readable or coherent as narrative. She characterized two basic "types" according to their "habits of attention," which she regarded as "reflexes of the complete character of the individual." Type I was high-strung and imaginative, while Type II was phlegmatic and sentimental. In different degrees and admixtures, these two types determined what she called the "bottom nature" of any given individual character.[6] Thus, the outcome of events fictionalized in Q.E.D. led Stein to conclude that Helen (curious, fast, intuitive) and Adele (regular, slow, rational) had incompatible "bottom natures" under the conditions of the powerful narrative control imposed by Mabel, who separates the would-be lovers. Their mismatched bottom natures lack the force to bypass the external (or "environmental") obstacle Mabel presents. Characters such as Helen, who reacted strongly to external stimuli, or characters such as Adele, who focused strongly on internal perceptions, had to expend much time and effort to refocus their accustomed habits of attention. In the complex context of real time, place, and event—as opposed to that of the laboratory—such refocusing usually occurs too late to rescue the characters from the miscommunication and mistiming resulting from their acquired habits. Alternately, the very process of refocusing becomes devoid of meaning through sheer repetition and the appearance of new environmental stimuli requiring new habits of attention.

For Larsen, the consequences of the discontinuities fostered by the binary decorum of the "Veil" extend everywhere, from the coerced efforts of the Naxos administrators to cut black people to "the white man's pattern" to Helga Crane's final self-abnegation to the authority of "the white man's God" (pp. 39, 157). Although Stein does not critique monotheism directly, she likewise attacks the habits of mind that allow scientists to classify people as "normal" or "abnormal" according to this binary decorum, thus playing "God,"

---

6. See James R. Mellow, *Charmed Circle: Gertrude Stein and Company* (New York, 1975), for an excellent discussion of the influence of Stein's early scientific experiments on her practice of "experimental" narration.

as it were, by positioning themselves as the authoritative control. The classifying schema developed by Western scientists testifies not to their knowledge but to their power to dispose of a wide variety of human subjects, often with distinctly different languages, dialects, occupations, religions, classes, races, ethnicities, sexualities, histories, and cultures, into the mega-category of the Other. For example, Sander Gilman asserts that the "protean" quality of the Other enables "various signs of difference to be linked without any recognition of inappropriateness." This linkage in dominant discourse transforms various Others into an interlocking system of metaphor:

> Patterns of association are mostly commonly based on a combination of real-life experience (as filtered through the models of perception) and the world of myth, and the two intertwined to form fabulous images, neither entirely of this world nor of the realm of myth. . . . Since analogies are rooted in a habitual perception of the world, they are understood as an adequate representation of reality. . . . Analogy thus becomes the basis for the association between otherwise disparate categories.[7]

Thus Jews become types of blacks, lesbians become types of mulattas, and prostitutes, women, bohemians, and even cosmopolitans become associated in a web of analogy. Literary artists from these groups who seek cultural legitimacy must stress their sameness with a highly suspicious dominant discourse, while they simultaneously endeavor to express their rapport with an often equally suspicious minority discourse. Unfortunately and ironically, the epistemology underlying these classifications has the further consequence of making the dominant group and discourse immune to the disastrous results of constructing unitary standards of "verbal correctness." Rather, blame for miscommunication devolves upon those among the marginalized who attempt to be heard and attempt to gain access to an otherwise closed system, rather than upon those in the dominant discourse whose power enables them to remain oblivious to their rhetorical duplicity.

African Masks, Lesbian Sexuality, and Cubist Aesthetics

Writers like Stein and Larsen who sought to both challenge and gain entry into the dominant literary discourse had to speak in two voices and employ subterfuge, including the transformation of binary categories and character typologies into subversive masquerades. Thus, rather than merely substituting black for white, male for female, or

---

7. Sander L. Gilman, *Difference and Pathology: Stereotypes of Sexuality, Race, and Madness* (Ithaca, NY, 1985), p. 21.

heterosexual for lesbian, in "Melanctha" Stein creates a triadic oscillation among the categories of the social, the natural, and the artful, which results in the disruption and confounding of stable binarisms.[8] Furthermore, while Stein employs hermetic metaphors throughout her work, she does not rely solely upon encoded language systems to construct character or sexuality.[9] Rather, her use of ever-shifting repetition dismantles systems of verbal decorum that dictate that an aggregate of inherent traits equals a predetermined character.

Soon after moving permanently to Paris in the wake of her abortive affair with May Bookstaver, Stein began to purchase experimental art and became a close friend of Pablo Picasso's. Their joint employment of African sculpture enabled them to revolutionize their respective fields and to effect a break with mimetic theories of literary and pictorial representation. As Stein first deployed her literary strategies of masking in "Melanctha," she simultaneously became the subject of an artistic experimentation in pictorial masking. During the time she created the portrait of the "complex and desiring" Melanctha Herbert, Picasso rendered the mask-like painting that has become the iconographic representation of Stein. The portrait shows her leaning slightly forward in an armchair, her voluminous figure dominating its surroundings. Picasso, who claimed he could no longer "see" her when looking at her actual face, finished the portrait without her, painting out the original head and giving her an artificially white, sphinx-like face with prominent eyes, a large and sharply angled nose, and a straight, determined mouth. In *The Autobiography of Alice B. Toklas*, Stein comments that for Picasso, this portrait marked the transition "from the harlequin, the charming early italian period to the intensive struggle which was to end in cubism."[1] Similarly, Stein felt that "Melanctha" marked her own movement from nineteenth-century realism to twentieth-century modernist experimentation. Her deployment of the mask as a metaphor for modern culture relates to the affinity Stein perceived between American and Spanish cultures, both of which combined features of African, Latin, Anglo, and Jewish cultural traditions, and whose forms and language

8. Such triple oscillations are also characteristic of the gay-lesbian rhetoric of "camp," which destabilizes binary categories of gender and sexuality through such devices as grotesque exaggeration, the defiant camp laugh, and inversions of serious and trivial and high and low subject matter and style.

9. Stein's short story, "Miss Furr and Miss Skeene," provides an excellent example of how Stein employs repetition to encode words with special (that is, lesbian and gay) meanings. Stein strategically repeats the words "regular" (to show that gays and lesbians are not "irregular"), "cultivate" (to suggest the pedagogical and socially constructed nature of homosexual identity), and "gay" (to indicate that gays and lesbians are not "morbid") in her campy and tongue-in-cheek portrait of the lives and adventures of two lesbians. See "Miss Furr and Miss Skeene" in Gertrude Stein, *Selected Writings of Gertrude Stein*, ed. Carl Van Vechten (1946; rpt. New York, 1990), pp. 563–68.

1. Gertrude Stein, *The Autobiography of Alice B. Toklas*, in ibid., p. 50.

tended toward "elemental abstraction" because of their racially, verbally, and visually "composite" or "mulatto" character.[2] Although Stein later denied that African sculpture exerted any influence on her cubist writing, the language and method of "Melanctha," like her other works dealing with racial difference, depend heavily upon the three-dimensional African mask. But Stein states that whereas Europeans such as Matisse regarded African sculpture as primitive, naive, and exotic, she and Picasso, by contrast, regarded the mask as "natural, direct and civilized."[3]

In "Melanctha," Stein employs the African mask as an abstract persona that embodies the principle of abstraction and conducts the reader-audience through the imbricated narrative significations of race, gender, sexuality, education, and "environment." This mask defamiliarizes and denaturalizes mimetic Western modes of narrative representation and therefore radically alters conventional assumptions regarding the interrelationships among stereotype, character, voice, and discourse. Henry Louis Gates, Jr., explains that certain African cultures regard the mask as nothing more than "a doll in wood" until the artist carries it before his choral audience, at which point it functions as "mask in motion." Governed by "laws of cohesive interiority" and neutral to exterior norms and mores, the mask represents "the essence of immobility fused with the essence of mobility; fixity with transience; order with chaos; permanence with the transitory; the substantial with the evanescent."[4]

The narrator functions as the voice behind the mask, bringing before the audience what Gates describes as "a dialectic embracing potentially unresolvable social forms, notions of origin, and issues of value."[5] By encompassing the issues that divide and disarray the audience, the masked artist functions to unify the community by dramatizing the contradictions which comprise the whole. In "Melanctha," Stein represents this "bridging" function in the name of the town in which the action occurs, Bridgepoint. The mask simul-

---

2. Ibid., p. 60.

3. Ibid., p. 61. Cubist works such as Picasso's *Les demoiselles d'Avignon* modified older European artistic traditions of including blacks in paintings as signs of sensuality. Picasso used blacks and African masks in abstract representations of suffering and sexuality and linked the presence of women and nonwhites to these themes. Even the supposedly "revolutionary" dadaists and surrealists continued the practice of juxtaposing the white female with African masks, creating a collage of white female body (or head) against African head (or body), as in Man Ray's *Kiki*, Hannah Hoch's *Monument to Vanity II*, or Max Ernst's *Elephant of the Celebes*.

4. Henry Louis Gates, Jr., "Dis and Dat: Dialect and the Descent," in *Afro-American Literature: The Reconstruction of Instruction*, ed. Dexter Fisher and Robert B. Stepto (New York, 1979), p. 89. The comments of traditional African sculptors, such as the Baule carvers of the Yamoussoukro area of the Ivory Coast, indicate that the mask is not an aesthetic object d'art cut off from action and isolated from display; rather, it *is* action. For further discussion of Western misinterpretations of non-Western art, see Marianna Torgovnick, *Gone Primitive: Savage Intellects, Modern Lives* (Chicago, 1990).

5. Ibid., pp. 89–90.

taneously impinges upon and provides a vehicle for voices that respond to complex and ever-changing oppositions between their interior states and the intersecting exterior "labels" the masks bear.

The story explores the abstract dialectic of the African mask most forcibly through the relationship between Melanctha Herbert and Rose Johnson. Rose, whose character exemplifies the power to maintain stable selfhood through cunning manipulations of the mask, lacks the selflessness required to nourish and care for her newborn baby. Her friend Melanctha, whose inability to remain in any one place demonstrates the chaos of the mask in perpetual motion, leaves to "wander," and the baby dies. The narrator comments that since such deaths are "common" in this world, it is soon forgotten. Nevertheless, the death of the baby becomes a metaphor for the lapse of the nourishing bond between Melanctha and Rose, and for the various types of carelessness and inattentiveness that not only make Melanctha "blue" about "the way her world was made" (p. 87) but that eventually result in her own death as well.

The structure of the narrative reinforces the encompassing theme of private and public forgetfulness and speechlessness through a circular, repetitive pattern that begins with Rose and Melanctha, then moves back in time to describe Melanctha's unhappy childhood, her early "wanderings" in search of sexual and intellectual "wisdom," her passionate initiatory relationship with Jane Harden, her frustrated romance with Jeff Campbell, the history of her friendship with Rose, and her brief engagement to the gambler Jem Richards. Shortly after the death of the baby, the event that simultaneously marks the beginning and the ending of the narrative, both Jem and Rose break with Melanctha and thus sever her tenuous bonds with the community. Melanctha subsequently dies alone in a hospital from consumption, literally consumed by "wandering" through worlds in which she could not discover her "right position."

The opening pages of "Melanctha," however, seem to confirm the judgment of many critics that the text is simply racist.[6] The narrator describes Rose Johnson, a shrewdly successful if hardly ideal character, in terms so bumptiously stereotypical and naively reductive that they seem intentionally to mock their own claims to authority and reliability:

> Rose Johnson was a real black, tall, well built, sullen, stupid, childlike, good looking negress. She laughed when she was

6. See Richard Bridgman, "Melanctha," *American Literature* 33 (1961): 350–59; Sonia Saldívar-Hull, "Wrestling Your Ally: Stein, Racism, and Feminist Critical Practice," in *Women's Writing in Exile*, ed. Mary Lynn Broe and Angela Ingram (Chapel Hill, NC, 1989), pp. 182–95; Aldon Nielsen, *Reading Race: White American Poets and the Racial Discourse* (Athens, GA, 1988); and Milton A. Cohen, "Black Brutes and Mulatto Saints: The Racial Hierarchy of Stein's 'Melanctha,'" *Black American Literature Forum* 26 (1986): 119–21. (See pp. 358–67 for Saldívar-Hull.)

happy and grumbled and was sullen with everything that troubled. . . . Rose was careless and was lazy, but she had been brought up by white folks and she needed decent comfort. Her white training had only made for habits, not for nature. Rose had the simple, promiscuous unmorality of the black people. [pp. 85–86].

Because all of her seemingly positive attributes are physical while her negative ones are psychological or behavioral, this description clearly links the "blackness" or "real" blackness in "negresses" such as Rose Johnson with sexual unmorality.[7] Nevertheless, because the mask functions to jam the machinery of received stereotypes, slight discrepancies begin to appear among her various attributes as the narrative progresses and Rose animates the static "doll-like" mask she wears in the opening description. The narrator, for example, describes Rose as "coarse, decent, sullen, ordinary, good looking, black [and] childish," but "coarse" does not quite complement "decent" or "good looking" (p. 86). The descriptions of Rose, like those of the other characters, simultaneously remain stable and shift slightly from iteration to iteration. As the narrative contexts, the events, and the relationships among the characters develop and permutate, the function, meaning, and value of stereotype and attribute undergo constant revision. Therefore Rose, described at the beginning of the narrative as "unmoral, promiscuous, shiftless," becomes at the end of the story "always so simple, solid, decent," although the narrative itself has returned to the time and place where it began (pp. 86, 214).

The shifting vocabulary intrudes a disjunctive quality into the narrative, giving the story the impression of having two simultaneous but radically incompatible purposes in mind. What appears, divorced from context, as the Lockean opposition between her "black" nature and her "white" upbringing becomes the process through which Rose manipulates the perceived difference between habit and nature to acquire power within her community and secure her material and social position. Rose has not naturalized her white training, and thus these external habits do not operate, as the "Veil" does for Helga Crane, to inwardly divide Rose from her "nature." Rather, they simply make Rose shrewdly aware of the practical social advantage or value of maintaining appearances considered respectable, so she takes care to marry well and live "regular." Rose seems aware that the mask-like attributes of her "white habits" and "real black" nature have real power and reality only in the context of her membership

7. The description leaves uncertain whether "real" black connotes "very," "really," or "truly." The use of this descriptor, however, implies the "reality" of an "unreal" black or blackness. Like the use of "unmorality" rather than "immorality," the word "real" dismantles the mechanisms that stabilize any unitary notion of "real" (that is, authentic) black identity.

in the black community, not as an outsider in the white community. Rose's capacity to ground herself within her "nature" and heterosexual black community explains why Melanctha feels "lost" once Rose casts her away, and why Rose eventually "worked in to be the deepest of all of Melanctha's emotions" (pp. 233–34).

Unlike Rose, Melanctha Herbert falls victim to her ability to perceive contradictions and her inability to manipulate them to her advantage. The mask of silence she wears concerning her private memory and history connects to her desire to remove or reduce the mask itself to verbal illusion. In essence, Melanctha wishes to speak a "dialect" of private desire that is voiceless and invisible because her public world has no language, form, or memory for it. For Stein, Melanctha's inability to articulate her desires coherently symbolizes the problems of constructing an adequate language of lesbian sexuality in the absence of a historical record of lesbian community. Her wandering becomes emblematic of her search for wisdom and power that transcend the abstract essences of race and sex, and thus of her homelessness, her ungrounded condition, and the "blues" evoked in her at "the thought of how all her world was made" (p. 87). The disparate fates of Rose and Melanctha demonstrate that stereotype has harsh consequences for those who, bereft of history and community, cannot find the means to differentiate between "essence" as contextualized identity and "essence" as internalized label. By repeatedly posing the riddle of the enigmatic and seemingly incongruous nature of the relationship between Rose and Melanctha, the narrator challenges the reader to unravel the mystery at the heart of the story:

> Why did the subtle, intelligent, attractive, half white girl Melanctha Herbert love and do for and demean herself in service to this coarse, decent, sullen, ordinary, black childish Rose, and why was this unmoral, promiscuous, shiftless Rose married, and that's not so common either, to a good man of the negroes, while Melanctha with her white blood and attraction and her desire for a right position had not yet been really married. [p. 86]

The answer to this riddle proves as "complex and desiring" as Melanctha herself and compels the reader to wander down many pathways, which commence with the differences between the treatments Rose and Melanctha receive during childhood, and how race and gender influence personal and collective perceptions of the cultural significations of "blood," family, community, and sexuality. While Rose has a childhood marked by differences of race but unmarked by emotional turmoil, Melanctha finds her childhood "bitter to remember" and torn by parental neglect and conflict (p. 90). Melanctha, the perennial social outsider, despite her presumed advantages of education and skin color, has far less social grounding and community support than Rose, by whom Melanctha ultimately wishes to be loved and mothered.

Milton Cohen, who treats race as the only significant marker in his literalized analysis of the text, and thereby divorces race from the interior reality of the characters, argues that racism makes "Melanctha" artistically flawed because the incongruous representations of the characters "cast considerable doubt on the depth and acuity of [Stein's] perceptions of human nature."[8] To illustrate the "ominously schematic" nature of Stein's "racial hierarchy," he himself employs a schematic diagram correlating character roles, skin color, and characteristics. But because Cohen does not read the text as narrative and does not discuss equally pertinent factors such as individual history, gender, sexuality, or social status, discrepancies appear in his own schema. For instance, he confuses the consequences of genetic inheritance with those of parental conflict, arguing that "Melanctha's contradictory behavior derives from the *genetic* opposition of her black father's violent impulsiveness and attraction to power and experience, and her pale yellow mother's 'sweet, mysterious, uncertain, and pleasant' character."[9] But Stein does not equate the science of genetics with cultural interpretations of difference, and Chidi Ikonne astutely notes that it would "take courses in genetics and genealogy" to understand how Melanctha, the daughter of a "very black man" and a "pale yellow colored woman," can be elsewhere described as "having been half made with real white blood."[1]

The spirit of the Yoruban trickster figure, Esu-Elegbara, seems to animate the mask and launches a triadic oscillation between nature, society, and art that explodes stable binary categories.[2] For example, readers who assume that the mask-like narrator associates whiteness with abstract value will then assume that the redeeming characteristics of Rose derive from her "white training" and those of Melanctha from her "pale yellow" skin color or her "real white blood." The same readers will associate the "near whiteness" of Jane Harden with the education and cultural privilege she shares with Melanctha but will have trouble reconciling her white value with her bisexuality, alcoholism, and recklessness, or explaining why Jane shares most of her attributes with James Herbert, Melanctha's "big black virile" father (p. 90). What does an angry, virile, very black heterosexual

---

8. Cohen, p. 121.
9. Ibid., p. 120 (italics mine).
1. Chidi Ikonne, *From Du Bois to Van Vechten: The Early New Negro Literature, 1903–1926* (Westport, CT, 1981), p. 22.
2. For discussions of the importance of the dual-gendered "trickster figure" to African American literature and culture, see Robert Farris Thompson, *Flash of the Spirit: African and Afro-American Art and Philosophy* (New York, 1983); and Henry Louis Gates, Jr., *The Signifying Monkey: A Theory of African-American Literary Criticism* (New York, 1988).

man have in common with an abrasive, rebellious, nearly white bisexual woman? Both live on the margins of respectable community, whether black or white, yet both possess the power to sustain their outlaw status with relative impunity. While Melanctha respects the power which her angry father and her reckless female lover both possess, her "complex and desiring" character does not comport with the narrow forcefulness that empowers her two role models. By labeling the same traits of character "white" at one point and "black" at another, the narrator demonstrates how factors such as gender, sexuality, and social status destabilize interpretations of the meaning of race and make membership within a stable community essential for all but the most extreme or powerful characters.

After the period of initiatory sexual and social education in which her lover Jane Harden "loved Melanctha hard and made Melanctha feel it very deeply . . . [and] . . . made Melanctha understand what everybody wanted, and what one did with power when one had it" (p. 106), the relationship becomes "different" as Melanctha acquires greater equality through learning the social rhetoric and etiquette of power.[3] The fact that Melanctha leaves Jane once she gains equal power with her lover reveals the status of their relationship in Melanctha's mind as intrinsically temporary and youthful—a stage (much like formal education or the "immature" stage posited by Freud) to "pass" through on the way to heterosexual adulthood. But her limited conception of her lesbian relationship with Jane points to a fundamental impasse in her thinking, which leads to her eventual downfall. While Melanctha cannot conceptualize her lesbian rite de passage with Jane as her permanent "right position," she also cannot discover an appropriate language or "right position" within relations structurally based on unequal power. "Right position" has obvious sexual connotations, and since Melanctha cannot imagine something other than sexual submission or domination, she is bound to find her experiment in an adult lesbian relationship based on the "right position" of sexual and social equality unsatisfactory or confusing.

This central contradiction becomes exhaustively dramatized after Melanctha leaves Jane and starts a heterosexual relationship with Jefferson Campbell, the "serious, earnest, good young joyous doctor" who "loved his own colored people" and laughed with the "free abandoned laughter that gives the warm broad glow to negro sunshine" (pp. 110–11). Stein transfers the heterosexist paradigms that limited the relationship between Adele and Helen in *Q.E.D.* to the similar clash between Jeff and Melanctha over middle-class morality and

3. Stein links Jane's characteristic mode of loving Melanctha "hard" not to any supposedly inherent genetic abnormality or degeneracy, but to her last name, which she has obviously "acquired" from her father.

bohemian mores. Unlike the other major characters, all of whom bear conflicting attributes, Jeff Campbell appears *almost* seamlessly consistent, in his "proper" gender attributes, his "mulatto" racial mixture, and in the "light brown" and "pale brown" parental types that form and inform his character. This consistency seems connected with his cheerful but doctrinaire espousal of racial uplift, which involves adhering to the rules of regulated existence and avoiding "running around" and "excitements." Ironically, Jeff seems to embody the stereotype of the "happy darkie" associated with uneducated rural blacks, but here his "negro sunshine" represents his naive conceptions of racial identity, his lack of sexual "wisdom," and the comforts of his middle-class existence. Protected from the contradictory nature of experience within "his" community, Jeff both deplores and obsesses over the thirst for "excitements" among the "colored people":

> No I ain't got any use for all the time being in excitements and wanting to have all kinds of experience all the time. I got plenty of experience just living regular and quiet and with my family, and doing my work, and taking care of people, and trying to understand it. I don't believe much in this running around business and I don't want to see the colored people do it. I am a colored man and I ain't sorry, and I want to see the colored people want what is good and what I want them to have, and that's to live regular and work hard and understand things, and that's enough to keep any decent man excited. [p. 117]

Melanctha, the proponent of "experience" and "real wisdom," exposes the contradictory and unintelligible logic that characterizes his polemic and creates a chasm between his abstract values and concrete experience. While Jeff deplores the wayward behaviors that hinder the progress of the "colored people," his profession allows him to enjoy these excitements vicariously rather than living them directly. For example, Melanctha astutely observes that while Jeff befriends and admires Jane Harden, the "good people" he lavishly extols regard her as a deplorably "bad woman:"

> Seems to me Dr. Campbell you find her to have something in her, and you go there very often, and you talk to her much more than you do to the nice girls that stay at home with their people, the kind you say you are really wanting. It don't seem to me Dr. Campbell, that what you say and what you do seem to have much to do with each other. . . . It seems to me, Dr. Campbell you want to have a good time just like all us others, and then you just keep on saying that it's right to be good and you ought not to have excitements, and yet you really don't want to do it Dr. Campbell, no more than me or Jane Harden. No, Dr. Camp-

bell, it certainly does seem to me you don't know very well yourself, what you mean, when you are talking. [pp. 117–18]

Jeff and Melanctha now launch into an even more elaborate and
exhaustive version of the seemingly endless disputations and struggles between Adele and Helen in *Q.E.D.* In the process of debating
the relative values of sensation and direct experience, on the one
hand, and reason and deliberation on the other, their positions
become to some extent enmeshed, but the relationship finally col-
lapses under the sheer weight of accumulated verbal baggage. Furthermore, Melanctha loses her patience with Jeff when she begins
to gain equal power with him and hence begins to "trust" him. She
remains interested in Jeff only so long as she can oppose him and
hence retain her autonomy, difference, and distance from him.
Despite all his attractive and stable qualities, Jeff is, at last, an enormous bore, and Melanctha, like the reader, escapes from the tedium
of his company with relief. Melanctha wanders back once more to
Rose, in search of a stable mask, female-centered community, and
maternal home that will prove more that is "real" than an evanescent
verbal illusion.

The self-protective silence Melanctha stoically maintains around
her innermost personal history serves as her enduring mask, and it
not only accounts for the apparent gaps in her memory but also for
her inability "to tell a story wholly . . . to leave out big pieces which
make a story very different, for when it came to what had happened
and what she had said and what it was that she had really done,
Melanctha never could remember right" (p. 100). Her urgent need
to camouflage her history becomes manifest in her desire for complete experiential immersion in a continual present tense. The fact
that Melanctha feels obliged to mask herself to evade the social
stigma of her unhappy history forms the most viable critique of
"Melanctha" as a racist text, for without an active history to explain
herself to herself, Melanctha and those around her are to some
extent obliged to regard their conditions as immutable if incongruous
"facts of nature." Nevertheless, the silence of Melanctha as character
serves as the mask of silence for Stein as author as well. Stein clearly
wished to transcend the painful and distorting aspects of her relationship with May Bookstaver, but in the complex translation of personal memory into narrative, she transfers her dilemma over
enunciating her personal history and private language onto her fictional character. The absence of a history of lesbian existence, like
the absence of a coherent history of racial oppression, reduces cultural differences to biological essences in the perceptions of the culture at large. For Stein and Melanctha the modernist philosophy of
the "continuous present" not only becomes a mode of bringing

coherence to otherwise disconnected personal histories, but also of foregrounding the invisibility or unintelligibility of lesbian sexuality within an economy that recognizes and legitimates only one (male) desiring subjectivity.

"Real wisdom" becomes the function of the language Stein creates to establish an equivalence between the abstract attributes of the mask and the formal features of the spoken language the characters employ. The "bottom nature" and "bottom rhythm" of each character becomes manifest in the distinct patterns of repetition, syntax, phrasing, and diction of their speech. Stein, unlike other white authors of her day, broke from the minstrel tradition of rendering black vernacular speech through orthographic distortions, such as mutilated spelling and elision, designed to reinforce the sense of linguistic caricature and parody by making the language comically or pathetically aberrant and broken. Rather, Stein deploys the African mask to disassemble the system of verbal correctness that creates the distinction between "normal" and "deviant" language. For example, the durable Rose, who has no interest in "wandering" and little patience with the "blues" that fill Melanctha with despair, speaks in direct and simple patterns of emphatic repetition that express her rooted determination to survive:

> I don't see Melanctha why you should talk like you would kill yourself just because you're blue. I'd never kill myself Melanctha just 'cause I was blue. I'd maybe kill somebody else Melanctha 'cause I was blue, but I'd never kill myself. If I ever killed myself Melanctha it'd be by accident, and if I ever killed myself by accident Melanctha, I'd be awful sorry. [p. 89]

In contrast, the "blues" evoked in Melanctha at "the thought of how all her world was made" (p. 89) evinces her recognition that the limitation resides not within her, but within the structures that inhibit her powers of expression. The highly evocative terms associated with Melanctha—"blues," "wisdom," "desiring," "power," "wandering," "complex," "experience," "trouble," "right position"— constellate resonant clusters of emotive and mythic association whose meaning neither the narrative persona nor Melanctha herself ever clearly articulates, but whose very indeterminacy augment their connotative charge. The sublime object of her complex desire eludes her grasp, and because her aspirations have no concrete verbal or visual reality within her community, Melanctha finally loses her foothold in the world and dies.

Racial Masquerade, African Art, and Lesbian Panic

The theme and plot of *Passing* reveal that Nella Larsen not only comprehended the dilemmas of silence and self-division that confronted both Melanctha as character and Stein as author, but also that she experienced these dilemmas as an African American woman writer who embodied the intersections of racial difference and gender. Whereas for Stein racial identity was primarily, in the case of "Melanctha," a metaphor, for Larsen race was ontologically inseparable from day-to-day existence and, by extension, from literary aesthetics. In Clare Kendry, Larsen creates a character who, while faced with many of the same problems as Melanctha Herbert, nonetheless addresses them with more determination and self-conscious irony than does Stein's protagonist. Oscillating between what Houston A. Baker terms the "cryptic" mask of self-disguise and the "phaneric" mask of self-display, Clare does not internalize the sexual and racial self-divisions of the "Veil," but rather becomes highly adept at subverting the expectations and eluding the domination of others through selective shape-shifting and camouflage.[4]

*   *   *

Minority Consciousness and Interracial "Queer" Culture

In voluntary exile in Paris, Gertrude Stein not only freed herself from the repressive ethos of American society but also found the means to create an experimental literary language that, based on simple oral diction and repetition-within-variation, challenged traditional Western conceptions of character and representation. In "Melanctha," Stein employs the African mask in what represents one of the first and most ambitious attempts to articulate the minority consciousness of lesbians by imbricating the issues of sexual orientation, gender identification, and racial difference with those of historical absence, cultural invisibility, and social taboo. Stein wrote "Melanctha" at a time when blacks and lesbians, if mentioned or recognized at all, were portrayed by others as infantile, prurient, sensational, decadent, criminal, or insane creatures beyond the pale of Western civilization. Legal discourse did not recognize the existence of lesbians and relegated blacks to segregation under cover of a "separate but equal" interpretation of the Fourteenth Amendment.[5] Scientific

4. Houston A. Baker, *Modernism and the Harlem Renaissance* (Chicago, 1987), pp. 51–52. Baker derives the term "phaneric" from the zoologist H. B. Cott, who uses "phaneric" to designate one of the "allaesthetic" characteristics designed to enhance self-preservation and survival through aggressive self-advertisement (H. B. Cott, "Animal Form in Relation to Appearance," in *Aspects of Form: A Symposium on Form in Art and Nature*, ed. Lancelot Law Whyte [Bloomington, IN, 1951], pp. 122–23). As Baker notes, "Rather than concealing or disguising in the manner of the *cryptic* mask (a colorful mastery of codes), the phaneric mask is meant to advertise. It distinguishes rather than conceals. It secures territorial advantage and heightens a group's survival possibilities" (p. 51).

5. In *Plessy v. Ferguson* (1896), Justice Henry B. Brown, writing for a majority of seven, institutionalized racial segregation by establishing a specious distinction between the "political" and "cultural" rights of the two races. "The object of the [Fourteenth] amend-

discourses of medical sexology and eugenics treated both groups as biologically inferior entities or social problems to solve or, at best, tolerate. Rejecting both the scientific models of female sexuality she had imbibed at medical school and the fin-de-siècle literary representations of lesbians, Stein seized upon the African mask as an artifact from what she perceived as civilized African cultures to challenge and explore dominant Western conceptions of the primitive. For Stein, the cult of primitivism was a Western romantic notion, derived from Rousseau, of "uncivilized" wildness, suffering, and sexuality that revealed much more about the displaced fears and fantasies of contemporary Europeans than it did about non-Western cultures. Thus, in "Melanctha" Stein domesticates the issues of cultural difference and historical absence raised by the African mask by exploring the consciousness of racial and sexual minorities who are colonized *within* Western culture by projections of primitivism.

In *Passing*, Larsen further subverts the modernist appropriation of the African mask by exploring the colonized consciousness of her unreliable narrator Irene Redfield, who internalizes the "Veil" of sexual and racial self-division. Upholding the seemingly contrary principles of cultural assimilation and racial segregation, Irene projects onto her childhood friend Clare Kendry the tropes of exoticism and primitivism that Europeans projected onto African cultures. Larsen thus reveals that such tropes have their basis in *unspeakable* racial and sexual taboos, which, in turn, are generated by dominant conceptions of bourgeois propriety and morality. American society transforms Clare into an illicit object of desire for Irene, who ultimately acts to preserve her sense of identity and place by destroying Clare through the agency of lesbian panic.

The fates of both Larsen and Stein on the literary marketplace have thus far been separate but unequal, because, while Stein employed the African mask as an artistic vehicle, Larsen literally inhabited the mask of racial difference. Nonetheless, an examination of issues of sexuality and gender in the works of both of these ground-breaking artists reveals, as Jurgen Habermas has argued, that the project of modernity is not exhausted but merely unfinished. An examination of the history of interracial gay and lesbian culture not only reveals the process by which lesbians and gays constructed a minority identity and consciousness but also uncovers the extent to which racial prejudice and sexual taboos inevitably operate in tandem.

---

ment was undoubtedly to enforce the absolute equality of the two races before the law, but, in the nature of things, it could not have been intended to abolish distinctions based upon color, or to enforce social, as distinguished from political, equality, or a commingling of the two races upon terms unsatisfactory to either. Laws permitting, and even requiring, their separation, in places where they are liable to be brought into contact, do not necessarily imply the inferiority of either race to the other" (*The Supreme Court Reporter*, *Vol. 16* [St. Paul, MN, 1896], pp. 1138–48).

MICHAEL NORTH

[Stein, Picasso, and African Masks]†

Not long after the publication of *The Nigger of the "Narcissus,"* European artists were attracted en masse to an African art they knew virtually nothing about and were mesmerized by the way that African masks and statues dislocated all conventional artistic strategies.[1] A 1924 *Opportunity* editorial described this new influence as a "forcible entry" and an invasion, promising or warning, it is hard to tell, "Soon primitive Negro art will invade this country as it has invaded Europe. It is inevitable." For aesthetes like Alain Locke and Albert Barnes, the African vogue that influenced Picasso, Apollinaire, Cendrars, Stravinsky, Satie, and many others augured a new prominence for African-American creativity as well, a rise in attention, if not estimation, that Matheus later compared to Wait's arrival and domination.[2]

The questions raised by Conrad's preface and novel are also relevant to this wider African influence on modern art. What is the role of race, of racial prejudice, stereotyping, and romantic identification, in the crisis of representation that Picasso purposely provoked in paintings like *Les Demoiselles d'Avignon*? Was this new interest primarily ethnographic, fixated on the culture that could be rather luridly imagined behind a single African artifact, or was it aesthetic, with the artifact seen as a new arrangement of shapes in space? Was it part of an escapist daydream or a radical disruption of European representational conventions?

One way of answering these questions is to examine the role of Africa in one of the most celebrated relationships in European mod-

---

† From *The Dialect of Modernism: Race, Language, and Twentieth-Century Literature* (New York: Oxford University Press, 1994), pp. 59–62, 70–71, 72–75. Copyright © 1994 by Michael North. Used by permission of Oxford University Press, Inc.

1. "The modern movement in art gets its inspiration undoubtedly from African art, and it could not be otherwise." Paul Guillaume, "African Art at the Barnes Foundation," *Opportunity* 2 (May 1924): 140–41. Quoted in Chidi Ikonné, *From Du Bois to Van Vechten: The Early New Negro Literature, 1903–1926* (Westport, Conn.: Greenwood Press, 1981), pp. 3–4. Though current scholarly opinion is a good deal cooler on the subject, it still acknowledges the force of European fascination with African masks and statues. See the catalogue of the Museum of Modern Art exhibition *"Primitivism" in 20th Century Art: Affinity of the Tribal and the Modern*, ed. William Rubin (New York: Museum of Modern Art, 1984), in which Rubin takes issue with previous opinions like Guillaume's but also argues at length for an important but rather vaguely defined "affinity" between "tribal" art and the modern. The controversy surrounding this exhibition gives a good indication of current opinion about this "affinity." See, for example, James Clifford, "Histories of the Tribal and the Modern," *Art in America* 73 (April 1985): 164–77, 215; reprinted in *The Predicament of Culture* (Cambridge, Mass.: Harvard University Press, 1988); Hal Foster, "The 'Primitive' Consciousness of Modern Art," *October* 34 (Fall 1985): 45–70; and Rosalind Krauss, "Preying on 'Primitivism,' " *Art & Text* 17 (April 1985): 58–62.

2. "Dr. Barnes," *Opportunity* 2 (May 1924): 133; Alain Locke, "A Note on African Art," *Opportunity* 2 (May 1924): 134–38.

ernism, namely, that of Pablo Picasso and Gertrude Stein. Their
meeting took place at a crucial moment both for them and for the
arts they practiced, with Stein just beginning to write under the influence of postimpressionism and Picasso on the verge of disrupting
his canvases with actual words. This crossing of old boundaries had
a lot to do with the beginnings of modernism, but it was accompanied
by another, rather different, crossing, as Stein and Picasso simultaneously discovered African art. Though the first of these "transgressions" seems aesthetic and the second ethnographic, it may be that
their relationship is more than coincidental.

Both Stein and Picasso came to resent the myth that modernism
began on the day Matisse showed them an African figurine he had
found in a secondhand shop.[3] Late in his life, Picasso strenuously
denied that he had been crucially influenced by African art, and
Stein said of herself in *The Autobiography of Alice B. Toklas*: "She
was not at any time interested in African sculpture."[4] And yet the
original frontispiece of this very work shows Stein ensconced behind
her writing desk, awaiting Alice, with a piece of African sculpture
prominently displayed before her. This is perhaps one of a group of
objects Stein purchased for Picasso at Nîmes in 1918.[5] Her acting
as Picasso's agent in this case is emblematic, despite the disclaimers,
of their collaborative use of African models in inventing modernism.

One of the most important episodes in the birth of that movement
occurred shortly before Matisse brought his find to Stein's studio. In
the winter of 1906 Picasso ended a long struggle with his portrait of
Stein by repainting a likeness he had labored over for as many as
ninety-two sittings. On this generally realistic portrait he superimposed a flat, expressionless mask with two eye slits cut against the
angle of the rest of the face and body, a mask derived from ancient
Iberian reliefs he had seen at the Louvre. This portrait was the first

3. There is a good deal of dispute about the timing and significance of this discovery. For
   Stein's account, in which Matisse surprises Picasso with an African statue, see *The Autobiography of Alice B. Toklas* (1933; rpt. New York: Random House/Vintage, 1960), p. 63.
   For the most minute investigation see William Rubin, "Picasso," in Rubin, ed., esp.
   pp. 337, n. 86 and 339, n. 138.
4. Stein, *Autobiography of Alice B. Toklas*, p. 64. See the critical commentary on this and
   other passages in Stein's work in Aldon Lynn Nielsen, *Reading Race: White American
   Poets and the Racial Discourse in the Twentieth Century* (Athens: University of Georgia
   Press, 1988), pp. 22–24. Picasso's later dismissals of African art as an influence are con-
   sidered strategic by William Rubin. See his "From Narrative to 'Iconic' in Picasso: The
   Buried Allegory in *Bread and Fruitdish on a Table* and the Role of *Les Demoiselles
   D'Avignon*," Art Bulletin 65 (December 1983): 645; and "Picasso," p. 335, n. 52. See also
   Gertrude Stein, *Picasso: The Complete Writings*, ed. Edward Burns (1970; rpt. Boston:
   Beacon, 1985), p. 47.
5. Rubin, "Picasso," pp. 297–98. In the surviving correspondence Picasso asks Stein to look
   for "les statues negres" for him and then refers to the objects Stein subsequently purchased
   as "les negres." Pablo Picasso to Gertrude Stein, December 1917 (letter 101), and April
   26, 1918 (letter 104), Stein correspondence, American Literature Collection, Beinecke
   Rare Book and Manuscript Library, Yale University.

Man Ray: Gertrude Stein and Alice B. Toklas (ca. 1922). Frontispiece, *The Autobiography of Alice B. Toklas* (New York: Random House, 1933). © 2006 Man Ray Trust/Artists Rights Society (ARS), NY/ADAGP, Paris.

in a series of paintings, all featuring rock-solid figures with impassive faces, that culminated in the women of *Les Demoiselles d'Avignon*, some of whom have faces much like the mask Picasso had fashioned for Stein, some of whom wear masks inspired by his visit to the Musée d'Ethnographie at the Palais du Trocadéro. In its finished state, therefore, *Les Demoiselles* is a virtual map of Picasso's progress from 1905 to 1907, from the Stein portrait, through Africa, to the first intimations of "what two years later would become Cubism."[6]

Even while sitting for Picasso, Stein was composing the work she herself would call, with a disarming lack of modesty, "the first definite step away from the nineteenth century and into the twentieth century in literature."[7] Stein took this step in a way remarkably like that of Picasso, for she composed this crucial work by covering a failed self-portrait with an ethnic mask. Having struggled unsuccessfully to account for an unhappy love affair in *Q.E.D.*, a book that remained unpublished until after her death, Stein rewrote the story, sometimes leaving whole lines of dialogue nearly intact, as "Melanctha," the story of a young black woman's emotional trials.[8]

Thus, Stein and Picasso take the first steps into cubism and literary modernism by performing uncannily similar transformations on the figure of Gertrude Stein herself. Placing a painted mask over his naturalistic portrait, Picasso duplicates the linguistic mask Stein was just devising for herself. By rewriting her own story for black characters, Stein anticipates, and perhaps even motivates, Picasso's use of African masks in *Les Demoiselles d'Avignon*. In each case, in painting and in literature, the step away from conventional verisimilitude into abstraction is accomplished by a figurative change of race.

Of course, Picasso's immediate models are not the same as Stein's, but the fact that Stein drew her inspiration from black Baltimoreans she encountered as a medical student and not from African art would not have mattered much at the time.[9] "Melanctha" was composed in a time of growing pan-Africanism, from the international pan-African conference in London in 1900 to the collapse of Marcus Garvey's movement in the early 1920s.[1] Stylized African masks drawn by the American Aaron Douglas figure prominently in the decorative artwork of *The New Negro*, and similar masks were at one time commissioned for Carl Van Vechten's *Nigger Heaven*.[2] In that

---

6. Rubin, "Picasso," pp. 247–48. For Stein's account of her sittings for the portrait see *The Autobiography of Alice B. Toklas*, pp. 46–47, 49, 53.

7. Stein, *The Autobiography of Alice B. Toklas*, p. 54.

8. Among many accounts of the similarities between these two works, the most interesting is still Richard Bridgman's "Melanctha," *American Literature* 33 (November 1961): 350–59. See also Bridgman's *Gertrude Stein in Pieces* (New York: Oxford University Press, 1970); and Jayne L. Walker, *Gertrude Stein: The Making of a Modernist* (Amherst: University of Massachusetts Press, 1984), pp. 27–38. (See pp. 346–55 for Walker.)

9. James R. Mellow, *Charmed Circle: Gertrude Stein & Company* (New York: Praeger, 1974), p. 44.

1. Cary D. Wintz, *Black Culture and the Harlem Renaissance* (Houston: Rice University Press, 1988), pp. 45–47.

2. Ikonné, pp. 27–28. It should be noted that the exact relationship between African art and African-American art and literature was discussed from a number of different points of view in *The New Negro*. Alain Locke himself was at least ambivalent on the subject, as shown by his own essay "The Legacy of the Ancestral Arts," which he significantly bracketed with Countee Cullen's poem "Heritage," which begins, "What is Africa to me?" *The New Negro*, ed. Alain Locke (1925; rpt. New York: Atheneum, 1968), pp. 250–67.

work itself the main character, who fitted Van Vechten's image of an up-to-date young black woman, collects African sculpture and quotes a long stretch of "Melanctha" from memory.[3]

* * *

3. Carl Van Vechten, *Nigger Heaven* (1926; rpt. New York: Octagon, 1980), pp. 55, 57. Van Vechten's curious preface to *Three Lives* is worth noting here, because in it he praises Stein as "so distinguished, so instinct with *race* and force and character . . . [original emphasis]" *Three Lives* (Norfolk: New Directions, 1933), p. viii.

Stein created a version of this mask for herself in "Melanctha." Just as Picasso had performed a sex change on one of his own alter egos to produce *Les Demoiselles*, Stein, in rewriting *Q.E.D.*, transformed Adele, her mouthpiece, into Dr. Jeff Campbell. On one hand, this change provides a convenient mask for the sexual feelings that disorder *Q.E.D.*, since it changes the lesbian relationships of that book into heterosexual ones. On the other hand, the revisionary masquerade sets up an uncanny oscillation, especially in that all of Adele's most conventional fears and prejudices have been transferred to Dr. Jeff, as if Stein chose to represent the more retrograde parts of her own psyche as male. Certainly, much of the shock value of "Melanctha" comes from the blithe reversal by which the woman "wanders" while the man fidgets at home.

One of the most objectionable aspects of "Melanctha" is certainly its fixation on the sexual lives of its subjects, as if African-American characters are to be understood primarily in sensual terms. Yet the shift of race seemed to make it easier for Stein to see the senses, even the body itself, as ruled by convention. Perhaps Stein, like her publishers, invites her predominantly white readership to identify with the characters and thus play a black role, and yet presenting race *as* a role seems an open invitation to consider it as culturally constituted and perhaps to consider gender a role as well. The residual ambiguity created by the racial masquerade makes gender and then finally the body itself seem a mask. Once again, then, the mask is not a cover for an unconventional sexuality but a revelation of it; even a means of achieving it. Like other forms of masquerade, particularly cross-dressing, the racial mask highlights what Kaja Silverman calls "the dislocation between subjectivity and the role."[4] The ambiguous relationship between mask and face, costume and body, makes it impossible to see biology as destiny.

Like the Arab robes of T. E. Lawrence or the Indian regalia of E. M. Forster, the racial masks that Stein and Picasso give to their own sexual ambiguity have a complex motivation and effect. There is, no doubt in each case, a longing for a certain kind of sensual freedom, found in Africa or Arabia or India because such freedom is always found "elsewhere," just as the natural is always found "elsewhere."[5] On the other hand, the mask maintains a tension between nature and convention, essence and accident, that expresses, even

4. Silverman, p. 11. See also Suleri, p. 142.
5. See Patrick Brantlinger on India as "a realm of imaginative license . . . a place where the fantastic becomes possible in ways that are carefully circumscribed at home." *Rule of Darkness: British Literature and Imperialism, 1830–1914* (Ithaca, N.Y.: Cornell University Press, 1988), p. 13. But this is not entirely a European mode of thought. See the discussion in Michael Taussig, *Shamanism, Colonialism, and the Wild Man: A Study in Terror and Healing* (Chicago: U of Chicago P, 1987) of the fact that "wherever you go, the great *brujos* [magicians or sorcerers] are elsewhere" (p. 179).

if it does not explain, the very process of displacement that simultaneously links and separates the two halves of each pair. The virtue of works like *Les Demoiselles* and "Melanctha" is that they bring out into the open the dialectical relationship between the mask as raw nature and the mask as cultural convention, and thus approximate the power of the African mask in its own context.

According to Henry Louis Gates, Jr., the African mask is a dialectical synthesis of all sorts of discordant qualities: "Mask is the essence of immobility fused with the essence of mobility, fixity with transience, order with chaos, permanence with the transitory, the substantial with the evanescent."[6] Picasso seems to have sensed in the African art he found in Paris similar possibilities, since he spoke of that art as both "raisonnable," that is to say, formally ordered, and "magicaux," uncanny, mysterious, occult.[7] Stein also spoke of African art as "natural, direct and civilised" as if to defy the usual contrast between the natural and the civilized.[8] These modernists were attracted to African art because it seemed to promise direct access to nature but also because it broke down the whole dichotomy between nature and culture.

Thus the mask that Picasso gives first to Stein is both ancient and impersonal while somehow also being a perfectly individual likeness, "the only reproduction of me which is always I, for me," as Stein put it.[9] A representation that is so obviously a "reproduction" can hardly be a perfect likeness as well, but Stein's insistence that the portrait *is* her is more than merely playful. What the portrait most faithfully represents is the tension, the slippage, between mask and face, between impersonality and individuality, conventional representation and likeness, which it was Stein's program in life and art to explore. Picasso's mask presents this program by only indirectly representing Stein's face.

*   *   *

According to Adam Gopnick, the mask that Picasso painted over the Stein portrait became, in its mixture of styles and forms, "a kind of creole." The beginnings of modernism are thus compared to what happens when two different dialect groups exchange vocabularies. The same comparison between mask and dialect is frequently made from the other direction. For example, Gates has used the African

---

6. Henry Louis Gates, Jr., *Figures in Black: Words, Signs, and the "Racial" Self* (New York: Oxford University Press, 1987), p. 168. See also Dennis Duerden, *The Invisible Present: African Art & Literature* (New York: Harper & Row, 1975), esp. p. 117.
7. Rubin, "Picasso," pp. 255; 335, n. 53.
8. Stein, *Picasso*, p. 52.
9. Ibid., p. 34. Note also Picasso's famous comment, quoted in Mellow (p. 93) among other places, that, though Stein does not now resemble her portrait, "She will."

mask as a metaphor for certain American linguistic and literary tactics. According to Gates, the literary version of the mask is dialect,
which he calls "a verbal mask."[1]

Yet the "self-conscious switch of linguistic codes" that Gates identifies as one of the primary strategies of dialect speakers is a mask
that does more than just cover or obscure. Under this definition
dialect is not a particular kind of language, not a mere deviation or
deformation, but a particular *use* of language. It puts the standard
language in conflict with itself, "constructing a continuum of variation," to quote Deleuze and Guattari, "negotiating all of the variables
both to constrict the constants and to expand the variables. . . ."[2]
Social linguists such as Shirley Brice Heath have discovered a similar
conflict in the course of empirical studies: different social and ethnic
groups use language for different purposes, call on it for different
reasons, and only a very few of these have to do with correctness of
expression.[3] Dialect is most like "a verbal mask" when it plays against
such correctness because then it approximates the mask's uncanny
power to focus the natural and the arbitrary in a single spot. Instead
of merely setting up a screen behind which nonstandard speakers
might plot or smirk, dialect actively contrasts what poses as natural
to its own conventions. It is this play *between* dialect and the standard language that resembles the tension the mask creates between
the face and its facsimile.

It is in this sense that Stein creates a mask of dialect in "Melanctha." The language in this work has been called "photographically
exact."[4] Though this may seem a bit extreme, the first publishers of
the story did send a representative to Stein's studio to determine if
she were in fact an educated native speaker, the language apparently
coming a bit too close to crude reality for perfect comfort.[5] But when
Stein wanted to write in dialect, as she did rather frequently in her
letters, she used the same phonological and syntactical conventions
that white American writers had been using for decades: "The cakes

1. Gates, *Figures in Black*, pp. 169, 171. See also the discussion of dialect and mask in
   Benedict R. O'G. Anderson, *Language and Power: Exploring Political Cultures in Indonesia*
   (Ithaca, N.Y.: Cornell University Press, 1990), pp. 129–31, 144, 149–51.
2. Gilles Deleuze and Félix Guattari, *A Thousand Plateaus: Capitalism and Schizophrenia*,
   trans. Brian Massumi (Minneapolis: University of Minnesota Press, 1987), p. 104. See
   also Deleuze and Guattari's *Kafka: Toward a Minor Literature*, trans. Dana Polan (Minneapolis: University of Minnesota Press, 1986).
3. Shirley Brice Heath, *Ways with Words: Language, Life, and Work in Communities and
   Classrooms* (Cambridge: Cambridge University Press, 1983).
4. George F. Whicher, quoted in Bridgman, "Melanctha," p. 356. This has been said in more
   recent criticism as well: "The syntactical devices Stein uses to probe the psyches of her
   characters, recorded in black English, are authentic." Bettina L. Knapp, *Gertrude Stein*
   (New York: Continuum, 1990), p. 86. And see the lengthy, quite favorable, discussion in
   Sylvia Wallace Holton, *Down Home and Uptown: The Representation of Black Speech in
   American Fiction* (London and Toronto: Associated University Presses, 1984), pp. 96–98.
5. Mellow, p. 87; Stein, *Autobiography of Alice B. Toklas*, p. 68. There is an intriguing resemblance between this episode and Edward Garnett's expectation that because he wrote of
   the East Conrad might be Asian himself.

did arrive and dey was damn good," or "We is doin business too."[6] There is very little of this sort of dialect in "Melanctha" itself.[7] What Stein does instead is to create a dialect in which conventions of verbal verisimilitude are played against themselves so that the speech seems simultaneously concrete and highly artificial.

The first readers of "Melanctha" were promised photographic realism because it was inconceivable in the atmosphere created by the dialect literature of the time that writing about black people could have any other purpose than photographic realism. Dialect was concrete language made and used by down-to-earth literalists, which is precisely why it appealed to—indeed, why it was most often created by—people who felt a surfeit of connotation. Thus R. Emmett Kennedy presented to his audience "crude, semi-barbarous poetry, if you will, but savoring of the real, original essence."[8]

Stein seems to feed the same appetite for the real and concrete by trapping her characters within a round of numbing repetition. In his study of colloquial language in American literature, Richard Bridgman observes, "In the dialogue of uninstructed characters, iteration is understood to result from their inability or superstitious unwillingness to substitute synonyms, pronouns or verbal auxiliaries for the concrete terms of their discussion. This steady, relentless hewing to a line of particulars suggests then that material reality is all that is trusted, all that can be depended upon to convey meaning."[9] Stein seems to make the same point by choosing a particular class of words for repeated repetition, words like *real*, *regular*, and *certainly*. Particularly in the speech of Jeff Campbell, reliance on these words suggests a desire to stabilize reality by fastening language to it ineluctably.

Yet this technique has the curious power to complicate even as it reiterates. As Kenneth Burke observes, "The most clear-sounding of words can be used for the vaguest of reference, quite as we speak of 'a certain thing' when we have no particular thing in mind." Burke points out that when we say that something is "essentially" true we often mean that it is not true at all.[1] In the same way, when we protest that something is "really" true, our emphasis suggests that there is some reason for doubt. Stein wedges an entire argument

6. Mellow, pp. 69, 64. See also p. 77.
7. A few exceptions might be found, such as the invariant *be* in Melanctha's promise to Jeff: "I be home Jeff to-night to see you" (p. 196). Yet even here the usage is incorrect, because the invariant *be* usually expresses an ongoing condition.
8. R. Emmett Kennedy, *Black Cameos* (New York: Albert & Charles Boni, 1924), p. xiv. This was a claim made over and over at the time. For a summary statement see C. Alphonso Smith, "Dialect Writers," in *The Cambridge History of American Literature*, ed. W. P. Trent et al. (New York: Putnam, 1918), p. 356.
9. Richard Bridgman, *The Colloquial Style in America* (New York: Oxford University Press, 1966), p. 92.
1. Kenneth Burke, *A Grammar of Motives* (1945; rpt. Berkeley: University of California Press, 1969), p. 52.

into the minute space between the adjective and its adverbial qualification. What does it mean, for example, that Rose Johnson is "married really" to her husband? (p. 88). Why is it necessary for her to
assure her friends that she is not married "falsely"? There are even
more possibilities in the negative case, as, for example, when the
narrator assures us that for all her wandering Melanctha never did
anything "really wrong" (p. 96).

In such cases, it seems that the very effort to nail language to a
single unequivocal reality defeats itself, as if the very act of invoking
the real over and over actually multiplied it. "It was all so nearly alike
it must be different and it is different," as Stein says elsewhere.[2]
Repetition of simple, basic words often has this effect in Stein, as,
for example, when Melanctha accuses Jeff Campbell: "[Y]ou want to
have a good time just like all us others, and then you just keep on
saying that it's right to be good . . ." (p. 118). To have "a good time"
is obviously the very opposite of being "good," as becomes clear at
the end of the story when Rose Johnson observes that Melanctha
"never come to no good" because she insisted on her right "to have
a good time" (p. 235). If "good" can mean both bad and good, then
it seems that very little is stable in the system of language or in the
morality it supports.

By taking the real and the good and transforming them into terms
of qualification, Stein raises a general suspicion about the way that
language attaches attributes to things. Several times in the course
of this story, Stein calls Jane Harden "a roughened woman" (pp. 104,
107). Thus, it would seem that her name is an appropriate one, des-
ignating some essential hardness in her nature. Yet she is called
"roughened," not "rough," and, if what Stein says elsewhere is true
and "people can be made by their names"[3] then perhaps Jane was
roughed up by her own name. Perhaps her "roughness" is merely an
impression that others have about her. Or perhaps it designates her
ability to "harden" others. But when Jeff Campbell accuses Melanctha of having "hard" ways like Jane, he exclaims, "I can't believe you
mean them hardly" (p. 138) so that "hardly" means both hardly and
hardly at all.

Thus the paradox on which Stein constructs the peculiar dialect
of "Melanctha." A patois with a very restricted vocabulary and a repetitious, looping sentence structure, it seems on the surface to correspond to Bridgman's description of a kind of speech that sticks
almost superstitiously to the known and familiar. And yet the more
Stein's speakers reiterate the few simple words allotted to them, the
more unstable those words become. Even in the act of assuring their

---

2. Gertrude Stein, *Selected Writings*, ed. Carl Van Vechten (1962; rpt. New York: Random/
Vintage, 1972), p. 519.
3. Gertrude Stein, *Lectures in America* (1935; rpt. Boston: Beacon Press, 1985), p. 210.

hearers that they can speak the truth, speakers like Jeff Campbell convict themselves of lying: "It's easy enough for me always to be honest, Miss Melanctha. All I got to do is always just to say right out what I am thinking. I certainly never have got any real reason for not saying it right out like that to anybody" (p. 128). The more he uses *certainly*, *real*, and *right* as magical intensifiers, the more one begins to doubt what he is saying. In fact, Jeff has just admitted, in the very same paragraph, "I just can't say that right out that way to you" (p. 128).

So much of the drama of "Melanctha" is about what characters say, instead of what they do, that this conflict between the sayable and the unsayable comes to dominate the story. It is Jeff's destructive habit of using words to pull intimate emotions to the surface that threatens and destroys his relationship with Melanctha. "You always wanting to have it all clear out in words always, what everybody is always feeling," Melanctha complains. "I certainly don't see a reason, why I should always be explaining to you what I mean by what I am just saying" (p. 171). The phraseology here clarifies the conflict between the characters. Jeff demands words that justly represent habitual feelings, words that commit the speaker. For Melanctha, however, words are something that she is "just saying." If Jeff maintains that it is easy "just to say" what he is thinking, Melanctha counters that whatever she is "just saying" need not represent her innermost thoughts.

This sexual conflict might also be seen as an interracial difference of the kind Heath documents in her study of language acquisition. The white families Heath describes emphasize saying "the right thing." One way that parents school their children in this discipline is by rejecting "children's descriptions of things by their attributes before they have learned to respond with the *name* of the item."[4] This clears away the inessential, the attribute, and emphasizes the single essential designation, the name. But, as Stein says, "the reason that slang exists is to change the nouns which have been names for so long."[5] The dialect Stein puts in the mouths of her black speakers does correspond to the black speech Heath describes in her study in that it multiplies attributes and uses them, moreover, to undermine the solidity of the name.[6]

Long before Stein came to it, the conflict between dialect and the rigidity of the standard language was fought across lines of race and

---

4. Heath, *Ways with Words*, p. 141.
5. Stein, *Lectures in America*, p. 214.
6. Thus Heath herself has cited Stein as an inspiring literary example of oral or unplanned discourse rebelling against the standard language. Shirley Brice Heath, "Literacy and Language Change," *Georgetown University Round Table on Language and Linguistics* 1985: 282–93. Her primary example here is William Carlos William's *Spring and All*. See chapter 7 of the present volume.

gender. Dialect that could trace itself back to Anglo-Saxon was always referred to as "manly."[7] Its concrete reliability corresponded to a sacred myth of sturdy yeomanry. On the other hand, the dialects of foreigners and, most especially, of blacks, were seen as effeminate. The Italian language itself, according to G. P. Marsh, was "inconsistent with being bold and manly and generous and truthful."[8] And it was no accident that the influence of slave speech was so often perceived as coming through the domestic household, through the idle women who prattled thoughtlessly with their servants.[9]

In "Melanctha," however, the male and the female use the same words: only tiny differences of arrangement separate what Jeff wants so badly "just to say" from what Melanctha is "just saying." How can the difference between truth and falsehood, concrete reality and fantasy, male and female, hinge on such minute differences? By making her dialect both direct and indirect, distinct and very slippery, Stein also undermines the associated differences of race and gender. The masks worn by her characters, which transform Stein herself into Dr. Jeff, correspond to these verbal masks. Like the dislocations of Picasso's finished canvas, which preserve in altered form the secret history of race and sex change, Stein's verbal dislocations represent in the final text the indeterminacy that made her hover between male and female, white and black.

PRISCILLA WALD

[Immigration and "The Anxiety of Identity"]†

Stein is typically read in a modernist rather than an American cultural context. Her affiliation with avant-garde art movements in Paris, where she lived her adult life, is a well-known context for her language experiments. Those interested in earlier sources of her stylistic innovation attend to the theories of perception offered by her adored professor William James and the research done in the psychology laboratory of Hugo Münsterberg, where a young Gertrude Stein prepared for medical school.[1] Under James and Münsterberg's

7. Henry Alford, *A Plea for the Queen's English* (London: A. Strahan, 1864), p. 244.
8. Quoted in Edward Finegan, *Attitudes Toward English Usage: The History of a War of Words* (New York: Teacher's College of Columbia University Press, 1980), p. 67.
9. Dennis E. Baron, *Grammar and Good Taste: Reforming the American Language* (New Haven, Conn.: Yale University Press, 1982), p. 26.
† From *Constituting Americans: Cultural Anxiety and Narrative Form* (Durham: Duke University Press, 1995), 237–43. Reprinted by permission of the publisher.
1. I have found Wendy Steiner's discussions of Stein's laboratory work especially useful. See Steiner, "The Steinian Portrait: The History of a Theory," in *Exact Resemblance to Exact Resemblance: The Literary Portraiture of Gertrude Stein* (New Haven: Yale University Press, 1978). Steiner is interested in the relationship of Stein's evolving theory of identity

direction, she conducted experiments that explored how and why
habit diminished attention and influenced what could be seen. James
called habit society's "most precious conserving agent."[2] Yet experience did not always conform to or accommodate habit, and, James
explained, situations where habits proved insufficient, where there
was "hesitation," awakened "explicit thought."[3] In her language
experiments, Stein sought to prolong that awakening, to disrupt habits of attention in order to gain insight into the unseen.

Aesthetic and psychological contexts, however, do not fully explain
why Stein chose to develop her characteristic style in a work entitled
The Making of Americans. Exclusive attention to the aesthetic context and stylistic experimentation of the work have obscured her
engagement with the cultural issues reflected in the subject of the
work.[4] The project grew out of Stein's fictionalized account—and
analysis—of the failed marriage of her New York German-Jewish
cousin and expanded into a study of culture and character centering
on immigrant grandparents and their descendants. Americanization
initiatives were well under way in all facets of United States culture,
from education to medicine, law to the emerging social sciences,
before Stein left for Europe and before she began her magnum opus.
And, in her words, "any one is of one's period."[5] Additionally, in the
cross-cultural experience of immigrants, Stein could extend her
exploration of the disruptions in the habits of attention that had
intrigued her as a student of psychology.

Immigrants, for Stein, were selves in transit, between narratives
as much as between geopolitical locations. Their status at once manifested and provoked an anxiety of identity that Stein represented as
a transition between states of consciousness and that corresponded,
in her work, to other experiences involving similar transitions. At the
beginning of *The Making of Americans*, the narrator describes the
feeling of being old to oneself (the narrative of aging) as "a horrid

---

to her portraiture. See also "Gertrude Stein in the Psychological Laboratory," appended
to Michael Hoffman's *The Development of Abstractionism in the Writings of Gertrude Stein*
(Philadelphia: University of Pennsylvania Press, 1965).

2. William James, *The Principles of Psychology* (Cambridge, Mass.: Harvard University Press,
1983), p. 279. Subsequent text references are designated *PP*. One thinks here of Thomas
Jefferson's claim that "mankind are more disposed to suffer while evils are sufferable, than
to right themselves by abolishing the forms to which they are accustomed" *The Complete
Jefferson: Containing His Major Writings, Published and Unpublished, Except His Letters*,
arr. Saul K. Padover (New York: Duell, Sloan, & Pearce, 1943), 19).

3. William James, "The Chicago School," in *William James: Writings, 1902–1910* (New York:
Library of America, 1987), pp. 1136–40, p. 1137. The essay identifies a philosophical
school of thought associated with John Dewey and colleagues and students at the University of Chicago. Originally published in *The Psychological Bulletin*, January 15, 1904.

4. For an example of *The Making of Americans* in an American cultural context—read as a
generational narrative—see Mary Dearborn, *Pocahontas's Daughters: Gender and Ethnicity
in American Culture* (New York: Oxford University Press, 1986).

5. "Portraits and Repetition," in *Lectures in America* (Boston: Beacon Press, 1985), pp. 163–
206, p. 177. Subsequent text references are designated *PR*.

losing-self sense . . . a horrid feeling, like the hard leaving of our sense when we are forced into sleeping or the coming to it when we are just waking."[6] The "horrid feeling" of these moments grows out of a sense that the self is not coextensive with experience, that the body does not fully represent—or embody—the subject (the "I"): while my body was sleeping, I was somewhere else. The experience is one of alienation rather than transcendence: subjectivity experienced as something other than the body but without the transcendence offered by the concept of the soul. With the drugged, visionary moment between sleeping and wakefulness, Stein theorizes a state of consciousness that explains what is at stake in the making of Americans. To the longing for comprehensibility, for coherence, she traces both the need to accommodate the immigrants within a familiar narrative of cultural identity and the eagerness of many immigrants to be thus accommodated.

In Stein, the frustration caused by endless disruptions forces readers to confront their own longing for the narrative conventions that make a work comprehensible. Asking what we are "refusing when we label a text unreadable," one Stein reader suggests that Stein so thoroughly draws her reader into her work that the reader is threatened with a "loss of identity (fear of failure to differentiate from the mother)."[7] The desire for meaning is, in this formulation, a desire for the distance and boundaries that ensure individuation. In the context supplied by Stein's title, however, the boundaries are marked nationally as well as personally. Character and culture come together not in the fear of merging but in the fear of disappearing into incomprehensibility—into an identification not with a mother (or maternal metaphor) but with an immigrant divested of the cultural narratives, and the familiar terms, that mark personhood. To the *anxiety of identity* that arises from this identification, Stein turns her own and her readers' attention.

Throughout *The Making of Americans*, Stein associates a longing for comprehensibility with a longing for narrative. For her characters, that longing leads to a conformity with internalized cultural expectations that confine them; they find themselves inexplicably unable to make productive choices in their lives. The narrator manifests a similar longing, which compromises her ability to tell a story—and especially to tell the story of the making of Americans. Yet that difficulty is the story of *The Making of Americans*; the disrupted narrative shows what has been repressed and suppressed by that process.

6. Gertrude Stein, *The Making of Americans, being a History of a family's progress* (New York: Something Else Press, 1966), p. 5. Subsequent text references are designated *MA*.
7. Ellen Berry, "On Reading Gertrude Stein," *Genders* 5 (Summer 1989): 1–20, pp. 13–14. Berry advocates "being more attentive to the ways in which narrative as a structure itself may act to obscure difference" (17).

Stein began writing *The Making of Americans* in 1903 but stopped later that year; she did not resume composition until 1906, after she had written the novellas *Q.E.D.* (1903) and *Fernhurst* (1904–1905) and the three character sketches published as *Three Lives* (1906).[8] A letter to her friend Mabel Weeks probably written in 1906 offers some hints that may account for the interruption. She confides:

> I am afraid that I can never write the Great American novel. I don't know how to sell on a margin or to do anything with shorts and longs, so I have to content myself with niggers and servant girls and the foreign population generally. Leo he said there wasn't no art in Lovett's book and then he was bad and wouldn't tell me that there was in mine so I went to bed very missable but I don't care there ain't any Tchaikovfsky Pathetique or Omar Kayam or Wagner or Whistler or White Man's Burden or green burlap in mine at least not in the present ones. Dey is werry simple and werry wulgar and I don't think they will interest the great American publia.[9]

The "Great American novel" she had planned was her "long book," *The Making of Americans*; the alternative project described by "niggers and servant girls and the foreign population generally" refers to the character studies of a native-born white lower-class woman, a black woman, and an immigrant woman published as *Three Lives*. That work surfaces in this letter, descriptively at least, as a disruption of the narrative of *The Making of Americans*.

Following my formulation for such disruptions, *Three Lives*, in this letter, should mark the press of an untold story and the expression

---

8. Scholars attempting to document the dates of the text's composition have had to contend both with Stein's conflicting claims—notably, on the title page of the first edition where she describes the work as having been "written 1906–1908" and in "The Gradual Making of The Making of Americans," a lecture she gave in the United States in 1934, where she claims to have worked on the narrative over three years—and with the multiple revisions that the manuscript underwent. In "The Making of *The Making of Americans*," Donald Gallup posits 1903 as the beginning, 1906 as the recommencement (after Stein had finished *Three Lives*), and 1911 as the date of completion. Leon Katz, who originally claimed 1902 as the beginning, later decided that while Stein may have begun work on the narrative in 1902, she did not begin to write until 1903. The notebooks Stein kept as she drafted the manuscript show a marked change in style in 1908, the year she read Otto Weininger's *Sex and Character*. See especially Katz's "The First Making of *The Making of Americans*: A Study Based on Gertrude Stein's Notebooks and Early Versions of Her Novel (1902–1908)" (Ph.D. dissertation, Columbia University, 1963); and Katz's introduction to *Fernhurst, Q.E.D., and other early writings by Gertrude Stein* (New York: Liveright, 1971), pp. ix–xlii. Subsequent text references are designated FM and FQ respectively. Gallup's "The Making of *The Making of Americans*" is included as an appendix to *Fernhurst, Q.E.D., and other early writings by Gertrude Stein*. It is also interesting that Stein dates the *end* of her composition 1908, as though, she might say, beginning writing is an ending.

9. Letter, Gertrude Stein to Mabel Weeks, early 1906, Yale Collection of American Literature, Beinecke Rare Book and Manuscript Library, Yale University. For discussions of this letter, see John Malcolm Brinnin, *The Third Rose: Gertrude Stein and Her World* (New York: Addison-Wesley, 1987), pp. 99–100; and Katz, "The First Making of *The Making of Americans*," p. 76.

of an ill-fitting selfhood. Indirectly, it does both. Stein describes turning from the Great American Novel she had planned to write upon discovering that the Great American Novel is both about business and is itself a business venture prescribed by politics and fashion. In a conscious and defiant gesture, she rejects the speculation of the market for her observation of the margins from and about which she writes: instead of selling on a margin, she offers the margins themselves. The pressing story of those margins is *Three Lives*. Hers is a different kind of story, she tells Weeks, a story that will tell simply all that the abstractions of the socioeconomic system do not represent. But she is also aware of the lack of audience for her stories. The margins from which she writes hardly constitute the vision of the nation that its most powerful potential readers wish to have. And with no "credit" among the American public—no name on which she can cash in—Stein doubts that she can earn the "interest" of that public, which her wordplay casts in Latinate nonsense, "publia."[1]

The American public she describes longs for a self-representation more compatible with the center of power than with the margins of culture. The reference to "Lovett's book" in the Weeks letter probably alludes to the *History of English Literature* by an acquaintance of the Steins, Robert Morss Lovett, a former student of William James and a favorite classmate of Du Bois. Lovett's literary history, which might be more in the interest of the publia's self-representation than Stein's own projects, is antithetical to everything Stein claims she wants to foreground in her own work.[2] By contrast,

1. Stein's wordplay in this letter is, typically, tantalizing. Although the word "publia" has conventionally been cited as "public," my own analysis of Stein's handwriting yields "publia." Stein's general linguistic playfulness, as exhibited in this letter, cannot preclude sheer nonsensical wordplay, part of her jouissance. Yet the sexuality frequently associated with Stein's wordplay offers a tempting alternative. "Publia" is richly evocative, suggestive perhaps of "publica," literally "public woman"—or prostitute. The American public in this image, made pretentious by the Latinate term, is readily flattered and easily swayed, coquettish more than professional and subject to blandishments. Stein knows that she will present to the public—or publia—an image that "she," the public, does not wish to confront in her mirror; hence, an ill-fitting selfhood.

2. Of all the Lovetts living and writing during this period, Robert Morss Lovett seems the most likely candidate. Not only was he at Harvard (as a student and professor) while Leo and Gertrude Stein were there, but he was also in Europe—and a particular friend of Stein intimate Bernard Berenson—at the end of the nineteenth and again at the beginning of the twentieth centuries. During this time Lovett coauthored the *History of English Literature*, the kind of book the Steins could very well have been sent—perhaps in manuscript. Lovett's coauthor, William Vaughn Moody, was Stein's English composition instructor (she seems, in fact, to have made use of a few of her compositions in *The Making of Americans*). Gertrude and Leo could also have read a manuscript that was never published and subsequently lost. In his autobiography, *All Our Years* (New York: Viking Press, 1948), Lovett describes a (much later) debate with Gertrude Stein, in which he acknowledges having "fared badly," about property and literature (93). (In *The Autobiography of W.E.B. Du Bois*, Du Bois describes Lovett as "perhaps the closest white friend I made at Harvard" [p. 288].) Another possibility is Eva Lovett, who wrote *The Making of a Girl* (1902), a manners guide for young ladies published by J. F. Taylor and Company. While

Stein's experience working in Baltimore while a medical student at Johns Hopkins University had brought her into contact with another America and with Americans whose stories were poorly served by the official narratives. *Three Lives* determinedly presses the margins on a presumably reluctant audience—not to mention a demonstrably reluctant publishing industry, a possible referent for "publia."

But the ill-fitting selfhood expressed by *Three Lives* was not wholly—or even primarily—political. *Three Lives* supposedly takes the reader into the daily lives and minds of black, lower-class, and immigrant characters. Yet contemporary readers of Stein have seen in these stories evidence of her attempt to project elements of her own forbidden stories—such as her own lesbian love triangle chronicled in her 1903 novella *Q.E.D.*, a story either lost or willfully suppressed until it reemerged in a reference in her 1933 *The Autobiography of Alice B. Toklas*—onto characters whose race, class, or ethnicity made cultural transgressions less threatening to the white middle-class readers presumed to be the largest audience for the Great American Novel.[3]

In the Weeks letter itself, Stein's use of dialect enacts a similar displacement. With her brother Leo's rebuff, she moves into pronunciations that mark a speaker's race, class, or immigrant status, beginning with "missable," which captures her anxiety. She is afraid of being not only miserable but miss-able, negligible, like the margins about which she writes. Clearly she wondered, in spite of her irony, whether she had assumed a lesser portion, and Leo would not reassure her otherwise. His reticence, in particular with reference to Lovett's book, provoked an uncertainty that she could not quite dismiss.

The letter reenacts a disturbance in the process of writing *The Making of Americans* created by Stein's need to come to terms with her own sense of exclusion. The undifferentiated populations, dialect, and racist language strikingly illustrate Toni Morrison's claim that "the fabrication of an Africanist persona is reflexive; an extraordinary meditation on the self; a powerful exploration of the fears and desires that reside in the writerly conscious. It is an astonishing revelation of longing, of terror, of perplexity, of shame, of magnanimity."[4] Stein's letter is just such a revelation, although lower-class and

---

this work offers intriguing possibilities for spoof on the part of both Leo and Gertrude, I have found nothing that links Eva Lovett or her book to the Steins.

3. See especially Katz, introduction to *Fernhurst, Q.E.D.*; Catharine R. Stimpson, "The Mind, the Body, and Gertrude Stein," *Critical Inquiry* 3 (1977): 489–506; and Lisa Ruddick, *Reading Gertrude Stein: Body, Text, Gnosis* (Ithaca, N.Y.: Cornell University Press, 1990). Subsequent text references to Ruddick are designated LR.

4. Toni Morrison, *Playing in the Dark: Whiteness and the Literary Imagination* (Cambridge: Harvard UP, 1992), p. 17.

foreign characters join Africanist personae. Her racism and classism are evident, as many readers have observed, in her use of these characters to express her own feelings of estrangement.[5] With her substitution of "niggers and servant girls and the foreign population generally" for her sense of her own marginality, she actually stresses her differences from more than her similarity to those populations, in effect re-placing herself more centrally within a (normalized) white middle-class narrative by those differences. Yet, as the letter suggests, *Three Lives* marked her inability to write the Great American novel. As oppressed groups trouble official stories, Stein's depiction of margins signals her unease with the "middle-class narrative" she claims to be writing in *The Making of Americans*.

Three Lives, and perhaps the Weeks letter, were productive disruptions for *The Making of Americans*. Although there is no indication that she acknowledged her racism or classism, she returned to her original project with a more determined focus on depictions of her own estrangement and her difficulty telling the story she wanted to tell. In *The Making of Americans*, she writes self-consciously from within her limitations. She was indeed a white, middle-class woman of her times, but she was also engaged in an important struggle with herself. *The Making of Americans* grapples with the writer's sense of her complicity in the irresistible pull of the cultural narrative, and the limitations of *Three Lives* and of the sentiments expressed in the Weeks letter are an intrinsic part of that story. *The Making of Americans* demonstrates—and, I shall argue, was intended to demonstrate—that no one can tolerate the kind of incomprehensibility necessary for an ongoing disruption of habits of attention—or of the cultural narrative that reinforces them.

Stein risked ugliness and ridicule to explore what those habits made it nearly impossible to see. In "The Making of Americans," according to the character Alice B. Toklas, Stein "was struggling with her sentences, those long sentences that had to be so exactly carried out."[6] This reference to Stein's precision answers charges of arbitrariness and automatism so frequently leveled against her as it calls attention to her authorship. That authorship entails struggling with *sentences*, with the compulsory regulations of conventional grammatical units and the culture they reflect. Stein shows how disruptions of those conventions precipitate an incomprehensibility symbolically tantamount to nonexistence, a "horrid losing-self

---

5. See especially Sonia Saldívar-Hull, "Wrestling Your Ally: Stein, Racism, and Feminist Critical Practice," in *Women's Writing in Exile*, ed. Mary Lynn Broe and Angela Ingram (Chapel Hill: University of North Carolina Press, 1989), pp. 182–98.
6. *The Autobiography of Alice B. Toklas*, in *Selected Writings of Gertrude Stein*, ed. Carl Van Vechten (New York: Vintage Books, 1962), pp. 2–237, p. 38. Subsequent text references are designated *ABT*.

sense." The fear of self-loss corresponds, in this work, to the fear of not being comprehended or comprehensible: the estrangement of a terrain that is more than alien, that simply makes no sense. *The Making of Americans* charts that terrain, asking readers to look deeply into the terror of displacement and to understand that terror as intrinsic to a conception of selfhood rendered almost unquestionable by the fear of incomprehensibility.

JAIME HOVEY

Sapphic Primitivism in Gertrude Stein's *Q.E.D.*†

Feminist critics have long seen Gertrude Stein's writing as a dialectical negotiation of patriarchal language and social conventions, an attempt to change the terms of masculine signification in order to represent the feminine, the lesbian, and the unconventional.[1] Eager to celebrate once-silenced white female—and especially lesbian—writers as progressive foremothers, however, many white feminist critics have also exercised a measure of "unknowing" concerning racial stereotypes in Gertrude Stein's early writing, allowing her a certain freedom from accountability. As Eve Sedgwick[2] points out in the case of the homosexual closet, a "powerful unknowing" (77) can "collude or compete with" organizing knowledges that help to structure or buttress oppression (4). Indeed, even the critics who do attempt to address and unravel the elaborate racial taxonomies that structure Stein's early narratives seem to fall into the trap of the racial categories as Stein sets them up, replicating the very illogical

---

† From *MFS Modern Fiction Studies*, Volume 42, number 3, Fall 1996. Copyright © for the Purdue Research Foundation by the Johns Hopkins University Press.

1. See Marianne DeKoven's *A Different Language: Gertrude Stein's Experimental Writing* (Madison U of Wisconsin P, 1983), where she argues that experimental writing is "partly explicitly female, of the mother," a "dialectic of gender modes" which "can liberate, for both genders, the nonlinearity, pluridimensionality, free play of the signifier, the continuity of the order of things with the order of symbols—in sum, our preOedipal experience of language" (22). Shari Benstock, in "Expatriate Modernism" (in *Women's Writing in Exile*, eds. Mary Lynn Broe and Angela Ingram, [Chapel Hill: U of North Carolina P, 1989, pp. 21–39] also sees Stein's language as an essentialist dialectic, with the "hidden seam of female writing" which subverts conventional forms, "not merely resisting the grammatical law but writing itself in, around, against, and through that law" (30). Catharine Stimpson (in "The Mind the Body, and Gertrude Stein, from *Critical Inquiry* 3 [1977], pp. 499–502), argues that *Q.E.D.* and "Melanctha" are closeted—or, as she puts it, "coded"—texts. For Stimpson, Stein's dialectic is one between conventional and unconventional sexual identities, her early texts reflecting both her semi-closeted social existence and the "conventional and heterosexual terms" with which she tried to legitimate "the unconventional and then the homosexual" (496).

2. In *Epistemology of the Closet* (Berkeley: U California P, 1990).

equivalences which form the core of discursive racial "knowledge" in texts such as *Q.E.D.* and "Melanctha."[3]

To complicate these byzantine tangles of unknowing, critics must consider the fundamental instability and ambivalence of the racial stereotypes from which this unknowing proceeds. Stein's "overtly" lesbian novel *Q.E.D.* (1903), which later became the "overtly" racialized "Melanctha" in her 1909 *Three Lives*, took up various scientific discourses which attributed sexual deviance to non-white peoples, dramatizing the signifying gestures through which such discourses consolidated knowledge as power. Yet Stein's professed "forgetfulness" concerning the autobiographical *Q.E.D.*, which she never published, and her decision to rearticulate that text's sexual concerns through black characters for publication in "Melanctha," strongly suggests that the "unknowing" of her lesbian closet was structured at least in part by a racist cultural closet in which white female desire could be expressed only through displacement onto racial drag. The persistence of this problem of how to read Stein's racial stereotypes suggests that feminist critics must begin recontextualizing lesbian modernist writers such as Stein in light of their use of national and colonial racial discourses. Such a recontextualization might explore, in part, the degree to which the articulation of lesbian subjectivity and polymorphous sexuality within modernism's self-conscious discursivity contests these discourses.[4]

Defined in the work of Michel Foucault[5] as "regimes" of knowl-

---

3. Sonia Saldívar-Hull in "Wrestling Your Ally: Stein, Racism, and Feminist Critical Practice" in *Women's Writing in Exile*, eds. Mary Lynn Broe and Angela Ingram [Chapel Hill: U of North Carolina P. pp. 181–98], for example, has strongly criticized feminist critics who read over Stein's racist and classist stereotypes; others like Stimpson have attempted to sift through Stein's conscious motives, maintaining that Stein's conscious motives, maintaining that Stein's aversion to "raw racial injustice" was something that "must be balanced against the fact that racial stereotypes help to print out the narrative" (501). Similarly granting Stein a privileged "unknowing," Milton A. Cohen (in "Black Brutes and Mulatto Saints: The Racial Hierarchy of Gertrude Stein's 'Melanctha,'" in *Black American Literature Forum* 18.3 (1984), pp. 119–21) argues that Stein "merely incorporated these racial stereotypes unthinkingly into her real concern with character and consciousness" (121). Lisa Ruddick (in *Reading Gertrude Stein: Body, Text, Gnosis* [Ithaca: Cornell UP, 1990]) has suggested that using psychologist William James's theory of "habits of attention" and setting *Three Lives* among Baltimore's working class might have helped Stein distance herself from her own internalized homophobia, yet as Ruddick herself points out, James considered indiscriminate attention a characteristic of children, and so one must therefore wonder how this image of the childlike negro can be read as other than a racist stereotype. Most recently, Karin Cope (in "'Moral Deviancy' and Contemporary Feminism: The Judgement of Gertrude Stein" in *Feminism Beside Itself*, eds. Diane Elam and Robyn Wiegman (New York: Routledge, 1995, pp. 155–78) has concluded that feminist bewilderment in the face of the ethical dilemma posed by Stein's use of intersecting race and gender taxonomies has served to forestall feminist analysis both of Stein and of the differences within the feminist "community."

4. Both Ruddick and DeKoven (in *Rich and Strange*) have attempted to correct this oversight, but critics are only just beginning to see more clearly how race operates in this text. Corinne Blackmer, for example, suggests that the contradictory nature of the text's racial attributes reveal race as a surface only, a mask at odds with the characters' "interior reality" (246).

5. French Postmodernist theorist and philosopher (1926–1984). [*Editor's note.*]

edge which help to police and normalize entire populations, the notion of discursive formations has proven enormously influential to scholars exploring colonialist texts, as well as those concerned with sexuality. Discourses such as the those Edward Said[6] identifies in European thought as "Orientalist," and which Toni Morrison[7] asserts structure American identity by means of "a distancing Africanism" (8), have been central to the constitution of modern national and gendered identities. Many lesbian or bisexual modernist writers—Stein, Radclyffe Hall, Virginia Woolf, Nella Larsen, and Djuna Barnes, to name a few—deployed colonizing "primitivist" tropes in part to suggest a history for the queer, polymorphously perverse female subject, grounding her nature as precivilized or, after Freud, pre-Oedipal. These tropes rendered lesbian sexuality intelligible, perpetuating in literary discourse the nineteenth-century practice by sexologists and scientists of racializing nonnormative sexual practices. Sander Gilman[8] has shown how throughout the nineteenth century the scientific and medical establishments drew equivalences between those people deemed to be racial and sexual outsiders, labeling and policing homosexuals, non-European peoples, and white women by producing discourses fixing them as "deviant." Gilman points out that in the peculiar logic of nineteenth-century pseudo-scientific racism, black female sexuality was pathologized in gynecology textbooks as both deviant and lesbian: "By 1877 it was a commonplace that the Hottentot's anomalous sexual form was similar to other errors in the development of the labia . . . leading to those 'excesses' which are called 'lesbian love' " (89).[9]

I should like to contextualize Stein's writing both as part of a scientific discursive tradition of racialized sexuality and as marking the beginning of a certain strain of modernist writing I will term "sapphic primitivism." This term owes quite a bit both to Shari Benstock's notion of "sapphic modernism,"[1] which makes strong claims for reading the work of lesbian writers as a particular genre of modernist writing, and to Marianna Torgovnik's observation[2] that the modern

---

6. Literary theorist and Palestinian activist (1935–2003). [*Editor's note.*]

7. In *Playing in the Dark: Whiteness and the Literary Imagination* (New York: Random House, 1992).

8. In *Difference and Pathology: Stereotypes of Sexuality, Race, and Madness* (Ithaca: Cornell UP, 1985.)

9. Gilman's work on the "scientific" exploitation and display of the unfortunate Sarah Barton, the infamous "Hottentot Venus," documents the scientific racism of the nineteenth-century European medical discourse later imported by American schools such as Johns Hopkins and University of Chicago. Gilman underscores the pervasive tendencies of this discourse to pathologize difference, arguing that "[i]n the nineteenth century, the black female was widely perceived as possessing not only a 'primitive' sexual appetite but also the external signs of this temperament—'primitive' genitalia" (89).

1. Explicated in "Expatriate Sapphic Modernism: Entering Literary History" in *Lesbian Texts and Contexts: Radical Revisions*, eds. Joanne Glasgow and Karla Jay (New York: New York UP, 1990), pp. 183–203.

2. In *Gone Primitive: Savage Intellects, Modern Lives* (Chicago: U of Chicago P, 1990).

West's fascination with the figure of the "primitive" reflects, after Lukács, a "transcendental homelessness," an American and Anglo-European anxiety about origins and place.[3] As both its lesbian content and its colonialist discursive tropes might suggest, sapphic primitivist writing is fundamentally ambivalent, wanting to "have it both ways" in terms of its national, racial, and class belonging. In modernist sapphic primitivism, which reached its heyday between the World Wars, the polymorphous female subject vacillates between her identifications with a colonizing authority and with a colonized sexual/racial subject. On the one hand, sapphic primitivism celebrates a "foreign" sexuality as dark, other, earthy, and outside bourgeois codes; on the other, such writing invokes the whiteness, wealth, and bourgeois respectability of the lesbian body in order to demand a social—and even national—niche for the polymorphously perverse woman. Homi Bhabha argues in *The Location of Culture*[4] that stereotypes in colonial discourse are always ambivalent and unstable because the authority of colonial discourse is undermined by the hybridity, the " 'other' knowledge," which circulates within that discourse (88). Stein's writing articulates a liminal lesbian sexual subjectivity by means of tropes which play with the discursive equivalences and experiential disparities between racial and sexual knowledges, and while both *Q.E.D.* and "Melanctha" are structured around the narrator's will to know the lesbian subject by means of her racialized attributes, the incommensurability between the white lesbian and her "primitive" sexual nature serves to contest the racialized otherness with which scientific discourses characterized lesbian sexual desire.

Although Stein plays discourses of race and sex off of one another, it is racial stereotypes which sexualize the white lesbian in *Q.E.D.*, and not the reverse. As Foucault points out in *The History of Sexuality, Volume I*,[5] pleasure is an important factor in the operation of power; his notion of a discursive "power-knowledge-pleasure regime" (II) refuses to separate one element out from the other. Stein's obvious delight in what she terms in *Q.E.D.* the "double meaning" of lesbian identity, the sensual relish with which she stirs up racial stereotypes in order to separate the white lesbian from her closet of bourgeois respectability, ultimately colludes with colonialist authority in celebrating and reifying images of the hypersexualized racial "other" while "unknowing" that collusion. In her early writing, Stein borrows a sexual essence from the "primitive" but seems far less interested in granting the latter, for example, intellectual complexity.

Stein's sapphic primitivism, its ambivalent sexual resistance refracted through a nostalgic longing for groundedness, reflects not only her own barely acknowledged racially and sexually liminal identity as a white Jewish lesbian, but larger social concerns about social identity and the production of "home" as a racially and morally homogenous national and domestic space. Torgovnik characterizes the Anglo-European journey to "primitive" regions as "an individual journey"—actual or imaginative—to join with a "universal mankind" (187). Such a formulation is paradoxical; the "primitive," a figure or state usually associated with a white western fantasy of racial, cultural, sexual, and historical alterity, is both foreign and local, both "other" and universal.[6] This contradiction allows the "primitive" to both mark and cover over the site of colonization in the texts which use it. That the "primitive" trope can smooth over these contradictions by embodying a fantasy of wholeness suggests that an active "unknowing" is intrinsic to its discursive operation and must be colluded with by writers and readers both.

This strange movement between ideological strategies of "internal" racist formations, (carrying within them assumptions of racial homogeneity), and of "external" xenophobia, (the foreignness of the "other" outside national borders),[7] can be mapped in Stein's text by examining the primitivizing tropes which function as psychosexual "reminiscences," not unlike those Freud ascribed to hysterics. French Lacanians Jean Laplanche and Jean-Bertrand Pontalis[8] characterize hysterical reminiscences as a kind of "internalized exteriority" rooted in the geography of a fantasy world, as fantasies which function "not unlike the nature reserves which are set up to preserve the original natural state of the country" (7). Stein was no hysteric; rather, the sexually excessive hysteric's "nature preserve" suggests the social constructedness of "nature" as it operates ideologically and unconsciously in the imperial context. Nature in colonial discourse

---

6. David Theo Goldberg (in *Racist Culture: Philosophy and the Politics of Meaning* [Cambridge: Blackwell, 1993]) points out the paradox of creating as a sign for history a subject whose own history has been obliterated and "frozen" (157); he also critiques Torgovnik for being seduced by primitivist discourse into believing that "the primitive" has a real referent—one which, apparently, does not constitute the reading audience of Torgovnik's book (159).

7. Such primitivist "unknowing" seems to resemble the ideological strategies which Etienne Balibar (in "Racism and Nationalism" in *Race, Nation, Class: Ambiguous Identities*, eds. Etienne Balibar and Immanuel Wallerstein [London: Verso, 1992, pp. 37–67]) argues make false distinctions between internal racist formations, such as slavery and anti-Semitism, and those racisms considered external and xenophobic, such as colonialist oppression. Both types of racism, as Etienne Balibar maintains, are produced within certain historical moments, with the "heritage of colonialism" operating in fact as "a fluctuating combination of continued exteriorization and 'internal exclusion' " (43).

8. In "Fantasy and the Origins of Sexuality" in *Formations of Fantasy*, eds. Victor Burgin, James Donald, and Cora Kaplan (New York: Routledge, 1986, pp. 5–34).

is intimately linked to the primitive, functioning as a mythical, "orig-inal" groundedness which covers over the oppressive and usually rac-ist and sexually normative context within which the fantasy of "home" operates. Laplanche and Pontalis's striking image of the nature reserve provides a useful way to look at Stein's internalized correspondence of her inner nature with the African presence in America as a colonialist "reminiscence," a correspondence which is both a recognition and repression of the primal scene of American slavery's forced patriation. The repressed "event" or trauma in Stein's writing is the colonizing moment, long past but still felt in its effects; the pleasure she uncovers is her fantasy of kinship with the colonized "other."

Indeed, primitivist tropes figure prominently in Stein's early attempt to schematize her own relation to a local, rural American identity. While a college student at Radcliffe in Boston, she not only viewed Baltimore through a nostalgic lens, but seems to have begun to identify her own indolent proclivities as simultaneously black and Baltimorean. Stein's earthy "negroes singing" naturalizes an African presence by grounding it in a connection to the land. Stein's opening up of the meaning of racist associations takes her early prose on wild associative rides which she seems uninterested in directing or reining in. As is clear in her Radcliffe themes, written long before she began Q.E.D., such stereotypes offer her a point of phantasmatic identifi-cation, as well as a colonialist vocabulary which renders sensuality and transgressive sexuality as a local, racialized, essential feature of "home":

> It is disheartening to come back to Cambridge after a week of the delicious, dreamy south. Baltimore, sunny Baltimore, where no one is in a hurry and the voices of the negroes singing as their carts go lazily by, lull you into drowsy reveries. It is a strangely silent city, even its busiest thoroughfares seem still and the clanging car-bells only blend with the peaceful silence and do but increase it. To lie on the porch, to listen to the weird strains of Grieg's spring-song, to hear the negro voices in the distance and to let your mind wander idly as it listeth, that is happiness. The lotus-eaters knew not the joys of calm more completely than a Baltimorean. Let us alone for we have the essence of contentment, quiet dreamy, slothful ease in the full sensuous sunshine.[9]

Baltimore, an American city, is the location of contentment in this passage, a site outside of history, modernity, and nation by virtue of

---

9. March 21, 1895; from "The Radcliffe Manuscripts" in *Gertrude Stein: Form and Intelli-gibility*, ed. Rosalind S. Miller (New York: Exposition, 1949), pp. 108–55.

its local, rural, and primitive qualities.[1] Stein's language exemplifies what Frantz Fanon characterizes in *The Wretched of the Earth*[2] as the typical colonizing mentality which knows its subject through racist stereotypes: "that mob without beginning or end, those children who seem to belong to nobody, that laziness stretched out in the sun, that vegetative rhythm of life—all this forms part of the colonial vocabulary" (43). Stein's production of herself in her Radcliffe themes as an educated colonial subject with her own heart of darkness is a complex move. Stein's "negro voices" ground the natural setting, aboriginal to it rather than forcibly relocated, present before civilization and modern urban life. These "primitive" voices enhance the "high" art of Grieg's romantic pastoral music; Stein herself becomes the site of American hybridity, uniquely poised to hear and apprehend the significance of the juxtaposition of European and African-American culture.

As Stein aligns herself with culturally legible representations of unconstrained sensuality, she also draws a line of inclusion around herself as a Baltimorean, racializing that essence. While she still appears as the lazy colonist in another country, her identifications are beginning to shift, as are her allegiances to bourgeois sexual propriety. Not only does she identify with the authentic, mysterious, more physical experience of the "native," but she makes readers complicit with the pleasures of primitivist discourse by enticing them into this lotus-eating bliss formally, offering the aesthetic yield of primitivism's fruits as "quiet dreamy" and "slothful . . . sensuous sunshine." Marianne DeKoven, writing of Stein's use of such stereotypes in the revision of *Q.E.D.* as "Melanctha" in *Three Lives*, perceptively suggests that Stein was "quite literally" excited by these racial stereotypes, which helped her "unleash her new writing" by means of the repetition of such terms as " '*abandoned* laughter,' 'earth-born, *boundless* joy,' 'promiscuous unmorality.' "[3] In her play with the language of racialized sexuality, Stein revels in the doubled pleasure of power and shifting identification, a doubled pleasure which her identity as both white American and lesbian "other" afforded her.

---

1. Oscar Cargill, unable to read Stein except as a "primitivist," suggested (in *Intellectual America* [New York: Macmillan, 1941]) that her authorial role was akin to that of an anthropologist searching for the origins of a universal human character: "What Gertrude Stein perceived was not only the universality of this primitive mind (the 'unconscious' is her name for it) but also the fact that, if the conscious mind could be eliminated, this subconscious mind would most clearly represent the instinctive or 'mechanical' mental processes of the savage—the processes which governed him and were his 'thought' before he had reason or 'intelligence' " (313).
2. New York: Grove, 1963.
3. Pp. 71–72 in *Rich and Strange: Gender, History, Modernism* (Princeton: Princeton UP, 1991).

It is important to note that Stein completed college and began medical school in the last decade of the nineteenth century, a high-water mark of American colonial expansion during which—as Walter Benn Michaels[4] succinctly writes of 1898—the United States "annexed Hawaii, went to war in Cuba, seized the Philippines from Spain, and emerged as a national power" (655). The scientific and sociological debates concerning primitivism and degeneration which reached a crescendo in the 1890s, just prior to Stein's writing *Q.E.D.*, provide striking examples of colonialist interior exclusions. Degeneration discourse usually articulates a white racial panic; degeneration itself had long been ascribed to the "primitive," its physiognomy of racial alterity seen by Europeans as a sign of lower development and an inability to survive a Darwinian universe. Max Nordau[5] identifies this fear of degeneration as a fin de siècle malaise influenced by Norse mythology. "The Twilight of the Gods" thus becomes a prevalent fear of a "Dusk of the Nations," where western man "with all its institutions and creations is perishing in the midst of a dying world" (2). Stein plays with two kinds of degeneration discourses in her first novel. In her writing, racial stereotypes and primitivist assertions produce an ambiguous nationality for the desiring woman by anchoring the local in the features of bodies that are simultaneously familiar and threatening, their physiognomies both legible and inscrutable, harboring dangerous pathologies. One argument of these discourses, such as that articulated by Brooks Adams in his anti-Semitic, neo-feudal *Law of Civilization and Decay* (1898),[6] is that primitive rural "folk" needed to intermarry with the weary, overcivilized European races fallen from "martial" to "monied" types in order to reinvigorate Western civilization (353). Another side of degeneration discourse, rooted in nineteenth-century evolutionary pseudo-science, argued that "primitive" races were prone to atavism and decay, the hidden pathology which would eventually surface and become "readable" as mental instability, sterility, and early death.

Gay historian George Chauncey[7] links German sexologist Richard von Krafft-Ebing's use of degeneracy to explain sexual inversion in his *Psychopathia Sexualis* (published in America in 1892) to an upsurge in medical studies of "primitive" sexual morality in the first part of the century—studies which defined the terms of the debate until well into the teens (133–34). In addition, as lesbian historian

---

4. In "Race into Culture: A Critical Genealogy of Cultural Identity" in *Critical Inquiry* 18 (1992), pp. 655–85.
5. In *Degeneration* (originally published 1895; rpt. Lincoln: U of Nebraska P, 1993).
6. New York: Macmillan, 1898.
7. In "From Sexual Inversion to Homosexuality: Medicine and the Changing Conceptualization of Female Deviance," from *Salmagundi* 58–59 (1982–83), pp. 114–46.

Lillian Faderman points out,[8] such studies also discouraged feminism by linking the women's movement to sexual abnormality (48).
Krafft-Ebing was convinced that deviant sexuality was a product of
civilization and urban life. "It is a remarkable fact," he writes, "that
among savages and half-civilized races, sexual intemperance is not
observed" (3). Not only does Krafft-Ebing advocate the elevating
benefits of Christian monogamy as against the "eternal harem" of
Mohammedan "sensual gratification" (3), but he also cautions
against migration and mixing. Krafft-Ebing applauded the "Egyp-
tians," the "Israelites," the "Greeks," and "the Teutonic races,"
which, unlike darker peoples such as "Aleutians and the Oriental
and Nama-Hottentot women who practice masturbation," had
achieved the moral high ground of heterosexual domesticity "wherever nomadic habits yield to the spirit of colonization, where man
. . . feels the necessity for a companion in life, a housewife in a settled home" (4). His "scientific" treatise is, in fact, framed as an imperialist moral crusade against the sexual pathology of the dark-skinned
and nomadic sexual infidel lurking in the modern metropolis, an
infidel which reveals its pathology through sexual deviancy: "Careful
observation among the ladies of large cities soon convinces one that
homosexuality is by no means a rarity. Uranism may nearly always
be suspected in females wearing their hair short, or who dress in the
fashion of men" (263).

British sexologist Havelock Ellis in his 1897 *Sexual Inversion* additionally exteriorized domestic "uncultured" sexual deviance by class
as well as race; in noting a tolerance for homosexual practices among
Europeans of the "lower classes," Ellis concluded that "[i]n this matter, as folklore shows in so many other matters, the uncultured man
of civilization is linked to the savage" (9). Fascinated by lesbians,
determined to see inverted sexual attraction as still retaining an
impulse towards difference, be it between the "subtle masculinity"
of the mannish lesbian and her feminine lover or "in an attraction
between persons of different race and colour" (120), he linked the
frequency of interracial lesbian relationships in American prisons by
inference to the presence of violent—and thus to his mind seemingly
more masculine—"negresses" (121).

Gertrude Stein's exposure to the imperialist anxieties of such scientific and medical discourses was both cultural and institutional,
coming to her in large part through such famous scientists as her
obstetrics professor at Johns Hopkins, the eminent John Whitridge
Williams, who supervised, as she wrote in *The Autobiography of Alice
B. Toklas*, "her turn in the delivering of babies" (82) in Baltimore's

8. In *Odd Girls and Twilight Lovers: A History of Lesbian Life in Twentieth-Century America*
(New York: Columbia UP, 1991).

African-American community. A pioneer in medical obstetrics, Williams also adopted contemporary theories conflating nonnormative sexuality with peoples of a non-Anglo-Saxon racial extraction. The 1903 version of his widely used textbook *Obstetrics*[9] instructs medical students to note that "[c]onsiderable variations may be observed in the form of the pelvis in various races, and especially upon comparing those obtained from aboriginal and civilized peoples" (15). Williams and his students studied the lesbian, Jew, and Hottentot in relation to their low position on the evolutionary ladder, each linked to the other by a lack of civilization and "rudimentary" sexuality. Williams interprets the then-standard types of pelvic classifications—Turner's three categories ranging from narrow to broad (dolichopellic, found in men; mesatipellic, and platypellic)—as providing specific scientific evidence that the "higher" races are those most fitted to reproduce:

> The mesatipellic variety is observed in the women of the lower races, notably among the Bushmen, Hottentots, and the lower classes of negroes; while the platypellic forms are found in all the higher races. But even among civilized whites considerable racial differences are not infrequently noted, and it is generally stated that the pelvises of the English and Holstein women are broader than those of other nationalities; while the Jewesses living in the vicinity of Dorpat have extremely small pelvises (15–16).

The sexually "undifferentiated" or androgynous woman, with her in-between-the-sexes mesatipellic pelvis, is conveniently non-Teutonic, her physiognomy clearly readable as physiologically primitive. Typical of his time, Williams also remarks on the hypertrophied labia of Hottentots (25) and the generally "rudimentary" nature of the female clitoris (26); scientific and detached, he seems merely to "note" that the Teutonic English and German races are marked as "higher" by nature, their more feminine bodies better fit to reproduce than those of their darker sisters.

For Stein, both Jewish and lesbian, such theories defined her sexual desires and behaviors in racial terms; transgressive sexual practices indicated non-Teutonic racial attributes, and vice versa. The link for Stein between the white lesbian and the "dark" degenerate was not only the hidden sexual pathology common to both, but also a simultaneous sexual and national liminality. Stein must have found it highly amusing that the body of the "wandering" expatriate Jew was also that of the genderless sexual invert, and it is no wonder that she became interested in her writing in interrogating the terms of national belonging by separating the threads of national and racial

9. New York: D. Appleton and Company, 1903.

identity out from each other. Her interest in the intersection between bodily destiny and the agency of imaginary processes continued throughout her expatriate lifetime, privileging the fantasy of national identification over an essentialized, embodied national self. "Writers have to have two countries," she wrote in 1940 in *Paris France*, "the one where they belong and the one in which they live really. The second one is romantic, it is separate from themselves, it is not real but it is really there."[1]

Written in 1903 under the title *Q.E.D.*,[2] Stein's first novel is mainly concerned with the role race and lesbian desire plays in rendering the polymorphous female subject intelligible. Both *Q.E.D.* and "Melanctha" suggest that the experience of love itself produces other ways of knowing; *Q.E.D.* is a text which refuses to resolve its deep distrust of discourse, and the protagonist's voice in "Melanctha" is silenced by more powerful discourses which seek to read her life only as proof of a naturalistic tale of atavism and degeneration. In both *Q.E.D.* and "Melanctha," feminine sexuality, whether lesbian, bisexual, or heterosexually promiscuous, alienates the desiring woman from her community, race, and nation. By narrating the story of this sexually dissident woman as a drama about her national and racial affiliations, rather than her sexual proclivities, Stein exposes these scientific discourses as contradictory knowledges.

Stein's emphasis on language and discourse, its unruliness as well as its ideological complicities, is central to her exploration of the intelligibility of the lesbian body. *Q.E.D.* opens with a passage from Shakespeare's *As You Like It* that emphasizes the impossibility of "tell[ing] this youth what 'tis to love" from a closet of secrets and disguises (Stein 52). In Shakespeare's play, the double entendres of his cross-dressing character Rosalind are read one way by those characters in the play who cannot see through her disguise as a man and another way, as a code, by the audience "knowing" her transvestite disguise. Stein's use of this play as a frame foregrounds her autobiographical protagonist Adele's powerful desire to escape from an urban world of marginalization and hypocritical secrets into a pastoral Arden of freedom and rustic simplicity, and in the course of *Q.E.D.* Adele does escape, having been exiled because of her awakening sexuality from a puritan and urban American moral universe into a more sensual and democratic European pastoral. Stein's frame strongly suggests that any attempt to make sense of her lesbian passion verbally will end in the aporia of primitivist signification, her love for another woman as displaced and unintelligible as, in the words Stein cites from Shakespeare's cross-dressing Rosalind, "the

---

1. P. 2 in *Paris France* (originally published 1940; rpt. London: Peter Owen, 1970).
2. *Fernhurst, Q.E.D., and Other Early Writings by Gertrude Stein*, ed. Leon Katz (New York: Liveright, 1971).

howling of Irish wolves against the moon" (Stein 52). While Adele's
new sexual knowledge helps her unearth an older, less repressed,
and, significantly, "darker" self buried under layers of proper immigrant upward mobility and white bourgeois respectability, the restrictions of the language through which she imagines her sexuality, the
terms of colonialist stereotypes, dictate that she escape into a world
she characterizes as beyond language, as silent.

Q.E.D. is about the white American lesbian's "discovery" of the
sexual and racial "other" buried within her, as if this primitive "foreign body" (Laplanche and Pontalis 10–13) is quite literally that
which Stein, as a lesbian writer, must stop simultaneously repress-
ing/expelling in order to experience her own sensuality and render
that sensuality intelligible. In Q.E.D. the protagonist Adele falls in
love with Helen, whose lesbian lover Mabel pretends not to notice
their affair. Adele is torn by the incommensurability of her sexual
desires with the values of American society. Her desire for a more
straightforward correspondence between her feelings and words, her
inner and outer worlds, conflicts with Helen and Mabel's habitual
secrecy and social respectability. Adele and Helen wander the city
together in a kind of transcendental homelessness, exiled because of
their affair from proper society, family, and even mutual lesbian
friends. Ultimately, Mabel's hold over Helen prevents Helen from
leaving with Adele, and Adele's search for an easier correspondence
between her transgressive desires and the social world exiles her to
the silent spaces of an orientalized Europe.

It is now well known that Stein based Q.E.D. on her affair with
May Bookstaver while the two of them were students at Johns Hopkins, but Q.E.D.'s editor Leon Katz reads the novel as pure autobiography, as if Stein's characterization of herself as the upright Adele
is an authentic rendering of the "real" Gertrude Stein. He argues
that Stein was too naive and conventional to understand her lover's
sophisticated ways, that with only her "four-square moral pieties" to
guide her, Stein "understood neither the language of sign and gesture that May was using nor the precise moral significance of what
either of them was doing. Not talking the same language, neither
could begin to understand what the other's genuine feeling was"
(xiv). Katz's summation of Stein's "character system" is striking: "a
'clean,' 'Anglo-Saxon,' courageously attacking Siegfried opposes a
'dirty,' 'earthy,' cowardly Alberich" (xvi).

Although Katz passes over the problematic nature of a Jewish les-
bian using Wagner to frame the story of her first affair with a woman,
Stein's logic seems at first to be both racist and homophobic. Since
Wagner's Alberich was often played as the stereotypical miserly Jew,
Stein's use of a Wagnerian take on Norse mythology appears initially
to celebrate the anti-Semitic and sex-phobic attitudes of her auto-

biographical character Adele. In *Q.E.D.*, however, it is Mabel Neathe, a woman who caters to ideologies of bourgeois sexual respectability by keeping her lesbianism closeted, who is the sneaky "Alberich." This villainous characterization of Mabel seems to attack her for being a closeted lesbian rather than take into any account the larger world which dictates her invisibility. Stein sets up Mabel Neathe as a pathologized object of scientific scrutiny: her Alberich traits suggest Nordau's linking of fin de siècle degeneration fears to the popularity of Norse mythology, her atavistic physiognomy citing Brooks Adams's argument mourning the fall of the martial races into hoarding economic types.

Stein's fascination with such theories suggests that, at first, she might have seen the difficulty of representing lesbian sexuality as a problem caused by the imprecise narrative of the lesbian body itself, rather than as a problem of representation born of larger social or symbolic constraints. Daniel Pick[3] has argued that scientists of the period viewed a diagnosis of degeneration as "the condition of conditions, the ultimate signifier of pathology . . . the resolution to a felt imprecision of language and diagnosis" which "suggested at once a technical diagnosis and a racial prophecy" (8). In Stein's *Q.E.D.* all of the characters are introduced as watered-down versions of their European forebears, suggesting that the novel is interested both in atavistic liminal identities and hidden narratives, and in the rejuvenating possibilities of migration and mixing which might free the lesbian to become something new. Critics have often interpreted Stein's title—*Quod Erat Demonstrandum*, indicating a kind of academic proof—as a signal to readers of the text's interest in working out theories about love. Yet clearly, race plays a major role in such a proof; Mabel Neathe, Stein's most legible lesbian character, embodies a sexual and cultural duality, her subjectivity a dramatic conflict between "white" femininity and "dark" sensuality. Stein's scientific, rational style in her first novel is strikingly similar to that of the anthropologist studying a native specimen: "It is one of the peculiarities of American womanhood that the body of a coquette often encloses the soul of a prude and the angular form of a spinster is possessed by the nature of the tropics. Mabel Neathe had the angular body of a spinster but the face told a different story" (55). Stein draws Mabel as a kind of sexual mulatto, "pale yellow brown in complexion and . . . heavy about the mouth, not with the weight of flesh but with the drag of unidealized passion, continually sated and continually craving" (55). Mabel is at war with her "nature of the tropics" (55), her body likened to a country engaged in the process of attempting to engulf its own "foreign" yet local tropical neigh-

3. In *Faces of Degeneration: A European Disorder c. 1848–c. 1918* (Cambridge: Cambridge UP, 1989).

bors. Mabel's "nature of the tropics" appears both selfish and sensual, her addiction to passion a handicap and an outward sign of decadence. Stein makes Mabel's physiognomy both lacking in intelligence and possessing a mixed racial heritage, but this depiction seems meant to emphasize her decadent hypocrisy rather than her racial extraction. Like America itself, busily trying to gobble up its neighbors, Mabel's greedy cravings, her atavistic gluttony and secret addictions, are all the more terrible because of the just and democratic face she presents to the world. The incommensurability of Mabel's face with her ascetic-seeming body tell the "real" story of a nature torn between her body and social respectability, whose inner and outer personalities lack correspondence.

Since Mabel is a specimen of "American womanhood," her vices are not a product of the Italy with which she shares a "purely spiritual" kinship, but of the secret hypocrisies of the American moneyed classes. Rather than suggesting that the corruption of this class is somehow Jewish in its essence—Mabel is not Jewish, but a Jamesian American *haute bourgeoise*—it seems likely that Stein is using her character to play with racial stereotypes. Stein's taking up of racist stereotypes through a kind of "tragic mulatto" protagonist creates *Q.E.D.* as a novel—as later is true of "Melanctha"—in which racism is both deployed and ventriloquized as a staging of debates concerning the effect of degeneration on an individual character with a conflicted nature, desirous on the one hand of bourgeois respectability but bound to follow the proclivities of an essentially pathological predisposition.

Stein's obfuscating prose suggests the power of language to render unintelligible that which it seems to reveal: "The subtlety and impersonality of her atmosphere which in a position of recognized power would have had compelling attraction, here in a community of equals where there could be no mystery as the seeker had complete liberty in seeking she lacked the vital force necessary to win" (71). Mabel is the constraint on the romance between Adele and Helen; her nature with its sexual contradictions and social hypocrisies upholds respectability in public while subverting it in secret. Though a lesbian, she upholds the status quo of decency which exiles Adele and Helen in their search for a home. Mabel physically resembles Ellis's and Krafft-Ebing's tailored, mannish lesbian, but her money insulates her, allowing her to financially manipulate financially Helen's fidelity, while she remains quite comfortable in the role of a well-to-do bourgeois man whose woman is his "property" to be hoarded. Indeed, ethnicity often seems to function in Mabel's character as a red herring, because her real character flaw is not a racially determined nature but her embrace of socially constructed middle-class notions of respectable sexual behavior.

If Mabel's power is that of the bourgeois male, then it is Adele's notion that "respectability and decency" also constitute her own nature which both constrains her and lends legitimacy to Mabel's claims on Helen. In a position later echoed in "Melanctha" by the medical doctor Jeff Campbell, Adele ventriloquizes a subject position which is simultaneously masculine-identified and "respectably" bourgeois: "I simply contend that the middle-class ideal which demands that people be affectionate, respectable, honest and content, that they avoid excitements and cultivate serenity is the ideal that appeals to me, is in short the ideal of affectionate family life, of honorable business methods" (59). Adele's allegiance to what she calls "the Calvinist influence which dominates my American training" (103) reveals itself as ambivalent when she admonishes Helen that "when one goes out of bounds one has no claim to righteous indignation if one is caught" (108). Whiteness, hardness, and the secure boundedness of absolute knowing offer Adele an easily apprehended path to proper behavior, yet that path is institutional and disciplinary. Adele strikes up her intimacy with Helen by praising whiteness, domesticity, and unyielding distinctions: "Being on the ocean is like being placed under a nice clean white inverted saucer. All the boundaries are so clear and hard. There is no escape from the knowledge of the limits of your prison" (58).

Adele's language eroticizes both the constraint and its transgression; while claiming to resent such limitations, Adele's language lovingly caresses the simple emphatic masculine strength of the words "nice," "white," "clear," and "hard." Language itself becomes a masculine constraint, and Adele allies herself with a position which is other than feminine in order to explore its sinews. She ridicules Mabel and Helen's mannered exchanges and disavows their conventional feminine smalltalk by declaring " 'I always did thank God I wasn't born a woman' " (58). Adele distances herself from Mabel's stereotypically Semitic miserliness by invoking the male Jewish morning prayer, ridiculing their femininity by invoking yet denying her own gender and ethnicity. By using language against itself, Adele foregrounds its doubleness and insists on her own power as a language user, turning its agency into fuel for her own resistance to identity and its discourses.

Adele's flight from England back to America is a last attempt to escape from her own "fallen" and transgressive feminine sexuality, which she imagines as polluted, déclassé, and as physically marked by sin as are the English prostitutes "with bedraggled, frayed out skirts, their faces swollen and pimply with sordid dirt ground into them until it has become a natural part of their ugly surface" (100). In order to renew herself, Adele searches for a naive, childlike national character formed in simplicity rather than decadence—a phantasmatic, masculine white American home "without mystery and complexity" more like a Calvinist church than a place "clean and straight and meagre and hard and white and high" (101). Fleeing England, Adele seeks American identity in the simple monosyllables of the American language itself. She thinks she sees this childlike national primitivism in the "passionless intelligence" of the democratic Boston crowds, without the "double meanings" (101) which have characterized her lesbian—and by implication, decadent and un-American—relationship with Helen. Yet this primitive "home" seems the complete opposite of the ideal "home" of Stein's Radcliffe themes, and sure enough, Adele eventually realizes that "clear eyed Americanism" is "not earthy enough to be completely satisfying" (101). While the asceticism of such an ideal still retains its appeal, only the "earthy" stains of a "deepest understanding" will now satisfy her. In choosing "stains" and earthiness, Adele comes out as a transnational subject, exiled by her own desiring body to the browner and more sensual continents of the Old World. Rather than flee double meanings, she decides to embody them.

Stein's narrator becomes more and more excited by the suggestive possibilities of this racist vocabulary as the novel progresses, unironically deploying such stereotypes to suggest that Adele's awakening nature is more sensual, more emotional, and darker than her respectable American self. The lesbian passion consisting of physical sensation and silences with which Helen upsets Adele's carefully schematized world of "views and theories" eventually opens Adele to transnational experiences where she surrenders to the silent world of brown bodies, "feeling entirely at home with the Moors" (67) in Tangiers (67). With the Spanish girl in Granada Adele is—conveniently!—spared the trivialities of convention, "their intercourse saved from the interchange of commonplaces by their ignorance of each other's language" (68). Silence suspends recognition of difference and conflict; "unknowing" may not overcome "double meanings," but neither is the impossibility of knowing the truth rendered articulate and disturbing. This silent moment together is deep and intimate, made possible, it is implied, by the more profound emotional nature of brown people. Adele's insistent attempts to articulate and discursively apprehend the nature of her physical fumblings with Helen seem, by comparison, quite awkward and unnatural.

After battling her own "many revulsions" (88) and "puritan instincts" (103), Adele finds a "community of equals" in the more elemental "alien mass of earthy spontaneity whose ideal expression is enthusiasm" (118). The appeal of such a mass for Adele seems to be in its undifferentiated otherness, as well as its tolerance for emotional and sexual expression. Yet Stein contradicts this characterization: confronting Helen about her submissiveness to Mabel's financial manipulations allows Adele to choose a more democratic "European sisterhood" over the rigidly respectable "lack of individual imagination" exemplified by Helen and Mabel. The "individual imagination" Stein is suggesting is really an emotional expressiveness; Adele is allowed to extract the suggestive possibilities of this "alien mass" in order to embody a more elemental sensuality *without* becoming subsumed by its otherness. Adele "goes primitive," becoming earthier, aboriginal, and more native: "large, abundant, full-busted and joyous"; a "brown and white and clean" Aphrodite "just sprung out of the sea" (118). This revitalizing, mythic strain of primitivism allows Adele to be both white and brown, both sensual and unproblematically clean. The conjunctions which join these characteristics together, refusing to hierarchize them, suggest the fantasy of a psychic wholeness which Adele constructs out of these qualities. Adele transfers her allegiance from American puritanism to Italy's landscape and public spaces, "coming home" to the simplicity of her ascetic "big desert spaces," "huge ugly dignified buildings," and "great friendly church halls" (124).

This transition is not, apparently, as full of contradictions for Stein as it might seem to her reader; doubleness or lack of correspondence between Adele's internal feelings and the values of her external society is no longer a problem for Adele in Europe. The obvious fact that the things Adele now loves about Italy aren't all that different in character from the places she left in America is dissolved in the text's conflation of brownness, hotness, and earthiness, signifying a corresponding freedom from emotional repression. In confronting Helen about her subjection to Mabel's economic manipulation, Adele refuses to take up a respectable—and male—class alliance, or "pass"—as do Mabel and Helen—as a conventional heterosexual bourgeois white woman in America. Her refusal to lead a "double" life of hypocrisy frees her to become part of the wandering brown masses in Italy and Spain, ironically more democratic and tolerant than the rigid hierarchies of the American society she leaves behind. Shifting from an emphasis on degenerative pathologies to a revitalizing, unrepressed primitivist incorporation, Stein's text—like her protagonist Adele—surrenders to the "other," relaxing the vigilant borders which protect her national, racial, and sexual identity from being engulfed and transformed by the primitive.

Stein's language itself becomes rhythmic, polysyllabic, and lyrical as she describes Adele in a setting which evokes the "oriental" in order to suggest the psychic totality of exotic sensual experience: "Sitting in the court of the Alhambra watching the swallows fly in and out of the crevices of the walls, bathing in the soft air filled with the fragrance of myrtle and oleander and letting the hot sun burn her face and the palms of her hands" (68). This passage suggests

Stein's own appreciation of Flaubert, whose version of the Orient Edward Said critiques in *Orientalism*[4] as "watched" and "a living tableau of queerness" (103). For Stein this "queerness" is not all externalized; her orientalism includes a notion of internal correspondence. Although *Q.E.D.* ends in romantic frustration for Adele and Helen, Stein's use of this vocabulary of racist colonizing tropes allows her to free Adele's "natural temperament" (103) from its Calvinist American superego, and her own writing from its stiff empiricism. Paradoxically, Adele's quest to find a country which corresponds to her own "nature of the tropics" (55) also begins to contest the moral codes which exile her interior sexual desires from her exterior social world of white, upper-middle-class America.

Rather than use race to signal sexuality, as she did in *Q.E.D.*, Stein decides next in "Melanctha" to use sexuality to signal race. The colonialist vocabulary with which she begins to construct a nomadic and liminal national, racial, and sexual subject in *Q.E.D.* combines with her own libidinal and discursive pleasure in the fantasies such language invokes to thoroughly inform the later version of *Q.E.D.* she published as "Melanctha." Stein should be held accountable for these choices, as well as celebrated for the instances when she appears to advocate multiple and simultaneous positions. The resistance to discursive knowledges about racialized sexual pathologies offered by *Q.E.D.*'s "white" lesbian triangle disappears in "Melanctha"; when Stein rewrites her "lesbian" text as a "black" text, scrambling any correspondence between racial appearance and sexual desire, dissident sexuality operates to buttress racial stereotypes rather than contest them. The American Africanist version of Stein's sexual awakening in "Melanctha" neutralizes *Q.E.D.*'s resisting, physically grounded bodily narrative of polymorphous lesbian "knowing," lodging such knowledge instead within larger deterministic racial stereotypes. Yet by refusing to tell her readers where to stand, undermining the possibility that "truth" can be arrived at through language, and occupying as many positions as possible, her textual play also directs readers back to their own dubious cultural values and cultural heritage, slyly holding up a discursive mirror that continues to infuriate, perplex, and intrigue them.

---

4. New York: Vintage, 1979.

CARLA L. PETERSON

["Melanctha" and African-American Music]†

Shortly after completing *Three Lives* in 1906, Gertrude Stein wrote a letter of lament from Paris to her friend Mabel Weeks: "I am afraid that I can never write the great American novel. I don't know how to sell on a margin or do anything with shorts or longs, so I have to content myself with niggers and servant girls and the foreign population generally." To explain her aesthetic choices and to underscore her affinity with such "foreign" peoples, Stein appropriated the language of the uneducated and in particular of black dialect: "Leo he said there wasn't no art in Lovett's book and then he was bad and wouldn't tell me that there was in mine so I went to bed very missable but I don't care there ain't any Tschaikowsky Pathetique or Omar Kayam or Wagner or Whistler or White Man's Burden or green burlap in mine at least not in the present ones. Dey is very simple and very vulgar and I don't think they will interest the great American public. I am very sad Mamie."[1]

What Stein's lament first addresses is her early ambition to write a *great* novel that would be *American*, and to do so from a position abroad in France. Stein would later attribute her inspiration for *Three Lives* to two great European modernists—Flaubert, author of the composite *Trois contes* and obsessed pursuer of *le mot juste*, and Cézanne, innovator of a new technique of heavy block brush strokes. In *The Autobiography of Alice B. Toklas*, Stein recalled: "She had begun not long before as an exercise in literature to translate Flaubert's *Trois Contes* and then she had this Cézanne [portrait of a woman] and she looked at it and under its stimulus she wrote *Three Lives*."[2] Still later she asserted that it was the aesthetic sensibility of these two Frenchmen that had enabled her to put into practice a new "realism of composition": distinctions between central and subordinate ideas disappear, "one thing [becomes] as important as another thing [and] each part is as important as the whole." In the literary text, such realism of composition is characterized by "a constant recurring . . . a marked direction in the direc-

† From "The Remaking of Americans: Gertrude Stein's "Melanctha" and African-American Musical Traditions" in *Criticism and the Color Line: Desegregating American Literary Studies*, ed. Henry B. Wonham (Piscataway: NJ, 1996), pp. 140–57. Copyright © 1996 by Rutgers, The State University. Reprinted by permission of Rutgers University Press.

1. Quoted in James R. Mellow, *Charmed Circle: Gertrude Stein & Company* (New York: Praeger, 1974), 77.

2. Gertrude Stein, *The Autobiography of Alice B. Toklas* (New York: Vintage Books, 1960), 34. All further references are to this edition and will be placed parenthetically within the text.

tion of being in the present" that results in the creation of a "prolonged present."[3]

Critics have argued that Stein's development of such modernist literary techniques converged with modernist painters' new interest in African art, in particular the mask that flattens out surfaces and abstracts individual features.[4] I would argue, however, that in *Three Lives* Stein's aesthetic inspiration is equally American, as Grant Richards, a British publisher who rejected her manuscript, was all too well aware: "Moreover, there is the question of scene and atmosphere, both in this case so very American that the ordinary English reader would be a little at a loss."[5] I would further argue that this inspiration derives quite specifically from Baltimore and, in the case of "Melanctha," from African-American Baltimore. Indeed, Stein in her *Autobiography* acknowledged African-American culture as an important source of her own modernist beginnings: "Gertrude Stein had written the story of Melanctha the negress, . . . which was the first definite step away from the nineteenth century and into the twentieth century in literature" (54).

Adopting the critical paradigm elaborated by Raymond Williams in *The Politics of Modernism*, I suggest that Stein in Paris occupied the modernist situation of the emigré. For Williams, modernism can be explained only in terms of its specific historical moment. This moment is characterized by the end of organic community and the development of global socioeconomic transformations that encourage massive international migrations of peoples, whether forced or voluntary, to ever expanding imperial and capitalist metropoli. As a consequence the city attains increasing importance, first as a geographic borderland where disparate groups of peoples live together in strange propinquity and where the dislocation of individuals often results in isolation and loneliness, and second as a site in which immigration leads to an estrangement and denaturalization of language, which is no longer perceived as customary but as arbitrary and conventional. Thus the imperial metropolis extends "over a new range of disparate, often wholly alien and exotic, cultures and languages."[6]

3. Gertrude Stein, "A Transatlantic Interview 1946," in *Gertrude Stein: A Primer for the Gradual Understanding of Gertrude Stein*, ed. Robert Bartlett Haas (Los Angeles: Black Sparrow Press, 1971), 15–16; "Composition as Explanation," in *A Stein Reader, Gertrude Stein*, ed. Ulla F. Dydo (Evanston, Ill.: Northwestern University Press, 1993), 498.
4. See, for example, Michael North, *The Dialect of Modernism: Race, Language, and Twentieth-Century Literature* (New York: Oxford University Press, 1994), 59–65.
5. Quoted in *The Flowers of Friendship: Letters Written to Gertrude Stein*, ed. Donald Gallup (New York: Octagon Books, 1979), 54.
6. Raymond Williams, *The Politics of Modernism: Against the New Conformists* (London: Verso, 1989), 77–78; for a similar application of Williams's theories to Pound and Eliot, see North, *The Dialect of Modernism*, ch.4.

Such an analysis of modernism's historical moment aptly describes the migratory pattern of Daniel Stein's family from Allegheny, Pennsylvania, where Gertrude was born in 1874, to Austria, France, and then to Baltimore and Oakland, as well as Stein's self-imposed exile to Paris in 1903; and it may well explain the perception by others of Stein's "foreign" use of the English language.[7] But I would also contend that it accurately portrays the city of Baltimore at the turn of the century and hence of Bridgepoint, the fictionalized Baltimore of *Three Lives* inhabited by "niggers and servant girls and the foreign population generally." Indeed, from the 1880s on Baltimore was a fast-growing city, workers drawn to it because of its rapid expansion of manufacturing and industry. By the mid-1880s its population included a large number of factory workers in the coal and oyster industries, in canning, glass blowing, brickwork, carpentry, electrification, and in clothing sweatshops; in addition, women labored as domestics, laundresses, and needle workers. Given the sharp increase in transatlantic migration in the last decades of the nineteenth century, many of these workers were ethnically Irish, German, Italian, and Eastern European immigrants, as well as African Americans who constituted approximately 15 percent of Baltimore's population in 1890; religiously, they were Catholic, Protestant, and Jewish.[8] According to a 1907 study of housing conditions in Baltimore, this working population lived not only in segregated tenement and alley districts, but also in mixed ones: "In the [Albermarle street] tenement district the large majority of the inhabitants were Russian Jews, with a smaller number of Italians, and a sprinkling of other nationalities. . . . The [Biddle] alley district . . . is occupied largely by negroes with a sprinkling of native white families, and a remnant of the colony of clean, hard-working, thrifty Germans, who seem to have constituted the original inhabitants."[9]

Stein herself lived in Baltimore, first with her aunt and uncle, the Bachrachs, from 1892 to 1893, then with her brother, Leo, and later with a friend, Emma Lootz, from the fall of 1897 to early 1902, when she was a student at the Johns Hopkins medical school. As her biographers have noted, Stein had direct contact with the city's immigrant and African-American population. According to a cousin, "everybody was attracted to Gertrude—men, women and children, our German maids, the negro laundresses." More specifically, Gertrude and Leo's housekeeper was a German immigrant named Lena Lebender who in *Three Lives* is fictionalized as "the good Anna" and

7. Richard Bridgman, *Gertrude Stein in Pieces* (New York: Oxford University Press, 1970), 6.
8. Sherry H. Olson, *Baltimore: The Building of an American City* (Baltimore: Johns Hopkins University Press, 1980), 200–229.
9. Association for the Improvement of the Condition of the Poor, *Housing Conditions in Baltimore* (Baltimore: Charity Organization Society, 1907), 12, 16.

gives her name to "the gentle Lena." Finally, Stein's choice of residence during her medical school years suggests a necessary acquaintance with this minority population. Rather than confine herself to the solidly middle-class German Jewish enclave around Eutaw Place in the northwestern part of the city where the Bachrachs and the Cone sisters lived, Stein established herself to the east in a more heterogeneous neighborhood, first at 215 East Biddle Street, then at 220 East Eager Street, a street Lootz remembered as "nice enough . . . except for the hens floating down the gutter." These residences were not far from the black middle-class neighborhood of West Biddle Street beyond which lay the Biddle alley district; and the Hopkins medical school was located in the middle of another poor black area through which Stein was obliged to pass in order to reach the hospital and in which she delivered babies to fulfill the requirements for her course in obstetrics.[1]

In *Q.E.D.*, Stein's first sustained fictional effort written in 1903 after she had abandoned medical school and moved to Paris, she appears to have deliberately turned her back on Baltimore; thus her protagonist and fictional self, Adele, remarks: " 'We are all agreed that Baltimore isn't much of a town to live in.' "[2] The novella appears to be exclusively preoccupied with Stein's dilemma over her own psychosexual situation; as critics have noted, the triangular lesbian relationship of Adele, Helen Thomas, and Mabel Neathe is a reenactment of Stein's own tormented relationship with May Bookstaver and Mabel Haynes that took place between 1901 and 1903.

Q.E.D., however, also hints at larger modernist concerns that are later foregrounded in *Three Lives*. The text's point of departure is geographic displacement, here the transatlantic voyage, which becomes the enabling condition of modernist psychological experience but also reaffirms the vital "need of the country to which one belongs, . . . for the particular air that is native" (99). More specifically, the native place for the working out of such experience is the American city, Baltimore, but especially New York and Boston; and it is Stein's fictional self, Adele, who comes to typify the modernist individual lost in the urban crowd and reveling in it as a space of potential liberation. Finally, the novella enacts the search to define native character, in this case American womanhood: the female protagonists are "distinctly American but each one at the same time bore definitely the stamp of one of the older civilisations, incomplete

1. Quoted in Elizabeth Sprigge, *Gertrude Stein: Her Life and Work* (New York: Harper and Brothers, 1957), 23, 39; Robert Crunden, *American Salons: Encounters with European Modernism* (New York: Oxford University Press, 1993), 165–177.
2. Gertrude Stein, *Q.E.D.* in *Fernhurst, Q.E.D., and Other Early Writing* (New York: Liveright, 1971), 72. All further references are to this edition and will be placed parenthetically within the text.

and frustrated in this American version but still always insistent"
(54). If Helen is "the American version of the English handsome
girl" (54) and Mabel "sufficiently betray[s] her New England origin"
(55), Adele is denied any form of relationship to an older civilization
but suggests "a land of laziness and sunshine" (55–56), a description
that will reappear in "Melanctha" in association with "the negro."

By the time she started writing *Three Lives*, Stein's imagination
had drifted back to Baltimore, which, fictionalized as Bridgepoint,
becomes the central site of experience in all three stories. The good
Anna and the gentle Lena of the first and last stories respectively
represent Stein's "servant girls and the foreign population generally,"
and through them the narrative explores issues of geographic displacement and European immigration. Both Anna and Lena come
from Germany to America and enter into service; Anna and her
mother "came second-class, but it was for them a long and dreary
journey"; Lena is "patient, gentle, sweet and german. She had been
a servant for four years and had liked it very well."[3] As immigrants,
Anna's and Lena's relationship to their older native language is suddenly ruptured and their use of the new dominant language remains
strange and unnatural. As menial workers in an urban environment,
both women suffer acutely from their dependent situation and its
ensuing loneliness; they can survive neither the harshness of
working-class conditions in a rapidly developing capitalist metropolis
nor the compulsory heterosexuality that patriarchy enforces on
them.

Both "The Good Anna" and "The Gentle Lena" thus explicitly
point to the ways in which nationality, class, and gender shape the
lives of their protagonists. Yet, issues of race lurk just below the
surface as Stein's fictional narratives echo the contemporary racial
discourse that had become increasingly virulent as a consequence of
the widespread immigration of the European poor in the 1880s and
1890s. Emerging Anglo-Saxon nativist ideologies affirmed the separation of Europeans into different biological types and ultimately
races, asserting the inherent inferiority and progressive degeneration
of Eastern and Southern European immigrants and the consequent
need to maintain Anglo-Saxon racial purity in the interest of national
survival.[4] In "The Gentle Lena," Lena's American cousins resort to
racial analogy to mock their immigrant cousin's social inferiority:
"They hated to have a cousin, who was to them, little better than a
nigger" (246). But it is only in "Melanctha," the last of the stories
written, that Stein chose to represent "niggers" fully.

3. Gertrude Stein, *Three Lives* (New York: Vintage Books, 1936), 24, 239. All further references are to this edition and will be placed parenthetically within the text.
4. For a full discussion of Anglo-Saxon nativist ideologies at the turn of the century, see John
Higham, *Strangers in the Land* (New York: Atheneum, 1975), ch. 6.

I suggest that to write "Melanctha" Stein turned to black popular cultural forms with which she had come into contact during her Baltimore years. In analyzing these appropriations, I am following Toni Morrison's injunction that we need to investigate what she has called "Africanism" in American literary texts.[5] Such critical activity forms part of a larger cultural project committed to the deconstruction of racial categories. According to this project, race can no longer be viewed as a biological construct, since human genetic variability between "races" is no greater than that within a given "race," and since the term "race" is often used to describe what are in fact ethnic experiences—historically acquired—of blacks in the United States. Rather, race must be seen as an ideological construct conditioned by social, cultural, and historical factors. As Aldon Nielsen has argued, race is "a consummately empty signifier, that is constituted out of a people's desire . . . to name themselves as not-other"; an "empty signifier," race acquires meaning only when invested with particular social and cultural constructions by given groups or individuals.[6]

In studies of African-American culture, critics such as myself have worked to assess the ways in which African Americans have negotiated "blackness" throughout our history, creating social institutions, economic networks, and cultural forms that have enabled the emergence of black subjectivity and historical agency. In turning to white writers, however, we need to look at how blackness has served as a strategy for their definition and redefinition of themselves as white Americans. To quote Aldon Nielsen once again: "In writing themselves into history *as* white writers . . . white authors of our past . . . were founding their essential subjectivity upon, depended for their very being upon, the existence of black people."[7] White identity is revealed to be dependent on blackness in some fundamental way, and hence blackness becomes an inescapable condition of Americanness. This blackness is most often not historically contextualized, however, but exists as something other, that which Michael Rogin has called "the surplus symbolic value of blacks," whether born of fear, desire, or aspiration to power and control.[8] Yet paradoxically, what this symbolic value points to is the existence in the United States of a complex racial borderland where blood lines are often blurred and cultural traditions merged. African-American critics need, then, to analyze the ways in which this borderland gestures

5. Toni Morrison, *Playing in the Dark: Whiteness and the Literary Imagination* (Cambridge: Harvard University Press, 1993), 6.
6. Aldon L. Nielsen, *Writing Between the Lines: Race and Intertextuality* (Athens: University of Georgia Press, 1994), 16.
7. Ibid., 11.
8. Michael Rogin, "Blackface, White Noise: The Jewish Jazz Singer Finds His Voice," *Critical Inquiry* 18 (Spring 1992): 417.

toward a shared culture but also reaffirms existing hierarchies and power relations.

I want to argue that in "Melanctha" Stein appropriated African-American musical traditions to assert her Americanness in opposition to the European high culture of Flaubert and Cézanne, while at the same time marking her distance and alienation from the dominant American culture—that which forced her admission: "I don't know how to sell on a margin or do anything with shorts or longs." A newly-arrived emigré in Paris, Stein occupied the position of outsider, the immigrant stranger who is both unassimilated and unassimilable. Linguistically, she found herself, to paraphrase Williams, liberated from the dominance of the "old, settled language" and in the presence of a "new, dynamic language." Yet Williams himself warns against any rigid opposition between these two languages, noting that the "uses of a language of connection and of forms of intended communication remained an emphasis and an intention of [those] social groups . . . whose specific existence had been blurred or contained within the imposed 'national' forms," while the new language could be "deliberately manipulative and exploiting."[9]

Indeed, in "Melanctha" Stein invented a modernist discourse that was rooted more in the geographic and linguistic borderland culture of the American metropolis than in the "dynamic" languages of Europe. To create this new language, Stein worked toward, in Williams's words, "a deliberate running-together, cross-fertilization, even integration of what had been hitherto seen as different arts, aspir[ing] to develop language towards the condition of music, or towards the immediacy and presence of visual imagery or performance."[1] And she was able to achieve her purposes by turning to contemporary musical traditions—coon songs, early folk-blues, and ragtime music—of African Americans, one of those "social groups" whose "specific existence" the dominant culture had hoped to "blur or contain within the imposed 'national' language." As we shall see, however, not all of these musical traditions can be said to be purely African-American either in origin or in practice. They are, in fact, inextricably linked to other American ethnicities, underscoring the incredible complexity of race and race relations at the turn of the century.

Stein appropriated these African-American musical forms because their images were useful to her as she sought to work out her sense of both her Jewishness, which, she increasingly felt, differentiated and isolated her from her larger social community, and her lesbianism, which, as *Q.E.D.* attests, she was slowly coming to acknowledge. As many critics have noted, Stein projected herself most

9. Williams, *Politics of Modernism*, 79.
1. Ibid., 70.

explicitly into "Melanctha" as the light-skinned doctor, Jeff Campbell, the "whitest" of all the characters in terms of his values and
behavior and the most critical of black working-class mores. Yet,
Stein also made use of her black lower-class characters—Rose Johnson, James Herbert, and Melanctha herself—to explore personal,
sexual, and familial conflicts; in the text, blackness functions as a
means of both self-expression and denial.[2] Stein's exploitation of
these images is thus double-edged, encompassing a repulsion against
blacks as foreign and primitive, on the one hand, and an attraction
to them as emblematic of free sexuality and vibrant womanhood on
the other. In short, if we need to question Stein's total adherence to
Flaubert's and Cézanne's "realism of composition" and modernist
criticism's exclusive focus on the experimental quality of her writings, we also need to avoid the caricaturing of Stein as a "white
supremacist" guilty of offensive racial stereotyping.[3]

Musical history indicates that Baltimore was a central site for the
development of African-American musical culture at the turn of the
century. Although Stein nowhere makes specific reference to this
music, both the external evidence provided by her proximity to black
neighborhoods and the internal evidence of her prose suggest her
acute awareness of it. Furthermore, we know that Stein was
intensely attuned to the sound of voices, commenting in the *Autobiography* that "I don't hear a language, I hear tones of voice and
rhythms" (70). More particularly, in a Radcliffe theme of 1895 Stein
recorded the strong impression made on her by the "negro" sounds
of Baltimore: "Baltimore, sunny Baltimore, where no one is in a
hurry and the voices of the negroes singing as their carts go lazily
by, lull you into (the) drowsy (wakin) reveries. . . . To hear the negro
voices in the distance and to let your mind wander idly as it listeth,
that is happiness. The lotus-eaters knew not the joys of calm more
completely than a Baltimorean."[4] It was Stein's rendering of these
sounds that Richard Wright was responding to when he wrote that
"while turning the pages of 'Melanctha,' I suddenly began to *hear*

2. See also Lisa Ruddick, *Reading Gertrude Stein: Body, Text, Gnosis* (Ithaca: Cornell University Press, 1990), 33.
3. On Stein's racism, see Sonia Saldívar-Hull, "Wrestling Your Ally: Stein, Racism, and Feminist Critical Practice," in *Women's Writing in Exile*, ed. Mary Lynn Broe and Angela
Ingram (Chapel Hill: University of North Carolina Press, 1989), 185; on Stein as an
experimental writer, see Marianne DeKoven, *A Different Language: Gertrude Stein's Experimental Writing* (Madison: University of Wisconsin Press, 1983). In a later study, DeKoven
seeks to correct her earlier "oversight" of Stein's racial stereotyping by analyzing Stein's
reference to "Melanctha" as the first step into twentieth-century literature, *Rich and
Strange: Gender, History, Modernism* (Princeton: Princeton University Press, 1991), 229,
68.
4. Quoted in Rosalind S. Miller, *Gertrude Stein: Form and Intelligibility* (New York: The
Exposition Press, 1949), 139.

the English *language* for the first time in my life. . . . English as
Negroes spoke it: simple, melodious, tolling, rolling, rough, infectious."[5]

Perhaps the earliest negro sound that Stein would have heard in
Baltimore in the 1890s was the coon song, sung by whites and blacks
alike, that had developed out of earlier minstrel and road show
traditions. Its lyrics relied on caricature and racist stereotyping in
order to ridicule and lampoon blacks as uncivilized and primitive
people. In such songs as "All Coons Look Alike to Me," "My Coal
Black Lady," "May Irwin's 'Bully' Song," or "Mister Johnson Turn
Me Loose," black men, in Edward Berlin's words, "are portrayed as
ignorant, gluttonous, thieving (stealing chickens, watermelons, and
pork pies), gambling, cowardly, shiftless, and violent (most often
wielding a razor); the women are sexually promiscuous and merce-
nary, often leaving one 'honey' (which rhymes with 'money') for
another." The racism of the language and imagery is overt and unde-
niable. In "May Irwin's 'Bully' Song," for example, the male protagonist boasts about his successful confrontation with the "bully" in
the following terms: "I riz up like a black cloud and took a look aroun'
/ There was dat new bully standin' on the ground / I've been lookin'
for you nigger and I've got you found / Razors 'gun a flyin', niggers
'gun to squawk."[6]

Tremendously popular at the turn of the century, coon song shows
were a readily available form of entertainment as individual performers and companies toured widely, stopping in all major cities, including of course Baltimore. It is to this tradition, I suggest, that Stein
turned in order to portray Melanctha's father, James Herbert, her
last lover, Jem Richards, and her friend, Rose Johnson, characters
who appear at the beginning and the end of the story, thereby providing its frame. Jem is the typical "young buck" of coon songs (216);
the description of the fight between Herbert, "fierce, suspicious, . . .
look[ing] very black and evil," and the coachman John is strongly
reminiscent of the tradition's representations of black men: "Suddenly between them there came a moment filled full with strong
black curses, and then sharp razors flashed in the black hands that
held them flung backward in the negro fashion, and then for some
minutes there was fierce slashing" (94); finally, Rose Johnson, "a real
black, tall, well built, sullen, stupid, childlike, good looking negress
. . . [who] had the simple, promiscuous unmorality of the black people" (85–86) may well bring to mind the burlesque heroine of "My

5. Quoted in *Richard Wright: Books and Writers*, ed. Michel Fabre (Jackson: University Press of Mississippi, 1990), 151.
6. Edward A. Berlin, "Ragtime Songs," in *Ragtime: Its History, Composers, and Music*, ed. John Edward Hasse (New York: Schirmer Books, 1985), 72; Edward A. Berlin, *Ragtime: A Musical and Cultural History* (Berkeley: University of California Press, 1980), 33.

Coal Black Lady": "This coal black lady, She is my baby, . . . Her color's shady, But she's a lady."[7]

It is important to remember, however, that despite its racist content, the coon song tradition was not a purely white form, but was born of mixed blood lines. Its origins lay in an earlier minstrel tradition that itself combined Euro-American art forms—dances such as the Irish jig and clog, Scottish and Irish folk songs, musical instruments like the tambourine and fiddle, songs and stories of the American frontier—with African-American elements such as dance-steps, folk expressions, and instruments like the banjo and the jawbone.[8] Similarly, coon songs were written and performed not only by whites but by blacks as well; one of the earliest songs, "All Coons Look Alike to Me," was written and first sung by the famous black entertainer, Ernest Hogan. Yet black performers such as Hogan, Billy Kersands, Bob Cole, Billy Johnson, and J. Rosamund Johnson did not simply adapt themselves unthinkingly to the coon song tradition but subverted it, seeking, following Houston Baker's formulation, *"the mastery of form"* in order then to engage in *"the deformation of mastery,"* so that the minstrel mask ultimately became "a governing object in a ritual of *non-sense"* composed of mere sounds. This deformation of mastery is perhaps nowhere more evident than in black performers' subversive questioning of the authenticity of both the tradition and its practitioners; Bert Williams and George Walker underscored the fraudulent identity of white performers when they advertised themselves as "Two *real* Coons," while Ernest Hogan's claim to being "the unbleached American" implicitly hinted at the alien status of all those other bleached Americans.[9]

It is quite possible that Stein patterned the characters of Rose and Sam Johnson after the protagonists of the antebellum minstrel song "Coal Black Rose," whose lines echo faintly in "My Coal Black Lady." According to music historians, the plot of "Coal Black Rose" was developed into an Ethiopian opera entitled *Oh Hush! or the Virginny Cupids* that was first performed in 1833 and subsequently became "one of the most frequently revived pieces in the entire repertoire of American minstrelsy."[1] This piece portrays the rivalry between the bootblack, Sambo Johnson, and his boss, Cuff, in their courtship of "coal black Rose," and the ultimate success of Sambo, although Cuff does get his revenge at the end in his physical assault on Sambo.

7. W. T. Jefferson, "My Coal Black Lady" (M. Witmark & Sons, 1896).
8. Robert C. Toll, *Blacking Up: The Minstrel Show in Nineteenth-Century America* (New York: Oxford University Press, 1974), 27–51; Eric Lott, *Love and Theft: Blackface Minstrelsy and the American Working Class* (New York: Oxford University Press, 1993), 92–96.
9. Houston A. Baker, Jr., *Modernism and the Harlem Renaissance* (Chicago: University of Chicago Press, 1987), 15, 21, 20; *The Afro-American*, April 11, 1903.
1. Gary Engle, ed., *This Grotesque Essence: Plays from the American Minstrel State* (Baton Rouge: Louisiana State University Press, 1978), 1.

Sambo and Rose are held up to ridicule as black characters who are foolish enough to try to ape middle-class conventions of courtship; it is easy to see how they might function as prototypes of Stein's Sam and Rose Johnson. Significantly, although the lyrics of "Coal Black Rose" were American, the music derived from British folk tradition.[2] Such a mixed genealogy underscores the inextricable entanglement of white and black cultural forms in the nineteenth century and invites us to reinterpret with renewed seriousness Stein's narrator's insistence that the "real black" Rose Johnson "had been brought up quite like their own child by white folks" (86).

I would argue that Stein's creation of these frame characters, born of mixed racial heritage, allowed her to articulate highly charged childhood family conflicts that continued to haunt her, enabling her both to discharge anger against, and reconstitute understanding of, past events and individuals by means of projection, disguise, and displacement. For example, as Richard Bridgman has noted, many of Stein's fictional fathers, including James Herbert, are "domineering, suspicious, impatient and brutal" and may be seen as projections of Daniel Stein.[3] Further, Rose Johnson may be viewed as Stein's imaginative response to the figure of the ineffectual, victimized wife/mother (both Stein's and Melanctha's own); deliberately rejecting both housewifery and motherhood to ensure her own survival, Rose transfers her domestic obligations onto Melanctha and neglects her own child until it dies: "Rose Johnson was careless and negligent and selfish, and when Melanctha had to leave for a few days, the baby died. . . . Rose and Sam her husband were very sorry but . . . neither of them thought about it very long" (85).

In the late 1890s composers began to put coon songs to syncopated rhythms, giving rise to a new musical form, ragtime, which, from its beginnings, was intimately associated with Baltimore, birthplace of the great rag pianist Eubie Blake. Although originally merely an instrumental accompaniment to the coon song, ragtime rhythms gradually came to dominate the lyrics, which became less explicitly racial in content, and then disappeared altogether. Syncopation has been considered a distinctly African-American form that improvisationally disrupts the regularity of the stressed beats of a musical composition by emphasizing a normally unstressed beat or by delaying, pushing, or interpolating a beat; counterpoint is created when the right hand imposes such rhythmic irregularities upon the left. If ragtime began as the instrumental accompaniment of coon songs, it soon gained wider currency as composers started applying syncopated rhythms to classical music. In such situations, rag became dependent on European musical expression, whose regularity it worked to disrupt; once again the blood lines between black and white cultural forms became blurred. Given its African-American rhythmic and improvisational nature, however, rag remained an expression of freedom and subversion.[4]

Blake, who has left us a fascinating first-hand account of the development of ragtime, started his musical career in 1898 at the age of fifteen playing the piano in such Baltimore "bawdy houses" as Aggie Shelton's and Annie Gilly's, as well as at Alfred Greenfeld's saloon. In his reminiscences he recounts how ragtime music was one of those negro sounds that permeated the atmosphere of Baltimore, and we may speculate that it eventually reached Stein herself. Annie Gilly's, for example, was located on East Street, some blocks to the west of the Johns Hopkins hospital; furthermore, according to Blake, African-American street bands accompanying funerals often passed the corner of Jefferson and Ann streets directly in front of the hospital: "Well, the people would sing and the band would play, you know, funeral music, dirges. Now on the way back, see, they play the very same melodies—he's buried now, see—in ragtime. Oh, how they'd swing!"[5] Finally, we may wonder whether Eubie Blake's real name, James Hubert, does not find itself echoed in the name of Melanctha's father, James Herbert.

Eubie Blake's reminiscences are especially significant for their perception of how race, ethnicity, and sexuality shaped the practice and performance of ragtime and how boundaries between different racial and ethnic groups at times weakened and became blurred, illustrating once again the borderland nature of the modernist metropolis. Aggie Shelton's, for example, was located in a black neighborhood, but Aggie herself was of German background and spoke in a "thick Teutonic accent"; if Eubie, the entertainer, was black, "the girls were all *white*, and of course so were the customers." Finally, different rags were seen to appeal to different social groups; Jesse Pickett, composer of "The Dream Rag," a piece that Blake himself learned to play, "often called it 'The Bull Dyke's Dream' because of its strong impact on the lesbians who worked in sporting houses, who crowded around the piano wherever he went, crying 'Hey, Mr. Pickett!! Play The Dream.' "[6]

Heightened awareness of the syncopated rhythms of ragtime music invites us to rethink and rephrase the many incisive analyses made by Stein scholars concerning the modernist experimental style of "Melanctha." Thus, Marianne DeKoven's and Lisa Ruddick's ref-

4. Terry Waldo, *This Is Ragtime* (New York: Hawthorn Books, 1976), 34–35.
5. Quoted in Al Rose, *Eubie Blake* (New York: Schirmer Books, 1979), 12–13.
6. Ibid., 21, 22; Robert Kimball and William Bolcom, *Reminiscing with Sissle and Blake* (New York: Viking Press, 1973), 42.

erences to the story's narrator as "obtuse" may in fact intimate the presence of syncopation. According to these critics, the narrator is "obtuse" because she is unable to tell her story properly and give her narrative direction, because she fails to provide an internal logic to her narration of events, so that linear causality is noticeably absent. More specifically, the narrator shows signs of a "collapse of emphasis"; consequently, "the dramatic outlines are flattened." Finally, she reveals herself incapable of subordination, of placing in the background those events that are less important than others.[7] I would suggest that rather than being "obtuse," the narrator of "Melanctha" may in fact be ragging on conventional notions of narrative logic, causality, emphasis, and subordination that are the hallmark of the dominant literary tradition. The peculiarity of the narrative style of "Melanctha" is confirmed by DeKoven's comment on the degree to which it differs from that of both "The Good Anna" and "The Gentle Lena"; the "compact, evenly stressed rhythms" of the two earlier composed stories "are transformed by repetition in 'Melanctha' into a wavelike cadence with phrases or measures emphasized by rhymes." To support her argument DeKoven quotes a narrative passage in which the prose "rushes forward freely and then halts at each '-er' rhyme," creating a strange push-and-stop effect:

> Now when her father began fiercely to assail her, she did not really know what it was that he was so furious to force from her. In every way that he could think of in his anger, he tried to make her say a thing she did not really know. She held out and never answered anything he asked her, for Melanctha had a breakneck courage and she just then badly hated her black father.
>
> When the excitement was all over, Melanctha began to know her power, the power she had so often felt stirring within her and which she now knew she could use to make her stronger. (95)

Such a combination of abrupt shift in rhythm, repetition of "-er" syllables, and accumulation of staccato rhymes contradicts traditional Western notions of prose regularity and hints at the presence of syncopation.[8]

As Ruddick has pointed out, Melanctha and the narrator share many stylistic traits, given their similar tendency toward a form of mind-wandering marked by repetition, offbeat stresses, and lack of subordination.[9] Melanctha is prone to syncopated rhythms as well, and her use of syncopation is particularly effective in her conversations with Jeff Campbell, contributing in important ways to the evo-

7. DeKoven, A Different Language, 28, 37; Ruddick, Reading Gertrude Stein, 33–37.
8. DeKoven, A Different Language, 42–43.
9. Ruddick, Reading Gertrude Stein, 33–35.

lution of Jeff's character. As noted earlier, Stein's foremost identification is with the logical, bookish, scientific Jeff, who stands outside black popular culture, offering the reader a distanced perspective on it as he decries the tendency of "colored people" toward "excitements" and "this running around business" (117). Yet if Jeff insists on his disgust with such irregular living, Melanctha quite rightly points out the degree to which he is also attracted to "queer folks": " 'I can't say as I see just what you mean when you say you want to be good and real pious, because I am very certain Dr. Campbell that you ain't that kind of a man at all, and you ain't never ashamed to be with queer folks Dr. Campbell' " (120). Jeff's dissociation from this urban culture of excitements leads him ironically to participate in another world of the senses, that of the pastoral: "Jeff always loved to watch everything as it was growing, and he loved all the colors in the trees and on the ground, and the little, new, bright colored bugs he found in the moist ground and in the grass he loved to lie on" (149). Much as in the case of the sensuous Adele in *Q.E.D.*, Jeff's affinity to nature suggests his openness to a world that is neither rational nor scientific, but rather appeals directly to senses that are capable of being excited.

It falls to the sexually adventurous Melanctha, whose experiences include both the heterosexual and the homoerotic, to open Jeff up to this world of sensual excitement, and she does so in their many lengthy conversations which play themselves out in a counterpoint of voices as Melanctha responds to the regularity of Jeff's discourse by means of syncopation. When Jeff comments that religion is "a good way for many people to be good and regular" (118–119), she questions his use of these terms and reminds him of his willingness to associate with "queer folks." Jeff initially resists shifting rhythm, complaining that she goes too "fast" for his "slow way of doing" (163). But he eventually gives up his regular rhythm to syncopate, hesitating, repeating words, interpolating additional phrases—"you see," "really," "it's like this way with me"—in his search for greater emotional knowledge:

> "You see, Melanctha, really, it's just like this way always with me. You see, Melanctha, its like this way now all the time with me. You remember, Melanctha, what I was once telling to you, when I didn't know you very long together, about how I certainly never did know more than just two kinds of ways of loving, one way the way it is good to be in families and the other kind of way, like animals are all the time just with each other, and how I didn't ever like that last kind of way much for any of the colored people. You see Melanctha, it's like this way with me. I got a new feeling now, you been teaching to me." (158)

If Melanctha may be loosely associated with the syncopated rhythms of ragtime, she can be linked even more closely with the early folk-blues. In contrast to the coon songs, blues music and lyrics are more purely African-American and exhibit strikingly different perspectives on, and attitudes toward, the African-American folk. Although the blues as a formal musical structure (a twelve-bar, three-line, AAB form) was not known until around 1910, folk-blues originated much earlier out of the vernacular music of Southern blacks—hollers, work songs, love songs, and spirituals; these were simple one-verse oral compositions consisting of a single line repeated three times that expressed the singer's intense feelings of sadness, lonesomeness, and abandonment, as for example in the line "Got no mo' home dan a dog, Lawd." Many early singers and composers have insisted that it is impossible to locate a specific time and place for the origin of the blues—" 'The blues? Ain't no first blues! The blues always been' "—especially since early blues singers were wanderers who carried their music from place to place via the railroad, the river, and the road. Ma Rainey recalled that she heard the blues for the first time quite by accident in a small town in Missouri in 1902, while Eubie Blake is said to have exclaimed: " 'Blues in Baltimore? Why, Baltimore is the blues!' "[1]

As critics have noted, the protagonists of the blues—both male and female—are individuals who are down on their luck, perhaps because they have lost their money or job, or more often because they have been betrayed by a wife/girlfriend or husband/boyfriend; sexual desire, fulfillment, and betrayal are central to the blues. Friendless and alone in the world, these individuals may turn to drink to numb their pain or leave home to wander about aimlessly and sing the blues; railways, dockyards, and roads become important settings of their experience. In the lyrics the representation of black womanhood is complex and sometimes contradictory. Women are sexually experienced, highly adept at "rolling" their "jelly"; and they are hard-drinking, connoisseurs of whiskey, gin, and rum. But if women singers tend to lament their victimization at the hands of two-timing men, male singers regard women as manipulative and duplicitous. Internalizing the racist aesthetics of the dominant culture, these men often prefer brown or yellow women to black as objects of sexual desire; yet they sometimes also acknowledge that these lighter-skinned women are not as trustworthy, and ultimately turn back to black women. Finally, particular suspicion is directed toward women who choose to spend time together and "don't think about no man":

1. Abbe Niles, *Blues: An Anthology*, ed. W. C. Handy, rev. Jerry Silverman (New York: Da Capo Paperback, 1990), 12, 20, 61; quoted in Eileen Southern, *The Music of Black Americans*, 2nd ed. (New York: W. W. Norton, 1983), 330.

"Ketch two women runnin' togedder long, / You can bet yo' life dere's somethin' gwine wrong."[2]

A blues sensibility permeates "Melanctha," determining the story's geographic setting and shaping the destinies of both Melanctha and Jane Harden, who, as critics have noted, are fictional projections and reconfigurations of May Bookstaver / Helen Thomas and Mabel Haynes / Mable Neathe, respectively. As Melanctha gradually detaches herself from her family shortly after her father's razor fight with John, she starts to wander, much like her own creator Stein. Blues fashion, she strays "sometimes by railroad yards, sometimes on the docks or around new buildings" (96). In these places she meets black workers who are not hesitant to name female sexuality in the language of the blues: " 'Hullo sis, do you want to sit on my engine,' and, 'Hullo, that's a pretty lookin' yaller girl, do you want to come and see him cookin' " (98); or " 'Do you think you would make a nice jelly?' " (102). As blues women, Melanctha and Jane Harden are headstrong, passionate, and deliberately flout social convention to insist on their geographic mobility and freedom to express their sexuality as they please. If both of them are "yaller," it is because in the world of the blues it is the light-skinned women who are the most self-sufficient and unpredictable. Moreover, in blues lyrics the name Jane is often attached to women who make sure they get their own way: "My Jane's a gal gits all she can, / If you ain't got it, she hunts another man."[3] Jane Harden's independence is evident in the narrator's description of her vast worldly experience, her hard drinking ("Jane Harden had many bad habits. She drank a great deal, and she wandered widely" [104]), and of course in her suggested lesbianism, expressed through her strong attachment to Melanctha: "Jane grew always fonder of Melanctha. Soon they began to wander, more to be together than to see men and learn their various ways of working" (105).

It is Melanctha, however, whose very name suggests the blues, who is the primary blues figure of the story. She rambles in such blues sites as the railroad yard and the docks, hoping to gain "real experience" by getting to know the "natures" and "various ways of working" of the men who labor there (97, 95); and for a time she challenges traditional sexual mores as she and Jane choose to "run together." But Melanctha's blues nature is embodied above all in her "complex, desiring" personality that draws her first to Jane, then to Jeff Campbell, and finally to Jem Richards, in search of "real, strong, hot love" (87, 122); and it is her consequent disappointment in this

2. *The Blues Line*, ed. Eric Sackheim (Hopewell, N.J.: Ecco Press, 1993), 288; Niles, *Blues*, 13.
3. Howard W. Odum and Guy B. Johnson, *Negro Workaday Songs* (New York: Negro Universities Press, 1969), 144.

search that leads her to name herself as a blues woman in a conversation with Rose that occurs at the beginning of the story and is then recalled twice at the end:

> Sometimes the thought of how all her world was made, filled the complex, desiring Melanctha with despair. She wondered, often, how she could go on living when she was so blue.
>
> Melanctha told Rose one day how a woman whom she knew had killed herself because she was so blue. Melanctha said, sometimes, she thought this was the best thing for her herself to do.
>
> Rose Johnson did not see it the least bit that way.
>
> "I don't see Melanctha why you should talk like you would kill yourself just because you're blue. I'd never kill myself Melanctha just 'cause I was blue." (87)

Stein's text here indeed sings the blues.

As critics have noted, Stein was aware from a very early period in her life of the sensual side of her nature; one of her Radcliffe themes portrays a "dark-skinned girl" who is filled with "passionate yearnings" and "wild moods," and a notebook entry comments on "the Rabelaisian, nigger abandonment . . . bitter taste fond of it" to which she was clearly attracted.[4] Thus, even though Stein projects herself in "Melanctha" into the more sober character of Jeff Campbell, she nonetheless betrays a strong identification with those "complex, desiring" aspects of her female protagonist, an identification kept carefully veiled within the culture of the blues. Indeed, sexual ideologies of this period viewed the homosexual, in particular the lesbian, as a hybrid (neither woman nor man) and thus as degenerate; furthermore, according to these ideologies, it is the black woman who, through the supposed malformation of her genitalia, comes to embody the lesbian most fully: "the overdevelopment of the clitoris . . . lead[s] to those 'excesses' which are called 'lesbian love.' The concupiscence of the black is thus associated also with the sexuality of the lesbian."[5] Seen from the perspective of the dominant culture, the vital image of black womanhood in the blues lyrics from which Stein constructed her portrayal of Melanctha is transformed into one of degeneracy.

The foregoing analysis is meant to suggest the possibility of Stein's deep familiarity with both coon songs, descended from mixed blood

---

4. Miller, *Gertrude Stein*, 141–142; Linda Wagner-Martin, *"Favored Strangers": Gertrude Stein and her Family* (New Brunswick: Rutgers University Press, 1995), 80.
5. Sander L. Gilman, "Black Bodies, White Bodies: Toward an Iconography of Female Sexuality in Late Nineteenth-Century Art, Medicine, and Literature," *Critical Inquiry* 12 (Autumn 1985): 218.

lines, and ragtime music, performed in ethnically mixed settings and appealing to diverse sexualities, as well as her attraction to the representation of blues women as independent and sexually experimental. In imaginatively appropriating these African-American musical traditions with which she had become familiar while living in Baltimore, Stein turned to a culture that offered her representations of masculinity, femininity, and sexuality through which she could explore personal, familial, and social issues that had followed her on her transatlantic migration.[6] Yet from the point of view of the dominant culture, these musical traditions were perceived as degenerate because of their association with blackness and also with deviant lesbian sexuality, itself linked, as we have seen, to blackness. Thus, if "Melanctha" suggests Stein's fascination with African-American popular music, it also reflects her need to distance herself from it, out of fear of being assimilated to blackness, of actually being identified as a "nigger." The story embodies modernism's ambivalence over the loss of organic community and the flowering of borderland cultures in which the liberating fluidity of personal identity also becomes a source of anxiety.

Such fears were not entirely implausible to a Jewish woman who had inhabited an American metropolis at the turn of the century. Sander Gilman has argued that European anti-Semitic traditions had for centuries identified Jews as blacks, first through religious iconography that portrayed Jews as the Antichrist, and then through interpretations that asserted the physical similarity between Jews and blacks. Gilman has further shown how the physical reality of "plica polonica," a disease that plagued Eastern European Jews living in conditions of filth and poverty and blackened their skin, became a marker of their unhygienic nature, hypersexuality, and ugliness, linking them to blacks. In the United States, the massive immigration of foreign populations in the 1890s transformed American cities into geographic borderlands, and recently arrived Eastern European Jews came to be regarded by the dominant culture as little different from blacks. In this moment of social change, according to Michael Dobkowski, the Jew was readily perceived as the racial Other, the unwholesome and filthy slumdweller, the uncivilized and morally

---

6. Stein's awareness of her acts of cultural appropriation, as well as her anxiety over their legitimacy, are fully intimated in a passage in her later *Autobiography* in which she suggested that Negro culture does not necessarily belong to the Negro, but should be presumed to be universal, while at the same time accusing this culture of "nothingness": "Gertrude Stein did not like hearing him [Paul Robeson] sing spirituals. They do not belong to you any more than anything else, so why don't she claim them, she said. He did not answer. . . . Gertrude Stein concluded that negroes were not suffering from persecution, they were suffering from nothingness" (238). I thank Sterling Stuckey for pointing this passage out to me.

degraded foreigner who is ultimately incapable of being assimilated into Anglo-Saxon society.[7]

Even more radical were those views that asserted Jews to be of non-European origin; most typically, Jews were believed to be descended from an Asiatic race, specifically the Mongoloid Khazars.[8] At the extreme, a few race theorists even speculated on the historical admixture of Negro blood with the Jewish race. In a 1910 monograph, Arthur T. Abernethy asserted that "the Jew of to-day is essentially Negro in habits, physical peculiarities and tendencies." Such theories would eventually culminate in the better-known writings of Lothrop Stoddard, who argued that "it was also probably during their Egyptian sojourn that the Jews picked up their first traces of Negro blood. A Negroid strain undoubtedly exists in Jewry; to it the frizzy or woolly hair, thick lips, and prognathous jaws appearing in many Jewish individuals are probably due." Jews and blacks are further linked through the visible signs of physical degeneracy, marked by "deformed skulls, protruding jaws, and low brain weights," proving them to be races out of their proper place, and promising their eventual extinction.[9] Degeneracy has occurred because by the end of the nineteenth century neither of these displaced races is pure but rather hybridized. Jews continue to carry the stain of their early infusion of Negro blood while more recent racial miscegenation has given rise to the mongrelized mulatto. As these theories continued to assimilate Jews to blacks, many racial characteristics originally ascribed to blacks became attributed to Jews, in particular that of unrestrained and deviant sexuality. Here, finally, theories of racial degeneracy converged with those of sexual degeneracy.

It was from these images of degeneration that Stein ultimately sought to distance herself. Indeed, such standard conflations of racial and sexual deviancy may well explain her curious endorsement of Otto Weininger's treatise *Sex and Character*, published in 1906, in which the intersections of race and sexuality are very differently configured. Weininger condemns the Jewish race, which bears the mark of the Negro particularly in its "readily curling hair," since,

7. Sander L. Gilman, *Difference and Pathology: Stereotypes of Sexuality, Race, and Madness* (Ithaca: Cornwell University Press, 1985), 31–32, and *The Jew's Body* (New York and London: Routledge, 1991), 172–173; Michael N. Dobkowski, *The Tarnished Dream: The Basis of American Anti-Semitism* (Westport, Ct.: Greenwood Press, 1979), 146–147.

8. Robert Singerman, "The Jew as Racial Alien: The Genetic Component of American Anti-Semitism," in *Anti-Semitism in American History*, ed. David A. Gerber (Urbana: University of Illinois Press, 1986), 116.

9. Arthur T. Abernethy, *The Jew a Negro, Being a Study of the Jewish Ancestry from an Impartial Standpoint* (Moravian Falls, N.C., 1910), 105; Lothrop Stoddard, "The Pedigree of Judah," *The Forum* 75 (March 1926): 326; Nancy Stepan, "Biological Degeneration: Races and Proper Places," in *Degeneration: The Dark Side of Progress*, ed. J. Edward Chamberlain and Sander L. Gilman (New York: Columbia University Press, 1985), 98–99.

according to him, this race is "saturated with femininity" and lacking in individuality, dignity, ethical sensibility, self-control, and genius. In contrast, Weininger praises the homosexual, rejecting sexual inversion as psycho-pathological and symptomatic of degeneration, and asserting that such inversion is "merely the sexual condition of these intermediate sexual forms that stretch from one ideally sexual condition to the other sexual condition." The "ideally sexual condition" is of course that of the male, and thus the homosexual woman who contains a large proportion of maleness in her becomes the subject of Weininger's intense admiration.[1]

One of the strategies through which some turn-of-the-century Jewish performers such as Al Jolson, Eddie Cantor, and Sophie Tucker sought to deal with the dominant culture's assimilation of Jewishness to blackness was by means of blackface, a representational strategy that emphasized the instability and volatility of the two groups' relationship to one another. When such Jewish performers assumed blackface, they were assimilating themselves to blacks; blackface then also became a means through which they could hide their real identities as Jews.[2] Yet, female blackface entertainers like Sophie Tucker also betrayed a real fear of identification with blacks and a need for racial reassurance when they insisted on revealing their true identity at the end of the performance. Forced to adopt blackface when a booking agent found her "so big and ugly," Tucker came to value the make-up; it functioned as a protective mask, freeing and enabling her to become the "World-renowned Coon Shouter." Yet her deliberate distance from blackness is all too obviously asserted in her compulsion at the end of the act "to peel off a glove and wave to the crowd to show I was a white girl," and in her obsessive investment in her own whiteness: "My own hair under the wig was a mass of burnished gold curls. Nature and my Crimean ancestors had done that for me. They had given me, too, my smooth, fine skin, that was pleasingly white now, since I had learned how to care for it."[3] Finally, as Michael Rogin has pointed out, such a revelation of what lies beneath blackface also functioned as part of a process of Americanization whereby Jewish performers hoped to assert their racial distance from blacks and embark on a path of upward mobility.[4]

Much like these Jewish entertainers, Stein may be said to adopt a form of blackface performance in writing "Melanctha." To the extent that she projected herself into the characters of Jeff and Melanctha, Stein was both identifying with blacks and using blackface as a pro-

---

1. Otto Weininger, *Sex and Character* (1906; rpt. London: William Heinemann, 1975), 303, 306, 48.
2. Rogin, "Blackface, White Noise," 420, 439.
3. Sophie Tucker, *Some of These Days* (Garden City, N.Y.: Doubleday, 1945), 33, 35, 60.
4. Rogin, "Blackface, White Noise," 440, 447.

tective mask behind which to explore personal dangers; blackface came then to function as a distancing mask behind which Stein flaunted her own whiteness. If racial distancing is unequivocal in Stein's stereotyping of certain of the frame characters, a more complex ambivalence is at work in the triumphant survival of Rose Johnson at the end. And if the story concludes with the demise of the two blues women—the disappearance of Jane Harden from the narrative and the death of Melanctha—the lessons of the blues live on in Jeff Campbell: "Jeff always had strong in him the meaning of all the new kind of beauty Melanctha Herbert once had shown him, and always more and more it helped him with his working for himself and for all the colored people" (207); and finally, the syncopated rhythms of ragtime endure beyond the narrated events in the style of the narrator herself.

In writing "Melanctha" Stein found herself caught in a complex web of racial contradictions. She was both powerfully drawn to African-American popular musical culture at the turn of the century, which offered her representations of strong, vibrant women unavailable to her in other artistic traditions, and she was repulsed by these images out of fear of being assimilated to them through her double identity as a Jew and a lesbian. These dual tendencies are fully inscribed in the racial discourse of "Melanctha."

M. LYNN WEISS

[Stein and Richard Wright]†

> I do not think there has been anything done like it [Wright's *Uncle Tom's Children*] since I wrote *Three Lives*.
>
> GERTRUDE STEIN

The relationship between Gertrude Stein and Richard Wright is generally noted, but its implications are rarely explored. In the context of American literary history where Stein's friendships with Ernest Hemingway and Thornton Wilder or Wright's with James Baldwin and Ralph Ellison are central, the invisibility of the Stein/Wright relationship is suggestive. In most expatriate studies Stein and Wright are rarely considered in the same book, a reluctance perhaps to cross boundaries created by the critical practice of feminist, African-American, and ethnic studies. Such studies have made important contributions to American literary history, but their Lin-

† From *Gertrude Stein and Richard Wright: The Poetics and Politics of Modernism* (Jackson: University Press of Mississippi, 1998), pp. 1–21. Reprinted by permission of the publisher.

naean impulse can obscure significant features of a writer's life and work. Richard Wright's work grew out of his experience as a black man from Mississippi who began his apprenticeship in Chicago; but as a thinker and a writer, he took lessons from Americans (such as Gertrude Stein) and Europeans, men and women on both sides of the color line. Similarly Gertrude Stein's *Three Lives* owes as much to black Baltimore and immigrant narratives as it does to Paul Cézanne, William James, or Gustave Flaubert. Our blindness to the Stein/Wright relationship and its implications for American literary history is related to the perception that these writers have very little in common.

Indeed Gertrude Stein and Richard Wright occupy opposite ends of the American spectrum. Stein was a white woman from the upper middle class, a graduate of Radcliffe College, who also completed four years of medical school at Johns Hopkins. Raised in a nonobservant Jewish household, Stein had lived in Vienna, Paris, Baltimore, and Oakland before she was ten years old. By 1908, the year Wright was born, Stein was thirty-four years old and had already completed *Three Lives* and was well into the composition of *The Making of Americans*.

Richard Wright, the son of a sharecropper, was born in rural Mississippi. The family's meager circumstances were made worse by the father's desertion and the mother's chronic illness. From a very early age, Wright worked at odd jobs and, because of his mother's frail health, his early schooling was marked by constant interruption; his formal education ended after the eighth grade. And although resistant to religious teachings, Wright was raised with the orthodoxy of his Seventh-Day Adventist grandmother.

These biographical differences between Gertrude Stein and Richard Wright are further demonstrated through a comparison of their work. Stein's radical experiments with language, best illustrated in *Three Lives*, *The Making of Americans*, and *Tender Buttons*, share little in common with Wright's *Uncle Tom's Children*, *Native Son*, or *Black Boy*. Apart from featuring an African-American community in "Melanctha," Stein's work is little concerned with such social realities, much less the social protest that drives Wright's fiction. Indeed these writers have come to represent two opposite tendencies in twentieth-century American literature; Stein is the avatar of art-for-art's-sake, while Wright is the politically conscious artiste engagé. Given such differences, the two should not have even liked each other.

Quite the opposite was true. Despite the silence that surrounds this friendship, both writers were very public in their mutual praise. In a 1945 article for the *New York Times Magazine*, Stein wrote, "when one Negro can write as Richard Wright does, writing as a Negro about Negroes writes not as a Negro but as a man, well the minute that happens, the relation between the white and the Negro is no longer a difference of races but a minority question and ends . . . in persecution. That is the trouble, when people have equality there can be differences but no persecution."[1] When asked about her relationship with Wright during a 1946 interview, Stein reiterated her praise: "he has a great mastery of the English language and . . . to my mind, he has succeeded in doing the most creative work . . . done in many a year."[2] Stein concluded this interview by paying Wright the highest compliment: she compared his work to her own. Stein's enthusiasm for Wright's work prompted her to befriend him as well. In addition to their lively correspondence, Gertrude Stein played an important role in his first visit to France. When the U.S. State Department refused to grant him a passport, she helped obtain an invitation for him from the French government.

In her last two letters to Carl Van Vechten, Stein expressed some reservation in her estimation of Richard Wright. On June 12, 1946, she wrote, "he interests me immensely, he is strange, I have a lot of theories about him and sometime when it all gets straightened out I'll tell you . . . he has made quite clear to me the whole question of the Negro problem, the black white the white black, are they white or are they black . . . in his particular case it is very interesting, more so than in any of the others I have ever met."[3] In her next letter dated June 27, 1946, she does not commit herself any further except to say that there is a strange "materialism" about him that was not "Negro." The context does not clarify her meaning. She does seem a bit jealous of the attention Wright was getting from the French, which was very much in character, but she never retracted or qualified her praise of Wright's work.

Richard Wright's admiration for Gertrude Stein is equally well documented. It began when he read *Three Lives* in the early 1930s. Wright was in Chicago by this time and recalls having read an unflattering review of Stein's work. Stein's work was in the papers because she was on a lecture tour of the United States between the fall of 1934 and the spring of 1935. She gave a two-week seminar at the University of Chicago in the spring of 1935. Wright's published praise of Stein includes the piece, "Why I Chose Melanctha"[4] and reviews of Stein's *Wars I Have Seen*[5] and

1. Stein, "The New Hope Is 'Our Sad Young Man' " (*New York Times Magazine*, June 3, 1945: 15, 38).
2. Robert Haas, ed., *A Primer for the Gradual Understanding of Gertrude Stein* (Los Angeles: Black Sparrow P, 1971, 31–32).
3. Edward Burns, ed. *The Letters of Gertrude Stein and Carl Van Vechten, 1913–1946.* (New Haven: Yale UP, 1986, 823, 827).
4. Richard Wright, "Why I Chose 'Melanctha.' " in *I Wish I'd Written That*, Whit Burnett, ed. (New York: McGraw Hill, 1946).
5. Richard Wright, "Gertrude Stein's Story is Drenched in Hitler's Horrors," review of *Wars I Have Seen* (*PM* 11, March 1945, 5).

Brewsie and Willie.[6] In the unpublished essay, "Memories of my Grandmother," Wright explores more fully Stein's influence on his thinking. In *American hunger*,[7] Wright cites Stein's influence on his early attempts to write, and in *Lawd Today!*,[8] a novel attentive to the experimental prose and poetry of high modernism, one of the characters compares Stein's "rose is a rose is a rose" to a Cab Calloway scat. More privately, in an October 1945 letter to Stein in which he had enclosed a copy of *Black Metropolis*,[9] Wright indicated where her essay "What Are Masterpieces" had influenced his introduction to that study. In January 1945, Wright wrote in his journal, "Am reading Stein's *Narration* and find it fascinating. . . . How odd that this woman who is distrusted by everyone can remind me of the most basic things in my life. . . . Yes, she's got something, but I'd say that one could live and write like that only if one lived in Paris or in some out of the way spot where one could claim one's own soul" Journal, Jan. 1945.[1] Indeed Wright admired the way Stein had, after years of expatriation, remained an original American voice.

In spite of the obvious and important differences in education, economic backgrounds, race, religion, and gender, Gertrude Stein and Richard Wright shared a similar intellectual landscape: they began their careers as marginals within already marginalized communities; their commitment to writing and their desire to live peacefully in unorthodox marriages led to permanent self-exile. The circumstances that led each writer to live abroad were qualitatively different, but both needed a distant haven. Even though the roads they traveled were not at all the same, Paris guaranteed a certain social and aesthetic freedom for both Stein and Wright. Stein left the United States, in part, to recover from a broken heart and a failed career in medicine. Paris offered a haven from the pressures and constraints of a highly educated woman struggling to come to terms with the heresy of her sexuality. The financial and moral support of her brothers, already in Paris, made the transition easier.

When Wright came to Paris in 1946, he was at the height of his career. In a letter to Stein dated May 27, 1945, he gleefully reported that *Black Boy* had sold 450,000 copies in eleven weeks. Despite the fame and fortune, which enabled him to purchase a home for his

---

6. Richard Wright, "American GIs' Fears Worry Gertrude Stein," review of *Brewsie and Willie* (*PM* 21, July 1946, 15–16).
7. New York: Harper and Row, 1977. (Reprinted as *Black Boy* [*American Hunger*] [New York: Perennial Classics, 1998])
8. 1960, rpt. in *Richard Wright: Early Works* (New York: Library of America, 1991).
9. St. Clair Drake, and Horace Cayton, *Black Metropolis: A Study of Negro Life in a Northern City* (New York: Harcourt Brace, 1945).
1. Journal typescript in the James Weldon Johnson Collection, Beinecke Library, Yale University.

mother in Chicago and for his family in Greenwich Village, Wright
was unable to escape the daily insults of his deeply racist native land:
he was served salted coffee in neighborhood cafes when accompanied by his wife; neighborhood youths shouted racial epithets as he
walked to and from home; his daughter was refused access to a
toilet.[2] Wright knew that, in 1947, were he and Gertrude Stein to
meet for coffee at a lunch counter in Mississippi it would provoke
violence. Wright needed the refuge of a foreign land if he were to
continue to write. Each writer made only one trip back to the United
States in all their years of expatriation; Stein spent forty-three years
abroad and Richard Wright spent thirteen. Unlike most expatriate
writers, Stein and Wright died and are buried in Paris. And despite
the decades away from their native land and the critique this absence
implies, both writers insisted upon their American identity; indeed
expatriation enabled them to be Americans in ways inaccessible to
them back home.

During their separate apprenticeships, both writers had to struggle
against a domineering influence upon which they were dependent.
Gertrude Stein's unusually close relationship to her brother Leo
began to fracture when she persisted in her literary experimentation.
Although Stein was reticent on this subject, Leo's assessment of his
sister as "basically stupid" supports her telegraphic account of the
relationship in *The Autobiography*;[3] Leo ridiculed her every effort. In
his autobiography, Leo Stein expressed his objections to both
Picasso's cubism and his sister's writing: "Both he and Gertrude are
using their intellects, which they ain't got, to do what would need
the finest critical tact, which they ain't got either, and they are in
my belief turning out the most Godalmighty rubbish that is to be
found" (53).

Richard Wright's battle to become a writer began in childhood.
Black Boy-American Hunger chronicles many of these conflicts, and
although Wright did exaggerate some of the details, one can easily
imagine the ways a black boy from rural Mississippi in the early
decades of this century would have been discouraged from a career
as a writer. Among the conflicts Wright includes are his grandmother's refusal to let him read anything but books approved by her
church; the racism of the white South and black complicity when
the school principal gives Richard the speech he is to read for com-
mencement in lieu of the one he had written; the librarians who
would not have let him borrow books, much less anything by
Mencken. To the problem of race, add class; Richard Wright did not

2. Michel Fabre, *The Unfinished Quest of Richard Wright*, trans. Isabel Barzun. (New York: Morrow, 1971), 312.
3. Stein, *The Autobiography of Alice B. Toklas* (New York: Random House, 1933).

come from the middle-class milieu of W.E.B. Du Bois or James Weldon Johnson. Finally Wright includes the American Communist Party's censure for his failing to toe the line.

Wright's conflict with the American Communist Party should not be underestimated. Although he was bright and ambitious, his dream of becoming a writer would have been impossible in the context of the Great Depression without the help of party affiliates such as the John Reed Club or the *Daily Worker*. Richard Wright did not have the intellectual or financial support that such writers as Zora Neale Hurston, Langston Hughes, and Ralph Ellison acquired through their college experiences. Instead the Chicago branch of the John Reed Club and later the New York office of the *Daily Worker* provided cultural, intellectual, and financial support, and ultimately through the journals *Left Front* and *New Masses*, the party published Wright's early work. For a number of years Richard Wright flourished in that milieu. He became the John Reed Club's executive secretary and organized a lecture series that brought several progressive professors from the University of Chicago to lecture. Wright met Professor Louis Wirth through his wife Mary Wirth because she was the Wright family's social worker. But only in his capacity as the club's secretary would Wright have been able to encounter scholars such as Melville Herskovits, John Strachey, and Robert Morss Lovett (Fabre, *Unfinished* 100–130). The break was inevitable; the party expected Wright to produce party-line literature and to recognize that party politics were more important than writing. The most important event leading to this break turned on the issue of race. Wright objected to the party's decision to withhold support from any effort to combat government discrimination in the courts in the guise of wartime solidarity. Wright expressed much of his frustration with the party in "I Tried to Be a Communist"[4] and in *American Hunger*.

Each writer fought a war on two fronts: where the uncertainty of her/his literary ambitions lived, and in the daily struggle to be free from the support that had once been vital. These battles were inevitable and prolonged. Even though Stein's writing and the arrival of Alice Toklas had begun to separate them as early as 1908, Leo Stein did not leave 27 rue de Fleurus until 1913. And although Richard Wright knew that he would have to leave the party as early as 1935, he did not officially sever his ties until 1942 (Fabre, *Unfinished* 207–46). There was a finality to these breaks; Stein never again spoke to Leo after their separation nor did Wright ever forgive the American Communist Party.

Our efforts to appreciate the affinities between Gertrude Stein and Richard Wright are further frustrated by apparently irreconcilable

4. Richard Wright, "I Tried to Be A Communist" in *The God That Failed*, ed. Richard Crossman (New York: Harper's, 1949).

differences between the modernisms of black and white American writers. Houston Baker's *Modernism and the Harlem Renaissance*[5] and Paul Gilroy's *Small Acts: Thoughts on the Politics of Black Cultures*[6] speak to the important differences in the black writer's use of modernism. For Houston Baker any cultural form that is "designated 'modernist' for Afro-America is also, and by dint of adequate historical accounts, always, co-extensively labeled popular, economic and liberating" (101). Unlike white writers, the African-American writer's modernist "anxiety" is produced by the daunting task of having to use "audible extant forms" to move beyond the legacy of slavery (101). Developing this point further, Gilroy argues that it is possible to reconcile the "aesthetics of personalism and the matching politics of radical individualism" and that this reconciliation is best expressed by the idea of a "populist modernism," developed by Werner Sollors to describe the work of Leroi Jones/Amiri Baraka.[7] This apparent oxymoron acknowledges black writers' roles as creators and critics of modernism who are also aware of their obligations to the history of the black Atlantic in the making of modernity. Gilroy defines populist modernism in these terms:

> This distinctive aesthetic and ethico-political approach requires a special gloss on terms like reason, justice, freedom, and "communicative ethics." It starts from the recognition of the African diaspora's peculiar position as "step-children" of the West and of the extent to which our imaginations are conditioned by an enduring proximity to regimes of racial terror. It seeks deliberately to exploit the distinctive quality of perception that Du Bois identified long ago as "double consciousness." Whether this is viewed as an effect of oppression or a unique moral burden, it is premised on some sense of black cultures . . . as counter-cultures of modernity forged in the quintessentially modern condition of racial slavery. (*Small Acts* 103)

In the manifesto, "Blueprint for Negro Writing," Richard Wright emphasizes these points.[8] African-American writers had to create with an awareness of the history of slavery and racial terror; "Negro writers must have in their consciousness the foreshortened picture of the *whole*, nourishing culture from which they were torn in Africa, of the long, complex . . . struggle to regain in some form and under alien conditions of life a *whole* again" (47). Moreover, to preserve the creative perspective, black writers had to connect this history to

5. Houston Baker, *Modernism and the Harlem Renaissance* (Chicago: U of Chicago P, 1987).
6. Paul Gilroy, *Small Acts: Thoughts on the Politics of Black Cultures.* (London: Serpent's Tail, 1993).
7. Werner Sollors, *Amiri Baraka/Leroi Jones: The Quest for a Populist Modernism* (New York: Columbia UP, 1978).
8. Richard Wright, "Blueprint for Negro Writers" in *The Richard Wright Reader*, ed. Michel Fabre and Ellen Wright (New York: Harper and Row, 1978).

a global history, to see the lives of African Americans in New York and Chicago with the awareness that "one sixth of the earth's surface belongs to the working class" (46). Wright's position argues for a modernism that draws on both African-American folk traditions and the modernist discursive strategies of Stein, Proust, and Hemingway.

Richard Wright's first novel, *Lawd Today!*, is an early example of a populist modernism. Published posthumously in 1960, *Lawd Today!* makes explicit references to Stein, Dos Passos, and Joyce. The story takes place on a single day, February 12, a holiday celebrating the birth of Abraham Lincoln. The narrative is continually interrupted by blaring newspaper headlines, advertisements, and radio. In this example, Jake, the protagonist is reading the morning paper:

> He stirred his cup and read again
> EINSTEIN SAYS SPACE BENDS
> "Humph! Now this is what I call crazy! Yes, siree, just plumb crazy!
> This guy takes the prize. What in hell do he know about space bending." (32)

When the discussion turns to the relative sanity of white people, one of the characters cites Stein's "rose is a rose is a rose" as proof of their insanity, but another compares this phrase to jazz scats (174). Linking this most famous of Stein's reiterations to a jazz scat, Wright suggests that such artists might drink from the same well. Even as it playfully evokes modernist literary strategies, *Lawd Today!* never veers from its serious subject; black life in America. The African-American writer's need for a populist modernism is argued again in Wright's brilliant story "The Man Who Lived Underground."

Richard Wright's sense of the relationship between Calloway's scat jazz and the poetics of highly experimental formalism of Stein, Joyce, or the surrealists turns on the idea that "forced exclusion from this conventional world has led black Americans to: the production of an obliqueness of vision, a different way of looking at the world, of conceiving and feeling it."[9] The odd and disturbing poetics of high modernism began in the writer's sense of uncertainty and alienation. And while the sense of standing on shaky ground may have been new to white writers (although perhaps to a lesser degree for Joyce and Stein than for Eliot and Pound), it was familiar terrain for black writers. Although Wright could agree with the disruptive dimension of modernist poetics, unless these were grounded in a historical consciousness the road would lead to Freddy Daniels's cave.

"The Man Who Lived Underground" was written in 1942 in the

9. Eugene Miller, *The Voice of a Native Son: The Poetics of Richard Wright* (Jackson: UP of Mississippi, 1990), 82.

important interval between *Native Son* and *Black Boy*. The story is familiar: Freddy Daniels is falsely accused of murdering a white woman. The police beat him until he signs a confession, but remarkably he escapes, taking refuge in the sewer. Once underground, the narrative moves from the naturalist world of *Native Son* to an eerily disturbing other world; indeed it is *le monde à l'envers*.[1] As Eugene Miller has noted, the composition of this piece coincided with Wright's reading Freudian dream theory and surrealism. The forced exclusion from life and the alienation this produces in Freddy is evoked through the antirational strategies of surrealism: "the dead world of sunshine" and "obscene sunshine," "the dark sunshine aboveground," and the placement of familiar objects out of context. A furtive interloper, Freddy steals gems, currency, tools, a radio, and a typewriter from the aboveground. Here too the surrealist aesthetic is invoked: Freddy uses hundred-dollar bills to paper the walls of his cave and then nails up wristwatches and a meat cleaver. Diamonds become encrusted in the dirt of the cave's floor and remind Freddy of the starry night sky.

Carla Cappetti has argued persuasively that "The Man Who Lived Underground" criticizes the hermetically sealed universe of the radically experimental formalism of the surrealists, including the more obscure work of Gertrude Stein.[2] "The Man Who Lived Underground" illustrates the limits of experimental formalism for Richard Wright. The extent to which the "complex simplicity" of black American life could be expressed through such radical formalism was limited by its narrow focus on the subjective (Cappetti, *"Black Boy"*). (Besides which, as Wright knew so well, jazz was black America's radical formalism.) In a 1938 interview for *Columbia University Writers Club Bulletin*, Wright makes this point: "All of us young writers were influenced by Hemingway ... We liked the simple, direct way in which he wrote, but a great many of us wanted to write about social problems ... Hemingway's style is so concentrated upon naturalistic detail that there is no room for social comment."[3] Which is not to argue that Richard Wright sacrificed aesthetics for the social and political commitment. Indeed the enduring power of his work is its ability to use these forms, as Houston Baker suggests, "in ways that move clearly up, masterfully and resoundingly away from slavery" (101). More important, Richard Wright did not so much learn from white modernists as he recognized in their poetics the sense of alienation and estrangement with which he and most black Americans were quite familiar.

1. "The world upside down" [*Editor's note*].
2. Carla Cappetti, *"Black Boy ... Who Lived Underground*: Richard Wright Beyond Realism and Aestheticism," paper delivered at Black Boy at Fifty Conference (Washington U, November 18, 1995).
3. Michel Fabre, *Richard Wright: Books and Writers* (Jackson: UP of Mississippi, 1990).

Eugene Miller makes a solid case for the influence of the formally radical modernists during Wright's apprenticeship. Miller's discussion includes passages from an unpublished story, "Tarbaby's Dawn," which resonates with the language of "Melanctha." Note this striking example: "Gradually he began to see and feel it all and he felt her helping him to feel her and then he had her, feeling him and her coming to a dark red point of hotness and blazing red and red and red" (63). Even though Wright did not employ these formal strategies in his canonical work, Stein's prose helped him to see literary style as not "merely . . . external and decorative but as interior and integral . . . the form chosen to make the work perceivable" (66). Wright ultimately chose the narrative strategies of naturalism and realism because, as Cappetti argues, he needed forms that would best convey the stories of black American life he hoped to tell. In Emile Zola's novels of the desperately poor in pitiless urban squalor, *Nana* and *L'Assommoir*, Wright found a parallel to the story of Chicago's black ghetto. Recall too that the earliest sociological studies depended on many Zola-inspired narratives, or "life stories." In the United States, this was the practice of the Chicago School—to keep theory about human migration and social change grounded in human experience (20–31). Naturalism, realism, and the highly formal modernism of Joyce and Stein share a sense of the displacement of a religious for a secular worldview, of alienation, and a focus on human consciousness, perception, and cognition. Gertrude Stein and Richard Wright were influenced by the social sciences engaged in the study of human consciousness in a strange new world.

David Hollinger rightly challenges the conventional notion of literary modernism as being in opposition to modern science. Hollinger notes that the term "modernism" is most closely associated with early twentieth-century literature, which is characterized by an "anti-rational, alienated and experimental style." But this "dominant reading of modernism as anti-rational, experimental and alienated" obscures the rational and scientific aspect of modernity and what we think of as the Modern (38). We need not deny the term "modernism" to this literary and artistic movement, but we need to recall that it represents one of many responses to modernity. Another, as important, response is that of the scientist; we are as much the children of Charles Darwin as of William Butler Yeats. One of the features of "modernism" for the artist as well as for the scientist is the celebration of the "cognitive capability of human beings." Indeed, "many of the careers we normally take to be major episodes in the intellectual history of the last century were responsive to both" (42–45). This certainly describes Gertrude Stein and Richard Wright and further illuminates their intellectual and temperamental affinities.

Intellectually, Stein and Wright were influenced by the new social sciences of psychology and sociology. Both disciplines articulate two important theories associated with modernism that were fundamental to their work: the focus on human consciousness informed by new scientific theories of the self and the alienation of the self in the modern urban setting. For Gertrude Stein there was nothing more important than "the relationship of the self to the self." In the early decades of this century, sociology offered a persuasive paradigm for understanding the major upheavals in American society provoked by mass immigration from Europe as well as the Great Migration of black Americans from the rural South to northern cities. Richard Wright's encounter with the theories of Louis Wirth and Robert Park enabled him to see the African-American experience in the context of a global transformation that is the hallmark of modernity. In this context, an individual life could not be adequately understood outside his/her conflict with community both large and small.

At Harvard between 1894 and 1896, Gertrude Stein was present at the beginning of an entirely new discipline in American higher education: William James's courses in psychology. Stein's scientific training, first as an undergraduate at Harvard and later as a medical student, made her extremely attentive to states of consciousness as revealed through speech. Her insights for narrative, that is, repetition and the continuous present, are grounded in this scientific training. Stein's first publication, "Normal Motor Automatism,"[4] which she coauthored with Leon Solomons, reported the results of an experiment to measure responses to fatigue. Even after her career in medical school came to an end, Stein spent another semester in the laboratory doing brain research.[5] This background, particularly Jamesian psychology, enabled Stein to think and to write with a new kind of subjectivity.

The idea that gave impetus to *The Making of Americans*, to "describe the bottom nature of everyone who was ever living," had its origins in her scientific background. But just as important, another of Stein's objectives in writing *The Making of Americans* was to show "the old world in the new or more exactly the new world all made out of the old." In her mind, psychology that revealed the subject in new ways was linked to the prototypical American form. All that is familiar in the immigrant family narrative of assimilation is sabotaged by the novel's form, which creates a modernist aesthetic as it expresses the modernity of the American experience. For Gertrude Stein, the narrative of her American experience runs aground on available forms. Or as Pricilla Wald has argued, "Stein's telling differs from conventional immigrant narratives because she wants to tell the story of that telling-of the difference between what the nar-

4. Stein with Leon Solomons, in *Harvard Psychological Review* (Sept. 1896), 495–512.
5. Richard Bridgman, *Gertrude Stein in Pieces* (New York: Oxford UP, 1970), 37.

rator *means* to tell and of what she can actually tell" (257). All of Stein's formal innovations worked (borrowing an expression from jazz) to "worry," to question, the relationship between sign and signified, noun and referent, lived experience and its representation. This is echoed in the title, where process is privileged over fixity. Process, that which is evolving and therefore indeterminate was, for Stein, key to her own identity as an artist and an American. Stein's modernism came out of her scientific training and the dialectic of her experience as both an American and, like Richard Wright, an outsider. With the exception of Henry James, no writer at the turn of the century illustrates more vividly the artist's struggle to make cognitive process part of the artistic production than does Gertrude Stein. *Three Lives* (1906), *The Making of Americans* (1911), and *Tender Buttons* (1914) are the founding texts of American literary modernism.

In *Writing Chicago: Modernism, Ethnography, and the Novel*,[6] Carla Cappetti has demonstrated the extent to which Richard Wright's thinking was influenced by the Chicago School of Sociology. Much of Wright's prose, fiction and nonfiction, would ultimately be shaped by the idea of the Marginal Man, the peasant who migrates from the rural Past to the urban Now. It is the paradigm developed by Robert Park and the Chicago School of Sociology. Wright accounts for the centrality of this paradigm to his work in his introduction to St. Clair Drake and Horace Cayton's *Black Metropolis: A Study of Negro Life in a Northern City*: "I did not know what my story was, and it was not until I stumbled upon science that I discovered some of the meanings of the environment that battered and taunted me . . . The huge mountains of fact piled up by the Department of Sociology at the University of Chicago gave me my first concrete vision of the forces that molded the urban Negro's body and soul" (Drake and Cayton 18–19). The sociological model kept Wright's modernist perspective grounded in the world he was committed to making visible.

Richard Wright appropriated two concepts from Robert Park's essay "Human Migration and the Marginal Man" that catalyzed his thinking and writing about the African-American experience, including his own. In this essay, Park argues that social change comes out of catastrophe and from the social chaos (the Great Migration from the South to the northern urban centers, or the vast influx of immigrants from eastern Europe) there emerges a new man (and woman) who culturally embodies both the old order and the new. He is "a man on the margin of two cultures." Marginal Man is freed from the

6. New York: Columbia University Press, 1993.

"local bonds . . . from the culture of the tribe and folk . . . from the sacred order of tribal custom" (345–56). Louis Wirth focuses on a related problem: a sociological definition of the city. Wirth begins with a design that contrasts the rural (the world of kinship and unity, of emotional attachment) with the urban (the world of freedom, sophistication, and tolerance but also alienation, insecurity, and powerlessness). Park's Marginal Man lives on the bridge spanning these two worlds (60–83).

The Chicago School of Sociology provided Wright with a powerful model from which he created one of the century's most enduring metaphors: the marginal, alienated black boy. The structure of *Black Boy-American Hunger* owes much to the sociological model of conflict "between groups and individuals, community and society, tradition and modernity, nature time and clock time" (Cappetti, *Writing* 196). Wright also drew on the slave narrative and the portrait-of-the-artist genres to tell his story. But what made *Black Boy* more than another portrait of the artist or neo-slave narrative was his incorporation of the conflict around which both sociological theory and literary modernism, in the United States and Europe, had developed (196). Wright's genius lay in his ability to see that the black American experience was an extraordinarily rich instance of the conflict between tradition and modernity, between the individual and the community as the hallmark of modernity. Richard Wright's gift to world literature was to move the Other from the circumference to the center of modern life. To understand modernity, in all its complexity, white Americans had to come to terms with the black American; "the Negro" he argued, "is America's metaphor."[7] In most of his expatriate writing, Wright extended the discussion of what W. E. B. Du Bois referred to as the problem of the twentieth century beyond America's borders to include the entire world.

These new models of self and society enabled Gertrude Stein and Richard Wright to express substantively and stylistically their own complex alienation. The psychological and sociological paradigms contributed to and formalized each writer's psychological and emotional distance from his/her material. This distance enables what I call the modernist impulse to make visible the ways in which social forms (Jim Crow) and literary practices (syntax) are culturally determined and culturally relative. As such, Wright's metaphors and Stein's discursive strategies are important instances of cultural critique. Marianne DeKoven argues that Stein's encrypted narratives were in part a response to disturbing feelings about her sexuality but that "Stein did not merely stifle or deny her anger, her sense that

7. Richard Wright, *White Man, Listen!* (New York: Harper's, 1957), 72.

she did not fit and that the deficiency was not hers but rather that of the structure which excluded her."[8]

In the unpublished essay "Memories of My Grandmother," Wright recalls an incident that captures the quality he most appreciated in the prose of Gertrude Stein. One summer day during the Loeb-Leopold trial, Wright's family had gathered on the porch to listen to an uncle read a newspaper account. Young Wright was struck by the fact that these men could speak several languages. He then announced to the elders, "I wish I could forget English for a few minutes, just so I could listen to it and hear how it sounds" (Journal 16). Years later, when Wright describes how Stein's *Three Lives* had enabled him to hear English as never before, that childhood wish is evoked; "I heard English as Negroes spoke it: . . . melodious, tolling, rough, infectious, subjective, laughing, cutting . . . Words which I'd know all of my life but . . . never really heard. . . . And not only the words, but the winding psychological patterns that lay back of them!" (Journal 19). Eugene Miller raises the point many critics and writers have observed over the years; Melanctha doesn't sound black, at least not by conventional/stereotypical standards, then or now. So what was it in "Melanctha" that so reminded him of Grandmother Wilson? In part Wright heard the repetitions that are intrinsic to the African-American folkloric tradition. And as important, Wright, "heard . . . not what Stein's characters were saying but rather Stein's attitude toward language. . . . she made him aware of a validity in language that was not in the scientific mode . . . but in its sensory qualities, as music or incantation" (Miller 72).

The meaning of the words or an odd syntax are less important than "the intonation of her voice, the rhythm of her simple, vivid sentences. . . . 'Melanctha' was written in such a manner that I could actually stand outside of the English language and hear it" (Journal 20). The ability to "stand outside of the English language" is key to the linguistic innovations of high modernism. Making it new meant in part making it strange.

In *The Dialect of Modernism*, Michael North's discussion of Malinowski's theory of language illuminates Wright's desire to stand outside of the English language.[9] Malinowski's experiences as an anthropologist led him to conceive of language as that which enables "phatic communion." Meaning is secondary: "the primary function of language, all language, is not to convey meaning at all but to facilitate the social communion without which it has no existence" (46). (This is North's paraphrase of Bonislaw Malinowski, "The

---

8. Marianne DeKoven, *A Different Language: Gertrude Stein's Experimental Writing* (Madison: U of Wisconsin Press, 1983), 36. (See p. 317.)
9. Michael North, *The Dialect of Modernism: Race, Language, and Twentieth Century Literature* (New York: Oxford UP, 1994). (See p. 429.)

Problem of Meaning in Primitive Languages.") North argues for the centrality of this concept in the work of Joseph Conrad. For Conrad, who referred to "phatic communion" as solidarity, "the power of sound has always been greater than the power of sense" (47). This "solidarity" is inaccessible to the linguistic outsider; conversely, those within the magic circle are unaware of it. Through Stein's *Three Lives*,[1] Wright becomes a linguistic outsider long enough to hear the "solidarity" of southern, rural, Christian, black America in his grandmother's voice. The implications are important; Wright could apperceive this solidarity only to the extent he already felt himself outside of it. The modernism of Richard Wright's work, its striking prescience and insurgency, grew out of his being the insider who is simultaneously the outsider.

Richard Wright's reading of *Three Lives* influenced the way he would represent the African-American experience. In "Memories" he links the Conradian sense of the "solidarity" of language to the "surreal" quality of black American life that is characterized by *"psychological distance*—even when it deals with realistic subject matter" (Journal 20). For black Americans this distance is *"enforced severance* . . . through unemployment, oppression from the functional meaning of society" (20). The link between what Wright called his grandmother's "abstract" way of living in but not of the world because of her religious beliefs and Stein's highly stylized prose is an emotional and psychological distance. It is that quality in Stein's work that he describes as being possible only "if one lived in Paris or in some out of the way spot where one could claim one's own soul." Wright and Stein did, in part, achieve that distance through expatriation. But expatriation simply completes and confirms the existing psychological and perhaps spiritual alienation.

In *Paris France*[2] and elsewhere Stein insisted on the artist's need for two countries. Especially in France, she was content to have been "left alone with my eyes and my english." But in "Melanctha" Stein had also achieved an emotional distance by locating the story of her own failed love affair in Baltimore's African-American community. North argues that Stein's assumption of an African-American persona also functioned as a kind of cultural expatriation and helped to further free her, psychologically and formally, from her bourgeois origins (59–76). Ironically, Stein's need for distance to narrate an episode of personal crisis prompted her to approximate an African-American idiom that would someday enable a striving young black writer to embrace, from a distance, a troubled relationship of his own. "Melanctha" as much as Mencken or the Chicago School of Sociology helped Richard Wright to find his voice.

1. Stein, *Three Lives* (New York: Grafton, 1909).
2. Stein, *Paris France* (London: Batsford, 1940).

Unlike T. S. Eliot or Ezra Pound, Stein appropriated a black voice as much from an identification with the blues of black folk, particularly as a Jew and a lesbian, as from its function as a distancing strategy. Gertrude Stein's interest in Richard Wright and his work grew out of her attentiveness to the African-American presence and experience in America. In a 1945 interview for the *Baltimore Afro-American*, Gertrude Stein told journalist Vincent Tubbs, "I am interested in the cultural products of the world like Richard Wright's *Black Boy* which I think heralds an evolution from intellectual defensiveness to intellectual offensiveness." And toward the end of the interview Stein stated, "The things we have talked about today we did not talk about twenty five years ago and what you say is interesting and I could see it in Wright's book which I think is really epochal because it means the colored race is no longer the white man's burden and is conversing himself about himself and magnificently too" (5). During the last months of her life, between April 1945 and July 1946, Gertrude Stein read, corresponded with, and finally met Richard Wright.

This period coincided with the euphoric end of World War II, and, given her experience of that war, it is not surprising that Stein would be impressed by *Black Boy* and its young author. Racist propaganda, aimed primarily at Jews, gypsies, and foreigners, had dominated the French media during the war. Rather than quit their adopted country, Stein and Toklas spent the period between 1939 and 1944 in two small rural villages in eastern France. Like the French majority, Stein had initially backed Philippe Pétain's Vichy government. Pétain's overwhelming popular support was owing to his astounding heroism in the decisive World War I battle of Verdun. Pétain's victory had encouraged Stein and Toklas to return to France, where between 1916 and 1918 they were volunteers with the "American Fund for French Wounded." For their work, which involved driving supplies all over the south of France, Stein and Toklas were awarded le Médaille de la Reconnaissance Française in 1922.[3]

That Gertrude Stein actually translated 180 pages of the marshal's speeches and kept her friendship with Bernard Faÿ, an Americanist who became head of the Bibliothéque Nationale during the Vichy regime, continues to be troubling. It is unclear, as Edward Burns and Ulla Dydo note, why, once Pétain's anti-Semitic policies began to result in deportations, Stein continued to work on the speeches.[4] Stein and Toklas were protected by Pétain through Faÿ, and perhaps this impaired her judgment. However much we must fault Stein and

3. John Malcolm Brinnin, *The Third Rose: Gertrude Stein and Her World* (Boston: Little, Brown, 1959), 220–31.
4. Edward Burns and Ulla Dydo, eds., *The Letters of Gertrude Stein and Thornton Wilder* (New York: Columbia UP, 1996), 401–21.

Toklas for their conservative politics, we are obligated to distinguish between conservative politics and Nazi collaboration. Stein and Toklas had seen the consequences of World War I, "when all the men were dead or badly wounded" (Van Vechten 633). In retrospect can one fault them or the French if they preferred a negotiated peace to another war? Should she have refused Faÿ's protection, whom she had known since 1926, of not just herself but her art collection in Paris? Might we be more forgiving had she, like Joyce, gone to Switzerland? It made more sense to stay in France; Stein and Toklas were well integrated into the small rural communities in Belley and Culoz and had spent every summer in that region for the previous twenty years. In addition, both women were in their mid- to late sixties during the war. It can be argued that Stein simply followed the example of her own government; the United States never severed its ties to the Vichy government either.

This history is further complicated by Stein's contributions, in 1942–43, to a monthly arts journal, *Confluences*. It was published in Lyons, as opposed to Paris, and enjoyed a certain amount of independence because of it. *Confluences'* critics complained that it published the work of "Jews, communists and pederasts." During that somber period, it was among few journals open to the increasingly numerous anti-Vichy writers. Stein's poem, "Ballade" appeared in the famous July 1942 edition in which Louis Aragon published "Nymphée," a thinly disguised critique of the French and the Vichy government. For this offense, the publication of *Confluences* was suspended for two months. Stein's "Ballade" also takes up the idea of the necessity of resistance by the weaklings against the stronger bullies. In August 1943, René Tavernier, *Confluences'* editor wrote to inform Stein that her name appeared on the list "OTTO," those writers whose work could not be published in France. Stein's status as a Jewish writer earned her this distinction (Burns and Dydo 419–20). Having read Gertrude Stein's letters to René Tavernier at Institut Mémoires de l'Edition Contemporaine in Paris, I could not determine how she responded to this news; her correspondence with Tavernier, which had up to that point been fairly regular, stopped abruptly for one year.

After the war, Stein and Toklas went to Germany for *Life* magazine. The two women made a tour of the American army bases, and, along with a troop of American soldiers, they visited Hitler's mountain retreat in Berchtesgarten, Austria. There Stein and the soldiers had their photo taken on the terrace in mock Third Reich salute. During this tour, a black soldier approached Stein and recited her poetry, an incident that moved her. The Third Reich's racist ideology that had driven World War II, combined with its reflection in America's Jim Crow army, prompted Gertrude Stein to "meditate" on the race problem. In the *Life* article, Stein chastises Americans who must learn to appreciate the "Other" to learn to think for themselves, and she points to defeated Germany as an example of all that was wrong in the world. So explicit was her social criticism that the sergeant presented her with a card that read "to Gertie, another Radical."[5] There is a photo that puts a finer point on Stein's own criticism of American racism; in it she is standing among a group of African-American soldiers in occupied Germany (the photo is the property of the Beinecke Library, Yale University).[6] Stein's meditations on race and racism dominated her thinking until her death.

Stein had initially written to Wright to praise *Black Boy*, which she read after his favorable review of *Wars I Have Seen*. She also asked that he send copies of his other work that were still unavailable in postwar Paris. Wright happily complied and, in addition, sent her a copy of Dan Burly's *Handbook to Harlem Jive* and some of Father Divine's speeches. Stein plied Wright with questions about racism in America; Stein's interest in the subject had taken on new intensity. By July she was reading Gunnar Myrdal's landmark study, *An American Dilemma*. In a July 6, 1945, letter to Carl Van Vechten, she asked for any work by black educator Kelly Miller (Burns, *Letters of Stein and Van Vechten* 782–83). By August, Stein had received and read *Uncle Tom's Children* and wrote, "I'm mad about it, there is a tremendous mastery in the thing" (789). Vincent Tubbs interviewed Stein for the *Baltimore Afro-American* because she had made it publicly known that she wanted to talk to black servicemen. "This correspondent went to see Miss Stein because I believe anybody who wants to know colored people should be given the opportunity" (Tubbs 5). And in *Brewsie and Willie*,[7] a novel that features American GIs, the black soldiers surpass the white soldiers in creativity and ambition.

In a 1993 essay on Gertrude Stein and Nella Larsen, Corinne Blackmer found it remarkable that, despite the shared concerns and masking strategies of "Melanctha" and *Passing*, there had been no comparative study of these texts. Blackmer suggests that this critical silence stemmed, in part, from the taboo surrounding lesbian fiction, and she notes, "that exclusive focus on one category of difference tends to inhibit analysis of how overlapping differences operate in syncopation" (232).[8] This is not to argue that the race, gender, class, and education differences between them were unimportant. The experience as outsider shaped their lives and work, but neither Stein

---

5. Stein, "Off We All Went to See Germany," *Life* 6 Aug. 1945: 54–58.
6. Renate Stendhal, ed., *Gertrude Stein in Words and Pictures* (Chapel Hill, N.C.: Algonquin, 1994), 248–49.
7. Stein, *Brewsie and Willie* (New York: Random House, 1946).
8. Corinne Blackmer, "African Masks and the Arts of Passing in Gertrude Stein's 'Melanctha' and Nella Larsen's *Passing*," *Journal of the History of Sexuality* 4.2 (1993): 230–63.

nor Wright could be bound by categories of race, gender, or class in life or art. I proceed with two premises in mind: I take seriously their friendship, however brief or mediated, and I assume that their over-lapping differences make it possible to discuss their work together.
* * *

BARBARA WILL

[Race and Jewishness]†

* * * I am interested in the role that the category of "race" might be said to play in the ambiguities of Stein's intellectual trajectory at this time: in her attention to the self-doubling of "Normal Motor Autom-atism," and in her investment in typological essentialism in "Culti-vated Motor Automatism." As a Jewish woman working in a predominantly Protestant male environment—first Harvard, and then Johns Hopkins University, where she was a medical student from 1897 to 1901—Stein would perforce find herself located in the interstices between discourses and institutions, a tenuous position-ing that would in turn affect the kinds of positionings presented in her two scientific articles. But I am also interested in how the traces of these positionings are inscribed in the problematics of race in Stein's remarkable novella *Melanctha*—the middle story of her col-lection entitled *Three Lives*, composed 1905–6—written several years after she had left medical school and America to take up life as a writer and art collector in Paris. To what extent is Stein's por-trayal of African-Americans in that work an effect of her early anx-ieties over the relationship between knowledge, authority, and a racialized "bottom nature"? To what extent is *Melanctha* an effort "to study (the otherness of) oneself by attending to the otherness of an/other Other"?[1]

"Race" is clearly an issue in *Melanctha*, but that this issue might emerge from Stein's fraught relationship to her own racial identity is a potentially contentious point. One could argue that Stein's rela-tionship to her Jewishness is, if anything, notable by its absence.[2]

† From *Gertrude Stein, Modernism, and the Problem of "Genius"* (Edinburgh: Edinburgh University Press, 2000), pp. 34–43. Copyright © 2000 by Barbara Will. Reprinted by permission of the publisher.

1. Maria Damon, "Gertrude Stein's Jewishness, Jewish Social Scientists, and the 'Jewish Question,' " *Modern Fiction Studies* 42:3 (Fall 1996): 489–506. [Will references the 1990 Penguin reissue of *Three Lives*.—*Editor*.]
2. "There has been very little attention paid to Gertrude Stein as a Jewish writer," Linda Wagner-Martin rightly observes, locating Stein's own lack of emphasis on her Jewishness in her desire for "universalism": "The modernist writer aimed to be universal, above polit-ical alliances, washed clean in the purity of serious and innovative aesthetics, and Gertrude certainly wanted to play that game well. She would have gained nothing in high modernist

Despite her embeddedness in a close-knit Jewish family at Harvard, in Baltimore, and in the early Paris years, Stein was throughout her life a secular Jew: she was not religiously observant, did not observe dietary laws, and was not interested in Zionism.[3] After her move to Paris and with the start of her literary career, Stein made few explicit references to Jews or Judaism, even in her private notebooks; her occasional nickname for Alice Toklas, "my little Hebrew," suggests that it was Toklas who for Stein carried the "Jewish" traits. Recent revelations about Stein's endorsement of the Vichy regime during World War II further support the contention by many critics that Stein had little interest in Jewish solidarity.[4] This rejection of religion and distancing from community in turn problematizes the extent to which Stein could be said to consider herself Jewish, or to feel herself part of a "racialized" identity. Does race matter for Stein?

In charting Stein's early development as a scientist, an intellectual, and a writer, it is possible to locate the attenuation of her tie to Judaism in the period during the composition of *The Making of Americans* (1902–11)—a text initially concerned with Jewish immigrants, who in successive revisions become "Germans" and then "middle-class."[5] But as a student at Radcliffe and in the Harvard Psychological Laboratory in the 1890s, being seen as part of the "Jewish race" was clearly for Stein both a constraining social reality and a point of pride. As Brenda Wineapple has recently argued about Harvard and Radcliffe during this period, "Jewish students . . . knew they were a group apart."[6] "Allosemitism"—the practice "of setting the Jews apart as people radically different from all the others, needing separate concepts to describe and comprehend them and special treatment in all or most social intercourse"[7]—was widespread within elite American institutions like Harvard. Charles William Eliot, Harvard's president from 1869 to 1909, set the tone by speaking of his desire to greet "all the new races and to do its best for them," Jews included.[8] Although Eliot felt Jews to be "the most resistant and

Paris by describing herself as a Jewish American lesbian." In Linda Wagner-Martin, "Gertrude Stein," in *Jewish American Women Writers: A Bio-Bibliographical and Critical Sourcebook*, ed. Ann Shapiro (London: Greenday Press, 1994), 431–39.

3. Damon, "Stein's Jewishness," 492. Wineapple also discusses Stein and Jewishness (*Sister Brother*, 56–8, and *passim*), in Brenda Wineapple, *Sister Brother: Gertrude and Leo Stein* (New York: G. P. Putnam's Sons, 1996).

4. In "Portrait of a National Fetish: Gertrude Stein's 'Introduction to the Speeches of Maréchal Pétain' (1942)," *Modernism/Modernity* 3:3 (September 1996), 69–96, Wanda Van Dusen reprints and interprets Stein's 'Introduction to the Speeches of Maréchall Pétain' (1942).

5. Richard Bridgman makes this observation in *Gertrude Stein in Pieces* (New York: Oxford UP, 1970), 161.

6. Wineapple, *Sister Brother*, 51.

7. Zygmunt Bauman, "Allosemitism: Premodern, Modern, Postmodern," in Cheyette and Marcus (eds), *Modernity, Culture and 'the Jew'* (Stanford: Stanford UP, 1998), 143.

8. By the time Eliot stepped down as president, only 2.5 per cent of the student body was composed of students of Jewish descent. Yet Jews under Eliot's tenureship generally fared

prepotent race in the world," he encouraged "racial" separatism and discouraged intermarriage on the grounds that Jews might well come to "dominate."[9] Many distinguished professors on Eliot's Harvard faculty—including the typologists to whom Stein was so attracted as a young intellectual—also viewed the whole of Jewry as belonging to a discrete and decidedly foreign "race."[1] Their racialist "research" into the nature of "the Jew" was often, although not always, discriminatory. Those who were aligned with anti-immigrant groups used their typological claims to denounce blacks and Jews especially "in an attempt to defend what they considered truly 'American.' "[2] Henry Adams, in *The Education* (recently voted the best English-language book of nonfiction to appear in the twentieth century),[3] referred to the Jew as "reeking," "snarling," and "weird," with "a freer hand than he—American of Americans." His brother Brooks Adams wrote in *The Law of Civilization and Decay* that Jews, in modern economic times, were part of "a favoured aristocracy of the craftiest and subtlest types." Others like Nathaniel Shaler, dean of the Lawrence Scientific School at the turn of the century, used the example of the "typical Jew" to suggest the need for Americans (that is, non-Jews) to recognize qualities of superior intelligence even in an "alien race."[4] As Sander Gilman has recently written in *Smart Jews: The Construction of the Image of Jewish Superior Intelligence*: "the racialist notion of Jewish identity at the turn of the century" was inseparable from concerns over whether the presumed "superiority" of Jewish intelligence was in fact "degenerate": "[W]as their intelligence of the correct quality to enter into the gentility of the American educational system?"[5] Turn-of-the-century critics in Europe and America alike warned that "the greatest number of the decadents are Semites, at

---

better socially and institutionally at Harvard than they did under Eliot's successor, A. Lawrence Lowell, who favored admission quotas for Jews. See Kim Townsend, *Manhood at Harvard: William James and Others* (New York: W. W. Norton, 1996), 92; also see Marcia Graham Synott,*The Half-Opened Door: Discrimination and Admissions at Harvard, Yale, and Princeton, 1900–1970* (Westport, CT: Greenwood Press, 1979), 44–47.

9. Eliot quoted in Synnott, *Half-Opened Door*, 47.

1. Petersen discusses the history of this perception in "Jews as a Race," 35–7.

2. Townsend, *Manhood*, 231. Among the professors Townsend cites are Henry Adams, Charles Eliot Norton, Evert Wendell, Nathaniel Shaler, and Albert Bushnell Hart, W.E.B. DuBois's thesis adviser. Even William James, who called for a "typology" as specific as each unique individual, and who publicly criticized the anti-semitism and imperialism of his colleagues, was less than consistent in his private remarks to students and colleagues (Wineapple, *Sister Brother*, 51). For James's criticism of his colleagues' anti-Semitism, see Townsend, *Manhood*, 236.

3. Dinitia Smith, "Another Top 100 List: Now It's Nonfiction," *The New York Times* E:2 (30 April 1999), 45.

4. Henry Adams quoted in Louise A. Mayo, *The Ambivalent Image: Nineteenth-Century America's Perception of the Jew* (Cranbury, NJ: Associated UP, 1988), 58; Brooks Adams refers to Jews in *The Law of Civilization and Decay: An Essay on History* (1896; rpt. New York: Vintage, 1955), 292. Shaler quoted in Townsend, *Manhood*, 23–3.

5. Sander L. Gilman, *Smart Jews: The Construction of the Image of Jewish Superior Intelligence* (Lincoln: U of Nebraska P, 1996), 54; 58.

least according to their descent, and Jewry today finds itself at the stage of a physical and psychic decadence."[6] Being identified as Jewish, and especially being labeled a "smart Jew," thus carried with it the potential valence of "degeneracy."

Stein's authorial position as a young intellectual was marked by the institutions and discourses of which she was a part, and by their investment in making her visible as a "racialized" Jew. Strongly attracted herself to the typologizing impulse, Stein would largely affirm her own "bottom nature" in the terms provided by her peers and professors. In papers and letters from Radcliffe, Stein would claim that she was "a Jew first and an American only afterwards," insisting that the Jews are "a Chosen People chosen for high purposes," for "noble aims and great deeds." She would aver that Jews have "a covenant with God which has made them endure" and would note the specificity of their "ethical . . . and spiritual nature." And in a passionate essay written for a Harvard forensics course, Stein would champion "race feeling" and Jewish cultural separatism.[7] Yet the young Stein would also resist being interpellated as a "smart Jew." Wineapple recounts a telling anecdote concerning Stein and a non-Jewish Radcliffe student in which the latter claimed "I had never known a Jew; thought they were something different. I remember her [Stein] saying, 'I'm the top of the heap,' and I said, 'The top of your heap.' She was much offended."[8] Stein's taking "offense" is presumably linked in large part to the stigma attached to "Jewish"—that is, "degenerate"—intelligence. Throughout her life, Stein would claim that she was just like everybody, and at the same time "more" than everybody. One need only recall Stein's authorial claim, in "Normal Motor Automatism," to being both "perfectly normal" and capable of extraordinary acts of consciousness at one and the same time. Being "the top of the heap" was not the same as being the top of the *Jewish* heap; asserting Jewish racial difference—especially concerning intelligence—meant that Stein could not lay claim to either representative normality or universal genius.

After abandoning her psychological studies and moving to Paris, Stein would increasingly repudiate racial identification. In the notebooks to *The Making of Americans*, Stein would refer to Jews as having "good minds but not great minds."[9] She would refute the

---

6. Ibid., 133.
7. Wineapple, *Sister Brother*, 57; Linda Wagner-Martin, *"Favored Strangers": Gertrude Stein and Her Family* (New Brunswick, NJ: Rutgers UP, 1995), 34. In this essay, entitled "The Modern Jew who Has Given Up the Faith of His Fathers Can Reasonably and Consistently Believe in Isolation," Stein argued that "in the sacred precincts of the home, in the close union of family and of kinsfolk [one] must be a Jew with Jews; the Gentile has no place there" (quoted in Wagner-Martin, *"Favored Strangers"*, 34).
8. Wineapple, *Sister Brother*, 56.
9. Notebook A-3 in Stein's Notebooks in Yale American Literature Collection, Beinecke Library, Yale University. (Notebooks hereafter referred to as NB.)

presumed essentialism of Jewish character, arguing that non-Jews like Goethe and Frederick the Great could be Jewish "because they persistently and consciously educated themselves, consciously ran themselves by their minds" (NB, C-20). Most problematically, she would embrace as a fellow traveler the anti-Semitic philosopher Otto Weininger, who in his own massive typology argued that both "the Jew" and "the woman" were the negation of the ideal and universal type of "genius." In reading herself through Weininger, Stein imagined herself able to shed the ties of both race and gender and to assert the universality of her own type. Clearly, here, Stein could only be a genius—in the typological terms that made sense to her—by not identifying herself as Jewish. But it is worth considering whether this process of e-racing in order to re-type herself was not already being performed in the composition of a text that Stein wrote two years before she discovered Weininger in 1908 and came to the recognition that she was a genius: *Melanctha*. Written during a hiatus in the eight-year-long composition of *The Making of Americans*, *Melanctha* was a stylistic and thematic departure from the former, which was still at that point a fairly conventional novel of German-Jewish assimilation or American-making. Returning to an early unpublished *roman-à-clef* (*Q.E.D.* [composed 1903]), Stein decided to rewrite this story of a lesbian triangle as a narrative of the heterosexual relationship between two African-Americans. Out of this effort was born Stein's first identifiably "modernist" text, whose noted stylistic strangeness is embodied in the social and semantic "wandering" of its eponymous female protagonist. In the challenge she poses to habitual or automatic action and thought, Melanctha arguably represents the "genius" that Stein would soon lay claim to herself. In her *a*typicality, in her refusal to be "normal" or to act in "regular" or "habitual" ways, Melanctha represents a force of newness, disruption, and modernity. Yet Melanctha is also a racial "type" that would have been instantly recognizable to Stein's readers: the tragic mulatta, drawn by the one-drop rule into an essential (and fatal) association with bottom blackness. In her typicality *and* in her strangeness, Melanctha thus inscribes Stein's conflicted effort—evident in both the early psychological experiments and in her first literary experiments—to think about the human subject as both objectively "knowable" and always already in excess of epistemological and symbolic containments. Crucially, "race" becomes the carrier of these conflicts.

Many critics have focused on the way *Melanctha* treats sexuality and gender, rewriting the homosexual dynamic of *Q.E.D.* as a heterosexual plot yet encoding the otherness of queer desire within Melanctha's mysterious "wandering." Melanctha's refusal of normative femininity and her unconfined bisexuality are thus often read as projections of Stein's own "dissident sexuality."[1] Yet few critics have considered *Melanctha* as a rewriting of Jewish difference or "dissidence" as African-American otherness (it would take the Harlem Renaissance writer Claude McKay to point out that "Melanctha, the mulatress, might have been a Jewess"[2]). This, despite the fact that within *Three Lives* as a whole, *Melanctha* is sandwiched between two non-Jewish German-immigrant stories: *The Good Anna* and *The Gentle Lena*. As the in-between, the liminal, the middleman (a role often played by Jews), *Melanctha* is the story that could be said to supply the "racial" term missing from the German context. Furthermore, as with *Q.E.D.*, Stein makes it clear from the start of *Melanctha* that "race" is central to the character "types" with which both narratives are so centrally concerned. In its effort to render a mathematical proof based upon the relationship between various character types as a naturalist narrative, *Q.E.D.* clearly identifies Adele— the figure for Stein in the text—as Jewish, and figures Mabel Neathe, Adele's lesbian antagonist, as "a kind of sexual mulatto."[3] Similarly, in the opening pages of *Melanctha* "race" and "type" are inextricable. Intelligence, curiosity, sensuality, and "sweetness" are linked to lighter skin tones, while "real black[ness]" is correlated with coarseness, virility, stupidity, laziness, and childishness. Where these traits are mixed, as in Rose, brought up by a white family, "character" still comes down to a fundamentally racialized "bottom nature": "Her white training had only made for habits, not for nature. Rose had the simple, promiscuous unmorality of the black people." (TL, 60). To be sure, the "excessive literalism"[4] of blackness within the typology of *Melanctha* is problematized by the presence of the mulatto characters, such as Melanctha herself, described as a "graceful, pale yellow, intelligent, attractive negress" (TL, 60). Here, the clarity of an embodied "bottom nature" is obscured precisely because the mulatta's body is seen to be at once white and an imitation of whiteness. Yet Melanctha too is initially presented in naturalistic terms, as living out the inevitably fatal consequences of her "type." While she has a share of "real white blood" that denotes her superiority to Rose, she still bears the mark of miscegenation and thus of degeneration, and despite her "intelligent, attractive" traits, she seems

---

1. For example, see Jaime Hovey, "Sapphic Primitivism in Gertrude Stein's *Q.E.D.*" in *Modern Fiction Studies* 42:3 (Fall 1996), 547–68 (see p. 457).
2. McKay quoted in Milton Hindus, "Ethnicity and Sexuality in Gertrude Stein" in *Midstream* 20:1 (January 1974), 69–76.
3. Adele's Jewishness is marked in the conversational terms through which Stein would later define "genius" ("talking and listening"): "I never seem to know how to keep still, but you both know already that I have the failing of my tribe," she announces to Mabel and Helen, "I believe in the sacred rites of conversation even when it is a monologue" (QED, 57). On Mabel Neathe as "sexual mulatto," see Hovey, "Sapphic Primitivism," 559.
4. The phrase is Sara Suleri's, quoted in Michael North, *The Dialect of Modernism: Race, Language, and Twentieth-Century Literature* (New York: Oxford UP, 1994), 65.

doomed to downward racial and class mobility. In this, she represents the typical tragic mulatta.[5]

Drawn from dominant turn-of-the-century assumptions about the deterministic meaning of blackness, such characterizations have led readers either to condemn Stein as a racist or to forgive her for unthinkingly reiterating "the clichés of the age."[6] Yet one could also argue that the racist clichés in *Melanctha* are the effect of a category crisis for Stein during these early years of authorial self-fashioning, and that what might be called her performance of "blackface" in this text is an attempt both to displace and to resolve this crisis. Stein's crisis about Jewishness, authority, and difference could be both clarified and mediated through projection onto African-Americans, whose racialization was more relentlessly constructed by turn-of-the-century cultural discourses than even that of Jews. As the Yiddish press of the day pointed out, "blacks were in America what Jews were in Europe—the most oppressed, the most despised, and the most victimized segment of the population."[7] "Scientific" racial typing "located signs of contamination on black and Jewish bodies" alike, but the former were seen as even more "alien" than the latter.[8] The Harvard intellectual Nathaniel Shaler, who had advocated Jewish assimilation, would draw the line with Negroes, pronouncing them "ineradicably alien."[9] The anthropologist Franz Boas noted that "The Negro of our times carries even more heavily the burden of his racial descent than did the Jew of an earlier period."[1] Jewish voices, too, contributed to this effort to differentiate their own relative "whiteness" from the resolute "blackness" of African-Americans. Stein's friend Israel Zangwill, Jewish playwright and author of the *echt*-assimilationist drama *The Melting Pot*, a play that emphasized the

5. For a discussion of the figure of the tragic mulatto/a and of the one-drop rule see Eric J. Sundquist, *To Wake the Nations: Race in the Making of American Literature* (Cambridge: Harvard UP, 1993), esp. 249–63; also Hazel Carby, *Reconstructing Womanhood: The Emergence of the Afro-American Woman Novelist* (New York: Oxford UP, 1987), 88–91.

6. Milton A. Cohen, "Black Brutes and Mulatto Saints: The Racial Hierarchy of Stein's 'Melanctha,'" in *Black American Literature Forum* 18:3 (Fall 1984): 119–21. Much has been written since Cohen's formative article on Stein's alleged or actual racism; see especially Cope, "'Moral Deviency,'" for a brilliant analysis of Stein's work and the politics of interpretation. For other critiques of racism in *Melanctha*, see Sonia Saldívar-Hull, "Wrestling Your Ally: Stein, Racism, and Feminist Critical Practice," in *Women's Writing in Exile*, ed. Mary Lynn Broe and Angela Ingram (Chapel Hill: U of North Carolina P, 1989), 189–98 (see p. 000); also Hovey, "Sapphic Primitivism."

7. Quoted in Hasia R. Diner, *In the Almost Promised Land: American Jews and Blacks, 1915–1935* (Westport, CT: Greenwood Press, 1977), 74.

8. Michael Rogin suggests that parallels can be made between racism toward African Americans in America and anti-Semitism directed at Jews in European ghettos (Michael Rogin, *Blackface, White Noise: Jewish Immigrants in the Hollywood Melting Pot* [Berkeley: U of California P, 1996], 45–70). Yet Jews who came to the United States never shared the same burden of racism as blacks: "in the United States African Americans substituted for Jews as the dominant targets of racial nationalism . . . [t]he people who came to be ghettoized—who had to be stopped from changing their identities, from passing, integrating, and assimilating—were blacks rather than Jews" (ibid., 63).

9. Townsend, *Manhood*, 233.

1. Rogin, *Blackface, White Noise*, 17.

successful resolution of the Jewish-Gentile marriage plot, would in 1914 note the "justifiab[ility]" of avoiding "physical intermarriage with the negro."[2]

For the young Gertrude Stein desiring epistemological certainty, the African-American Other would have seemed a typologist's ideal subject—primitive, authentic, knowable, *readable*. Yet such problematically unproblematic racial "typing," especially in a writer so sensitive to the complexities of her own racial identification, suggests that Stein's African-American types are also projections and displacements, carriers of her contradictory desires for both identification with and distance from the category of race. In this, *Melanctha* can arguably be located within the long American tradition of blackface minstrelsy: the practice by non-black actors (and some blacks) of darkening their faces in order to perform, in exaggerated and often caricatural ways, "typical" African-American roles.[3] Significantly, Jewish-American entertainers were the main blackface performers at the turn of the century.[4] As Michael Rogin has recently argued in his study of blackface and Jewish-American actors, such performance worked for Jews in two ways: as "appropriative identification" (identifying with and ventriloquizing black otherness) and as dissociation from the category of race altogether (emphasizing through black caricature that Jews had assimilated, that "they were not black"). Blackface, Rogin suggests, serves to "loosen . . . up white identities by taking over black ones, by underscoring the line between white and black."[5] Insofar as *Melanctha* represents the "blacking up" of an autobiographical account of sexual and racial difference (*Q.E.D.*), it can be seen to offer Stein two contradictory modes of compensation. On the one hand, telling her story in African-American terms could allow Stein to emphasize an identification with blackness, its marginality and difference. In this, it is interesting how much Melanctha's "typically mulatta" characteristics could also be seen as "typically Jewish": her light skin, her intelligence, even—or especially—her propensity to "wander."[6] On the other hand, "blacking up" would allow Stein to cast her story as Other, to "loosen" it from self-identification. As blackface, *Melanctha* serves to "underscore the line between white and black": if African-Americans embody racial and sexual otherness, then Jewish-Americans do not need to. By performing her story as "black," in

---

2. Ibid., 6.
3. North suggests as much when he writes of Stein's and Picasso's "racial role-playing" in *Melanctha* and *Les Demoiselles d'Avignon*: "Stein and Picasso act out twenty years in advance the other side of *The Jazz Singer* . . . donning the African mask to make a break with their own cultural past" (North, *Dialect of Modernism*, 66).
4. Rogin, *Blackface, White Noise*, 11.
5. Ibid., 66; 34.
6. I am grateful to Susannah Heschel for emphasizing these points of similarity.

short, Stein can mark a distance from the performance of her identity as Jewish.

But if *Melanctha* represents Stein in blackface, then the racial mask that Stein adopts in this text is also what occludes epistemological certainty, including knowledge about "race" and "type." Blackface makes easy stereotypes visible; but as masking it also points to the invisible and the unknowable that lies below the visible surface of the "racial type." What is curious about *Melanctha* is that its African-American protagonist both embodies "racial type" and ultimately resists the gaze that would "know" her *as* a type; she eludes "knowing" even as she is presented as knowable in her racialization. In fact, it is precisely Melanctha's mulatta "melancholy" that marks her both as a "type" *and* as a mysteriously split subject: "melancholia," in Freud's terms, being the condition of "ambivalence . . . in which hate and love contend with each other."[7] Drawn to a bourgeois male lover yet desiring "excitement," Melanctha is "typically" mulatto—the tragic product of mixed blood. Yet she is also the site of ambivalence, of unreadability, of semantic disruption: in short, a mask. She both attracts and unsettles those who watch and analyze her—the narrator, Rose, James Herbert, John, the Bishops' coachman, Jane Harden, and her lover Jeff Campbell. Rose herself laments that "you certainly never can noways learn to act right Melanctha" (TL, 161); Jane Harden claims that "Melanctha Herbert never had any sense of how to act to anybody" (TL, 78); and all men feel her mysterious "power." In the face of Jeff Campbell's middle-class, normative credo—that "being good and careful and always honest and living always just as regular as can be" is best (TL, 85)—Melanctha remains a mystery even to herself: "always she did not know what it was that really held her" (TL, 67). In her changing, desiring restlessness, Melanctha appears to act without intention, will, conscious thought, or the sense of personal identity, and this in turn problematizes any efforts to locate her within a framework of knowledge, of typicality. In this, Melanctha's ultimate narrative function could be said to lie not in proving the veracity of "type" but in confusing and refusing the (sexual, racial, epistemological, narrative) desire of the subjects who would type her.

This refusal is most evident in the protracted passages of dialogue between Melanctha and Jeff which make up the long, middle section of the narrative, and which stage both an epistemological and a lin-

7. "In melancholia, the relation to the object is no simple one; it is complicated by the conflict due to ambivalence . . . [C]ountless separate struggles are carried on over the object, in which hate and love contend with each other; the one seeks to detach the libido from the object, the other to maintain this position of the libido against the assault" (Freud, "Mourning and Melancholia," in *The Standard Edition of the Complete Psychological Works of Sigmund Freud*, trans. and ed. James Strachey [London: The Hogarth Press, 1957], vol. XIV, 256). See also my Ch. 4, 114–15.

guistic crisis in the text. The Melanctha—Jeff opposition can be understood as a struggle between words that "commit the speaker" and words that work to "undermine the solidity of the name"; between an understanding of signification as productive (of knowledge, meaning, and so on) or as disruptive (resisting the epistemophilic or regulatory gaze).[8] In one dialogue, Jeff enters into a long excursus on the essential difference between "thinking" and "feeling," only to find in Melanctha's response an inversion of his terms of signification:

> "No, I don't stop thinking much Miss Melanctha and if I can't ever feel without stopping thinking, I certainly am very much afraid Miss Melanctha that I never will do much with that kind of feeling . . . I certainly do think I feel as much for you Miss Melanctha, as you ever feel about me, sure I do. I don't think you know me right when you talk like that to me. Tell me just straight out how much do you care about me, Miss Melanctha." "Care about you Jeff Campbell," said Melanctha slowly. "I certainly do care for you Jeff Campbell less than you are always thinking and much more than you are ever knowing." (TL, 92–3)

Jeff expects a clarity from language which Melanctha refuses to mirror: in responding to his request to "tell me just straight out" her feelings, Melanctha reiterates Jeff's words and at the same time implodes the careful semantic structure of his argument. Melanctha's inversion of Jeff's terms deauthorizes the hierarchical relationship between thinking and feeling which his repeated invocation of these terms has attempted to set up, and in so doing reveals that his "sure" definition of reality is itself a shifting discursive construct. Even a slightly altered repetition such as she effects when reordering Jeff's "care about" to the more prosaic (and condescending) "care for" serves to disrupt and expose the direction he attempts to impose upon their mutual discourse, and to call into question the "solidity" of his signifying ground. As Butler writes, "reiterations are never simply replicas of the same"; in reiterating Jeff's words in order to foreground their non-replicatability, their *failure* to repeat "the same," Melanctha implicitly challenges Jeff's belief that one can remain "good and regular" in language as in life. While Jeff represents the regulatory and normativizing forces of habitual or automatic action, Melanctha works to expose this action as a contingent and *in*essential performance whose claim to "goodness" is ultimately repressive and deadening.

As Lisa Ruddick concludes, Melanctha "has what James in a fan-

---

8. The terms of this opposition are taken from North's deft analysis of dialect in *Melanctha* (*Dialect of Modernism*, 74–5).

ciful moment labels genius—'the faculty of perceiving in an unhabitual way'."[9] Ruddick's dismissal of the significance of the label
"genius" as "fanciful" limits her relevance to this analysis beyond the
striking fact that she correlates Melanctha with a Jamesian notion
of "genius" in the first place. As the *un*habitual, Melanctha embodies
James's definition of "genius; as the *un*automatic, constituted
through her resistant discursive exchanges with the "normal" Jeff,
Melanctha is like the "consciousness without memory" that Stein
and Solomons discuss in "Normal Motor Automatism." Significantly,
Melanctha "never could remember right when it came to what she
had done and what had happened" (TL, 75). Lacking the sense of a
past that would enable a "self" to emerge as a consistent presence,
signifying desire and resistance toward the automatic, habitual world
around her, Melanctha both reinstantiates the "excessive" subject of
"Normal Motor Automatism" and anticipates what Stein herself
would shortly come to call "genius." Yet precisely in her disruptive,
anti-identitarian, genial "wandering," Melanctha also represents a
challenge to the typological schema, and to the discourse of "race,"
which underwrites her story. In arresting Jeff's desire, in resisting
"the solidity of the name," Melanctha also dismantles the larger narrative effort to literalize "bottom nature" by locating it in the racialized body. In the end, Melanctha's disruptiveness toward Jeff and
others is also a disruption of the entire Steinian typological endeavor
and its culminating desire for epistemological certainty through displacement and projection onto "blackness." That Melanctha "all her
life did not know how to tell a story wholly" (TL, 70) suggests that
the narrative that bears her name also contains an excess that defies
both "knowledge" and closure. After over a hundred pages of "wandering," the almost arbitrary ending to this story—Melanctha falls
ill and dies within two paragraphs—speaks to the failure of the narrative to resolve its contradictory trajectories; the brutality of this
ending suggests Stein's own ambivalence toward a figure too radical
and unknowable for its narrative frame. That Stein attributes to
Melanctha an unfathomable power that lies outside all determinant
characteristics—race, gender, sexuality, "type"—is, however, a sign
of something to come.

9. Lisa Ruddick, *Reading Gertrude Stein: Body, Text, Gnosis* (Ithaca: Cornell UP, 1990), 19.
(See p. 374.)

514

DAYLANNE K. ENGLISH

[Eugenics in "Melanctha"]†

Unlike her earlier texts, *Fernhurst, Q.E.D.*, and *The Making of Americans, Three Lives* insists on the legitimacy of working-class, black, and ethnic immigrant American women as literary subjects. But it also relies on dangerous racial and cultural stereotypes to describe them. *Three Lives* challenges, in clearly feminist terms, oppressive, modern-male-authored medical and literary models, yet it treats the black female body as the object of an authoritative and relentless literary-medical gaze. In sum, *Three Lives* worries about conventional literary and medical treatments of laboring (in both senses) female bodies, but it also worries about the presence and proliferation of those bodies in the modern, urban United States. It is this racially and ethnically inflected, and literary, medicalization of her subjects that discloses the eugenic anxiety attending Stein's participation in a modern, Poundian, "diagnosis and cure" aesthetic model (set forth in the second epigraph of this chapter).[1] Put more simply, the book's literary-medical experimentation engages racialist and eugenic, along with feminist, thinking. One biographer observes that Stein can "seem not to be an artist at all, but a scientist elaborately constructing metaphors in a laboratory of words."[2] Many kinds of women entered Stein's literary laboratory, especially in *Three Lives*, but not all survived her experiments.

Three Lives consists of stories about the lives, illnesses, hospitalizations, and deaths of three women: two immigrant German domestic servants, Anna and Lena, and one "mulatto" woman, Melanctha. Stein's first published book, *Three Lives* (1909) carries out many of her characteristically unconventional literary experiments, especially her use of rhythmic repetition and vernacular speech. Stein doubted that the book, with its unconventional protagonists and literary techniques, would reach a wide readership. As James Mellow notes, Stein once wrote that her "very simple and very vulgar" characters would not "interest the great American public."[3] Stein might have been right that her protagonists did not at first seem compelling, or at

† From *Unnatural Selections: Eugenics in American Modernism and the Harlem Renaissance* (Chapel Hill: The University of North Carolina Press, 2004), pp. 98–114. Copyright © 2004 the University of North Carolina Press. Reprinted by permission of the publisher.

1. Here I am adopting Juan León's term "eugenic anxiety," which he coined to describe T. S. Eliot's participation in the modern period's eugenic discourse. See Juan Enrique León, "A Literary History of Eugenic Terror in England and America," Ph.D. diss. (Cambridge: Harvard University, 1989). [English refers to the 1985 Penguin reprint of *Three Lives* and to the James R. Mellow Introduction therein.—*Editor's note.*]

2. John Malcolm Brinnin, *The Third Rose: Gertrude Stein and Her World* (1959, rpt. Reading, MA: Addison-Wesley, 1987), 49.

3. Mellow, introduction to *Three Lives*, xi.

least conventional, subjects for high modernist literary experiment. Anna, a housekeeper modeled after Stein's own immigrant housekeeper during her medical school days in Baltimore, is a domineering yet not particularly articulate woman. The narrator periodically reminds us that "Anna led an arduous and troubled life."[4] Melanctha, an unstable and "melancholy" mulatto woman, is characterized chiefly by her vague desires: "Melanctha did not know what it was she so badly wanted" (93). Finally, Lena, a pathologically passive servant, is relentlessly characterized by the narrator as "gentle" and "patient." All three women eventually become ill and die. Anna, worn down by constant labor and anxiety, dies in the hospital after an operation. Melanctha contracts tuberculosis and dies "in a home for consumptives" (236). Lena dies in the hospital while giving birth to her fourth baby (280).

Stein began writing *Three Lives* shortly after abandoning her study of medicine in 1902, and the book unquestionably reflects Stein's experiences among the poor, largely African American and immigrant urban population for whom she provided care during her clinical rotations at Johns Hopkins. Set in Bridgepoint, a thinly veiled Baltimore, the book effectively blends medical documentation and literary experimentation; William Carlos Williams once aptly described "Melanctha" as a "thrilling clinical record."[5] And, indeed, Stein was writing *Three Lives* just as the "individual folder system for maintaining records" was "replacing the single, continuous record book that had been the mainstay of many institutions."[6] She was, then, both witnessing and contributing to new forms of medical and literary discourse. Her original title for *Three Lives, Three Histories*, suggests that the three lives might well function as fictional medical histories, as charts.[7] Generic hybrids, they occupy a discursive space between modern medical and literary authority—partaking of and, at times, resisting both. Suggestively, as physician-author, Stein frequently exerts the greatest clinical authority precisely where she appears most formally experimental, with African American and immigrant women the subjects, perhaps victims, of some of her most radical early experiments.

In *Three Lives*, Stein's very denomination of immigrant and black heroines, however progressive in terms of white modernists' construction of literary subjectivity, becomes imbricated with their med-

4. Stein, *Three Lives*, 3, 5; further citations will be parenthetical in the text.
5. William Carlos Williams, "The Work of Gertrude Stein" (1930), in *Gertrude Stein*, ed. Harold Bloom (New York: Chelsea House, 1986), 19–24, p. 23.
6. Jeffrey L. Geller and Maxine Harris, eds., *Women of the Asylum: Voices from Behind the Walls, 1840–1945* (New York: Anchor, 1994), 179.
7. As Jayne L. Walker has noted, Stein's original title was probably also intended as an acknowledgment of the literary influence of Flaubert and his *Trois Contes*. See *The Making of a Modernist: Gertrude Stein from Three Lives to Tender Buttons* (Amherst: U of Massachusetts P, 1984), 19. (See p. 339.)

icalization, indeed their pathologization. First, "The Good Anna" and "The Gentle Lena," the first and third of the three stories/lives, are conjoined by their titles to their diagnoses. Anna's goodness and Lena's gentleness stand for the laboring and the passivity that eventually lead to their deaths. "Melanctha," by contrast, remains conspicuously unmodified, as if to suggest that her essential racial identity, her "melan" (with its dual connotations of *blackness/melanin* and *melancholy*), is her pathology. Just so, it is Melanctha's racial and psychological makeup that apparently leads to her death. Second, Stein's experimental narrative chronology, what she termed a "continuous present," links *Three Lives* at once with literary-formal radicalism and with clinical authority. Just like medical charts, the three lives consist of encounters that are narrated retrospectively but are also informed by the present that invariably distinguishes the clinical relationship. Medical charts document a series of face-to-face encounters which, by definition, take place in the present. Conventionally written shortly after the clinical encounter, the chart, with its always present-tense verbs, encompasses the patient's past experiences along with the most recent encounter. To put this another way, only through an accumulation of recorded clinical observations made in the (continuous) presence of the patient can a medical chart be constructed. This temporal correspondence to a chart suggests a medical source for the Steinian literary technique of a "prolonged" or "continuous present."[8] For example, the narrator of "The Good Anna" assesses the title character's physical and emotional states in precise clinical terms: "At this time, Anna, about twenty-seven years of age, was not yet all thin and worn. The sharp bony edges and corners of her head and face were still rounded out with flesh, but already the temper and the humor showed sharply in her clear blue eyes, and the thinning was begun about the lower jaw, that was so often strained with the upward pressure of resolve. Today, alone there in the carriage, she was all stiff and yet all trembling with the sore effort of decision and revolt" (21–22). In this passage, the narrator acts as diagnostician, noting "temper" and "humor" like a medieval physician. At the same time, the tension in the passage (bodily and grammatical) between "Today" and the past verb tense ("was") matches the temporal dynamic of medical case histories. Admittedly, Stein's narrator here actually possesses temporal authority and knowledge beyond those of the physician. In its awareness of what *will* come to pass ("Anna was . . . not yet all thin and worn"), the narrative voice mirrors Stein's selection of literary over medical authority in her career. Literary authority actually grants Stein greater power; as author, she can manipulate the pres-

8. Stein, "Composition as Explanation" (1926), in *Selected Writings of Gertrude Stein*, ed. Carl Van Vechten (New York: Random House, 1946), 453–61, p. 457.

ent and the future of characters in a way that Stein as physician certainly would never have been able to with her patients.

Yet Stein still finds modern medical-narrative models useful for her literary innovations in *Three Lives*. Stein's modernist narrative experiment offered new ways to establish character just as the chart offered physicians a new clinical genre through which to describe (even construct) the individual patient.[9] The narrator of Anna's history introduces her as "a small, spare german woman at this time about forty years of age" (5). Anna "presents," then, with the potential (medical) problems of gender, age, and ethnicity. Moreover, like each of the three lives, "The Good Anna" ends (as ongoing medical histories eventually must) with the death of the patient. In "The Death of the Good Anna," the final section of Anna's story, physician and narrator together command and oversee her death, first linguistically—"the doctor said she simply could not live on so"—then literally: "In a few days they had Anna ready. Then they did the operation, and then the good Anna with her strong, strained, worn-out body died" (77–78). Such careful attention to, and recording of, Anna's condition apparently establishes the text's participation in a classically Foucauldian model of medically authoritative discourse, wherein "doctor and patient are caught up in ever greater proximity."[1] Harriet Chessman, noting that increasing proximity between Anna and the narrator, has pointed out that they "share . . . narrative space."[2] But in "The Good Anna," character-patient and narrator-doctor actually merge into a dialectical narrative even more intimate than free indirect discourse. As a result, Stein seems initially to depend on but ultimately subverts a clinical gaze in "The Good Anna." For example, in the following passage, the subjectivities of narrator and character converge: "To Anna alone there in the carriage . . . the warmth, the slowness, the jolting over stones, the steaming from the horses, the cries of men and animals and birds, and the new life all around were simply maddening. 'Baby! if you don't lie still, I think I kill you. I can't stand any more like this' " (21). The bodily experience here is shared by Anna and the narrator,

9. The modern medical chart emerged out of physicians' need for efficient, standardized assessment and diagnosis of ever-increasing numbers (and types) of patients. But, as of 1909, the publication date of *Three Lives*, the chart itself was still in an experimental stage; it represented a new genre highly susceptible to Stein's narrative innovations. *Three Lives* experiments with the chart's conventional categories of subjective information (supplied by the patient), objective information (observed by the clinician), assessment (diagnosis), and plan (prescription). By charting her characters via the medical gaze of a narrator-diagnostician, Stein at first appears to participate in a literary version of the epistemological hierarchy implied by the conventions of medical charting. However, her narrative technique also challenges such categorical assignment of authoritative knowledge by blurring the boundaries between "subjective" (patient) and "objective" (physician).

1. Michel Foucault, *The Birth of the Clinic*, trans. A. M. Sheridan Smith (New York: Pantheon, 1973), 15.

2. Harriet Chessman, *The Public Is Invited to Dance: Representation, the Body, and Dialogue in Gertrude Stein* (Stanford: Stanford UP, 1989), 28.

while Anna's angry speech to her dog follows without break from the charting of her "simply maddened" emotional state. By sharing narrative space with Anna in this instance, the narrator temporarily relinquishes a diagnostic stance so as to see through the character's eyes. Stein's narrative technique thus destabilizes the power relations encoded in a potentially oppressive clinical encounter, while it establishes mutually constitutive relationships between physician and patient and between narrator and character. Stein's sympathy for immigrant, working-class women and their bodily realities leads her to a literary merging of perspectives that in turn mirrors her own relinquishment of medical authority and her selection of women as paradigmatic modern subjects.

But Stein reinvokes that authority, at least to a degree, in the second of the three lives, "Melanctha." Here Stein projects her ambivalence about the exertion of medical-literary authority onto racialized female bodies as either sites of resistance (as with the half-white Melanctha) or of clinical inscription (as with Melanctha's "black" friend Rose Johnson). Without a titular diagnosis beyond her identity as tragic mulatto, Melanctha presents the narrator with questions, but no answers: "Why did the subtle, intelligent, attractive, half white girl Melanctha Herbert love and do for and demean herself in service to this coarse, decent, sullen, ordinary, black childish Rose, and why was this immoral, promiscuous, shiftless Rose married, and that's not so common either, to a good man of the negroes, while Melanctha with her white blood and attraction and desire for a right position had not yet been really married" (83). The narrator explains that Melanctha "always loved too hard and much too often" and "was always full with mystery and subtle movements and denials and vague distrusts and complicated disillusions" (86). It is just her "complex, desiring" (83) nature that resists the text's impulse to fix Melanctha either temporally ("always") or diagnostically ("too").

As female patient/subject, Melanctha frustrates the diagnostic efforts of both the narrator and her physician-lover, Jeff Campbell.[3] The narrator's diagnostic impulse is associated with a (male) medical desire to know, to circumscribe and describe Melanctha: "Some man would learn a good deal about her in the talk, never altogether truly, for Melanctha all her life did not know how to tell a story wholly.

---

3. Critics have frequently observed that Jeff Campbell functions as a fictional stand-in for Stein herself, in a more veiled (by race and gender) version of the real-life love affair she had rendered earlier in *Q.E.D.* See Katz, introduction to *Fernhurst, Q.E.D., and Other Early Writings*, and Walker, *Making of a Modernist*. Lisa Ruddick, in *Reading Gertrude Stein*, persuasively argues that the "two lovers in the story, Melanctha and Jeff, are the products of Stein's imaginative self-splitting" (13). Ruddick goes on to suggest that Melanctha is "the locus of ambiguity in the story" (13). But Jeff Campbell represents an equally powerful site of narrative ambiguity. He clearly serves as another racialized locus of ambivalence around medical-literary authority.

. . . Melanctha never could remember right" (97). Jeff Campbell later concurs with the narrator's diagnosis: "You certainly Melanctha, you ain't got down deep loyal feeling, true inside you, and when you ain't just that moment *quick with feeling*, then you certainly ain't got anything more there to keep you. . . . You certainly Melanctha, never can remember right, when it comes to what you have done and what you think happens to you" (179, emphasis added). Jeff acts at once as internist and obstetrician by assessing Melanctha's "inside" as pathologically non-impregnated ("ain't . . . quick"). Analogously, the narrator has already told us that Melanctha cannot reproduce experience via normal narrative production ("for Melanctha all her life did not know how to tell a story wholly"). As Marianne DeKoven has suggested, in "Melanctha," "race, class, and childbirth figure together in the disruption of traditional narrative form."[4]

Melanctha, by insisting on her own version of the narrative, challenges the ostensibly normative clinical and narrative diagnoses imposed by both the narrator and Jeff Campbell. As a result, both encounter "trouble with Melanctha's meaning" (127). Janice Doane has pointed out that Melanctha is "incapable of assimilation into [her] own narrative history."[5] She will not fully ("altogether truly") reveal herself to either a medical or a narrative gaze. She replies to Jeff's assessment: "You remember right, because you don't remember nothing till you get home with your thinking everything over, but I certainly don't think much ever of that kind of way of remembering right, Jeff Campbell. I certainly do call it remembering right Jeff Campbell to remember right just when it happens to you, so you have a right kind of feeling" (180). In this passage, "Melanctha," as story, rejects Jeff's diagnostic "remembering" as a kind of Wordsworthian poetics (conventional literary memory).[6] Melanctha, as character, likewise rejects his universalized prescriptions: "Melanctha did not feel the same as he did about being good and regular in life, and not having excitements all the time, which was the way that Jefferson Campbell wanted that *everybody should be*" (113, emphasis added). Melanctha (along with "Melanctha") thereby devalues the traditional sort of storytelling performed by (male) physicians and narrators.

Despite that feminist challenge to conventional institutional (literary and medical) memory, Stein fails to divest herself fully of a potentially oppressive medical gaze, along with its documentation of pathology, particularly in the racially "other." "Melanctha" offers a

4. Marianne DeKoven, *Rich and Strange: Gender, History, Modernism* (Princeton: Princeton UP, 1991), 67.
5. Janice L. Doane, *Silence and Narrative: The Early Novels of Gertrude Stein* (Westport, CT: Greenwood Press, 1986), 54.
6. I am referring here to Wordsworth's well-known description of poetry as originating "from emotion recollected in tranquillity" (Preface to *Lyrical Ballads*).

version of blackness that presents with clear symptoms, and thus represents an all too familiar diagnostic field. The "very black" Rose Johnson was "careless and was lazy," and she "had the simple, promiscuous unmorality of the black people" (82). Rose's "white training" had "only made for habits, not for nature" (82). Melanctha, by contrast, was "a graceful, pale yellow, intelligent, attractive negress" who "had been half made with real white blood" (82). The narrator here uses a spectrum of essentialized racial biology to perform differential diagnoses for Rose and Melanctha. "Melanctha" describes "naturally" complex mulattoes and fully legible black characters, thus participating quite resoundingly in the (unreconstructed) racialism of its day.[7] Just as in Eliot's Bolo verse, here pure blackness represents unleashed sexuality and pure vitality.

Also like Eliot, Stein associates racial mixture with morbidity. The narrator describes Melanctha as "pale yellow and mysterious and a little pleasant like her mother," while "the real power in Melanctha's nature came through her robust and unpleasant and very unendurable black father" (86). Stein here racializes the model of genetic individual identity she had advanced in *The Making of Americans*: "So now we begin again this history of us and always we must keep in us the knowledge of the men and women and parents and grandparents who came together and mixed up to make us and we must always have in us a lively sense of these mothers and these fathers, of how they lived and married and then they had us and we came to be inside us in us" (67). At the same time, in describing Melanctha's "nature," Stein also sounds more than a bit like the eugenicist Lothrop Stoddard, who confidently observed that in "ethnic crosses, the negro strikingly displays his prepotency, for black blood, once entering a human stock, seems never really bred out again."[8] But, in a classic eugenical paradox, it is Melanctha's white blood, with its own "prepotency," that complicates (elevates) her nature and establishes her as the tragic mulatto, "with her white blood and attraction and desire for a right position. . . . Sometimes the thought of how all her world was made, filled the complex, desiring Melanctha with despair" (83). Stoddard similarly describes the genetically determined fate of mulattoes: "These unhappy beings, every cell of whose bodies is a battle-ground of jarring heredities, express their souls in acts of hectic violence and aimless instability" (120).

Melanctha's "aimless instability" corresponds to her inability to

---

7. As Toni Morrison has pointed out in *Playing in the Dark: Whiteness and the Literary Imagination* (Cambridge : Harvard UP, 1992), "For American writers generally, this Africanist other became the means of thinking about the body, mind, chaos, kindness, and love; provided the occasion for exercises in the absence of restraint [and] the presence of restraint" (47).

8. Lothrop Stoddard, *The Rising Tide of Color against White World-Supremacy* (New York: Scribner, 1920); further citations will be parenthetical in the text.

fulfill the marriage plot: she cannot, finally, live happily ever after. Her "wandering" (Stein's euphemism for Melanctha's sexual experimentation) leads in the end to her death and the termination of her story. Unlike the lesbianism of the characters in Q.E.D., Melanctha's straying from racial, sexual, and narrative normativity ultimately translates into pathology, both literal and literary. Non-middle-class, non-college-educated, nonwhite women apparently cannot survive outside the marriage plot in Stein's early work. Just so, after her final wandering with Jem Richards does not result in marriage ("Jem Richards never could want to marry any girl while he had trouble," 221), Melanctha runs out of story. But the narrative does not permit her even the fallen heroine's conventional ending: "But Melanctha Herbert never really killed herself because she was so blue, though often she thought this would be really the best way for her to do. Melanctha never killed herself, she only got a bad fever and went into the hospital where they took good care of her and cured her" (235). Although the hospital initially cures Melanctha (unlike Anna and Lena), her pathology persists. Melanctha's fate is determined not by medical intervention, but by her own pathological, hybrid identity. In the end, as with the good Anna, the doctors must pronounce Melanctha's death: "Melanctha went back to the hospital, and there the Doctor told her she had the consumption, and before long she would surely die" (236).

In contrast to the tragic and sickly mulatto figures in "Melanctha," the "sullen, childish, cowardly, black" (222) Rose Johnson thrives explicitly by *not* wandering.[9] Unlike Melanctha, Rose "had the sense for decent comfort, Rose had strong the sense for proper conduct, Rose had the sense to get straight always what she wanted, and she always knew what was the best thing she needed, and always Rose got what she wanted" (214). Rose, who "was a real black negress" (82), does not stray from racial normativity. Thus she can fulfill the marriage plot, for, as the narrator informs us, Rose is "married, and that's not so common either, to a good man of the negroes" (83). As products of miscegenation (an inviable mixture for this version of eugenics), the "tragic" mulattoes in *Three Lives* apparently have access neither to Rose's well-aimed stability nor to her unmixed vitality.

Just as "Melanctha" assigns an essential unfitness to mulattoes, "The Good Anna" and "The Gentle Lena" essentialize the laboring immigrant ("german") character. For Stein's immigrant characters, class, along with ethnicity, forms part of their pathology. "The Good Anna" meticulously identifies all its working-class characters accord-

---

9. All the mulatto characters in "Melanctha" are "sick": "Melanctha's pale yellow mother was very sick and in this year she died" (106). Jane Harden, "who was so white that hardly anyone would guess it" (100), was "very sick almost all day" (140).

ing to ethnicity: Lizzie, "a pretty, cheerful irish girl" (6); Molly, "born
in America of german parents" (6); and, extraordinarily specifically,
Anna herself, who "was of solid, lower middle-class south german
stock" (17). In contrast to such precise ethnic identification, the
narrative's description of the employing class suggests that they are
racially and ethnically unmarked. Miss Mathilda, Anna's employer
(generally considered a stand-in for Stein herself), apparently possesses neither race nor nationality; she is, simply, "a large and careless woman" (14). According to the narrator, "Anna's superiors
always must be these large helpless women, or be men, for none
others could give themselves to be made so comfortable and free"
(18). The socio-anatomical hierarchy here is clear: the "small, spare
german" Anna naturally serves the "large" and "helpless."

"The Gentle Lena," too, constructs an immigrant apparently biologically fit for servitude. Lena's life story begins like the others, with
an authoritative assessment: "Lena was patient, gentle, sweet, and
german. She had been a servant for four years and liked it very well"
(239). As in "The Good Anna," the tone here matches that of a medical history. The narrator continues, describing Lena, precisely, as
"a brown and pleasant creature, brown as blonde races often have
them brown, brown not with the yellow or red or the chocolate brown
of sun burned countries, but brown with the clear color laid flat on
the light toned skin beneath, the plain, spare brown that makes it
right to have been made with hazel eyes" (240–41). Not only Lena's
plain brownness, but her very anatomy (like Anna's) reflects a
working-class destiny: "Lena had the flat chest, straight back and
forward falling shoulders of the patient and enduring working
woman" (241). Indeed, the "gentle Lena" embodies the eugenicist's
paradoxical anxiety: like all the less genetically "worthy" European
immigrants, her reproductive success signals the unnatural selection
that, according to eugenicists, characterized modernity.[1] Lothrop
Stoddard asserted that the "white race divides into three main subspecies—the Nordics, the Alpines, and the Mediterraneans" (162),
with "no question that the Nordic is far and away the most valuable
type" (162). But, he claimed, the "cramped factory and the crowded
city" have "weeded out the big, blond Nordic . . . whereas the little

---

1. The combination of anxiety over working-class fecundity and insistence on white, middle-
class genetic superiority represents the central eugenic paradox. Only through an ideologically tailored (fractured) Darwinism could the eugenicists simultaneously insist on their
own greater fitness while fretting about what the Reverend James Marchant termed, in
his introduction to C. W. Saleeby's *The Methods of Race Regeneration* (New York: Moffat,
Yard, 1911), "the uncontrolled multiplication of the degenerate, who threatened to swamp
in a few generations the purer elements of our race" (4). According to "pure" Darwinian
logic, the more reproductively successful species is, in fact, the "fitter" species. The upper
class will shrink, therefore, only if selected against. Of course, the underlying flaw in the
eugenicists' twisted Darwinism lies in their application of species theory to class and
race—neither of which has any biological or genetic reality.

brunet Mediterranean, in particular, [has] adapted himself to the operative's bench or the clerk's stool, prospered—and reproduced his kind" (164–65). Lena embodies his fertile "little brunet Mediterranean," one who, despite her relative unfitness and inferiority to Nordics, repeatedly "reproduces her kind." When viewed through the lens of its ethnic and racial typing, *Three Lives* thus emerges less as a progressive feminist text and more as an anxiously eugenic one.

Three Lives paints an urban landscape populated by "mysterious mulattoes," "careless Negroes," and immigrant servants—characters who are, to Stein, racially and culturally "other." Of course, as my prior chapters have shown, Stein was not alone in her representation of modern urban space as overpopulated by the racial and ethnic other. The 1910s and 1920s witnessed a kind of cultural consensus that the United States needed to protect and improve its national stock by correcting for the unnatural selection that its urbanization and modernity had produced. As the prominent U.S. eugenicist Harry Laughlin put it in 1914, if "America is to escape the doom of nations generally, it must breed good Americans."[2] Unprecedented levels of immigration to the United States between 1880 and 1920 represent perhaps the clearest stimulus for the period's eugenic thinking. Roughly 28 million immigrants came to the United States during that time.[3] Along with this massive foreign immigration, the period witnessed dramatic levels of domestic migration as well. Between 1890 and 1920, over 1.2 million African Americans migrated from the southern to the northern United States.[4] At the same time, medical and public health professionals (who were observing, treating, and regulating the new arrivals) were emerging in large numbers.[5]

The changing population profile of the United States, along with advances in medical knowledge (such as the acceptance of germ theory), called for new strategies on the part of the new health and social service professionals. Among these "members of the new social

2. Harry Laughlin, *Bulletin No. 10A: Report of the Committee to Study and to Report on the Best Practical Means of Cutting off Defective Germ-Plasm in the American Population* (Cold Spring Harbor, NY: Eugenics Record Office, 1914), 59.

3. Ann Douglas, *Terrible Honesty: Mongrel Manhattan in the 1920s* (New York: Farrar, Straus and Giroux, 1995), 304.

4. Suzanne W. Model, "Work and Family: Blacks and Immigrants from South and East Europe" in *Immigration Reconsidered: History, Sociology, Politics*, ed. Virginia Yans-McLaughlin (New York: Oxford UP, 1990), 130–59, pp. 138, 141.

5. Stein entered the medical profession at a particularly significant historical moment—and at an equally significant institution. Johns Hopkins was, as public health historian John Duffy notes in *The Sanitarians: A History of American Public Health* (Urbana: U of Illinois P, 1990), at the forefront of the professionalization of medicine at the turn of the century and opened the first permanent U.S. school of public health in 1918. Duffy observes that Johns Hopkins "established the formula for public health schools" and was a leading force in the institutionalization of public health in the United States (253). The establishment of the Johns Hopkins School of Public Health and Hygiene stands as a symbolic culmination of a public health movement with roots in the mid-nineteenth century.

control professions," as Nicole Rafter terms them, middle-class ima-
ginings about the reproductive capacities of the newly mobile—along
with a very real concern about their suffering—promoted positive
public health (as well as disturbing eugenic) measures designed to
aid (but also to contain) the urban poor.[6] For example, in the first
decade of the twentieth century in the United States, plumbing and
sanitation in many cities were being improved, but the nation's first
compulsory sterilization laws (along with increasingly restrictive
immigration acts) were also being passed. Literary critic T. Hugh
Crawford identifies in William Carlos Williams's poetry just such a
tension between progressive compassion for the poor and reactionary
desires for both literal and figurative urban purification. As Crawford
puts it, the "doctor cannot have both cleanliness and contact simultaneously."[7] Some doctors chose cleanliness over contact; eugenics
historian Daniel Kevles notes that the foremost eugenic "enthusi-
asts" in the United States "tended to be well-to-do rather than rich,
and many were professionals—physicians, social workers, clerics,
writers, and numerous professors, notably in the biological and social
sciences."[8] This specifically medical version of eugenic anxiety was
perhaps nowhere more clearly expressed than in the field of obstetrics.

   Modern obstetrics was "born" in the late 1800s (when Stein was
attending Johns Hopkins Medical School), but the first modern U.S.
obstetricians, unlike other new medical specialists, encountered
competition from a well-established lay tradition. As one medical
historian describes it, the "decade from about 1908 began the contest between the increasingly self-conscious obstetrical specialist and
his adversaries, the midwife and her advocates. . . . The result [was]
the complete defeat of the United States' variety of midwife and the
essential triumph of a 'single standard of obstetrics.' "[9] As evidenced
by the proliferation during the 1910s in medical journals of
physician-authored articles with titles such as "Control of Midwives"
and "The Elimination of the Midwife," many obstetricians were wag-
ing an overt economic and professional war on midwifery.[1] We must

6. Nicole Rafter, *White Trash: The Eugenic Family Studies, 1877–1919* (Boston: Northeast-
   ern UP, 1988), 15.
7. T. Hugh Crawford, *Modernism, Medicine, and William Carlos Williams* (Norman: U of
   Oklahoma P, 1993), 110.
8. I. Daniel Kevles, *In the Name of Eugenics: Genetics and the Uses of Human Heredity* (New
   York: Knopf, 1985), 64; further citations will be parenthetical in the text.
9. Frances E. Kobrin, "The American Midwife Controversy: A Crisis of Professionalization"
   in *Sickness and Health in America*, ed. Judith Leavitt and Ronald Numbers (Madison: U
   of Wisconsin P, 1978), 217–25, p. 197.
1. Harold Bailey, "Control of Midwives" in *The American Journal of Obstetrics* 6 (September
   1923): 293–98; Charles Ziegler, "The Elimination of the Midwife," in *The Journal of the
   American Medical Association* 60 (January 1913): 32–38. Ziegler declared himself "unal-
   terably and uncompromisingly opposed to any plan which seeks to give [the midwife] a
   permanent place in the practice of medicine" (32). One of his primary arguments for
   obstetricians' elimination of midwifery baldly discloses the contest's economic underpin-

realize that the medical profession's suppression of midwifery between 1900 and 1924 in the United States correlates directly with the period's (eugenic) restrictions on immigration. As exclusionary measures, both disclose the intense and complex struggle that was taking place over the nature of modern American nativity (with both its figurative-national and literal-birth meanings)—that is, the "making of Americans." A 1916 physicians' forum on midwifery printed in the *Journal of the American Medical Association* quotes Dr. J. M. Baldy, who asserts that the United States "contains several groups of foreigners who have been accustomed to the midwife, and until immigration ceases and these peoples have evolved into Americans, the midwife will be demanded."[2] Here, assimilation—authentic national subjectivity—is associated with a higher degree of both evolution and medical-obstetrical professionalism. Indeed, as Richard Wertz and Dorothy Wertz have pointed out, by the late nineteenth century, midwives in U.S. cities were disproportionately immigrants.[3] Thus immigration restriction was equally effective as a restriction of midwifery. In 1910, 50 percent of all births in the United States were reported by midwives, and, as medical historian Frances Kobrin observes, "the percentage for large cities was often higher," because midwives were consulted primarily by African American and immigrant women, who were concentrated in urban population centers, and who "usually shared race, nationality and language" with their midwives.[4] But the percentage of midwife-attended births dropped over the following three decades (along with immigration levels), until midwifery was all but eradicated by the 1940s.[5]

Three Lives registers both structurally and thematically the period's national anxieties over the imagined fecundity of immigrant

---

nings: he cites the "$5,000,000 which it is estimated is collected [annually] by midwives in this country and which should be paid to physicians and nurses for doing the work properly" (34). By contrast, for examples of physician support for midwives during the period, see S. Josephine Baker, "Schools for Midwives" in *The American Journal of Obstetrics* 65 (1912): 256–70; Clara D. Noyes, "Training of Midwives in Relation to the Prevention of Infant Mortality," in *The American Journal of Obstetrics* 66 (1912): 1051–59.

2. J. M. Baldy, "The Midwife," in *The Journal of the American Medical Association* 61 (January 1916): 56. Likewise, pioneering Boston obstetrician J. B. Huntington observed, in a 1912 issue of the *American Journal of Obstetrics and Gynecology*, that "as soon as the immigrant is assimilated, then the midwife is no longer a factor in his home" (quoted in Kobrin, "American Midwife Controversy," 200). One obstetrician frankly assessed the situation in 1907, declaring that midwives "are un-American": see Mabbott, "Regulation of Midwives," 526.

3. Richard W. Wertz and Dorothy C. Wertz, *Lying-In: A History of Childbirth in America* (1977; rpt. New Haven: Yale UP, 1989), 211, 215–17.

4. Kobrin, "American Midwife Controversy," 197.

5. Ibid., and Judith Leavitt, " 'Science' Enters the Birthing Room: Obstetrics in America since the Eighteenth Century," in Judith Leavitt and Ronald Numbers, eds., *Sickness and Health in America* (Madison: U of Wisconsin P, 1985), 81–97, 97. Leavitt notes in *Brought to Bed* that by 1930 midwife-attended births had dropped to 15 percent of the total number (268).

and non-white women and the control of their births, but the book's politics surrounding these matters are not simple.[6] *Three Lives* does assign a central role to African American and immigrant women's fertility, but the text's competing and complementary ideologies—eugenics, racialism, and feminism—complicate its representation of that fertility. "Melanctha," for example, depends, at a structural level, on childbirth. The story begins with, and in the end returns to, Rose Johnson's delivery. The birth represents the temporal touchstone within the narrative's continuous present; it provides the parentheses between which Melanctha's story unfolds. "Melanctha" in fact begins with a sentence that makes grammatical sense only from an obstetrical point of view: "Rose Johnson made it very hard to bring her baby to its birth" (81). The following passage suggests that the absence of Melanctha (and her "white blood") quite literally leads to death for Rose's baby: "The child though it was healthy after it was born, did not live long. Rose Johnson was careless and negligent and selfish, and when Melanctha had to leave for a few days, the baby died. Rose Johnson had liked the baby well enough and perhaps just forgot it for awhile, anyway the child was dead and Rose and Sam her husband were sorry but then these things came so often in the negro world in Bridgepoint, that neither of them thought about it very long" (81). Here, the inadequacy of "negro" memory is associated with morbidity, even mortality. The text seems to suggest that the black (non-mulatto) community pathologically lacks conventional literary-medical memory. In an inversion of a statistically based model of public health, the high incidence of "negro" infant mortality ("these things came so often") *actually prevents* documentation and inscription of memory within the "negro" community ("neither of them thought about it very long"). Therefore, from the public health professional's point of view, as from the obstetrician's, Rose and her fertility are difficult to regulate and record.

Indeed, each of the stories emerges out of a preoccupation with fertility and its failed regulation. The good Anna represents the absence of desire and the urge to suppress sexuality and reproduction. Anna even "had high ideals for canine chastity and discipline," so "she always took great care to seclude the bad dogs from each

---

6. In 1920 Lothrop Stoddard described the "negro" as the "quickest of the breeders" (*Rising Tide*, 90), while Harry Laughlin (probably the foremost U.S. eugenicist during the 1910s and 1920s) cautioned in 1914 that the "Federal Government" must undertake the task of "preventing the landing of inferior breeding stock" (*Bulletin No. 10A*, 62). At the same time (but not coincidentally), medical discourse was perfecting what Michel Foucault termed the "thorough medicalization" of white, middle-class women's bodies and sexuality, a process "carried out in the name of the responsibility they owed to the health of their children, the solidity of the family institution, and the safeguarding of society" (*The History of Sexuality, Volume I*, trans. A. M. Sheridan Smith [New York: Pantheon, 1973], 146–47). As C. W. Saleeby, a leading eugenicist of the day, put it, in "all times and places, women's primal and supreme function is or should be that of choosing the fathers of the future" (*Methods of Race Regeneration*, 36).

other when she had to leave the house" (4–5). And, significantly, Mrs. Lehntman's adoption of a baby boy temporarily estranges Anna from her friend (36–37). But, despite Anna's attempts to curb others' familial and sexual desires, her dog Peter does impregnate a neighbor's dog, and Mrs. Lehntman does keep the baby. In Anna's immigrant community, as in the "negro" community in "Melanctha," fertility is difficult to regulate. That suggests why the fecundity of the nonnative, the poor, and the working class constituted the primary target of the nation's eugenic policies of immigration restriction and compulsory sterilization. On the other hand, *Three Lives* does not advance a thoroughgoing version of such mainline eugenic ideology. White supremacist and nativist eugenicists of the period, such as Lothrop Stoddard and Harry Laughlin, worried primarily about the toll of immigrant, poor, and nonwhite reproduction on the national body.[7] Stein, by contrast, worries about the particular toll of labor—both manual and reproductive—on immigrant (if not black) women's bodies. This double meaning of labor for working-class women forms the core of the text of *Three Lives*. As a result, Stein's reservations about medical and eugenic prescriptions emerge as feminist, although not antiracist, in all three women's lives, particularly in "The Good Anna."

Stein represents in "The Good Anna" an alternative, (immigrant) woman-authored model of medical care in an allegory of the obstetrician-midwife contest that was taking place at the time of its publication at around the turn of the century in the United States. In "The Good Anna," the presumably immigrant Mrs. Lehntman, who is "the romance in Anna's life" (24), is also a midwife. The narrator describes her practice as a benevolent women's refuge: "Mrs. Lehntman in her work loved best to deliver young girls who were in trouble. She would take these into her own house and care for them in secret, till they could guiltlessly go home or back to work" (24). So Mrs. Lehntman provides absolution as well as deliverance; her intervention actually removes "guilt." But, as the following passage suggests, Mrs. Lehntman's female idyll is disrupted by a male physician in a narrative reenactment of the actual institutional contest then taking place between the native U.S. doctor and the immigrant midwife:

> Anna did not fail to see that Mrs. Lehntman had something on her mind that was new. What was it? What was it that disturbed Mrs. Lehntman so? . . .
> Through the fog and dust and work and furnishing in the new

7. Kevles argues, correctly, for the existence of two strains of eugenics in the United States and Britain—one espoused by "social-radical eugenicists" such as George Bernard Shaw and Havelock Ellis, the other by eugenicists "of a conservative bent" such as Lothrop Stoddard and Karl Pearson (*In the Name of Eugenics*, 86–88).

house, and through the disturbed mind of Mrs. Lehntman, there loomed up to Anna's sight a *man*, a *new doctor* that Mrs. Lehntman knew. (50, emphasis added)

According to this passage, the advent of the male medical professional obscures, at least partially, the woman's diagnostic gaze. Anna is never quite clear about the trouble the doctor causes Mrs. Lehntman: he was "a mystery that Anna had not the strength just then to vigorously break down" (50). But Anna knows that he "was too certainly an evil as well as a mysterious man, and he had power over the widow and midwife, Mrs. Lehntman" (58).

Anna's worries may well be justified on a literal, bodily level. As one historian of the advance of obstetrics observes, "Rather than making childbirth safer, physicians in the 1920s and 1930s . . . were responsible for maintaining high rates of maternal mortality."[8] Moreover, despite the "widely held medical opinion" that in the United States the use of midwives by poor women was responsible for the relatively high rate of maternal mortality in the early decades of the century, the lowest maternal mortality figures in the 1910s and 1920s were "frequently found in cities with the highest percentage of births attended by midwives."[9] "The Good Anna," as obstetrical allegory, suggests that Stein resists modern medical authority as a result of its potentially dangerous treatment of the female body, as well as its displacement of the female medical expert.[1] In other words, assimilation to a national, professionalized (medical) narrative could prove lethal to the immigrant, working-class female subject.

Lena, in the last of the three lives, enacts that fatal assimilationist narrative, but she simultaneously enacts the eugenicist's anxious story about the fecundity of working-class, immigrant women. Admittedly, Stein invites the reader to think of the overly "gentle" Lena as a passive victim, rather than as one of the mainline eugen-

---

8. Leavitt, " 'Science' Enters the Birthing Room," 91.

9. Joyce Antler and Daniel M. Fox, "The Movement toward a Safe Maternity: Physician Accountability in New York City, 1915–1940," in Leavitt and Numbers, *Sickness and Health in America*, 375–92 p. 492. For period defenses by physicians of the safety of midwifery, see Julius Levy, "The Maternal and Infant Mortality in Midwifery Practice in Newark, New Jersey," in *The American Journal of Obstetrics* 77 (January 1918): 41–53 and Zinke, Gustav, and William Humiston, "Discussion on the Papers of Drs. Harrar and Levy," in *The American Journal of Obstetrics* 77 (January 1918): 114–16. In " 'Science' Enters the Birthing Room," Leavitt explains the failure of early-twentieth-century obstetricians to improve on rates of maternal mortality as being a result of their readiness to intervene in the birth process. She argues that "when physician-directed obstetrics finally became master of the birthing room" (89), a "direct relationship existed between anesthesia and forceps" (91). Overuse and lack of skilled use of such interventions actually "increased the number of maternal deaths" (91).

1. Stein's allegorical rendition of the displacement of the female medical expert may also serve as an early critique of the emerging gender politics of modernism. In other words, she is anxious to maintain her own status as the central figure of the modernist literary avant-garde, the expert of the experimental.

icist's "swarming, prolific aliens,"[2] who demographically and genetically victimize the employing class. Lena actually emerges as a
relatively appealing and sympathetic character. The narrator
observes "the rarer strain there was in Lena" (246). This "strain"
(with its associations of lineage, ancestry, genetic trait) engenders
Lena's heroine status along with reader sympathy. Semantically,
then, she possesses a quasi-biological uniqueness that, ironically,
helps bring about her tragic ending. Lena stands as a kind of maladaptive mutation in both Germany and the United States. She is
never quite *fit* for her family (or nation) of origin or affiliation: "Lena
did not like her german life very well. It was not the hard work but
the roughness that disturbed her" (246). This "rarer strain" that
makes Lena "not an important daughter in the family" also makes
her worthy of readerly and narrative attention. We care about Lena
in a way that we can't care about her brutish cousin Mathilda, who
"was an overgrown, slow, flabby, blonde, stupid, fat girl, just beginning as a woman; thick in her speech and dull and simple in her
mind" (248). Lena, by contrast, is "dreamy," "not there," and possessed of a "rarer feeling" (245, 241).

Yet the degree to which Lena behaves as a normal "german" determines her fitness, if not as a heroine, then as a domestic laborer in
a U.S. family (and therefore her survival as an immigrant). Sometimes, Lena behaves like a model immigrant domestic: "Lena's
german patience held no suffering. . . . She stood in the hallway
every morning a long time in her unexpectant and unsuffering german patience calling to the young ones to get up" (239–40).
Although Lena's "german patience" here forestalls suffering in her
domestic labor, it cannot save her from the suffering that accom-
panies obstetrical labor. Lena's fate is biologically determined as
much by *re*production as by production. Stein may inscribe Lena as
quasi-biologically special in a minor way, but, as a fertile immigrant
female, she cannot rise above her dual role as laborer. Gentle Lena's
interminable labor is assured when she agrees to a marriage arranged
by her domineering aunt: " 'I do whatever you tell me it's right for
me to do. I marry Herman Kreder, if you want me'. . . . And so for
Lena Mainz the match was made" (253). With that final declarative
sentence, Lena's fate is not only determined, but overdetermined, by
the combined weight of her "rarer strain," her class, and her gender.

For Lena, marriage signals the beginning of the end. She and her
new husband move in with his parents, "and Lena began soon with
[their move] to look careless and dirty, and to be more *lifeless* with
it" (270, emphasis added). Lena's first pregnancy accelerates her
decline: "Poor Lena was not feeling any joy to have a baby. . . . She

2. Stoddard, *Rising Tide*, 164–65.

was scared and lifeless, and sure that every minute she would die"
(277). With each successive pregnancy, "Lena was always more and
more lifeless and Herman now mostly never thought about her"
(280). The "only things Herman ever really cared for were his babies.
. . . He more and more took all the care of their three children" (279–
80). All that remains for the unfit and "lifeless" Lena is labor; and,
as the "good german cook" explains, "That's the only way a german
girl can make things come out right Lena" (274). Lena ultimately
dies in childbirth, leaving Herman "very well content" and "always
alone now with his three good, gentle children" (281). Their children
thus carry both the dominant german "good" (Anna) and "gentle"
(Lena) traits, with no hint of Lena's recessive and maladaptive "rarer
strain." The narrative does, then, "come out right," with only the
fittest surviving to live happily ever after.

Paradoxically, although the children's dominant strains of "goodness" and "gentleness" may indeed be adaptive for tolerating domestic labor, those traits may, in the end, lead (like their mother's "rarer
strain") to premature mortality. The only old immigrant in the book
is the far from gentle "Old Katy," with her "uncouth and aged peasant
hide" (9). Within the textual world of *Three Lives*, the niche occupied
by the immigrant domestic laborer is itself associated with premature
morbidity; goodness and gentleness simply serve to accelerate the
process. Good, gentle workers like Anna and Lena die in labor. And
yet we are never sure what exactly kills these immigrant women.
After she marries and has her babies, "patient" Lena promptly
becomes "lifeless": "Then there was to come to them, a fourth baby.
Lena went to the hospital nearby to have the baby. Lena seemed to
be going to have trouble with it. When the baby came out at last, it
was like its mother lifeless. While it was coming, Lena had grown
very pale and sicker. When it was all over Lena had died, too, and
nobody knew just how it had happened to her" (280). As Jayne Walker puts it, Stein's "discourse effectively blurs the moment of passage
from figurative to literal lifelessness."[3] "The Good Anna," too, ends
with neither an explicit cause of death nor even a clear-cut diagnosis:
"Then they did the operation, and then the good Anna with her
strong, strained, worn-out body died" (78). This narrative gap, like
an unfilled blank on a medical chart, undermines the medical-
statistical containment of patient Lena and good Anna. Stein thus
exploits poetic, rather than medical, license to reveal the inadequacy
of conventional modern treatments of women patients/characters.
Lena is rendered lifeless by the U.S. literary-medical prescription:
the hospital (and, presumably, the obstetrician), in conjunction with
the marriage plot, kills the female patient. Apparently, conformity to

3. Walker, *Making of a Modernist*, 27.

the narrative of the laboring, assimilating immigrant kills both Anna and Lena: domestic work for Anna; obstetrical labor for Lena.

The Stein who literally (or perhaps literarily) kills the good Anna and the gentle Lena clearly has reservations about the beneficence, at least for immigrant women, of both literal and literary operations. Along with their immigrant, laboring status, Anna's goodness and Lena's gentleness ensure that they will survive neither Stein's literary experimentation nor more conventional plotting. Just so, the "mulatto" Melanctha dies despite her resistance to traditional inscriptions and prescriptions, whereas her "black" friend Rose Johnson chooses and survives both the marriage plot and childbirth. Both the working-class immigrant and the racial hybrid thereby emerge in *Three Lives* as essentially unfit for long-term survival either as patients or as modernist literary subjects. Lena's rarer strain does suggest, however, that she might have been able to survive, given access to less conventional—that is, more feminist and egalitarian—plots and medicine.

According to Stein's other writings from the early 1900s through the 1920s, a rarer strain compels only the immigrant or mulatto woman to enact a tragic drama of gender- and class-specific "unfitness." Stein's own rarer strain marks her as a genius. As she declares in *Everybody's Autobiography*: "I know that I am the most important writer writing today."[4] Stein, along with the heroines of *Three Lives*, may fail to conform to racial, sexual, or cultural norms of early-twentieth-century America; but, unlike them, she, along with the characters of *Q.E.D.*, is *not* selected against as a result. As middle-class, college-educated "new" women, they have the requisite access to unconventional literary and social forms. Indeed, Stein herself conceives of and delivers those forms. Thus, immigrant servants and black women may perform literal labor, but Stein's authentically "new" women will provide the literary and cultural labor for modernist literary and social experimentation in the early twentieth century. * * *

4. Stein, *Everybody's Autobiography* (New York: Random House, 1937), 28.

Gertrude Stein: A Chronology

1872   Leo Stein born.

1874   Gertrude Stein born February 3 in Allegheny, Pennsylvania, fifth and last living child of Daniel and Amelia Stein.

1880   Stein family moves to Oakland, California, where Daniel works for a streetcar line.

1888   Amelia Stein dies of cancer, having been ill for several years.

1891   Daniel Stein dies; family, headed and supported by eldest son Michael, moves to San Francisco, where Michael works for the street railway.

1892   Gertrude, brother Leo, and sister Bertha move to maternal aunt's house in Baltimore; Leo enters Harvard.

1893   Gertrude follows Leo to Harvard, entering what was then called the Harvard Annex, renamed Radcliffe College in 1894.

1894–97   Studies with William James and Hugo Münsterberg, eminent Harvard psychologists, and George Santayana, distinguished philosopher; highly successful student.

1897   Joins Leo in Baltimore, where he is studying biology; enters the Johns Hopkins Medical School.

1898   Awarded Bachelor of Arts Degree from Radcliffe College, after passing a required Latin exam she had failed in 1897.

1900   Meets May Bookstaver in Baltimore; spends summer in Italy and France with Leo, who has left Baltimore and has given up the study of biology.

1901   Depressed about stalemate of affair with May Bookstaver; leaves Johns Hopkins Medical School before completing her degree; joins Leo in Paris.

1902   Lives first in Italy and then in London with Leo; ends affair with May Bookstaver; reads extensively at British Library; Leo leaves for Paris in December.

1903   Moves to New York in February; begins preliminary version of *The Making of Americans* and writes *Q.E.D.*; joins Leo in Paris at 27 rue de Fleurus in fall, after spending summer traveling with him in Italy; Michael and wife Sally move to Paris; the Stein family begins to collect modern art.

1904 Spends winter in America; returns to Europe in June; spends summer with Leo in Fiesole, near Florence, Italy. Salons begin at 27 rue de Fleurus.

1905 Begins translation of Flaubert's *"Un coeur simple"* and then begins *Three Lives*, writing "The Good Anna"; meets Pablo Picasso.

1906 Sits for Picasso portrait, walking back and forth to his Montmartre studio; finishes *Three Lives* and attempts to find a publisher for it; spends summer in Fiesole, resuming work on *The Making of Americans*.

1907 Alice B. Toklas arrives in Paris from San Francisco, meets Gertrude Stein; they begin a relationship that lasts until Gertrude's death.

1908 Alice, with her friend Harriet Levy, spends summer near Gertrude and Leo in Italy; Alice learns to type and begins transcribing *The Making of Americans*, will type all of Gertrude's work for the rest of Gertrude's life; from 1908–1912, Gertrude writes *TWO: Gertrude Stein and Her Brother*, *Two Women*, *A Long Gay Book*, and *GMP* (*Matisse, Picasso and Gertrude Stein*), (all published posthumously), and some of the short experimental pieces collected in *Geography and Plays* (*G&P*, published 1922).

1909 Alice moves in with Gertrude and Leo in Paris; *Three Lives* is published at Stein's expense and is well reviewed; Gertrude writes "Matisse," "Picasso," "Manguin A Painter," and "Play," all collected in *Portraits and Prayers* (*P&P*, published 1934).

1911 Finishes *The Making of Americans*; writes several short pieces that will appear in *P&P*.

1912 Spends summer with Alice in Spain, where she moves toward a more experimental, cubist-inspired style; works on *TWO*, writes *Tender Buttons* and portraits collected in *P&P*; "Matisse" and "Picasso" published in photographer Alfred Stieglitz's modernist journal *Camera Work*.

1913 Armory Show introduces modernist art and Gertrude Stein's experimental writing to New York; separates from Leo, who moves to Italy; Gertrude and Alice take over household together at 27 rue de Fleurus; summer together again in Spain; writes many short works to be collected in *G&P, P&P, Selected Writings of Gertrude Stein* (*SW*, published in 1934), and posthumous publications.

1914   *Tender Buttons* published; writes many short pieces, most of them collected in posthumous publications; the portrait "Marsden Hartley" published for the Marsden Hartley Exhibition, Little Gallery of Photo-Secession; travels with Alice to England where, as guests of Alfred North Whitehead and his family, they are stranded when the Great War begins in August; return to Paris in October.

1915   Frightened by German zeppelin raids, leaves Paris with Alice for temporary residence in Mallorca, Spain; writing shifts to focus on voices in dialogue; writes less than before war; almost all works published posthumously.

1916   Encouraged by outcome of Battle of Verdun, returns to Paris with Alice; productivity increases; writes many short pieces that will appear in *G&P*, many published posthumously; publishes "Mrs. Th———y" in *Soil I* (December).

1917   Has Ford car shipped from America, names it "Auntie"; volunteers for American Fund for French Wounded, driving "Auntie" as supply vehicle; productivity diminishes, but publishes "Relief Work in France" in *Life* LXX December 27).

1918   Does civilian relief work in Alsace; productivity up again; publishes "The Great American Army" in *Vanity Fair* X (June).

1919   Returns to Paris; writes several works published posthumously; also publishes short works "J.R.," "J.R. II," "The Meaning of the Bird," and "A Deserter" in *Vanity Fair* XI (March).

1920   Buys new Ford, names it "Godiva"; writes many short pieces, with great productivity and in a variety of experimental styles and genres that characterize her 1920s work, collected in *G&P* and published posthumously.

1921   Meets Sherwood Anderson; modernist artist Jacques Lipschitz does bronze sculpture of her head; writes short pieces collected in *P&P, Operas and Plays* (*O&P*, published 1932), and several others that are published posthumously.

1922   Meets Ernest Hemingway; awarded Médaille de la Reconaissance Française for volunteer work during war; *Geography and Plays*, anthology of experimental work written since 1908, published; also publishes 1920 piece "Marie Claire Suggests a Meadow. And The Use of Thought" in *Little Review* VIII (Spring 1922); other short pieces collected in *P&P*, *O&P*, and published posthumously.

1923   First trip to Belley, in the rural Rhône Valley, where Gertrude and Alice will eventually spend most of their time; nature, or "landscape," becomes increasingly important in her work; publishes 1914 piece "Wear" in *Broom* IV (January 1923); writes works collected in *P&P*, *O&P*, *SW*, and published posthumously.

1924   A section of *The Making of Americans* serialized in *Transatlantic Review*, April–December; "Mildred's Thoughts" published in *The American Caravan*; 1923 piece "An Indian Boy" published in *The Reviewer* IV (January 1924); short pieces collected in *P&P*, *O&P*, and published posthumously.

1925   *The Making of Americans* published; publishes "Review: Troubadour" in *Ex Libris* (June 1925) and 1920 piece "Ireland" in *Der Querschnitt* (March 1925); writes *A Novel of Thank You*, published posthumously, and short pieces all but one (that appears in *P&P*, the portrait "Sitwell Edith Sitwell"), published posthumously.

1926   Lecture "Composition as Explanation" delivered at Oxford and Cambridge and published; will be included in *SW*; meets composer Virgil Thomson, who will collaborate with her on the operas *Four Saints in Three Acts* and *The Mother of Us All*; meets Bernard Faÿ, controversial Vichy collaborator who will protect Gertrude and Alice from the Nazis; publishes 1918 piece "One Has Not Lost One's Marguerite" in *Black and Blue Jay* VI (April 1926) and *A Book Concluding With As a Wife Has a Cow: a Love Story*; three pieces collected in *P&P*, three published posthumously.

1927   Writes one piece to appear in *O&P*, three in *P&P*, thirteen published posthumously; publishes 1914 piece "Mrs. Emerson" in *Close up* 2 (August 1927), 1916 piece "Water Pipe" in *larus* I (February 1927), 1923 pieces "Are There Arithmetics" in *Oxford 1927* (28 May 1927) and "Studies in Conversation" in *transition* 6 (September 1927), and 1924 piece "Made a Mile Away" in *transition* 8 (November 1927).

1928   Acquires first standard poodle, named Basket: dogs and cars appear throughout her subsequent work; publishing steadily in important modernist journal *transition*: 1924 piece "Descriptions of Literature" in *transition* 13 (Summer 1928), and "Answer: Why I Do Not Live in America" in *transition* 14 (Fall 1928).

1929   Leases country house in Bilignin, France; writes pieces that will appear in *P&P* and *O&P*; publishes *Useful Knowledge*, 1928 piece "J. H. Jane Heap" and "Letter to *Little Review*" in *Little Review* XII (May 1929), and "Bibliography" in *transition* 15 (February 1929).

1930   Has productive year; writes many pieces to appear in *P&P* and *O&P* and to be published posthumously; publishes 1929 piece "Five Words in a Line" in *Pagany* I (Winter 1930), long poem *Before the Flowers of Friendship Faded Friendship Faded*, and "Genuine Creative Ability" in *Creative Art* VI (February 1930).

1931   Her 1927 narrative *Lucy Church Amiably*, inspired by Bilignin countryside, published; publishes *How to Write*, "We Came a History" in *Readies for Bob Brown's Machine*; writes pieces to appear in *O&P*, *P&P* and posthumously.

1932   Writes *The Autobiography of Alice B. Toklas* at Bilignin; publishes *O&P*, including several pieces written this year, the 1931 piece "Grant or Rutherford B. Hayes" in *Americans Abroad*, "Thoughts on American Contemporary Feeling" in *Creative Age* X (February 1932), and "Preface," *Picabia, Chez Léonce Rosenberg*.

1933   *The Autobiography of Alice B. Toklas* published, first popular success; her subsequent writing retains modernist, experimental forms but becomes more accessible; writes *Four in America*, not published until 1947, and *Blood on the Dining-Room Floor*, published in 1948; publishes 1931 piece "Left to Right" in *Story* III (November 1933), "Story of a Book," *Wings* VII (September 1933), "Page IX" in *The Observer* II:1 (1933); writes many pieces published posthumously.

1934–5   *Four Saints in Three Acts* published and performed first in Hartford, CT, then in New York, with all black cast; Gertrude and Alice arrive in New York in October, Gertrude's first return to the United States since visit in 1904; sees performance of *Four Saints* in Chicago during highly successful lecture tour of United States; returns to France in May; writes *What Are Masterpieces and Why Are There So Few of Them*, not published until 1940; publishes *Lectures in America* and *Narration* based on her lecture tour; has many pieces published in various mainstream and modernist journals and collections.

1936   Publishes *The Geographical History of America or the Relation of Human Nature to the Human Mind*, written in 1935; lectures at Oxford and Cambridge; continues to publish widely in major American magazines, newspapers and intellectual journals, including *Vanity Fair, Saturday Evening Post, Atlantic Monthly, Cosmopolitan, The Chicago Daily Tribune* and *The Partisan Review*.

1937   Goes to premiere of ballet *A Wedding Bouquet* at Sadlers Wells in London; meets Thornton Wilder; evicted from Paris home at 27 rue de Fleurus; productivity low through 1938; publishes a few pieces in exhibition catalogs and small literary journals; one piece in *Harper's Bazaar*; publishes 1937 *Everybody's Autobiography*, containing the infamous characterization of Oakland, "There is no there there."

1938   Moves to apartment on rue Christine, Paris; publishes *Picasso* in French and English.

1939   Leaves Paris at approach of war and rampant anti-Semitism; moves to Bilignin; writes about wartime France.

1940   Paris occupied by Germany; advised by American consul in Bilignin to stay there, protected by Bernard Faÿ; publishes 1935 *What Are Masterpieces and Why Are There So Few of Them*; writes *Mrs. Reynolds: A Novel*, published posthumously, an experimental, anti-Nazi novel about Hitler.

1941   Publishes *Ida: A Novel*, written the year before; productivity low throughout war.

1942   Publishes *Wars I Have Seen*.

1943   Lease expires on Bilignin house; Gertrude and Alice move to house in Culoz, where German and Italian troops are briefly billetted; Gertrude sympathetic to the *Maquis*, the French resistance.

1944   American soldiers arrive, to Gertrude's and Alice's great rejoicing; they return to Paris, where they entertain many American GIs.

1945   Visits American Army bases in occupied Germany; lectures in Brussels; writes *The Mother of Us All*, 1945–46.

1946   Play *Yes Is For a Very Young Man* premieres at Pasadena Playhouse; publishes 1945 *Brewsie and Willie*, about American GIs; writes "Reflections on the Atomic Bomb," published in *Yale Poetry Review* 7 (December 1947);

"Transatlantic Interview 1946" also published posthumously; becomes ill en route to Bernard Faÿ's country house; admitted to hospital July 19, makes will July 23, dies July 27 following operation for cancer; final words: "What is the answer? But then, what is the question?"; buried at Père Lachaise Cemetery in Paris.

1947	Leo dies in Florence.
1967	Alice dies.

Selected Bibliography

•indicates a work included or excerpted in this Norton Critical Edition.

BOOKS

Benstock, Shari. *Women of the Left Bank: Paris, 1900–1940.* U of Texas P, 1986.

Bernstein, Charles. *My Way: Speeches and Poems.* U of Chicago P, 1999.

•Bloom, Harold, ed. *Gertrude Stein.* Modern Critical Views. New York: Chelsea House Publishers, 1986.

•Broe, Mary Lynn, and Angela Ingram, eds. *Women's Writing in Exile.* Chapel Hill: U of North Carolina P, 1989.

•Bridgman, Richard. *Gertrude Stein in Pieces.* New York: Oxford UP, 1971.

Brinnin, John Malcolm. *The Third Rose: Gertrude Stein and Her World.* Radcliffe Biography Series. Reading, MA: Addison-Wesley, 1987.

Caramello, Charles. *Henry James, Gertrude Stein, and the Biographical Act.* Chapel Hill: U of North Carolina P, 1996.

Chessman, Harriet. *The Public Is Invited to Dance: Representation, the Body, and Dialogue in Gertrude Stein.* Stanford: Stanford UP, 1989.

Curnutt, Kirk, ed. *The Critical Response to Gertrude Stein.* Westport, CT: Greenwood, 2000.

•DeKoven, Marianne. *A Different Language: Gertrude Stein's Experimental Writing.* Madison: U of Wisconsin P, 1983.

———. *Rich and Strange: Gender, History, Modernism.* Princeton: Princeton UP, 1991.

Doane, Janice. *Silence and Narrative: The Early Novels of Gertrude Stein.* Westport, CT: Greenwood, 1986.

Dubnick, Randa K. *The Structure of Obscurity: Gertrude Stein, Language and Cubism.* Urbana: U of Illinois P, 1984.

Dydo, Ulla E. *Gertrude Stein: The Language That Rises: 1923–1934.* Evanston: Northwestern UP, 2003.

———, ed. *A Stein Reader.* Evanston: Northwestern UP, 1993.

•English, Daylanne K. *Unnatural Selections: Eugenics in American Modernism and the Harlem Renaissance.* Chapel Hill: U of North Carolina P, 2004.

Gass, William H. *Fiction and the Figures of Life: Essays.* New York: Alfred A. Knopf, 1970. Reprint, Boston: David R. Godine, 1978.

Grahn, Judy, ed. *Really Reading Gertrude Stein: A Selected Anthology with Essays by Judy Grahn.* Freedom, CA: Crossing Press, 1989.

Hobhouse, Janet. *Everybody Who Was Anybody: A Biography of Gertrude Stein.* NY: Putnam, 1975. Reprint, New York: Bookthrift, 1978.

Hoffman, Michael J. *Critical Essays on Gertrude Stein.* Boston: G.K. Hall, 1986.

———. *The Development of Abstractionism in the Work of Gertrude Stein.* Philadelphia: U of Pennsylvania P, 1965.

James, William. *Psychology: Briefer Course.* Reprint, Harvard UP, 1984.

Kellner, Bruce, ed. *A Gertrude Stein Companion: content with the example.* New York: Greenwood Press, 1988.

Knapp, Bettina L. *Gertrude Stein: Literature and Life.* New York: Continuum, 1990.

Luhan, Mabel Dodge. *Intimate Memories: The Autobiography of Mabel Dodge Luhan.* 4 vols. New York: Harcourt, Brace, 1933–37.

Mellow, James R. *Charmed Circle: Gertrude Stein and Company.* New York: Avon Books, 1974. Reprint, New York: Owl Books, 2003.

•North, Michael. *The Dialect of Modernism: Race, Language & Twentieth-Century Literature.* New York: Oxford UP, 1994.

Pavloska, Susanna. *Modern Primitives: Race and Language in Gertrude Stein, Ernest Hemingway, and Zora Neale Hurston.* New York: Garland Publishing, 1999.

Perelman, Bob. *The Trouble with Genius: Reading Pound, Joyce, Stein, and Zukofsky*. U of California P, 1994.

Perloff, Marjorie. *The Poetics of Indeterminacy: Rimbaud to Cage*. Princeton: Princeton UP, 1981. Reprint, Evanston: Northwestern UP, 2000.

•Ruddick, Lisa. *Reading Gertrude Stein: Body, Text, Gnosis*. Ithaca: Cornell UP, 1990.

Scott, Bonnie Kime, ed. *The Gender of Modernism: A Critical Anthology*. Bloomington: Indiana UP, 1990.

Simon, Linda. *Gertrude Stein: A Composite Portrait*. New York: Avon, 1974.

Stewart, Allegra. *Gertrude Stein and the Present*. Cambridge, MA: Harvard UP, 1967.

Stimpson, Catharine. *Where the Meanings Are: Feminism and Cultural Spaces*. New York: Routledge, 1990.

Souhami, Diana. *Gertrude and Alice*. San Francisco: Pandora, 1991.

•Sutherland, Donald. *Gertrude Stein: A Biography of Her Work*. New Haven: Yale UP, 1951. Reprint, Westport, CT: Greenwood, 1971.

•Wagner-Martin, Linda. *"Favored Strangers": Gertrude Stein and Her Family*. New Brunswick: Rutgers UP, 1995.

•Wald, Priscilla. *Constituting Americans: Cultural Anxiety and Narrative Form*. Duke UP, 1995.

•Walker, Jayne L. *The Making of a Modernist: Gertrude Stein, from* Three Lives *to* Tender Buttons. Amherst, MA: U of Massachusetts P, 1984.

•Weininger, Otto. *Sex and Character*. 1903. Reprint, New York: AMS, 1975.

Weinstein, Norman. *Gertrude Stein and the Literature of Modern Consciousness*. New York: Frederick Ungar, 1970.

•Weiss, M. Lynn. *Gertrude Stein and Richard Wright: The Poetics and Politics of Modernism*. Jackson: The UP of Mississippi, 1998.

•Will, Barbara. *Gertrude Stein, Modernism, and the Problem of "Genius."* Edinburgh: Edinburgh UP, 2000.

•Williams, William Carlos. *Selected Essays*. New York: Random House, 1954.

Wilson, Edmund. *Axel's Castle: A Study in the Imaginative Literature of 1870–1930*. New York: Charles Scribner's Sons, 1931. Reprint, New York: Farrar, Straus & Giroux, 2004.

Wineapple, Brenda. *Sister Brother: Gertrude & Leo Stein*. New York: G.P. Putnam's Sons, 1996.

ARTICLES

•Blackmer, Corinne E. "African Masks and the Art of Passing in Gertrude Stein's 'Melanctha' and Nella Larsen's *Passing*." *Journal of the History of Sexuality* 4:2 (1993): 230–63.

Farber, Lawren. "Fading: A Way: Gertrude Stein's Sources for *Three Lives*." *Journal of Modern Literature* 5 (1976): 463–80.

•Hovey, Jaime. "Sapphic Primitivism in Gertrude Stein's *Q.E.D.*" *Modern Fiction Studies* 42: 3 (Fall 1996): 547–68.

Miller, Eugene E. "Richard Wright and Gertrude Stein." *Black American Literature Forum* 16:3 (1982): 107–12.

•Peterson, Carla. "The Remaking of Americans: Gertrude Stein's 'Melanctha' and African-American Musical Traditions." *Criticism and the Color Line: Desegregating American Literary Studies*. Ed. Henry B. Wonham. New Brunswick, NJ: Rutgers UP, 1996, 140–57.

•Saldívar-Hull, Sonia. "Wrestling Your Ally: Stein, Racism, and Feminist Critical Practice." *Women's Writing in Exile*. Eds. Mary Lynn Broe and Angela Ingram. Chapel Hill: U of North Carolina P, 1989, 181–98.

Saunders, Judith P. "Bipolar Conflict in Stein's 'Melanctha.' " *Modern Language Studies* 15: 2 (1985): 55–64.

Silverman, Debra B. "Nella Larsen's *Quicksand*: Untangling the Webs of Exoticism." *African American Review* 27 (1993): 599–614.

Simmons, Diane. "The Mother Mirror in Jamaica Kincaid's *Annie John* and Gertrude Stein's " 'The Good Anna.' " *The Anna Book: Searching for Anna in Literary History*. Ed. Mickey Pearlman. Westport, CT: Greenwood Press, 1992, 99–104.

Spahr, Juliana. "A, B, C: Reading Against Emily Dickinson and Gertrude Stein." *A Poetics of Criticism*. Eds. Juliana Spahr, Mark Wallace, Kristin Prevallet, and Pam Rehm. Buffalo: Leave, 1994, 281–92.

•Stimpson, Catharine. "The Mind, the Body and Gertrude Stein." *Critical Inquiry* 3:3 (Spring 1977): 489–506.

•Wood, Carl. "Continuity of Romantic Irony: Stein's Homage to LaForgue in *Three Lives*." *Comparative Literature Studies* 12 (1975): 147–58.